WEISSENBERGER'S OHIO CIVIL PROCEDURE
2003 LITIGATION MANUAL

Weissenberger's

OHIO CIVIL PROCEDURE

2003 Litigation Manual

A.J. STEPHANI

J.D., University of Cincinnati

GLEN WEISSENBERGER

Dean and Professor of Law
DePaul University College of Law

ANDERSON PUBLISHING CO.

CINCINNATI

WEISSENBERGER'S OHIO CIVIL PROCEDURE 2003 LITIGATION MANUAL

© 2002 by Anderson Publishing Co.
2035 Reading Road/Cincinnati, Ohio 45202
Telephone: 800 582-7295
Fax: 513 562-8110
E-mail: mail@andersonpublishing.com
World Wide Web: http://www.andersonpublishing.com (catalog site)
http://www.apohiolaw.com (legal research site)

ISBN 1-58360-566-5

DEDICATION

To C.G.D.,
A.J.S.

To my children,
G.W.

CONTENTS

OHIO RULES OF CIVIL PROCEDURE

TITLE I
SCOPE OF RULES—ONE FORM OF ACTION

TITLE II
COMMENCEMENT OF ACTION AND VENUE; SERVICE OF PROCESS; SERVICE AND FILING OF PLEADINGS AND OTHER PAPERS SUBSEQUENT TO THE ORIGINAL COMPLAINT; TIME

TITLE III
PLEADINGS AND MOTIONS

vii

CONTENTS

TITLE VII
JUDGMENT

TITLE VIII
PROVISIONAL AND FINAL REMEDIES

TITLE IX
SPECIAL PROCEEDINGS

TITLE X
GENERAL PROVISIONS

APPENDIX

PREFACE

This manual is designed to provide a thorough, yet concise, analysis of the Ohio Rules of Civil Procedure. It is intended to aid the practitioner, judge, and student alike in understanding the operation and application of the Rules in situations that recur throughout the course of litigation. Although this manual is not exhaustive of every procedural issue in Ohio, it is anticipated that it will function both to identify other additional sources on Ohio law as well as to resolve problems frequently engendered by the application of the Rules.

Each Chapter in this manual contains the full text of each Rule in a format that lends itself to easier examination and dissection than any other currently available. Practical commentary on each Rule is also provided, as are hundreds of illustrations of possible applications. Each Chapter also includes a list of additional Ohio authorities and a carefully-selected list of leading cases. These cases are intended to serve as starting points for additional research; comprehensive annotations are beyond the scope of this manual.

This manual also contains a host of other useful features, including a directory of all clerks of court within the state of Ohio, a note on judicial rulemaking in Ohio, an appellate district map, official forms, and a table used to calculate the number of days between two dates, as well as the full text of the Ohio Rules of Appellate Procedure and the Federal Rules of Civil Procedure. A quick-reference index is located on the inside front cover and a section locator on the back cover will direct the user to the section of the book where the desired information is found.

WEISSENBERGER'S OHIO CIVIL PROCEDURE: LITIGATION MANUAL is published annually and will inevitably benefit from refinement in future editions. Corrections, comments and suggestions are always welcome and may be directed to the authors at their e-mail addresses listed below.

A.J. Stephani
AJ.Stephani@juno.com

Glen Weissenberger
gweissen@depaul.edu

ACKNOWLEDGMENTS

The authors would like to acknowledge and extend thanks to student research editors Theresa Nelson, Jeff God, and Brian Schultz, without whom this manual would not have been possible. The authors would also like to acknowledge Mike Frey for his expertise in book concept and design and Connie Miller for her efforts in putting the pieces of this manual together.

TABLE OF AUTHORITIES

Full citations of sources are presented below in the order they are listed in the Additional Authority section of each Chapter.

CHARLES A. WRIGHT & ARTHUR R. MILLER, FEDERAL PRACTICE AND PROCEDURE, Vols. 4-12 (2d. ed., West Pub. Co.), *hereinafter* _____ WRIGHT & MILLER § _____

JAMES W. MOORE ET AL., MOORE'S FEDERAL PRACTICE, Vols. 1-14 (3d ed., Matthew Bender Pub. Co.), *hereinafter* _____ MOORE'S FEDERAL PRACTICE § _____

STANLEY E. HARPER, JR. & MICHAEL E. SOLIMINE, ANDERSON'S OHIO CIVIL PRACTICE, Vol. 4 (Anderson Pub. Co. 1996 & Supp.), *hereinafter* 4 ANDERSON'S OHIO CIVIL PRACTICE § _____

MICHAEL E. SOLIMINE, ANDERSON'S OHIO CIVIL PRACTICE, Vol. 5 (Anderson Pub. Co. 1996 & Supp.), *hereinafter* 5 ANDERSON'S OHIO CIVIL PRACTICE § _____

JAMES P. BOTTI ET AL., ANDERSON'S OHIO CIVIL PRACTICE, Vol. 6 (Anderson Pub. Co. 1996 & Supp.), *hereinafter* 6 ANDERSON'S OHIO CIVIL PRACTICE § _____

KLEIN DARLING CIVIL PRACTICE Vols. 1-2 (Banks-Baldwin Law Pub. Co. 1997), *hereinafter* _____ KLEIN DARLING _____

TEREZ CIVIL PRACTICE, Vol. 3 (Banks-Baldwin Law Pub. Co. 1997), *hereinafter* _____ TEREZ _____

OHIO JURISPRUDENCE PLEADING AND PRACTICE FORMS, Vol. 1-8 (James A. Lowe ed., Lawyers Coop. Pub., looseleaf current through 9/96), *hereinafter* _____ OH. JUR. PL. AND PRAC. FORMS, ch. _____

WILLIAM W. MILLIGAN, OHIO FORMS OF PLEADING AND PRACTICE, CIVIL PROCEDURE, Vols. 1-7 (Matthew Bender & Co., Inc., looseleaf current through 7/97), *hereinafter* _____ MILLIGAN Forms _____

HOWARD P. FINK ET AL., OHIO RULES OF CIVIL PROCEDURE WITH COMMENTARY, Vols. 1-2 (The Michie Co., 1992 and Supp.), *hereinafter* _____ FINK § _____

OHIO LITIGATION CHECKLISTS, Vol. 1 (General Practice) (Lonnie E. Griffith, Jr. editorial director, Lawyers Coop. Pub., 1993), *hereinafter* OHIO LITIGATION CHECKLISTS, [subsection], § _____

NOTE ON JUDICIAL RULEMAKING IN OHIO

Despite the structural and schematic similarity between the Federal Rules of Civil Procedure and the Ohio Rules of Civil Procedure, they differ markedly both with respect to the process through which they were promulgated and with regard to their legal effect. Unlike the United States Supreme Court, which derives its authority to create rules of procedure in federal court from the Rules Enabling Act, 28 U.S.C. § 2072, the Ohio Supreme Court's authority to pass rules of procedure is vested in the Ohio Constitution itself.

Rulemaking Authority

Article IV, § 5(B) of the Ohio Constitution confers upon the Ohio Supreme Court oversight authority over all state courts and empowers it to prescribe rules of practice and procedure. However, the Ohio Supreme Court does not have unfettered control over the promulgation of rules of procedure. Instead, § 5(B) takes the unusual step of providing the General Assembly of Ohio with veto power over rules prescribed by the Ohio Supreme Court.

Rulemaking Procedure

Proposed rules must be submitted to the General Assembly by January 15 of the year in which they take effect, with May 1 operating as the final deadline for any amendments to those rules. If the General Assembly of Ohio does nothing, the rules take effect on July 1 of the same year. The General Assembly may, however, adopt a concurrent resolution of disapproval no later than June 30, and the resolution operates to defeat the rules and send the proposal back to the Ohio Supreme Court. Notice of and a public comment period on proposed rules is also typical, though no such period is required by the Ohio Constitution.

Veto Power of Ohio General Assembly

The mechanics of the rulemaking procedure in Ohio are similar to those established by Congress under the Rules Enabling Act, but significant differences exist. For one, the veto power provided to the Ohio General Assembly is not selective. In other words, the General Assembly may defeat proposed sets of rules in toto, but not in part. This power is in contrast to that held by Congress, who, of course, retains final authority over proposed rules of procedure and may elect to preempt the operation of certain rules while allowing others to take effect.

Final Authority on Rules of Procedure

Another feature of the rulemaking authority of the Ohio Supreme Court and a significant difference from that in the federal system is implied from the nature of the authority conferred upon the Ohio Supreme Court to prescribe rules of procedure. This authority is granted to the Ohio Supreme Court by the Ohio Constitution, as opposed to the delegation of that authority to the United States Supreme Court by Congress. Accordingly, rules of procedure promulgated by the Ohio Supreme Court supersede any conflicting Ohio statutory provision, a point made explicitly in § 5(B) of the Constitution itself. Ohio courts have routinely held that statutes that merely supplement or complement rules of procedure are still permitted, so the authority granted to the Ohio Supreme Court in § 5(B) is apparently nonexclusive.

Procedural Rules Must Be Nonsubstantive

The familiar proscription that rules of procedure may not "abridge, enlarge, or modify any substantive right" operates in Ohio as it does in the federal system. Thus, a rule of procedure that amends or expands upon a substantive right is void, and any conflicting statutory provision controls. Such rules should be carefully distinguished from nonsubstantive procedural rules, which supersede contrary statutory provisions. However, this proscription functions in Ohio as a constitutional mandate, as opposed to the analogous proscription on the United States Supreme Court, which functions as a limit on the delegation of authority by Congress under the Rules Enabling Act.

Local Rules and Rules of Superintendence

Procedural rules established by local courts are permitted under the Ohio Constitution provided that they are consistent with other rules of procedure and they do not, of course, affect the substantive rights of parties. Finally, rules of practice and procedure passed pursuant to § 5(B) of the Ohio Constitution should be distinguished from rules of superintendence passed pursuant to § 5(A)(1); rules of superintendence are neither subject to a veto power of the Ohio General Assembly nor do they correlatively supersede conflicting statutory provisions.

OHIO RULES OF CIVIL PROCEDURE

Effective July 1, 1970
Complete with amendments through June 30, 2003

TITLE I
SCOPE OF RULES —
ONE FORM OF ACTION

RULE 1. Scope of rules: applicability; construction; exceptions

(A) Applicability. These rules prescribe the procedure to be followed in all courts of this state in the exercise of civil jurisdiction at law or in equity, with the exceptions stated in subdivision (C) of this rule.

(B) Construction. These rules shall be construed and applied to effect just results by eliminating delay, unnecessary expense and all other impediments to the expeditious administration of justice.

(C) Exceptions. These rules, to the extent that they would by their nature be clearly inapplicable, shall not apply to procedure (1) upon appeal to review any judgment, order or ruling, (2) in the appropriation of property, (3) in forcible entry and detainer, (4) in small claims matters under Chapter 1925, Revised Code, (5) in uniform reciprocal support actions, (6) in the commitment of the mentally ill, (7) in all other special statutory proceedings; provided, that where any statute provides for procedure by a general or specific reference to the statutes governing procedure in civil actions such procedure shall be in accordance with these rules.

(Amended, eff 7-1-71; 7-1-75)

RULE 2. One form of action

There shall be only one form of action, and it shall be known as a civil action.

TITLE II
COMMENCEMENT OF ACTION AND VENUE; SERVICE OF PROCESS; SERVICE AND FILING OF PLEADINGS AND OTHER PAPERS SUBSEQUENT TO THE ORIGINAL COMPLAINT; TIME

RULE 3. Commencement of action; venue

(A) Commencement. A civil action is commenced by filing a complaint with the court, if service is obtained within one year from such filing upon a named defendant, or upon an incorrectly named defendant whose name is later corrected pursuant to Civ. R. 15(C), or upon a defendant identified by a fictitious name whose name is later corrected pursuant to Civ. R. 15(D).

(B) Venue: where proper. Any action may be venued, commenced, and decided in any court in any county. When applied to county and municipal courts, "county," as used in this rule, shall be construed, where appropriate, as the territorial limits of those courts. Proper venue lies in any one or more of the following counties:

(1) The county in which the defendant resides;

(2) The county in which the defendant has his or her principal place of business;

(3) A county in which the defendant conducted activity that gave rise to the claim for relief;

(4) A county in which a public officer maintains his or her principal office if suit is brought against the officer in the officer's official capacity;

(5) A county in which the property, or any part of the property, is situated if the subject of the action is real property or tangible personal property;

(6) The county in which all or part of the claim for relief arose; or, if the claim for relief arose upon a river, other watercourse, or a road, that is the boundary of the state, or of two or more counties, in any county bordering on the river, watercourse, or road, and opposite to the place where the claim for relief arose;

(7) In actions described in Civ. R. 4.3, in the county where plaintiff resides;

(8) In an action against an executor, administrator, guardian, or trustee, in the county in which the executor, administrator, guardian, or trustee was appointed;

(9) In actions for divorce, annulment, or legal separation, in the county in which the plaintiff is and has been a resident for at least ninety days immediately preceding the filing of the complaint;

(10) In actions for a civil protection order, in the county in which the petitioner currently or temporarily resides;

(11) If there is no available forum in divisions (B)(1) to (B)(10) of this rule, in the county in which plaintiff resides, has his or her principal place of business, or regularly and systematically conducts business activity;

(12) If there is no available forum in divisions (B)(1) to (B)(11) of this rule:

(a) In a county in which defendant has property or debts owing to the defendant subject to attachment or garnishment;

(b) In a county in which defendant has appointed an agent to receive service of process or in which an agent has been appointed by operation of law.

(C) Change of venue.

(1) When an action has been commenced in a county other than stated to be proper in division (B) of this rule, upon timely assertion of the defense of improper venue as provided in Civ. R. 12, the court shall transfer the action to a county stated to be proper in division (B) of this rule.

(2) When an action is transferred to a county which is proper, the court may assess costs, including reasonable attorney fees, to the time of transfer against the party who commenced the action in a county other than stated to be proper in division (B) of this rule.

(3) Before entering a default judgment in an action in which the defendant has not appeared, the court, if it finds that the action has been commenced in a county other than stated to be proper in division (B) of this rule, may transfer the action to a county that is proper. The clerk of the court to which the action is transferred shall notify the defendant of the transfer, stating in the notice that the defendant shall have twenty-eight days from the receipt of the notice to answer in the transferred action.

(4) Upon motion of any party or upon its own motion the court may transfer any action to an adjoining county within this state when it appears that a fair and impartial trial cannot be had in the county in which the suit is pending.

(D) Venue: no proper forum in Ohio. When a court, upon motion of any party or upon its own motion, determines: (1) that the county in which the action is brought is not a proper forum; (2) that there is no other proper forum for trial within this state; and (3) that there exists a proper forum for trial in another jurisdiction outside this state, the court shall stay the action upon condition that all defendants consent to the jurisdiction, waive venue, and agree that the date of commencement of the action in Ohio shall be the date of commencement for the application of the statute of limitations to the action in that forum in another jurisdiction which the court deems to be the proper forum. If all defendants agree to the conditions, the court shall not dismiss the action, but the action shall be stayed until the court receives notice by affidavit that plaintiff has recommenced the action in the out-of-state forum within sixty days after the effective date of the order staying the original action. If the plaintiff fails to recommence the action in the out-of-state forum within the sixty day period, the court shall dismiss the action without prejudice. If all defendants do not agree to or comply with the conditions, the court shall hear the action.

If the court determines that a proper forum does not exist in another jurisdiction, it shall hear the action.

(E) Venue: multiple defendants and multiple claims for relief. In any action, brought by one or more plaintiffs against one or more defendants involving one or more claims for relief, the forum shall be deemed a proper forum, and venue therein shall be proper, if the venue is proper as to any one party other than a nominal party, or as to any one claim for relief.

Neither the dismissal of any claim nor of any party

except an indispensable party shall affect the jurisdiction of the court over the remaining parties.

(F) Venue: notice of pending litigation; transfer of judgments.

(1) When an action affecting the title to or possession of real property or tangible personal property is commenced in a county other than the county in which all of the real property or tangible personal property is situated, the plaintiff shall cause a certified copy of the complaint to be filed with the clerk of the court of common pleas in each county or additional county in which the real property or tangible personal property affected by the action is situated. If the plaintiff fails to file a certified copy of the complaint, third persons will not be charged with notice of the pendency of the action.

To the extent authorized by the laws of the United States, division (F)(1) of this rule also applies to actions, other than proceedings in bankruptcy, affecting title to or possession of real property in this state commenced in a United States District Court whenever the real property is situated wholly or partly in a county other than the county in which the permanent records of the court are kept.

(2) After final judgment, or upon dismissal of the action, the clerk of the court that issued the judgment shall transmit a certified copy of the judgment or dismissal to the clerk of the court of common pleas in each county or additional county in which real or tangible personal property affected by the action is situated.

(3) When the clerk has transmitted a certified copy of the judgment to another county in accordance with division (F)(2) of this rule, and the judgment is later appealed, vacated or modified, the appellant or the party at whose instance the judgment was vacated or modified must cause a certified copy of the notice of appeal or order of vacation or modification to be filed with the clerk of the court of common pleas of each county or additional county in which the real property or tangible personal property is situated. Unless a certified copy of the notice of appeal or order of vacation or modification is so filed, third persons will not be charged with notice of the appeal, vacation, or modification.

(4) The clerk of the court receiving a certified copy filed or transmitted in accordance with the provisions of division (F) of this rule shall number, index, docket, and file it in the records of the receiving court. The clerk shall index the first certified copy received in connection with a particular action in the indices to the records of actions commenced in the clerk's own court, but may number, docket, and file it in either the regular records of the court or in a separate set of records. When the clerk subsequently receives a certified copy in connection with that same action, the clerk need not index it, but shall docket and file it in the same set of records under the same case number previously assigned to the action.

(5) When an action affecting title to registered land is commenced in a county other than the county in which all of such land is situated, any certified copy required or permitted by this division (F) of this rule shall be filed with or transmitted to the county recorder, rather than the clerk of the court of common pleas, of each county or additional county in which the land is situated.

(G) Venue: collateral attack; appeal. The provisions of this rule relate to venue and are not jurisdictional. No order, judgment, or decree shall be void or subject to collateral attack solely on the ground that there was improper venue; however, nothing here shall affect the right to appeal an error of court concerning venue.

(Amended, eff 7-1-71; 7-1-86; 7-1-91; 7-1-98)

RULE 4. Process: summons

(A) Summons: issuance. Upon the filing of the complaint the clerk shall forthwith issue a summons for service upon each defendant listed in the caption. Upon request of the plaintiff separate or additional summons shall issue at any time against any defendant.

(B) Summons: form; copy of complaint. The summons shall be signed by the clerk, contain the name and address of the court and the names and addresses of the parties, be directed to the defendant, state the name and address of the plaintiff's attorney, if any, otherwise the plaintiff's address, and the times within which these rules or any statutory provision require the defendant to appear and defend, and shall notify him that in case of his failure to do so, judgment by default will be rendered against him for the relief demanded in the complaint. Where there are multiple plaintiffs or multiple defendants, or both, the summons may contain, in lieu of the names and addresses of all parties, the name of the first party on each side and the name and address of the party to be served.

A copy of the complaint shall be attached to each summons. The plaintiff shall furnish the clerk with sufficient copies.

(C) Summons: plaintiff and defendant defined. For the purpose of issuance and service of summons "plaintiff" shall include any party seeking the issuance and service of summons, and "defendant" shall include any party upon whom service of summons is sought.

(D) Waiver of service of summons. Service of summons may be waived in writing by any person entitled thereto under Rule 4.2 who is at least eighteen years of age and not under disability.

(E) Summons: time limit for service. If a service of the summons and complaint is not made upon a defendant within six months after the filing of the complaint and the party on whose behalf such service was required cannot show good cause why such service was not made within that period, the action shall be dismissed as to that defendant without prejudice upon the court's own initiative with notice to such party or upon motion. This division shall not apply to out-of-state service pursuant to Rule 4.3 or to service in a foreign country pursuant to Rule 4.5

(Amended, eff 7-1-71; 7-1-73; 7-1-75; 7-1-84)

RULE 4.1 Process: methods of service

All methods of service within this state, except service by publication as provided in Civ. R. 4.4(A) are described in this rule. Methods of out-of-state service and for service in a foreign country are described in Civ. R. 4.3 and 4.5.

(A) Service by certified or express mail. Evidenced by return receipt signed by any person, service of any process shall be by certified or express mail unless otherwise permitted by these rules. The clerk shall place a copy of the process and complaint or other document to be served in an envelope. The clerk shall address the envelope to the person to be served at the address set forth in the caption or at the address set forth in written instructions furnished to the clerk with instructions to forward. The clerk shall affix adequate postage and place the sealed envelope in the United States mail as certified or express mail return receipt requested with instructions to the delivering postal employee to show to whom delivered, date of delivery, and address where delivered.

The clerk shall forthwith enter the fact of mailing on the appearance docket and make a similar entry when the return receipt is received. If the envelope is returned with an endorsement showing failure of delivery, the clerk shall forthwith notify, by mail, the attorney of record or, if there is no attorney of record, the party at whose instance process was issued and enter the fact of notification on the appearance docket. The clerk shall file the return receipt or returned envelope in the records of the action.

All postage shall be charged to costs. If the parties to be served by certified or express mail are numerous and the clerk determines there is insufficient security for costs, the clerk may require the party requesting service to advance an amount estimated by the clerk to be sufficient to pay the postage.

(B) Personal service. When the plaintiff files a written request with the clerk for personal service, service of process shall be made by that method.

When process issued from the Supreme Court, a court of appeals, a court of common pleas or a county court is to be served personally, the clerk of the court shall deliver the process and sufficient copies of the process and complaint, or other document to be served, to the sheriff of the county in which the party to be served resides or may be found. When process issues from the municipal court, delivery shall be to the bailiff of the court for service on all defendants who reside or may be found within the county or counties in which that court has territorial jurisdiction and to the sheriff

of any other county in this state for service upon a defendant who resides in or may be found in that other county. In the alternative, process issuing from any of these courts may be delivered by the clerk to any person not less than eighteen years of age, who is not a party and who has been designated by order of the court to make service of process. The person serving process shall locate the person to be served and shall tender a copy of the process and accompanying documents to the person to be served. When the copy of the process has been served, the person serving process shall endorse that fact on the process and return it to the clerk who shall make the appropriate entry on the appearance docket.

When the person serving process is unable to serve a copy of the process within twenty-eight days, the person shall endorse that fact and the reasons therefor on the process and return the process and copies to the clerk who shall make the appropriate entry on the appearance docket. In the event of failure of service, the clerk shall follow the notification procedure set forth in division (A) of this rule. Failure to make service within the twenty-eight day period and failure to make proof of service do not affect the validity of the service.

(C) Residence service. When the plaintiff files a written request with the clerk for residence service, service of process shall be made by that method.

Residence service shall be effected by leaving a copy of the process and the complaint, or other document to be served, at the usual place of residence of the person to be served with some person of suitable age and discretion then residing therein. The clerk of the court shall issue the process, and the process server shall return it, in the same manner as prescribed in division (B) of this rule. When the person serving process is unable to serve a copy of the process within twenty-eight days, the person shall endorse that fact and the reasons therefor on the process and return the process and copies to the clerk who shall make the appropriate entry on the appearance docket. In the event of failure of service, the clerk shall follow the notification procedure set forth in division (A) of this rule. Failure to make service within the twenty-eight day period and failure to make proof of service do not affect the validity of service.

(Amended, eff 7-1-71; 7-1-80; 7-1-97)

RULE 4.2 Process: who may be served

Service of process, except service by publication as provided in Civ. R. 4.4(A), pursuant to Civ. R. 4 through Civ. R. 4.6 shall be made as follows:

(A) Upon an individual, other than a person under sixteen years of age or an incompetent person, by serving the individual;

(B) Upon a person under sixteen years of age by serving either the person's guardian or any one of the following persons with whom the person to be served lives or resides: father, mother, or the individual having the care of the person; or by serving the person if the person neither has a guardian nor lives or resides with a parent or a person having his or her care;

(C) Upon an incompetent person by serving either the incompetent's guardian or the person designated in division (E) of this rule, but if no guardian has been appointed and the incompetent is not under confinement or commitment, by serving the incompetent;

(D) Upon an individual, confined to a penal institution of this state or of a subdivision of this state, by serving the individual, except that when the individual to be served is a person under sixteen years of age, the provisions of division (B) of this rule shall be applicable;

(E) Upon an incompetent person who is confined in any institution for the mentally ill or mentally deficient or committed by order of court to the custody of some other institution or person by serving the superintendent or similar official of the institution to which the incompetent is confined or committed or the person to whose custody the incompetent is committed;

(F) Upon a corporation either domestic or foreign: by serving the agent authorized by appointment or by law to receive service of process; or by serving the corporation by certified or express mail at any of its usual places of business; or by serving an officer or a managing or general agent of the corporation;

(G) Upon a partnership, a limited partnership, or a limited partnership association by serving the entity by certified or express mail at any of its usual places of business or by serving a partner, limited partner, manager, or member;

(H) Upon an unincorporated association by serving it in its entity name by certified or express mail at any of its usual places of business or by serving an officer of the unincorporated association;

(I) Upon a professional association by serving the association in its corporate name by certified or express mail at the place where the corporate offices are maintained by or serving a shareholder;

(J) Upon this state or any one of its departments, offices and institutions as defined in division (C) of section 121.01 of the Revised Code, by serving the officer responsible for the administration of the department, office or institution or by serving the attorney general of this state;

(K) Upon a county or upon any of its offices, agencies, districts, departments, institutions or administrative units, by serving the officer responsible for the administration of the office, agency, district, department, institution or unit or by serving the prosecuting attorney of the county;

(L) Upon a township by serving one or more of the township trustees or the township clerk or by serving the prosecuting attorney of the county in which the township is located, unless the township is organized under Chapter 504. of the Revised Code, in which case

service may be made upon the township law director;

(M) Upon a municipal corporation or upon any of its offices, departments, agencies, authorities, institutions or administrative units by serving the officer responsible for the administration of the office, department, agency, authority, institution or unit or by serving the city solicitor or comparable legal officer;

(N) Upon any governmental entity not mentioned above by serving the person, officer, group or body responsible for the administration of that entity or by serving the appropriate legal officer, if any, representing the entity. Service upon any person who is a member of the "group" or "body" responsible for the administration of the entity shall be sufficient.

(Amended, eff 7-1-71; 7-1-96; 7-1-97)

RULE 4.3 Process: out-of-state service

(A) When service permitted. Service of process may be made outside of this state, as provided in this rule, in any action in this state, upon a person who, at the time of service of process, is a nonresident of this state or is a resident of this state who is absent from this state. "Person" includes an individual, an individual's executor, administrator, or other personal representative, or a corporation, partnership, association, or any other legal or commercial entity, who, acting directly or by an agent, has caused an event to occur out of which the claim that is the subject of the complaint arose, from the person's:

(1) Transacting any business in this state;

(2) Contracting to supply services or goods in this state;

(3) Causing tortious injury by an act or omission in this state, including, but not limited to, actions arising out of the ownership, operation, or use of a motor vehicle or aircraft in this state;

(4) Causing tortious injury in this state by an act or omission outside this state if the person regularly does or solicits business, engages in any other persistent course of conduct, or derives substantial revenue from goods used or consumed or services rendered in this state;

(5) Causing injury in this state to any person by breach of warranty expressly or impliedly made in the sale of goods outside this state when the person to be served might reasonably have expected the person who was injured to use, consume, or be affected by the goods in this state, provided that the person to be served also regularly does or solicits business, engages in any other persistent course of conduct, or derives substantial revenue from goods used or consumed or services rendered in this state;

(6) Having an interest in, using, or possessing real property in this state;

(7) Contracting to insure any person, property, or risk located within this state at the time of contracting;

(8) Living in the marital relationship within this state

notwithstanding subsequent departure from this state, as to all obligations arising for spousal support, custody, child support, or property settlement, if the other party to the marital relationship continues to reside in this state;

(9) Causing tortious injury in this state to any person by an act outside this state committed with the purpose of injuring persons, when the person to be served might reasonably have expected that some person would be injured by the act in this state;

(10) Causing tortious injury to any person by a criminal act, any element of which takes place in this state, that the person to be served commits or in the commission of which the person to be served is guilty of complicity.

(B) Methods of service.

(1) Service by certified or express mail. Evidenced by return receipt signed by any person, service of any process shall be by certified or express mail unless otherwise permitted by these rules. The clerk shall place a copy of the process and complaint or other document to be served in an envelope. The clerk shall address the envelope to the person to be served at the address set forth in the caption or at the address set forth in written instructions furnished to the clerk with instructions to forward. The clerk shall affix adequate postage and place the sealed envelope in the United States mail as certified or express mail return receipt requested with instructions to the delivering postal employee to show to whom delivered, date of delivery, and address where delivered.

The clerk shall forthwith enter the fact of mailing on the appearance docket and make a similar entry when the return receipt is received. If the envelope is returned with an endorsement showing failure of delivery, the clerk shall forthwith notify, by mail, the attorney of record or, if there is no attorney of record, the party at whose instance process was issued and enter the fact of notification on the appearance docket. The clerk shall file the return receipt or returned envelope in the records of the action. If the envelope is returned with an endorsement showing failure of delivery, service is complete when the attorney or serving party, after notification by the clerk, files with the clerk an affidavit setting forth facts indicating the reasonable diligence utilized to ascertain the whereabouts of the party to be served.

All postage shall be charged to costs. If the parties to be served by certified or express mail are numerous and the clerk determines there is insufficient security for costs, the clerk may require the party requesting service to advance an amount estimated by the clerk to be sufficient to pay the postage.

(2) Personal service. When ordered by a court, a "person" as defined in division (A) of this rule may be personally served with a copy of the process and complaint or other document to be served. Service under this division may be made by any person not less than eighteen years of age who is not a party and who has been designated by order of the court. On request, the clerk shall deliver the summons to the plaintiff for transmission to the person who will make service.

Proof of service may be made as prescribed by Civ. R. 4.1(B) or by order of the court.

(Amended, eff 7-1-71; 7-1-80; 7-1-88; 7-1-91; 7-1-97)

RULE 4.4 Process: service by publication

(A) Residence unknown. (1) Except in an action governed by division (A)(2) of this rule, if the residence of a defendant is unknown, service shall be made by publication in actions where such service is authorized by law. Before service by publication can be made, an affidavit of a party or his counsel shall be filed with the court. The affidavit shall aver that service of summons cannot be made because the residence of the defendant is unknown to the affiant, all of the efforts made on behalf of the party to ascertain the residence of the defendant, and that the residence of the defendant cannot be ascertained with reasonable diligence.

Upon the filing of the affidavit, the clerk shall cause service of notice to be made by publication in a newspaper of general circulation in the county in which the complaint is filed. If no newspaper is published in that county, then publication shall be in a newspaper published in an adjoining county. The publication shall contain the name and address of the court, the case number, the name of the first party on each side, and the name and last known address, if any, of the person or persons whose residence is unknown. The publication also shall contain a summary statement of the object of the complaint and demand for relief, and shall notify the person to be served that he or she is required to answer within twenty-eight days after the publication. The publication shall be published at least once a week for six successive weeks unless publication for a lesser number of weeks is specifically provided by law. Service shall be complete at the date of the last publication.

After the last publication, the publisher or its agent shall file with the court an affidavit showing the fact of publication together with a copy of the notice of publication. The affidavit and copy of the notice shall constitute proof of service.

(2) In a divorce, annulment, or legal separation action, if the plaintiff is proceeding *in forma pauperis* and if the residence of the defendant is unknown, service by publication shall be made by posting and mail. Before service by posting and mail can be made, an affidavit of a party or the party's counsel shall be filed with the court. The affidavit shall contain the same averments required by division (A)(1) of this rule and, in addition, shall set forth the defendant's last known address.

Upon the filing of the affidavit, the clerk shall cause service of notice to be made by posting in a conspicuous place in the courthouse or courthouses in which the general and domestic relations divisions of the court of common pleas for the county are located and in two additional public places in the county that have been designated by local rule for the posting of notices pursuant to this rule. The notice shall contain the same information required by division (A)(1) of this rule to be contained in a newspaper publication. The notice shall be posted in the required locations for six successive weeks.

The clerk shall also cause the complaint and summons to be mailed by ordinary mail, address correction requested, to the defendant's last known address. The clerk shall obtain a certificate of mailing from the United States Postal Service. If the clerk is notified of a corrected or forwarding address of the defendant within the six-week period that notice is posted pursuant to division (A)(2) of this rule, the clerk shall cause the complaint and summons to be mailed to the corrected or forwarding address. The clerk shall note the name, address, and date of each mailing in the docket.

After the last week of posting, the clerk shall note on the docket where and when notice was posted. Service shall be complete upon the entry of posting.

(B) Residence known. If the residence of a defendant is known, and the action is one in which service by publication is authorized by law, service of process shall be effected by a method other than by publication as provided by:

(1) Rule 4.1, if the defendant is a resident of this state,

(2) Rule 4.3(B), if defendant is not a resident of this state, or

(3) Rule 4.5, in the alternative, if service on defendant is to be effected in a foreign country.

If service of process cannot be effected under the provisions of this subdivision or Rule 4.6(C) or Rule 4.6(D), service of process shall proceed by publication.

(Amended, eff 7-1-71; 7-1-91)

RULE 4.5 Process: alternative provisions for service in a foreign country

(A) Manner. When Civ. R. 4.3 or Civ. R. 4.4 or both allow service upon a person outside this state and service is to be effected in a foreign country, service of the summons and complaint may also be made:

(1) In the manner prescribed by the law of the foreign country for service in that country in an action in any of its courts of general jurisdiction when service is calculated to give actual notice;

(2) As directed by the foreign authority in response to a letter rogatory when service is calculated to give actual notice;

(3) Upon an individual by delivery to him personally;

(4) Upon a corporation or partnership or association by delivery to an officer, a managing or general agent;

(5) By any form of mail requiring a signed receipt,

when the clerk of the court addresses and dispatches this mail to the party to be served;

(6) As directed by order of the court.

Service under division (A)(3) or (A)(6) of this rule may be made by any person not less than eighteen years of age who is not a party and who has been designated by order of the court, or by the foreign court. On request the clerk shall deliver the summons to the plaintiff for transmission to the person or the foreign court or officer who will make the service.

(B) Return. Proof of service may be made as prescribed by Civ. R. 4.1(B), or by the law of the foreign country, or by order of the court. When mail service is made pursuant to division (A)(5) of this rule, proof of service shall include a receipt signed by the addressee or other evidence of delivery to the addressee satisfactory to the court.

(Amended, eff 7-1-97)

RULE 4.6 Process: limits; amendment; service refused; service unclaimed

(A) Limits of effective service. All process may be served anywhere in this state and, when authorized by law or these rules, may be served outside this state.

(B) Amendment. The court within its discretion and upon such terms as are just, may at any time allow the amendment of any process or proof of service thereof, unless the amendment would cause material prejudice to the substantial rights of the party against whom the process was issued.

(C) Service refused. If service of process is refused, and the certified or express mail envelope is returned with an endorsement showing such refusal, or the return of the person serving process states that service of process has been refused, the clerk shall forthwith notify, by mail, the attorney of record or, if there is no attorney of record, the party at whose instance process was issued. If the attorney, or serving party, after notification by the clerk, files with the clerk a written request for ordinary mail service, the clerk shall send by ordinary mail a copy of the summons and complaint or other document to be served to the defendant at the address set forth in the caption, or at the address set forth in written instructions furnished to the clerk. The mailing shall be evidenced by a certificate of mailing which shall be completed and filed by the clerk. Answer day shall be twenty-eight days after the date of mailing as evidenced by the certificate of mailing. The clerk shall endorse this answer date upon the summons which is sent by ordinary mail. Service shall be deemed complete when the fact of mailing is entered of record. Failure to claim certified or express mail service is not refusal of service within the meaning of division (C) of this rule.

(D) Service unclaimed. If a certified or express mail envelope is returned with an endorsement showing that the envelope was unclaimed, the clerk shall forthwith notify, by mail, the attorney of record or, if there is no attorney of record, the party at whose instance process was issued. If the attorney, or serving party, after notification by the clerk, files with the clerk a written request for ordinary mail service, the clerk shall send by ordinary mail a copy of the summons and complaint or other document to be served to the defendant at the address set forth in the caption, or at the address set forth in written instructions furnished to the clerk. The mailing shall be evidenced by a certificate of mailing which shall be completed and filed by the clerk. Answer day shall be twenty-eight days after the date of mailing as evidenced by the certificate of mailing. The clerk shall endorse this answer date upon the summons which is sent by ordinary mail. Service shall be deemed complete when the fact of mailing is entered of record, provided that the ordinary mail envelope is not returned by the postal authorities with an endorsement showing failure of delivery. If the ordinary mail envelope is returned undelivered, the clerk shall forthwith notify the attorney, or serving party, by mail.

(E) Duty of attorney of record or serving party. The attorney of record or the serving party shall be responsible for determining if service has been made and shall timely file written instructions with the clerk regarding completion of service notwithstanding the provisions in Civ. R. 4.1 through 4.6 which instruct a clerk to notify the attorney of record or the serving party of failure of service of process.

(Amended, eff 7-1-71; 7-1-78; 7-1-97)

RULE 5. Service and filing of pleadings and other papers subsequent to the original complaint

(A) Service: when required. Except as otherwise provided in these rules, every order required by its terms to be served, every pleading subsequent to the original complaint unless the court otherwise orders because of numerous defendants, every paper relating to discovery required to be served upon a party unless the court otherwise orders, every written motion other than one which may be heard ex parte, and every written notice, appearance, demand, offer of judgment, and similar paper shall be served upon each of the parties. Service is not required on parties in default for failure to appear except that pleadings asserting new or additional claims for relief or for additional damages against them shall be served upon them in the manner provided for service of summons in Civ. R. 4 through Civ. R. 4.6.

(B) Service: how made. Whenever under these rules service is required or permitted to be made upon a party who is represented by an attorney of record in the proceedings, the service shall be made upon the attorney unless service upon the party is ordered by the court. Service upon the attorney or party shall be made by delivering a copy to the person to be served, transmitting it to the office of the person to be served by facsimile transmission, mailing it to the last known address of the person to be served or, if no address is known, leaving it with the clerk of the court. The served copy shall be accompanied by a completed copy of the proof of service required by division (D) of this rule. "Delivering a copy" within this rule means: handing it to the attorney or party; leaving it at the office of the person to be served with a clerk or other person in charge; if there is no one in charge, leaving it in a conspicuous place in the office; or, if the office is closed or the person to be served has no office, leaving it at the dwelling house or usual place of abode of the person to be served with some person of suitable age and discretion then residing in the dwelling house or usual place of abode. Service by mail is complete upon mailing. Service by facsimile transmission is complete upon transmission.

(C) Service: numerous defendants. In any action in which there are unusually large numbers of defendants, the court, upon motion or of its own initiative, may order that service of the pleadings of the defendants and replies thereto need not be made as between the defendants and that any cross-claim, counterclaim, or matter constituting an avoidance or affirmative defense contained therein shall be deemed to be denied or avoided by all other parties and that the filing of any such pleading and service thereof upon the plaintiff constitutes due notice of it to the parties. A copy of every such order shall be served upon the parties in such manner and form as the court directs.

(D) Filing. All papers, after the complaint, required to be served upon a party shall be filed with the court within three days after service, but depositions upon oral examination, interrogatories, requests for documents, requests for admission, and answers and responses thereto shall not be filed unless on order of the court or for use as evidence or for consideration of a motion in the proceeding. Papers filed with the court shall not be considered until proof of service is endorsed thereon or separately filed. The proof of service shall state the date and manner of service and shall be signed in accordance with Civ. R. 11.

(E) Filing with the court defined. The filing of documents with the court, as required by these rules, shall be made by filing them with the clerk of court, except that the judge may permit the documents to be filed with the judge, in which event the judge shall note the filing date on the documents and transmit them to the clerk. A court may provide, by local rules adopted pursuant to the Rules of Superintendence, for the filing of documents by electronic means. If the court adopts such local rules, they shall include all of the following:

(1) Any signature on electronically transmitted documents shall be considered that of the attorney or party it purports to be for all purposes. If it is established that the documents were transmitted without authority, the court shall order the filing stricken.

(2) A provision shall specify the days and hours during which electronically transmitted documents will be received by the court, and a provision shall specify when documents received electronically will be considered to have been filed.

(3) Any document filed electronically that requires a filing fee may be rejected by the clerk of court unless the filer has complied with the mechanism established by the court for the payment of filing fees.

(Amended, eff 7-1-71; 7-1-84; 7-1-91; 7-1-94; 7-1-01)

RULE 6. Time

(A) Time: computation. In computing any period of time prescribed or allowed by these rules, by the local rules of any court, by order of court, or by any applicable statute, the date of the act, event, or default from which the designated period of time begins to run shall not be included. The last day of the period so computed shall be included, unless it is a Saturday, a Sunday, or a legal holiday, in which event the period runs until the end of the next day which is not a Saturday, a Sunday, or a legal holiday. When the period of time prescribed or allowed is less than seven days, intermediate Saturdays, Sundays, and legal holidays shall be excluded in the computation. When a public office in which an act, required by law, rule, or order of court, is to be performed is closed to the public for the entire day which constitutes the last day for doing such an act, or before its usual closing time on such day, then such act may be performed on the next succeeding day which is not a Saturday, a Sunday, or a legal holiday.

(B) Time: extension. When by these rules or by a notice given thereunder or by order of court an act is required or allowed to be done at or within a specified time, the court for cause shown may at any time in its discretion (1) with or without motion or notice order the period enlarged if request therefor is made before the expiration of the period originally prescribed or as extended by a previous order, or (2) upon motion made after the expiration of the specified period permit the act to be done where the failure to act was the result of excusable neglect; but it may not extend the time for taking any action under Rule 50(B), Rule 59(B), Rule 59(D) and Rule 60(B), except to the extent and under the conditions stated in them.

(C) Time: unaffected by expiration of term. The period of time provided for the doing of any act or the taking of any proceeding is not affected or limited by the continued existence or expiration of a term of court. The existence or expiration of a term of court in no way affects the power of a court to do any act or take any proceeding in any civil action consistent with these rules.

(D) Time: motions. A written motion, other than one which may be heard ex parte, and notice of the hearing thereof shall be served not later than seven days before the time fixed for the hearing, unless a different period is fixed by these rules or by order of the court. Such an order may for cause shown be made on ex parte application. When a motion is supported by affidavit, the affidavit shall be served with the motion; and, except as otherwise provided in Rule 59(C), opposing affidavits may be served not later than one day before the hearing, unless the court permits them to be served at some other time.

(E) Time: additional time after service by mail. Whenever a party has the right or is required to do some act or take some proceedings within a prescribed period after the service of a notice or other paper upon him and the notice or paper is served upon him by mail, three days shall be added to the prescribed period. This subdivision does not apply to responses to service of summons under Rule 4 through Rule 4.6.

(Amended, eff 7-1-78)

TITLE III
PLEADINGS AND MOTIONS

Rule
    (F) Motion to strike
    (G) Consolidation of defenses and objections
    (H) Waiver of defenses and objections
  13. Counterclaim and cross-claim
    (A) Compulsory counterclaims
    (B) Permissive counterclaims
    (C) Counterclaim exceeding opposing claim
    (D) Counterclaim against this state
    (E) Counterclaim maturing or acquired after pleading
    (F) Omitted counterclaim
    (G) Cross-claim against co-party
    (H) Joinder of additional parties
    (I) Separate trials; separate judgments
    (J) Certification of proceedings
  14. Third-party practice
    (A) When defendant may bring in third party
    (B) When plaintiff may bring in third party
  15. Amended and supplemental pleadings
    (A) Amendments
    (B) Amendments to conform to the evidence
    (C) Relation back of amendments
    (D) Amendments where name of party unknown
    (E) Supplemental pleadings
  16. Pretrial procedure

RULE 7. Pleadings and motions

(A) Pleadings. There shall be a complaint and an answer; a reply to a counterclaim denominated as such; an answer to a cross-claim, if the answer contains a cross-claim; a third-party complaint, if a person who was not an original party is summoned under the provisions of Rule 14; and a third-party answer, if a third-party complaint is served. No other pleading shall be allowed, except that the court may order a reply to an answer or a third-party answer.

(B) Motions.

(1) An application to the court for an order shall be by motion which, unless made during a hearing or a trial, shall be made in writing. A motion, whether written or oral, shall state with particularity the grounds therefor, and shall set forth the relief or order sought. The requirement of a writing is fulfilled if the motion is stated in a written notice of the hearing of the motion.

(2) To expedite its business, the court may make provision by rule or order for the submission and determination of motions without oral hearing upon brief written statements of reasons in support and opposition.

(3) The rules applicable to captions, signing, and other matters of form of pleading apply to all motions and other papers provided for by these rules.

(4) All motions shall be signed in accordance with Rule 11.

(C) Demurrers abolished. Demurrers shall not be used.

(Amended, eff 7-1-84)

RULE 8. General rules of pleading

(A) Claims for relief. A pleading that sets forth a claim for relief, whether an original claim, counterclaim, cross-claim, or third-party claim, shall contain (1) a short and plain statement of the claim showing that the party is entitled to relief, and (2) a demand for judgment for the relief to which the party claims to be entitled. If the party seeks more than twenty-five thousand dollars, the party shall so state in the pleading but shall not specify in the demand for judgment the amount of recovery sought, unless the claim is based upon an instrument required to be attached pursuant to Civ. R. 10. At any time after the pleading is filed and served, any party from whom monetary recovery is sought may request in writing that the party seeking recovery provide the requesting party a written statement of the amount of recovery sought. Upon motion, the court shall require the party to respond to the request. Relief in the alternative or of several different types may be demanded.

(B) Defenses; form of denials. A party shall state in short and plain terms the party's defenses to each claim asserted and shall admit or deny the averments upon which the adverse party relies. If the party is without knowledge or information sufficient to form a belief as to the truth of an averment, the party shall so state and this has the effect of a denial. Denials shall fairly meet the substance of the averments denied. When a pleader intends in good faith to deny only a part or a qualification of an averment, the pleader shall specify so much of it as is true and material and shall deny the remainder. Unless the pleader intends in good faith to controvert all the averments of the preceding pleading, the pleader may make the denials as specific denials or designated averments or paragraphs, or the pleader may generally deny all the averments except the designated averments or paragraphs as the pleader expressly admits; but, when the pleader does intend to controvert all its averments, including averments of the grounds upon which the court's jurisdiction depends, the pleader may do so by general denial subject to the obligations set forth in Civ. R. 11.

(C) Affirmative defenses. In pleading to a preceding pleading, a party shall set forth affirmatively accord and satisfaction, arbitration and award, assumption of risk, contributory negligence, discharge in bankruptcy, duress, estoppel, failure of consideration, want of consideration for a negotiable instrument, fraud, illegality, injury by fellow servant, laches, license, payment, release, res judicata, statute of frauds, statute of limitations, waiver, and any other matter constituting an avoidance or affirmative defense. When a party has mistakenly designated a defense as a counterclaim or a counterclaim as a defense, the court, if justice so requires, shall treat the pleading as if there had been a proper designation.

(D) Effect of failure to deny. Averments in a pleading to which a responsive pleading is required, other than those as to the amount of damage, are admitted when not denied in the responsive pleading. Averments in a pleading to which no responsive pleading is required or permitted shall be taken as denied or avoided.

(E) Pleading to be concise and direct; consistency.

(1) Each averment of a pleading shall be simple, concise, and direct. No technical forms of pleading or motions are required.

(2) A party may set forth two or more statements of a claim or defense alternatively or hypothetically, either in one count or defense or in separate counts or defenses. When two or more statements are made in the alternative and one of them if made independently would be sufficient, the pleading is not made insufficient by the insufficiency of one or more of the alternative statements. A party may also state as many separate claims or defenses as he has regardless of consistency and whether based on legal or equitable grounds. All statements shall be made subject to the obligations set forth in Rule 11.

(F) Construction of pleadings. All pleadings shall be so construed as to do substantial justice.

(G) Pleadings shall not be read or submitted. Pleadings shall not be read or submitted to the jury, except insofar as a pleading or portion thereof is used in evidence.

(H) Disclosure of minority or incompetency. Every pleading or motion made by or on behalf of a minor or an incompetent shall set forth such fact unless the fact of minority or incompetency has been disclosed in a prior pleading or motion in the same action or proceeding.

(Amended, eff 7-1-94)

RULE 9. Pleading special matters

(A) Capacity. It is not necessary to aver the capacity of a party to sue or be sued or the authority of a party to sue or be sued in a representative capacity or the legal existence of an organized association of persons that is made a party. When a party desires to raise an issue as to the legal existence of any party or the capacity of any party to sue or be sued or the authority of a party to sue or be sued in a representative capacity, he shall do so by specific negative averment, which shall include such supporting particulars as are peculiarly within the pleader's knowledge.

(B) Fraud, mistake, condition of the mind. In all averments of fraud or mistake, the circumstances constituting fraud or mistake shall be stated with particularity. Malice, intent, knowledge, and other condition of mind of a person may be averred generally.

(C) Conditions precedent. In pleading the performance or occurrence of conditions precedent, it is sufficient to aver generally that all conditions precedent have been performed or have occurred. A denial of performance or occurrence shall be made specifically and with particularity.

(D) Official document or act. In pleading an official document or official act it is sufficient to aver that the document was issued or the act done in compliance with law.

(E) Judgment. In pleading a judgment or decision of a court of this state or a foreign court, judicial or quasi-judicial tribunal, or of a board or officer, it is sufficient to aver the judgment or decision without setting forth matter showing jurisdiction to render it.

(F) Time and place. For the purpose of testing the sufficiency of a pleading, averments of time and place are material and shall be considered like all other averments of material matter.

(G) Special damage. When items of special damage are claimed, they shall be specifically stated.

RULE 10. Form of pleadings

(A) Caption; names of parties. Every pleading shall contain a caption setting forth the name of the court, the title of the action, the case number, and a designation as in Rule 7(A). In the complaint the title of the action shall include the names and addresses of all the parties, but in other pleadings it is sufficient to state the name of the first party on each side with an appropriate indication of other parties.

(B) Paragraphs; separate statements. All averments of claim or defense shall be made in numbered paragraphs, the contents of each of which shall be limited as far as practicable to a statement of a single set of circumstances; and a paragraph may be referred to by number in all succeeding pleadings. Each claim founded upon a separate transaction or occurrence and each defense other than denials shall be stated in a separate count or defense whenever a separation facilitates the clear presentation of the matters set forth.

(C) Adoption by reference; exhibits. Statements in a pleading may be adopted by reference in a different part of the same pleading or in another pleading or in any motion. A copy of any written instrument attached to a pleading is a part thereof for all purposes.

(D) Copy must be attached. When any claim or defense is founded on an account or other written instrument, a copy thereof must be attached to the pleading. If not so attached, the reason for the omission must be stated in the pleading.

(E) Size of paper filed. All pleading, motions, briefs, and other papers filed with the clerk, including those filed by electronic means, shall be on paper not exceeding $8\frac{1}{2}$ x 11 inches in size and without backing or cover.

(Amended, eff 7-1-85; 7-1-91)

RULE 11. Signing of pleadings, motions, or other documents

Every pleading, motion, or other document of a party represented by an attorney shall be signed by at least one attorney of record in the attorney's individual name, whose address, attorney registration number, telephone number, telefax number, if any, and business e-mail address, if any, shall be stated. A party who is not represented by an attorney shall sign the pleading, motion, or other document and state the party's address. Except when otherwise specifically provided by these rules, pleadings need not be verified or accompanied by affidavit. The signature of an attorney or *pro se* party constitutes a certificate by the attorney or party that the attorney or party has read the document; that to the best of the attorney's or party's knowledge, information, and belief there is good ground to support it; and that it is not interposed for delay. If a document is not signed or is signed with intent to defeat the purpose of this rule, it may be stricken as sham and false and the action may proceed as though the document had not been served. For a willful violation of this rule, an attorney or *pro se* party, upon motion of a party or upon the court's own motion, may be subjected to appropriate action, including an award to the opposing party of expenses and reasonable attorney fees incurred in bringing any motion under this rule. Similar action may be taken if scandalous or indecent matter is inserted.

(Amended, eff 7-1-94; 7-1-95; 7-1-01)

RULE 12. Defenses and objections—when and how presented—by pleading or motion—motion for judgment on the pleadings

(A) When answer presented.

(1) Generally. The defendant shall serve his answer within twenty-eight days after service of the summons and complaint upon him; if service of notice has been made by publication, he shall serve his answer within twenty-eight days after the completion of service by publication.

(2) Other responses and motions. A party served with a pleading stating a cross-claim against him shall serve an answer thereto within twenty-eight days after the service upon him. The plaintiff shall serve his reply to a counterclaim in the answer within twenty-eight days after service of the answer or, if a reply is ordered by the court, within twenty-eight days after service of the order, unless the order otherwise directs. The service of a motion permitted under this rule alters these periods of time as follows, unless a different time is fixed by order of the court: (a) if the court denies the motion, a responsive pleading, delayed because of service of the motion, shall be served within fourteen days after notice of the court's action; (b) if the court grants the motion, a responsive pleading, delayed because of service of the motion, shall be served within fourteen days after service of the pleading which complies with the court's order.

(B) How presented. Every defense, in law or fact, to a claim for relief in any pleading, whether a claim, counterclaim, cross-claim, or third-party claim, shall be asserted in the responsive pleading thereto if one is required, except that the following defenses may at the option of the pleader be made by motion: (1) lack of jurisdiction over the subject matter, (2) lack of jurisdiction over the person, (3) improper venue, (4) insufficiency of process, (5) insufficiency of service of process, (6) failure to state a claim upon which relief can be granted, (7) failure to join a party under Rule 19 or Rule 19.1. A motion making any of these defenses shall be made before pleading if a further pleading is permitted. No defense or objection is waived by being joined with one or more other defenses or objections in a responsive pleading or motion. If a pleading sets forth a claim for relief to which the adverse party is not required to serve a responsive pleading, he may assert at the trial any defense in law or fact to that claim for relief. When a motion to dismiss for failure to state a claim upon which relief can be granted presents matters outside the pleading and such matters are not excluded by the court, the motion shall be treated as a motion for summary judgment and disposed of as provided in Rule 56. Provided, however, that the court shall consider only such matters outside the pleadings as are specifically enumerated in Rule 56. All parties shall be given reasonable opportunity to present all materials made pertinent to such a motion by Rule 56.

(C) Motion for judgment on the pleadings. After the pleadings are closed but within such time as not to delay the trial, any party may move for judgment on the pleadings.

(D) Preliminary hearings. The defenses specifically enumerated (1) to (7) in subdivision (B) of this rule, whether made in a pleading or by motion, and the motion for judgment mentioned in subdivision (C) of this rule shall be heard and determined before trial on application of any party.

(E) Motion for definite statement. If a pleading to which a responsive pleading is permitted is so vague or ambiguous that a party cannot reasonably be required to frame a responsive pleading, he may move for a definite statement before interposing his responsive pleading. The motion shall point out the defects complained of and the details desired. If the motion is granted and the order of the court is not obeyed within fourteen days after notice of the order or within such other time as the court may fix, the court may strike the pleading to which the motion was directed or make such order as it deems just.

(F) Motion to strike. Upon motion made by a party before responding to a pleading, or if no responsive pleading is permitted by these rules, upon motion made by a party within twenty-eight days after the service of the pleading upon him or upon the court's own initiative at any time, the court may order stricken from any pleading any insufficient claim or defense or any redundant, immaterial, impertinent or scandalous matter.

(G) Consolidation of defenses and objections. A party who makes a motion under this rule must join with it the other motions herein provided for and then available to him. If a party makes a motion under this rule and does not include therein all defenses and objections then available to him which this rule permits to be raised by motion, he shall not thereafter assert by motion or responsive pleading, any of the defenses or objections so omitted, except as provided in subdivision (H) of this rule.

(H) Waiver of defenses and objections.

(1) A defense of lack of jurisdiction over the person, improper venue, insufficiency of process, or insufficiency of service of process is waived (a) if omitted from a motion in the circumstances described in subdivision (G), or (b) if it is neither made by motion under this rule nor included in a responsive pleading or an amendment thereof permitted by Rule 15(A) to be made as a matter of course.

(2) A defense of failure to state a claim upon which relief can be granted, a defense of failure to join a party indispensable under Rule 19, and an objection of failure to state a legal defense to a claim may be made in any pleading permitted or ordered under Rule 7(A), or by motion for judgment on the pleadings, or at the trial on the merits.

(3) Whenever it appears by suggestion of the parties or otherwise that the court lacks jurisdiction of the subject matter, the court shall dismiss the action.

(Amended, eff 7-1-83)

RULE 13. Counterclaim and cross-claim

(A) Compulsory counterclaims. A pleading shall state as a counterclaim any claim which at the time of serving the pleading the pleader has against any opposing party, if it arises out of the transaction or occurrence that is the subject matter of the opposing party's claim and does not require for its adjudication the presence of third parties of whom the court cannot acquire jurisdiction. But the pleader need not state the claim if (1) at the time the action was commenced the claim was the subject of another pending action, or (2) the opposing party brought suit upon his claim by attachment or other process by which the court did not acquire jurisdiction to render a personal judgment on that claim, and the pleader is not stating any counterclaim under this Rule 13.

(B) Permissive counterclaims. A pleading may state as a counterclaim any claim against an opposing party not arising out of the transaction or occurrence that is the subject matter of the opposing party's claim.

(C) Counterclaim exceeding opposing claim. A counterclaim may or may not diminish or defeat the recovery sought by the opposing party. It may claim relief exceeding in amount or different in kind from that sought in the pleading of the opposing party.

(D) Counterclaim against this state. These rules shall not be construed to enlarge beyond the limits now fixed by law the right to assert counterclaims or to claim credits against this state, a political subdivision or an officer in his representative capacity or agent of either.

(E) Counterclaim maturing or acquired after pleading. A claim which either matured or was acquired by the pleader after serving his pleading may, with the permission of the court, be presented as a counterclaim by supplemental pleadings.

(F) Omitted counterclaim. When a pleader fails to set up a counterclaim through oversight, inadvertence, or excusable neglect, or when justice requires, he may by leave of court set up the counterclaim by amendment.

(G) Cross-claim against co-party. A pleading may state as a cross-claim any claim by one party against a co-party arising out of the transaction or occurrence that is the subject matter either of the original action or of a counterclaim therein or relating to any property that is the subject matter of the original action. Such cross-claim may include a claim that the party against whom it is asserted is or may be liable to the cross-claimant for all or part of a claim asserted in the action against the cross-claimant.

(H) Joinder of additional parties. Persons other than those made parties to the original action may be made parties to a counterclaim or cross-claim in accordance with the provisions of Rule 19, Rule 19.1, and Rule 20. Such persons shall be served pursuant to Rule 4 through Rule 4.6

(I) Separate trials; separate judgments. If the court orders separate trials as provided in Rule 42(B), judgment on a counterclaim or cross-claim may be rendered in accordance with the terms of Rule 54(B) when the court has jurisdiction so to do, even if the claims of the opposing party have been dismissed or otherwise disposed of.

(J) Certification of proceedings. In the event that a counterclaim, cross-claim, or third-party claim exceeds the jurisdiction of the court, the court shall certify the proceedings in the case to the court of common pleas.

(Amended, eff 7-1-71)

RULE 14. Third-party practice

(A) When defendant may bring in third party. At any time after commencement of the action a defending party, as a third-party plaintiff, may cause a summons and complaint to be served upon a person not a party to the action who is or may be liable to him for all or part of the plaintiff's claim against him. The third-party plaintiff need not obtain leave to make the service if he files the third-party complaint not later than fourteen days after he serves his original answer. Otherwise he must obtain leave on motion upon notice to all parties to the action. The person served with the summons and third-party complaint, hereinafter called the third-party defendant, shall make his defenses to the third-party plaintiff's claim as provided in Rule 12 of his counterclaims against the third-party plaintiff and cross-claims against other third-party defendants as provided in Rule 13. The third-party defendant may assert against the plaintiff any defenses which the third-party plaintiff has to the plaintiff's claim. The third-party defendant may also assert any claim against the plaintiff arising out of the transaction or occurrence that is the subject matter of the plaintiff's claim against the third-party plaintiff. The plaintiff may assert any claim against the third-party defendant arising out of the transaction or occurrence that is the subject matter of the plaintiff's claim against the third-party plaintiff, and the third-party defendant thereupon shall assert his defenses as provided in Rule 12 and his counterclaims and cross-claims as provided in Rule 13. Any party may move to strike the third-party claim, or for its severance or separate trial. If the third-party defendant is an employee, agent, or servant of the third-party plaintiff, the court shall order a separate trial upon the motion of any plaintiff. A third-party defendant may proceed under this rule against any person not a party to the action who is or may be liable to him for all or part of the claim made in the action against the third-party defendant.

(B) When plaintiff may bring in third party. When a counterclaim is asserted against a plaintiff, he may cause a third party to be brought in under circumstances which under this rule would entitle a defendant to do so.

RULE 15. Amended and supplemental pleadings

(A) Amendments. A party may amend his pleading once as a matter of course at any time before a responsive pleading is served or, if the pleading is one to which no responsive pleading is permitted and the action has not been placed upon the trial calendar, he may so amend it at any time within twenty-eight days after it is served. Otherwise a party may amend his pleading only by leave of court or by written consent of the adverse party. Leave of court shall be freely given when justice so requires. A party shall plead in response to an amended pleading within the time remaining for response to the original pleading or within fourteen days after service of the amended pleading, whichever period may be the longer, unless the court otherwise orders.

(B) Amendments to conform to the evidence. When issues not raised by the pleadings are tried by express or implied consent of the parties, they shall be treated in all respects as if they had been raised in the pleadings. Such amendment of the pleadings as may be necessary to cause them to conform to the evidence and to raise these issues may be made upon motion of any party at any time, even after judgment. Failure to amend as provided herein does not affect the result of the trial of these issues. If evidence is objected to at the trial on the ground that it is not within the issues made by the pleadings, the court may allow the pleadings to be amended and shall do so freely when the presentation of the merits of the action will be subserved thereby and the objecting party fails to satisfy the court that the admission of such evidence would prejudice him in maintaining his action or defense upon the merits. The court may grant a continuance to enable the objecting party to meet such evidence.

(C) Relation back of amendments. Whenever the claim or defense asserted in the amended pleading arose out of the conduct, transaction, or occurrence set forth or attempted to be set forth in the original pleading, the amendment relates back to the date of the original pleading. An amendment changing the party against whom a claim is asserted relates back if the foregoing provision is satisfied and, within the period provided by law for commencing the action against him, the party to be brought in by amendment (1) has received such notice of the institution of the action that he will not be prejudiced in maintaining his defense on the merits, and (2) knew or should have known that, but for a mistake concerning the identity of the proper party, the action would have been brought against him.

The delivery or mailing of process to this state, a municipal corporation or other governmental agency, or the responsible officer of any of the foregoing, subject to service of process under Rule 4 through Rule 4.6, satisfies the requirements of clauses (1) and (2) of the preceding paragraph if the above entities or officers thereof would have been proper defendants upon the original pleading. Such entities or officers thereof or both may be brought into the action as defendants.

(D) Amendments where name of party unknown. When the plaintiff does not know the name of a defendant, that defendant may be designated in a pleading or proceeding by any name and description. When the name is discovered, the pleading or proceeding must be amended accordingly. The plaintiff, in such case, must aver in the complaint the fact that he could not discover the name. The summons must contain the words "name unknown," and a copy thereof must be served personally upon the defendant.

(E) Supplemental pleadings. Upon motion of a party the court may, upon reasonable notice and upon such terms as are just, permit him to serve a supplemental pleading setting forth transactions or occurrences or events which have happened since the date of the pleading sought to be supplemented. Permission may be granted even though the original pleading is defective in its statement of a claim for relief or defense. If the court deems it advisable that the adverse party plead to the supplemental pleading, it shall so order, specifying the time therefor.

RULE 16. Pretrial procedure

In any action, the court may schedule one or more conferences before trial to accomplish the following objectives:

(1) The possibility of settlement of the action;

(2) The simplification of the issues;

(3) Itemizations of expenses and special damages;

(4) The necessity of amendments to the pleadings;

(5) The exchange of reports of expert witnesses expected to be called by each party;

(6) The exchange of medical reports and hospital records;

(7) The limitation of the number of expert witnesses;

(8) The imposition of sanctions as authorized by Civ. R. 37;

(9) The possibility of obtaining:

(a) Admissions of fact;

(b) Admissions into evidence of documents and other exhibits that will avoid unnecessary proof;

(10) Other matters as may aid in the disposition of the action.

The producing by any party of medical reports or hospital records does not constitute a waiver of the privilege granted under section 2317.02 of the Revised Code.

The court may, and on the request of either party shall, make a written order that recites the action taken at the conference. The court shall enter the order and submit copies to the parties. Unless modified, the order shall control the subsequent course of the action.

The court may require that parties, or their representatives or insurers, attend a conference or otherwise participate in pretrial proceedings, in which case the court shall give reasonable advance notice to the parties of the conference or proceedings.

(Amended, eff 7-1-93)

TITLE IV
PARTIES

RULE 17. Parties plaintiff and defendant; capacity

(A) Real party in interest. Every action shall be prosecuted in the name of the real party in interest. An executor, administrator, guardian, bailee, trustee of an express trust, a party with whom or in whose name a contract has been made for the benefit of another, or a party authorized by statute may sue in his name as such representative without joining with him the party for whose benefit the action is brought. When a statute of this state so provides, an action for the use or benefit of another shall be brought in the name of the state. No action shall be dismissed on the ground that it is not prosecuted in the name of the real party in interest until a reasonable time has been allowed after objection for ratification of commencement of the action by, or joinder or substitution of, the real party in interest. Such ratification, joinder, or substitution shall have the same effect as if the action had been commenced in the name of the real party in interest.

(B) Minors or incompetent persons. Whenever a minor or incompetent person has a representative, such as a guardian or other like fiduciary, the representative may sue or defend on behalf of the minor or incompetent person. If a minor or incompetent person does not have a duly appointed representative the minor may sue by a next friend or defend by a guardian ad litem. When a minor or incompetent person is not otherwise represented in an action the court shall appoint a guardian ad litem or shall make such other order as it deems proper for the protection of such minor or incompetent person.

(Amended, eff 7-1-75; 7-1-85)

RULE 18. Joinder of claims and remedies

(A) Joinder of claims. A party asserting a claim to relief as an original claim, counterclaim, cross-claim, or third-party claim, may join, either as independent or as alternate claims, as many claims, legal or equitable, as he has against an opposing party.

(B) Joinder of remedies; fraudulent conveyances. Whenever a claim is one heretofore cognizable only after another claim has been prosecuted to a conclusion, the two claims may be joined in a single action; but the court shall grant relief in that action only in accordance with the relative substantive rights of the parties. In particular, a plaintiff may state a claim for money and a claim to have set aside a conveyance fraudulent as to him, without first having obtained a judgment establishing the claim for money.

RULE 19. Joinder of persons needed for just adjudication

(A) Persons to be joined if feasible. A person who is subject to service of process shall be joined as a party in the action if (1) in his absence complete relief cannot be accorded among those already parties, or (2) he claims an interest relating to the subject of the action and is so situated that the disposition of the action in his absence may (a) as a practical matter impair or impede his ability to protect that interest or (b) leave any of the persons already parties subject to a substantial risk of incurring double, multiple, or otherwise inconsistent obligations by reason of his claimed interest, or (3) he has an interest relating to the subject of the action as an assignor, assignee, subrogor, or subrogee. If he has not been so joined, the court shall order that he be made a party upon timely assertion of the defense of failure to join a party as provided in Rule 12(B)(7). If the defense is not timely asserted, waiver is applicable as provided in Rule 12(G) and (H). If he should join as a plaintiff but refuses to do so, he may be made a defendant, or, in a proper case, an involuntary plaintiff. In the event that such joinder causes the relief sought to exceed the jurisdiction of the court, the court shall certify the proceedings in the action to the court of common pleas.

(B) Determination by court whenever joinder not feasible. If a person as described in subdivision (A)(1), (2), or (3) hereof cannot be made a party, the court shall determine whether in equity and good conscience the action should proceed among the parties before it, or should be dismissed, the absent person being thus regarded as indispensable. The factors to be considered by the court include: first, to what extent a judgment rendered in the person's absence might be prejudicial to him or those already parties; second, the extent to which, by protective provisions in the judgment, by the shaping of relief, or other measures, the prejudice can be lessened or avoided; third, whether a judgment rendered in the person's absence will be adequate; fourth, whether the plaintiff will have an adequate remedy if the action is dismissed for nonjoinder.

(C) Pleading reasons for nonjoinder. A pleading asserting a claim for relief shall state the names, if known to the pleader, of any persons as described in subdivision (A)(1), (2), or (3) hereof who are not joined, and the reasons why they are not joined.

(D) Exception of class actions. This rule is subject to the provisions of Rule 23.

RULE 19.1 Compulsory joinder

(A) Persons to be joined. A person who is subject to service of process shall be joined as a party in the action, except as provided in division (B) of this rule, if the person has an interest in or a claim arising out of the following situations:

(1) Personal injury or property damage to the person or property of the decedent which survives the decedent's death and a claim for wrongful death to the same decedent if caused by the same wrongful act;

(2) Personal injury or property damage to a husband or wife and a claim of the spouse for loss of consortium or expenses or property damage if caused by the same wrongful act;

(3) Personal injury or property damage to a minor and a claim of the parent or guardian of the minor for loss of consortium or expenses or property damage if caused by the same wrongful act;

(4) Personal injury or property damage to an employee or agent and a claim of the employer or principal for property damage if caused by the same wrongful act.

If he has not been so joined, the court, subject to subdivision (B) hereof, shall order that he be made a party upon timely assertion of the defense of failure to join a party as provided in Rule 12(B)(7). If the defense is not timely asserted, waiver is applicable as provided in Rule 12(G) and (H). If he should join as a plaintiff but refuses to do so, he may be made a defendant, or, in a proper case, an involuntary plaintiff. In the event that such joinder causes the relief sought to exceed the jurisdiction of the court, the court shall certify the proceedings in the action to the court of common pleas.

(B) Exception to compulsory joinder. If a party to the action or a person described in subdivision (A) shows good cause why that person should not be joined, the court shall proceed without requiring joinder.

(C) Pleading reasons for nonjoinder. A pleading asserting a claim for relief shall state the names, if known to the pleader, of any persons as described in subdivision (A)(1), (2), (3), or (4) hereof who are not joined, and the reasons why they are not joined.

(D) Exception to class actions. This rule is subject to the provisions of Rule 23.

(Amended, eff 7-1-96)

RULE 20. Permissive joinder of parties

(A) Permissive joinder. All persons may join in one action as plaintiffs if they assert any right to relief jointly, severally, or in the alternative in respect of or arising out of the same transaction, occurrence, or succession or series of transactions or occurrences and if any question of law or fact common to all these persons will arise in the action. All persons may be joined in one action as defendants if there is asserted against them jointly, severally, or in the alternative, any right to relief in respect of or arising out of the same transaction, occurrence, or succession or series of transactions or occurrences and if any question of law or fact common to all defendants will arise in the action. A plaintiff or defendant need not be interested in obtaining or defending against all the relief demanded. Judgment may be given for one or more of the plaintiffs according to their respective rights to relief, and against one or more defendants according to their respective liabilities.

(B) Separate trials. The court may make such orders as will prevent a party from being prejudiced, delayed, or put to expense by the inclusion of a party against whom he asserts no claim and who asserts no claim against him, and may order separate trials or make other orders to prevent prejudice or delay.

RULE 21. Misjoinder and nonjoinder of parties

Misjoinder of parties is not ground for dismissal of an action. Parties may be dropped or added by order of the court on motion of any party or of its own initiative at any stage of the action and on such terms as are just. Any claim against a party may be severed and proceeded with separately.

RULE 22. Interpleader

Persons having claims against the plaintiff may be joined as defendants and required to interplead when their claims are such that the plaintiff is or may be exposed to double or multiple liability. It is not ground for objection to the joinder that the claims of the several claimants or the titles on which their claims depend do not have a common origin or are not identical but are adverse to and independent of one another, or that the plaintiff avers that he is not liable in whole or in part to any or all of the claimants. A defendant exposed to similar liability may obtain such interpleader by way of cross-claim or counterclaim. The provisions of this rule supplement and do not in any way limit the joinder of parties permitted in Rule 20.

In such an action in which any part of the relief sought is a judgment for a sum of money or the disposition of a sum of money or the disposition of any other thing capable of delivery, a party may deposit all or any part of such sum or thing with the court upon notice to every other party and leave of court. The court may make an order for the safekeeping, payment or disposition of such sum or thing.

RULE 23. Class actions

(A) Prerequisites to a class action. One or more members of a class may sue or be sued as representative

parties on behalf of all only if (1) the class is so numerous that joinder of all members is impracticable, (2) there are questions of law or fact common to the class, (3) the claims or defenses of the representative parties are typical of the claims or defenses of the class, and (4) the representative parties will fairly and adequately protect the interests of the class.

(B) Class actions maintainable. An action may be maintained as a class action if the prerequisites of subdivision (A) are satisfied, and in addition:

(1) the prosecution of separate actions by or against individual members of the class would create a risk of

(a) inconsistent or varying adjudications with respect to individual members of the class which would establish incompatible standards of conduct for the party opposing the class; or

(b) adjudications with respect to individual members of the class which would as a practical matter be dispositive of the interests of the other members not parties to the adjudications or substantially impair or impede their ability to protect their interests; or

(2) the party opposing the class has acted or refused to act on grounds generally applicable to the class, thereby making appropriate final injunctive relief or corresponding declaratory relief with respect to the class as a whole; or

(3) the court finds that the questions of law or fact common to the members of the class predominate over any questions affecting only individual members, and that a class action is superior to other available methods for the fair and efficient adjudication of the controversy. The matters pertinent to the findings include: (a) the interest of members of the class in individually controlling the prosecution or defense of separate actions; (b) the extent and nature of any litigation concerning the controversy already commenced by or against members of the class; (c) the desirability or undesirability of concentrating the litigation of the claims in the particular forum; (d) the difficulties likely to be encountered in the management of a class action.

(C) Determination by order whether class action to be maintained; notice; judgment; actions conducted partially as class actions.

(1) As soon as practicable after the commencement of an action brought as a class action, the court shall determine by order whether it is to be so maintained. An order under this subdivision may be conditional, and may be altered or amended before the decision on the merits.

(2) In any class action maintained under subdivision (B)(3), the court shall direct to the members of the class the best notice practicable under the circumstances, including individual notice to all members who can be identified through reasonable effort. The notice shall advise each member that (a) the court will exclude him from the class if he so requests by a specified date; (b) the judgment, whether favorable or not, will include all members who do not request exclusion; and (c) any member who does not request exclusion may, if he

desires, enter an appearance through his counsel.

(3) The judgment in an action maintained as a class action under subdivision (B)(1) or (B)(2), whether or not favorable to the class, shall include and describe those whom the court finds to be members of the class. The judgment in an action maintained as a class action under subdivision (B)(3), whether or not favorable to the class, shall include and specify or describe those to whom the notice provided in subdivision (C)(2) was directed, and who have not requested exclusion, and whom the court finds to be members of the class.

(4) When appropriate (a) an action may be brought or maintained as a class action with respect to particular issues, or (b) a class may be divided into subclasses and each subclass treated as a class, and the provisions of this rule shall then be construed and applied accordingly.

(D) Orders in conduct of actions. In the conduct of actions to which this rule applies, the court may make appropriate orders: (1) determining the course of proceedings or prescribing measure to prevent undue repetition or complication in the presentation of evidence or argument; (2) requiring, for the protection of the members of the class or otherwise for the fair conduct of the action, that notice be given in such manner as the court may direct to some or all of the members of any step in the action, or of the proposed extent of the judgment, or of the opportunity of members to signify whether they consider the representation fair and adequate, to intervene and present claims or defenses, or otherwise to come into the action; (3) imposing conditions on the representative parties or on intervenors; (4) requiring that the pleadings be amended to eliminate therefrom allegations as to representation of absent persons, and that the action proceed accordingly; (5) dealing with similar procedural matters. The orders may combine with an order under Rule 16, and may be altered or amended as may be desirable from time to time.

(E) Dismissal or compromise. A class action shall not be dismissed or compromised without the approval of the court, and notice of the proposed dismissal or compromise shall be given to all members of the class in such manner as the court directs.

(F) Aggregation of claims. The claims of the class shall be aggregated in determining the jurisdiction of the court.

RULE 23.1 Derivative actions by shareholders

In a derivative action brought by one or more legal or equitable owners of shares to enforce a right of a corporation, the corporation having failed to enforce a right which may properly be asserted by it, the complaint shall be verified and shall allege that the plaintiff was a shareholder at the time of the transaction of which he complains or that his share thereafter devolved on him by operation of law. The complaint shall also allege with particularity the efforts, if any, made by the plaintiff

to obtain the action he desires from the directors and, if necessary, from the shareholders and the reasons for his failure to obtain the action or for not making the effort. The derivative action may not be maintained if it appears that the plaintiff does not fairly and adequately represent the interests of the shareholders similarly situated in enforcing the right of the corporation. The action shall not be dismissed or compromised without the approval of the court, and notice of the proposed dismissal or compromise shall be given to shareholders in such manner as the court directs.

RULE 24. Intervention

(A) Intervention of right. Upon timely application anyone shall be permitted to intervene in an action: (1) when a statute of this state confers an unconditional right to intervene; or (2) when the applicant claims an interest relating to the property or transaction that is the subject of the action and the applicant is so situated that the disposition of the action may as a practical matter impair or impede the applicant's ability to protect that interest, unless the applicant's interest is adequately represented by existing parties.

(B) Permissive intervention. Upon timely application anyone may be permitted to intervene in an action: (1) when a statute of this state confers a conditional right to intervene; or (2) when an applicant's claim or defense and the main action have a question of law or fact in common. When a party to an action relies for ground of claim or defense upon any statute or executive order administered by a federal or state governmental officer or agency or upon any regulation, order, requirement or agreement issued or made pursuant to the statute or executive order, the officer or agency upon timely application may be permitted to intervene in the action. In exercising its discretion the court shall consider whether the intervention will unduly delay or prejudice the adjudication of the rights of the original parties.

(C) Procedure. A person desiring to intervene shall serve a motion to intervene upon the parties as provided in Civ.R. 5. The motion and any supporting memorandum shall state the grounds for intervention and shall be accompanied by a pleading, as defined in Civ.R. 7(A), setting forth the claim or defense for which intervention is sought. The same procedure shall be followed when a statute of this state gives a right to intervene.

(Amended, eff 7-1-99)

RULE 25. Substitution of parties
(A) Death.
(1) If a party dies and the claim is not thereby extinguished, the court shall, upon motion, order substitution of the proper parties. The motion for substitution may be made by any party or by the successors or representatives of the deceased party and, together with the notice of hearing, shall be served on the parties as provided in

Rule 5 and upon persons not parties in the manner provided in Rule 4 through Rule 4.6 for the service of summons. Unless the motion for substitution is made not later than ninety days after the death is suggested upon the record by service of a statement of the fact of the death as provided herein for the service of the motion, the action shall be dismissed as to the deceased party.

(2) In the event of the death of one or more of the plaintiffs or of one or more of the defendants in an action in which the right sought to be enforced survives only to the surviving plaintiffs or only against the surviving defendants, the action does not abate. The death shall be suggested upon the record and the action shall proceed in favor of or against the surviving parties.

(B) Incompetency. If a party is adjudged incompetent, the court upon motion served as provided in subdivision (A) of this rule shall allow the action to be continued by or against his representative.

(C) Transfer of interest. In case of any transfer of interest, the action may be continued by or against the original party, unless the court upon motion directs the person to whom the interest is transferred to be substituted in the action or joined with the original party. Service of the motion shall be made as provided in subdivision (A) of this rule.

(D) Public officers; death or separation from office.

(1) When a public officer is a party to an action in his official capacity and during its pendency dies, resigns, or otherwise ceases to hold office, the action does not abate and his successor is automatically substituted as a party. Proceedings following the substitution shall be in the name of the substituted party, but any misnomer not affecting the substantial rights of the parties shall be disregarded. An order of substitution may be entered at any time, but the omission to enter such an order shall not affect the substitution.

(2) When a public officer sues or is sued in his official capacity, he may be described as a party by his official title rather than by name. The court however may require the addition of his name.

(E) Suggestion of death or incompetency. Upon the death or incompetency of a party it shall be the duty of the attorney of record for that party to suggest such fact upon the record within fourteen days after he acquires actual knowledge of the death or incompetency of that party. The suggestion of death or incompetency shall be served on all other parties as provided in Rule 5.

TITLE V
DISCOVERY

RULE 26. General provisions governing discovery

(A) Policy; discovery methods. It is the policy of these rules (1) to preserve the right of attorneys to prepare cases for trial with that degree of privacy necessary to encourage them to prepare their cases thoroughly and to investigate not only the favorable but the unfavorable aspects of such cases and (2) to prevent an attorney from taking undue advantage of his adversary's industry or efforts.

Parties may obtain discovery by one or more of the following methods: deposition upon oral examination or written questions; written interrogatories; production of documents or things or permission to enter upon land or other property, for inspection and other purposes; physical and mental examinations; and requests for admission. Unless the court orders otherwise, the frequency of use of these methods is not limited.

(B) Scope of discovery. Unless otherwise ordered by the court in accordance with these rules, the scope of discovery is as follows:

(1) In general. Parties may obtain discovery regarding any matter, not privileged, which is relevant to the subject matter involved in the pending action, whether it relates to the claim or defense of the party seeking discovery or to the claim or defense of any other party, including the existence, description, nature, custody, condition and location of any books, documents, or other tangible things and the identity and location of persons having knowledge of any discoverable matter. It is not ground for objection that the information sought will be inadmissible at the trial if the information sought appears reasonably calculated to lead to the discovery of admissible evidence.

(2) Insurance agreements. A party may obtain discovery of the existence and contents of any insurance agreement under which any person carrying on an insurance business may be liable to satisfy part or all of a judgment which may be entered in the action or to indemnify or reimburse for payments made to satisfy the judgment. Information concerning the insurance agreement is not by reason of disclosure subject to comment or admissible in evidence at trial.

(3) Trial preparation: materials. Subject to the provisions of subdivision (B)(4) of this rule, a party may obtain discovery of documents and tangible things prepared in anticipation of litigation or for trial by or for another party or by or for that other party's representative (including his attorney, consultant, surety, indemnitor, insurer, or agent) only upon a showing of good cause therefor. A statement concerning the action or its subject matter previously given by the party seeking the statement may be obtained without showing good cause. A statement of a party is (a) written statement signed or otherwise adopted or approved by the party, or (b) a stenographic, mechanical, electrical, or other recording, or a transcription thereof, which is a substantially verbatim recital of an oral statement which was made by the party and contemporaneously recorded.

(4) Trial preparation: experts.
(a) Subject to the provisions of subdivision (B)(4)(b) of this rule and Rule 35(B), a party may discover facts known or opinions held by an expert retained or specially employed by another party in anticipation of litigation or preparation for trial only upon a showing that the party seeking discovery is unable without undue hardship to obtain facts and opinions on the same subject by other means or upon a showing of other exceptional circumstances indicating that denial of discovery would cause manifest injustice.

(b) As an alternative or in addition to obtaining discovery under subdivision (B)(4)(a) of this rule, a party by means of interrogatories may require any other party (i) to identify each person whom the other party expects to call as an expert witness at trial, and (ii) to state the subject matter on which the expert is expected to testify. Thereafter, any party may discover from the expert or the other party facts known or opinions held by the expert which are relevant to the stated subject matter. Discovery of the expert's opinions and the grounds therefor is restricted to those previously given to the other party or those to be given on direct examination at trial.

(c) The court may require that the party seeking discovery under subdivision (B)(4)(b) of this rule pay the expert a reasonable fee for time spent in responding to discovery, and, with respect to discovery permitted under subdivision (B)(4)(a) of this rule, may require a party to pay another party a fair portion of the fees and expenses incurred by the latter party in obtaining facts and opinions from the expert.

(C) Protective orders. Upon motion by any party or by the person from whom discovery is sought, and for good cause shown, the court in which the action is pending may make any order that justice requires to protect a party or person from annoyance, embarrassment, oppression, or undue burden or expense, including one or more of the following: (1) that the discovery not be had; (2) that the discovery may be had only on specified terms and conditions, including a designation of the time or place; (3) that the discovery may be had only by a method of discovery other than that selected by the party seeking discovery; (4) that certain matters not be inquired into or that the scope of the discovery be limited to certain matters; (5) that discovery be conducted with no one present except persons designated by the court; (6) that a deposition after being sealed be opened only by order of the court; (7) that a trade secret or other confidential research, development, or commercial information not be disclosed or be disclosed only in a designated way; (8) that the parties simultaneously file specified documents or information enclosed in sealed envelopes to be opened as directed by the court.

If the motion for a protective order is denied in whole or in part, the court, on terms and conditions as are just, may order that any party or person provide or permit discovery. The provisions of Civ. R. 37(A)(4) apply to the award of expenses incurred in relation to the motion.

Before any person moves for a protective order under this rule, that person shall make a reasonable effort to resolve the matter through discussion with the attorney or unrepresented party seeking discovery. A motion for a protective order shall be accompanied by a statement reciting the effort made to resolve the matter in accordance with this paragraph.

(D) Sequence and timing of discovery. Unless the court upon motion, for the convenience of parties and witnesses and in the interests of justice, orders otherwise, methods of discovery may be used in any sequence and the fact that a party is conducting discovery, whether by deposition or otherwise, shall not operate to delay any other party's discovery.

(E) Supplementation of responses. A party who has responded to a request for discovery with a response that was complete when made is under no duty to supplement his response to include information thereafter acquired, except as follows:

(1) A party is under a duty seasonably to supplement his response with respect to any question directly addressed to (a) the identity and location of persons having knowledge of discoverable matters, and (b) the identity of each person expected to be called as an expert witness at trial and the subject matter on which he is expected to testify.

(2) A party who knows or later learns that his response is incorrect is under a duty seasonably to correct the response.

(3) A duty to supplement responses may be imposed by order of the court, agreement of the parties, or at any time prior to trial through requests for supplementation of prior responses.

(Amended, eff 7-1-94)

RULE 27. Perpetuation of testimony—depositions before action or pending appeal

(A) Before action.

(1) Petition. A person who desires to perpetuate his own testimony or the testimony of another person regarding any matter that may be cognizable in any court may file a petition in the court of common pleas in the county of the residence of any expected adverse party. The petitioner shall verify that he believes the facts stated in the petition are true. The petition shall be entitled in the name of the petitioner and shall show:

(a) That the petitioner or his personal representatives, heirs, beneficiaries, successors, or assigns may be parties to an action or proceeding cognizable in a court but is presently unable to bring or defend it;

(b) The subject matter of the expected action or proceeding and his interest therein (if the validity or construction of any written instrument connected with the subject matter of the deposition may be called in question a copy shall be attached to the petition);

(c) The facts which he desires to establish by the proposed testimony and his reasons for desiring to perpetuate it;

(d) The names or, if the names are unknown, a description of the persons he expects will be adverse parties and their addresses so far as known;

(e) The names and addresses of the persons to be examined and the subject matter of the testimony which he expects to elicit from each.

The petition shall then ask for an order authorizing the petitioner to take the depositions of the persons to be examined named in the petition, for the purpose of perpetuating their testimony.

(2) Notice and service. The petitioner shall thereafter serve a notice upon each person named in the petition as an expected adverse party, together with a copy of the petition, stating that the petitioner will apply to the court, at a time and place named therein, for the order described in the petition. At least twenty-eight days before the date of hearing, unless the court upon application and showing of extraordinary circumstances prescribes a hearing on shorter notice, the notice shall be served either within or outside of this state by a method provided in Rule 4 through Rule 4.6 for service of summons, or in any other manner affording actual notice, as directed by order of the court. But if it appears to the court that an expected adverse party cannot be given actual notice, the court shall appoint a competent attorney to cross-examine the deponent; such attorney shall be allowed reasonable fees therefor which shall be taxed as costs. If any expected adverse party is a minor or incompetent the provisions of Rule 17(B) apply.

(3) Order and examination. If the court is satisfied that the allowance of the petition may prevent a failure or delay of justice, and that the petitioner is unable to bring or defend the contemplated action, the court shall order the testimony perpetuated, designating the deponents, the subject matter of the examination, when, where, and before whom their deposition shall be taken, and whether orally or upon written questions. The depositions may then be taken in accordance with these rules; and the court may make orders of the character provided for by Rule 34, Rule 35 and Rule 37. For the purpose of applying these rules to depositions for perpetuating testimony, each reference therein to the court in which the action is pending shall be deemed to refer to the court in which the petition for such deposition was filed.

(4) Use of deposition. Subject to the same limitations and objections as though the deponent were testifying at the trial in person, and to the provisions of Rule 26 and Rule 32(A) a deposition taken in accordance with this rule may be used as evidence in any action subsequently brought in any court, where the deposition is that of a party to the action, or where the issue is such that an interested party in the proceedings in which the deposition was taken had the right and opportunity for cross-examination with an interest and motive similar to that which the adverse party has in the action in which the deposition is offered. But, except where the deposition is that of a party to the action and is offered against the party, the deposition may not be used as evidence unless the deponent is unavailable as a witness at the trial.

(B) Pending appeal. If an appeal has been taken from a judgment of any court, a party who desires to perpetuate testimony may make a motion in the court where the action was tried, for leave to take depositions upon the same notice and service thereof as provided in (A)(2) of this rule. The motion shall show the names and addresses of the persons to be examined, the subject matter of the testimony which he expects to elicit from each, and the reasons for perpetuating their testimony. If the court is satisfied that the motion is proper to avoid a failure or delay of justice, it may make an order allowing the deposition to be taken and may make orders of the character provided for by Rule 34, Rule 35, and Rule 37. The depositions may be taken and used in the same manner and under the same conditions as are prescribed for depositions in Rule 26 and Rule 32(A).

(C) Perpetuation by actions. This rule does not limit the inherent power of a court to entertain an action to perpetuate testimony.

(D) Filing of depositions. Depositions taken under this rule shall be filed with the court in which the petition is filed or the motion is made.

(E) Costs of deposition. The party taking any deposition under this rule shall pay the costs thereof and of all proceedings hereunder, unless otherwise ordered by the court.

(F) Depositions taken in other states. A deposition taken under similar procedure of another jurisdiction is admissible in this state to the same extent as a deposition taken under this rule.

(G) Construction of rule. This rule shall be so construed as to effectuate the general purpose to make uniform the law of those states which have similar rules or statutes.

(Amended, eff 7-1-72)

RULE 28. Persons before whom depositions may be taken

(A) Depositions within state. Depositions may be taken in this state before: a person authorized to administer any oath by the laws of this state, a person appointed by the court in which the action is pending, or a person agreed upon by written stipulation of all the parties.

(B) Depositions outside state. Depositions may be taken outside this state before: a person authorized to administer oaths in the place where the deposition is taken, a person appointed by the court in which the action is pending, a person agreed upon by written stipulation of all the parties, or, in any foreign country, by any consular officer of the United States within his consular district.

(C) Disqualification for interest.
Unless the parties agree otherwise as provided in Civ. R. 29, depositions shall not be taken before a person who:
(1) is a relative or employee of or attorney for any of the parties, or
(2) is a relative or employee of an attorney for any of the parties, or
(3) is financially interested in the action.

(D) Prohibited contracts.
(1) Any blanket contract for private court reporting services, not related to a particular case or reporting incident, shall be prohibited between a private court reporter or any other person with whom a private court reporter has a principal and agency relationship, and any attorney, party to an action, party having a financial interest in an action, or any entity providing the services of a shorthand reporter.
(2) "Blanket contract" means a contract under which a court reporter, court recorder, or court reporting firm agrees to perform all court reporting or court recording services for a client for two or more cases at a rate of compensation fixed in the contract.
(3) Negotiating or bidding reasonable fees, equal to all parties, on a case-by-case basis is not prohibited.
(4) Division (D) of this rule does not apply to the courts or the administrative tribunals of this state.

(Amended, eff 7-1-01)

RULE 29. Stipulations regarding discovery procedure

Unless the court orders otherwise, the parties may by written stipulation (1) provide that depositions may be taken before any person, at any time or place, upon any notice, and in any manner and when so taken may be used like other depositions; and (2) modify the procedures provided by these rules for other methods of discovery.

RULE 30. Depositions upon oral examination

(A) When depositions may be taken. After commencement of the action, any party may take the testimony of any person, including a party, by deposition upon oral examination. The attendance of a witness deponent may be compelled by the use of subpoena as provided by Civ.R. 45. The attendance of a party deponent may be compelled by the use of notice of examination as provided by division (B) of this rule. The deposition of a person confined in prison may be taken only by leave of court on such terms as the court prescribes.

(B) Notice of examination; general requirements; nonstenographic recording; production of documents and things; deposition of organization; deposition by telephone.

(1) A party desiring to take the deposition of any person upon oral examination shall give reasonable notice in writing to every other party to the action. The notice shall state the time and place for taking the deposition and the name and address of each person to be examined, if known, and, if the name is not known, a general description sufficient to identify the person or the particular class or group to which the person belongs. If a subpoena duces tecum is to be served on the person to be examined, a designation of the materials to be produced shall be attached to or included in the notice.

(2) If any party shows that when the party was served with notice the party was unable, through the exercise of diligence, to obtain counsel to represent the party at the taking of the deposition, the deposition may not be used against the party.

(3) If a party taking a deposition wishes to have the testimony recorded by other than stenographic means, the notice shall specify the manner of recording, preserving, and filing the deposition. The court may require stenographic taking or make any other order to ensure that the recorded testimony will be accurate and trustworthy.

(4) The notice to a party deponent may be accompanied by a request made in compliance with Civ.R. 34 for the production of documents and tangible things at the taking of the deposition.

(5) A party, in the party's notice, may name as the deponent a public or private corporation, a partnership, or an association and designate with reasonable particularity the matters on which examination is requested. The organization so named shall choose one or more of its proper employees, officers, agents, or other persons duly authorized to testify on its behalf. The persons so designated shall testify as to matters known or available to the organization. Division (B)(5) does not preclude taking a deposition by any other procedure authorized in these rules.

(6) The parties may stipulate in writing or the court may upon motion order that a deposition be taken by telephone. For purposes of this rule, Civ. R. 28, and Civ. R. 45(C), a deposition taken by telephone is taken in the county and at the place where the deponent is to answer questions propounded to the deponent.

(C) Examination and cross-examination; record of examination; oath; objections. Examination and cross-examination of witnesses may proceed as permitted at the trial. The officer before whom the deposition is to be taken shall put the witness on oath or affirmation and personally, or by someone acting under the officer's direction and in the officer's presence, shall record the testimony of the witness. The testimony shall be taken stenographically or recorded by any other means designated in accordance with division (B)(3) of this rule. If requested by one of the parties, the testimony shall be transcribed.

All objections made at the time of the examination to the qualifications of the officer taking the deposition, or to the manner of taking it, or to the evidence presented, or to the conduct of any party, and any other objection to the proceedings, shall be noted by the officer upon the deposition. Evidence objected to shall be taken subject to the objections. In lieu of participating in the oral examination, parties may serve written questions on the party taking the deposition and require him to transmit them to the officer, who shall propound them to the witness and record the answers verbatim.

(D) Motion to terminate or limit examinations. At any time during the taking of the deposition, on motion of any party or of the deponent and upon a showing that the examination is being conducted in bad faith or in such manner as unreasonably to annoy, embarrass, or oppress the deponent or party, the court in which the action is pending may order the officer conducting the examination to cease forthwith from taking the deposition, or may limit the scope and manner of the taking of the deposition as provided in Civ. R. 26(C). If the order made terminates the examination, it shall be resumed thereafter only upon the order of the court in which the action is pending. Upon demand of the objecting party or deponent, the taking of the deposition shall be suspended for the time necessary to make a motion for an order. The provisions of Civ. R. 37 apply to the award of expenses incurred in relation to the motion.

(E) Submission to witness; changes; signing. When the testimony is fully transcribed, the deposition shall be submitted to the witness for examination and shall be read to or by the witness, unless examination and reading are waived by the witness and by the parties. Any changes in form or substance that the witness desires to make shall be entered upon the deposition by the officer with a statement of the reasons given by the witness for making them. The deposition shall then be signed by the witness, unless the parties by stipulation waive the signing or the witness is ill, cannot be found, or refuses to sign. If the deposition is not signed by the witness within seven days of its submission to the witness, or within such longer period, not exceeding twenty-eight days, to which the parties agree, the officer shall sign it and state on the record the fact of the waiver or of the illness or absence of the witness or the fact of the refusal to sign together with the reason, if any, given therefor; and the deposition may then be used as fully as though signed, unless on a motion to suppress the court holds that the reasons given for the refusal to sign require rejection of the deposition in whole or in part.

(F) Certification and filing by officer; exhibits; copies; notice of filing.

(1) Upon request of any party or order of the court, the officer shall transcribe the deposition. Provided the officer has retained an archival-quality copy of the officer's notes, the officer shall have no duty to retain paper notes of the deposition testimony beyond five years from the date of the deposition. The officer shall certify on the transcribed deposition that the witness was fully sworn or affirmed by the officer and that the transcribed deposition is a true record of the testimony given by the witness. If any of the parties request or the court orders, the officer shall seal the transcribed deposition in an envelope endorsed with the title of the action and marked "Deposition of (here insert name of witness)" and, upon payment of the officer's fees, promptly shall file it with the court in which the action is pending or send it by certified or express mail to the clerk of the court for filing.

Unless objection is made to their production for inspection during the examination of the witness, documents and things shall be marked for identification and annexed to and returned with the deposition. The materials may be inspected and copied by any party, except that the person producing the materials may substitute copies to be marked for identification, if the person affords to all parties fair opportunity to verify the copies by comparison with the originals. If the person producing the materials requests their return, the officer shall mark them, give each party an opportunity to inspect and copy them, and return them to the person producing them, and the materials may then be used in the same manner as if annexed to and returned with the deposition.

(2) Upon payment, the officer shall furnish a copy of the deposition to any party or to the deponent.

(3) The party requesting the filing of the deposition shall forthwith give notice of its filing to all other parties.

(G) Failure to attend or to serve subpoena; expenses.

(1) If the party giving the notice of the taking of a deposition fails to attend and proceed with the deposition and another party attends in person or by attorney pursuant to the notice, the court may order the party giving the notice to pay to the other party the amount of the reasonable expenses incurred by the other party and the other party's attorney in so attending, including reasonable attorney's fees.

(2) If the party giving the notice of the taking of a deposition of a witness fails to serve a subpoena upon the witness and the witness because of the failure does not attend, and another party attends in person or by attorney because the other party expects the deposition of that witness to be taken, the court may order the party giving the notice to pay to the other party the amount of the reasonable expenses incurred by the other party and the other party's attorney in so attending, including reasonable attorney's fees.

(Amended, eff 7-1-76; 7-1-85; 7-1-92; 7-1-94; 7-1-97)

RULE 31. Depositions of witnesses upon written questions

(A) Serving questions; notice. After commencement of the action, any party may take the testimony of any person, including a party, by deposition upon written questions. The attendance of witnesses may be compelled by the use of subpoena as provided by Rule 45. The deposition of a person confined in prison may be taken only by leave of court on such terms as the court prescribes.

A party desiring to take a deposition upon written questions shall serve them upon every other party with a notice stating (1) the name and address of the person who is to answer them, if known, and if the name is not known, a general description sufficient to identify him or the particular class or group to which he belongs, and (2) the name and descriptive title and address of the officer before whom the deposition is to be taken. A deposition upon written questions may be taken of a public or private corporation or a partnership or association in accordance with the provisions of Rule 30(B)(5).

Within twenty-one days after the notice and written questions are served, a party may serve cross questions upon all other parties. Within fourteen days after being served with cross questions, a party may serve redirect questions upon all other parties. Within fourteen days after being served with redirect questions, a party may serve recross questions upon all other parties. The court may for cause shown enlarge or shorten the time.

(B) Officer to take responses and prepare record. A copy of the notice and copies of all questions served shall be delivered by the party taking the deposition to the officer designated in the notice, who shall proceed promptly, in the manner provided by Rule 30(C), (E), and (F), to take the testimony of the witness in response to the questions and to prepare, certify, and file or mail the deposition, attaching thereto the copy of the notice and the questions received by him.

(C) Notice of filing. The party requesting the filing of the deposition shall forthwith give notice of its filing to all other parties.

RULE 32. Use of depositions in court proceedings

(A) Use of depositions. Every deposition intended to be presented as evidence must be filed at least one day before the day of trial or hearing unless for good cause shown the court permits a later filing.

At the trial or upon the hearing of a motion or an interlocutory proceeding, any part or all of a deposition, so far as admissible under the rules of evidence applied as though the witness were then present and testifying, may be used against any party who was present or represented at the taking of the deposition or who had reasonable notice thereof, in accordance with any one of the following provisions:

(1) Any deposition may be used by any party for the purpose of contradicting or impeaching the testimony of deponent as a witness.

(2) The deposition of a party or of anyone who at the time of taking the deposition was an officer, director, or managing agent, or a person designated under Rule 30(B)(5) or Rule 31(A) to testify on behalf of a public or private corporation, partnership or association which is a party may be used by an adverse party for any purpose.

(3) The deposition of a witness, whether or not a party, may be used by any party for any purpose if the court finds: (a) that the witness is dead; or (b) that the witness is beyond the subpoena power of the court in which the action is pending or resides outside of the county in which the action is pending unless it appears that the absence of the witness was procured by the party offering the deposition; or (c) that the witness is unable to attend or testify because of age, sickness, infirmity, or imprisonment; or (d) that the party offering the deposition has been unable to procure the attendance of the witness by subpoena; or (e) that the witness is an attending physician or medical expert, although residing within the county in which the action is heard; or (f) that the oral examination of a witness is not required; or (g) upon application and notice, that such exceptional circumstances exist as to make it desirable, in the interest of justice and with due regard to the importance of presenting the testimony of witnesses orally in open court, to allow the deposition to be used.

(4) If only part of a deposition is offered in evidence by a party, an adverse party may require him to introduce all of it which is relevant to the part introduced, and any party may introduce any other parts.

Substitution of parties pursuant to Rule 25 does not affect the right to use depositions previously taken. When another action involving the same subject matter is or has been brought between the same parties or their representatives or successors in interest, all depositions lawfully taken in the one action may be used in the other as if originally taken therefor.

(B) Objections to admissibility. Subject to the provisions of subdivision (D)(3) of this rule, objection may be made at the trial or hearing to receiving in evidence any deposition or part thereof for any reason which would require the exclusion of the evidence if the witness were then present and testifying. Upon the motion of a party, or upon its own initiative, the court shall decide such objections before the deposition is read in evidence.

(C) Effect of taking or using depositions. A party does not make a person his own witness for any purpose by taking his deposition. The introduction in evidence of the deposition or any part thereof for any purpose other than that of contradicting or impeaching the deponent makes the deponent the witness of the party introducing the deposition, but this shall not apply to the use by an adverse party of a deposition as described in subdivision (A)(2) of this rule. The use of subdivision (A)(3)(e) of this rule does not preclude any party from calling such a witness to appear personally at the trial nor does it preclude the taking and use of any deposition otherwise provided by law. At the trial or hearing any party may rebut any relevant evidence contained in a deposition whether introduced by him or by any other party.

(D) Effect of errors and irregularities in depositions.

(1) As to notice. All errors and irregularities in the notice for taking a deposition are waived unless written objection stating the grounds therefor, is promptly served upon the party giving the notice.

(2) As to disqualification of officer. Objection to taking a deposition because of disqualification of the officer before whom it is to be taken is waived unless made before the taking of the deposition begins or as soon thereafter as the disqualification becomes known or could be discovered with reasonable diligence.

(3) As to taking of depositions.

(a) Objections to the competency of a witness or to the competency, relevancy, or materiality of testimony are not waived by failure to make them before or during the taking of the deposition, unless the ground of the objection is one which might have been obviated or removed if presented at that time.

(b) Errors and irregularities occurring at the oral examination in the manner of taking the deposition, in the form of the questions or answers, in the oath or affirmation, or in the conduct of parties and errors of any kind which might be obviated, removed, or cured if promptly presented, are waived unless reasonable objection thereto is made at the taking of the deposition.

(c) Objections to the form of written questions submitted under Rule 31 are waived unless served in writing upon the party propounding them within the time allowed for serving the succeeding cross or other questions and within seven days after service of the last questions authorized.

(4) As to completion and return of deposition. Errors and irregularities in the manner in which the testimony is transcribed or the deposition is prepared, signed, certified, sealed, indorsed, transmitted, filed, or otherwise dealt with by the officer under Rule 30 and Rule 31 are waived unless a motion to suppress the deposition or some part thereof is made with reasonable promptness after such defect is, or with due diligence might have been, ascertained.

(Amended, eff 7-1-72)

RULE 33. Interrogatories to parties

(A) Availability; procedures for use. Any party, without leave of court, may serve upon any other party up to forty written interrogatories to be answered by the party served. A party shall not propound more than forty interrogatories to any other party without leave of court. Upon motion, and for good cause shown, the court may extend the number of interrogatories that a party may serve upon another party. For purposes of this rule, any subpart propounded under an interrogatory shall be considered a separate interrogatory.

If the party served is a public or private corporation or a partnership or association, the organization shall choose one or more of its proper employees, officers, or agents to answer the interrogatories, and the employee, officer, or agent shall furnish information as is known or available to the organization.

Interrogatories, without leave of court, may be served upon the plaintiff after commencement of the action and upon any other party with or after service of the summons and complaint upon the party.

Each interrogatory shall be answered separately and fully in writing under oath, unless it is objected to, in which event the reasons for objection shall be stated in lieu of an answer. When the number of interrogatories exceeds forty without leave of court, the party upon whom the interrogatories have been served need only answer or object to the first forty interrogatories. The answers are to be signed by the person making them, and the objections signed by the attorney making them. The party upon whom the interrogatories have been served shall serve a copy of the answers and objections within a period designated by the party submitting the interrogatories, not less than twenty-eight days after the service of the interrogatories or within such shorter or longer time as the court may allow. The party submitting the interrogatories may move for an order under Civ.R. 37 with respect to any objection to or other failure to answer an interrogatory.

(B) Scope and use at trial. Interrogatories may relate to any matters that can be inquired into under Civ.R. 26(B), and the answers may be used to the extent permitted by the rules of evidence.

The party calling for such examination shall not thereby be concluded but may rebut it by evidence.

An interrogatory otherwise proper is not objectionable merely because an answer to the interrogatory involves an opinion, contention, or legal conclusion, but the court may order that such an interrogatory be answered at a later time, or after designated discovery has been completed, or at a pretrial conference.

(C) Option to produce business records. Where the answer to an interrogatory may be derived or ascertained from the business records of the party upon whom the interrogatory has been served or from an examination, audit, or inspection of the business records, or from a compilation, abstract, or summary based on the business records, and the burden of deriving or ascertaining the answer is substantially the same for the party serving the interrogatory as for the party served, it is a sufficient answer to the interrogatory to specify the records from which the answer may be derived or ascertained and to afford to the party serving the interrogatory reasonable opportunity to examine, audit, or inspect the records and to make copies of the records or compilations, abstracts, or summaries from the records.

(D) Form of answers and objections to interrogatories. The party submitting interrogatories shall arrange them so that there is sufficient space after each interrogatory in which to type the answer or objections to that interrogatory. The minimum vertical space between interrogatories shall be one inch.

(Amended, eff 7-1-72; 7-1-89; 7-1-99)

RULE 34. Production of documents and things for inspection, copying, testing and entry upon land for inspection and other purposes

(A) Scope. Subject to the scope of discovery provisions of Civ.R. 26(B), any party may serve on any other party a request to produce and permit the party making the request, or someone acting on the requesting party's behalf (1) to inspect and copy, any designated documents (including writings, drawings, graphs, charts, photographs, phonorecords, and other data compilations from which intelligence can be perceived, with or without the use of detection devices) that are in the possession, custody, or control of the party upon whom the request is served; (2) to inspect and copy, test, or sample any tangible things that are in the possession, custody, or control of the party upon whom the request is served; (3) to enter upon designated land or other property in the possession or control of the party upon whom the request is served for the purpose of inspection and measuring, surveying, photographing, testing, or sampling the property or any designated object or operation on the property.

(B) Procedure. Without leave of court, the request may be served upon the plaintiff after commencement of the action and upon any other party with or after service of the summons and complaint upon that party. The request shall set forth the items to be inspected either by individual item or by category and describe each item and category with reasonable particularity. The request shall specify a reasonable time, place, and manner of making the inspection and performing the related acts.

The party upon whom the request is served shall

serve a written response within a period designated in the request that is not less than twenty-eight days after the service of the request or within a shorter or longer time as the court may allow. With respect to each item or category, the response shall state that inspection and related activities will be permitted as requested, unless it is objected to, in which event the reasons for objection shall be stated. If objection is made to part of an item or category, the part shall be specified. The party submitting the request may move for an order under Civ. R. 37 with respect to any objection to or other failure to respond to the request or any part of the request, or any failure to permit inspection as requested.

A party who produces documents for inspection shall, at its option, produce them as they are kept in the usual course of business or organized and labeled to correspond with the categories in the request.

(C) Persons not parties. Subject to the scope of discovery provisions of Civ.R. 26(B) and 45(F), a person not a party to the action may be compelled to produce documents or tangible things or to submit to an inspection as provided in Civ.R. 45. A party seeking production under this division shall give reasonable notice in writing to every other party to the action. The notice shall state the time and place for production and the name and address of each person subpoenaed. A designation of the materials to be produced shall be attached to or included in the notice.

(D) Prior to filing of action.

(1) Subject to the scope of discovery provisions of Civ.R. 26(B) and 45(F), a person who claims to have a potential cause of action may file a petition to obtain discovery as provided in this rule. Prior to filing a petition for discovery, the person seeking discovery shall make reasonable efforts to obtain voluntarily the information from the person from whom the discovery is sought. The petition shall be captioned in the name of the person seeking discovery and be filed in the court of common pleas in the county in which the person from whom the discovery is sought resides, the person's principal place of business is located, or the potential action may be filed. The petition shall include all of the following:

(a) A statement of the subject matter of the petitioner's potential cause of action and the petitioner's interest in the potential cause of action;

(b) A statement of the efforts made by the petitioner to obtain voluntarily the information from the person from whom the discovery is sought;

(c) A statement or description of the information sought to be discovered with reasonable particularity;

(d) The names and addresses, if known, of any person the petitioner expects will be an adverse party in the potential action;

(e) A request that the court issue an order authorizing the petitioner to obtain the discovery.

(2) The petition shall be served upon the person from whom discovery is sought and, if known, any person the petitioner expects will be an adverse party in the

potential action, by one of the methods provided in these rules for service of summons.

(3) The court shall issue an order authorizing the petitioner to obtain the requested discovery if the court finds all of the following:

(a) The discovery is necessary to ascertain the identity of a potential adverse party;

(b) The petitioner is otherwise unable to bring the contemplated action;

(c) The petitioner made reasonable efforts to obtain voluntarily the information from the person from whom the discovery is sought.

(Amended, eff 7-1-93; 7-1-94)

RULE 35. Physical and mental examination of persons

(A) Order for examination. When the mental or physical condition (including the blood group) of a party, or of a person in the custody or under the legal control of a party, is in controversy, the court in which the action is pending may order the party to submit himself to a physical or mental examination or to produce for such examination the person in the party's custody or legal control. The order may be made only on motion for good cause shown and upon notice to the person to be examined and to all parties and shall specify the time, place, manner, conditions, and scope of the examination and the person or persons by whom it is to be made.

(B) Examiner's report.

(1) If requested by the party against whom an order is made under Rule 35(A) or the person examined, the party causing the examination to be made shall deliver to such party or person a copy of the detailed written report submitted by the examiner to the party causing the examination to be made. The report shall set out the examiner's findings, including results of all tests made, diagnoses and conclusions, together with like reports of all earlier examinations of the same condition. After delivery, the party causing the examination shall be entitled upon request to receive from the party against whom the order is made a like report of any examination, previously or thereafter made, of the same condition, unless, in the case of a report of examination of a person not a party, the party shows that he is unable to obtain it. The court on motion may make an order against a party to require delivery of a report on such terms as are just. If an examiner fails or refuses to make a report, the court on motion may order, at the expense of the party causing the examination, the taking of the deposition of the examiner if his testimony is to be offered at trial.

(2) By requesting and obtaining a report of the examination so ordered or by taking the deposition of the examiner, the party examined waives any privilege he may have in that action or any other involving the same controversy, regarding the testimony of every other per-

son who has examined or may thereafter examine him in respect of the same mental or physical condition.

(3) This subdivision 35(B), applies to examinations made by agreement of the parties, unless the agreement expressly provides otherwise.

RULE 36. Requests for admission

(A) **Request for admission.** A party may serve upon any other party a written request for the admission, for purposes of the pending action only, of the truth of any matters within the scope of Rule 26(B) set forth in the request that relate to statements or opinions of fact or of the application of law to fact, including the genuineness of any documents described in the request. Copies of documents shall be served with the request unless they have been or are otherwise furnished or made available for inspection and copying. The request may, without leave of court, be served upon the plaintiff after commencement of the action and upon any other party with or after service of the summons and complaint upon that party.

Each matter of which an admission is requested shall be separately set forth. The matter is admitted unless, within a period designated in the request, not less than twenty-eight days after service thereof or within such shorter or longer time as the court may allow, the party to whom the request is directed serves upon the party requesting the admission a written answer or objection addressed to the matter, signed by the party or by his attorney. If objection is made, the reasons therefor shall be stated. The answer shall specifically deny the matter or set forth in detail the reasons why the answering party cannot truthfully admit or deny the matter. A denial shall fairly meet the substance of the requested admission, and when good faith requires that a party qualify his answer or deny only a part of the matter of which an admission is requested, he shall specify so much of it as is true and qualify or deny the remainder. An answering party may not give lack of information or knowledge as a reason for failure to admit or deny unless he states that he has made reasonable inquiry and that the information known or readily obtainable by him is insufficient to enable him to admit or deny. A party who considers that a matter of which an admission has been requested presents a genuine issue for trial may not, on that ground alone, object to the request; he may, subject to the provisions of Rule 37(C), deny the matter or set forth reasons why he cannot admit or deny it.

The party who has requested the admission may move for an order with respect to the answers or objections. Unless the court determines that an objection is justified, it shall order that an answer be served. If the court determines that an answer does not comply with the requirements of this rule, it may order either that the matter is admitted or that an amended answer be served. The court may, in lieu of these orders, determine that final disposition of the request be made at a pretrial conference or at a designated time prior to trial. The provisions of Rule 37(A)(4) apply to the award of expenses incurred in relation to the motion.

(B) **Effect of admission.** Any matter admitted under this rule is conclusively established unless the court on motion permits withdrawal or amendment of the admission. Subject to the provisions of Rule 16 governing modification of a pretrial order, the court may permit withdrawal or amendment when the presentation of the merits of the action will be subserved thereby and the party who obtained the admission fails to satisfy the court that withdrawal or amendment will prejudice him in maintaining his action or defense on the merits. Any admission made by a party under this rule is for the purpose of the pending action only and is not an admission by him for any other purpose nor may it be used against him in any other proceeding.

(C) **Form of answers and objections to requests for admissions.** The party submitting requests for admissions shall arrange them so that there is sufficient space after each request for admission in which to type the answer or objections to that request for admission. The minimum vertical space between requests for admissions shall be one inch.

(Amended, eff 7-1-72; 7-1-76)

RULE 37. Failure to make discovery: sanctions

(A) **Motion for order compelling discovery.** Upon reasonable notice to other parties and all persons affected thereby, a party may move for an order compelling discovery as follows:

(1) **Appropriate court.** A motion for an order to a party or a deponent shall be made to the court in which the action is pending.

(2) **Motion.** If a deponent fails to answer a question propounded or submitted under Rule 30 or Rule 31, or a party fails to answer an interrogatory submitted under Rule 33, or if a party, in response to a request for inspection submitted under Rule 34, fails to respond that inspection will be permitted as requested or fails to permit inspection as requested, the discovering party may move for an order compelling an answer or an order compelling inspection in accordance with the request. On matters relating to a deposition on oral examination, the proponent of the question may complete or adjourn the examination before he applies for an order.

(3) **Evasive or incomplete answer.** For purposes of this subdivision an evasive or incomplete answer is a failure to answer.

(4) **Award of expenses of motion.** If the motion is granted, the court shall, after opportunity for hearing, require the party or deponent who opposed the motion or the party or attorney advising such conduct or both of them to pay to the moving party the reasonable expenses incurred in obtaining the order, including at-

torney's fees, unless the court finds that the opposition to the motion was substantially justified or that other circumstances make an award of expenses unjust.

If the motion is denied, the court shall, after opportunity for hearing, require the moving party or the attorney advising the motion or both of them to pay to the party or deponent who opposed the motion the reasonable expenses incurred in opposing the motion, including attorney's fees, unless the court finds that the making of the motion was substantially justified or that other circumstances make an award of expenses unjust.

If the motion is granted in part and denied in part, the court may apportion the reasonable expenses incurred in relation to the motion among the parties and persons in a just manner.

(B) Failure to comply with order.

(1) If a deponent fails to be sworn or to answer a question after being directed to do so by the court, the failure may be considered a contempt of that court.

(2) If any party or an officer, director, or managing agent of a party or a person designated under Rule 30(B)(5) or Rule 31(A) to testify on behalf of a party fails to obey an order to provide or permit discovery, including an order made under subdivision (A) of this rule and Rule 35, the court in which the action is pending may make such orders in regard to the failure as are just, and among others the following:

(a) An order that the matters regarding which the order was made or any other designated facts shall be taken to be established for the purposes of the action in accordance with the claim of the party obtaining the order;

(b) An order refusing to allow the disobedient party to support or oppose designated claims or defenses, or prohibiting him from introducing designated matters in evidence;

(c) An order striking out pleadings or parts thereof, or staying further proceedings until the order is obeyed, or dismissing the action or proceeding or any part thereof, or rendering a judgment by default against the disobedient party;

(d) In lieu of any of the foregoing orders or in addition thereto, an order treating as a contempt of court the failure to obey any orders except an order to submit to a physical or mental examination;

(e) Where a party has failed to comply with an order under Rule 35(A) requiring him to produce another for examination, such orders as are listed in subsections (a), (b), and (c) of this subdivision, unless the party failing to comply shows that he is unable to produce such person for examination.

In lieu of any of the foregoing orders or in addition thereto, the court shall require the party failing to obey the order or the attorney advising him or both to pay the reasonable expenses, including attorney's fees, caused by the failure, unless the court expressly finds that the failure was substantially justified or that other circumstances make an award of expenses unjust.

(C) Expenses on failure to admit. If a party, after being served with a request for admission under Rule 36, fails to admit the genuineness of any documents or the truth of any matter as requested, and if the party requesting the admissions thereafter proves the genuineness of the document or the truth of the matter, he may apply to the court for an order requiring the other party to pay him the reasonable expenses incurred in making that proof, including reasonable attorney's fees. Unless the request had been held objectionable under Rule 36(A) or the court finds that there was good reason for the failure to admit or that the admission sought was of no substantial importance, the order shall be made.

(D) Failure of party to attend at own deposition or serve answers to interrogatories or respond to request for inspection. If a party or an officer, director, or a managing agent of a party or a person designated under Rule 30(B)(5) or Rule 31(A) to testify on behalf of a party fails (1) to appear before the officer who is to take his deposition after being served with a proper notice, or (2) to serve answers or objections to interrogatories submitted under Rule 33, after proper service of the interrogatories, or (3) to serve a written response to a request for inspection submitted under Rule 34, after proper service of the request, the court in which the action is pending on motion and notice may make such orders in regard to the failure as are just, and among others it may take any action authorized under subsections (a), (b), and (c) of subdivision (B)(2) of this rule. In lieu of any order or in addition thereto, the court shall require the party failing to act or the attorney advising him or both to pay the reasonable expenses, including attorney's fees, caused by the failure, unless the court expressly finds that the failure was substantially justified or that other circumstances make an award of expenses unjust.

The failure to act described in this subdivision may not be excused on the ground that the discovery sought is objectionable unless the party failing to act has applied for a protective order as provided by Rule 26(C).

(E) [Duty to resolve.] Before filing a motion authorized by this rule, the party shall make a reasonable effort to resolve the matter through discussion with the attorney, unrepresented party, or person from whom discovery is sought. The motion shall be accompanied by a statement reciting the efforts made to resolve the matter in accordance with this section.

(Amended, eff 7-1-94)

TITLE VI
TRIALS

Rule

    (A) By jury
    (B) By the court
    (C) Advisory jury and trial by consent
40. Pre-recorded testimony
41. Dismissal of actions
    (A) Voluntary dismissal: effect thereof
        (1) By plaintiff; by stipulation
        (2) By order of court
    (B) Involuntary dismissal: effect thereof
        (1) Failure to prosecute
        (2) Dismissal; non-jury action
        (3) Adjudication on the merits; exception
        (4) Failure other than on the merits
    (C) Dismissal of counterclaim, cross-claim, or third-party claim
    (D) Costs of previously dismissed action
42. Consolidation; separate trials
    (A) Consolidation
    (B) Separate trials
43. [Reserved]
44. Proof of official record
    (A) Authentication
        (1) Domestic
        (2) Foreign
    (B) Lack of record
    (C) Other proof
44.1 Judicial notice of certain law; determination of foreign law
    (A) Judicial notice of certain law
    (B) Determination of foreign law
45. Subpoena
    (A) Form; issuance
    (B) Service
    (C) Protection of persons subject to subpoenas
    (D) Duties in responding to subpoena
    (E) Sanctions
    (F) Privileges
46. Exceptions unnecessary
47. Jurors
    (A) Examination of jurors
    (B) Challenges to jury
    (C) Alternate jurors
48. Juries: majority verdict; stipulation of number of jurors
49. Verdicts; interrogatories
    (A) General verdict
    (B) General verdict accompanied by answer to interrogatories
    (C) Special verdicts abolished
50. Motion for a directed verdict and for judgment notwithstanding the verdict
    (A) Motion for directed verdict
        (1) When made
        (2) When not granted
        (3) Grounds
        (4) When granted on the evidence
        (5) Jury assent unnecessary
    (B) Motion for judgment notwithstanding the verdict
    (C) Conditional rulings on motion for judgment notwithstanding verdict
    (D) Denial of motion for judgment notwithstanding verdict
    (E) Statement of basis of decision
51. Instructions to the jury; objection
    (A) Instructions; error; record

Rule

    (B) Cautionary instructions
52. Findings by the court
53. Magistrates
    (A) Appointment
    (B) Compensation
    (C) Reference and powers
        (1) Order of reference
        (2) General powers
        (3) Power to enter orders
    (D) Proceedings
    (E) Decisions in referred matters
        (1) Magistrate's decision
        (2) Findings of fact and conclusions of law
        (3) Objections
        (4) Court's action on magistrate's decision

RULE 38. Jury trial of right

(A) Right preserved. The right to trial by jury shall be preserved to the parties inviolate.

(B) Demand. Any party may demand a trial by jury on any issue triable of right by a jury by serving upon the other parties a demand therefor at any time after the commencement of the action and not later than fourteen days after the service of the last pleading directed to such issue. Such demand shall be in writing and may be indorsed upon a pleading of the party. If the demand is indorsed upon a pleading the caption of the pleading shall state "jury demand indorsed hereon." In an action for appropriation of a right of way brought by a corporation pursuant to Article XIII, Section 5, of the Ohio Constitution, the jury shall be composed of twelve members unless the demand specifies a lesser number; and in the event of timely demand by more than one party in such action the jury shall be composed of the greater number not to exceed twelve. In all other civil actions the jury shall be composed of eight members unless the demand specifies a lesser number; and in the event of timely demand by more than one party in such actions the jury shall be composed of the greater number not to exceed eight.

(C) Specification of issues. In his demand a party may specify the issues which he wishes so tried; otherwise he shall be deemed to have demanded trial by jury for all the issues so triable. If he has demanded trial by jury for only some of the issues, any other party within fourteen days after service of the demand or such lesser time as the court may order, may serve a demand for trial by jury of any other or all of the issues of fact in the action.

(D) Waiver. The failure of a party to serve a demand as required by this rule and to file it as required by Rule 5(D) constitutes a waiver by him of trial by jury. A demand for trial by jury made as herein provided may not be withdrawn without the consent of the parties.

(Amended, eff 7-1-72; 7-1-76)

RULE 39. Trial by jury or by the court

(A) By jury. When trial by jury has been demanded as provided in Rule 38, the action shall be designated upon the docket as a jury action. The trial of all issues so demanded shall be by jury, unless (1) the parties or their attorneys of record, by written stipulation filed with the court or by an oral stipulation made in open court and entered in the record, consent to trial by the court sitting without a jury or (2) the court upon motion or of its own initiative finds that a right of trial by jury of some or all of those issues does not exist. The failure of a party or his attorney of record either to answer or appear for trial constitutes a waiver of trial by jury by such party and authorizes submission of all issues to the court.

(B) By the court. Issues not demanded for trial by jury as provided in Rule 38 shall be tried by the court; but, notwithstanding the failure of a party to demand a jury in an action in which such a demand might have been made of right, the court in its discretion upon motion may order a trial by a jury of any or all issues.

(C) Advisory jury and trial by consent. In all actions not triable of right by a jury (1) the court upon motion or on its own initiative may try any issue with an advisory jury or (2) the court, with the consent of both parties, may order a trial of any issue with a jury, whose verdict has the same effect as if trial by jury had been a matter of right.

(Amended, eff 7-1-71)

RULE 40. Pre-recorded testimony

All of the testimony and such other evidence as may be appropriate may be presented at a trial by videotape, subject to the provisions of the Rules of Superintendence.

(New, eff 7-1-72)

RULE 41. Dismissal of actions

(A) Voluntary dismissal: effect thereof.

(1) By plaintiff; by stipulation. Subject to the provisions of Civ. R. 23(E), Civ. R. 23.1, and Civ. R. 66, a plaintiff, without order of court, may dismiss all claims asserted by that plaintiff against a defendant by doing either of the following:

(a) filing a notice of dismissal at any time before the commencement of trial unless a counterclaim which cannot remain pending for independent adjudication by the court has been served by that defendant;

(b) filing a stipulation of dismissal signed by all parties who have appeared in the action.

Unless otherwise stated in the notice of dismissal or stipulation, the dismissal is without prejudice, except that a notice of dismissal operates as an adjudication upon the merits of any claim that the plaintiff has once dismissed in any court.

(2) By order of court. Except as provided in division (A)(1) of this rule, a claim shall not be dismissed at the plaintiff's instance except upon order of the court and upon such terms and conditions as the court deems

proper. If a counterclaim has been pleaded by a defendant prior to the service upon that defendant of the plaintiff's motion to dismiss, a claim shall not be dismissed against the defendant's objection unless the counterclaim can remain pending for independent adjudication by the court. Unless otherwise specified in the order, a dismissal under division (A)(2) of this rule is without prejudice.

(B) Involuntary dismissal: effect thereof.

(1) Failure to prosecute. Where the plaintiff fails to prosecute, or comply with these rules or any court order, the court upon motion of a defendant or on its own motion may, after notice to the plaintiff's counsel, dismiss an action or claim.

(2) Dismissal; non-jury action. After the plaintiff, in an action tried by the court without a jury, has completed the presentation of the plaintiff's evidence, the defendant, without waiving the right to offer evidence in the event the motion is not granted, may move for a dismissal on the ground that upon the facts and the law the plaintiff has shown no right to relief. The court as trier of the facts may then determine them and render judgment against the plaintiff or may decline to render any judgment until the close of all the evidence. If the court renders judgment on the merits against the plaintiff, the court shall make findings as provided in Civ. R. 52 if requested to do so by any party.

(3) Adjudication on the merits; exception. A dismissal under division (B) of this rule and any dismissal not provided for in this rule, except as provided in division (B)(4) of this rule, operates as an adjudication upon the merits unless the court, in its order for dismissal, otherwise specifies.

(4) Failure other than on the merits. A dismissal for either of the following reasons shall operate as a failure otherwise than on the merits:

(a) lack of jurisdiction over the person or the subject matter;

(b) failure to join a party under Civ. R. 19 or Civ. R. 19.1.

(C) Dismissal of counterclaim, cross-claim, or third-party claim. The provisions of this rule apply to the dismissal of any counterclaim, cross-claim, or third-party claim. A voluntary dismissal by the claimant alone pursuant to division (A)(1) of this rule shall be made before the commencement of trial.

(D) Costs of previously dismissed action. If a plaintiff who has once dismissed a claim in any court commences an action based upon or including the same claim against the same defendant, the court may make such order for the payment of costs of the claim previously dismissed as it may deem proper and may stay the proceedings in the action until the plaintiff has complied with the order.

(Amended, eff 7-1-71; 7-1-72; 7-1-01)

RULE 42. Consolidation; separate trials

(A) Consolidation. When actions involving a common question of law or fact are pending before a court, that court after a hearing may order a joint hearing or trial of any or all the matters in issue in the actions; it may order some or all the actions consolidated; and it may make such orders concerning proceedings therein as may tend to avoid unnecessary costs or delay.

(B) Separate trials. The court, after a hearing, in furtherance of convenience or to avoid prejudice, or when separate trials will be conducive to expedition and economy, may order a separate trial of any claim, cross-claim, counterclaim, or third-party claim, or of any separate issue or of any number of claims, cross-claims, counterclaims, or third-party claims, or issues, always preserving inviolate the right to trial by jury.

RULE 43. [Reserved]

RULE 44. Proof of official record

(A) Authentication.

(1) Domestic. An official record, or an entry therein, kept within a state or within the United States or within a territory or other jurisdiction of the United States, when admissible for any purpose, may be evidenced by an official publication thereof or by a copy attested by the officer having the legal custody of the record, or by his deputy, and accompanied by a certificate that such officer has the custody. The certificate may be made by a judge of a court of record in which the record is kept or may be made by any public officer having a seal of office and having official duties in the political subdivision in which the record is kept, authenticated by the seal of his office.

(2) Foreign. A foreign official record, or an entry therein, when admissible for any purpose, may be evidenced by an official publication thereof; or a copy thereof, attested by a person authorized to make the attestation, and accompanied by a final certification as to the genuineness of the signature and official position (a) of the attesting person or (b) of any foreign official whose certificate of genuineness of signature and official position relates to the attestation or is in a chain of certificates of genuineness of signature and official position relating to the attestation. A final certification may be made by a secretary of embassy or legation, consul general, consul, vice consul, or consular agent of the United States, or a diplomatic or consular official of the foreign country assigned or accredited to the United States. If reasonable opportunity has been given to all parties to investigate the authenticity and accuracy of the documents, the court may, for good cause shown, (a) admit an attested copy without final certification or (b) permit the foreign official record to be evidenced by an attested summary with or without a final certification.

(B) Lack of record. A written statement that after diligent search no record or entry of a specified tenor is found to exist in the records designated by the statement, authenticated as provided in subdivision (A)(1)

of this rule in the case of a domestic record, or complying with the requirements of subdivision (A)(2) of this rule for a summary in the case of a foreign record, is admissible as evidence that the records contain no such record or entry.

(C) Other proof. This rule does not prevent the proof of official records or of entry or lack of entry therein by any other method authorized by law.

RULE 44.1 Judicial notice of certain law; determination of foreign law

(A) Judicial notice of certain law.

(1) Judicial notice shall be taken of the rules of the supreme court of this state and of the decisional, constitutional, and public statutory law of this state.

(2) A party who intends to rely on a municipal ordinance, a local rule of court, or an administrative regulation within this state shall give notice in his pleading or other reasonable written notice. The court in taking judicial notice of a municipal ordinance, a local rule of court, or an administrative regulation within this state may inform itself in such manner as it deems proper, and may call upon counsel to aid in obtaining such information. The court's determination shall be treated as a ruling on a question of law and shall be made by the court and not the jury. A court may, however, take judicial notice of its own rules or of a municipal ordinance within the territorial jurisdiction of the court without advance notice in the pleading of a party or other written notice.

(3) A party who intends to rely on the decisional, constitutional, public statutory law, rules of court, municipal ordinances, or administrative regulations of any other state, territory, and jurisdiction of the United States shall give notice in his pleading or other reasonable notice. The court in taking judicial notice of the decisional, constitutional, public statutory law, rules of court, municipal ordinances, or administrative regulations of any other state, territory, and jurisdiction of the United States may inform itself in such manner as it deems proper, and may call upon counsel to aid in obtaining such information. The court's determination shall be treated as a ruling on a question of law, and shall be made by the court and not the jury.

(B) Determination of foreign law. A party who intends to rely on the law of a foreign country shall give notice in his pleadings or other reasonable written notice. The court in determining the law of a foreign country may consider any relevant material or source, including testimony, whether or not submitted by a party. The court's determination shall be treated as a ruling on a question of law and shall be made by the court and not the jury.

RULE 45. Subpoena

(A) Form; issuance.

(1) Every subpoena shall do all of the following:

(a) state the name of the court from which it is issued, the title of the action, and the case number;

(b) command each person to whom it is directed, at a time and place specified in the subpoena, to:

(i) attend and give testimony at a trial, hearing, or deposition;

(ii) produce documents or tangible things at a trial, hearing, or deposition;

(iii) produce and permit inspection and copying of any designated documents that are in the possession, custody, or control of the person;

(iv) produce and permit inspection and copying, testing, or sampling of any tangible things that are in the possession, custody, or control of the person; or

(v) permit entry upon designated land or other property that is in the possession or control of the person for the purposes described in Civ. R. 34(A)(3).

(c) set forth the text of divisions (C) and (D) of this rule.

A command to produce and permit inspection may be joined with a command to attend and give testimony, or may be issued separately.

A subpoena may not be used to obtain the attendance of a party or the production of documents by a party in discovery. Rather, a party's attendance at a deposition may be obtained only by notice under Civ. R. 30, and documents may be obtained from a party in discovery only pursuant to Civ. R. 34.

(2) The clerk shall issue a subpoena, signed, but otherwise in blank, to a party requesting it, who shall complete it before service. An attorney who has filed an appearance on behalf of a party in an action may also sign and issue a subpoena on behalf of the court in which the action is pending.

(3) If the issuing attorney modifies the subpoena in any way, the issuing attorney shall give prompt notice of the modification to all other parties.

(B) Service. A subpoena may be served by a sheriff, bailiff, coroner, clerk of court, constable, or a deputy of any, by an attorney at law, or by any other person designated by order of court who is not a party and is not less than eighteen years of age. Service of a subpoena upon a person named therein shall be made by delivering a copy of the subpoena to the person, by reading it to him or her in person, or by leaving it at the person's usual place of residence, and by tendering to the person upon demand the fees for one day's attendance and the mileage allowed by law. The person serving the subpoena shall file a return of the subpoena with the clerk. If the witness being subpoenaed resides outside the county in which the court is located, the fees for one day's attendance and mileage shall be tendered without demand. The return may be forwarded through the postal service or otherwise.

(C) Protection of persons subject to subpoenas.

(1) A party or an attorney responsible for the issuance and service of a subpoena shall take reasonable steps to avoid imposing undue burden or expense on a person subject to that subpoena.

(2)(a) A person commanded to produce under divisions (A)(1)(b)(ii), (iii), (iv), or (v) of this rule need not appear in person at the place of production or inspection unless commanded to attend and give testimony at a deposition, hearing, or trial.

(b) Subject to division (D)(2) of this rule, a person commanded to produce under divisions (A)(1)(b)(ii), (iii), (iv), or (v) of this rule may, within fourteen days after service of the subpoena or before the time specified for compliance if such time is less than fourteen days after service, serve upon the party or attorney designated in the subpoena written objections to production. If objection is made, the party serving the subpoena shall not be entitled to production except pursuant to an order of the court by which the subpoena was issued. If objection has been made, the party serving the subpoena, upon notice to the person commanded to produce, may move at any time for an order to compel the production. An order to compel production shall protect any person who is not a party or an officer of a party from significant expense resulting from the production commanded.

(3) On timely motion, the court from which the subpoena was issued shall quash or modify the subpoena, or order appearance or production only under specified conditions, if the subpoena does any of the following:

(a) Fails to allow reasonable time to comply;

(b) Requires disclosure of privileged or otherwise protected matter and no exception or waiver applies;

(c) Requires disclosure of a fact known or opinion held by an expert not retained or specially employed by any party in anticipation of litigation or preparation for trial as described by Civ.R. 26(B)(4), if the fact or opinion does not describe specific events or occurrences in dispute and results from study by that expert that was not made at the request of any party;

(d) Subjects a person to undue burden.

(4) Before filing a motion pursuant to division (C)(3)(d) of this rule, a person resisting discovery under this rule shall attempt to resolve any claim of undue burden through discussions with the issuing attorney. A motion filed pursuant to division (C)(3)(d) of this rule shall be supported by an affidavit of the subpoenaed person or a certificate of that person's attorney of the efforts made to resolve any claim of undue burden.

(5) If a motion is made under division (C)(3)(c) or (C)(3)(d) of this rule, the court shall quash or modify the subpoena unless the party in whose behalf the subpoena is issued shows a substantial need for the testimony or material that cannot be otherwise met without undue hardship and assures that the person to whom the subpoena is addressed will be reasonably compensated.

(D) Duties in responding to subpoena.

(1) A person responding to a subpoena to produce documents shall, at the person's option, produce them as they are kept in the usual course of business or organized and labeled to correspond with the categories in the subpoena. A person producing documents pursuant to a subpoena for them shall permit their inspection

and copying by all parties present at the time and place set in the subpoena for inspection and copying.

(2) When information subject to a subpoena is withheld on a claim that it is privileged or subject to protection as trial preparation materials under Civ.R. 26(B)(3) or (4), the claim shall be made expressly and shall be supported by a description of the nature of the documents, communications, or things not produced that is sufficient to enable the demanding party to contest the claim.

(E) Sanctions. Failure by any person without adequate excuse to obey a subpoena served upon that person may be deemed a contempt of the court from which the subpoena issued. A subpoenaed person or that person's attorney who frivolously resists discovery under this rule may be required by the court to pay the reasonable expenses, including reasonable attorney's fees, of the party seeking the discovery. The court from which a subpoena was issued may impose upon a party or attorney in breach of the duty imposed by division (C)(1) of this rule an appropriate sanction, which may include, but is not limited to, lost earnings and reasonable attorney's fees.

(F) Privileges. Nothing in this rule shall be construed to authorize a party to obtain information protected by any privilege recognized by law, or to authorize any person to disclose such information.

(Amended, eff 7-1-71; 7-1-72; 7-1-93; 7-1-94)

RULE 46. Exceptions unnecessary

An exception at any stage or step of the case or matter is unnecessary to lay a foundation for review whenever a matter has been called to the attention of the court by objection, motion, or otherwise and the court has ruled thereon.

(Amended, eff 7-1-75)

RULE 47. Jurors

(A) Examination of jurors. Any person called as a juror for the trial of any cause shall be examined under oath or upon affirmation as to his qualifications. The court may permit the parties or their attorneys to conduct the examination of the prospective jurors or may itself conduct the examination. In the latter event, the court shall permit the parties or their attorneys to supplement the examination by further inquiry.

(B) Challenges to jury. In addition to challenges for cause provided by law, each party peremptorily may challenge three jurors. If the interests of multiple litigants are essentially the same, "each party" shall mean "each side."

Peremptory challenges may be exercised after the minimum number of jurors allowed by the rules has been passed for cause and seated on the panel. Peremptory challenges shall be exercised alternately, with the first challenge exercised by the plaintiff. The failure of a party to exercise a peremptory challenge constitutes a waiver of that challenge. If all parties or both sides, alternately and in sequence, fail to exercise a peremptory challenge, the joint failure constitutes a waiver of all peremptory challenges.

A prospective juror peremptorily challenged by either party shall be excused and another juror shall be called who shall take the place of the juror excused and be sworn and examined as other jurors. The other party, if he has peremptory challenges remaining, shall be entitled to challenge any juror then seated on the panel.

(C) Alternate jurors. The court may direct that no more than four jurors in addition to the regular jury be called and impanelled to sit as alternate jurors. Alternate jurors in the order in which they are called shall replace jurors who, prior to the time the jury retires to consider its verdict, become or are found to be unable or disqualified to perform their duties. Alternate jurors shall be drawn in the same manner, shall have the same qualifications, shall be subject to the same examination and challenges, shall take the same oath, and shall have the same functions, powers, facilities, and privileges as the regular jurors. An alternate juror who does not replace a regular juror shall be discharged after the jury retires to consider its verdict. Each party is entitled to one peremptory challenge in addition to those otherwise allowed by law if one or two alternate jurors are to be impanelled, and two peremptory challenges if three or four alternate jurors are to be impanelled. The additional peremptory challenges may be used against an alternate juror only, and the other peremptory challenges allowed shall not be used against an alternate juror.

(Amended, eff 7-1-71; 7-1-72; 7-1-75)

RULE 48. Juries: majority verdict; stipulation of number of jurors

In all civil actions, a jury shall render a verdict upon the concurrence of three-fourths or more of their number. The verdict shall be in writing and signed by each of the jurors concurring therein. All jurors shall then return to court where the judge shall cause the verdict to be read and inquiry made to determine if the verdict is that of three-fourths or more of the jurors. Upon request of either party, the jury shall be polled by asking each juror if the verdict is that of the juror; if more than one-fourth of the jurors answer in the negative, or if the verdict in substance is defective, the jurors must be sent out again for further deliberation. If three-fourths or more of the jurors answer affirmatively, the verdict is complete and the jury shall be discharged from the case. If the verdict is defective in form only, with the assent of the jurors and before their discharge, the court may correct it.

The parties may stipulate that the jury shall consist of any number less than the maximum number provided by Rule 38(B). For the purpose of rendering a verdict, whenever three-fourths of the jury does not consist of an integral number, the next higher number shall be construed to represent three-fourths of the jury. For juries with less than four members, the verdict must be unanimous.

(Amended, eff 7-1-71; 7-1-72)

RULE 49. Verdicts; interrogatories

(A) General verdict. A general verdict, by which the jury finds generally in favor of the prevailing party, shall be used.

(B) General verdict accompanied by answer to interrogatories. The court shall submit written interrogatories to the jury, together with appropriate forms for a general verdict, upon request of any party prior to the commencement of argument. Counsel shall submit the proposed interrogatories to the court and to opposing counsel at such time. The court shall inform counsel of its proposed action upon the requests prior to their arguments to the jury, but the interrogatories shall be submitted to the jury in the form that the court approves. The interrogatories may be directed to one or more determinative issues whether issues of fact or mixed issues of fact and law.

The court shall give such explanation or instruction as may be necessary to enable the jury both to make answers to the interrogatories and to render a general verdict, and the court shall direct the jury both to make written answers and to render a general verdict.

When the general verdict and the answers are consistent, the appropriate judgment upon the verdict and answers shall be entered pursuant to Rule 58. When one or more of the answers is inconsistent with the general verdict, judgment may be entered pursuant to Rule 58 in accordance with the answers, notwithstanding the general verdict, or the court may return the jury for further consideration of its answers and verdict or may order a new trial.

(C) Special verdicts abolished. Special verdicts shall not be used.

(Amended, eff 7-1-80)

RULE 50. Motion for a directed verdict and for judgment notwithstanding the verdict

(A) Motion for directed verdict.

(1) When made. A motion for a directed verdict may be made on the opening statement of the opponent, at the close of the opponent's evidence or at the close of all the evidence.

(2) When not granted. A party who moves for a directed verdict at the close of the evidence offered by an opponent may offer evidence in the event that the motion is not granted, without having reserved the right so to do and to the same extent as if the motion had not been made. A motion for a directed verdict which is not granted is not a waiver of trial by jury even though all parties to the action have moved for directed verdicts.

(3) Grounds. A motion for a directed verdict shall state the specific grounds therefor.

(4) When granted on the evidence. When a motion for a directed verdict has been properly made, and the trial court, after construing the evidence most strongly in favor of the party against whom the motion is directed, finds that upon any determinative issue reasonable minds could come to but one conclusion upon the evidence submitted and that conclusion is adverse to such party, the court shall sustain the motion and direct a verdict for the moving party as to that issue.

(5) Jury assent unnecessary. The order of the court granting a motion for a directed verdict is effective without any assent of the jury.

(B) Motion for judgment notwithstanding the verdict. Whether or not a motion to direct a verdict has been made or overruled and not later than fourteen days after entry of judgment, a party may move to have the verdict and any judgment entered thereon set aside and to have judgment entered in accordance with his motion; or if a verdict was not returned such party, within fourteen days after the jury has been discharged, may move for judgment in accordance with his motion. A motion for a new trial may be joined with this motion, or a new trial may be prayed for in the alternative. If a verdict was returned, the court may allow the judgment to stand or may reopen the judgment. If the judgment is reopened, the court shall either order a new trial or direct the entry of judgment, but no judgment shall be rendered by the court on the ground that the verdict is against the weight of the evidence. If no verdict was returned the court may direct the entry of judgment or may order a new trial.

(C) Conditional rulings on motion for judgment notwithstanding verdict.

(1) If the motion for judgment notwithstanding the verdict, provided for in subdivision (B) of this rule, is granted, the court shall also rule on the motion for a new trial, if any, by determining whether it should be granted if the judgment is thereafter vacated or reversed. If the motion for a new trial is thus conditionally granted, the order thereon does not affect the finality of the judgment. In case the motion for a new trial has been conditionally granted and the judgment is reversed on appeal, the new trial shall proceed unless the appellate court has otherwise ordered. In case the motion for a new trial has been conditionally denied, the appellee on appeal may assert error in that denial; and if the judgment is reversed on appeal, subsequent proceedings shall be in accordance with the order of the appellate court.

(2) The party whose verdict has been set aside on motion for judgment notwithstanding the verdict may serve a motion for a new trial pursuant to Rule 59 not later than fourteen days after entry of the judgment notwithstanding the verdict.

(D) Denial of motion for judgment notwithstanding verdict. If the motion for judgment notwithstanding the verdict is denied, the party who prevailed on that motion may, as appellee, assert grounds entitling him to a new trial in the event the appellate court concludes that the trial court erred in denying the motion for judgment notwithstanding the verdict. If the appellate court reverses the judgment, nothing in this rule precludes it from determining that the appellee is entitled to a new trial, or from directing the trial court to determine whether a new trial shall be granted.

(E) Statement of basis of decision. When in a jury trial a court directs a verdict or grants judgment without or contrary to the verdict of the jury, the court shall state the basis for its decision in writing prior to or simultaneous with the entry of judgment. Such statement may be dictated into the record or included in the entry of judgment.

RULE 51. Instructions to the jury; objection

(A) Instructions; error; record. At the close of the evidence or at such earlier time during the trial as the court reasonably directs, any party may file written requests that the court instruct the jury on the law as set forth in the requests. Copies shall be furnished to all other parties at the time of making the requests. The court shall inform counsel of its proposed action on the requests prior to counsel's arguments to the jury and shall give the jury complete instructions after the arguments are completed. The court also may give some or all of its instructions to the jury prior to counsel's arguments. The court need not reduce its instructions to writing.

On appeal, a party may not assign as error the giving or the failure to give any instruction unless the party objects before the jury retires to consider its verdict, stating specifically the matter objected to and the grounds of the objection. Opportunity shall be given to make the objection out of the hearing of the jury.

(B) Cautionary instructions. At the commencement and during the course of the trial, the court may give the jury cautionary and other instructions of law relating to trial procedure, credibility and weight of the evidence, and the duty and function of the jury and may acquaint the jury generally with the nature of the case.

(Amended, eff 7-1-72; 7-1-75; 7-1-92)

RULE 52. Findings by the court

When questions of fact are tried by the court without a jury, judgment may be general for the prevailing party unless one of the parties in writing requests otherwise before the entry of judgment pursuant to Civ. R. 58, or not later than seven days after the party filing the request has been given notice of the court's announcement of its decision, whichever is later, in which case, the court shall state in writing the conclusions of fact found separately from the conclusions of law.

When a request for findings of fact and conclusions of law is made, the court, in its discretion, may require any or all of the parties to submit proposed findings of fact and conclusions of law; however, only those findings of fact and conclusions of law made by the court shall form part of the record.

Findings of fact and conclusions of law required by this rule and by Rule 41(B)(2) are unnecessary upon all other motions including those pursuant to Rule 12, Rule 55 and Rule 56.

An opinion or memorandum of decision filed in the action prior to judgment entry and containing findings of fact and conclusions of law stated separately shall be sufficient to satisfy the requirements of this rule and Rule 41(B)(2).

(Amended, eff 7-1-71; 7-1-89)

RULE 53. Magistrates

(A) Appointment. A court of record may appoint one or more magistrates who shall be attorneys at law admitted to practice in Ohio. A magistrate appointed under this rule may also serve as a magistrate under Crim. R. 19 or as a traffic magistrate.

(B) Compensation. The compensation of the magistrate shall be fixed by the court, and no part of the compensation shall be taxed as costs.

(C) Reference and Powers.

(1) Order of reference.

(a) A court of record may by order refer any of the following to a magistrate:

(i) any pretrial or post-judgment motion in any case;

(ii) the trial of any case that will not be tried to a jury; and

(iii) upon the unanimous written consent of the parties, the trial of any case that will be tried to a jury.

Except as provided in division (C)(1)(a)(iii) of this rule, the effect of a magistrate's order or decision is the same regardless of whether the parties have consented to the order of reference.

(b) Subject to division (C)(1)(a)(ii) and (iii) of this rule, an order of reference may be specific to a particular case or may refer categories of motions or cases.

(c) The order of reference to a magistrate may do all of the following:

(i) specify or limit the magistrate's powers;

(ii) direct the magistrate to report only upon particular issues, do or perform particular acts, or receive and report evidence only;

(iii) fix the time and place for beginning and closing the hearings and for the filing of the magistrate's decision.

(2) General powers. Subject to the specifications and limitations stated in the order of reference, the magistrate shall regulate all proceedings in every hearing as if by the court and do all acts and take all measures necessary or proper for the efficient performance of the magistrate's duties under the order. The magistrate may do all of the following:

(a) issue subpoenas for the attendance of witnesses and the production of evidence;

(b) rule upon the admissibility of evidence, unless otherwise directed by the order of reference;

(c) put witnesses under oath and examine them;

(d) call the parties to the action and examine them under oath.

(e) In cases involving direct or indirect contempt of court, and when necessary to obtain the alleged contemnor's presence for hearing, issue an attachment for the alleged contemnor and set bail to secure the alleged contemnor's appearance, considering the conditions of release prescribed in Crim. R. 46.

(3) Power to enter orders.

(a) Pretrial orders. Unless otherwise specified in the order of reference, the magistrate may enter orders without judicial approval in pretrial proceedings under Civ. R. 16, in discovery proceedings under Civ. R. 26 to 37, temporary restraining orders under Civ. R. 75(I), in hearings under Civ. R. 75(N), and other orders as necessary to regulate the proceedings.

(b) Appeal of pretrial orders. Any person may appeal to the court from any order of a magistrate entered under division (C)(3)(a) of this rule by filing a motion to set the order aside, stating the party's objections with particularity. The motion shall be filed no later than ten days after the magistrate's order is entered. The pendency of a motion to set aside does not stay the effectiveness of the magistrate's order unless the magistrate or the court grants a stay.

(c) Contempt in the magistrate's presence. In cases of contempt in the presence of the magistrate, the magistrate may impose an appropriate civil or criminal contempt sanction. Contempt sanctions under division (C)(3)(c) of this rule may be imposed only by a written order that recites the facts and certifies that the magistrate saw or heard the conduct constituting contempt. The contempt order shall be filed and a copy provided by the clerk to the appropriate judge of the court forthwith. The contemnor may by motion obtain immediate review of the magistrate's contempt order by a judge, or the judge or magistrate may set bail pending judicial review.

(d) Other orders. Unless prohibited by the order of reference, a magistrate shall continue to be authorized to enter orders when authority is specifically conveyed by statute to magistrates.

(e) Form of magistrate's orders. All orders of a magistrate shall be in writing, signed by the magistrate, identified as a magistrate's order in the caption, filed with the clerk, and served on all parties or their attorneys.

(D) Proceedings.

(1) All proceedings before the magistrate shall be in accordance with these rules and any applicable statutes, as if before the court.

(2) Except as otherwise provided by law, all proceedings before the magistrate shall be recorded in accordance with procedures established by the court.

(E) Decisions in referred matters. Unless specifically required by the order of reference, a magistrate is not required to prepare any report other than the magistrate's decision. Except as to those matters on which magistrates are permitted to enter orders without judicial approval pursuant to division (C)(3) of this rule, all matters referred to magistrates shall be decided as follows:

(1) Magistrate's decision. The magistrate promptly shall conduct all proceedings necessary for decision of referred matters. The magistrate shall prepare, sign, and file a magistrate's decision of the referred matter with the clerk, who shall serve copies on all the parties or their attorneys.

(2) Findings of fact and conclusions of law. If any party makes a request for findings of fact and conclusions of law under Civ. R. 52 or if findings and conclusions are otherwise required by law or by the order of reference, the magistrate's decision shall include findings of fact and conclusions of law. If the request under Civ. R. 52 is made after the magistrate's decision is filed, the magistrate shall include the findings of fact and conclusions of law in an amended magistrate's decision.

(3) Objections.

(a) Time for filing. Within fourteen days of the filing of a magistrate's decision, a party may file written objections to the magistrate's decision. If any party timely files objections, any other party may also file objections not later than ten days after the first objections are filed. If a party makes a request for findings of fact and conclusions of law under Civ. R. 52, the time for filing objections begins to run when the magistrate files a decision including findings of fact and conclusions of law.

(b) Form of objections. Objections shall be specific and state with particularity the grounds of objection. If the parties stipulate in writing that the magistrate's findings of fact shall be final, they may object only to errors of law in the magistrate's decision. Any objection to a finding of fact shall be supported by a transcript of all the evidence submitted to the magistrate relevant to that fact or an affidavit of that evidence if a transcript is not available. A party shall not assign as error on appeal the court's adoption of any finding of fact or conclusion of law unless the party has objected to that finding or conclusion under this rule.

(4) Court's action on magistrate's decision.

(a) When effective. The magistrate's decision shall be effective when adopted by the court. The court may adopt the magistrate's decision if no written objections are filed unless it determines that there is an error of law or other defect on the face of the magistrate's decision.

(b) Disposition of objections. The court shall rule on any objections. The court may adopt, reject, or modify the magistrate's decision, hear additional evidence, recommit the matter to the magistrate with instructions, or hear the matter. The court may refuse to consider additional evidence proffered upon objections unless the objecting party demonstrates that with reasonable diligence the party could not have produced that evidence for the magistrate's consideration.

(c) Permanent and interim orders. The court may adopt a magistrate's decision and enter judgment without waiting for timely objections by the parties, but the filing of timely written objections shall operate as an automatic stay of execution of that judgment until the court disposes of those objections and vacates, modifies, or adheres to the judgment previously entered. The court may make an interim order on the basis of a magistrate's decision without waiting for or ruling on timely objections by the parties where immediate relief is justified. An interim order shall not be subject to the automatic stay caused by the filing of timely objections. An interim order shall not extend more than twenty-eight days from the date of its entry unless, within that time and for good cause shown, the court extends the interim order for an additional twenty-eight days.

(Amended, eff 7-1-75; 7-1-85; 7-1-92; 7-1-93; 7-1-95; 7-1-96; 7-1-98)

TITLE VII
JUDGMENT

RULE 54. Judgment; costs

(A) Definition; form. "Judgment" as used in these rules includes a decree and any order from which an appeal lies as provided in section 2505.02 of the Revised Code. A judgment shall not contain a recital of pleadings, the magistrate's decision in a referred matter, or the record of prior proceedings.

(B) Judgment upon multiple claims or involving multiple parties. When more than one claim for relief is presented in an action whether as a claim, counterclaim, cross-claim, or third-party claim, and whether arising out of the same or separate transactions, or when multiple parties are involved, the court may enter final judgment as to one or more but fewer than all of the claims or parties only upon an express determination that there is no just reason for delay. In the absence of a determination that there is no just reason for delay, any order or other form of decision, however designated, which adjudicates fewer than all the claims or the rights and liabilities of fewer than all the parties, shall not terminate the action as to any of the claims or parties, and the order or other form of decision is subject to revision at any time before the entry of judgment adjudicating all the claims and the rights and liabilities of all the parties.

(C) Demand for judgment. A judgment by default shall not be different in kind from or exceed in amount that prayed for in the demand for judgment. Except as to a party against whom a judgment is entered by default, every final judgment shall grant the relief to which the party in whose favor it is rendered is entitled, even if the party has not demanded the relief in the pleadings.

(D) Costs. Except when express provision therefor is made either in a statute or in these rules, costs shall be allowed to the prevailing party unless the court otherwise directs.

(Amended, eff 7-1-89; 7-1-92; 7-1-94; 7-1-96)

RULE 55. Default

(A) Entry of judgment. When a party against whom a judgment for affirmative relief is sought has failed to plead or otherwise defend as provided by these rules, the party entitled to a judgment by default shall apply in writing or orally to the court therefor; but no judgment by default shall be entered against a minor or an incompetent person unless represented in the action by a guardian or other such representative who has appeared therein. If the party against whom judgment by default is sought has appeared in the action, he (or, if appearing by representative, his representative) shall be served with written notice of the application for judgment at least seven days prior to the hearing on such application. If, in order to enable the court to enter judgment or to carry it into effect, it is necessary to take an account or to determine the amount of damages or to establish the truth of any averment by evidence or to make an investigation of any other matter, the court may conduct such hearings or order such references as it deems necessary and proper and shall when applicable accord a right of trial by jury to the parties.

(B) Setting aside default judgment. If a judgment by default has been entered, the court may set it aside in accordance with Rule 60(B).

(C) Plaintiffs, counterclaimants, cross-claimants. The provisions of this rule apply whether the party entitled to the judgment by default is a plaintiff, a third-party plaintiff or a party who has pleaded a cross-claim or counterclaim. In all cases a judgment by default is subject to the limitations of Rule 54(C).

(D) Judgment against this state. No judgment by default shall be entered against this state, a political subdivision, or officer in his representative capacity or agency of either unless the claimant establishes his claim or right to relief by evidence satisfactory to the court.

(Amended, eff 7-1-71)

RULE 56. Summary judgment

(A) For party seeking affirmative relief. A party seeking to recover upon a claim, counterclaim, or cross-claim or to obtain a declaratory judgment may move with or without supporting affidavits for a summary judgment in the party's favor as to all or any part of the claim, counterclaim, cross-claim, or declaratory judgment action. A party may move for summary judgment at any time after the expiration of the time permitted under these rules for a responsive motion for pleading by the adverse party, or after service of a motion for summary judgment by the adverse party. If the action has been set for pretrial or trial, a motion for summary judgment may be made only with leave of court.

(B) For defending party. A party against whom a claim, counterclaim, or cross-claim is asserted or a declaratory judgment is sought may, at any time, move with or without supporting affidavits for a summary judgment in the party's favor as to all or any part of the claim, counterclaim, cross-claim, or declaratory judgment action. If the action has been set for pretrial or trial, a motion for summary judgment may be made only with leave of court.

(C) Motion and proceedings. The motion shall be served at least fourteen days before the time fixed for hearing. The adverse party, prior to the day of hearing may serve and file opposing affidavits. Summary judgment shall be rendered forthwith if the pleadings, depositions, answers to interrogatories, written admissions, affidavits, transcripts of evidence, and written stipulations of fact, if any, timely filed in the action, show that there is no genuine issue as to any material fact and that the moving party is entitled to judgment as a matter of law. No evidence or stipulation may be considered except as stated in this rule. A summary judgment shall not be rendered unless it appears from the evidence or stipulation, and only from the evidence or stipulation, that reasonable minds can come to but one conclusion and that conclusion is adverse to the party against whom the motion for summary judgment is made, that party being entitled to have the evidence or stipulation construed most strongly in the party's favor. A summary judgment, interlocutory in character, may be rendered on the issue of liability alone although there is a genuine issue as to the amount of damages.

(D) Case not fully adjudicated upon motion. If on motion under this rule summary judgment is not rendered upon the whole case or for all the relief asked and a trial is necessary, the court in deciding the motion, shall examine the evidence or stipulation properly before it, and shall if practicable, ascertain what material facts exist without controversy and what material facts are actually and in good faith controverted. The court shall thereupon make an order on its journal specifying the facts that are without controversy, including the extent to which the amount of damages or other relief is not in controversy, and directing such further proceedings in the action as are just. Upon the trial of the action the facts so specified shall be deemed established and the trial shall be conducted accordingly.

(E) Form of affidavits; further testimony; defense required. Supporting and opposing affidavits shall be made on personal knowledge, shall set forth such facts as would be admissible in evidence, and shall show affirmatively that the affiant is competent to testify to the matters stated in the affidavit. Sworn or certified copies of all papers or parts of papers referred to in an affidavit shall be attached to or served with the affidavit. The court may permit affidavits to be supplemented or opposed by depositions or by further affidavits. When a motion for summary judgment is made and supported as provided in this rule, an adverse party may not rest upon the mere allegations or denials of the party's pleadings, but the party's response, by affidavit or as otherwise provided in this rule, must set forth specific facts showing that there is a genuine issue for trial. If the party does not so respond, summary judgment, if appropriate, shall be entered against the party.

(F) When affidavits unavailable. Should it appear from the affidavits of a party opposing the motion for summary judgment that the party cannot for sufficient reasons stated present by affidavit facts essential to justify the party's opposition, the court may refuse the application for judgment or may order a continuance to permit affidavits to be obtained or discovery to be had or may make such other order as is just.

(G) Affidavits made in bad faith. Should it appear to the satisfaction of the court at any time that any of the affidavits presented pursuant to this rule are presented in bad faith or solely for the purpose of delay, the court shall forthwith order the party employing them to pay to the other party the amount of the reasonable expenses which the filing of the affidavits caused the other party to incur, including reasonable attorney's fees, and any offending party or attorney may be adjudged guilty of contempt.

(Amended, eff 7-1-76; 7-1-97; 7-1-99)

RULE 57. Declaratory judgments

The procedure for obtaining a declaratory judgment pursuant to Sections 2721.01 to 2721.15, inclusive, of the Revised Code, shall be in accordance with these rules. The existence of another adequate remedy does not preclude a judgment for declaratory relief in cases where it is appropriate. The court may advance on the trial list the hearing of an action for a declaratory judgment.

RULE 58. Entry of judgment

(A) Preparation; entry; effect. Subject to the provisions of Rule 54(B), upon a general verdict of a jury, upon a decision announced, or upon the determination of a periodic payment plan, the court shall promptly cause the judgment to be prepared and, the court having signed it, the clerk shall thereupon enter it upon the journal. A judgment is effective only when entered by the clerk upon the journal.

(B) Notice of filing. When the court signs a judgment, the court shall endorse thereon a direction to the clerk to serve upon all parties not in default for failure to appear notice of the judgment and its date of entry upon the journal. Within three days of entering the judgment upon the journal, the clerk shall serve the parties in a manner prescribed by Civ. R. 5(B) and note the service in the appearance docket. Upon serving the notice and notation of the service in the appearance docket, the service is complete. The failure of the clerk to serve notice does not affect the validity of the judgment or the running of the time for appeal except as provided in App. R. 4(A).

(C) Costs. Entry of the judgment shall not be delayed for the taxing of costs.

(Amended, eff 7-1-71; 7-1-89)

RULE 59. New trials

(A) Grounds. A new trial may be granted to all or any of the parties and on all or part of the issues upon any of the following grounds:

(1) Irregularity in the proceedings of the court, jury, magistrate, or prevailing party, or any order of the court or magistrate, or abuse of discretion, by which an aggrieved party was prevented from having a fair trial;

(2) Misconduct of the jury or prevailing party;

(3) Accident or surprise which ordinary prudence could not have guarded against;

(4) Excessive or inadequate damages, appearing to have been given under the influence of passion or prejudice;

(5) Error in the amount of recovery, whether too large or too small, when the action is upon a contract or for the injury or detention of property;

(6) The judgment is not sustained by the weight of the evidence; however, only one new trial may be granted on the weight of the evidence in the same case;

(7) The judgment is contrary to law;

(8) Newly discovered evidence, material for the party applying, which with reasonable diligence he could not have discovered and produced at trial;

(9) Error of law occurring at the trial and brought to the attention of the trial court by the party making the application.

In addition to the above grounds, a new trial may also be granted in the sound discretion of the court for good cause shown.

When a new trial is granted, the court shall specify in writing the grounds upon which such new trial is granted.

On a motion for a new trial in an action tried without a jury, the court may open the judgment if one has been entered, take additional testimony, amend findings of fact and conclusions of law or make new findings and conclusions, and enter a new judgment.

(B) Time for motion. A motion for a new trial shall be served not later than fourteen days after the entry of judgment.

(C) Time for serving affidavits. When a motion for a new trial is based upon affidavits they shall be served with the motion. The opposing party has fourteen days after such service within which to serve opposing affidavits, which period may be extended for an additional period not exceeding twenty-one days either by the court for good cause shown or by the parties by written stipulation. The court may permit supplemental and reply affidavits.

(D) On initiative of court. Not later than fourteen days after entry of judgment the court of its own initiative may order a new trial for any reason for which it might have granted a new trial on motion of a party.

The court may also grant a motion for a new trial, timely served by a party, for a reason not stated in the party's motion. In such case the court shall give the parties notice and an opportunity to be heard on the matter. The court shall specify the grounds for new trial in the order.

(Amended, eff 7-1-96)

RULE 60. Relief from judgment or order

(A) Clerical mistakes. Clerical mistakes in judgments, orders or other parts of the record and errors therein arising from oversight or omission may be corrected by the court at any time on its own initiative or on the motion of any party and after such notice, if any, as the court orders. During the pendency of an appeal, such mistakes may be so corrected before the appeal is docketed in the appellate court, and thereafter while the appeal is pending may be so corrected with leave of the appellate court.

(B) Mistakes; inadvertence; excusable neglect; newly discovered evidence; fraud; etc. On motion and upon such terms as are just, the court may relieve a party or his legal representative from a final judgment, order or proceeding for the following reasons: (1) mistake, inadvertence, surprise or excusable neglect; (2) newly discovered evidence which by due diligence could not have been discovered in time to move for a new trial under Rule 59(B); (3) fraud (whether heretofore denominated intrinsic or extrinsic), misrepresentation or other misconduct of an adverse party; (4) the judgment has been satisfied, released or discharged, or a prior judgment upon which it is based has been reversed or otherwise vacated, or it is no longer equitable that the judgment should have prospective application; or (5) any other reason justifying relief from the judgment. The motion shall be made within a reasonable time, and for reasons (1), (2) and (3) not more than one year after the judgment, order or proceeding was entered or taken. A motion under this subdivision (B) does not affect the finality of a judgment or suspend its operation.

The procedure for obtaining any relief from a judgment shall be by motion as prescribed in these rules.

RULE 61. Harmless error

No error in either the admission or the exclusion of evidence and no error or defect in any ruling or order or in anything done or omitted by the court or by any of the parties is ground for granting a new trial or for setting aside a verdict or for vacating, modifying or otherwise disturbing a judgment or order, unless refusal to take such action appears to the court inconsistent with substantial justice. The court at every stage of the proceeding must disregard any error or defect in the proceeding which does not affect the substantial rights of the parties.

RULE 62. Stay of proceedings to enforce a judgment

(A) Stay on motion for new trial or for judgment. In its discretion and on such conditions for the security of the adverse party as are proper, the court may stay the execution of any judgment or stay any proceedings to enforce judgment pending the disposition of a motion for a new trial, or of a motion for relief from a judgment or order made pursuant to Rule 60, or of a motion for judgment notwithstanding the verdict made pursuant to Rule 50.

(B) Stay upon appeal. When an appeal is taken the appellant may obtain a stay of execution of a judgment or any proceedings to enforce a judgment by giving an adequate supersedeas bond. The bond may be given at or after the time of filing the notice of appeal. The stay is effective when the supersedeas bond is approved by the court.

(C) Stay in favor of the government. When an appeal is taken by this state or political subdivision, or administrative agency of either, or by any officer thereof acting in his representative capacity and the operation or enforcement of the judgment is stayed, no bond, obligation or other security shall be required from the appellant.

(D) Power of appellate court not limited. The provisions in this rule do not limit any power of an appellate court or of a judge or justice thereof to stay proceedings during the pendency of an appeal or to suspend, modify, restore, or grant an injunction during the pendency of an appeal or to make any order appropriate to preserve the status quo or the effectiveness of the judgment subsequently to be entered.

(E) Stay of judgment as to multiple claims or multiple parties. When a court has ordered a final judgment under the conditions stated in Rule 54(B), the court may stay enforcement of that judgment until the entering of a subsequent judgment or judgments and may prescribe such conditions as are necessary to secure the benefit thereof to the party in whose favor the judgment is entered.

RULE 63. Disability of a judge

(A) During trial. If for any reason the judge before whom a jury trial has been commenced is unable to proceed with the trial, another judge, designated by the administrative judge, or in the case of a single-judge division by the chief justice of the supreme court, may proceed with and finish the trial upon certifying in the record that he has familiarized himself with the record of the trial; but if such other judge is satisfied that he cannot adequately familiarize himself with the record, he may in his discretion grant a new trial.

(B) [After verdict or findings.] If for any reason the judge before whom an action has been tried is unable to perform the duties to be performed by the court after a verdict is returned or findings of fact and conclusions of law are filed, another judge designated by the administrative judge, or in the case of a single-judge division by the Chief Justice of the Supreme Court, may perform those duties; but if such other judge is satisfied that he cannot perform those duties, he may in his discretion grant a new trial.

(Amended, eff 7-1-72; 7-1-73; 7-1-94)

TITLE VIII
PROVISIONAL AND FINAL REMEDIES

RULE 64. Seizure of person or property

At the commencement of and during the course of an action, all remedies providing for seizure of person or property for the purpose of securing satisfaction of the judgment ultimately to be entered in the action are available under the circumstances and in the manner provided by law. The remedies thus available include arrest, attachment, garnishment, replevin, sequestration, and other corresponding or equivalent remedies, however designated and regardless of whether the remedy is ancillary to an action or must be obtained by independent action.

RULE 65. Injunctions

(A) Temporary restraining order; notice; hearing; duration. A temporary restraining order may be granted without written or oral notice to the adverse party or his attorney only if (1) it clearly appears from specific facts shown by affidavit or by the verified complaint that immediate and irreparable injury, loss or damage will result to the applicant before the adverse party or his attorney can be heard in opposition, and (2) the applicant's attorney certifies to the court in writing the efforts, if any, which have been made to give notice and the reasons supporting his claim that notice should not be required. The verification of such affidavit or verified complaint shall be upon the affiant's own knowledge, information or belief; and so far as upon information and belief, shall state that he believes this information to be true. Every temporary restraining order granted without notice shall be filed forthwith in the clerk's office; shall define the injury and state why it is irreparable and why the order was granted without notice; and shall expire by its terms within such time after entry, not to exceed fourteen days, as the court fixes, unless within the time so fixed the order, for good cause shown, is extended for one like period or unless the party against whom the order is directed consents that it may be extended for a longer period. The reasons for the extension shall be set forth in the order of extension. In case a temporary restraining order is granted without notice, the motion for a preliminary injunction shall be set down for hearing at the earliest possible time and takes precedence over all matters except older matters of the same character. When the motion comes on for hearing the party who obtained the temporary restraining order shall proceed with the application for a preliminary injunction and, if he does not do so, the court shall dissolve the temporary restraining order. On two days' notice to the party who obtained the temporary restraining order without notice or on such shorter notice to that party as the court may prescribe, the adverse party may appear and move its dissolution or modification, and in that event the court shall proceed to hear and determine such motion as expeditiously as the ends of justice require.

(B) Preliminary injunction.

(1) Notice. No preliminary injunction shall be issued without reasonable notice to the adverse party. The application for preliminary injunction may be included in the complaint or may be made by motion.

(2) Consolidation of hearing with trial on merits. Before or after the commencement of the hearing of an application for a preliminary injunction, the court may order the trial of the action on the merits to be advanced and consolidated with the hearing of the application. Even when this consolidation is not ordered, any evidence received upon an application for a preliminary injunction which would be admissible upon the trial on the merits becomes part of the record on the trial and need not be repeated upon the trial. This subdivision (B)(2) shall be so construed and applied as to save to the parties any rights they may have to trial by jury.

(C) Security. No temporary restraining order or preliminary injunction is operative until the party obtaining it gives a bond executed by sufficient surety, approved by the clerk of the court granting the order or injunction, in an amount fixed by the court or judge allowing it, to secure to the party enjoined the damages he may sustain, if it is finally decided that the order or injunction should not have been granted.

The party obtaining the order or injunction may deposit, in lieu of such bond, with the clerk of the court granting the order or injunction, currency, cashier's check, certified check or negotiable government bonds in the amount fixed by the court.

Before judgment, upon reasonable notice to the party who obtained an injunction, a party enjoined may move the court for additional security. If the original security is found to be insufficient, the court may vacate the injunction unless, in reasonable time, sufficient security is provided.

No security shall be required of this state or political subdivision, or agency of either, or of any officer thereof acting in his representative capacity.

A surety upon a bond or undertaking under this rule submits himself to the jurisdiction of the court and irrevocably appoints the clerk of the court as his agent upon whom any papers affecting his liability on the bond or undertaking may be served. His liability as well as the liability of the party obtaining the order or injunction may be enforced by the court without jury on motion without the necessity for an independent action. The motion and such notice of the motion as the court prescribes may be served on the clerk of the court who shall forthwith mail copies to the persons giving the security if their addresses are known.

(D) Form and scope of restraining order or injunction. Every order granting an injunction and every restraining order shall set forth the reasons for its issuance; shall be specific in terms; shall describe in reasonable detail, and not by reference to the complaint or other document, the act or acts sought to be restrained; and is binding upon the parties to the action, their officers, agents, servants, employees, attorneys and those persons in active concert or participation with them who receive actual notice of the order whether by personal service or otherwise.

(E) Service of temporary restraining orders and injunctions. Restraining orders which are granted ex parte shall be served in the manner provided for service of process under Rule 4 through Rule 4.3 and Rule 4.6, or in a manner directed by order of the court. If the restraining order is granted upon a pleading or motion accompanying a pleading the order may be served with the process and pleading. When service is made pursuant to Rule 4 through Rule 4.3 and Rule 4.6, the sheriff or the person designated by order of the court shall forthwith make his return.

Restraining orders or injunctions which are granted with notice may be served in the manner provided under Rule 4 through Rule 4.3 and Rule 4.6, in the manner provided in Rule 5 or in the manner designated by order of the court. When service is made pursuant to Rule 4 through Rule 4.3 and Rule 4.6, the sheriff or the person designated by order of the court shall forthwith make his return.

RULE 66. Receivers

An action wherein a receiver has been appointed shall not be dismissed except by order of the court.

Receiverships shall be administered in the manner provided by law and as provided by rules of court.

RULE 67. [Reserved]

RULE 68. Offer of judgment

An offer of judgment by any party, if refused by an opposite party, may not be filed with the court by the offering party for purposes of a proceeding to determine costs.

This rule shall not be construed as limiting voluntary offers of settlement made by any party.

NOTE: The 1997 *PROPOSED* amendment to Civ. R. 68 was withdrawn.

RULE 69. Execution

Process to enforce a judgment for the payment of money shall be a writ of execution, unless the court directs otherwise. The procedure on execution, in proceedings supplementary to and in aid of a judgment, and in proceedings on and in aid of execution shall be as provided by law. In aid of the judgment or execution, the judgment creditor or his successor in interest when that interest appears of record, may also obtain discovery from any person, including the judgment debtor, in the manner provided in these rules.

RULE 70. Judgment for specific acts; vesting title

If a judgment directs a party to execute a conveyance of land, to transfer title or possession of personal property, to deliver deeds or other documents, or to perform any other specific act, and the party fails to comply within the time specified, the court may, where necessary, direct the act to be done at the cost of the disobedient party by some other person appointed by the court, and the act when so done has like effect as if done by the party. On application of the party entitled to performance, the clerk shall issue a writ of attachment against the property of the disobedient party to compel obedience to the judgment. The court may also in proper cases adjudge the party in contempt. If real or personal property is within this state, the court in lieu of directing a conveyance thereof may enter a judgment divesting the title of any party and vesting it in others, and such judgment has the effect of a conveyance executed in due form of law. When any order or judgment is for the delivery of possession, the party in whose favor it is entered is entitled to a writ of execution upon application to the clerk.

RULE 71. Process in behalf of and against persons not parties

When an order is made in favor of a person who is

not a party to the action, he may enforce obedience to the order by the same process as if he were a party; and, when obedience to an order may be lawfully enforced against a person who is not a party, he is liable to the same process for enforcing obedience to the order as if he were a party.

RULE 72. [Reserved]

TITLE IX
PROBATE, JUVENILE, AND DOMESTIC RELATIONS PROCEEDINGS

RULE 73. Probate division of the court of common pleas

(A) Applicability. These Rules of Civil Procedure shall apply to proceedings in the probate division of the court of common pleas as indicated in this rule. Additionally, all of the Rules of Civil Procedure, though not specifically mentioned in this rule, shall apply except to the extent that by their nature they would be clearly inapplicable.

(B) Venue. Civ. R. 3(B) shall not apply to proceedings in the probate division of the court of common pleas, which shall be venued as provided by law. Proceedings under Chapters 2101. through 2131. of the Revised Code, which may be venued in the general division or the probate division of the court of common pleas, shall be venued in the probate division of the appropriate court of common pleas.

Proceedings that are improperly venued shall be transferred to a proper venue provided by law and division (B) of this rule, and the court may assess costs, including reasonable attorney fees, to the time of transfer against the party who commenced the action in an improper venue.

(C) Service of summons. Civ. R. 4 through 4.6 shall apply in any proceeding in the probate division of the court of common pleas requiring service of summons.

(D) Service and filing of pleadings and papers subsequent to original pleading. In proceedings requiring service of summons, Civ. R. 5 shall apply to the service and filing of pleadings and papers subsequent to the original pleading.

(E) Service of notice. In any proceeding where any type of notice other than service of summons is required by law or deemed necessary by the court, and the statute providing for notice neither directs nor authorizes the court to direct the manner of its service, notice shall be given in writing and may be served by or on behalf of any interested party without court intervention by one of the following methods:

(1) By delivering a copy to the person to be served;

(2) By leaving a copy at the usual place of residence of the person to be served;

(3) By certified or express mail, addressed to the person to be served at the person's usual place of residence with instructions to forward, return receipt requested, with instructions to the delivering postal employee to show to whom delivered, date of delivery, and address where delivered, provided that the certified or express mail envelope is not returned with an endorsement showing failure of delivery;

(4) By ordinary mail after a certified or express mail envelope is returned with an endorsement showing that it was refused;

(5) By ordinary mail after a certified or express mail envelope is returned with an endorsement showing that it was unclaimed, provided that the ordinary mail envelope is not returned by the postal authorities with an endorsement showing failure of delivery;

(6) By publication once each week for three consecutive weeks in some newspaper of general circulation in the county when the name, usual place of residence, or existence of the person to be served is unknown and cannot with reasonable diligence be ascertained; provided that before publication may be utilized, the person giving notice shall file an affidavit which states

that the name, usual place of residence, or existence of the person to be served is unknown and cannot with reasonable diligence be ascertained;

(7) By other method as the court may direct.

Civ. R. 4.2 shall apply in determining who may be served and how particular persons or entities must be served.

(F) Proof of service of notice; when service of notice complete. When service is made through the court, proof of service of notice shall be in the same manner as proof of service of summons.

When service is made without court intervention, proof of service of notice shall be made by affidavit. When service is made by certified or express mail, the certified or express mail return receipt which shows delivery shall be attached to the affidavit. When service is made by ordinary mail, the prior returned certified or express mail envelope which shows that the mail was refused or unclaimed shall be attached to the affidavit.

Service of notice by ordinary mail shall be complete when the fact of mailing is entered of record except as stated in division (E)(5) of this rule. Service by publication shall be complete at the date of the last publication.

(G) Waiver of service of notice. Civ. R. 4(D) shall apply in determining who may waive service of notice.

(H) Forms used in probate practice. Forms used in proceedings in the probate division of the courts of common pleas shall be those prescribed in the rule applicable to standard probate forms in the Rules of Superintendence. Forms not prescribed in such rule may be used as permitted in that rule.

Blank forms reproduced for use in probate practice for any filing to which the rule applicable to specifications for printing probate forms of the Rules of Superintendence applies shall conform to the specifications set forth in that rule.

(I) Notice of filing of judgments. Civ. R. 58(B) shall apply to all judgments entered in the probate division of the court of common pleas in any action or proceeding in which any party other than a plaintiff, applicant, or movant has filed a responsive pleading or exceptions. Notice of the judgment shall be given to each plaintiff, applicant, or movant, to each party filing a responsive pleading or exceptions, and to other parties as the court directs.

(J) Filing with the court defined. The filing of documents with the court, as required by these rules, shall be made by filing them with the probate judge as the *ex officio* clerk of the court. A court may provide, by local rules adopted pursuant to the Rules of Superintendence, for the filing of documents by electronic means. If the court adopts such local rules, they shall include all of the following:

(1) any signature on electronically transmitted documents shall be considered that of the attorney or party it purports to be for all purposes. If it is established that the documents were transmitted without authority, the court shall order the filing stricken.

(2) a provision shall specify the days and hours during which electronically transmitted documents will be received by the court, and a provision shall specify when documents received electronically will be considered to have been filed.

(3) any document filed electronically that requires a filing fee may be rejected by the clerk of court unless the filer has complied with the mechanism established by the court for the payment of filing fees.

(Amended, eff 7-1-71; 7-1-75; 7-1-77; 7-1-80; 7-1-96; 7-1-97; 7-1-01)

RULE 74. Juvenile proceedings

Abrogated, eff 7-1-77.

RULE 75. Divorce, annulment, and legal separation actions

(A) Applicability. The Rules of Civil Procedure shall apply in actions for divorce, annulment, legal separation, and related proceedings, with the modifications or exceptions set forth in this rule.

(B) Joinder of parties. Civ.R. 14, 19, 19.1, and 24 shall not apply in divorce, annulment, or legal separation actions, however:

(1) A person or corporation having possession of, control of, or claiming an interest in property, whether real, personal, or mixed, out of which a party seeks a division of marital property, a distributive award, or an award of spousal support or other support, may be made a party defendant;

(2) When it is essential to protect the interests of a child, the court may join the child of the parties as a party defendant and appoint a guardian ad litem and legal counsel, if necessary, for the child and tax the costs;

(3) When child support is ordered, the court, on its own motion or that of an interested person, after notice to the party ordered to pay child support and to his or her employer, may make the employer a party defendant.

(C) Trial by court or magistrate. In proceedings under this rule there shall be no right to trial by jury. All issues may be heard either by the court or by a magistrate as the court, on the request of any party or on its own motion, may direct. Civ. R. 53 shall apply to all cases or issues directed to be heard by a magistrate.

(D) Investigation. On the filing of a complaint for divorce, annulment, or legal separation, where minor children are involved, or on the filing of a motion for the modification of a decree allocating parental rights and responsibilities for the care of children, the court may cause an investigation to be made as to the character, family relations, past conduct, earning ability, and financial worth of the parties to the action. The report of the investigation shall be made available to either party or their counsel of record upon written request not less than seven days before trial. The report shall be signed by the investigator and the investigator shall be subject to cross-examination by either party concerning the contents of the report. The court may tax as costs all or any part of the expenses for each investigation.

(E) Subpoena where custody involved. In any case involving the allocation of parental rights and responsibilities for the care of children, the court, on its own motion, may cite a party to the action from any point within the state to appear in court and testify.

(F) Judgment. The provisions of Civ. R. 55 shall not apply in actions for divorce, annulment, legal separation, or civil protection orders. For purposes of Civ. R. 54(B), the court shall not enter final judgment as to a claim for divorce, dissolution of marriage, annulment, or legal separation unless one of the following applies:

(1) The judgment also divides the property of the parties, determines the appropriateness of an order of spousal support, and, where applicable, either allocates parental rights and responsibilities, including payment of child support, between the parties or orders shared parenting of minor children;

(2) Issues of property division, spousal support, and allocation of parental rights and responsibilities or shared parenting have been finally determined in orders, previously entered by the court, that are incorporated into the judgment;

(3) The court includes in the judgment the express determination required by Civ. R. 54(B) and a final determination that either of the following applies:

(a) The court lacks jurisdiction to determine such issues;

(b) In a legal separation action, the division of the property of the parties would be inappropriate at that time.

(G) Civil protection order. A claim for a civil protection order based upon an allegation of domestic violence shall be a separate claim from a claim for divorce, dissolution of marriage, annulment, or legal separation.

(H) Relief pending appeal. A motion to modify, pending appeal, either a decree allocating parental rights and responsibilities for the care of children, or a spousal or other support order, shall be made to the trial court in the first instance, whether made before or after a notice of appeal is filed. The trial court may grant relief upon terms as to bond or otherwise as it considers proper for the security of the rights of the adverse party and in the best interests of the children involved. Civ. R. 62(B) does not apply to orders allocating parental rights and responsibilities for the care of children or a spousal or other support order. An order entered upon motion under this rule may be vacated or modified by the appellate court. The appellate court has authority to enter like orders pending appeal, but an application to the appellate court for relief shall disclose what has occurred in the trial court regarding the relief.

(I) Temporary restraining orders.

(1) Restraining order: exclusion. The provisions of Civ. R. 65(A) shall not apply in divorce, annulment, or legal separation actions.

(2) Restraining order: grounds, procedure. When it is made to appear to the court by affidavit of a party sworn to absolutely that a party is about to dispose of or encumber property, or any part thereof of property, so as to defeat another party in obtaining an equitable division of marital property, a distributive award, or spousal or other support, or that a party to the action or a child of any party is about to suffer physical abuse, annoyance, or bodily injury by the other party, the court may allow a temporary restraining order, with or without bond, to prevent that action. A temporary restraining order may be issued without notice and shall remain in force during the pendency of the action unless the court or magistrate otherwise orders.

(J) Continuing jurisdiction. The continuing jurisdiction of the court shall be invoked by motion filed in the original action, notice of which shall be served in the manner provided for the service of process under Civ. R. 4 to 4.6. When the continuing jurisdiction of the court is invoked pursuant to this division, the discovery procedures set forth in Civ. R. 26 to 37 shall apply.

(K) Hearing. No action for divorce, annulment, or legal separation may be heard and decided until the expiration of forty-two days after the service of process or twenty-eight days after the last publication of notice of the complaint, and no action for divorce, annulment, or legal separation shall be heard and decided earlier than twenty-eight days after the service of a counterclaim, which under this rule may be designated a cross-complaint, unless the plaintiff files a written waiver of the twenty-eight day period.

(L) Notice of trial. In all cases where there is no counsel of record for the adverse party, the court shall give the adverse party notice of the trial upon the merits. The notice shall be made by regular mail to the party's last known address, and shall be mailed at least seven days prior to the commencement of trial.

(M) Testimony. Judgment for divorce, annulment, or legal separation shall not be granted upon the testimony or admission of a party not supported by other credible evidence. No admission shall be received that the court has reason to believe was obtained by fraud, connivance, coercion, or other improper means. The parties, notwithstanding their marital relations, shall be competent to testify in the proceeding to the same extent as other witnesses.

(N) Allowance of spousal support, child support, and custody pendente lite.

(1) When requested in the complaint, answer, or counterclaim, or by motion served with the pleading, upon satisfactory proof by affidavit duly filed with the clerk of the court, the court or magistrate, without oral hearing and for good cause shown, may grant spousal support pendente lite to either of the parties for the party's sustenance and expenses during the suit and may make a temporary order regarding the

support, maintenance, and allocation of parental rights and responsibilities for the care of children of the marriage, whether natural or adopted, during the pendency of the action for divorce, annulment, or legal separation.

(2) Counter affidavits may be filed by the other party within fourteen days from the service of the complaint, answer, counterclaim, or motion, all affidavits to be used by the court or magistrate in making a temporary spousal support order, child support order, and order allocating parental rights and responsibilities for the care of children. Upon request, in writing, after any temporary spousal support, child support, or order allocating parental rights and responsibilities for the care of children is journalized, the court shall grant the party so requesting an oral hearing within twenty-eight days to modify the temporary order. A request for oral hearing shall not suspend or delay the commencement of spousal support or other support payments previously ordered or change the allocation of parental rights and responsibilities until the order is modified by journal entry after the oral hearing.

(O) Delay of decree. When a party who is entitled to a decree of divorce or annulment is ordered to pay spousal support or child support for a child not in his or her custody, or to deliver a child to the party to whom parental rights and responsibilities for the care of the child are allocated, the court may delay entering a decree for divorce or annulment until the party, to the satisfaction of the court, secures the payment of the spousal support or the child support for the child, or delivers custody of the child to the party to whom parental rights and responsibilities are allocated.

(Amended, eff 7-1-71; 7-1-72; 7-1-77; 7-1-78; 7-1-91; 7-1-96; 7-1-97; 7-1-98; 7-1-01)

RULE 76. Time for perfecting appeal stayed [Abrogated]

Reserved, 7-1-72.

RULES 77–80.   [Reserved]

RULE 81. References to Ohio Revised Code

A reference in these rules to a section of the Revised Code shall mean the section as amended from time to time including the enactment of additional sections the numbers of which are subsequent to the section referred to in the rules.

TITLE X
GENERAL PROVISIONS

RULE 82.   Jurisdiction unaffected

These rules shall not be construed to extend or limit the jurisdiction of the courts of this state.

RULE 83.   Local rules of practice

(A) A court may adopt local rules of practice which shall not be inconsistent with these rules or with other rules promulgated by the Supreme Court and shall file its local rules of practice with the Clerk of the Supreme Court.

(B) Local rules of practice shall be adopted only after the court gives appropriate notice and an opportunity for comment. If a court determines that there is an immediate need for a rule, it may adopt the rule without prior notice and opportunity for comment, but promptly shall afford notice and opportunity for comment.

(Amended, eff 7-1-94; 7-1-00)

RULE 84.   Forms

The forms contained in the Appendix of Forms which the supreme court from time to time may approve are sufficient under these rules and are intended to indicate the simplicity and brevity of statement which these rules contemplate.

RULE 85.   Title

These rules shall be known as the Ohio Rules of Civil Procedure and may be cited as "Civil Rules" or "Civ. R. ___."

(Amended, eff 7-1-71)

RULE 86.   Effective date

(A) Effective date of original rules. These rules shall take effect on the first day of July, 1970. They govern all proceedings in actions brought after they take effect and also all further proceedings in actions then pending, except to the extent that in the opinion of the court their application in a particular action pending when the rules take effect would not be feasible or would work injustice, in which event the former procedure applies.

(B) Effective date of amendments. The amendments submitted by the Supreme Court to the General Assembly on January 15, 1971, on April 14, 1971, and on April 30, 1971, shall take effect on the first day of July, 1971. They govern all proceedings in actions brought after they take effect and also all further proceedings in actions then pending, except to the extent that in the opinion of the court their application in a particular action pending when the rules take effect would not be feasible or would work injustice, in which event the former procedure applies.

(C) Effective date of amendments. The amendments submitted by the Supreme Court to the General Assembly on January 15, 1972, and on May 1, 1972, shall take effect on the first day of July, 1972. They govern all proceedings in actions brought after they take effect and also all further proceedings in actions then pending, except to the extent that their application in a particular action pending when the rules take effect would not be feasible or would work injustice, in which event the former procedure applies.

(D) Effective date of amendments. The amendments submitted by the Supreme Court to the General Assembly on January 12, 1973, shall take effect on the first day of July, 1973. They govern all proceedings in actions brought after they take effect and also all further proceedings in actions then pending, except to the extent that their application in a particular action pending when the amendments take effect would not be feasible or would work injustice, in which event the former procedure applies.

(E) Effective date of amendments. The amendments submitted by the Supreme Court to the General Assembly on January 10, 1975 and on April 29, 1975, shall take effect on July 1, 1975. They govern all proceedings in actions brought after they take effect and also all further proceedings in actions then pending, except to the extent that their application in a particular action pending when the amendments take effect would not be feasible or would work injustice, in which event the former procedure applies.

(F) Effective date of amendments. The amendments submitted by the Supreme Court to the General Assembly on January 9, 1976 shall take effect on July 1, 1976. They govern all proceedings in actions brought after they take effect and also all further proceedings in actions then pending, except to the extent that their application in a particular action pending when the amendments take effect would not be feasible or would work injustice, in which event the former procedure applies.

(G) Effective date of amendments. The amendments submitted by the Supreme Court to the General Assembly on January 12, 1978, and on April 28, 1978, shall take effect on July 1, 1978. They govern all proceedings in actions brought after they take effect and also all further proceedings in actions then pending, except to the extent that their application in a particular action pending when the amendments take effect would not be feasible or would work injustice, in which event the former procedure applies.

(H) Effective date of amendments. The amendments submitted by the Supreme Court to the General Assembly on January 14, 1980 shall take effect on July 1, 1980. They govern all proceedings in actions brought after they take effect and also all further proceedings in actions then pending, except to the extent that their application in a particular action pending when the amendments take effect would not be feasible or would work injustice, in which event the former procedure applies.

(I) Effective date of amendments. The amendments submitted by the Supreme Court to the General Assembly on January 12, 1983 shall take effect on July 1, 1983. They govern all proceedings in actions brought after they take effect and also all further proceedings in actions then pending, except to the extent that their application in a particular action pending when the amendments take effect would not be feasible or would work injustice, in which event the former procedure applies.

(J) Effective date of amendments. The amendments submitted by the Supreme Court to the General Assembly on January 12, 1984 shall take effect on July 1, 1984. They govern all proceedings in actions brought after they take effect and also all further proceedings in actions then pending, except to the extent that their application in a particular action pending when the amendments take effect would not be feasible or would work injustice, in which event the former procedure applies.

(K) Effective date of amendments. The amendments submitted by the Supreme Court to the General Assembly on December 24, 1984 and January 8, 1985 shall take effect on July 1, 1985. They govern all proceedings in actions brought after they take effect and also all further proceedings in actions then pending, except to the extent that their application in a particular action pending when the amendments take effect would not be feasible or would work injustice, in which event the former procedure applies.

(L) Effective date of amendments. The amendments submitted by the Supreme Court to the General Assembly on January 9, 1986 shall take effect on July 1, 1986. They govern all proceedings in actions brought after they take effect and also all further proceedings in actions then pending, except to the extent that their application in a particular action pending when the amendments take effect would not be feasible or would work injustice, in which event the former procedure applies.

(M) Effective date of amendments. The amendments submitted by the Supreme Court to the General Assembly on January 14, 1988 shall take effect on July 1, 1988. They govern all proceedings in actions brought after they take effect and also all further proceedings in actions then pending, except to the extent that their application in a particular action pending when the amendments take effect would not be feasible or would work injustice, in which event the former procedure applies.

(N) Effective date of amendments. The amendments submitted by the Supreme Court to the General Assembly on January 6, 1989 shall take effect on July 1, 1989. They govern all proceedings in actions brought after they take effect and also all further proceedings in actions then pending, except to the extent that their application in a particular action pending when the amendments take effect would not be feasible or would work injustice, in which event the former procedure applies.

(O) Effective date of amendments. The amendments submitted by the Supreme Court to the General Assembly on January 10, 1991 and further revised and submitted on April 29, 1991, shall take effect on July 1, 1991. They govern all proceedings in actions brought after they take effect and also all further proceedings in actions then pending, except to the extent that their application in a particular action pending when the amendments take effect would not be feasible or would work injustice, in which event the former procedure applies.

(P) Effective date of amendments. The amendments filed by the Supreme Court with the General Assembly on January 14, 1992 and further revised and filed on April 30, 1992, shall take effect on July 1, 1992. They govern all proceedings in actions brought after they take effect and also all further proceedings in actions then pending, except to the extent that their application in a particular action pending when the amendments take effect would not be feasible or would work injustice, in which event the former procedure applies.

(Q) Effective date of amendments. The amendments submitted by the Supreme Court to the General Assembly on January 8, 1993 and further revised and filed on April 30, 1993 shall take effect on July 1, 1993. They govern all proceedings in actions brought after they take effect and also all further proceedings in actions then pending, except to the extent that their application in a particular action pending when the amendments take effect would not be feasible or would work injustice, in which event the former procedure applies.

(R) Effective date of amendments. The amendments submitted by the Supreme Court to the General Assembly on January 14, 1994 shall take effect on July 1, 1994. They govern all proceedings in actions brought after they take effect and also all further proceedings in actions then pending, except to the extent that their application in a particular action pending when the amendments take effect would not be feasible or would work injustice, in which event the former procedure applies.

(S) Effective date of amendments. The amendments to Rules 11 and 53 filed by the Supreme Court with the General Assembly on January 11, 1995 and refiled on April 25, 1995 shall take effect on July 1, 1995. They govern all proceedings in actions brought after they take effect and also all further proceedings in actions then pending, except to the extent that their application in a particular action pending when the amendments take effect would not be feasible or would work injustice, in which event the former procedure applies.

(T) Effective date of amendments. The amendments to Rules 4.2, 19.1, 53, 54, 59, 73, and 75 filed by the Supreme Court with the General Assembly on January 5, 1996 and refiled on April 26, 1996 shall take effect on July 1, 1996. They govern all proceedings in actions brought after they take effect and also all further proceedings in actions then pending, except to the extent that their application in a particular action pending when the amendments take effect would not be feasible or would work injustice, in which event the former procedure applies.

(U) Effective date of amendments. The amendments to Rules 4.1, 4.2, 4.3, 4.5, 4.6, 30, 56, 73, and 75 filed by the Supreme Court with the General Assembly on January 10, 1997 and refiled on April 24, 1997 shall take effect on July 1, 1997. They govern all proceedings in actions brought after they take effect and also all further proceedings in actions then pending, except to the extent that their application in a particular action pending when the amendments take effect would not be feasible or would work injustice, in which event the former procedure applies.

(V) Effective date of amendments. The amendments to Rules 3, 53, and 75 filed by the Supreme Court with the General Assembly on January 15, 1998 and further revised and refiled on April 30, 1998, shall take effect on July 1, 1998. They govern all proceedings in actions brought after they take effect and also all further proceedings in actions then pending, except to the extent that their application in a particular action pending when the amendments take effect would not be feasible or would work injustice, in which event the former procedure applies.

(W) Effective date of amendments. The amendments to Rules 24, 33, and 56 filed by the Supreme Court with the General Assembly on January 13, 1999 shall take effect on July 1, 1999. They govern all proceedings in actions brought after they take effect and also all further proceedings in actions then pending, except to the extent that their application in a particular action pending when the amendments take effect would not be feasible or would work injustice, in which event the former procedure applies.

(X) Effective date of amendments. The amendments to Civil Rule 83 filed by the Supreme Court with the General Assembly on January 13, 2000 and refiled on April 27, 2000 shall take effect on July 1, 2000. They govern all proceedings in actions brought after they take effect and also all further proceedings in actions then pending, except to the extent that their application in a particular action pending when the amendments take effect would not be feasible or would work injustice, in which event the former procedure applies.

(Y) Effective date of amendments. The amendments to Civil Rules 5, 11, 28, 41, 73, and 75 filed by the Supreme Court with the General Assembly on January 12, 2001, and revised and refiled on April 26, 2001, shall take effect on July 1, 2001. They govern all proceedings in actions brought after they take effect and also all further proceedings in actions then pending, except to the extent that their application in a particular action pending when the amendments take effect would not be feasible or would work injustice, in which event the former procedure applies.

(Amended, eff 7-1-71; 7-1-72; 7-1-73; 7-1-75; 7-1-76; 7-1-78; 7-1-80; 7-1-83; 7-1-84; 7-1-85; 7-1-86; 7-1-88; 7-1-89; 7-1-91; 7-1-92; 7-1-93; 7-1-94; 7-1-95; 7-1-96; 7-1-97; 7-1-98; 7-1-99; 7-1-00; 7-1-01)

I
SCOPE OF RULES—
ONE FORM OF ACTION

CHAPTER 1

Rule 1. Scope of Rules: Applicability; Construction; Exceptions

Rule 1 reads as follows:

(A) Applicability. These rules prescribe the procedure to be followed in all courts of this state in the exercise of civil jurisdiction at law or in equity, with the exceptions stated in subdivision (C) of this rule.

(B) Construction. These rules shall be construed and applied to effect just results by eliminating delay, unnecessary expense and all other impediments to the expeditious administration of justice.

(C) Exceptions. These rules, to the extent that they would by their nature be clearly inapplicable, shall not apply to procedure

    (1) upon appeal to review any judgment, order or ruling,

    (2) in the appropriation of property,

    (3) in forcible entry and detainer,

    (4) in small claims matters under Chapter 1925, Revised Code,

    (5) in uniform reciprocal support actions,

    (6) in the commitment of the mentally ill,

    (7) in all other special statutory proceedings; provided, that where any statute provides for procedure by a general or specific reference to the statutes governing procedure in civil actions such procedure shall be in accordance with these rules.

COMMENTARY

Rule 1 addresses the applicability and construction of the Ohio Rules of Civil Procedure. The Rules, which were promulgated by the Ohio Supreme Court, replaced the statutory civil pleading and practice system originally adopted by Ohio in 1853. They became effective on July 1, 1970. Because the Ohio Constitution vests in the Ohio Supreme Court primary authority over rules of practice and procedure in Ohio courts, the Ohio Rules of Civil Procedure control over conflicting statutory provisions.

Applicability of Rules

Rule 1 creates a broad rule of general applicability of the Ohio Rules of Civil Procedure. Under subsection (A), the Rules are applicable in all civil actions in Ohio courts, subject only to the provisions of subsection (C). In certain instances, however, individual Rules draw distinctions between certain types of cases.

Illustration 1-1

Rule 23, which sets forth the procedure to be used in class actions, differentiates between class actions in which injunctive relief is the primary remedy being sought and those class actions in which monetary damages is the primary kind of relief being sought.

Exceptions to Applicability of Rules

Subsection (C) lists exceptions to the rule of general applicability of the Rules set forth in subsection (A). The proper construction of subsection (C) is tricky, however, because it does *not* state that the Rules are inapplicable in the proceedings listed in that subsection. Instead, subsection (C) provides that the Rules are inoperative in those proceedings only "to the extent that they would by their nature be clearly inapplicable." In other words, the Rules are a default in those proceedings, and Ohio courts have applied the Rules in land appropriation actions, forcible entry and detainer proceedings, and small claims litigation. Because Rule 1 is specifically directed to "courts," the Rules are not binding on adjudicatory proceedings before administrative agencies.

As with any other Rule, Rule 1(C) is properly interpreted when construed to promote the goals listed in subsection (B). The Rule was amended in 1971 to permit a broader application of the Rules to special statutory proceedings.

Purpose and Construction

Subsection (B) of Rule 1 directs courts to apply a construction that will attain the stated goals of eliminating delay, unnecessary expense, and all other impediments to the expeditious administration of justice. A liberal construction of the Rules is therefore preferred over a technical interpretation.

Subsection (B) provides trial court judges with a considerable amount of inherent discretion to fashion practices that are consistent with the Rules, acts of the Ohio Legislature, and the Ohio Constitution. In light of the vagaries and variabilities inevitably infusing the multiplicity of disputes faced by trial courts, the affirmative provision of such discretion is prudent as well as provident.

ADDITIONAL AUTHORITY

4 Wright & Miller §§ 1011-1040
1 Moore's Federal Practice §§ 1.01-1.22
4 Anderson's Ohio Civil Practice §§ 147.01-147.03
1 Klein Darling AT 1-1 to AT 1-96
1 Milligan Forms 1-1 to 1-83
1 Fink §§ 1-1 to 1-7

LEADING CASES

Administrative Proceedings

Yoder v. Ohio State Bd. of Educ., 40 Ohio App. 3d 111, 531 N.E.2d 769 (the Rules are not binding on adjudicatory proceedings before the State Board of Education), *cause dismissed*, 38 Ohio St. 3d 709, 533 N.E.2d 359 (1988)

Applicability to Special Proceedings

Robinson v. B.O.C. Group, Gen. Motors Corp., 81 Ohio St. 3d 361, 691 N.E.2d 667 (1998) (a special statutory procedure renders a particular Rule of Civil Procedure "clearly inapplicable" only when its use alters the basic statutory purpose for which a specific procedure was originally provided)

Conflict with Statute

Fraiberg v. Cuyahoga County Court of Common Pleas, 76 Ohio St. 3d 374, 667 N.E.2d 1189 (1996) (the Rules control over conflicting statutes purporting to govern procedural matters)

Construction of Rules

Peterson v. Teodosio, 34 Ohio St. 2d 161, 297 N.E.2d 113 (1973) (the spirit of the Rules is the resolution of cases upon their merits, not upon pleading deficiencies)

Entry and Detainer Proceedings; Rules Applicable

Miele v. Ribovich, 90 Ohio St. 3d 439, 739 N.E.2d 333 (2000) (Rule 53 applies to forcible entry and detainer proceedings insofar as it authorizes a magistrate to prepare a decision without factual findings and enables the trial court to adopt the magistrate's decision without conducting an independent analysis)

Evictions; Rules Applicable

Talley v. Warner, 99 Ohio Misc. 2d 42, 715 N.E.2d 635 (M.C. 1999) (the Rules of Civil Procedure are applicable in eviction proceedings unless they are found to frustrate the summary nature of the proceedings)

Scope of Rules

Woodman v. Tubbs Jones, 103 Ohio App. 3d 577, 660 N.E.2d 520 (the Rules apply to all proceedings unless clearly inapplicable), *dismissed, appeal not allowed*, 74 Ohio St. 3d 1405, 655 N.E.2d 184 (1995)

CHAPTER 2

Rule 2. One Form of Action

Rule 2 reads as follows:

There shall be only one form of action, and it shall be known as a civil action.

COMMENTARY

Rule 2, with slight changes, is modeled after Federal Rule of Civil Procedure 2 and provides for a single action and mode of procedure in civil cases. However, actions in law and suits in equity were merged in Ohio long before the promulgation of Ohio Rule 2. Thus, Ohio Rule 2 is symbolically distinguishable from Federal Rule 2, which represents the incarnation of the merger of law and equity in federal courts. Ohio Rule 2 thus functions merely as a continuation of the elimination of any distinction between actions in law and suits in equity.

Nonetheless, the question whether an action would have been formerly characterized as "legal" or "equitable" is still significant. As with any other rule of procedure, Rule 2 can "neither abridge, enlarge nor modify the substantive rights of any litigant." The distinction between "legal" and "equitable" actions thus maintains its vitality for the right to jury trial as provided by article I, § 5 of the Ohio Constitution. The case law establishing the right to a jury trial is well-settled in Ohio, and cases decided prior to the adoption of Rule 2 remain binding on Ohio courts.

ADDITIONAL AUTHORITY

4 WRIGHT & MILLER §§ 1041-1050
1 MOORE'S FEDERAL PRACTICE §§ 2.01-2.06
1 KLEIN DARLING AT 2-1 to AT 2-3
2 OH. JUR. PL. AND PRAC. FORMS, ch. 7
1 MILLIGAN Forms 2-1 to 2-2
1 FINK §§ 2-1 to 2-5

LEADING CASES

One Form of Action

National Bank v. Haupricht Bros., 55 Ohio App. 3d 249, 564 N.E.2d 101 (1988)
(the Rules provide only one form of action, a civil action)

II

COMMENCEMENT OF ACTION
AND VENUE; SERVICE OF PROCESS;
SERVICE AND FILING OF PLEADINGS
AND OTHER PAPERS SUBSEQUENT
TO THE ORIGINAL COMPLAINT; TIME

CHAPTER 3

Rule 3. Commencement of Action; Venue

Rule 3 reads as follows:

(A) Commencement. A civil action is commenced by filing a complaint with the court, if service is obtained within one year from such filing upon a named defendant, or upon an incorrectly named defendant whose name is later corrected pursuant to Civ. R. 15(C), or upon a defendant identified by a fictitious name whose name is later corrected pursuant to Civ. R. 15(D).

(B) Venue: where proper. Any action may be venued, commenced, and decided in any court in any county. When applied to county and municipal courts, "county," as used in this rule, shall be construed, where appropriate, as the territorial limits of those courts. Proper venue lies in any one or more of the following counties:

(1) The county in which the defendant resides;

(2) The county in which the defendant has his or her principal place of business;

(3) A county in which the defendant conducted activity that gave rise to the claim for relief;

(4) A county in which a public officer maintains his or her principal office if suit is brought against the officer in the officer's official capacity;

(5) A county in which the property, or any part of the property, is situated if the subject of the action is real property or tangible personal property;

(6) The county in which all or part of the claim for relief arose; or, if the claim for relief arose upon a river, other watercourse, or a road, that is the boundary of the state, or of two or more counties, in any county bordering on the river, watercourse, or road, and opposite to the place where the claim for relief arose;

(7) In actions described in Civ. R. 4.3, in the county where plaintiff resides;

(8) In an action against an executor, administrator, guardian, or trustee, in the county in which the executor, administrator, guardian, or trustee was appointed;

(9) In actions for divorce, annulment, or legal separation, in the county in which the plaintiff is and has been a resident for at least ninety days immediately preceding the filing of the complaint;

(10) In actions for a civil protection order, in the county in which the petitioner currently or temporarily resides;

(11) If there is no available forum in divisions (B)(1) to (B)(10) of this rule, in the county in which plaintiff resides, has his or her principal place of business, or regularly and systematically conducts business activity;

(12) If there is no available forum in divisions (B)(1) to (B)(11) of this rule:

(a) In a county in which defendant has property or debts owing to the defendant subject to attachment or garnishment;

(b) In a county in which defendant has appointed an agent to receive service of process or in which an agent has been appointed by operation of law.

(C) Change of venue.

(1) When an action has been commenced in a county other than stated to be proper in division (B) of this rule, upon timely assertion of the defense of improper venue as provided in Civ. R. 12, the court shall transfer the action to a county stated to be proper in division (B) of this rule.

(2) When an action is transferred to a county which is proper, the court may assess costs, including reasonable attorney fees, to the time of transfer against the party who commenced the action in a county other than stated to be proper in division (B) of this rule.

(3) Before entering a default judgment in an action in which the defendant has not appeared, the court, if it finds that the action has been commenced in a county other than stated to be proper in division (B) of this rule, may transfer the action to a county that is proper. The clerk of the court to which the action is transferred shall notify the defendant of the transfer, stating in the notice that the defendant shall have twenty-eight days from the receipt of the notice to answer in the transferred action.

(4) Upon motion of any party or upon its own motion the court may transfer any action to an adjoining county within this state when it appears that a fair and impartial trial cannot be had in the county in which the suit is pending.

(D) Venue: no proper forum in Ohio. When a court, upon motion of any party or upon its own motion, determines: (1) that the county in which the action is brought is not a proper forum; (2) that there is no other proper forum for trial within this state; and (3) that there exists a proper forum for trial in another jurisdiction outside this state, the court shall stay the action upon condition that all defendants consent to the jurisdiction, waive venue, and agree that the date of commencement of the action in Ohio shall be the date of commencement for the application of the statute of limitations to the action in that forum in another jurisdiction which the court deems to be the proper forum. If all defendants agree to the conditions, the court shall not dismiss the action, but the action shall be stayed until the court receives notice by affidavit that plaintiff has recommenced the action in the out-of-state forum within sixty days after the effective date of the order staying the original action. If the plaintiff fails to recommence the action in the out-of-state forum within the sixty day period, the court shall dismiss the action without prejudice. If all defendants do not agree to or comply with the conditions, the court shall hear the action.

If the court determines that a proper forum does not exist in another jurisdiction, it shall hear the action.

(E) Venue: multiple defendants and multiple claims for relief. In any action, brought by one or more plaintiffs against one or more defendants involving one or more claims for relief, the forum shall be deemed a proper forum, and venue therein shall be proper, if the venue is proper as to any one party other than a nominal party, or as to any one claim for relief.

Neither the dismissal of any claim nor of any party except an indispensable party shall affect the jurisdiction of the court over the remaining parties.

(F) Venue: notice of pending litigation; transfer of judgments.

(1) When an action affecting the title to or possession of real property or tangible personal property is commenced in a county other than the county in which all of the real property or tangible personal property is situated, the plaintiff shall cause a certified copy of the complaint to be filed with the clerk of the court of common pleas in each county or additional county in which the real property or tangible personal property affected by the action is situated. If the plaintiff fails to file a certified copy of the complaint, third persons will not be charged with notice of the pendency of the action.

To the extent authorized by the laws of the United States, division (F)(1) of this rule also applies to actions, other than proceedings in bankruptcy, affecting title to or possession of real property in this state commenced in a United States District Court whenever the real property is situated wholly or partly in a county other than the county in which the permanent records of the court are kept.

(2) After final judgment, or upon dismissal of the action, the clerk of the court that issued the judgment shall transmit a certified copy of the judgment or dismissal to the clerk of the court of common pleas in each county or additional county in which real or tangible personal property affected by the action is situated.

(3) When the clerk has transmitted a certified copy of the judgment to another county in accordance with division (F)(2) of this rule, and the judgment

is later appealed, vacated or modified, the appellant or the party at whose instance the judgment was vacated or modified must cause a certified copy of the notice of appeal or order of vacation or modification to be filed with the clerk of the court of common pleas of each county or additional county in which the real property or tangible personal property is situated. Unless a certified copy of the notice of appeal or order of vacation or modification is so filed, third persons will not be charged with notice of the appeal, vacation, or modification.

(4) The clerk of the court receiving a certified copy filed or transmitted in accordance with the provisions of division (F) of this rule shall number, index, docket, and file it in the records of the receiving court. The clerk shall index the first certified copy received in connection with a particular action in the indices to the records of actions commenced in the clerk's own court, but may number, docket, and file it in either the regular records of the court or in a separate set of records. When the clerk subsequently receives a certified copy in connection with that same action, the clerk need not index it, but shall docket and file it in the same set of records under the same case number previously assigned to the action.

(5) When an action affecting title to registered land is commenced in a county other than the county in which all of such land is situated, any certified copy required or permitted by this division (F) of this rule shall be filed with or transmitted to the county recorder, rather than the clerk of the court of common pleas, of each county or additional county in which the land is situated.

(G) Venue: collateral attack; appeal. The provisions of this rule relate to venue and are not jurisdictional. No order, judgment, or decree shall be void or subject to collateral attack solely on the ground that there was improper venue; however, nothing here shall affect the right to appeal an error of court concerning venue.

COMMENTARY

Rule 3 has two functions: it specifies the point at which an action is deemed to have commenced, and it sets forth the provisions regarding venue in Ohio courts.

Commencement of Action

Under Rule 3(A), there are two requirements for the commencement of a civil action: (1) the filing of a complaint with the court; and (2) service of the complaint and summons on the defendant within one year of the filing of the complaint. Although service of the summons on the defendant is required for the commencement of an action, the filing date is used for determining whether the statute of limitations has run. Service of the summons on the defendant may occur after the statute of limitations has run, so long as the complaint was filed before the expiration of the relevant time period.

The time period specified in Rule 3(A) should be distinguished from the time period for serving a defendant with the summons and copy of the complaint set forth in Rule 4(E). Although Rule 3(A) contemplates service on the defendant at any time within one year of the date of filing of the complaint, Rule 4(E) requires that the summons be served within six months of the filing, unless good cause is shown. These provisions can be reconciled by interpreting Rule 3(A) as placing a limit on out-of-state service, service in a foreign country, or any extension granted by the court under Rule 4(E) for serving unknown or incorrectly named defendants.

Commencement by Filing of Other Papers

Although Rule 3(A) appears unambiguous with respect to the determination of when an action is deemed to have commenced, confusion frequently arises under certain kinds of statutory proceedings. For example, certain administrative appeals to trial courts may be initiated by the filing of a "petition" or "appeal," which may or may not have all of the characteristics of a formal complaint. Furthermore, the party filing the "petition" or "appeal" may not necessarily be considered the "plaintiff" for purposes of applying other Rules.

Illustration 3-1

Cindy, an employee of Seeview Corp., prevails on a workers' compensation claim in an administrative proceeding. Seeview then files a notice of appeal of the decision with the local court. As required by statute, Cindy then files a petition containing a statement of facts upon which the appeal of the administrative decision will proceed. Although the filing of Seeview's notice of appeal will be considered to have "commenced" the action under Rule 3, Cindy will be considered the "plaintiff" in the action and her "petition" is considered to be the initial "pleading" for purposes of applying particular Rules.

The confusion is resolved by understanding that Rule 3(A), like its federal analog, is concerned primarily with indicating the point in time at which an action is deemed to have commenced, not with the nature of the act pursuant to which the court has jurisdiction over the matter. It is intended to specify that "commencement" of the action, which, as noted, is used to determine whether the statute of limitations has tolled and to trigger certain time periods under the Rules, occurs upon the filing of a complaint or similar paper, not upon formal service of process on the defendant.

Relationship of Rule 3 to Savings Statute

Ohio's "savings statute" is located at OHIO REV. CODE ANN. § 2305.19 (1998). This provision operates when a decision is reversed on appeal or the action is dismissed or resolved other than on the merits of the case. In such a situation, a party may re-commence an action within one year after the date of dismissal, reversal, vacation, or failure of the action even if the applicable statute of limitations has run.

Properly construed and applied, the operation of the savings statute does not conflict with the provisions of Rule 3. Although the determination as to whether the statute of limitations has expired is made under Rule 3, the savings statute will not affect the date upon which the action is deemed to have commenced. A timely re-commencement of an action within the one-year time period under the savings statute will similarly be determined according to the provisions of Rule 3, *i.e.*, filing of a complaint with the court and subsequent service within one year of that filing.

Filing Requirements

The phrase "filing . . . with the court" is not defined in Rule 3; instead, Rule 5(E) sets forth the requirements for a proper filing with the court. Similarly, the list of allowable pleadings in a civil action is not the subject of Rule 3; instead, such a list is provided in Rule 7. The purpose of Rule 3 is simply to denominate the point at which an action is deemed to have been commenced.

Relation Back of Amendments

Rule 3(A) was changed in 1986 to allow for the amendment of complaints pursuant to Rule 15(C) and 15(D). Such amendments are necessary when a complaint is filed against defendants not yet known at the time of the filing. These amendments will relate back to the time of filing even if the identity of the defendants is discovered after the statute of limitations has expired.

Venue Not Jurisdictional; Objections

It is well-settled in Ohio that venue is a procedural question, not a jurisdictional one. Proper venue ensures that the defendant is provided with a convenient forum in which to defend an action, though improper venue will not deny a court's jurisdiction over an action. Judgments of Ohio courts are not subject to collateral attack solely on grounds of improper venue, a point made expressly in subsection (G).

Under subsection (C), if an objection to venue is properly raised under Rule 12(B)(3), a court must transfer the action to a proper venue as determined under the provisions of subsection (B). However, the failure to object to improper venue will constitute a waiver of that defense. Costs may be assessed against the party bringing the action in a court in which venue is improper. Subsection (C) also contains provisions relating to improper venue in cases in which a default judgment is about to be entered in the docket.

Venue Generally

Rule 3(B) sets forth the general provisions regarding venue in Ohio courts. Its initial statement that "[a]ny action may be venued, commenced, and decided in any court in any county of Ohio" should not be misconstrued as implying that venue is proper in any Ohio court. Actions must be brought according to the preferential scheme set forth in subsection (B). The word "county," as it is used in Rule 3, refers to the territorial limits of county or municipal courts, not the geographic limits of the counties themselves. In most cases, the territorial limits of county and municipal parallel the geographic boundaries of the counties in which the courts are located. In some cases, however, the territorial limits of certain courts may be broader or more restrictive than the geographic boundaries of the counties in which the courts are located.

The counties in which venue is proper are listed in subsection (B), and, as noted, the provision sets up a preferential scheme. Plaintiffs are required to bring actions in one of the counties specified in subsections (B)(1)-(10). If none of these choices is available, an action may be brought in the county in which the plaintiff resides, has a principal place of business, or regularly and systematically conducts business activity under subsection (B)(11). If this provision is likewise unavailable, subsection (B)(12) may be used in extreme cases to allow a plaintiff to bring an action in the counties specified in that subsection. Subsection (B)(11) and (B)(12) are not available to a plaintiff unless the options listed in subsections (B)(1)-(10) have been exhausted and no proper venue exists under those subsections.

Subsection (F) contains detailed provisions relating to the commencement of an action involving real or personal property in a county other than that in which the property is located. In such a circumstance, the clerk of the court in which the action was commenced should coordinate with the clerk of the county in which the property is located with regard to the filing of the complaint and any judgment rendered.

Venue in Actions for a Civil Protection Order

Subsection (B)(10) was added to Rule 3 in 1998. The new provision operates only in actions for civil protection orders, *e.g.*, domestic relations or family abuse cases. In these cases, venue must be laid in a court in the county where the petitioner currently or temporarily resides. The amended rule is unclear as to whether venue may be proper in another county in actions in which a civil protection order is but one form of relief requested, and the Staff Note concerning the amendment provides no guidance on the issue. Although proper venue in these cases will routinely overlap with the provisions in subsection (B)(9), additional clarification on this point is in order.

Additional amendments to Rule 3 in 1998 concerned the style used for references to Rules and subsections thereof, grammatical corrections, and other stylistic changes. No substantive amendments were intended.

Venue: No Proper Forum in Ohio

Subsection (D) sets forth the procedure to be used in Ohio courts when it is determined that no proper forum is available in Ohio but that a forum is available in another state. In this situation, the action may be stayed if all defendants agree to the following conditions: (1) the alternative venue has jurisdiction over all defendants; (2) objections to venue are waived by all parties; and (3) the parties agree that the date of commencement in Ohio for the application of the statute of limitations will apply in the forum of the alternate jurisdiction. Upon the satisfaction of these three requirements, a court must stay the action and allow the plaintiff to recommence the action in the out-of-state forum within 60 days. However, if the plaintiff fails to recommence the action within the 60 days, a court must dismiss the action without prejudice, and the applicable statute of limitations will begin to run as of the date of dismissal.

Multiple Parties or Claims

In an action involving multiple parties or multiple claims, venue is proper as to all parties and claims if venue is proper as to any one party so long as that party is not a nominal party. If any party is subsequently dismissed from the action, a court will retain its jurisdiction over all parties even if venue was established only by the dismissed party, unless the dismissed party was an indispensable party. Additionally, a forum that satisfies one of the venue choices of subsections (B)(1)-(9) as to a single defendant will be superior to venue under subsections (B)(10) and (B)(11) even if the venue chosen under subsections (B)(1)-(9) is improper as to the other defendants.

Forum Non Conveniens

The doctrine of *forum non conveniens*—that a court may resist imposition upon its jurisdiction even when jurisdiction is authorized by the letter of a general statute—is not specifically contemplated in the Ohio Rules. However, the doctrine may be employed by Ohio courts, pursuant to their inherent powers, to achieve the ends of justice and convenience of the parties or the witnesses. *Forum non conveniens*, like the Ohio Rules, is to be construed so that the mandates of Rule 1(B) are promoted. A variation on the doctrine—transfer of the action because a fair and impartial trial cannot be obtained in the county in which the action is pending—is specifically authorized by subsection (C)(4).

In considering a motion to dismiss for *forum non conveniens*, a trial court must weigh a number of public and private interests. Public interests include administrative difficulties and delay to other litigants caused by congested court dockets, the imposition of jury duty upon citizens of the jurisdiction, and the appropriateness of litigating a case in a forum familiar with the applicable law. Private interests to be considered include access to sources or proof, availability of compulsory process for attendance of unwilling witnesses, location of willing witnesses, and enforceability of a judgment if one is obtained.

ADDITIONAL AUTHORITY

4 WRIGHT & MILLER §§ 1051-1060
1 MOORE'S FEDERAL PRACTICE §§ 3.01-3.07
4 ANDERSON'S OHIO CIVIL PRACTICE §§ 148.01-148.30, 149.01-149.27
1 KLEIN DARLING AT 3-1 to AT 3-78
3 TEREZ F 3.2.1 to F 3.2.5, F 3.3.1 to F 3.3.5, F 4.12.1 to F 4.12.3
2 OH. JUR. PL. AND PRAC. FORMS, ch. 7-8
1 MILLIGAN Forms 3-1 to 3-126
1 FINK §§ 3-1 to 3-8
OHIO LITIGATION CHECKLISTS, Pleading and Process, §§ 20-22

LEADING CASES

Abuse of Discretion Standard on Motion to Change Venue

Railroad Ventures, Inc. v. Drake, 138 Ohio App. 3d 315, 741 N.E.2d 206 (2000) (a trial court's decision to change venue is reviewed on an abuse of discretion basis, which connotes more than an error of law or judgment; it implies that the trial court's attitude was unreasonable, arbitrary, or unconscionable)

Change of Venue

Romanchik v. Lucak, 44 Ohio App. 3d 215, 542 N.E.2d 699 (1988) (when venue is found to be improper, the court should transfer the cause of action to a county where venue lies)

Collateral Attack

Allied Chem. Co. v. Aurelius, 16 Ohio App. 3d 69, 474 N.E.2d 618 (1984) (writ of mandamus does not lie to compel a change of venue, as any error in venue is subject to appellate review)

Commencement of Action; Timing

Motorists Mut. Ins. Co. v. Huron Road Hosp., 73 Ohio St. 3d 391, 653 N.E.2d 235 (1995) (action is properly commenced if filed within the proscribed statutory period and service is obtained within one year from that filing)

Commencement Through Means Other than Filing of Complaint

Robinson v. B.O.C. Group, Gen. Motors Corp., 81 Ohio St. 3d 361, 691 N.E.2d 667 (1998) (the term "petition," as it is used in the statute governing appeals, is considered a "complaint" for purposes of applying the Rules of Civil Procedure; however, the action is deemed to have commenced when the employer files a notice of appeal, not when the employee files the statutorily required responding petition)

Costs

Atwood Resources, Inc. v. Lehigh, 98 Ohio App. 3d 293, 648 N.E.2d 548 (1994) (attorneys' fees may be assessed against a party who brings an action in a county where venue is improper), *appeal not allowed*, 71 Ohio St. 3d 1493, 646 N.E.2d 469 (1995)

Fictitious Defendants

Kramer v. Installations Unltd., 147 Ohio App. 3d 350, 770 N.E.2d 632 (2002) (under the one-year rule for commencement of an action, service does not have to be made within the statute of limitations on a former fictitious defendant, as long as the original complaint has been filed before the expiration of the statute of limitations)

No Proper Venue in Ohio

Singleton v. Denny's, Inc., 36 Ohio App. 3d 225, 522 N.E.2d 1097 (1987) (if venue is improper in Ohio, the court may stay the action to allow the plaintiff to recommence the action in a proper forum in another state)

Venue; Generally

Glover v. Glover, 66 Ohio App. 3d 724, 586 N.E.2d 159 (venue is equally proper in any county which satisfies one of the requirements of Rule 3(B)(1)-(9); however, specific provisions take precedence over general ones), *jurisdictional motion overruled*, 55 Ohio St. 3d 715, 563 N.E.2d 725 (1990)

Venue; Multiple Parties

Varketta v. General Motors Corp., 34 Ohio App. 2d 1, 295 N.E.2d 219 (1973) (if venue is proper as to any party in any county, that county is a proper forum as to all parties)

Venue; Waiver

Nicholson v. Landis, 27 Ohio App. 3d 107, 499 N.E.2d 1260 (1985) (failure to raise timely defense of improper venue in a responsive pleading or motion made prior to that pleading in accordance with Rule 12 constitutes a waiver as provided in Rule 12(H)(1))

CHAPTER 4

Rule 4. Process: Summons

Rule 4 reads as follows:

(A) Summons: issuance. Upon the filing of the complaint the clerk shall forthwith issue a summons for service upon each defendant listed in the caption. Upon request of the plaintiff separate or additional summons shall issue at any time against any defendant.

(B) Summons: form; copy of complaint. The summons shall be signed by the clerk, contain the name and address of the court and the names and addresses of the parties, be directed to the defendant, state the name and address of the plaintiff's attorney, if any, otherwise the plaintiff's address, and the times within which these rules or any statutory provision require the defendant to appear and defend, and shall notify him that in case of his failure to do so, judgment by default will be rendered against him for the relief demanded in the complaint. Where there are multiple plaintiffs or multiple defendants, or both, the summons may contain, in lieu of the names and addresses of all parties, the name of the first party on each side and the name and address of the party to be served.

A copy of the complaint shall be attached to each summons. The plaintiff shall furnish the clerk with sufficient copies.

(C) Summons: plaintiff and defendant defined. For the purpose of issuance and service of summons "plaintiff" shall include any party seeking the issuance and service of summons, and "defendant" shall include any party upon whom service of summons is sought.

(D) Waiver of service of summons. Service of summons may be waived in writing by any person entitled thereto under Rule 4.2 who is at least eighteen years of age and not under disability.

(E) Summons: time limit for service. If a service of the summons and complaint is not made upon a defendant within six months after the filing of the complaint and the party on whose behalf such service was required cannot show good cause why such service was not made within that period, the action shall be dismissed as to that defendant without prejudice upon the court's own initiative with notice to such party or upon motion. This division shall not apply to out-of-state service pursuant to Rule 4.3 or to service in a foreign country pursuant to Rule 4.5.

COMMENTARY

Rules 4-4.6 prescribe service of process requirements in Ohio courts. Rule 4 contains some of the general provisions regarding service of process, and it establishes the procedural framework within which Rules 4.1-4.6 operate. This framework is structurally more elegant than Federal Rule of Civil Procedure 4, which sets forth all the requirements for service of the summons within a single rule. Permissible methods of service are set forth in Rule 4.1.

Definition of Summons

A summons is the legal notification that a civil action has been commenced against the person or entity to whom the summons is addressed. Compliance with Rule 4 must be maintained whenever a person is joined as a party under Rules 14, 19, 20, and 22, and whenever a person is substituted as a party under Rule 25. Class actions have distinct service and notice requirements, and they are discussed in Chapter 23.

A subpoena is distinct from a summons. Service of subpoenas, which are directives from a court to non-party witnesses to appear in a particular place or take a particular action, is governed by Rule 45.

Service of Summons and Service of Process Distinguished

As noted, Rule 4 regulates the issuance and service of a summons and copy of the complaint on the defendants, the modern form of original process in virtually all domestic courts. It is well settled that the service of a properly executed and issued summons and copy of the complaint will satisfy constitutional due process requirements, or "service of process" requirements. The terms are thus often used interchangeably, and the term "service," as it is used in the Rules or in this manual, refers to either service of process generally or service of a summons accompanied by a copy of the complaint. The distinction between service of process and service of the summons and copy of the complaint as a form of service of process is reflected in the now almost archaic distinction between a motion under Rule 12(B)(4) to dismiss for insufficiency of process and a motion under Rule 12(B)(5) to dismiss for insufficiency of service of process. A motion under Rule 12(B)(4) attacks the summons or other process itself as insufficient in satisfying due process requirements. A motion under Rule 12(B)(5) attacks the manner in which the summons or other process was served upon the defendant or party raising the motion.

It should be noted that the service of a summons may not be the only form of process issued by Ohio courts. For example, persons who are subject to contempt orders or orders of civil commitment are not typically notified of such orders through a summons. Similarly, service of a summons may not be the exclusive manner in which "service of process" requirements may be satisfied. For example, service by publication, as set forth in Rule 4.4, does not typically result in an actual receipt of a summons by a defendant. Nonetheless, service by publication has been held to satisfy service of process requirements.

"Service" and "Delivery" Distinguished

To properly understand the operation of Rules 4-4.6 and the interrelationship of those Rules with Rule 5, it is crucial to distinguish between "service" of a document, such as a summons, and "delivery" of a document, such as a motion or discovery request. When a statute or rule specifies a method of *service* of process, that process must be conveyed by a person specifically authorized and in a manner in accordance with the terms of that statute or rule. Properly conceptualized, "delivery" of a document refers to a method of service of that document and may be used only when specifically authorized. For example, Rule 5 designates "delivery" as one method of service of documents falling within the purview of that Rule. On the other hand, Rule 4 does not contain provisions for "delivery" of a summons or any other kind of process. The effect of this distinction is that service of process under Rules 4-4.6 cannot be made merely by sending the summons by first-class mail or by hand-delivering the summons by anyone selected by the plaintiff. Instead, "service" of the summons must be effected through one of the methods or by a person specifically authorized by Rules 4.1-4.6.

Issuance of the Summons

Subsection (A) makes it clear that a plaintiff is responsible for ensuring service upon defendants by requiring that all defendants to be served are listed in the caption of a complaint filed with the clerk of courts. To avoid any ambiguity, the terms "plaintiff" and "defendant" are defined in subsection (C) in terms of who is seeking and to whom is directed the issuance and service of a summons. For example, a defendant who wishes to implead a third party under Rule 14 is considered a "plaintiff" for purposes of Rule 4 and must bear the responsibility for ensuring that the third party is properly served with a summons and copies of the pleadings.

A properly filed complaint will satisfy the requirements of Rule 10(A) for the contents of captions. Pursuant to a 1973 amendment, the clerk no longer has the obligation to read a complaint to determine if defendants, other than those listed in the caption, should also be served. The attorney for the plaintiff thus bears the responsibility of ensuring service by satisfying the requirements of Rule 4(A) and Rule 10(A). Service on named defendants satisfies the duty of the clerk of courts.

Contents of the Summons

Rule 4(B) lists the information that must be included in every summons. Crucially, it must contain the time period within which the defendant must appear and defend the action, and it must also notify the defendant that failure to do so will result in a default judgment against the defendant. Omission of any of the mandatory information listed in subsection (B) is a ground for a Rule 12(B)(4) motion for insufficiency of process.

Waiver

Subsection (D) provides for the waiver of service of the summons by any defendant who is at least 18 years old, not disabled, and deemed competent to receive process under Rule 4.2. The subsection requires that the waiver be in writing, but does not otherwise indicate how a waiver may be obtained.

In view of the broad range of methods in which a summons may be served under Rule 4.1, there appears to be little advantage in securing a waiver of that service. If waiver is nonetheless sought by a party, attorneys should seek a waiver by one of the methods specified in Rule 4.1 for actual service to avoid possible objections to the validity of the waiver. There is no incentive for defendants to waive service of process in Ohio as there is in the federal system.

It should be noted that the waiver provisions of subsection (D) do not correspond exactly with the provisions of Rule 4.2 as to who may be served. Under Rule 4.2, process may be served on any individual who is at least *16* years of age and not *"incompetent."* Though the term "not under disability" in Rule 4(D) may probably be interpreted synonymously with the term "incompetent" in Rule 4.2, it is clear that individual defendants who are 16 or 17 years old may not waive service of process and must be served personally under Rule 4.2.

Time Limit

Rule 4(E) provides that all defendants must be served with a summons and copy of the complaint within six months of the date that the complaint was filed, unless the plaintiff can show good cause as to why service has not been obtained within this period. This time period should be distinguished from the one-year time limit specified in Rule 3(A), which operates as a postcondition to the commencement of an action. These provisions can be reconciled by interpreting Rule 3(A) as placing a limit on any extension granted by the court under Rule 4(E) for out-of-state service, service in a foreign country, or for serving unknown or incorrectly named defendants.

ADDITIONAL AUTHORITY

4 WRIGHT & MILLER §§ 1061-1081

4A WRIGHT & MILLER §§ 1082-1140

1 MOORE'S FEDERAL PRACTICE §§ 4.01-4.121

4 ANDERSON'S OHIO CIVIL PRACTICE §§ 150.01-150.06

1 KLEIN DARLING AT 4-1 to AT 4-15

3 TEREZ F 1.1.1 to F 1.1.2

2 OH. JUR. PL. AND PRAC. FORMS, ch. 9

1 MILLIGAN Forms 4-1 to 4-83

1 FINK §§ 4-1 to 4-6

OHIO LITIGATION CHECKLISTS, Pleading and Process, §§ 20-22

LEADING CASES

Dismissal Improper

Bentz v. Carter, 55 Ohio App. 3d 120, 562 N.E.2d 925 (1988) (although service of process was not perfected within 6 months, dismissal of a complaint pursuant to Rule 4(E) was improper where plaintiff made attempts to effect process)

Effective Service; Generally

King v. Hazra, 91 Ohio App. 3d 534, 632 N.E.2d 1336 (1993) (effective service of process is not completed by filing a request to plead, nor by sending a courtesy copy of a complaint to the attorney of the opposing party), *jurisdictional motion overruled*, 69 Ohio St. 3d 1410, 629 N.E.2d 1371 (1994)

Good Cause for Failure to Effect Service

Thomas v. Freeman, 79 Ohio St. 3d, 680 N.E.2d 997 (1997) (the failure of a plaintiff to show good cause as to the lack of service within the requisite time period will justify an involuntary dismissal under Rule 41(B)(1))

Issuance of Summons

Scott v. Orlando, 2 Ohio App. 3d 333, 442 N.E.2d 96 (1981) (a cause of action will not be barred when the failure to obtain service within the proscribed time is caused by unreasonable delay on the part of the clerk of courts or the court itself)

Notice of Default Judgment

Furniture Sales Specialists, Inc. v. Thomas, 82 Ohio App. 3d 759, 613 N.E.2d 259 (1993) (where the summons did not notify the defendant that she could be found in default after 28 days, the summons is defective and default judgment is improper), *dismissed, appeal not allowed*, 72 Ohio St. 3d 1518, 649 N.E.2d 278 (1995)

Notice of Pretrial Hearing Insufficient

Harrell v. Guest, 33 Ohio App. 3d 163, 514 N.E.2d 1137 (1986) (service of summons is not satisfied by notice of a pretrial hearing)

Service on Attorney

Steiner v. Steiner, 85 Ohio App. 3d 513, 620 N.E.2d 152 (1993) (when service of process is required to be made upon a party represented by an attorney of record, service should be made upon the attorney unless the court expressly orders that it be made upon the party)

CHAPTER 4.1

Rule 4.1. Process: Methods of Service

Rule 4.1 reads as follows:

All methods of service within this state, except service by publication as provided in Civ. R. 4.4(A), are described in this rule. Methods of out-of-state service and for service in a foreign country are described in Civ. R. 4.3 and 4.5.

(A) **Service by certified or express mail.** Evidenced by return receipt signed by any person, service of any process shall be by certified or express mail unless otherwise permitted by these rules. The clerk shall place a copy of the process and complaint or other document to be served in an envelope. The clerk shall address the envelope to the person to be served at the address set forth in the caption or at the address set forth in written instructions furnished to the clerk with instructions to forward. The clerk shall affix adequate postage and place the sealed envelope in the United States mail as certified or express mail return receipt requested with instructions to the delivering postal employee to show to whom delivered, date of delivery, and address where delivered.

The clerk shall forthwith enter the fact of mailing on the appearance docket and make a similar entry when the return receipt is received. If the envelope is returned with an endorsement showing failure of delivery, the clerk shall forthwith notify, by mail, the attorney of record or, if there is no attorney of record, the party at whose instance process was issued and enter the fact of notification on the appearance docket. The clerk shall file the return receipt or returned envelope in the records of the action.

All postage shall be charged to costs. If the parties to be served by certified or express mail are numerous and the clerk determines there is insufficient security for costs, the clerk may require the party requesting service to advance an amount estimated by the clerk to be sufficient to pay the postage.

(B) **Personal service.** When the plaintiff files a written request with the clerk for personal service, service of process shall be made by that method.

When process issued from the Supreme Court, a court of appeals, a court of common pleas, or a county court is to be served personally, the clerk of the court shall deliver the process and sufficient copies of the process and complaint, or other document to be served, to the sheriff of the county in which the party to be served resides or may be found. When process issues from the municipal court, delivery shall be to the bailiff of the court for service on all defendants who reside or may be found within the county or counties in which that court has territorial jurisdiction and to the sheriff of any other county in this state for service upon a defendant who resides in or may be found in that other county. In the alternative, process issuing from any of these courts may be delivered by the clerk to any person not less than eighteen years of age, who is not a party and who has been designated by order of the court to make service of process. The person serving process shall locate the person to be served and shall tender a copy of the process and accompanying documents to the person to be served. When the copy of the process has been served, the person serving process shall endorse that fact on the process and return it to the clerk, who shall make the appropriate entry on the appearance docket.

When the person serving process is unable to serve a copy of the process within twenty-eight days, the person shall endorse that fact and the reasons therefor on the process and return the process and copies to the clerk who shall make the appropriate entry on the appearance docket. In the event of failure of service, the clerk shall follow the notification procedure set forth in division (A) of this rule. Failure to make service within the twenty-eight day period and failure to make proof of service do not affect the validity of the service.

(C) **Residence service.** When the plaintiff files a written request with the clerk for residence service, service of process shall be made by that method.

Residence service shall be effected by leaving a copy of the process and the complaint, or other document to be served, at the usual place of residence of the person to be served with some person of suitable age and discretion then residing therein. The clerk of the court shall issue the process, and the process server shall return it, in the same manner as prescribed in division (B) of this rule. When the person serving process is unable to serve a copy of the process within twenty-eight days, the person shall endorse that fact and the reasons therefor on the process, and return the process and copies to the clerk, who shall make the appropriate entry on the appearance docket. In the event of failure of service, the clerk shall follow the notification procedure set forth in division (A) of this rule. Failure to make service within the twenty-eight day period and failure to make proof of service do not affect the validity of service.

COMMENTARY

Rules 4-4.6 prescribe service of process requirements in Ohio courts. Rule 4.1

delineates permissible methods of service of process on in-state defendants, and should be read in conjunction with Rule 4.2, which specifies those persons on whom in-state process may be served. More general provisions regarding service of process are located in Rule 4, and this Rule should always be consulted when interpreting the specific provisions of Rule 4.3. Service of process by publication is an additional method of service permitted under Rule 4.4. It should be noted that Rule 4.1 is not applicable to service of process on out-of-state or foreign defendants.

Service by Mail

Rule 4.1 establishes service by mail as the preferred method of service within the state. A 1997 amendment to the Rule allows the use of express mail in addition to certified mail to effect the service of process by mail.

Service by mail is usually the most inexpensive method of service, and the procedure for effecting service by this method is set forth in subsection (A). Its provisions are self-explanatory. Proof of service by mail is ensured by the requirement of a return receipt, which the clerk is directed to retain and file with the other papers in the action. If service by mail fails, and the summons is returned undelivered, the plaintiff must effect service of process through one of the other methods listed in the Rule.

Rule 4.1 does not indicate when service of process is deemed to have been completed when effected by express or certified mail under subsection (A). The accurate determination of the date of service is important for, among other purposes, calculating the time period within which the defendant is required to serve an answer under Rule 12(A).

Four considerations militate in favor of the argument that service of process should be deemed complete when service of the summons and copy of the complaint is actually received by the defendant, as opposed to when the summons is placed in the mail by the clerk. First, the final two sentences of Rule 5(B), which govern the service of all documents in an action other than the original process, explicitly provide that service of papers by mail under that Rule is complete upon mailing or fax transmission. The absence of a similar provision in Rule 4.1 suggests that the drafters of the Rule intended a contrary result for service of the summons.

Second, the certainty provided by the return receipt of the express or certified mail is guaranteed by Rule 4.1's requirement that such methods of mail service be used for service of the summons. The necessity of a return receipt thus functions as superior proof of the date of actual service rather than the 3-day presumption of delivery by first-class mail employed by Rule 6(E).

Third, the final sentence of Rule 6(E), which generally provides for an automatic 3-day extension of any time period triggered by the service of a document by mail, expressly excepts responses to the service of a summons from its operation. This exception, which, properly conceived, functions as a complement to Rule 5(B)'s presumption that service by mail is complete upon mailing, implies that the time period within which responses to the service of a summons must be made should be measured in a different fashion than the time periods within which responses to other kinds of papers and documents must be made.

Finally, it should be recalled that Rules 4-4.6 must comply with state and federal constitutional considerations of due process that do not obtain to service of documents under Rule 5. The method most likely to result in actual notice of the pendency of an action against a particular person, a cornerstone of due process compliance, is insured by measuring the time period within which that person must take some kind of defensive action in the case from the date of actual receipt of the summons rather than from the date of an event that is marginally less likely to result in actual notice to the party.

Personal and Residence Service

Upon filing a written request with the clerk, personal service and residence service pursuant to Rule 4.1(B) and 4.1(C) may also be made. The process server is usually a sheriff of the county in which the court is located or a bailiff of the court in which the action is pending, but any non-party at least 18 years of age may be so designated by the court. If service of process fails under either of these two methods, the clerk must notify, by mail, the attorney of record or the party seeking service of process and enter the fact of notification on the appearance docket. Proof of service of process must be made by the person effecting the service, and the form must be returned to the clerk.

ADDITIONAL AUTHORITY

4 Wright & Miller §§ 1061-1081

4A Wright & Miller §§ 1082-1140

1 Moore's Federal Practice §§ 4.1.01-4.1.04

4 Anderson's Ohio Civil Practice §§ 150.17-150.28

Klein Darling AT 4.1-1 to AT 4.1-16

3 Terez F 1.1.1, F 1.2.1, F 1.2.2, F 1.3.1 to F 1.3.3

2 Oh. Jur. Pl. and Prac. Forms, ch. 9

1 Milligan Forms 4.1-1 to 4.1-23

1 Fink §§ 4.1-1 to 4.1-7

Ohio Litigation Checklists, Pleading and Process, §§ 20-22

LEADING CASES

Absent Defendants

Morrison v. Steiner, 32 Ohio St. 2d 86, 290 N.E.2d 841 (1972) (Rule 4.1(A) sets forth the method by which a municipal court may effect personal service upon a defendant found outside its territory)

Attorney General Service Mandatory for Constitutionality Challenge

In re Adoption of Coppersmith, 145 Ohio App. 3d 141, 761 N.E.2d 1163 (2001) (a party who challenges the constitutionality of a statute must: (1) raise the unconstitutionality claim in the complaint or amendment thereto; and (2) serve the Attorney General under the applicable Rules of Civil Procedure)

Cicco v. Stockmaster, 89 Ohio St. 3d 95, 728 N.E.2d 1066 (2000) (a party challenging the constitutionality of a statute must serve the pleading on the Attorney General in accordance with Rule 4.1)

Certified Mail; Generally

Schroeder v. Vigil-Escalera Perez, 76 Ohio Misc. 2d 25, 664 N.E.2d 627 (C.P. 1995) (service of process is sufficient when the return receipt is signed by any person at an address reasonably calculated to give notice to the defendant)

Entry and Detainer Actions; Service Requirements Invalid

Talley v. Warner, 99 Ohio Misc. 2d 42, 715 N.E.2d 635 (M.C. 1999) (the statute governing forcible entry and detainer actions, which permits the plaintiff to achieve service of process by ordinary mail when that service is accompanied by posting complaint at premises, conflicts with Rule 4.1, and is thus invalid; the use of certified or express mail, which is preferred under the Rules governing service of process, does not frustrate the summary nature of evictions)

Judgment Voided

O.B. Corp. v. Cordell, 47 Ohio App. 3d 170, 547 N.E.2d 1201 (1988) (judgment entered against an individual not served with process and who did not appear in the action is void)

Receipt of Certified Mail

Rite Rug Co. v. Wilson, 106 Ohio App. 3d 59, 665 N.E.2d 260 (1995) (service by certified mail does not require actual service by the party receiving notice)

Service at a Business

Bell v. Midwestern Educ. Servs., 89 Ohio App. 3d 193, 624 N.E.2d 196 (discussing elements for effective service at a place of business), *jurisdictional motion overruled*, 67 Ohio St. 3d 1456, 619 N.E.2d 424 (1993)

CHAPTER 4.2

Rule 4.2. Process: Who May Be Served

Rule 4.2 reads as follows:

Service of process, except service by publication as provided in Civ. R. 4.4(A), pursuant to Civ. R. 4 through 4.6 shall be made as follows:

(A) Upon an individual, other than a person under sixteen years of age or an incompetent person, by serving the individual;

(B) Upon a person under sixteen years of age by serving either the person's guardian or any one of the following persons with whom the person to be served lives or resides: father, mother, or the individual having the care of the person; or by serving the person if the person neither has a guardian nor lives or resides with a parent or a person having his or her care;

(C) Upon an incompetent person by serving either the incompetent's guardian or the person designated in division (E) of this rule, but if no guardian has been appointed and the incompetent is not under confinement or commitment, by serving the incompetent;

(D) Upon an individual confined to a penal institution of this state or of a subdivision of this state by serving the individual, except that when the individual to be served is a person under sixteen years of age, the provisions of division (B) of this rule shall be applicable;

(E) Upon an incompetent person who is confined in any institution for the mentally ill or mentally deficient or committed by order of court to the custody of some other institution or person by serving the superintendent or similar official of the institution to which the incompetent is confined or committed or the person to whose custody the incompetent is committed;

(F) Upon a corporation either domestic or foreign: by serving the agent authorized by appointment or by law to receive service of process; or by serving the corporation by certified or express mail at any of its usual places of business; or by serving an officer or a managing or general agent of the corporation;

(G) Upon a partnership, a limited partnership, or a limited partnership association by serving the entity by certified or express mail at any of its usual places of business or by serving a partner, limited partner, manager, or member;

(H) Upon an unincorporated association by serving it in its entity name by certified or express mail at any of its usual places of business or by serving an officer of the unincorporated association;

(I) Upon a professional association by serving the association in its corporate name by certified or express mail at the place where the corporate offices are maintained or by serving a shareholder;

(J) Upon this state or any one of its departments, offices and institutions as defined in division (C) of section 121.01 of the Revised Code, by serving the officer responsible for the administration of the department, office or institution or by serving the attorney general of this state;

(K) Upon a county or upon any of its offices, agencies, districts, departments, institutions or administrative units, by serving the officer responsible for the administration of the office, agency, district, department, institution or unit or by serving the prosecuting attorney of the county;

(L) Upon a township by serving one or more of the township trustees or the township clerk or by serving the prosecuting attorney of the county in which the township is located, unless the township is organized under Chapter 504. of the Revised Code, in which case service may be made upon the township law director;

(M) Upon a municipal corporation or upon any of its offices, departments, agencies, authorities, institutions or administrative units by serving the officer responsible for the administration of the office, department, agency, authority, institution or unit or by serving the city solicitor or comparable legal officer;

(N) Upon any governmental entity not mentioned above by serving the person, officer, group or body responsible for the administration of that entity or by serving the appropriate legal officer, if any, representing the entity. Service upon any person who is a member of the "group" or "body" responsible for the administration of the entity shall be sufficient.

COMMENTARY

Rules 4-4.6 prescribe service of process requirements in Ohio courts. Rule 4.2 specifies those persons eligible to receive process through one of the methods delineated in Rule 4.1. More general provisions regarding service of process are located in Rule 4, and this Rule should always be consulted when interpreting the specific provisions of Rule 4.2.

Who May Be Served

Rule 4.2 gathers together under a single rule all of the persons and entities who may be served, except those to whom service by publication under Rule 4.4 is the method of service being used. Rule 4.2 applies both to out-of-state defendants as well as in-state defendants. The specific provisions of Rule 4.2 are self-explanatory. Subsections (A)-(E) govern service of process upon individuals; subsections (F)-(H) provide for service of process upon private entities; and subsections (I)-(N) regulate service of process upon government entities.

ADDITIONAL AUTHORITY

4 Wright & Miller §§ 1061-1081
4A Wright & Miller §§ 1082-1140
1 Moore's Federal Practice §§ 4.01-4.121
4 Anderson's Ohio Civil Practice §§ 150.07-150.16
1 Klein Darling AT 4.2-1 to AT 4.2-24
3 Terez F 1.3.3 to F 1.3.5, F 1.3.8
2 Oh. Jur. Pl. and Prac. Forms, ch. 9
1 Milligan Forms 4.2-1 to 4.2-19
1 Fink §§ 4.2-1 to 4.2-11

LEADING CASES

Fictitious Names

Deaton v. Burney, 107 Ohio App. 3d 407, 666 N.E.2d 679 (1995) (a person may be joined as a defendant identified by use of a fictitious name, and will acquire the status of party when the action is filed), *dismissed, appeal not allowed*, 75 Ohio St. 3d 1509, 665 N.E.2d 679 (1996)

Service on a County

Picciuto v. Lucas County Bd. of Comm'rs, 69 Ohio App. 3d 789, 591 N.E.2d 1287 (1990) (Rule 4.2(K) requires that, to file suit against an agency of a county, the plaintiff must name the county agencies or administrators being sued), *motion to certify overruled*, 58 Ohio St. 3d 715, 570 N.E.2d 281 (1991)

Service on Shareholders

Bell v. Midwestern Educ. Servs., 89 Ohio App. 3d 193, 619 N.E.2d 424 (1993) (service of process on sole shareholders at a corporate address where the shareholders had no offices and rarely visited was not reasonably calculated to notify them of the action)

Service upon a Corporation

In re Estate of Popp, 94 Ohio App. 2d 640, 641 N.E.2d 739 (1994) (a corporation is served with process when the summons and complaint are served on a receptionist of the corporation)

Service upon an Incompetent Person

Newark Orthopedics, Inc. v. Brock, 92 Ohio App. 3d 117, 634 N.E.2d 278 (1994) (where a defendant has been adjudicated incompetent, service at the defendant's residence is not effective, because such service must be made upon a guardian), *dismissed, appeal not allowed*, 75 Ohio St. 3d 1448, 663 N.E.2d 330 (1996)

Service upon a Partnership

United Fairlawn, Inc. v. HPA Partners, 68 Ohio App. 3d 777, 589 N.E.2d 1344 (1990) (service of process on a partnership is not reasonably calculated to provide notice when service is made at a business address other than that set forth in a contract), *motion to certify overruled*, 58 Ohio St. 3d 710, 569 N.E.2d 512 (1991)

CHAPTER 4.3

Rule 4.3. Process: Out-of-State Service

Rule 4.3 reads as follows:

(A) **When service permitted.** Service of process may be made outside of this state, as provided in this rule, in any action in this state, upon a person who, at the time of service of process, is a nonresident of this state or is a resident of this state who is absent from this state. "Person" includes an individual, an individual's executor, administrator, or other personal representative, or a corporation, partnership, association, or any other legal or commercial entity, who, acting directly or by an agent, has caused an event to occur out of which the claim that is the subject of the complaint arose, from the person's:

(1) Transacting any business in this state;

(2) Contracting to supply services or goods in this state;

(3) Causing tortious injury by an act or omission in this state, including, but not limited to, actions arising out of the ownership, operation, or use of a motor vehicle or aircraft in this state;

(4) Causing tortious injury in this state by an act or omission outside this state if the person regularly does or solicits business, engages in any other persistent course of conduct, or derives substantial revenue from goods used or consumed or services rendered in this state;

(5) Causing injury in this state to any person by breach of warranty expressly or impliedly made in the sale of goods outside this state when the person to be served might reasonably have expected the person who was injured to use, consume, or be affected by the goods in this state, provided that the person to be served also regularly does or solicits business, engages in any other persistent course of conduct, or derives substantial revenue from goods used or consumed or services rendered in this state;

(6) Having an interest in, using, or possessing real property in this state;

(7) Contracting to insure any person, property, or risk located within this state at the time of contracting;

(8) Living in the marital relationship within this state notwithstanding subsequent departure from this state, as to all obligations arising for spousal support, custody, child support, or property settlement, if the other party to the marital relationship continues to reside in this state;

(9) Causing tortious injury in this state to any person by an act outside this state committed with the purpose of injuring persons, when the person to be served might reasonably have expected that some person would be injured by the act in this state;

(10) Causing tortious injury to any person by a criminal act, any element of which takes place in this state, that the person to be served commits or in the commission of which the person to be served is guilty of complicity.

(B) Methods of service.

(1) Service by certified or express mail. Evidenced by return receipt signed by any person, service of any process shall be by certified or express mail unless otherwise permitted by these rules. The clerk shall place a copy of the process and complaint or other document to be served in an envelope. The clerk shall address the envelope to the person to be served at the address set forth in the caption or at the address set forth in written instructions furnished to the clerk with instructions to forward. The clerk shall affix adequate postage and place the sealed envelope in the United States mail as certified or express mail return receipt requested with instructions to the delivering postal employee to show to whom delivered, date of delivery, and address where delivered.

The clerk shall forthwith enter the fact of mailing on the appearance docket and make a similar entry when the return receipt is received. If the envelope is returned with an endorsement showing failure of delivery, the clerk shall forthwith notify, by mail, the attorney of record or, if there is no attorney of record, the party at whose instance process was issued and enter the fact of notification on the appearance docket. The clerk shall file the return receipt or returned envelope in the records of the action. If the envelope is returned with an endorsement showing failure of delivery, service is complete when the attorney or serving party, after notification by the clerk, files with the clerk an affidavit setting forth facts indicating the reasonable diligence utilized to ascertain the whereabouts of the party to be served.

All postage shall be charged to costs. If the parties to be served by certified or express mail are numerous and the clerk determines there is insufficient security for costs, the clerk may require the party requesting service to advance an amount estimated by the clerk to be sufficient to pay the postage.

(2) Personal service. When ordered by the court, a "person" as defined in division (A) of this rule may be personally served with a copy of the process and complaint or other document to be served. Service under this division may be made by any person not less than eighteen years of age who is not a party and who has been designated by order of the court. On request, the clerk shall deliver the summons to the plaintiff for transmission to the person who will make the service.

Proof of service may be made as prescribed by Civ. R. 4.1(B) or by order of the court.

COMMENTARY

Rules 4-4.6 prescribe service of process requirements in Ohio courts. Rule 4.3 sets forth permissible methods of service of process on out-of-state defendants and should be read in conjunction with Rule 4.2, which specifies those persons on whom out-of-state process may be served. More general provisions regarding service of process are located in Rule 4, and this Rule should always be consulted when interpreting the specific provisions of Rule 4.3.

Permissible Service

The requirements for service of process on out-of-state defendants are set forth in Rule 4.3. Subsection (A) largely duplicates the provisions of OHIO REV. CODE ANN. § 2307.382, Ohio's long-arm statute, which authorizes the exercise of personal jurisdiction over non-resident defendants. Rule 4.3 provides for service of process to effectuate that jurisdiction, but it also applies to resident defendants who are not located within the state.

Methods of Service

Subsection (B) sets forth the methods of service for non-resident defendants and resident defendants who are absent from the state. The provisions of this subsection largely duplicate those in Rule 4.1, which set forth the methods of service for in-state defendants, with one salient exception. Residence service as described in Rule 4.1(C) is not available as a method of service on out-of-state defendants. Service by express or certified mail remains the preferred method of service, but personal service is also available under Rule 4.3(B)(2). Proof of out-of-state service is properly made as prescribed in Rule 4.1(B) or by order of the court. Rule 4.2 also applies to service on non-resident defendants and should be consulted to determine who may be served with process under the methods listed in subsection (B).

ADDITIONAL AUTHORITY

4 WRIGHT & MILLER §§ 1061-1081

4A WRIGHT & MILLER §§ 1082-1140

4 MOORE'S FEDERAL PRACTICE §§ 4.01-4.121

4 ANDERSON'S OHIO CIVIL PRACTICE §§ 150.29-150.49

1 KLEIN DARLING AT 4.3-1 to AT 4.3-93

3 TEREZ F 1.2.1, F 1.5.1

2 OH. JUR. PL. AND PRAC. FORMS, ch. 9

1 MILLIGAN Forms 4.3-1 to 4.3-33

1 FINK §§ 4.3-1 to 4.3-10

OHIO LITIGATION CHECKLISTS, Pleading and Process, §§ 20-22

LEADING CASES

Constitutionality of Long Arm Statute

Toma v. Corrigan, 92 Ohio St. 3d 589, 752 N.E.2d 281 (Ohio Aug 22, 2001) (in deciding if an Ohio court has personal jurisdiction over a nonresident defendant, court must determine: (1) whether Ohio's long-arm statute and the applicable Rule of Civil Procedure confer personal jurisdiction and, if so; (2) whether granting jurisdiction under the statute and rule would deprive the nonresident defendant of the right to due process of law under the Fourteenth Amendment to the United States Constitution)

Determination of Personal Jurisdiction

Sherry v. Geissler U. Pehr GmbH, 100 Ohio App. 3d 67, 651 N.E.2d 1383 (1995) (a court determining whether it may exercise personal jurisdiction over a nonresident defendant should (1) consider the plain language of the long-arm statute and applicable civil rule, and (2) if jurisdiction so lies, the court should determine whether exercising jurisdiction over the defendant comports with due process under the Fourteenth Amendment)

Dismissal for Lack of Personal Jurisdiction

Universal Coach, Inc. v. New York Transit Authority, Inc., 90 Ohio App. 3d 284, 629 N.E.2d 28 (1993) (when a court has no grounds for personal jurisdiction over a nonresident defendant, the court should grant a motion to dismiss)

Effects of Tortious Injury

Robinson v. Koch Refining Co., No. 98AP-900 (10th Dist.), 1999 Ohio App. LEXIS 2682 (1999) (decline in physical condition of a party due to the effects of a tortious injury sustained in another state does not confer personal jurisdiction, because a tortious injury is not considered to have occurred in Ohio where a party continues to suffer from the effects of the injury after returning to Ohio)

Jurisdiction by Marital Relationship

Fraiberg v. Cuyahoga County Court of Common Pleas, Domestic Relations Division, 76 Ohio St. 3d 374, 667 N.E.2d 1189, (1996) (a court should determine whether the defendant lived in a marital relationship within Ohio, such that the due process requirement of minimum contacts is satisfied)

Jurisdiction by Supplying Goods or Services

Cincinnati Art Galleries v. Fatzie, 70 Ohio App. 3d 696, 591 N.E.2d 1336 (1990) (nonresident defendants who contacted Ohio resident to sell artwork were within the personal jurisdiction of courts in Ohio)

Jurisdiction by Tortious Injury

Wayne County Bureau of Support v. Wolfe, 71 Ohio App. 3d 765, 595 N.E.2d 421 (1991) (a parent's failure to support his or her minor children residing in Ohio constitutes a tortious act or omission in Ohio, thus conferring personal jurisdiction)

Jurisdiction by Transacting Business

Hammill Mfg. Co. v. Quality Rubber Prod., 82 Ohio App. 3d 369, 612 N.E.2d 472 (1992) (a corporate nonresident that initiates and negotiates a contract and becomes obligated to make payments to an Ohio corporation has transacted business within Ohio)

Long-Arm Statute

Krutwosky v. Simonson, 109 Ohio App. 3d 367, 672 N.E.2d 219 (1996) (articulating the factors for determining whether a non-resident defendant falls within the reach of the long-arm statute)

Methods of Service; Left at Residence

Szabo v. Humphrey, 66 Ohio Misc. 2d 55, 642 N.E.2d 1173 (M.C. 1993) (service of process was improper when complaint was taped to defendant's door)

Methods of Service; Mail

United Home Fed. v. Rhonehouse, 76 Ohio App. 3d 115, 601 N.E.2d 138 (1991) (if service to a post office box is reasonably calculated to reach the addressee, service is sufficient)

Nonresident Jurisdiction

Mustang Tractor & Equip. Co. v. Sound Env't'l Serv., Inc., 104 Ohio Misc. 2d 1, 727 N.E.2d 977 (C.P. 1999) (to determine whether a court has personal jurisdiction over a nonresident, the trial court must determine: (1) whether

Ohio's long-arm statute and Rule 4.3, respectively, confer personal jurisdiction and permit service of process on the nonresident, and, if so; (2) whether the exercise of personal jurisdiction would deprive the defendant of the right to due process of law under the Fourteenth Amendment to the United States Constitution)

No Physical Presence of Corporation

Pharmed Corp. v. Biologies, Inc., 97 Ohio App. 3d 477, 646 N.E.2d 1167 (1994) (although it has no physical presence in Ohio, a nonresident corporate defendant has transacted business in Ohio where it conducted negotiations by telephone, facsimile, and mail for the sale of goods to an Ohio corporation for resale in Ohio)

Personal Jurisdiction Through Long-Arm Statute

Clark v. Connor, 82 Ohio St. 3d 309, 695 N.E.2d 751 (1998) (personal jurisdiction may be determined according to whether the applicable long-arm statute and corresponding rule of procedure function to confer personal jurisdiction over a defendant; statute and rule must also satisfy due process)

CHAPTER 4.4

Rule 4.4. Process: Service by Publication

Rule 4.4 reads as follows:

(A) Residence unknown.

   (1) Except in an action governed by division (A)(2) of this rule, if the residence of a defendant is unknown, service shall be made by publication in actions where such service is authorized by law. Before service by publication can be made, an affidavit of a party or his counsel shall be filed with the court. The affidavit shall aver that service of summons cannot be made because the residence of the defendant is unknown to the affiant, all of the efforts made on behalf of the party to ascertain the residence of the defendant, and that the residence of the defendant cannot be ascertained with reasonable diligence.

       Upon the filing of the affidavit, the clerk shall cause service of notice to be made by publication in a newspaper of general circulation in the county in which the complaint is filed. If no newspaper is published in that county, then publication shall be in a newspaper published in an adjoining county. The publication shall contain the name and address of the court, the case number, the name of the first party on each side, and the name and last known address, if any, of the person or persons whose residence is unknown. The publication also shall contain a summary statement of the object of the complaint and demand for relief, and shall notify the person to be served that he or she is required to answer within twenty-eight days after the publication. The publication shall be published at least once a week for six successive weeks unless publication for a lesser number of weeks is specifically provided by law. Service shall be complete at the date of the last publication.

       After the last publication, the publisher or its agent shall file with the court an affidavit showing the fact of publication together with a copy of the notice of publication. The affidavit and copy of the notice shall constitute proof of service.

   (2) In a divorce, annulment, or legal separation action, if the plaintiff is proceeding *in forma pauperis* and if the residence of the defendant is unknown, service by publication shall be made by posting and mail. Before service by posting and mail can be made, an affidavit of a party or the party's counsel shall be filed with the court. The affidavit shall contain the same averments required by division (A)(1) of this rule and,

43

in addition, shall set forth the defendant's last known address.

Upon the filing of the affidavit, the clerk shall cause service of notice to be made by posting in a conspicuous place in the courthouse or courthouses in which the general and domestic relations divisions of the court of common pleas for the county are located and in two additional public places in the county that have been designated by local rule for the posting of notices pursuant to this rule. The notice shall contain the same information required by division (A)(1) of this rule to be contained in a newspaper publication. The notice shall be posted in the required locations for six successive weeks.

The clerk shall also cause the complaint and summons to be mailed by ordinary mail, address correction requested, to the defendant's last known address. The clerk shall obtain a certificate of mailing from the United States Postal Service. If the clerk is notified of a corrected or forwarding address of the defendant within the six-week period that notice is posted pursuant to division (A)(2) of this rule, the clerk shall cause the complaint and summons to be mailed to the corrected or forwarding address. The clerk shall note the name, address, and date of each mailing in the docket.

After the last week of posting, the clerk shall note on the docket where and when notice was posted. Service shall be complete upon the entry of posting.

(B) **Residence known.** If the residence of a defendant is known, and the action is one in which service by publication is authorized by law, service of process shall be effected by a method other than by publication as provided by:

(1) Rule 4.1, if the defendant is a resident of this state,

(2) Rule 4.3(B) if defendant is not a resident of this state, or

(3) Rule 4.5, in the alternative, if service on defendant is to be effected in a foreign country.

If service of process cannot be effected under the provisions of this subdivision or Rule 4.6(C) or Rule 4.6(D), service of process shall proceed by publication.

COMMENTARY

Rules 4-4.6 prescribe service of process requirements in Ohio courts. Rule 4.4

establishes service by publication as a permissible method of satisfying service of process requirements for both in-state and out-of-state defendants. More general provisions regarding service of process are located in Rule 4, and this Rule should always be consulted when interpreting the specific provisions of Rule 4.4.

Service by Publication; Address Unknown

Rule 4.4 allows service of process by publication as a method of necessity or of last resort. Because notice by this method is not always a reliable means of notifying a defendant of the pendency of an action, the use of the method is carefully circumscribed.

Subsection (A) provides for service of process by publication when the address of the defendant is unknown. Service by this method is justified on the grounds that it is the only method of service available to a plaintiff when the location of the defendant cannot be ascertained. Plaintiffs should seek to exhaust every possibility in ascertaining the location of a defendant, as failure to receive notice of an action is a basis for a post-judgment motion to vacate the judgment under Rule 59(B)(5).

Before publication occurs, subsection (A) requires that an affidavit be filed, stating that the defendant's residence cannot be ascertained with reasonable diligence. The subsequent procedure of publication is detailed in that subsection.

Service by Publication; Address Known

Subsection (B) allows service by publication only as a last resort when the residence of a defendant is known to a plaintiff. The Rule specifies that service must be effected under the provisions of Rule 4.1, Rule 4.3, Rule 4.5, or Rule 4.6, whichever is applicable, before service by publication will be permitted.

ADDITIONAL AUTHORITY

4 WRIGHT & MILLER §§ 1061-1081
4A WRIGHT & MILLER §§ 1082-1140
1 MOORE's FEDERAL PRACTICE §§ 4.01-4.121
4 ANDERSON's OHIO CIVIL PRACTICE §§ 150.56-150.59
1 KLEIN DARLING AT 4.4-1 to AT 4.4-22
3 TEREZ F 1.4.1 to F 1.4.4
2 OH. JUR. PL. AND PRAC. FORMS, ch. 9
1 MILLIGAN Forms 4.4-1 to 4.4-28
1 FINK §§ 4.4-1 to 4.4-4
OHIO LITIGATION CHECKLISTS, Pleading and Process, §§ 20-22

LEADING CASES

Insufficient Service by Publication

Meadows v. Meadows, 73 Ohio App. 3d 316, 596 N.E.2d 1146 (1992) (pursuant to Rule 4.4(A), the failure to include the last known address of a defendant in the notice of publication renders such notice insufficient as a matter of law)

Service by Publication

In re T.C., 140 Ohio App. 3d 409, 747 N.E.2d 881 (2000) (in order to obtain service by publication, a party must submit affidavit stating that the residence of the opposing party is unknown and cannot be ascertained with reasonable diligence)

Service by Publication; General Circulation

Record Publishing Co. v. Kainrad, 49 Ohio St. 3d 296, 551 N.E.2d 1286 (1990) (a legal newspaper devoted to the publication of legal notices was not a newspaper "of general circulation" pursuant to Rule 4.3(A))

Service by Publication; Generally

Hrabak v. Collins, 108 Ohio App. 3d 117, 670 N.E.2d 281 (1995) (service on defendant by publication in daily legal news publication and by serving the Secretary of State was proper), *dismissed, appeal not allowed*, 76 Ohio St. 3d 1405, 666 N.E.2d 565 (1996)

Service by Publication; Reasonable Diligence

Kraus v. Maurer, 138 Ohio App. 3d 163, 740 N.E.2d 722 (2000) (to take advantage of the provisions permitting service by publication, plaintiff's counsel must first establish "reasonable diligence" in attempting to learn a defendant's address, which requires taking steps that an individual of ordinary prudence would reasonably expect to be successful in locating a defendant's address such as a check of telephone book or a call to telephone company, checking city directory, credit bureau, county records such as auto title department or board of elections, or inquiry of former neighbors)

In re Mullenax, 108 Ohio App. 3d 271, 670 N.E.2d 551 (1996) (upon a challenge to a party's exercise of reasonable diligence in discovering the address of the party to be served, the party seeking service must support its claim of exercise of reasonable diligence)

CHAPTER 4.5

Rule 4.5. Process: Alternative Provisions for Service in a Foreign Country

Rule 4.5 reads as follows:

(A) Manner. When Civ. R. 4.3 or Civ. R. 4.4 or both allow service upon a person outside this state and service is to be effected in a foreign country, service of the summons and complaint may also be made:

    (1)   In the manner prescribed by the law of the foreign country for service in that country in an action in any of its courts of general jurisdiction when service is calculated to give actual notice;

    (2)   As directed by the foreign authority in response to a letter rogatory when service is calculated to give actual notice;

    (3)   Upon an individual by delivery to him personally;

    (4)   Upon a corporation or partnership or association by delivery to an officer, a managing or general agent;

    (5)   By any form of mail requiring a signed receipt, when the clerk of the court addresses and dispatches this mail to the party to be served;

    (6)   As directed by order of the court. Service under division (A)(3) or (A)(6) of this rule may be made by any person not less than eighteen years of age who is not a party and who has been designated by order of the court, or by the foreign court. On request the clerk shall deliver the summons to the plaintiff for transmission to the person or the foreign court or officer who will make the service.

(B) Return. Proof of service may be made as prescribed by Civ. R. 4.1(B), or by the law of the foreign country, or by order of the court. When mail service is made pursuant to division (A)(5) of this rule, proof of service shall include a receipt signed by the addressee or other evidence of delivery to the addressee satisfactory to the court.

COMMENTARY

Rules 4-4.6 prescribe service of process requirements in Ohio courts. Rule 4.5 sets forth the provisions for service of process on foreign defendants. More general provisions regarding service of process are located in Rule 4, and this Rule should always be consulted when interpreting the specific provisions of Rule 4.5.

Service in a Foreign Country

Rule 4.5(A) establishes several alternate provisions for service of process on defendants located in foreign countries. The Rule is designed to permit service upon a foreign defendant in a manner that will provide actual notice and in a manner consonant with the customary method of service in the foreign country. It should also be noted that the Hague Convention on the Service Abroad of Judicial and Extrajudicial Documents sets forth methods of service for individuals in foreign countries. Subsection (B) sets forth the method according to which proof of service should be made.

ADDITIONAL AUTHORITY

4 WRIGHT & MILLER §§ 1061-1081
4A WRIGHT & MILLER §§ 1082-1140
1 MOORE'S FEDERAL PRACTICE §§ 4.01-4.121
4 ANDERSON'S OHIO CIVIL PRACTICE §§ 150.50-150.55
1 KLEIN DARLING AT 4.5-1 to AT 4.5-24
3 TEREZ F 1.5.2
2 OH. JUR. PL. AND PRAC. FORMS, ch. 9
1 MILLIGAN Forms 4.5-1 to 4.5-28
1 FINK §§ 4.5-1 to 4.5-3
OHIO LITIGATION CHECKLISTS, Pleading and Process, §§ 20-22

LEADING CASES

Personal Service in a Foreign Country

Schroeder v. Vigil-Escalera Perez, 76 Ohio Misc. 2d 25, 664 N.E.2d 627 (C.P. 1995) (because he could have been served by publication, personal service of process on a husband was proper)

Service in a Foreign Country; Method

Fieno v. Beaton, 68 Ohio App. 3d 13, 426 N.E.2d 203 (1980) (service of summons or complaint in a foreign country may be made by any form of mail that requires a signed receipt)

CHAPTER 4.6

Rule 4.6. Process: Limits; Amendment; Service Refused; Service Unclaimed

Rule 4.6 reads as follows:

(A) Limits of effective service. All process may be served anywhere in this state and, when authorized by law or these rules, may be served outside this state.

(B) Amendment. The court within its discretion and upon such terms as are just, may at any time allow the amendment of any process or proof of service thereof, unless the amendment would cause material prejudice to the substantial rights of the party against whom the process was issued.

(C) Service refused. If service of process is refused, and the certified or express mail envelope is returned with an endorsement showing such refusal, or the return of the person serving process states that service of process has been refused, the clerk shall forthwith notify, by mail, the attorney of record or, if there is no attorney of record, the party at whose instance process was issued. If the attorney, or serving party, after notification by the clerk, files with the clerk a written request for ordinary mail service, the clerk shall send by ordinary mail a copy of the summons and complaint or other document to be served to the defendant at the address set forth in the caption, or at the address set forth in written instructions furnished to the clerk. The mailing shall be evidenced by a certificate of mailing which shall be completed and filed by the clerk. Answer day shall be twenty-eight days after the date of mailing as evidenced by the certificate of mailing. The clerk shall endorse this answer date upon the summons which is sent by ordinary mail. Service shall be deemed complete when the fact of mailing is entered of record. Failure to claim certified or express mail service is not refusal of service within the meaning of division (C) of this rule.

(D) Service unclaimed. If a certified or express mail envelope is returned with an endorsement showing that the envelope was unclaimed, the clerk shall forthwith notify, by mail, the attorney of record or, if there is no attorney of record, the party at whose instance process was issued. If the attorney, or serving party, after notification by the clerk, files with the clerk a written request for ordinary mail service, the clerk shall send by ordinary mail a copy of the summons and complaint or other document to be served to the defendant at the address set forth in the caption, or at the address set forth in written instructions furnished to the clerk. The mailing shall be evidenced by a certificate of mailing which shall be completed and filed by the clerk. Answer day shall be twenty-eight days after the date of mailing as evidenced by the certificate of mailing. The clerk shall endorse this answer date upon the summons which is sent by ordinary mail. Service shall be deemed complete when the fact of mailing is entered of record, provided that the ordinary mail envelope is not returned by the postal authorities with an endorsement showing failure of delivery. If the ordinary mail envelope is returned undelivered, the clerk shall forthwith notify the attorney, or serving party, by mail.

(E) Duty of attorney of record or serving party. The attorney of record or the serving party shall be responsible for determining if service has been made and shall timely file written instructions with the clerk regarding completion of service notwithstanding the provisions in Civ. R. 4.1 through 4.6 which instruct a clerk to notify the attorney of record or the serving party of failure of service of process.

COMMENTARY

Rules 4-4.6 prescribe service of process requirements in Ohio courts. Rule 4.6 contains a miscellany of provisions concerning service of process and permissible methods for effecting that service. More general provisions regarding service of process are located in Rule 4, and this Rule should always be consulted when interpreting the specific provisions of Rule 4.6.

Limits and Amendment of Service

Subsection (A) sets forth the territorial limits of service of process. It provides that in-state service may be effected anywhere within the territorial borders of the state of Ohio. Out-of-state service may be effected according to the provisions of Rule 4.3.

Amendment of process is permitted under Rule 4.6(B) to prevent technical objections to the form of process or proof of service. Amendment is at the discretion of the court and should not be reversed unless the substantial rights of the parties are prejudiced.

Service Refused or Unclaimed

Subsection (C) sets forth alternate provisions for service of process if service under the other methods set forth under Rules 4.1-4.5 is refused. If service by certified mail under Rule 4.1(A) is refused, the plaintiff or the plaintiff's attorney must be notified by the clerk in accordance with subsection (C). Service may then be attempted by ordinary mail and evidenced by a certificate of mailing to be completed and filed by the clerk.

If service by certified mail is unclaimed, the process of notifying the attorney or party seeking service will commence as set forth in subsection (D). If service by ordinary mail is subsequently returned undelivered, the clerk will again notify the attorney or party seeking service. Ordinary mail service of process is complete under subsections (C) and (D) when the fact of mailing is entered of record, although ordinary mail service under subsection (D) will not be deemed complete if the ordinary mail service envelope is returned with an endorsement showing failure of delivery.

Ultimate Responsibility for Effective Service

Subsection (E) indicates that the ultimate responsibility for ensuring that effective service of process is made rests with the plaintiff or the plaintiff's attorney of record. Various provisions in Rules 4.1-4.6 relating to duties of the clerk of court are not intended to relieve the plaintiff of the plaintiff's attorney of this responsibility.

ADDITIONAL AUTHORITY

4 WRIGHT & MILLER §§ 1061-1081
4A WRIGHT & MILLER §§ 1082-1140
1 MOORE'S FEDERAL PRACTICE §§ 4.01-4.121
4 ANDERSON'S OHIO CIVIL PRACTICE §§ 150.60-150.61
1 KLEIN DARLING AT 4.6-1 to AT 4.6-25
3 TEREZ F 1.3.6 to F 1.3.8
2 OH. JUR. PL. AND PRAC. FORMS, ch. 9
1 MILLIGAN Forms 4.6-1 to 4.6-16
1 FINK §§ 4.6-1 to 4.6-5
OHIO LITIGATION CHECKLISTS, Pleading and Process, §§ 20-22

LEADING CASES

Refusal of Service; Postage Due

Lesowitz & Baskin v. Miller, 63 Ohio App. 3d 401, 579 N.E.2d 227 (1993) (the refusal to accept service by certified mail because postage was owed constitutes a refusal of service, thus permitting service by ordinary mail)

Service; Mail

United Home Fed. v. Rhonehouse, 76 Ohio App. 3d 115, 601 N.E.2d 138 (1991) (if service to a post office box is reasonably calculated to reach the addressee, service is sufficient)

Sufficiency of Service

> *King v. Hazra*, 91 Ohio App. 3d 534, 632 N.E.2d 1336 (1993) (effective service of process is not completed by filing a request to plead or by sending a courtesy copy of the complaint to the attorney of the defendant)

Unclaimed Service

> *United Home Fed. v. Rhonehouse*, 76 Ohio App. 3d 115, 601 N.E.2d 138 (1991) (upon the entry of the certificate of mailing in the record, service by ordinary mail is presumed to be complete, unless the envelope is returned marked "failure of delivery")

CHAPTER 5

Rule 5. Service and Filing of Pleadings and Other Papers Subsequent to the Original Complaint

Rule 5 reads as follows:

(A) Service: when required. Except as otherwise provided in these rules, every order required by its terms to be served, every pleading subsequent to the original complaint unless the court otherwise orders because of numerous defendants, every paper relating to discovery required to be served upon a party unless the court otherwise orders, every written motion other than one which may be heard ex parte, and every written notice, appearance, demand, offer of judgment, and similar paper shall be served upon each of the parties. Service is not required on parties in default for failure to appear except that pleadings asserting new or additional claims for relief or for additional damages against them shall be served upon them in the manner provided for service of summons in Civ. R. 4 through Civ. R. 4.6.

(B) Service: how made. Whenever under these rules service is required or permitted to be made upon a party who is represented by an attorney of record in the proceedings, the service shall be made upon the attorney unless service upon the party is ordered by the court. Service upon the attorney or party shall be made by delivering a copy to the person to be served, transmitting it to the office of the person to be served by facsimile transmission, mailing it to the last known address of the person to be served or, if no address is known, leaving it with the clerk of the court. The served copy shall be accompanied by a completed copy of the proof of service required by division (D) of this rule. "Delivering a copy" within this rule means: handing it to the attorney or party; leaving it at the office of the person to be served with a clerk or other person in charge; if there is no one in charge, leaving it in a conspicuous place in the office; or, if the office is closed or the person to be served has no office, leaving it at the dwelling house or usual place of abode of the person to be served with some person of suitable age and discretion then residing in the dwelling house or usual place of abode. Service by mail is complete upon mailing. Service by facsimile transmission is complete upon transmission.

(C) Service: numerous defendants. In any action in which there are unusually large numbers of defendants, the court, upon motion or of its own initiative, may order that service of the pleadings of the defendants and replies thereto need not be made as between the defendants and that any cross-claim, counterclaim, or matter constituting an avoidance or affirmative defense contained therein shall be deemed to be denied or avoided by all other parties and that the filing of any such pleading and service thereof upon the plaintiff constitutes due notice of it to the parties. A copy of every such order shall be served upon the parties in such manner and form as the court directs.

(D) Filing. All papers, after the complaint, required to be served upon a party shall be filed with the court within three days after service, but depositions upon oral examination, interrogatories, requests for documents, requests for admission, and answers and responses thereto shall not be filed unless on order of the court or for use as evidence or for consideration of a motion in the proceeding. Papers filed with the court shall not be considered until proof of service is endorsed thereon or separately filed. The proof of service shall state the date and manner of service and shall be signed in accordance with Civ. R. 11.

(E) Filing with the court defined. The filing of documents with the court, as required by these rules, shall be made by filing them with the clerk of court, except that the judge may permit the documents to be filed with the judge, in which event the judge shall note the filing date on the documents and transmit them to the clerk. A court may provide, by local rules adopted pursuant to the Rules of Superintendence, for the filing of documents by electronic means. If the court adopts such local rules, they shall include all of the following:

(1) Any signature on electronically transmitted documents shall be considered that of the attorney or party it purports to be for all purposes. If it is established that the documents were transmitted without authority, the court shall order the filing stricken.

(2) A provision shall specify the days and hours during which electronically transmitted documents will be received by the court, and a provision shall specify when documents received electronically will be considered to have been filed.

(3) Any document filed electronically that requires a filing fee may be rejected by the clerk of court unless the filer has complied with the mechanism established by the court for the payment of filing fees.

COMMENTARY

Rule 5 mandates that all the papers in a civil action listed in subsection (A) be served upon each of the parties in the action. Subsection (D) of the Rule also requires that each of these papers be filed with the court within 3 days after service on the parties, with exceptions for certain discovery documents that are discussed below.

Service of the papers upon the parties themselves is regarded as more important than service with the court, as reflected in the requirement that the time limitations on responses to filed papers are generally measured from the date of service of the papers to the parties, not from the date that they were actually filed with the court.

Rule 5 Distinguished from Rule 4

Rule 5 should not be confused with Rules 4-4.6, which govern service of process. Most noticeably, service under Rule 5 must be made to the attorney representing the party to be served under Rule 5(B), unless the court orders otherwise. Service under Rule 5 must be made in one of the methods set forth in subsection (B) and must be accompanied by sufficient proof of service according to subsection (D). Service of process under Rules 4-4.6 is more restrictive.

Illustration 5-1

Edgar sues Tom's Terrific Stadium Tours for $25,000 on a claim arising under a state false advertising statute, and promptly serves a summons and copy of the complaint on Tom, who owns the business. Tom quickly retains the services of an attorney, Jerry, to advise him on the matter. Under Rule 5, service of any pleading and papers subsequent to the original complaint must be served upon Jerry, unless the court orders otherwise.

Methods of Service

Permissible methods of service on the opposing attorney or party for the papers or documents described in subsection (A) are set forth in subsection (B). Under the subsection, service may be made in one of four ways: by "delivery," by fax, by mail, or if no address can be ascertained for a party, by leaving it with the clerk of court. Subsection (B) further delineates permissible methods of "delivery" as defined under the Rule.

Practitioners should use common sense in determining which method would be appropriate in a given instance. For large quantities of documents exchanged pursuant to discovery requests, service by delivery will usually be the most efficient method. For pleadings other than the complaint, motions, orders, and offers of judgment, service by mail may be preferred. If a large number of defendants would make service upon each one impracticable, subsection (C) permits the court to order service in a manner that would adequately apprise all parties of the document or paper without subjecting the party filing the document or paper to any unnecessary expense.

Service by Certified or Registered Mail Not Required

It should be noted that subsection (B) does not require registered or certified mail for service by mail to be effective. Certified or express mail *is* required if service of process is effected by mail under the provisions of Rule 4.1(A). However, practitioners serving documents under Rule 5 may nonetheless desire to use registered or certified mail to ensure actual receipt of the paper or document by the other parties.

Certain Discovery Materials Excepted

Subsection (D) provides that materials discovered pursuant to Rules 30, 33, 34, and 36 need not be filed with the court, unless the court orders otherwise or the materials are to be used at trial or to be considered as part of a motion.

Filing with the Clerk or with the Court

Subsection (E) of the Rule plainly states that "filing with the court" actually means filing with the clerk of the court, although the judge may personally accept the papers to be filed and transmit those papers to the clerk of the court.

Electronically Filed Documents

Subsection (E) was amended in 2001 as part of a group of amendments to other Rules of Procedure to establish minimum standards for the use of information systems, electronic signatures, and electronic filing. Under the Rule, local rules that provide for the electronic filing of documents may be adopted. However, local rules must contain, at a minimum, two provisions: a "signature provision" and a "time provision."

First, local rules must contain a "signature provision" that indicates that signatures on electronically transmitted documents shall be considered that of the attorney or party it purports to be for all purposes in an action. Evidence that a document filed electronically was done so without proper authority should be presented by motion, and if the court finds that such authority was absent, the filing must be stricken.

Second, local rules must contain a "time provision" that indicates the days and hours when documents may be submitted electronically and when such documents will be considered to have been filed. Local rules that provide for more than one method of electronic transmission for documents should adopt separate "time provisions" for each method.

The Rule also indicates that local rules may provide for the rejection of electronically filed documents if the appropriate filing fee has not been submitted. However, this provision is not required, and local rules may provide for the acceptance of such documents and alternative penalties, such as an increased fee.

ADDITIONAL AUTHORITY

4A Wright & Miller §§ 1141-1160
1 Moore's Federal Practice §§ 5.01-5.32
4 Anderson's Ohio Civil Practice §§ 150.62-150.64
1 Klein Darling AT 5-1 to AT 5-41
3 Terez F 4.4.1 to F 4.4.7
2 Oh. Jur. Pl. and Prac. Forms, ch. 11
1 Milligan Forms 5-1 to 5-50
1 Fink §§ 5-1 to 5-8

LEADING CASES

Certified Mail Not Required

Smith v. Fuerst, 89 Ohio St. 3d 456, 732 N.E.2d 983 (2000) (a writ of mandamus would not lie to compel the court clerk to use certified mail to send notice of dismissal of postconviction petition after a copy had been sent by regular mail)

Endorsement of Proof

Amiri v. Thropp, 80 Ohio App. 3d 44, 608 N.E.2d 828 (1992) (the court will not consider filed an answer that does not contain an endorsement of proof of service)

Filing Defined

Hecker v. Norfolk & W. Ry. Co., 86 Ohio App. 3d 543, 621 N.E.2d 601 (Rule providing that civil action is commenced by the filing of a complaint with the court if service is obtained within one year supersedes prior statute), *cause dismissed*, 66 Ohio St. 3d 1481, 612 N.E.2d 723 (1993)

Method of Service; Generally

Swander Ditch Landowners' Ass'n v. Joint Bd. of Huron & Seneca County Comm'rs, 51 Ohio St. 3d 131, 554 N.E.2d 1324 (1990) (service upon a party represented by an attorney of record should be made upon the attorney unless service upon the party is expressly ordered by the court)

Method of Service; Ordinary Mail

Quisenberry v. Quisenberry, 91 Ohio App. 3d 341, 632 N.E.2d 916 (1993) (service by mail of motion for appointment of receiver and for order requiring a party to vacate premises was sufficient to establish the court's jurisdiction)

Service of Notice of Death

Perry v. Eagle-Picher Indus., 52 Ohio St. 3d 168, 556 N.E.2d 484 (1993) (the filing of a statement of the fact of death of a party with the court and serving it on decedent's counsel and all other parties sufficiently enters, upon the record, the death of the party)

Service of Summary Judgment Notice

Brown v. Akron Beacon Journal Pub. Co., 81 Ohio App. 3d 135, 610 N.E.2d 507 (1991) (a party against whom summary judgment is sought must be given sufficient notice of the filing of the summary judgment motion), *dismissed, jurisdictional motion overruled*, 63 Ohio St. 3d 1404, 585 N.E.2d 426 (1992)

Service on Attorney

Steiner v. Steiner, 85 Ohio App. 3d 513, 620 N.E.2d 152 (1993) (service of an amended complaint on an attorney is appropriate where a party has appeared and has counsel of record)

Service Unnecessary on Party in Default

Shoup v. Holman, 81 Ohio App. 3d 127, 610 N.E.2d 502 (1991) (where a motion to vacate did not assert new or additional claims, and where a party was in default for failure to appear, service of notice on that party is not necessary)

CHAPTER 6

Rule 6. Time

Rule 6 reads as follows:

(A) **Time: computation.** In computing any period of time prescribed or allowed by these rules, by the local rules of any court, by order of court, or by any applicable statute, the date of the act, event, or default from which the designated period of time begins to run shall not be included. The last day of the period so computed shall be included, unless it is a Saturday, a Sunday, or a legal holiday, in which event the period runs until the end of the next day which is not a Saturday, a Sunday, or a legal holiday. When the period of time prescribed or allowed is less than seven days, intermediate Saturdays, Sundays, and legal holidays shall be excluded in the computation. When a public office in which an act, required by law, rule, or order of court, is to be performed is closed to the public for the entire day which constitutes the last day for doing such an act, or before its usual closing time on such day, then such act may be performed on the next succeeding day which is not a Saturday, a Sunday, or a legal holiday.

(B) **Time: extension.** When by these rules or by a notice given thereunder or by order of court an act is required or allowed to be done at or within a specified time, the court for cause shown may at any time in its discretion (1) with or without motion or notice order the period enlarged if request therefor is made before the expiration of the period originally prescribed or as extended by a previous order, or (2) upon motion made after the expiration of the specified period permit the act to be done where the failure to act was the result of excusable neglect; but it may not extend the time for taking any action under Rule 50(B), Rule 59(B), Rule 59(D) and Rule 60(B), except to the extent and under the conditions stated in them.

(C) **Time: unaffected by expiration of term.** The period of time provided for the doing of any act or the taking of any proceeding is not affected or limited by the continued existence or expiration of a term of court. The existence or expiration of a term of court in no way affects the power of a court to do any act or take any proceeding in any civil action consistent with these rules.

(D) **Time: motions.** A written motion, other than one which may be heard ex parte, and notice of the hearing thereof shall be served not later than seven days before the time fixed for the hearing, unless a different period is fixed by these rules or by order of the court. Such an order may for cause shown be made on ex parte application. When a motion is supported by affidavit, the affidavit shall be served with the motion; and, except as otherwise provided in Rule 59(C), opposing affidavits may be served not later than one day before the hearing, unless the court permits them to be served at some other time.

(E) Time: additional time after service by mail. Whenever a party has the right or is required to do some act or take some proceedings within a prescribed period after the service of a notice or other paper upon him and the notice or paper is served upon him by mail, three days shall be added to the prescribed period. This subdivision does not apply to responses to service of summons under Rule 4 through Rule 4.6.

COMMENTARY

Rule 6 covers various matters concerning the timing of certain actions taken under the Rules. The Rule is not intended to change any existing statute of limitations, but has served as a guideline for calculating whether the appropriate statute of limitations has been tolled. Other rules concerning time, such as Rule 14 of the Ohio Rules of Appellate Procedure, should also be consulted when appropriate.

Computation of Time Periods

Subsection (A) of the Rule, which is substantially the same as OHIO REV. CODE ANN. § 1.14, states that any time period under the Rules or applicable statute shall not include the day on which the act giving rise to the commencement of the time period occurs. The time period, however, does include the day in which the act is performed or the filing occurs, unless the final day happens to be a Saturday, Sunday, or "legal holiday" as defined in the Rule. If this occurs, the deadline is extended to the next day that is not a Saturday, Sunday, or "legal holiday" as defined in the Rule.

Illustration 6-1

On Friday, December 12, an Ohio trial court orders Snow Experts, Inc. to provide its shareholders with a copy of its tax returns within 30 days. This 30-day period begins on December 13 and ends on January 11. However, if January 11 happens to fall on a Saturday, Snow Experts, Inc. would have until Monday, January 13 to comply with the order.

Ordinarily, calendar days are used for computing any time period under the Rules or under local rules. However, Rule 6(A) makes an exception for periods of time of 6 days or less. In such situations, the applicable time period does not include Saturdays, Sundays, or legal holidays; *i.e.*, only business days are included.

Illustration 6-2

Under a local rule, parties must serve reply affidavits in response to a motion for summary judgment at least 3 days before a hearing on the motion. If a hearing on a summary judgment is scheduled for Monday, March 10, the parties must serve reply affidavits no later than Wednesday, March 5, as Saturday, March 8, and Sunday, March 9, are excluded from the computation.

Legal Holidays in Ohio

Rule 6 does not specify those days that are "legal holidays" for purposes of the Rule. However, under OHIO REV. CODE ANN. § 1.14, the analogous statutory provision for the computation of the time, the legal holidays are January 1 (New Year's Day), the third Monday in January (Martin Luther King Day), the third Monday in February (Washington-Lincoln Day), the day commemorated as Memorial Day, usually the last Monday in May, July 4 (Independence Day), the first Monday in September (Labor Day), the second Monday in October (Columbus Day), November 11 (Veterans Day), the fourth Thursday in November (Thanksgiving Day), December 25 (Christmas Day), and any other day appointed and recommended by the Governor of Ohio or the President of the United States as a holiday. Also, under § 1.14, when any of these holidays falls on a Sunday, the following Monday is considered to be a legal holiday. There is little reason to believe that Rule 6 should not be read in light of this statutory provision.

Enlargement of Time Periods

Subsection (B) governs the procedure according to which the court may extend the applicable time period. It distinguishes between situations in which the request for extension occurs before the time period has expired and situations in which the request occurs after the expiration of the time period. In the former case, the court may extend the time period for "cause shown," whether or not the request was made by motion or the opposing party was notified. If the request occurs after the time period has expired, the court may, upon motion only, extend the time period if the failure to act was "the result of excusable neglect," a considerably more stringent standard.

Illustration 6-3

Assume on the facts of Illustration 6-1 that Snow Experts, Inc. desires additional time, because of business reasons, in which to comply with the court order. If

Snow Experts, Inc. makes such a request before the deadline of January 11, the court should ordinarily grant the request. If, however, Snow Experts, Inc. makes the request after the deadline had passed, the court should deny the request. In the latter situation, if Snow Experts, Inc. was unable to comply with the court order because of the negligent misplacement of the returns by Unreliable Accounting Company, the court may extend the time period upon motion by Snow Experts, Inc. and notice to its shareholders.

Exception from Enlargement

The Rule excepts the time periods for taking actions under specified Rules from enlargement by the court. These Rules govern motions made by a party made after a judgment has been entered, such as a motion for a new trial under Rule 59 and a motion for post-judgment relief under Rule 60(B). Other Rules may also contain provisions relating to the enlargement or reduction of particular time periods. These specific provisions should take precedence over the more general provisions in this subsection.

Illustration 6-4

On Friday, December 12, Susan obtains a judgment against Devyn for $10,000 in a breach of contract action in an Ohio trial court. Under Rule 59, the parties have 14 days in which they may make a motion for a new trial. If either party fails to file a motion for a new trial within the requisite 14-day period, Rule 6 does not allow the court to grant the parties an extension.

Unaffected by Expiration of Term

Subsection (C) provides that the time provisions of the Rule are unaffected by the continued existence or expiration of a term of the court. Moreover, the existence or expiration of a term of the court does not affect the power of a court to take any action in a proceeding.

Notice of Hearing on a Motion; Reply Affidavits

Subsection (D) requires that the notice of a hearing on a motion other than an *ex parte* motion be served on the parties no later than 7 days before the hearing date. The subsection also requires that, when the motion is supported by an affidavit, the affidavits must also be filed with the motions. The opposing party may then serve opposing affidavits no later than 1 day before the hearing date, unless Rule 59(C) provides or the court permits otherwise.

Illustration 6-5

On April 1, Wanda files a complaint against Tim for personal injuries suffered in an automobile accident. After being served with a summons and copy of the complaint on April 5, Tim files a motion for summary judgment, accompanied by supporting affidavits, with the court on April 10. The court, in turn, orders a hearing on the motion for April 30. Wanda must be notified of the hearing no later than April 23, and any affidavits submitted by Tim in support of his motion must also be provided to Wanda by this date. Wanda must serve any affidavits in opposition to the motion on Tim by April 29, unless Rule 59(C) provides or the court permits otherwise.

Automatic 3-Day Extension if Service by Mail

Subsection (E) should be read in conjunction with Rule 5(B) and other Rules which permit the service of certain notices by mail. When service is effected in this manner, Rule 6(E) provides that any time period triggered by the service of those notices will be increased by 3 days. In effect, subsection (E) embodies the assumption that documents placed in the mail will be received 3 days later. For this reason, service of notices by overnight delivery service or courier should not activate the automatic 3-day extension.

Illustration 6-6

Assume on the facts on Illustration 6-5 that the court denies Tim's motion for summary judgment and that Tim thereafter mails an answer containing a counterclaim to Wanda on May 5. Under Rule 12(A)(2), Wanda ordinarily has 28 days in which to file a reply to Tim's answer. Because Tim mailed the answer, however, the time period is extended until June 5.

Properly construed, Rule 6(E) applies only to time periods that are triggered by the *service* of a document or notice. Time periods that are triggered by acts other than a service of a document or notice are not subject to the 3-day extension.

Illustration 6-7

Under Rule 59(B), a motion for a new trial must be made within 14 days after the entry of judgment. Although Rule 58(B) imposes a duty on the clerk to serve all parties with a notice of the entry of judgment, Rule 59(B) clearly denominates

> the entry of judgment as the date on which the time period in which a motion for a new trial may be made. For this reason, the 3-day extension of Rule 6(E) does not apply to this time period.

For time periods greater than 6 days, the additional 3 days are calendar days, not business days, and are simply added to the end of the prescribed time period. However, the final day relief set forth in subsection (A) remains available in such an instance.

> **Illustration 6-8**
> Assume on the facts of Illustration 6-6 that June 5 falls on a Saturday. In this instance, Wanda's deadline for filing a reply would be extended to June 7.

For time periods of 6 days or less, for which subsection (A) operates to exclude those Saturdays, Sundays, and legal holidays occurring within the 6-day period, it is uncertain whether the additional 3 days supplied by subsection (E) should similarly exclude intervening Saturdays, Sundays, or legal holidays. In view of the fact that mail service does not ordinarily occur on Sundays and legal holidays, logic would seem to dictate that those days should be similarly excluded from the additional 3-day extension, though commentators have reached the contrary conclusion.

ADDITIONAL AUTHORITY

4A WRIGHT & MILLER §§ 1161-1180
1 MOORE'S FEDERAL PRACTICE §§ 6.01-6.25
4 ANDERSON'S OHIO CIVIL PRACTICE §§ 152.1
1 KLEIN DARLING AT 6-1 to AT 6-45
3 TEREZ F 9.2.1 to F 9.2.9
2 OH. JUR. PL. AND PRAC. FORMS, ch. 12
1 MILLIGAN Forms 6-1 to 6-60
1 FINK §§ 6-1 to 6-9

LEADING CASES

Additional Time After Service by Mail

Pogacsnik v. Jewett, (9th Dist.), 1992 Ohio App. LEXIS 3914 (Rule 6(E) applies only where the period for response commences after the service of notice when notice is served by mail)

Computation from Date of Entry

Rinehart v. Rinehart, 87 Ohio App. 3d 325, 622 N.E.2d 359 (1993) (pursuant to computation of time, the "date of the act, event, or default" that triggers the court-imposed 21-day period for providing findings of fact and conclusions of law is the date the trial court's entry was file stamped)

Excusable Neglect; Constructive Notice

State ex rel. Weiss v. Industrial Comm'n, 65 Ohio St. 3d 470, 605 N.E.2d 37 (1992) (where a defendant had constructive notice of a complaint, no excusable neglect was shown)

Excusable Neglect; Good Faith

Fulwiler v. Schneider, 104 Ohio App. 3d 398, 662 N.E.2d 82 (1995) (a good faith belief that a defendant was not properly served and should have been dismissed from an action is sufficient to establish excusable neglect in failing to file a timely answer)

Excusable Neglect; Standard

State ex rel. Lindenschmidt v. Butler County Bd. of Comm'rs, 72 Ohio St. 3d 464, 650 N.E.2d 1343 (1995) (Rule 6(B)(2) test for excusable neglect is less stringent than that applied under Rule 60(B))

Extension; Commencing an Action

Fetterolf v. Hoffmann-LaRoche, Inc. 102 Ohio App. 3d 106, 656 N.E.2d 1020 (Rule 6(B) may not be used to extend the time under which an action may be brought pursuant to Rule 3(A)), *on reconsideration*, 104 Ohio App. 3d 272, 661 N.E.2d 811, *and dismissed, appeal not allowed*, 73 Ohio St. 3d 1411, 651 N.E.2d 1309 (1995)

Inexcusable Neglect; Definition

Davis v. Immediate Med. Servs., Inc., 80 Ohio St. 3d 10, 684 N.E.2d 292 (1997) (inexcusable neglect is defined as conduct that falls substantially below what is reasonable under the circumstances)

In-Term and Out-of-Term Distinction Abolished

McCue v. Buckeye Union Ins. Co., 61 Ohio App. 2d 101, 399 N.E.2d 127 (1979) (Rule 6(C) abolished the distinction between in-term and out-of-term)

Notice of Motions

McGlone v. Grimshaw, 86 Ohio App. 3d 279, 620 N.E.2d 935 (1993) (a defendant's motion to strike the plaintiff's reply to the answer just minutes after the motion was filed should not have been granted without notice to the plaintiff)

Seven-Day Period Extended by Local Rule

Hillabrand v. Drypers Corp., 87 Ohio St. 3d 517, 721 N.E.2d 1029 (2000) (Rule 7 confers upon the trial court the authority to enact a local rule modifying the seven-day period between the filing and hearing of a motion, and authorizing motion rulings without an oral hearing)

Three-Day Extension for Service Deadlines Only

Martin v. Lesko, 133 Ohio App. 3d 752, 729 N.E.2d 839 (1999) (the three-day extension under Rule 6(E) is applicable only when the time period is triggered by the service of a notice or paper upon the party against whom the time runs; it does not apply to time periods commenced by the filing of a document with the clerk)

III
PLEADINGS AND MOTIONS

CHAPTER 7

Rule 7. Pleadings and Motions

Rule 7 reads as follows:

(A) Pleadings. There shall be a complaint and an answer; a reply to a counter-claim denominated as such; an answer to a cross-claim, if the answer contains a cross-claim; a third-party complaint, if a person who was not an original party is summoned under the provisions of Rule 14; and a third-party answer, if a third-party complaint is served. No other pleading shall be allowed, except that the court may order a reply to an answer or a third-party answer.

(B) Motions.

    (1) An application to the court for an order shall be by motion which, unless made during a hearing or a trial, shall be made in writing. A motion, whether written or oral, shall state with particularity the grounds therefor, and shall set forth the relief or order sought. The requirement of writing is fulfilled if the motion is stated in a written notice of the hearing of the motion.

    (2) To expedite its business, the court may make provision by rule or order for the submission and determination of motions without oral hearing upon brief written statements of reasons in support and opposition.

    (3) The rules applicable to captions, signing, and other matters of form of pleading apply to all motions and other papers provided for by these rules.

    (4) All motions shall be signed in accordance with Rule 11.

(C) Demurrers abolished. Demurrers shall not be used.

COMMENTARY

Rule 7 specifies the pleadings that must be filed in any action. If claims are made by the plaintiff only, with no additional counterclaims, cross-claims, or third-party claims, the pleadings are limited to the complaint and an answer. The Rule also lists those pleadings that are required if additional claims are made in the action.

Significantly, the Rule does not permit a party to file additional pleadings without the permission of the court, and the Rule expressly excludes all other pleadings, including demurrers, which are re-denominated as motions to dismiss under Rule 12. Thus, a plaintiff is not even allowed to file a reply to the defendant's answer unless the defendant specifically includes a counterclaim in the answer, or unless the court orders a reply to the answer.

Illustration 7-1

Alex sues Bob for personal injuries suffered in a boating accident. Upon receipt of Alex's complaint, Bob files an answer, alleging that Alex was actually the negligent party. Under Rule 7, Alex cannot file a pleading in response to the allegations made in Bob's answer, unless the court orders a reply. If, however, Bob supplements his answer with a counterclaim, Alex must file a reply to respond to Bob's counterclaim.

Commencement of an Action Through Means Other than Pleadings

Although it is generally true that any paper filed with a court other than the pleadings specifically set forth in Rule 7(A) is deemed a "motion" by Rule 7(B), other kinds of filings are derived from the application of the Rules to certain proceedings specially provided for by statute. Administrative appeals to trial courts may be initiated by the filing of a "petition" or "appeal," which may or may not have all of the characteristics of a formal complaint. Furthermore, the consequences of filing such papers, *i.e.*, the applicability of particular Rules triggered by the filing of a "complaint" or a "pleading," may or may not apply in a particular instance. For example, the party whose act technically "commences" an action under Rule 3 may not be considered the "plaintiff" for purposes of applying other Rules. Specific case law should be consulted to determine the nuances of these kinds of special statutory proceedings and their relationship to the operation of the Rules.

Illustration 7-2

Cindy, an employee of Seeview Corp., prevails on a workers' compensation claim in an administrative proceeding. Seeview then files a notice of appeal of the decision with the local court. As required by statute, Cindy then files a petition containing a statement of facts upon which the appeal of the administrative decision will proceed. Although the filing of Seeview's notice of appeal will be considered to have "commenced" the action under Rule 3, Cindy will be considered the "plaintiff" in the action and her "petition" is considered to be the initial "pleading" for purposes of applying particular Rules.

Motion Practice Generally

Under Rule 7(B), any paper filed with the court other than the pleadings and which can be viewed as a request for the court to act in some way is deemed a "motion." Any such request must be made in writing other than a motion made at a hearing or trial, which may be made orally. The motion must state the relief or order desired by the party and must also state with particularity the grounds for the request. Under Rule 7(B)(2), a court, by local rule, may dispense with an oral hearing on motions relying on briefs written in support of the motions.

The Rules do not contain specific provisions concerning motion practice in Ohio. Rule 9 simply states that the Rule requires that all motions must comply with whatever caption, form, and Rule 11 signature requirements are applicable to pleadings.

Written Motions

Written motions should generally set forth with particularity the grounds for the order and the relief sought. Although the movant's reasons for the order are frequently explicated in a supporting brief or memorandum, Rule 7(B)(1) may be interpreted as requiring that the grounds appear in the motion itself. Practitioners should also consult with the clerk of the court in a particular litigation to determine if the judge has "standing orders" or rules governing motion practice.

Oral Motions

Oral motions are appropriate only during a hearing or trial. Although oral motions must also, in theory, satisfy the requirements of written motions (*i.e.*, specifying the grounds for the order and the relief sought), there is considerable more flexibility in the procedure for making oral motions in most courts.

Amendment of Motions

Although Rule 15 provides for the amendment of pleadings, Rule 7 indicates that motions are not to be considered "pleadings" for purposes of the Rules. Accordingly, there is no express provision in the Rules which permits motions to be amended or supplemented, and the practice is usually within the discretion of the court or may be provided for by local rule. However, in all cases the final amendment to a motion must comply with the seven-day time limitation set forth in Rule 6(D).

Motion Day

Motion days are specific days set aside on the court calendar for the making, arguing, and deciding of oral motions. Hearings are usually informal and do not allow for the calling of witnesses. Typically, the attorney for the moving party will schedule a time for the oral motion on motion day, notifying the opposing parties of the motion to be presented and the time scheduled for argument. The judge will frequently rule on the motions upon conclusion of the oral arguments or shortly thereafter. Once a favored device under code pleading practice, motion days have been largely abandoned by Ohio courts.

Notice of a Motion

The concepts of fairness and due process require that the party against whom a motion is made must be given notice of the motion to permit that party an opportunity to be heard on the matter. However, nothing in the Rules requires any kind of response to a motion, and the failure to attend oral argument on a motion is ordinarily not sanctionable. Although the notice requirement formally applies to both written and oral motions, it is usually satisfied by the presence of the opposing counsel at the time of the making of a motion in the latter instance.

Documentation Supporting a Motion

In general, a motion may be supported by any one of the six kinds of documents described in Rule 56(C) in support of a summary judgment motion. Such documents include affidavits, depositions, answers to interrogatories, written admissions, transcripts of testimony from a pending case, and written stipulations of fact. If a party desires to present the testimony of live witnesses, a hearing should be scheduled with the permission of the court.

Scope of the Ruling

The court has four theoretical options in responding to a motion. The motion may be granted, denied, stricken, or tabled. The action of the court with respect to the motion, however, should be made known to all parties.

In general, the scope of the court's decision is limited by the nature of the motion, though the court has vast discretion in this regard. All decisions should be memorialized in writing and signed by the judge. For purposes of computing time periods contained within rulings on motions, the decision on the motion should be deemed effective on the date that it is filed by the clerk.

ADDITIONAL AUTHORITY

5 Wright & Miller §§ 1181-1200

2 Moore's Federal Practice §§ 7.01-7.05

4 Anderson's Ohio Civil Practice §§ 151.01, 153.01, 153.14, 153.15

1 Klein Darling AT 7-1 to AT 7-22

2 Oh. Jur. Pl. and Prac. Forms, ch. 13

1 Milligan Forms 7-1 to 7-31

1 Fink §§ 7-1 to 7-14

Ohio Litigation Checklists, Pleading and Process, §§ 1-5, 12-14

LEADING CASES

Briefs in Support of Motions

P & O Containers, Ltd. v. Jamelco, Inc., 94 Ohio App. 3d 726, 641 N.E.2d 794 (1994) (a motion for summary judgment is normally supported by a memorandum or brief supplied by the movant; the non-movant then supplies a memorandum or brief opposing the motion)

Demurrers Abolished

State ex rel. Peto v. Thomas, 24 Ohio St. 2d 38, 263 N.E.2d 248 (1970) (the Rules abolished demurrers, which are now treated as motions to dismiss)

Hearing on Motions

Breeding v. Herberger, 81 Ohio App. 3d 419, 611 N.E.2d 374 (1994) (generally, a court should conduct a hearing before ruling on a motion, unless the motion can be heard ex parte)

Improper Labeling of Pleading

Perez v. Bush, 63 Ohio Misc. 2d 423, 631 N.E.2d 192 (C.P. 1993) (a document labeled "answer" and filed by a non-attorney corporate officer in response to a complaint was not an "answer" or "pleading" as contemplated by Rule 7(A) or Rule 55(A))

Motion for Attorneys Fees; Hearing

Wiltsie v. Teamor, 89 Ohio App. 3d 380, 624 N.E.2d 772 (1993) (upon the filing of a motion for attorney fees, the court should conduct a hearing, and the failure to do so constitutes an abuse of discretion)

Motions and Pleadings; Generally

Pollack v. Watts, No. 97CA0084 (5th Dist.), 1998 Ohio App. LEXIS 4052 (Rule 7(A) does not include motions as part of the definition of "pleadings," thus, the filing of motions for judgment on the pleadings, for relief from judgment, and for leave to file an answer instanter does not give the trial court the right to consider evidentiary material contained therein)

Motions and Pleadings; Sanctions

In re Estate of Cain, 92 Ohio App. 3d 835, 637 N.E.2d 362 (motions brought in connection with probate action were not "pleadings" for purposes of imposing sanctions for submitting frivolous pleadings), *jurisdictional motion overruled*, 69 Ohio St. 3d 1445, 632 N.E.2d 912 (1994)

Motions for Reconsideration

Woerner v. Mentor Exempted Village Sch. Dist. Bd. of Educ., 84 Ohio App.

3d 844, 619 N.E.2d 34 (1993) (generally, a motion of reconsideration should either call to the attention of the court obvious error in the court's decision or raise an issue for consideration that was not considered at all)

Notice of Motions

McGlone v. Grimshaw, 86 Ohio App. 3d 279, 620 N.E.2d 935 (1993) (a defendant's motion to strike the plaintiff's reply to the answer just minutes after the motion was filed should not have been granted without notice to the plaintiff of an order modifying the time requirements under Rule 6(D))

Seven-Day Period Extended by Local Rule

Hillabrand v. Drypers Corp., 87 Ohio St. 3d 517, 721 N.E.2d 1029 (2000) (Rule 7 confers upon the trial court the authority to enact a local rule modifying the seven-day period between the filing and hearing of a motion, and authorizing motion rulings without an oral hearing)

CHAPTER 8

Rule 8. General Rules of Pleading

Rule 8 reads as follows:

(A) Claims for relief. A pleading that sets forth a claim for relief, whether an original claim, counterclaim, cross-claim, or third-party claim, shall contain

  (1) a short and plain statement of the claim showing that the party is entitled to relief, and

  (2) a demand for judgment for the relief to which the party claims to be entitled.

  If the party seeks more than twenty-five thousand dollars, the party shall so state in the pleading but shall not specify in the demand for judgment the amount of recovery sought, unless the claim is based upon an instrument required to be attached pursuant to Civ. R. 10. At any time after the pleading is filed and served, any party from whom monetary recovery is sought may request in writing that the party seeking recovery provide the requesting party a written statement of the amount of recovery sought. Upon motion, the court shall require the party to respond to the request. Relief in the alternative or of several different types may be demanded.

(B) Defenses; form of denials. A party shall state in short and plain terms the party's defenses to each claim asserted and shall admit or deny the averments upon which the adverse party relies. If the party is without knowledge or information sufficient to form a belief as to the truth of an averment, the party shall so state and this has the effect of a denial. Denials shall fairly meet the substance of the averments denied. When a pleader intends in good faith to deny only a part or a qualification of an averment, the pleader shall specify so much of it as is true and material and shall deny the remainder. Unless the pleader intends in good faith to controvert all the averments of the preceding pleading, the pleader may make the denials as specific denials or designated averments or paragraphs, or the pleader may generally deny all the averments except the designated averments or paragraphs as the pleader expressly admits; but, when the pleader does intend to controvert all its averments, including averments of the grounds upon which the court's jurisdiction depends, the pleader may do so by general denial subject to the obligations set forth in Civ. R. 11.

(C) Affirmative defenses. In pleading to a preceding pleading, a party shall set forth affirmatively accord and satisfaction, arbitration and award, assumption of risk, contributory negligence, discharge in bankruptcy, duress, estoppel, failure of consideration, want of consideration for a negotiable instrument, fraud, illegality, injury by fellow servant, laches, license, payment, release, res judicata, statute of frauds, statute of limitations, waiver, and any other matter constituting an avoidance or affirmative defense. When a party has mistakenly designated a defense as a counterclaim or a counterclaim as a defense, the court, if justice so requires, shall treat the pleading as if there had been a proper designation.

(D) Effect of failure to deny. Averments in a pleading to which a responsive pleading is required, other than those as to the amount of damage, are admitted when not denied in the responsive pleading. Averments in a pleading to which no responsive pleading is required or permitted shall be taken as denied or avoided.

(E) Pleading to be concise and direct; consistency.

    (1)   Each averment of a pleading shall be simple, concise, and direct. No technical forms of pleading or motions are required.

    (2)   A party may set forth two or more statements of a claim or defense alternately or hypothetically, either in one count or defense or in separate counts or defenses. When two or more statements are made in the alternative and one of them if made independently would be sufficient, the pleading is not made insufficient by the insufficiency of one or more of the alternative statements. A party may also state as many separate claims or defenses as he has regardless of consistency and whether based on legal or equitable grounds. All statements shall be made subject to the obligations set forth in Rule 11.

(F) Construction of pleadings. All pleadings shall be so construed as to do substantial justice.

(G) Pleadings shall not be read or submitted. Pleadings shall not be read or submitted to the jury, except insofar as a pleading or portion thereof is used in evidence.

(H) Disclosure of minority or incompetency. Every pleading or motion made by or on behalf of a minor or an incompetent shall set forth such fact unless the fact of minority or incompetency has been disclosed in a prior pleading or motion in the same action or proceeding.

COMMENTARY

Rule 8 provides the rules and principles generally applicable to pleadings. Special pleading rules are also found in Rule 9. Rule 8(F), in conjunction with the liberal amendment procedures of Rule 15 and the construction provided by Rule 1(B), indicates that the merits of a case, rather than the technical rules governing code pleading, should dictate the tenor of a civil action.

Accordingly, Rule 8 is concerned primarily with a general formulation of the issues in a case. The theory of the Rules is that specific factual information will be obtained through the discovery rules, and such information need not be set forth in detail in the pleadings.

Contents of Pleadings

Subsection (A) also requires a general statement of the claim and the kind of relief sought. If damages are being claimed in an amount more than $25,000, the pleading must state this fact. However, the specific amount need not be stated unless it is an amount based upon a contract or other similar instrument required to be attached to the pleading under Rule 10. Additionally, a party against whom an unspecified amount is claimed in a pleading may request a written statement of the amount sought, but only after having received the pleading.

Subsection (B) requires a general statement of the party's defenses to a claim. General denials are permitted if made in good faith, and persons making such denials are subject to sanctions under Rule 11. Claims and defenses must be supported by some kind of factual basis; mere legal conclusions are not sufficient. The particularity required will vary with the specific claim or defense. The official forms accompanying the Rules, however, are indicative of the simplicity anticipated by Rule 8. Rule 8(E)(2) clearly contemplates pleading in the alternative, so that any number of hypothetical claims or defenses may be asserted in the pleadings.

Affirmative Defenses

Rule 8(C) lists the affirmative defenses that must be alleged in the pleadings. Failure to allege one of these defenses constitutes a waiver of that defense, and a court should not thereafter dismiss a claim on the basis of that defense. Likewise, an allegation of an affirmative defense that contains no factual basis will not support a dismissal supported by that defense.

Illustration 8-1

Jeanette commences a tort action against Curt in connection with an accident that occurred at Curt's place of business. In his answer, Curt alleges that Jeanette assumed the risk of injury, but fails to allege that Jeanette was contributorily negligent. Under Rule 8, Curt's failure to allege contributory negligence in his answer constitutes a waiver of the defense. Therefore, the court cannot dismiss Jeanette's action on the basis that she was contributorily negligent.

Improper Denomination of a Counterclaim or Defense

Subsection (C) also makes clear that a party's mistaken denomination of a defense or counterclaim as the other will not render a pleading insufficient on those grounds. The court, "if justice so requires, shall treat the pleading as if there had been a proper designation," *i.e.*, as if a "counterclaim" specified by a defending party had actually been specified as an "affirmative defense" or vice versa. A wrinkle not expressly covered under the Rules, however, is the effect of such a treatment by a court on the requirement of the adverse party to serve a responsive pleading. Because Rule 7 requires a party to make a reply "to a counterclaim denominated *as such*," the treatment by the court of a counterclaim denominated by a party as an "affirmative defense," but treated as a "counterclaim" under Rule 8(C), should not technically trigger the provisions of Rule 7(A). However, the final sentence of Rule 7(A), which allows the court to order a reply to an answer or a third-party answer, will provide courts the means for ordering a party to respond to an "affirmative defense" treated by the court "as if there had been a proper designation" of a counterclaim under Rule 8(C). If such an order is not made by the court, however, a party should not technically be required to file a responsive pleading to an "affirmative defense" treated as a counterclaim under Rule 8(C) under a strict interpretation of the Rules.

Illustration 8-2

Marion files an action against Al for negligence, claiming damages for injuries occurring in a restaurant fire. In his answer, Al states, as an affirmative defense, that Marion negligently caused the fire by carelessly smoking a cigar, and he claims $100,000 in damages to his restaurant. Although the court will undoubtedly treat Al's mistakenly denominated "affirmative defense" as a counterclaim, Marion will presumably not file a reply to Al's answer because Al has not specifically stated a counterclaim "as such." If Al then files a motion to dismiss Marion's original claim because she failed to file a reply, the court should deny Al's motion but order Marion to reply under Rule 7(A). Alternately, Al may amend his answer under Rule 15 and re-designate his counterclaim correctly. In this situation, Marion is required under Rule 15(A) to respond to Al's amended answer, which now contains a counterclaim denominated "as such."

Another puzzle created by the wording of Rule 8(C) is whether the court has the authority to "treat [a] pleading as if there had been a proper designation" with regard to cross-claims and third-party claims when a party makes a mistaken designation. Because the Rule refers only to mistaken designations of counterclaims and defenses, express authority appears to be lacking. Nevertheless, the liberal amendment provisions of Rule 15 supply an alternate remedy in this situation.

Effect of Failure to Deny

Rule 8(D) provides that any issues alleged in a pleading are deemed to have been admitted by the opposing party if they are not denied in a mandatory responsive pleading. This treatment entails especially harsh consequences when the issues to which a denial has not been made are demonstrably false but nonetheless regarded as true for purposes of litigation. It is thus imperative that all issues in a pleading be addressed specifically by the opposing party. Careful separation of the allegations into different counts pursuant to Rule 10(B) diminishes possible confusion engendered by the provisions of Rule 8(D).

Illustration 8-3

Diane commences a breach of contract action against Annette. In her complaint, Diane alleges that Annette failed to complete the repairs to her garage prior to the deadline specified in the contract. In addition, Diane alleges that Annette failed to comply with local building ordinances. Although Annette's answer specifically denies that the repairs failed to satisfy the requirements of the local building ordinances, Annette does not address whether the work was completed prior to the designated deadline. Because Annette did not deny the allegation regarding the contract deadline, the issue will be deemed to have been admitted by Annette, regardless of whether the allegation is actually true.

Pleadings Not to Be Read to Jury

Subsection (G) simply provides that pleadings occupy no special position in an action with regard to their admissibility at trial. Nothing in subsection (G) prevents the admission of pleadings or portions of pleadings at trial; however, such documents must still satisfy the requirements of admissibility established by the Ohio Rules of Evidence: relevancy, authentication, "best evidence" rule, and hearsay.

Disclosure of Minority or Incompetency

Subsection (H) simply ensures that the court and all parties are aware of the fact that one of the parties or interested persons in an action is a minor or incompetent person. Thus, any pleading or motion must reveal the fact of minority or incompetency unless a prior pleading or motion has made the fact evident.

ADDITIONAL AUTHORITY

5 WRIGHT & MILLER §§ 1201-1290

2 MOORE'S FEDERAL PRACTICE §§ 8.01-8.10

4 ANDERSON'S OHIO CIVIL PRACTICE §§ 151.03-151.08, 153.02-153.09

1 KLEIN DARLING AT 8-1 to AT 8-16

3 TEREZ F 4.11.1 to F 4.11.22

2 OH. JUR. PL. AND PRAC. FORMS, ch. 15

1 MILLIGAN Forms 8-1 to 266.2

2 MILLIGAN Forms 8-266.3 to 8-866

3 MILLIGAN Forms 8-866.1 to 8-1293

1 FINK §§ 8-1 to 8-9

OHIO LITIGATION CHECKLISTS, Pleading and Process, §§ 1-8

LEADING CASES

Affirmative Defenses; Waiver

Jim's Steak House, Inc. v. City of Cleveland, 81 Ohio St. 3d 18, 688 N.E.2d 506 (1998) (an affirmative defense is waived if not raised in the pleadings or in an amendment to the pleadings)

Affirmative Defenses; When Raised

Gallagher v. Cleveland Browns Football Co., 74 Ohio St. 3d 427, 659 N.E.2d 1232 (1996) (an affirmative defense of primary assumption of the risk must be raised before or during the trial)

Computation of Damages; Criminal Statute

Biomedical Innovations, Inc. v. McLaughlin, 103 Ohio App. 3d 122, 658 N.E.2d 1084 (1995) (a claim for civil damages based on the violation of a criminal statute under which criminal penalties are imposed is improper)

Contents of Claim for Relief

Mar-El Ass'n of Melville v. Picker Int'l, 100 Ohio App. 3d 667, 669 N.E.2d 313 (1995) (a claim for relief must contain a short and plain statement of the claim sufficient to give the defendant notice of the claim and the grounds upon which it is based)

Damages Must Be Alleged in Pleading

Diprima v. A.W. Tavern, Inc., 96 Ohio App. 3d 470, 645 N.E.2d 156 (dismissal of a counterclaim with prejudice was proper where defendant failed to allege an amount of damages), *appeal not allowed*, 70 Ohio St. 3d 1467, 640 N.E.2d 529 (1994)

Effect of Admissions in Pleadings

J. Miller Express, Inc. v. Pentz, 107 Ohio App. 3d 44, 667 N.E.2d 1018 (1995) (an admission in a pleading is equivalent to proof of the fact)

Effect of Failure to Deny

Huffer v. Cicero, 107 Ohio App. 3d 65, 667 N.E.2d 1031 (1995) (the defendant's failure to file a proper answer to a complaint essentially admitted issues regarding negligence and proximate cause)

Failure to Deny; Political Subdivisions

State ex rel. Bd. of Educ. of Youngstown Sch. Dist. v. City of Youngstown, 84 Ohio St. 3d 51, 701 N.E.2d 986 (1998) (because a default judgment may be entered against a political subdivision and its officers only if a claim or right to relief is established by evidence satisfactory to the court, the court looks beyond the simple admissions resulting from a failure to serve a responsive pleading)

Illegality of Contract Affirmative Defense

Stickovich v. Cleveland, 143 Ohio App. 3d 13, 757 N.E.2d 50 (2001) (a defense alleging the illegality of a contract is an affirmative defense and must be raised in a responsive pleading, or it is deemed to have been waived)

Legal Theory

Illinois Controls, Inc. v. Langham, 70 Ohio St. 3d 512, 639 N.E.2d 771 (1994) (Rule 8(A) does not require that a party plead either the legal theory of recovery upon which a claim is based, or the consequences flowing from the legal relationship of the parties by operation of law)

Operative Facts Not Pleaded with Particularity

Cincinnati v. Beretta U.S.A. Corp., 95 Ohio St. 3d 416, 768 N.E.2d 1136 (2002) (Ohio law does not ordinarily require a plaintiff to plead the operative facts of an action with particularity)

Pleadings Construed Liberally; Cause of Action

Wolf v. Lakewood Hosp., 73 Ohio App. 3d 709, 598 N.E.2d 160 (1991) (in determining whether a plaintiff has stated a cause of action, the court should look beyond the title given and examine the pleadings to determine if a cognizable claim has been stated)

Recoupment

Haddad v. English, 145 Ohio App. 3d 598, 763 N.E.2d 1199 (2001) (recoupment must be asserted as an affirmative defense or it will be deemed to have been waived)

Res Judicata and Collateral Estoppel Distinguished

Jackson v. Lou Cohen, Inc., 84 Ohio App. 3d 693, 618 N.E.2d 193 (1992) (res judicata, or claim preclusion, provides that a final judgment on the merits of a claim bars subsequent litigation on the same claim; collateral estoppel, or issue preclusion, prevents re-litigation of claims that were litigated and those that may properly have been litigated)

Statutory Immunity

Turner v. Cent. Local School Dist., 85 Ohio St. 3d 95, 706 N.E.2d 1261 (1999) (statutory immunity is an affirmative defense which is deemed to have been waived if it is not raised in a timely fashion)

Theory of Recovery Not Required to Be Pleaded

Leichliter v. Natl. City Bank of Columbus, 134 Ohio App. 3d 26, 729 N.E.2d 1285 (1999) (the purpose of the requirement that a pleading contain a short and plain statement of the claim and a demand for judgment is to provide the defendant fair notice of the claim and an opportunity to respond; the rule does not require the plaintiff to plead the legal theory of recovery, nor is the plaintiff bound by any particular theory of a claim)

CHAPTER 9

Rule 9. Pleading Special Matters

Rule 9 reads as follows:

(A) Capacity. It is not necessary to aver the capacity of a party to sue or be sued or the authority of a party to sue or be sued in a representative capacity or the legal existence of an organized association of persons that is made a party. When a party desires to raise an issue as to the legal existence of any party or the capacity of any party to sue or be sued or the authority of a party to sue or be sued in a representative capacity, he shall do so by specific negative averment, which shall include such supporting particulars as are peculiarly within the pleader's knowledge.

(B) Fraud, mistake, condition of the mind. In all averments of fraud or mistake, the circumstances constituting fraud or mistake shall be stated with particularity. Malice, intent, knowledge, and other condition of mind of a person may be averred generally.

(C) Conditions precedent. In pleading the performance or occurrence of conditions precedent, it is sufficient to aver generally that all conditions precedent have been performed or have occurred. A denial of performance or occurrence shall be made specifically and with particularity.

(D) Official document or act. In pleading an official document or official act it is sufficient to aver that the document was issued or the act done in compliance with law.

(E) Judgment. In pleading a judgment or decision of a court of this state or a foreign court, judicial or quasi-judicial tribunal, or of a board or officer, it is sufficient to aver the judgment or decision without setting forth matter showing jurisdiction to render it.

(F) Time and place. For the purpose of testing the sufficiency of a pleading, averments of time and place are material and shall be considered like all other averments of material matter.

(G) Special damage. When items of special damage are claimed, they shall be specifically stated.

COMMENTARY

Rule 9 contains rules relating to pleading in special circumstances. Although an exhaustive discussion of each of these circumstances is beyond the scope of this manual, a brief description of each situation is set forth below.

Capacity

Rule 9(A) sets forth the general rule that the capacity of a party to sue or to be sued in either a personal or a representative capacity need not be initially set forth in a pleading. In other words, the capacity to sue or to be sued in Ohio is assumed. A defense to a claim on grounds of lack of capacity must be raised specifically in a responsive pleading or by motion or the defense will be deemed to have been waived. Additional discussion concerning capacity can be found in Chapter 17 of this manual.

Fraud, Mistake, Condition of the Mind

Subsection (B) requires that allegations of fraud or mistake must be set forth with an added degree of particularity than that required for other kinds of allegations. In general, the time, place and content of the alleged misrepresentation, the specific act misrepresented, the identity of the person making the misrepresentation and the object of the fraud must be set forth in the pleading.

Malice, intent, knowledge and other conditions of mind may be alleged generally. In contrast to the particularity requirement for circumstances constituting fraud or mistake, the pleader need not allege specific facts to support a claim of malice or intent. The pleader need only allege that the party acted "maliciously" or "knowingly."

Conditions Precedent

Rule 9(C) draws a distinction between alleging the occurrence of a condition precedent and denying the occurrence of such a condition. Where the right to bring or maintain an action is dependent upon the occurrence of a condition precedent, the statement of claim may set forth a general allegation that such conditions did in fact occur. Obversely, if the opposing party seeks to deny the occurrence of the condition precedent, specific facts rebutting the general allegation are required.

Official Document or Act

Rule 9(D) must be followed when the issuance of an official document or the performance of an official act is pleaded. An official document is one issued either by a governmental agency of the United States or one of the individual States or a political subdivision thereof. A document is also considered to be "official" if it is issued by a public officer acting in an official capacity.

Judgment

Subsection 9(E) applies to judgments and decisions of courts, administrative agencies, or public officers acting in an official capacity. The rule obviates the need to plead jurisdictional facts.

Time and Place

Rule 9(F) is concerned primarily with ascertaining whether the applicable statute of limitations has run with respect to the claims presented in the pleadings.

Special Damages

Rule 9(G) states a special pleading requirement where "special damages" are claimed. The Rules distinguish between special damages, which must be specifically stated, and general damages, which can be either pleaded generally or not at all.

A precise definition of "special damages" is not located in the Rules, and the term has caused considerable confusion in Ohio courts. On the one hand, the Staff Notes to Rule 9 indicate that special damages are damages measurable by proof of market value or out-of-pocket expense. On the other hand, the Ohio Supreme Court has defined special damages as "damages of such a nature that they do not follow as a necessary consequence of the claimed injury." *Gennari v. Andres-Tucker Funeral Home, Inc.*, 21 Ohio St. 3d 102, 488 N.E.2d 174 (1986). To avoid any doubt, all damages should be alleged with as much specificity as possible. There is practically no adverse consequence in doing so, as Rule 54(C) expressly provides, in relevant part, that "every final judgment shall grant the relief to which the party in whose favor it is rendered is entitled, even if the party has not demanded the relief in the pleadings."

ADDITIONAL AUTHORITY

5 Wright & Miller §§ 1291-1320
2 Moore's Federal Practice §§ 9.01-9.11
4 Anderson's Ohio Civil Practice §§ 151.09-151.26
1 Klein Darling AT 9-1 to AT 9-8
3 Terez F 4.3.1 to F 4.3.16
2 Oh. Jur. Pl. and Prac. Forms, ch. 15
3 Milligan Forms 9-1 to 9-48
1 Fink §§ 9-1 to 9-8

LEADING CASES

Capacity Raised by Responsive Pleading

> *Frate v. Al-Sol, Inc.*, 131 Ohio App. 3d 283, 722 N.E.2d 185 (1999) (a party's capacity to sue may be raised by specific negative averment in a responsive pleading)

Definition of Special Damages

Gennari v. Andres-Tucker Funeral Home, Inc., 21 Ohio St. 3d 102, 488 N.E.2d 174 (1986) (special damages which must be specifically pled are those damages which are of such a nature that they do not follow as a necessary consequence of the claimed injury)

Failure to Raise Capacity Defense in Answer

Frate v. Al-Sol, Inc., 131 Ohio App. 3d 283, 722 N.E.2d 185 (1999) (the defendant's failure to raise the plaintiff's lack of capacity to sue in the answer waives the issue)

Fraud Claim Alleged with Specificity

Drozeck v. Lawyers Title Ins. Corp., 140 Ohio App. 3d 816, 749 N.E.2d 775 (2000) (a claim of fraud claim must be alleged with specificity, including averments concerning the applicable party's state of mind, and a failure to do so will render the claim invalid)

Official Versus Individual Capacity

Norwell v. Cincinnati, 133 Ohio App. 3d 790, 729 N.E.2d 1223 (1999) (where a party states expressly that the defendants are being sued in their official capacities, the action will not be deemed to have been commenced against the individuals in their personal capacities)

Pleading Fraud

Okocha v. Fehrenbacker, 101 Ohio App. 3d 309, 655 N.E.2d 744 (1995) (a claim of fraud must be specific enough so that the defendant is aware of the act complained of, and can prepare an effective response and defense)

Pleading Lack of Capacity

State v. Billings, 103 Ohio App. 3d 343, 659 N.E.2d 799 (1994) (a party's failure to raise by specific negative averment another party's corporate status, the defense of lack of capacity to sue was waived), *belated appeal granted*, 73 Ohio St. 3d 1412, 651 N.E.2d 1310, *and dismissed, jurisdictional motion overruled*, 74 Ohio St. 3d 1455, 656 N.E.2d 950 (1995)

CHAPTER 10

Rule 10. Form of Pleadings

Rule 10 reads as follows:

(A) Caption; names of parties. Every pleading shall contain a caption setting forth the name of the court, the title of the action, the case number, and a designation as in Rule 7(A). In the complaint the title of the action shall include the names and addresses of all the parties, but in other pleadings it is sufficient to state the name of the first party on each side with an appropriate indication of other parties.

(B) Paragraphs; separate statements. All averments of claim or defense shall be made in numbered paragraphs, the contents of each of which shall be limited as far as practicable to a statement of a single set of circumstances; and a paragraph may be referred to by number in all succeeding pleadings. Each claim founded upon a separate transaction or occurrence and each defense other than denials shall be stated in a separate count or defense whenever a separation facilitates the clear presentation of the matters set forth.

(C) Adoption by reference; exhibits. Statements in a pleading may be adopted by reference in a different part of the same pleading or in another pleading or in any motion. A copy of any written instrument attached to a pleading is a part thereof for all purposes.

(D) Copy must be attached. When any claim or defense is founded on an account or other written instrument, a copy thereof must be attached to the pleading. If not so attached, the reason for the omission must be stated in the pleading.

(E) Size of paper filed. All pleadings, motions, briefs, and other papers filed with the clerk, including those filed by electronic means, shall be on paper not exceeding 8½ x 11 inches in size and without backing or cover.

COMMENTARY

Rule 10 governs the form, as opposed to the content, of the pleadings. Subsection (A) mandates that all the parties to an action be named in the complaint, but subsequent pleadings and motions can be titled by reference to the first party on each side. All persons and entities named in the caption are parties to the action, even if additional references to the parties in the pleading omit one or more of the names included in the caption. The importance of an accurately prepared caption is emphasized in conjunction with the requirement in Rule 4(A) that a summons for service will only be issued upon defendants listed in the caption. Rule 10(A) does not provide for anonymous plaintiffs or defendants; however, specific exceptions have been allowed where, for example, the plaintiffs' need for privacy outweighs the concerns of disclosure in Rule 10.

Rule 10(B) anticipates separate counts in the pleadings in two circumstances. First, the Rule specifies that claims arising from a single set of circumstances be separated into different counts. Second, the Rule mandates separate counts whenever overlapping claims may arise from distinct transactions or occurrences, if the separation will facilitate the presentation of the claims.

Illustration 10-1

Linda files an action against Williams Construction, the general contractor who supervised the construction of Linda's home. Linda alleges that her gas furnace was installed improperly, and claims that Williams Construction is liable for the cost of repair, either on a breach of warranty theory or a negligence theory. In her complaint, Linda should set forth the breach of warranty and negligence theories in separate counts.

Illustration 10-2

Assume on the facts of Illustration 10-1 that two of Linda's neighbors join in her action against Williams Construction, each claiming that their furnace was installed improperly. The complaint should list each allegation of improper installation separately, as well as setting forth distinct theories of liability. Thus, the complaint should contain a minimum of six counts (three transactions times two theories of liability).

Subsection (C) allows for the adoption and incorporation of statements made in any pleading into any part of the same pleading, any other pleading, or any motion. Exhibits to a pleading are considered part of that pleading for all purposes and may also be incorporated by reference into other pleadings and motions.

Rule 10(D) requires that a pleading setting forth any claim or defense based upon a contract or other written instrument must contain a copy of the contract or written instrument. A failure to attach a copy must be explained in the pleading.

Finally, subsection (E) imposes a uniform standard for the size of papers filed with the clerk. Subsection (E) also applies to papers filed by electronic means, such as faxes.

ADDITIONAL AUTHORITY

5 Wright & Miller §§ 1321-1330

2 Moore's Federal Practice §§ 10.01-10.05

4 Anderson's Ohio Civil Practice §§ 151.02

1 Klein Darling AT 10-1 to AT 10-13

3 Terez F 4.3.62

Oh. Jur. Pl. and Prac. Forms, ch. 16

3 Milligan Forms 10-1 to 10-47

1 Fink §§ 10-1 to 10-9

Ohio Litigation Checklists, Pleading and Process, §§ 1-5

LEADING CASES

Addresses Not Required on Complaint

State ex rel. Crossman Communities of Ohio, Inc. v. Greene Cty. Bd. of Elections, 87 Ohio St. 3d 132, 717 N.E.2d 1091 (1999) (per curiam opinion of three judges with one judge concurring in judgment) (the failure of a party to list the addresses of all parties in their amended complaint did not require a dismissal of the action; the complaint complied with the Supreme Court rule governing the institution of original actions, which required only that the name, title and address of respondent be listed)

Attachments

Arthur v. Parentau, 102 Ohio App. 3d 302, 657 N.E.2d 284 (1995) (in an action on account, a copy of the account should be attached to the complaint pursuant to Rule 10(C))

Caption; Names of Parties

State ex rel. Hitchcock v. Cuyahoga County Court of Common Pleas, 97 Ohio App. 3d 600, 647 N.E.2d 208 (1994) (a complaint that failed to list in the caption the names of the party seeking a writ of prohibition, the names of respondents or the identity of the probate court judge was defective for not identifying proper parties before the court)

Failure to Name Defendants

Sherrills v. State, 91 Ohio St. 3d 133, 742 N.E.2d 651 (2001) (party who failed to name proper respondents and include their addresses in the complaint was properly dismissed)

Omission of Names and Addresses Grounds for Dismissal

State ex rel. Myocare Nursing Home, Inc. v. Cuyahoga Cty. Court of Common

Pleas, 145 Ohio App. 3d 22, 761 N.E.2d 1072 (2001) (the failure to include the names and addresses of all the parties in the caption of the complaint may be grounds for dismissal)

Paper Size Requirements

National Church Residences v. Timson, 78 Ohio App. 3d 798, 605 N.E.2d 1346 (1992) (the trial court's failure to insist on compliance with strict requirements on paper size was not reversible error)

Paragraphs; Separate Statements

Wright v. Ghee, 74 Ohio St. 3d 465, 659 N.E.2d 1261 (1996) (the appropriate remedy for the failure to comply with Rule 10(B)'s requirement of numbered paragraphs is granting a motion to separately state and number, not dismissal of the claim)

CHAPTER 11

Rule 11. Signing of Pleadings, Motions, or Other Documents

Rule 11 reads as follows:

Every pleading, motion, or other document of a party represented by an attorney shall be signed by at least one attorney of record in the attorney's individual name, whose address, attorney registration number, telephone number, telefax number, if any, and business e-mail address, if any, shall be stated. A party who is not represented by an attorney shall sign the pleading, motion, or other document and state the party's address. Except when otherwise specifically provided by these rules, pleadings need not be verified or accompanied by affidavit. The signature of an attorney or *pro se* party constitutes a certificate by the attorney or party that the attorney or party has read the document; that to the best of the attorney's or party's knowledge, information, and belief there is good ground to support it; and that it is not interposed for delay. If a document is not signed or is signed with intent to defeat the purpose of this rule, it may be stricken as sham and false and the action may proceed as though the document had not been served. For a willful violation of this rule, an attorney or *pro se* party, upon motion of a party or upon the court's own motion, may be subjected to appropriate action, including an award to the opposing party of expenses and reasonable attorney fees incurred in bringing any motion under this rule. Similar action may be taken if scandalous or indecent matter is inserted.

COMMENTARY

Rule 11 describes the conditions under which the court may impose sanctions on an attorney or a party for certain kinds of abuses of the litigation process, as well as the kinds of sanctions that may be imposed for such abuses. Rule 11 is loosely based on Federal Rule of Civil Procedure 11, but the Ohio version is greatly simplified.

Requirements Under the Rule

Rule 11 requires that every pleading, motion, or other document of a party must be signed by at least one attorney of record, who must include her address, attorney registration number, telephone number, and fax number and e-mail address, if any. An unrepresented party is required to sign all papers in an action, and the party's address must also be included with the signature. The Rule applies to all papers filed with the court as well as those papers served on any other party. The Rule abolishes any vestige of the common law requirement that pleadings must be verified or supported by an affidavit.

Representations by Attorneys or Parties

By signing a pleading or motion in accordance with Rule 11, an attorney or party makes three certifications with regard to that pleading or motion: (1) it has been read by the person signing it; (2) it is based on a good faith belief that there are grounds to support it; and (3) it has not been introduced for purposes of delay. The attorney or party signing the pleading or motion also impliedly certifies that the presentation of the document and signature is not intended to defeat the purpose of the Rule, as the fifth sentence of the Rule allows such documents to be stricken by the court.

Sanctions

The Rule permits the imposition of sanctions upon a showing that an attorney or party willfully violated the terms of the Rule. Inadvertent violations or documents submitted in good faith will not support the imposition of sanctions on that attorney or party. A motion for sanctions under Rule 11 may be brought by any party or may be ordered by the court *sua sponte*, though the court should allow the offending party an opportunity to explain the conduct or document under consideration.

Rule 11 makes clear that sanctions are discretionary with the court, even if the underlying conduct is undisputed. Additionally, the choice of the appropriate sanction is largely within the court's discretion, though some kinds of sanctions, such as outright dismissal, should be imposed only under exceptional circumstances. Under the Rule, sanctions may also be imposed upon the law firm employing a sanctionable attorney. The penultimate sentence of the Rule was added in 1994 to permit judges to award expenses and attorneys fees attributable to the filing of a Rule 11 motion.

ADDITIONAL AUTHORITY

5 WRIGHT & MILLER §§ 1331-1340
2 MOORE'S FEDERAL PRACTICE §§ 11.01-11.42
4 ANDERSON'S OHIO CIVIL PRACTICE §§ 151.23, 151.23a
1 KLEIN DARLING AT 11-1 to AT 11-10
3 TEREZ F 4.2.1 to F 4.2.4, F 4.18.4 to F 4.18.8, F 9.5.1, F 9.6.1, F 9.6.2
2 OH. JUR. PL. AND PRAC. FORMS, ch. 16
3 MILLIGAN Forms 11-1 to 11-12
1 FINK §§ 11-1 to 11-2
OHIO LITIGATION CHECKLISTS, Pleading and Process, §§ 1-5

LEADING CASES

Bad Faith Standard

Stone v. House of Day Funeral Serv., 140 Ohio App. 3d 713, 748 N.E.2d 1200 (2000) (the rule regarding sanctions for frivolous conduct employs a subjective bad faith standard)

Frivolous Claim

Jones v. Billingham, 105 Ohio App. 3d 8, 663 N.E.2d 657 (1995) (pursuant to Rule 11, a frivolous claim is one that is unsupported by facts in which complainant has a good faith belief)

Frivolous Lawsuits

Conley v. Brown Corp. of Waverly, Inc., 82 Ohio St. 3d 470, 696 N.E.2d 1085 (1998) (one solution to "frivolous" lawsuits brought pursuant to employer intentional tort theories is the use of Rule 11 which permits sanctions for abuse of the litigation process)

Hearing on Sanctions Collateral to Underlying Proceeding

Stone v. House of Day Funeral Serv., 140 Ohio App. 3d 713, 748 N.E.2d 1200 (2000) (although a voluntary dismissal generally divests a trial court of jurisdiction, a hearing on sanctions is considered collateral to the underlying proceedings and jurisdiction on the motion for sanctions is retained by the trial court)

Malpractice Certificate Filing Requirement Invalid

State ex rel. Ohio Academy of Trial Lawyers v. Sheward, 86 Ohio St. 3d 451, 715 N.E.2d 1062 (1999) (the statute requiring plaintiff bringing a malpractice action to file a certificate of merit within ninety days after the filing of a responsive pleading or compliance with discovery requests for the production of the appropriate medical or professional records, whichever is later, conflicted with Rule 11, and thus is invalid)

Sanctions Imposed; Dismissal

Schwartz v. General Accident Ins. of Am., 91 Ohio App. 3d 603, 632 N.E.2d 1379 (1993) (a court retains jurisdiction to grant sanctions under Rule 11, despite the voluntary dismissal of a complaint under Rule 41)

Sanctions on Law Firm

Lewis v. Celina Fin. Corp., 101 Ohio App. 3d 464, 655 N.E.2d 1333 (1995) (reliance on the representations of outside or forwarding counsel does not constitute "safe harbor" under Rule 11, and sanctions may be imposed on the signing attorney's law firm)

CHAPTER 12

Rule 12. Defenses and Objections—When and How Presented—By Pleading or Motion—Motion for Judgment on Pleadings

Rule 12 reads as follows:

(A) When answer presented.

(1) Generally. The defendant shall serve his answer within twenty-eight days after service of the summons and complaint upon him; if service of notice has been made by publication, he shall serve his answer within twenty-eight days after the completion of service by publication.

(2) Other responses and motions. A party served with a pleading stating a cross-claim against him shall serve an answer thereto within twenty-eight days after the service upon him. The plaintiff shall serve his reply to a counterclaim in the answer within twenty-eight days after service of the answer or, if a reply is ordered by the court, within twenty-eight days after service of the order, unless the order otherwise directs. The service of a motion permitted under this rule alters these periods of time as follows, unless a different time is fixed by order of the court:

(a) if the court denies the motion, a responsive pleading, delayed because of service of the motion, shall be served within fourteen days after notice of the court's action;

(b) if the court grants the motion, a responsive pleading, delayed because of service of the motion, shall be served within fourteen days after service of the pleading which complies with the court's order.

(B) How presented. Every defense, in law or fact, to a claim for relief in any pleading, whether a claim, counterclaim, cross-claim, or third-party claim, shall be asserted in the responsive pleading thereto if one is required, except that the following defenses may at the option of the pleader be made by motion:

(1) lack of jurisdiction over the subject matter,

(2) lack of jurisdiction over the person,

(3) improper venue,

(4) insufficiency of process,

(5) insufficiency of service of process,

(6)   failure to state a claim upon which relief can be granted,

(7)   failure to join a party under Rule 19 or Rule 19.1.

    A motion making any of these defenses shall be made before pleading if a further pleading is permitted. No defense or objection is waived by being joined with one or more other defenses or objections in a responsive pleading or motion. If a pleading sets forth a claim for relief to which the adverse party is not required to serve a responsive pleading, he may assert at the trial any defense in law or fact to that claim for relief. When a motion to dismiss for failure to state a claim upon which relief can be granted presents matters outside the pleading and such matters are not excluded by the court, the motion shall be treated as a motion for summary judgment and disposed of as provided in Rule 56. Provided however, that the court shall consider only such matters outside the pleadings as are specifically enumerated in Rule 56. All parties shall be given reasonable opportunity to present all materials made pertinent to such a motion by Rule 56.

(C)   **Motion for judgment on the pleadings.** After the pleadings are closed but within such time as not to delay the trial, any party may move for judgment on the pleadings.

(D)   **Preliminary hearings.** The defenses specifically enumerated (1) to (7) in subdivision (B) of this rule, whether made in a pleading or by motion, and the motion for judgment mentioned in subdivision (C) of this rule shall be heard and determined before trial on application of any party.

(E)   **Motion for definite statement.** If a pleading to which a responsive pleading is permitted is so vague or ambiguous that a party cannot reasonably be required to frame a responsive pleading, he may move for a definite statement before interposing his responsive pleading. The motion shall point out the defects complained of and the details desired. If the motion is granted and the order of the court is not obeyed within fourteen days after notice of the order or within such other time as the court may fix, the court may strike the pleading to which the motion was directed or make such order as it deems just.

(F)   **Motion to strike.** Upon motion made by a party before responding to a pleading, or if no responsive pleading is permitted by these rules, upon motion made by a party within twenty-eight days after the service of the pleading upon him or upon the court's own initiative at any time, the court may order stricken from any pleading any insufficient claim or defense or any redundant, immaterial, impertinent or scandalous matter.

(G)   **Consolidation of defenses and objections.** A party who makes a motion under this rule must join with it the other motions herein provided for and then available to him. If a party makes a motion under this rule and does not include therein all defenses and objections then available to him which this rule permits to be raised by motion, he shall not thereafter assert by motion or responsive pleading, any of the defenses or objections so omitted, except as provided in subdivision (H) of this rule.

(H) Waiver of defenses and objections.

(1) A defense of lack of jurisdiction over the person, improper venue, insufficiency of process, or insufficiency of service of process is waived

  (a) if omitted from a motion in the circumstances described in subdivision (G), or

  (b) if it is neither made by motion under this rule nor included in a responsive pleading or an amendment thereof permitted by Rule 15(A) to be made as a matter of course.

(2) A defense of failure to state a claim upon which relief can be granted, a defense of failure to join a party indispensable under Rule 19, and an objection of failure to state a legal defense to a claim may be made in any pleading permitted or ordered under Rule 7(A), or by motion for judgment on the pleadings, or at the trial on the merits.

(3) Whenever it appears by suggestion of the parties or otherwise that the court lacks jurisdiction of the subject matter, the court shall dismiss the action.

COMMENTARY

Rule 12 is one of the most important Rules; unfortunately, it is also one of the most complicated. Much of the confusion and interpretive difficulty surrounding the Rule stems from the fact that the framers of Rule 12 condensed the procedures of several different functions into a single Rule. Rule 12 is best conceptualized as performing no fewer than five distinct functions. The compression of these discrete functions into one Rule accounts for many of the issues discussed in this Chapter.

Overview of Functions of Rule 12

Subsection (A) is primarily a timing provision; it specifies the time periods, and their exceptions, within which a party must respond to a pleading. Subsection (B), the most familiar part of Rule 12, should be read in conjunction with subsections (G) and (H), which together govern how various defenses to an action may be presented, and how they may also be waived. The final sentences of subsection (B), along with subsection (C), specify a mechanism for disposing of an action before trial and delineate the operation of that mechanism in conjunction with Rule 56, which governs summary judgment. Subsection (D) provides for a preliminary hearing before trial in which to hear arguments concerning a motion pursuant to subsections (B) and (C). Finally, subsections (E) and (F) govern the motions that may be brought by a party to correct perceived defects in a pleading. These separate aspects of Rule 12, each delineating a discrete function, are explained in more detail below.

Time Periods in Which Responsive Pleadings Must Be Made

Rule 12(A) specifies the time periods in which an answer or other mandatory responsive pleading must be served. The Rule states that a party has 28 days from the service of a summons to answer the original complaint. If service by publication has been made pursuant to Rule 4.4, an answer must be served within 28 days after the final day on which the publication was made. The subsection contains no provision specifying the time period within which a party must serve an answer when that party has waived service of process under Rule 4(D). Such a party should serve an answer within 28 days of the date of waiver or seek the permission of the court for a longer time period.

Illustration 12-1

Paula commences a tort action against Dan for personal injuries resulting from an automobile accident. On February 26, Paula serves a summons and copy of the complaint on Dan by certified mail, which Dan receives on March 2. Dan has until March 30 to serve an answer on Paula.

Similarly, a party has 28 days after service of a pleading stating a cross-claim in which to respond. In addition, a party has 28 days after service of an answer stating a counterclaim in which to respond. Under subsection (A)(2), the court may extend these periods in its discretion.

The language of Rule 12(A) must be analyzed very carefully in conjunction with

---

Illustration 12-2

Assume on the facts of Illustration 12-1 that Dan serves an answer to Paula's original complaint by delivering the answer to Paula in person on March 30. In addition to denying the allegations contained in Paula's complaint, Dan's answer includes a counterclaim for the injuries he suffered in the automobile accident. Paula has until April 27 to file a reply to Dan's counterclaim.

---

the other Rules governing pleadings and service of process, and several points should be noted in this regard. First, under subsection (A), the 28-day time period for responding to a complaint is triggered by "service of the summons and complaint upon [a party]." This date is easily ascertained when service of process is effected through personal service under Rule 4.1(B) or residence service under Rule 4.1(C), as the date of "service" of the summons is the date that it was actually received by the party or left with a person of suitable age at the party's residence. However, Rule 4.1 does not indicate when service of process is deemed to have been completed when effected through express or certified mail under Rule 4.1(A).

As discussed in Chapter 4.1, four considerations militate in favor of the argument that service of process should be deemed complete when service of the summons and copy of the complaint is actually received by the defendant, as opposed to when the summons is placed in the mail by the clerk. The analysis provided in that Chapter supplies a persuasive argument that a proper construction of the term "service," as used in subsection (A) only, should refer to the date indicated by the return receipt of the certified or express mail as the actual date of service. The automatic 3-day extension for deadlines triggered by the service of a document by mail under Rule 6(E) is expressly made inapplicable to the service of a summons under Rules 4-4.6.

Illustration 12-3

Kaitlyn commences an action against Deidre on September 1 by filing a complaint in an Ohio trial court. The clerk sends the summons and copy of the complaint to Deidre by certified mail on September 2, and Deidre receives the summons and complaint the following day, September 3. Deidre should have until October 1 to serve an answer on Kaitlyn. Because actual service occurred on September 3, Rule 6(E) will not operate to extend the period by an additional 3 days.

Second, under subsection (A)(2), answers to cross-claims and replies to counter-claims are also triggered by the "service [of the pleading] upon [a party]." However, the arguments discussed in Chapter 4.1 which militate in favor of the argument that the date of service of the summons should be the date of actual receipt of the summons by the defendant are not applicable to the service of pleadings subsequent to the complaint. Service of these pleadings and other documents are governed by Rule 5, which does not require registered or certified mail for service under that Rule to be effective. Furthermore, the automatic 3-day extension of Rule 6(E) for deadlines triggered by the service of a document by mail applies to pleadings in which a cross-claim or counterclaim is presented. Thus, the date of the "service" of a pleading under subsection (A)(2) and the date from which the 28-day deadline for responding to that pleading begins to run should be measured by the date that the pleading was placed in the mail, even if certified or express mail is voluntarily chosen by a party.

> ### Illustration 12-4
>
> Assume on the facts of Illustration 12-3 that Deidre serves an answer containing a counterclaim by sending it by certified mail on September 5. Kaitlyn will have 28 days from the service of the answer in which to serve a reply. However, this period is extended by 3 days under Rule 6(E) because Kaitlyn is required to serve her reply within a prescribed period after the service of a notice or paper by mail. Thus, Kaitlyn should have until October 6 to serve a reply.

The third point that should be noted in this area relates to the date upon which the service of a pleading or paper other than the original process will be deemed to have been completed when service is effected by mail. Under Rule 5(B), the service of such papers is "complete upon mailing." This date is important not for determining the time period within which the opposing party must respond to the pleading, which is instead discussed in the preceding paragraphs, but rather for determining whether a response has been made in a timely fashion. Thus, a pleading mailed on the final day on which the applicable time period expires will be considered to be timely, even though the person to whom the pleading was sent will not be considered to have received the pleading until 3 days later under Rule 6(E). It is therefore possible for the exchange of pleadings to take longer than the 56 days implied by Rule 12(A).

> ### Illustration 12-5
>
> Assume on the facts of Illustration 12-3 that Deidre mails her answer containing a counterclaim to Kaitlyn on October 1. The answer is timely because Rule 5(B) provides that service is deemed complete upon mailing. Kaitlyn will have until November 1 to serve her reply, as 3 days will be added to the time period for replying to the counterclaim under Rule 6(E).

Finally, it should be noted that a court-ordered reply under the second sentence may not be subject to the automatic 3-day extension of Rule 6(E). This is because that provision clearly states that such a reply must be served within 28 days after service of the order of the court requiring the pleading. If the order is served by the court in any manner other than by mail, the 3-day extension will not apply.

Alteration of Time Periods

The service of a Rule 12 motion alters, and in most cases extends, the time periods explained above in two circumstances, as set forth in subsection (A)(2): (1) if the court denies the Rule 12 motion, the pleading shall be served within 14 days of notice of the court's denial; and (2) if the court grants the Rule 12 motion, the pleading must be served within 14 days of the service of a pleading in compliance with the grant of the motion. These alterations are inapplicable for motions made outside the ambit of Rule 12; *e.g.*, a motion for a jury demand will not alter the time period within which to respond to a pleading. However, it is unsettled whether a motion for summary judgment will alter the time periods, as such a motion is not a motion under Rule 12. A party seeking summary judgment before filing a responsive pleading should thus request from the court an extension of the time period in which that party is required to file a responsive pleading.

Illustration 12-6

Assume on the facts of Illustration 12-1 that, prior to filing an answer to Paula's original complaint, Dan files a Rule 12(B)(6) motion to dismiss for failure to state a claim upon which relief can be granted. If the court schedules a hearing for June 2 and then denies Dan's motion at the hearing, Dan is required to file an answer to Paula's complaint no later than June 16. If the court grants Dan's motion but grants Paula leave to amend her complaint, Dan must await the service of the amended pleading from Paula and file an answer within 14 days after the date of service. Thus, if Paula re-serves her complaint on July 7 by delivering it to Dan in person, Dan must file an answer by July 21.

In most cases, alteration of the time period under subsection (A)(2) will extend the period in which to respond to a pleading, as the party making a Rule 12 motion will not willingly decrease the time in which she is to respond, *i.e.*, she will want to serve the Rule 12 motion as close as possible to the expiration of the original time period in which she must respond. However, in the unusual event that a court denies a Rule 12 motion more than 14 days before the expiration of the original time period, it is uncertain whether the party should be allowed the additional time to respond between the end of the 14-day period under subsection (A)(2) and the end of the original 28-day time period. In any event, the court is given discretion in subsection (A)(2) to order a different time period in that rare circumstance.

Illustration 12-7

Assume on the facts of Illustration 12-6 that Dan makes the Rule 12(B)(6) motion on March 3, the day after receiving Paula's complaint. Instead of scheduling a hearing on the motion, the court immediately denies Dan's Rule 12(B)(6) motion and so notifies the parties on March 4. Under Rule 12(A)(2), Dan would have 14 days after notice of the denial of his motion in which to file an answer— March 18. However, Dan's original deadline for filing an answer was 28 days from the day after the date of the service of the summons—March 30. In this instance, the court should grant to Dan the additional time in which to file an answer.

Defenses in an Action Generally

The second function of Rule 12 is to set forth the manner in which all defenses to an action may be presented. Of course, the familiar litany of defenses in Rule 12(B) is the most salient part of the Rule. This list includes: 1) lack of subject matter jurisdiction; 2) lack of personal jurisdiction; 3) improper venue; 4) insufficient process; 5) insufficient service of process; 6) failure to state a claim upon which relief can be granted; and 7) failure to join a party under Rule 19 or Rule 19.1. Often overlooked, however, is the crucial first part of the sentence listing these defenses. It states, simply, that *"every defense, in law or fact, to a claim for relief in any pleading . . . shall be asserted in the responsive pleading thereto if one is required*, except that the following defenses may at the option of the pleader be made by motion: . . . ."* (emphasis added). The severe consequences of the failure to heed this directive are softened in some instances by the liberal amendment provisions in Rule 15, but the importance of explicitly setting forth all defenses should be evident. In addition, as discussed below, the failure to bring a defense listed in Rule 12(B) within the appropriate time period will sometimes also effect a waiver of those defenses. When a party fails to bring an enumerated defense under Rule 12, this may, at times, be unamendable by Rule 15.

Defenses; How Raised

Subsection (B) contains several other important provisions. First, the Rule makes clear that the listed defenses are not required to be made by motion; they may, at the option of a party, be raised in a responsive pleading. Second, the Rule states that, if a party chooses to raise any of the defenses by motion, the motion must be made before the next pleading is to be served. If a party fails to raise an enumerated defense by motion or in the responsive pleading to a claim, the defect can be cured only by amending the pleading as a matter of course pursuant to Rule 15(A). However, if the pleading is not amended as a matter of course pursuant to Rule 15(A), *i.e.*, if the court's permission is required to amend the pleading, the pleading may not be amended to include one of the enumerated defenses in Rule 12(B). It is thus crucial to raise the defenses listed in Rule 12(B) either by a motion before responding to the pleading or by raising the defense in the pleading itself.

Illustration 12-8

Eve sues Tim on a claim arising under an Ohio statute and serves Tim with a summons and copy of the complaint on July 22. Tim promptly serves an answer, which contains a general denial of all charges, on July 31. Although Eve's service of process upon Tim is insufficient because the summons was left with one of Tim's housekeepers, Tim fails to raise the defense by motion or in his answer to Eve's complaint. To raise the defense, Tim must amend his complaint before August 28. As the court's permission is required to amend Tim's answer after that date, the defense of insufficiency of service of process under Rule 12(B) will no longer be available to Tim in defending the action.

It should be noted that if a party is not required to make a responsive pleading and that party chooses not to make a motion under subsection (B), the party may still raise any defense at trial, including the ones listed in subsection (B). This provision ensures that a party cannot waive a defense simply by doing nothing before trial, if that party is, in fact, not required by the Rules to do anything. In essence, subsections (B), (G), and (H), read together, require a "triggering" mechanism, either a required pleading or permissive Rule 12 motion, in order for the waiver provisions of those subsections to take effect.

Joinder of Defenses

Finally, subsection (B) specifies that a defense is not waived by being joined with another defense in the same motion or pleading. This point is repeated in the first sentence of subsection (G) and made apparent by the severe consequences of failing to join together the specified defenses. Although perceived by some scholars as redundant of subsection (B), the consolidation provision of subsection (G) actually includes within its scope all the various motions described in Rule 12, whereas the consolidation provision of subsection (B) includes within its scope only those motions that can be brought under that subsection. Thus, subsection (G) indicates that, for example, a motion to strike under Rule 12(F) *can*, and as the waiver provision of subsection (G) makes clear, *must* be joined with any other motion brought under Rule 12.

Motions "Then Available to the Party"

The "then available to [the party]" language has a special application. If a party makes a Rule 12(E) motion for a more definite statement and the motion is granted, that party should still be allowed to bring another Rule 12 motion if the failure to bring the second motion was caused by the indefiniteness and lack of clarity in the pleading challenged in the first Rule 12(E) motion. The defense or objection that is the subject of the second motion would not have been "available to [the party]" at the time that the first motion was made. Notice that a Rule 12(E) motion does not automatically confer permission on the moving party to file another Rule 12 motion; whether a defense or objection is "available to a party" must be determined on a case-by-case basis.

Illustration 12-9

Rebecca commences an action against Andrea, but Andrea is unable to determine the nature of the lawsuit from Rebecca's complaint. Therefore, Andrea makes a Rule 12(E) motion for a more definite statement. The court grants Andrea's motion and orders Rebecca to issue a more definite statement within 20 days of the court's order. After Rebecca provides Andrea with a more definite statement of the nature of the lawsuit, Andrea may believe that Rebecca has now failed to state a claim upon which relief can be granted. Andrea should be allowed to make a second motion under 12(B), as Rebecca's lack of clarity in her original complaint prevented Andrea from consolidating both Rule 12 motions.

Consolidation and Waiver of Defenses Generally

The consolidation provisions of subsection (G) should be read in conjunction with subsection (H), which makes the waiver implications of failing to consolidate a motion under subsection (G) explicit. Subsection (H)(1) specifies that the defenses enumerated in subsections (B)(2)-(5) are waived if they are neither included in a Rule 12 motion nor raised in a responsive pleading or an amendment to that pleading under Rule 15(A) as a matter of course. As these defenses involve primarily the personal convenience of the party raising the motion, it is appropriate to require parties to raise those defenses at an early stage of the trial process.

Illustration 12-10

Cindy sues Roger for trespassing on her property, but fails to effect sufficient service of process upon Roger in accordance with Rules 4-4.6. Roger makes a Rule 12(B)(3) motion for improper venue, but fails to join with it a Rule 12(B)(5) motion for insufficiency of service of process. Because Roger has not joined all his Rule 12 defenses available to him at that time in a single motion, he may not thereafter raise the Rule 12(B)(5) defense. If, alternatively, Roger serves an answer to Cindy's complaint and does not include the Rule 12(B)(5) defense in his answer, the defense is lost unless Roger amends his answer within 28 days of its service on Cindy.

Because of the severe repercussions of omitting a defense or objection listed in Rule 12 from another Rule 12 motion or responsive pleading, the list of objections and defenses upon which the waiver and consolidation provisions of Rule 12 will operate should be strictly limited to those enumerated in the Rule.

Exceptions to Waiver of Defenses

Subsection (H)(2) specifies that the defenses enumerated in subsections (B)(6)-(7), as well as the objection of failure to state a legal defense to a claim (the opposing party's counterpart to a Rule 12(B)(6) motion), are not waived under the circumstances set forth above. Although these defenses may not be raised by an additional motion before responding to the pleading, they may be raised in the responsive pleading itself, in a motion for judgment on the pleadings, or at trial. These defenses are waived after the conclusion of the trial, and consequently, a party failing to raise these defenses during the trial stage of an action may not raise them for the first time on appeal. Because these defenses involve interests other than the personal convenience of the parties (*e.g.*, a motion for failure to join a party under Rule 19 or Rule 19.1 involves the interest of the non-joined party) it is appropriate to allow these defenses to be raised at later stages of an action.

Illustration 12-11

Robert commences an action against Hilary, a subcontractor employed to install the electrical system at the warehouse, for damages resulting from a fire at Robert's warehouse. During the course of discovery, Hilary arrives at the conclusion that Sally, an unrelated subcontractor employed to install the heating system at the warehouse, is actually the party responsible for the fire. Although Hilary had not raised a Rule 12(B) motion for failure to join a party under Rule 19 by motion or in a responsive pleading, Hilary may still raise the defense at trial. If, however, Hilary fails to raise the defense prior to the conclusion of the trial, Hilary has effectively waived the defense and cannot raise it for the first time on appeal.

Defense of Lack of Subject Matter Jurisdiction

Subsection (H)(3) distinguishes the defense of lack of subject matter jurisdiction under Rule 12(B)(1) from the other enumerated defenses. First, the issue may be raised at any time, including for the first time on appeal. Second, the objection need not be made by motion; the language indicates that objection may be made "by suggestion of the parties." Third, the subsection makes clear that the court may raise the issue *sua sponte*. Fourth, if the court finds that it does in fact lack subject matter jurisdiction, the court is divested of its usual discretion to fashion an appropriate remedy when granting a party's motion. Instead, the Rule states simply that "the court *shall* dismiss the action" (emphasis added).

The Relationship Between Rule 12 and Rule 56 Generally

The third function of Rule 12 is derived from an analysis of the interplay between the final 3 sentences of subsection (B) and Rule 56, which governs summary judgment. In order to properly understand this relationship, however, it is first necessary to examine the nature of the motions made pursuant to those Rules.

Nature of a Rule 12(B)(6) Motion

A motion to dismiss for failure to state a claim upon which relief can be granted under Rule 12(B)(6) is the Rule's analog to the general demurrer under code pleading. A party making a Rule 12(B)(6) motion denies that the allegations in the nonmoving party's pleading are legally sufficient to sustain an actionable claim. In making the determination of legal sufficiency under such a motion, a court will treat the factual allegations, in addition to all reasonable inferences therefrom, of the nonmoving party's pleading as having been admitted.

Illustration 12-12

Nathan commences an action against Kelly, alleging facts A, B, and C in his complaint. Kelly files a 12(B)(6) motion for failure to state a claim upon which relief may be granted, claiming that facts A, B, and C do not support a legally cognizable claim. The court will accept facts A, B, and C as true for purposes of ruling on Kelly's motion. If the court finds that fact D is a necessary element of the cause of action, it should grant Kelly's motion and dismiss the action. Alternatively, the court may grant Nathan leave to amend his pleading to correct the omission.

Conversion of Motions Under Rule 12 into Motions Under Rule 56

Motions made pursuant to Rule 12(B)(6) are automatically converted into motions for summary judgment under Rule 56 if materials outside of the pleadings are used by the court to determine the motion. Under Rule 56, both parties are allowed to present additional materials, such as affidavits or depositions, to support their claims, a prerogative not permitted with Rule 12 motions. In situations where summary judgment is a more appropriate method of disposing of an action than are judgments on the pleadings and Rule 12(B)(6) dismissals, Rule 12(B) provides for an easy transformation from those motions to one for summary judgment.

Illustration 12-13

Allan commences a breach of contract action against Deborah. After receiving the summons and copy of the complaint from Allan, Deborah makes a Rule 12(B)(6) motion for failure to state a claim upon which relief may be granted and submits a transcript of prior testimony from Allan to support her argument. The court should convert Deborah's motion into a motion for summary judgment and allow Allan to present additional materials that he feels would assist the court in ruling on the motion. The court should also make explicit whether the time in which Deborah is required to file a responsive pleading has been tolled by the conversion of the Rule 12 motion into a Rule 56 motion.

Preliminary Hearings on Rule 12 Motions

Rule 12(D) simply provides for preliminary hearings in which oral arguments may be heard both for and against a motion or pleading asserting a defense listed in subsection (B) or a motion for judgment on the pleadings. The preliminary hearing may be requested by any party, and should itself be requested by motion.

Ordinarily, Rule 12(E) motions for a more definite statement and Rule 12(D) motions to strike are ruled upon by the court without a preliminary hearing on the issue. By omitting these motions from those specifically mentioned in subsection (D), the Rule appears to require this result. Although Rule 12(D) does not specifically authorize a preliminary hearing on a motion for failure to state a legal defense to a claim (the converse of Rule 12(B)(6) motion described above), its preservation from waiver in subsection (H)(2) and categorical inclusion with the 12(B) defenses in that subsection lend support to the argument that a preliminary hearing on such an issue would be defensible under a liberal construction of the Rules.

Motions for a More Definite Statement and Motions to Strike

Finally, Rules 12(E) and (F) specify motions to correct alleged defects in a party's pleading. A Rule 12(E) motion for a more definite statement rarely has application today. A pleading that survives a Rule 12(B)(6) objection for failure to state a claim upon which relief can be granted will rarely be so vague or ambiguous such that a Rule 12(E) motion should be granted. Still, a Rule 12(E) motion is appropriate for vague or ambiguous answers, as those pleadings are not subject to Rule 12(B)(6) motions.

Rule 12(F) is the Rules' analog to the motion to expunge in code pleading. It should be used when there is redundant, immaterial, impertinent, or scandalous matter in a pleading. Although a party waives a Rule 12(F) motion in the same manner as the party waives other Rule 12 defenses or objections, the court may strike the material on its own initiative.

ADDITIONAL AUTHORITY

5 Wright & Miller §§ 1341-1400

2 Moore's Federal Practice §§ 12.01-12.51

4 Anderson's Ohio Civil Practice §§ 152.01-152.21

1 Klein Darling at 12-1 to at 12-14

3 Terez F 2.1.1 to F 2.1.3, F 3.1.1, F 4.7.1 to F 4.7.6, F 5.1.1 to F 5.1.5, F 7.4.4

2 Oh. Jur. Pl. and Prac. Forms, ch. 17

3 Milligan Forms 12-1 to 12-90

1 Fink §§ 12-1 to 12-9

Ohio Litigation Checklists, Pleading and Process, §§ 6-8, 12-14

LEADING CASES

Affirmative Defense Raised in Pleadings

Mankins v. Paxton, 142 Ohio App. 3d 1, 753 N.E.2d 918 (2001) (affirmative defenses ordinarily require a reference to materials outside complaint and thus cannot be raised by means of a motion to dismiss for failure to state a claim; however, an exception exists where the existence of an affirmative defense is obvious from face of complaint)

Evidence Outside of the Pleadings

State ex rel. Keller v. Cox, 85 Ohio St. 3d 279, 707 N.E.2d 931 (1999) (courts cannot rely on allegations or evidence outside of the pleadings complaint in determining a motion under Rule 12(B)(6))

Failure to Join a Party

State ex rel. Bush v. Spurlock, 42 Ohio St. 3d 77, 537 N.E.2d 641 (1989) (if a necessary party may still be joined under Rule 19, or if leave to amend a complaint can be granted, a complaint should not be dismissed for failure to join a necessary party)

Failure to State a Claim

Desenco, Inc. v. Akron, 84 Ohio St. 3d 535, 706 N.E.2d 323 (1999) (a claim may be dismissed under Rule 12(B)(6) when: (1) the factual allegations of the complaint and items properly incorporated therein must be accepted as true; (2) non-moving party must be afforded all reasonable inferences possibly derived from the factual allegations; and (3) it must appear beyond doubt that plaintiff can prove no set of facts entitling her to relief)

State ex rel. Fogle v. Steiner, 74 Ohio St. 3d 158, 656 N.E.2d 1288 (1995) (dismissal for failure to state a claim upon which relief could be granted is proper where it appears, beyond doubt, that the parties commencing the action could prove no set of facts warranting relief)

Improper Venue

Nicholson v. Landis, 27 Ohio App. 3d 107, 499 N.E.2d 1260 (1985) (the defendant's failure to raise the issue of improper venue in a timely manner will constitute a waiver of the defense)

Insufficiency of Service of Process

Rite Rug Co., Inc. v. Wilson, 106 Ohio App. 3d 59, 665 N.E.2d 260 (1995) (when effective service of process has not been made upon defendant, and the defendant has not appeared in the case or waived service, the court will lack jurisdiction to enter judgment against the defendant)

Lack of Personal Jurisdiction

Giachetti v. Holmes, 14 Ohio App. 3d 306, 471 N.E.2d 165 (1984) (to establish the personal jurisdiction of a court over a defendant without an evidentiary hearing, the plaintiff must only make a prima facie showing of jurisdiction sufficient to withstand a motion to dismiss)

Lack of Personal Jurisdiction; Waiver

Nehls v. Quad-K Advertising, Inc., 106 Ohio App. 3d 489, 666 N.E.2d 579 (personal jurisdiction may deemed to have been waived when not raised either in defendant's answer or by motion prior to the filing of the defendant's answer), *dismissed, appeal not allowed*, 74 Ohio St. 3d 1462, 656 N.E.2d 1298 (1995)

Lack of Subject Matter Jurisdiction; Standard

Kellon v. Cleveland Marshall College of Law, 102 Ohio App. 3d 684, 657 N.E.2d 835 (1995) (dismissal for lack of subject matter jurisdiction is proper where the court finds that no cause of action cognizable by the forum has been raised in the complaint)

Lack of Subject Matter Jurisdiction; When Raised

LTV Steel Co. v. Gibbs, 109 Ohio App. 3d 272, 671 N.E.2d 1360 (1996) (the lack of subject matter jurisdiction may be raised at any time by any party or by the court, sua sponte)

Material Outside Pleadings on Motion for Lack of Subject Matter Jurisdiction

McGuffey v. LensCrafters, Inc., 141 Ohio App. 3d 44, 749 N.E.2d 825 (2001) (when determining its own jurisdiction pursuant to a motion to dismiss for lack of jurisdiction over the subject matter, the trial court has the authority to consider any pertinent evidentiary materials and is not confined to the allegations of the complaint)

Motion for Dismissal; Generally

State ex rel. Midwest Pride IV, Inc. v. Pontious, 75 Ohio St. 3d 565, 664 N.E.2d 931 (1996) (a motion for dismissal of a complaint is properly granted when the court accepts all factual allegations as true, draws all reasonable inferences in favor of the nonmovant, and still concludes beyond doubt from the complaint that no provable set of facts warrants relief)

Motion for Judgment on the Pleadings

Schweizer v. Riverside Methodist Hosps., 108 Ohio App. 3d 539, 671 N.E.2d 312 (1996) (a motion for judgment on the pleadings is properly granted where no material factual issue exists, and the movant is entitled to judgment as a matter of law)

Motion to Strike

State ex rel. Neff v. Corrigan, 75 Ohio St. 3d 12, 661 N.E.2d 170 (1996) (a motion to strike should not be used as a substitute for a motion to dismiss for failure to state a claim upon which relief could be granted)

Notice Requirement Mandatory

State ex rel. Nelson v. Russo, 89 Ohio St. 3d 227, 729 N.E.2d 1181 (2000) (the court must notify all parties at least 14 days before the time fixed for hearing when it converts a motion to dismiss under Rule 12 into a motion for summary judgment under Rule 56)

Personal Jurisdiction Through Long-Arm Statute

Clark v. Connor, 82 Ohio St. 3d 309, 695 N.E.2d 751 (1998) (personal jurisdiction may be determined according to whether the applicable long-arm statute and corresponding rule of procedure function to confer personal jurisdiction over a defendant; statute and rule must also satisfy due process)

Sua Sponte Dismissal Permitted

State ex rel. Kreps v. Christiansen, 88 Ohio St. 3d 313, 725 N.E.2d 663 (2000) (a complaint for failure to state a claim may be dismissed sua sponte if the complaint is frivolous or the party obviously cannot prevail on the facts alleged in the complaint)

Subject Matter Jurisdiction; Waiver

Ivkovich v. Steubenville, 144 Ohio App. 3d 25, 759 N.E.2d 434 (2001) (subject matter jurisdiction may be raised *sua sponte* by the court at any stage of the proceedings, including for the first time on appeal)

In re Byard, 74 Ohio St. 3d 294, 658 N.E.2d 735 (1996) (subject matter jurisdiction cannot be waived, and can be raised at any time during the proceedings)

Untimely Answer

Turner v. Alexander, 107 Ohio App. 3d 853, 669 N.E.2d 565 (1995) (an untimely answer may only be filed upon a motion for leave and a showing of excusable neglect pursuant to Rule 6(B)(2))

Waiver of Defenses; Generally

State ex rel. The Plain Dealer Publishing Co. v. Cleveland, 75 Ohio St. 3d 31, 661 N.E.2d 187 (1996) (unless an affirmative defense is presented by motion before pleading, affirmatively in a responsive pleading, or by amendment, the defense will be deemed to have been waived)

CHAPTER 13

Rule 13. Counterclaim and Cross-Claim

Rule 13 reads as follows:

(A) Compulsory counterclaims. A pleading shall state as a counterclaim any claim which at the time of serving the pleading the pleader has against any opposing party, if it arises out of the transaction or occurrence that is the subject matter of the opposing party's claim and does not require for its adjudication the presence of third parties of whom the court cannot acquire jurisdiction. But the pleader need not state the claim if

    (1) at the time the action was commenced the claim was the subject of another pending action, or

    (2) the opposing party brought suit upon his claim by attachment or other process by which the court did not acquire jurisdiction to render a personal judgment on that claim, and the pleader is not stating any counterclaim under this Rule 13.

(B) Permissive counterclaims. A pleading may state as a counterclaim any claim against an opposing party not arising out of the transaction or occurrence that is the subject matter of the opposing party's claim.

(C) Counterclaim exceeding opposing claim. A counterclaim may or may not diminish or defeat the recovery sought by the opposing party. It may claim relief exceeding in amount or different in kind from that sought in the pleading of the opposing party.

(D) Counterclaim against this state. These rules shall not be construed to enlarge beyond the limits now fixed by law the right to assert counterclaims or to claim credits against this state, a political subdivision or an officer in his representative capacity or agent of either.

(E) Counterclaim maturing or acquired after pleading. A claim which either matured or was acquired by the pleader after serving his pleading may, with the permission of the court, be presented as a counterclaim by supplemental pleadings.

(F) Omitted counterclaim. When a pleader fails to set up a counterclaim through oversight, inadvertence, or excusable neglect, or when justice requires, he may by leave of court set up the counterclaim by amendment.

(G) Cross-claim against co-party. A pleading may state as a cross-claim any claim by one party against a co-party arising out of the transaction or occurrence that is the subject matter either of the original action or of a counterclaim therein or relating to any property that is the subject matter of the original action. Such cross-claim may include a claim that the party against whom it is asserted is or may be liable to the cross-claimant for all or part of a claim asserted in the action against the cross-claimant.

(H) Joinder of additional parties. Persons other than those made parties to the original action may be made parties to a counterclaim or cross-claim in accordance with the provisions of Rule 19, Rule 19.1, and Rule 20. Such persons shall be served pursuant to Rule 4 through Rule 4.6.

(I) Separate trials; separate judgments. If the court orders separate trials as provided in Rule 42(B) judgment on a counterclaim or cross-claim may be rendered in accordance with the terms of Rule 54(B) when the court has jurisdiction so to do, even if the claims of the opposing party have been dismissed or otherwise disposed of.

(J) Certification of proceedings. In the event that a counterclaim, cross-claim, or third-party claim exceeds the jurisdiction of the court, the court shall certify the proceedings in the case to the court of common pleas.

COMMENTARY

The labyrinth encompassing the joinder of claims and the joinder of parties begins with Rule 13. Rules 13 and 18, relating to the joinder of claims, Rules 19, 19.1 and 20, relating to the joinder of parties, and Rule 14, governing the joinder of parties and claims through third-party practice, are all interrelated, and a discussion of the complexities of any of these Rules necessarily entails reference to the others. Briefly, parties must be properly joined under Rule 19, Rule 19.1, or Rule 20 before counterclaims and cross-claims under Rule 13, third-party claims under Rule 14, and "conditional" claims under Rule 18 may be considered. Subsection (H) thus links Rule 13 with Rules 19, 19.1, and 20. Additionally, issues of claim-joinder and party-joinder should not be confused with the issue as to whether a court has jurisdiction over the parties, a statutory subject beyond the scope of this manual.

Definition of Counterclaims and Cross-Claims

Rule 13 governs counterclaims and cross-claims. Briefly, a counterclaim is a claim asserted by a party against an opposing party. Parties may be said to be "opposing" when they are situated in an adversarial posture in an action. A cross-claim, on the other hand, is a claim asserted by a party against a co-party. A co-party is a party with whom the relationship in an action cannot be said to be "opposing." Although it is possible for two parties to be both co-parties with respect to one claim in an action and opposing parties with respect to another, it makes sense to refer to the parties only as opposing parties for purposes of determining their rights and options under the Rules, as the rules governing counterclaims are more liberal than those governing cross-claims.

Compulsory Counterclaims Generally

Subsection (A) states that, if a party files a pleading in an action, all "compulsory" counterclaims a party may have against an opposing party must be asserted against that party. The Rule embodies the principle that all claims that are closely related should be resolved in a single action, avoiding the ineconomies of multiple litigation on the same issues. The Rule goes on to state two exceptions to this rule.

Illustration 13-1

Scott commences a tort action against David for personal injuries suffered in a rollerblading accident. Scott serves upon David a summons and copy of a complaint. David serves a timely answer on Scott. In his answer, David must assert all "compulsory" counterclaims that he may have against Scott at this time or the claims will be lost.

To properly understand the operation of Rule 13, it is helpful to analogize the structure of the Rule with the structure of the hearsay rules under the Ohio Rules of Evidence. As with the hearsay rules, Civil Rule 13 presents a definition of the pertinent term, an exception (or, in the case of the hearsay rules, exceptions) to the definition of the term, a mandatory rule employing the term, and exceptions to the rule. Civil Rule 13 also sets forth a precondition for the operation of the rule.

First, it should be noted that a counterclaim does need not to be asserted by a party unless the party files a pleading in the action. Thus, a party who files a Rule 12 motion or motion for summary judgment and files no other paper should not lose the ability to bring an otherwise "compulsory" counterclaim subject to the rule of mandatory assertion as an independent action. In the same way, a party that is the subject of a default judgment is not subject to the rule of mandatory assertion of counterclaims.

Illustration 13-2

Assume on the facts of Illustration 13-1 that, instead of serving an answer, David makes a Rule 12 motion to dismiss for lack of personal jurisdiction. If the court grants David's motion, David is then free to assert any claim he may have against Scott in a different forum.

Second, a "compulsory" counterclaim is defined by the Rule as a claim "aris[ing] out of the transaction or occurrence that is the subject matter of the opposing party's claim." This language appears in numerous procedural contexts and has been the subject of many cases. No one test has prevailed as the dominant standard. Some courts hold that a claim and counterclaim arise out of the same transaction or occurrence when they raise the same essential issues of fact and law, while other courts have stated that the appropriate test is whether res judicata would bar an independent action if the "compulsory" counterclaim rule did not exist. Still other courts have held that, if the same evidence would be used to either prove or refute the claim or counterclaim, the claim can be said to be "compulsory." Finally, many courts have stated that a counterclaim is "compulsory" if it is logically related to the original claim.

Illustration 13-3

Assume on the facts of Illustration 13-1 that David was also injured in the accident. Any claim for damages because of these injuries must be asserted in David's answer, as they clearly have arisen out of the occurrence that is the subject matter of Scott's claim.

Compulsory and Permissive Counterclaims Distinguished

The term "compulsory" has been placed in quotes because it is crucial to understand that the terms "compulsory" and "permissive," as they are used in the Rule, are legal terms of art that are not defined under the Rule according to their ordinary meanings. A "compulsory" counterclaim, despite the ordinary meaning of the word "compulsory," is not *defined* as a counterclaim that must be asserted by a party. Rather, counterclaims that are deemed as "compulsory" under one of the tests enumerated above are subject to the rule of mandatory assertion in Rule 13.

In the same way, "permissive" counterclaims are those counterclaims that are not "compulsory." "Permissive" counterclaims are, of course, permissive in the sense that a party is not required to assert them, but this fact arises from the word "may" in subsection (B) and not the ordinary meaning of the word "permissive." This distinction becomes consequential in the context of cross-claims. Only cross-claims that are "compulsory" may be asserted. Paradoxically, however, cross-claims are always permissive in the sense that they are not required to be asserted.

Illustration 13-4

Under the facts of Illustration 13-3, a counterclaim by David is deemed "compulsory" because of its relationship to the subject matter of the action. Under Rule 13(A), this claim must be asserted. If David has a breach of contract claim against Scott which is unrelated to the accident, the lack of a logical relationship between the claims will cause the breach of contract claim to be regarded as "permissive." Under Rule 13(B), such claims may, but need not be, asserted in the same action.

Counterclaims That Require Indispensable Parties

Rule 13(A) excepts from the definition of "compulsory" counterclaims those that "require for [their] adjudication the presence of third parties of whom the court cannot acquire jurisdiction." This means that counterclaims that require indispensable parties under Rule 19 or Rule 19.1 are not "compulsory" when jurisdiction over these parties cannot be obtained. Notice that Rule 13(A) does not say that "compulsory" counterclaims need not be asserted when jurisdiction over indispensable parties cannot be obtained; it simply says that such counterclaims are not "compulsory."

Illustration 13-5

Under the residuary clause of a will, Frank's Foundation, a struggling charity serving the needs of the poor, stands to receive $750,000. The Foundation sues Mary, the executrix of the will, to compel her to carry out the terms of the will with all due speed. Mary would like to counterclaim against the Foundation seeking to have the residuary clause declared invalid. James, a beneficiary under the will over whom the court does not have personal jurisdiction and who will not consent to such jurisdiction, stands to gain $50,000 if the residuary clause is declared invalid. Under these circumstances, Mary's counterclaim against Frank's Foundation is not "compulsory" under Rule 13 and is thus not subject to the rule of mandatory assertion of such claims.

Rule of Mandatory Assertion for Compulsory Counterclaims

Subsection (A) also sets forth the rule of mandatory assertion. It expressly provides that all "compulsory" counterclaims must be asserted by a party, providing that the pleading requirement has been met. A failure to assert a "compulsory" counterclaim will constitute a waiver of those claims, curable only through the provisions of subsection (F) or the more general amendment provisions in Rule 15.

Illustration 13-6

Larry, a renowned trumpet player, commences a breach of contract action against Max, an equally-renowned trombone player, alleging that Max intentionally sabotaged Larry's trumpet immediately prior to a performance. After receiving a summons and copy of the complaint from Larry, Max files an answer but fails to assert a "compulsory" counterclaim for assault and battery that Larry inflicted on Max upon discovering the sabotage to his trumpet. Max's failure to assert a "compulsory" counterclaim constitutes a waiver of any claim he may have arising from his injuries, unless he amends his pleading as a matter of course under Rule 15 or with the permission of the court under Rule 13(F).

Exceptions to the Rule of Mandatory Assertion

Subsection (A) goes on to state two exceptions to the rule that all "compulsory" counterclaims must be asserted. The second exception, which will be addressed here first, applies when jurisdiction in the action is *in rem* or *quasi in rem*, and the defendant chooses not to assert any other counterclaim. In such an instance, a defendant may defend the action without having to assert a "compulsory" counterclaim, and may bring the counterclaim as a subject of an independent action.

Illustration 13-7

Assume on the facts of Illustration 13-6 that Larry alleges that Max stole his trumpet and shipped it to another jurisdiction. If Larry brings an *in rem* action solely to recover his trumpet in the jurisdiction in which the trumpet is located and in which the court cannot assert personal jurisdiction over Max, Max may bring a claim for his injuries in a different forum.

The other exception to the general rule that "compulsory" counterclaims must be asserted is the circumstance in which the "compulsory" counterclaim is the subject of an independent action at the time the claim was filed. Of course, if the counterclaim in the latter action is asserted as a claim in an earlier independent action, the "compulsory" nature of the counterclaim in the latter action would seem to necessitate a finding that the original claim in the latter action was a "compulsory" counterclaim in the earlier action, and as such, subject to the rule of mandatory assertion. However, the fact that it was not asserted as a "compulsory" counterclaim in the earlier action should imply that it was waived, and the latter action should be dismissed.

Illustration 13-8

Lisa sues Heidi for personal injuries suffered in an automobile accident in an Ohio court. Heidi also suffers personal injuries in the accident. Rather than asserting her "compulsory" counterclaim against Lisa in her answer, Heidi commences an

> independent action against Lisa in the same court. Under these circumstances, Heidi's failure to assert her "compulsory" counterclaim against Lisa in Lisa's action implies that Heidi has waived any claim stemming from the accident. Accordingly, the court should dismiss Heidi's action against Lisa but may allow Heidi to amend her answer to include the claim.

Nonetheless, there are at least three circumstances in which "compulsory" counterclaims may legally be the subject of an independent action at the time an action is brought, thus excepting such "compulsory" claims from the rule of mandatory assertion. First, the court in the earlier action may have been unable to obtain jurisdiction over an indispensable party, whereas the court in the latter action may be able to do so.

Second, the party in the earlier action may not have filed a pleading in the action, so that the plaintiff is in the process of securing a default judgment. Third, if jurisdiction in the earlier action was *in rem* or *quasi in rem*, the party defending the action is not required to assert the "compulsory" counterclaim.

Permissive Counterclaims Generally

Subsection (B) covers "permissive" counterclaims, those claims by parties against opposing parties that are not "compulsory" counterclaims. "Permissive" counterclaims are not required to be asserted and cannot be asserted if doing so would destroy the jurisdictional basis of the action. The failure to assert a "permissive" counterclaim does not preclude the possibility of bringing an independent action on that claim. Subsection (I) permits the court to order separate trials on both "compulsory" and "permissive" counterclaims pursuant to Rule 42(B). Separate judgments must be entered by the court if separate trials are ordered.

Illustration 13-9

Tabitha commences a breach of contract action against Lauren, alleging that Lauren failed to comply with specific lease provisions regarding the maintenance of a building leased to Tabitha. In her answer to Tabitha's claim, Lauren alleges that Tabitha withheld rent in response to Lauren's alleged failure to maintain the property. Lauren is also considering suing Tabitha for unrelated damage to the building which occurred several months earlier. Under these circumstances, Lauren's counterclaim for the unpaid rent, a "compulsory" counterclaim, must be asserted in the same action. However, Lauren's counterclaim for the unrelated damage, a "permissive" counterclaim, may be brought as a separate action. If Lauren chooses to assert the "permissive" counterclaim in the same action and

> the court feels that a jury may be confused by the discrete issues involved, it may order separate trials. If this occurs, the court must enter separate judgments on each of Lauren's counterclaims.

Recoupment and Set-Off with Counterclaims and Cross-Claims

Subsection (C) incorporates the procedures of recoupment and set-off used by the former courts at common law and courts in equity. Although subsection (C), by its terms, applies only to counterclaims, there is little reason to suspect that the drafters did not intend for it to apply to cross-claims as well.

Counterclaims Against the State of Ohio

The scope of counterclaims against Ohio is delineated by statute. Subsection (D) reiterates and preserves this fact.

Immature Counterclaims

Subsection (E) provides that a "permissive" or "compulsory" counterclaim that is immature at the time the pleading giving rise to the counterclaim was filed may be presented as a counterclaim by a supplemental pleading. However, courts have typically required that immature claims be presented in independent actions.

Omitted Counterclaims

Subsection (F) complements the liberal provisions of Rule 15 by allowing the amendment of pleadings to assert counterclaims because of oversight, inadvertence, or excusable neglect. Although subsection (F) clearly contemplates that leave of court shall be given freely and as justice requires, courts denying a motion to amend pleadings in cases of extreme neglect or where an amendment would result in prejudice to the opposing party have been upheld.

Cross-Claims Generally

Cross-claims are governed by subsection (G), which is fortunately less complicated than subsection (A). As stated previously, cross-claims are claims filed by co-parties against one another. Co-parties are parties who are not in a adversarial posture in the action until, of course, the filing of a cross-claim. Cross-claims differ from counterclaims in several important respects. First, the assertion of all cross-claims is at the discretion of the parties. No party is required to assert a cross-claim, but a party may be required to assert a compulsory counterclaim against a party who asserts a cross-claim against that party.

Illustration 13-10

Aramis, Athos, and Porthos are all injured in a 3-way paintball accident. Porthos files an action against Aramis and Athos for personal injuries suffered in and dry cleaning expenses resulting from the accident. Aramis and Athos must assert their "compulsory" counterclaims against Porthos. However, neither Aramis nor Athos is required to assert a cross-claim against the other even though all the injuries occurred as part of the same occurrence. However, if Aramis chooses to do so, Athos will then be required to assert all claims arising out of the same transaction against Aramis.

Definition of Cross-Claim

All cross-claims under Rule 13(G) must "aris[e] out of the transaction or occurrence that is the subject matter either of the original action or of a counterclaim therein or relating to any property that is the subject matter either of the original action or of a counterclaim therein or relating to any property that is the subject matter of the original action." This language replicates in part the language defining a "compulsory" counterclaim in subsection (A). In this sense, the term "permissive" cannot be used to accurately describe cross-claims, as "permissive" counterclaims are defined in subsection (B) as those counterclaims "*not* arising out of the transaction or occurrence that is the subject of the opposing party's claim" (emphasis added). Cross-claims must always satisfy the test used to determine whether a counterclaim is "compulsory." Cross-claims are always "compulsory," as that term is defined in the Rule, but they are not subject to the rule of mandatory assertion in subsection (A).

Illustration 13-11

Assume on the facts of Illustration 13-10 that Aramis and Athos reach an oral agreement not to pursue cross-claims arising from the accident against one another, opting instead to consolidate their resources defending the action by Porthos. However, Aramis is considering bringing an unrelated breach of contract claim against Athos. Under Rule 13(G), the breach of contract claim cannot be joined as a cross-claim in the action because it is not related to the occurrence giving rise to the original action.

The final disjunctive phrase in the first sentence of subsection (G) indicates that cross-claims are available when the jurisdiction in the action is *in rem* or *quasi in rem*.

The second sentence of subsection (G) is designed to make clear that a party may "join" a third-party pleading under Rule 14 with a cross-claim under Rule 13.

Assertion of Cross-Claim Triggers Counterclaim Rules

As noted, a party that is the subject of a cross-claim is subject to the rule of mandatory assertion of "compulsory" counterclaims in subsection (A). Although co-parties are not required to make any claims against one another, even "compulsory" ones, once a cross-claim has been asserted, all "compulsory" counterclaims between the former co-parties in the action are then subject to the rule of mandatory assertion.

Furthermore, although a party is not permitted to bring a non-"compulsory" cross-claim against a co-party, the party may nevertheless bring it as a "conditional" claim under Rule 18 if the party also asserts a "compulsory" cross-claim. In other words, an unrelated cross-claim is not allowed unless it can be "joined" with a proper cross-claim.

Illustration 13-12

Assume on the facts of Illustration 13-11 that Aramis breaks his oral agreement with Athos and files a cross-claim claiming damages arising from the accident in question. Aramis may now join in the action his unrelated breach of contract claim against Athos under Rule 18. If this occurs, Athos must join as a "compulsory" counterclaim any claim he may have against Aramis arising out of the contract allegedly breached.

Certification of Proceedings to Court of Common Pleas

In Ohio, the jurisdiction of municipal and county courts is limited to claims under $10,000 and $3000, respectively. In the event that a counterclaim, cross-claim, or third-party claim is in an amount that divests a municipal or county court of its jurisdiction, subsection (J) provides that a record of the proceedings shall be certified and the action transferred to the court of common pleas in the county or territorial district in which the court is located.

ADDITIONAL AUTHORITY

6 WRIGHT & MILLER §§ 1401-1440
3 MOORE'S FEDERAL PRACTICE §§ 13.01-13.124
4 ANDERSON'S OHIO CIVIL PRACTICE §§ 155.01-155.18
1 KLEIN DARLING AT 13-1 to AT 13-40
3 TEREZ F 4.7.1 to F 4.7.10
2 OH. JUR. PL. AND PRAC. FORMS, ch. 18
4 MILLIGAN Forms 13-1 to 13-50

1 FINK §§ 13-1 to 13-14

OHIO LITIGATION CHECKLISTS, Pleading and Process, §§ 15-19

LEADING CASES

Compulsory Counterclaims; Res Judicata Effect

Westlake v. Rice, 100 Ohio App. 3d 438, 654 N.E.2d 181 (The failure to assert a compulsory counterclaim in a pending action will result in its being re-litigated in a subsequent action), *dismissed, appeal not allowed*, 72 Ohio St. 3d 1547, 650 N.E.2d 1367 (1995)

Co-Parties; Claims Are Permissive

United Capital Ins. Co. v. Brunswick Ins. Agency, 144 Ohio App. 3d 595, 761 N.E.2d 66 (2001) (claims against co-parties are permissive, and a failure to file a cross-claim will not result in a waiver of the claim)

Definition of Compulsory Counterclaim

Rettig Enters. v. Koehler, 68 Ohio St. 3d 274, 626 N.E.2d 99 (1994) ("logical relation" test provides that a compulsory counterclaim is one which is logically related to the opposing party's claim and where separate trials on each of their respective claims would involve a substantial duplication of effort and time by the parties)

Permissive Counterclaims Generally Permitted

Kirshner v. Shinaberry, 64 Ohio App. 3d 536, 582 N.E.2d 22 (1989) (Rule 13(B) permitted defendant to raise any counterclaim he had against the real party in interest, even though the claim did not arise from the transaction or occurrence that was the subject of the main claim)

Same Transaction or Occurrence

State ex rel. Barth v. Hamilton County Board of Elections, 65 Ohio St. 3d 219, 602 N.E.2d 1130 (1992) (although separate acts may have occurred at approximately the same time, those acts may not necessarily represent a single event for the purposes of Rule 13(G))

Small Claims Proceedings

Thirion v. Tutoki, 94 Ohio Misc.2d 77, 703 N.E.2d 378 (M.C. 1998) (because Rule 13(A) governing compulsory counterclaims is now applicable to small claims proceedings, res judicata bars litigation of issues that have been litigated at small claims court)

CHAPTER 14

Rule 14. Third-Party Practice

Rule 14 reads as follows:

(A) When defendant may bring in third party. At any time after commencement of the action a defending party, as a third-party plaintiff, may cause a summons and complaint to be served upon a person not a party to the action who is or may be liable to him for all or part of the plaintiff's claim against him. The third-party plaintiff need not obtain leave to make the service if he files the third-party complaint not later than fourteen days after he serves his original answer. Otherwise he must obtain leave on motion upon notice to all parties to the action. The person served with the summons and third-party complaint, hereinafter called the third-party defendant, shall make his defenses to the third-party plaintiff's claim as provided in Rule 12 and his counterclaims against the third-party plaintiff and cross-claims against other third-party defendants as provided in Rule 13. The third-party defendant may assert against the plaintiff any defenses which the third-party plaintiff has to the plaintiff's claim. The third-party defendant may also assert any claim against the plaintiff arising out of the transaction or occurrence that is the subject matter of the plaintiff's claim against the third-party plaintiff. The plaintiff may assert any claim against the third-party defendant arising out of the transaction or occurrence that is the subject matter of the plaintiff's claim against the third-party plaintiff, and the third-party defendant thereupon shall assert his defenses as provided in Rule 12 and his counterclaims and cross-claims as provided in Rule 13. Any party may move to strike the third-party claim, or for its severance or separate trial. If the third-party defendant is an employee, agent, or servant of the third-party plaintiff, the court shall order a separate trial upon the motion of any plaintiff. A third-party defendant may proceed under this rule against any person not a party to the action who is or may be liable to him for all or part of the claim made in the action against the third-party defendant.

(B) When plaintiff may bring in third party. When a counterclaim is asserted against a plaintiff, he may cause a third party to be brought in under circumstances which under this rule would entitle a defendant to do so.

COMMENTARY

The labyrinth encompassing the joinder of claims and the joinder of parties continues with Rule 14. As noted previously, Rules 13 and 18, relating to the joinder of claims, Rules 19, 19.1, and 20, relating to the joinder of parties, and Rule 14, governing the joinder of parties and claims through third-party practice, are all interrelated, and a discussion of the complexities of any of these Rules necessarily entails reference to the others.

Impleader Generally

Rule 14 covers third-party practice, and is sometimes referred to as "impleader." The Rule allows a party defending an action to join other entities that may be liable to that party for the claim or claims asserted against them. Although this license is initially afforded only to defendants, subsection (B) makes it clear that plaintiffs may also implead additional parties if a counterclaim has been asserted against them. Defendants who are the subject of cross-claims by other defendants are also allowed to implead third parties. Although the express terms of subsection (B) do not render the provisions of Rule 14 available to a co-plaintiff that has cross-claimed against another co-plaintiff, the language of subsection (A), making the Rule applicable to "a defending party," is broad enough to encompass all parties that are the subject of cross-claims, including co-plaintiffs.

Illustration 14-1

John and Jake commence a tort action against Wereckum Bus Company for injuries they sustained in an accident with a bus operated by that company. In addition to seeking relief from Wereckum Bus Company, Jake cross-claims against John, alleging that John is responsible for a portion of his injuries as well. John asserts that any liability apportioned to him should be paid by Brakes 'R Us, alleging that the accident was due in part to the negligent repair of his brakes by that company. John may join Brakes 'R Us as a party to the action by impleading it under Rule 14. If Wereckum Bus Company happens to have had the brakes on its bus repaired by Brakes 'R Us as well, it should also file a claim against that company under Rule 14(A).

Policy of Rule

The policy of Rule 14 is that a party defending a claim to whom an additional party is liable for that claim should not suffer the possibility of inconsistent results if that party is forced to litigate the action against the third party in a separate action. The Rule also allows a party defending a claim to avoid the inconvenience and expense of litigating the same issue twice. A defendant, of course, cannot force the plaintiff to join the third party as a defendant. Rule 14 provides a defendant with the means to effect substantially the same result. The provisions of Rule 14 are never mandatory, and the language of the Rule suggests that a party has an absolute right to implead a third party at any time not more than 14 days after service of the answer on the original plaintiff. Nonetheless, Ohio courts have typically held that the ability of a party to implead a third party is within the discretion of the court. The discretion is not absolute, however, and the court should be guided by a number of factors: the extent to which the joinder would promote judicial efficiency; avoid a duplication of testimony and evidence; avoid inconsistent verdicts; achieve fairness by consolidating actions that should be tried together.

It should also be noted that a court's refusal to allow a party to implead a third party is not a final appealable order absent certification by the court pursuant to Rule 54(B).

Operation of Rule 14

A party who initiates proceedings under Rule 14 is called a "third-party plaintiff," and the party defending a claim under the Rule is called a "third-party defendant." The Rule also allows parties who have been impleaded to further implead an additional party, the "fourth-party defendant," but on its face severs the extension of the Rule there.

Rule 14 states that any person "who is or may be liable to the third-party plaintiff for all or part of the plaintiff's claim against the third-party plaintiff" may be impleaded. This language restricts the scope of Rule 14 to situations involving "domino liability" among parties, and not to those situations involving mistaken defendants. In other words, if the claim asserted in third-party complaint does not arise *because of* the primary claim, or is not in some way derivative of it, then the claim is not properly asserted in third party complaint. Rule 14 is thus well-suited to indemnification actions, where an insurer is liable to an insured for actions arising under the terms of an insurance policy.

Illustration 14-2

Frederick sues Angelica for injuries suffered during an automobile collision. Angelica cannot implead a third party on the grounds that the third party was actually the person operating the vehicle. However, Angelica may implead the automobile maker on the grounds that, if she is found to be negligent, the brakes negligently manufactured by the automobile maker were actually the cause of the collision.

Process and Pleading Requirements for Impleaded Parties

Impleaded parties are subject to the same service and pleading requirements as defendants. Motions under Rule 12 are available to impleaded parties, and the time periods for responding to pleadings in Rule 12(A) apply to impleaded parties as well. Impleaded parties are also subject to the rule of mandatory assertion for "compulsory" counterclaims in Rule 13 against third-party plaintiffs, and are allowed to bring "compulsory" cross-claims against other impleaded parties. Impleaded parties may also assert defenses against the original plaintiff for the claim asserted against the original defendant and may also bring "compulsory" claims against the original plaintiff. If this latter event occurs, the plaintiff and the impleaded party are subject to the rule of mandatory assertion for "compulsory" counterclaims in Rule 13 and the provisions for "conditional" claims in Rule 18. However, the Rules do not appear to provide impleaded parties the ability to join additional parties with parties already involved in the action, unless an impleaded "third-party" wishes to implead a "fourth-party."

ADDITIONAL AUTHORITY

6 WRIGHT & MILLER §§ 1441-1470
3 MOORE'S FEDERAL PRACTICE §§ 14.01-14.59
4 ANDERSON'S OHIO CIVIL PRACTICE §§ 155.19-155.23
1 KLEIN DARLING AT 14-1 to AT 14-28
3 TEREZ F 4.1.18, F 4.6.1 to F 4.6.5, F 7.2.4
2 OH. JUR. PL. AND PRAC. FORMS, ch. 19
4 MILLIGAN Forms 14-1 to 14-54
1 FINK §§ 14-1 to 14-13
OHIO LITIGATION CHECKLISTS, Parties and Actions, §§ 2, 3

LEADING CASES

Dismissal of Third-Party Complaints

Stephens v. Crestview Cadillac, Inc., 64 Ohio App. 3d 129, 580 N.E.2d 842 (1989) (a third-party complaint filed by a defendant does not need to be dismissed when the action involving the original complaint is settled)

Third Party Action; When Appropriate

Renacci v. Martell, 91 Ohio App. 3d 217, 632 N.E.2d 536 (1993) (a third party action is proper where the right of the defendant to recover or the duty allegedly breached by the third-party defendant arose from the plaintiff's successful prosecution of the main action against the defendant), *jurisdictional motion overruled*, 68 Ohio St. 3d 1473, 628 N.E.2d 1391 (1994)

Third Party Practice; Generally

Cambridge Appliance & Serv., Inc. v. German, No. 95-CA-24 (5th Dist.), 1996
   Ohio App. LEXIS 2983 (Rule 14 provides for the treatment of multiple claims
   arising from a single set of facts in one action)

CHAPTER 15

Rule 15. Amended and Supplemental Pleadings

Rule 15 reads as follows:

(A) Amendments. A party may amend his pleading once as a matter of course at any time before a responsive pleading is served or, if the pleading is one to which no responsive pleading is permitted and the action has not been placed upon the trial calendar, he may so amend it at any time within twenty-eight days after it is served. Otherwise a party may amend his pleading only by leave of court or by written consent of the adverse party. Leave of court shall be freely given when justice so requires. A party shall plead in response to an amended pleading within the time remaining for response to the original pleading or within fourteen days after service of the amended pleading, whichever period may be the longer, unless the court otherwise orders.

(B) Amendments to conform to the evidence. When issues not raised by the pleadings are tried by express or implied consent of the parties, they shall be treated in all respects as if they had been raised in the pleadings. Such amendment of the pleadings as may be necessary to cause them to conform to the evidence and to raise these issues may be made upon motion of any party at any time, even after judgment. Failure to amend as provided herein does not affect the result of the trial of these issues. If evidence is objected to at the trial on the ground that it is not within the issues made by the pleadings, the court may allow the pleadings to be amended and shall do so freely when the presentation of the merits of the action will be subserved thereby and the objecting party fails to satisfy the court that the admission of such evidence would prejudice him in maintaining his action or defense upon the merits. The court may grant a continuance to enable the objecting party to meet such evidence.

(C) Relation back of amendments. Whenever the claim or defense asserted in the amended pleading arose out of the conduct, transaction, or occurrence set forth or attempted to be set forth in the original pleading, the amendment relates back to the date of the original pleading. An amendment changing the party against whom a claim is asserted relates back if the foregoing provision is satisfied and, within the period provided by law for commencing the action against him, the party to be brought in by amendment

(1) has received such notice of the institution of the action that he will not be prejudiced in maintaining his defense on the merits, and

(2)   knew or should have known that, but for a mistake concerning the identity of the proper party, the action would have been brought against him.

The delivery or mailing of process to this state, a municipal corporation or other governmental agency, or the responsible officer of any of the foregoing, subject to service of process under Rule 4 through Rule 4.6, satisfies the requirements of clauses (1) and (2) of the preceding paragraph if the above entities or officers thereof would have been proper defendants upon the original pleading. Such entities or officers thereof or both may be brought into the action as defendants.

(D)   Amendments where name of party unknown. When the plaintiff does not know the name of a defendant, that defendant may be designated in a pleading or proceeding by any name and description. When the name is discovered, the pleading or proceeding must be amended accordingly. The plaintiff, in such case, must aver in the complaint the fact that he could not discover the name. The summons must contain the words "name unknown," and the copy thereof must be served personally upon the defendant.

(E)   Supplemental pleadings. Upon motion of a party the court may, upon reasonable notice and upon such terms as are just, permit him to serve a supplemental pleading setting forth transactions or occurrences or events which have happened since the date of the pleading sought to be supplemented. Permission may be granted even though the original pleading is defective in its statement of a claim for relief or defense. If the court deems it advisable that the adverse party plead to the supplemental pleading, it shall so order, specifying the time therefor.

COMMENTARY

Rule 15 provides for amended and supplemental pleading in a manner that reflects the liberal policies of the Ohio Rules of Civil Procedure. The Rule also provides for amendments of pleadings to conform to the evidence presented. Subsection (C) sets forth the circumstances under which the date of an amendment of a pleading is treated as if it were made on the date of the original pleading, or the "relation back of amendments."

Amendment as of Right

Subsection (A) provides all parties with a right to amend their pleadings one time without the permission of the opposing party or the court under two circumstances. If a party has not been served with a required responsive pleading, amendment is permitted as of right. The term "responsive pleading" is to be construed literally, so the fact that a defendant has made a Rule 12 motion or motion for summary judgment but has not yet filed an answer does not preclude the plaintiff from amending the complaint as of right. Alternatively, if no responsive pleading is forthcoming, a party may amend its pleading within 28 days after that pleading was served on all the parties, providing that a trial date has not been fixed on the court's calendar.

Illustration 15-1

On May 1, Beth serves Jeff with a summons and copy of a complaint alleging that Jeff negligently caused property damage to her house while painting the exterior. Jeff files a motion to dismiss for failure to state a claim upon which relief can be granted under Rule 12(B)(6), arguing that Beth has not alleged facts sufficient to warrant an inference of causation, a necessary element of the cause of action. Beth may amend her complaint at this time to include the necessary allegation of facts, as Jeff has not filed a responsive pleading in the action.

A party may not amend the same pleading twice without the permission of the court or the opposing parties, but a party can amend two different pleadings one time each as of right.

Illustration 15-2

Assume on the facts of Illustration 15-1 that Beth now wishes to amend her complaint a second time to include a demand for punitive damages. Absent express permission from the court or the opposing parties, Beth cannot amend her complaint a second time.

When a pleading is amended, the opposing party is required to respond to the amended pleading within 14 days after being served with the amended pleading, unless a longer period remains in the time period in which the opposing party was required to respond to the original pleading.

Illustration 15-3

Assume on the facts of Illustration 15-1 that Beth serves the original summons and copy of the complaint upon Jeff on May 5 and the amended complaint on June 1. Jeff must file an answer no later than June 15.

When Leave to Amend Is Required

If a party has already amended a pleading and wishes to do so again, or if one of the conditions for amendment as of right is not met, then that party must obtain permission of the court or the opposing party. Typically, permission of the court is sought through a motion under Rule 7(B) with a copy of the amended pleading attached. Although judges have the discretion to deny an amendment when it would prejudice the opposing party, Rule 15 clearly contemplates that motions to amend a pleading should be granted in most circumstances.

Amendments to Conform to the Evidence

Subsection (B) allows amendments to pleadings to conform to the evidence presented at trial, and leave to make such amendments is freely and routinely given. This provision is applicable at any time during the course of an action, even on appeal. Although courts frequently exclude evidence at trial because it bears upon collateral matters not raised by the pleadings, these exclusions are compelled by the Ohio Rules of Evidence, not the Rules of Civil Procedure.

Relation Back of Amendments Generally

Subsection (C) provides for the relation back of the date of an amended pleading to the date of the original pleading in several circumstances. This provision is applicable primarily when a statute of limitations or the defense of laches is raised by the opposing party. The Rule distinguishes between amendments that alter the claim or defense in a pleading and those that change the parties to an action.

Relation Back of Amendments Changing a Claim or Defense

The first sentence of subsection (C) provides that an amendment that changes a claim or defense relates back to the date of the original pleading when the claim or defense sought to be added "arose out of the conduct, transaction, or occurrence set forth or attempted to be set forth in the original pleading." This test is essentially the same test used to determine the "compulsory" nature of counterclaims in Rule 13.

Relation Back of Amendments Changing a Party

Ordinarily, a new party may not be brought into the action after the applicable statute of limitations has run. However, the second sentence of subsection (C) provides for relation back of an amendment changing a party in an action if three conditions are satisfied. First, the "same transaction" test must be met with regard to the changed parties. Second, the party sought to be added must have been notified of the initiation of the action *within the original limitations period* under Ohio law. Unlike Federal Rule of Civil Procedure 15, it is not sufficient that the party against whom the action should have been filed received notice of the action within the six-month time period under Rule 4(E) for service of the summons and copy of the complaint after the filing of the complaint.

The kind of notice required under the Rule must also be such that the party to be added will not be prejudiced in maintaining a defense on the merits of the case. The final paragraph of subsection (C) provides clarification on that specific circumstance of the kind of notice that will be sufficient.

Illustration 15-4

Peter, Paul, and Mary are involved in a collision involving three speed boats. Three days before the statute of limitations expires, Peter commences an action against Mary for personal injuries stemming from the accident, and he promptly serves upon her a summons and copy of the complaint. However, Peter forgets to join Paul as a defendant. Ten days later, Peter discovers his mistake and makes a motion to add Paul as a defendant, and he notifies Paul of his intention by telephone. Because the statute of limitations has run with regard to Paul, the amendment will not relate back to the date on which the complaint was originally filed.

Finally, the party to be added must have known or should have known that the action should have been brought against it if it had not been for a mistake in the identity of the parties. This final condition is designed to ensure that a party who knows that the plaintiff made a mistake in naming the correct party in the pleading, and stands silently by, cannot take advantage of that mistake through a statute of limitations or laches defense.

Amendments Where Party Name Is Unknown

Rule 15(D) is a rule of convenience allowing a plaintiff to file an action against a defendant when the plaintiff does not know and is unable to discover the defendant's name. Upon discovering the name of the defendant, the pleading or proceeding must be amended to include the defendant's name. The complaint must still contain an identity or description of the defendant, however, to toll the statute of limitations with respect to that person.

Supplemental Pleadings

Subsection (E) allows for supplemental pleadings. These pleadings are different from amended pleadings in that supplemental pleadings are appropriate only in situations where pertinent occurrences or events have happened after the filing of the original pleading sought to be supplemented.

Illustration 15-5

Situations in which supplemental pleadings would be appropriate include new damages resulting after the filing of the pleading, res judicata stemming from the resolution of an action after the filing of the pleading, and the assertion of a claim previously immature at the time of the original pleading.

Matters of which a party is mistaken or ignorant, however, are properly added through amendment. Supplemental pleadings are within the discretion of the court, and must be requested by motion under Rule 7(B), with a copy of the supplemental pleading attached to the motion. Responsive pleadings to supplemental pleadings are not required, but may be ordered by the court. Opposing parties wishing to respond to supplemental pleadings should make a motion to that effect with the court.

Illustration 15-6

Randy sues Dave for personal injuries resulting from a skydiving accident. In his original complaint, Randy requests compensation for injuries to his neck. Two months later, Randy develops back problems and now wishes to recover damages for injuries to his back. In order to claim damages for his back injury, Randy must make a motion under Rule 7(B), seeking permission to file supplemental pleadings. If the court exercises its discretion and grants Randy's motion, Dave does not need to file a pleading in response to Randy's supplemental papers, unless the court directs otherwise.

ADDITIONAL AUTHORITY

6 WRIGHT & MILLER §§ 1471-1520
3 MOORE'S FEDERAL PRACTICE §§ 15.01-15.30
4 ANDERSON'S OHIO CIVIL PRACTICE §§ 156.01-156.12
1 KLEIN DARLING AT 15-1 to AT 15-16
3 TEREZ F 6.1.1 to F 6.1.5
2 OH. JUR. PL. AND PRAC. FORMS, ch. 20
4 MILLIGAN Forms 15-1 to 15-48
1 FINK §§ 15-1 to 15-7
OHIO LITIGATION CHECKLISTS, Pleading and Process, §§ 9-11, 20-22
OHIO LITIGATION CHECKLISTS, Trial, §§ 30

LEADING CASES

Affirmative Defense Waived

Spence v. Liberty Township Trustees, 109 Ohio App. 3d 357, 672 N.E.2d 213 (1996) (the failure to raise an affirmative defense by motion, responsive pleading, or by amending responsive pleadings will result in waiver of that defense)

Amended Pleading After Summary Judgment

Brannan v. Fowler, 100 Ohio App. 3d 577, 654 N.E.2d 434 (1995) (a motion to amend that was timely, identified the nature of the additional claim, and did not preclude ruling on the defendant's motion for summary judgment was proper even though the amendment was sought after the motion for summary judgment had been made)

Amendments Improper

Turner v. Central Local Sch. Dist., 85 Ohio St. 3d 95, 706 N.E.2d 1261 (1999) (although Rule 15(A) allows for liberal amendment of pleadings, a motion to amend should be refused upon a showing of bad faith, undue delay, or undue prejudice to the opposing party)

Amendments to Conform to the Evidence

MaCabe/Marra Co. v. Dover, 100 Ohio App. 3d 139, 652 N.E.2d 236 (when the proposed amendment would conform to the evidence and when the issue has been tried by express or implied consent of the parties, affirmative defenses which were not raised in the pleadings may be raised by implied amendment), *appeal not allowed*, 72 Ohio St. 3d 1529, 649 N.E.2d 839 (1995)

Discovery of Identity of Party

Hobbs v. Lopez, 96 Ohio App. 3d 670, 645 N.E.2d 1261 (1994) (amendments to name a defendant by her true name are permitted once the true identity is discovered)

Discretion of Court

Csejpes v. Cleveland Catholic Diocese, 109 Ohio App. 3d 533, 672 N.E.2d 724 (1996) (a trial court retains discretion in granting motion for leave to amend and will be reversed only upon a showing that the denial was unreasonable, arbitrary, or unconscionable)

Fictitious Names

Kramer v. Installations Unltd., 147 Ohio App. 3d 350, 770 N.E.2d 632 (2002) (the use of a fictitious defendant's name, with subsequent correction by amendment of the real name, relates back to the filing of the original complaint, and service must be obtained within one year of the filing of the original complaint)

Deaton v. Burney, 107 Ohio App. 3d 407, 669 N.E.2d 1 (1995) (a fictitious name may be used by a plaintiff to identify a defendant)

Implied Consent to Litigate an Issue

Frate v. Al-Sol, Inc., 131 Ohio App. 3d 283, 722 N.E.2d 185 (1999) (the question of whether the parties have impliedly consented to litigate an issue should be determined by a variety of factors, including: (1) whether the parties recognized that an unpleaded issue entered the case; (2) whether the opposing party had a fair opportunity to address the tendered issue or would offer additional evidence if the case were to be tried on a different theory; and (3) whether the witnesses were subjected to extensive cross-examination on the issue)

Motion to Dismiss Not a Responsive Pleading

State ex rel. Grendell v. Davidson, 86 Ohio St. 3d 629, 716 N.E.2d 704 (1999) (under Rule 15, a motion to dismiss is not a responsive pleading, and a party can amend its complaint as a matter of course even after a motion to dismiss has been filed)

Necessary Parties Joined by Amended Pleading

Plumbers & Steamfitters Local Union 83 v. Union Local Sch. Dist. Bd. of Edn., 86 Ohio St. 3d 318, 715 N.E.2d 127 (1999) (when it becomes apparent that not all interested persons have been made parties, the party seeking relief may join the absent party by amending its pleading; the fact that the requirement for joining all necessary parties is jurisdictional and cannot be waived does not preclude joinder by amendment)

New Matter Required for Amendment of Pleading

Martin v. Ohio Dept. of Rehab. & Corr., 140 Ohio App. 3d 831, 749 N.E.2d 787 (2001) (the party seeking leave to amend a complaint must at least demonstrate a prima facie showing that it can marshal support for the new matter sought to be pleaded)

Relation Back of Amendments; Generally

Megginson v. Song, No. 95-CA-2337 (4th Dist.), 1995 Ohio App. LEXIS 5680 (amended complaints relate back to the filing date of the original complaint where the defendant, after reading the complaint, should have known the action would have been brought against him but for technical errors), *appeal not allowed*, 75 Ohio St. 3d 1488, 664 N.E.2d 540 (1996)

Relation Back of Amendments; Identity of Parties

Kimble v. Pepsi-Cola Gen. Bottlers, 103 Ohio App. 3d 407, 658 N.E.2d 1135 (1995) (the relation back of amendments will be permitted where there is a mistake in the identity of the party originally named, and when the amendment will not prejudice the party to be added)

Relation Back of Amendments; Purpose

Dirksing v. Blue Chip Architectural Prods., 100 Ohio App. 3d 213, 653 N.E.2d 718 (1994) (the purpose of relation back of amendments is to preserve actions which have been mistakenly filed against the wrong person through confusion of identity or misnomer), *appeal allowed*, 71 Ohio St. 3d 1453, 644 N.E.2d 1026, *and appeal not allowed*, 71 Ohio St. 3d 1502, 646 N.E.2d 1126, *and appeal dismissed as improvidently allowed*, 72 Ohio St. 3d 1216, 651 N.E.2d 429 (1995)

Relationship to Rule 54(C)

Borges v. Everdry Waterproofing, Inc., 95 Ohio App. 3d 175, 642 N.E.2d 16 (1994) (the mandate of Rule 54(C) supersedes the Rule 15(B)'s more liberal pleading provisions, unless a compelling reason to establish an exception to the limitation is presented by the facts)

CHAPTER 16

Rule 16. Pretrial Procedure

Rule 16 reads as follows:

In any action, the court may schedule one or more conferences before trial to accomplish the following objectives:

(1) The possibility of settlement of the action;

(2) The simplification of the issues;

(3) Itemizations of expenses and special damages;

(4) The necessity of amendments to the pleadings;

(5) The exchange of reports of expert witnesses expected to be called by each party;

(6) The exchange of medical reports and hospital records;

(7) The limitation of the number of expert witnesses;

(8) The imposition of sanctions as authorized by Civ. R. 37;

(9) The possibility of obtaining:

    (a) Admissions of fact;

    (b) Admissions into evidence of documents and other exhibits that will avoid unnecessary proof;

(10) Other matters as may aid in the disposition of the action.

The producing by any party of medical reports or hospital records does not constitute a waiver of the privilege granted under section 2317.02 of the Revised Code.

The court may, and on the request of either party shall, make a written order that recites the action taken at the conference. The court shall enter the order and submit copies to the parties. Unless modified, the order shall control the subsequent course of the action.

The court may require that parties, or their representatives or insurers, attend a conference or otherwise participate in pretrial proceedings, in which case the court shall give reasonable advance notice to the parties of the conference or proceedings.

COMMENTARY

Rule 16 confers upon trial courts broad discretion to order and conduct pretrial conferences. The specific objectives listed in the Rule reflect the two primary goals of pretrial conferences: the simplification of issues and the promotion of settlement. In conjunction with Rule 83, Rule 16 contemplates that the schedule and ordering of pretrial conferences will be determined by local rule. Pretrial conferences are not mandatory under the Rule, but may be ordered by the court or required under local rules.

It should be noted that the Rule does not explicitly permit the imposition of sanctions on parties who fail to appear or refuse to attend a pretrial conference, as does Federal Rule of Civil Procedure 16. Whether a party may be sanctioned or held in contempt for refusing to obey a court order to that effect has not yet been resolved under Ohio case law.

Medical Information

The second paragraph of the Rule indicates that medical information that may be protected by a statutory privilege may nonetheless be compelled during discovery. The disclosure of otherwise privileged information is intended only to assist in the accomplishment of the dual goals specified above and will not operate as a waiver of an objection to the admissibility of the information at trial on grounds of privilege.

Pretrial Orders

Ordinarily, a pretrial conference produces a written order from the trial court. Such an order may be requested by any party or may be made by the court *sua sponte*. The order will then control the proceedings in the action after the conference, subject to modification in subsequent conferences or by order of the court. Failure to comply with the terms of an order made pursuant to a pretrial conference or to cooperate in any pretrial conference is sanctionable under Rule 37. Rule 16 was amended in 1993 to allow the court to require the attendance or participation of parties or their representatives or insurers. The provision allowing courts to require "participation" of parties includes the authority to direct counsel and parties to engage in settlement discussion, mediation, minitrials, and summary jury trials.

Alternative Dispute Resolution

A growing trend in Ohio courts is the promotion of settlement prior to trial through pretrial conferences. Mediation, arbitration, and other alternative dispute resolution procedures have thus become important topics of discussion in pretrial conferences. Such procedures are cheaper, faster, and they usually produce results that are more satisfactory to the parties than those achieved through traditional litigation. The three most common forms of alternative dispute resolution—settlement, mediation, and arbitration—are compared below.

A settlement is a private contract entered into by the parties with a stipulation of dismissal or acceptance of an offer of judgment usually supplying some or all of the consideration by one side. Although the court's signature is required in the latter instance, there is usually little to no court involvement in a settlement.

Mediation proceedings are most salient with respect to the compromise inherent in the process. Although a mediator will often set the tenor of the negotiation and encourage the parties to reach an amicable resolution to the conflict giving rise to the commencement of the action, whether the mediation process produces any kind of finality is ultimately within the control of the parties. Mediation is most appropriate when the parties are willing to entertain non-traditional solutions to their dispute or when neither party is adamant in having the action determined by an objective third party.

Arbitration proceedings resemble simplified bench trials. In most cases, the pertinent facts are presented to a third party, who then determines the most appropriate resolution of the controversy. However, arbitration proceedings are considerably less formal than courtroom trials, as rules of evidence and procedural mechanisms such as presumptions are typically not applicable. Arbitration is most appropriate when the parties simply do not agree as to a fact at issue in an action, the resolution of which would be effectively determinative of the outcome, making mediation unlikely to produce satisfactory results.

As the problem of congestion in the courts increases in magnitude, attempts to dispose of actions through such procedures have taken on added significance, and some courts have experimented by establishing a distinct court office through which alternative dispute resolution efforts are directed. Ohio has not yet adopted mandatory mediation proceedings as have several states, such as Michigan.

ADDITIONAL AUTHORITY

6 WRIGHT & MILLER §§ 1521-1540
3 MOORE'S FEDERAL PRACTICE §§ 16.01-16.94
5 ANDERSON'S OHIO CIVIL PRACTICE §§ 173.01-173.05
1 KLEIN DARLING AT 16-1 to AT 16-5
3 TEREZ F 13.1.1, F 13.1.2
2 OH. JUR. PL. AND PRAC. FORMS, ch. 21
1 FINK §§ 16-1 to 16-4
OHIO LITIGATION CHECKLISTS, Trial, §§ 10-13

LEADING CASES

Disclosure of Privileged Information in Discovery Not Waiver

Hollis v. Finger, 69 Ohio App. 3d 286, 590 N.E.2d 784 (1990) (the disclosure of privileged information may be required by the trial court for limited use in pretrial proceedings without requiring the waiver of privilege)

Discretion of Court

Lucas v. Gee, 104 Ohio App. 3d 423, 662 N.E.2d 382 (consideration of motions by the trial court and control of the court docket remain the province of the trial court's discretion in accordance with the Rules), *dismissed, appeal not allowed*, 74 Ohio St. 3d 1418, 655 N.E.2d 738 (1995)

Sanctions for Nondisclosure of Expert Witnesses

David v. Schwarzwald, Robiner, Wolf & Rock Co., 79 Ohio App. 3d 785, 607 N.E.2d 1173 (1992) (a trial court has the discretion to determine whether nondisclosure of an expert witness and her report, in violation of Rule 16, prevents testimony of the expert witness)

IV
PARTIES

CHAPTER 17

Rule 17. Parties Plaintiff and Defendant; Capacity

Rule 17 reads as follows:

(A) **Real party in interest.** Every action shall be prosecuted in the name of the real party in interest. An executor, administrator, guardian, bailee, trustee of an express trust, a party with whom or in whose name a contract has been made for the benefit of another, or a party authorized by statute may sue in his name as such representative without joining with him the party for whose benefit the action is brought. When a statute of this state so provides, an action for the use or benefit of another shall be brought in the name of this state. No action shall be dismissed on the ground that it is not prosecuted in the name of the real party in interest until a reasonable time has been allowed after objection for ratification of commencement of the action by, or joinder or substitution of, the real party in interest. Such ratification, joinder, or substitution shall have the same effect as if the action had been commenced in the name of the real party in interest.

(B) **Minors or incompetent persons.** Whenever a minor or incompetent person has a representative, such as a guardian or other like fiduciary, the representative may sue or defend on behalf of the minor or incompetent person. If a minor or incompetent person does not have a duly appointed representative the minor may sue by a next friend or defend by a guardian ad litem. When a minor or incompetent person is not otherwise represented in an action the court shall appoint a guardian ad litem or shall make such other order as it deems proper for the protection of such minor or incompetent person.

COMMENTARY

The proper litigation of an action depends upon the allegation of a viable claim by the appropriate party against the appropriate party. Rule 12(B)(6) protects against complaints that do not state a sufficient claim upon which relief can be granted; Rule 17 sets forth the rules protecting against the allegation of viable claims brought by or against the incorrect parties.

Real Party in Interest Rule/Capacity/Standing

The real party in interest rule should be distinguished from rules relating to capacity or standing. The real party in interest may be understood as the person who has an actual and substantial interest in the subject matter of the action rather than merely a formal or technical interest. In contrast, "capacity" refers to the eligibility of a person under applicable substantive law to commence an action. Capacity may hinge upon the age, legal competency, or mental fitness of a potential claimant. Capacity to sue or to be sued is governed by Ohio statutory law, whereas the real party in interest rule is embodied in Rule 15(A). Nonetheless, doctrinal distinctions between the real party in interest rule and the standing requirement are virtually nonexistent, as courts often interpret the two requirements synonymously.

Standing is an element of the constitutional case or controversy requirement which limits Ohio courts' subject matter jurisdiction. Although an extended discussion of this doctrine is beyond the scope of this manual, the standing requirement helps to ensure that justiciability of the controversy before the court by guaranteeing that a sufficient degree of adversity exists between the parties.

Real Party in Interest Rule

Subsection (A) sets forth the real party in interest rule. This rule applies only to plaintiffs and provides that every action must be prosecuted in the name of the person who has an enforceable right under the applicable law. It should be noted that Rule 17 does not, by itself, confer any substantive right to sue or be sued.

Illustration 17-1

Charles is the sole trustee of the Winthrop Family Trust, and he manages several income-producing assets held in that trust, including shares of stock in the Whiteglove Corporation. Under the terms of the trust, the present beneficiary of any trust income, as well as any distributions of the corpus of the trust, is the oldest surviving member of the Winthrop family, who at present is Hank Winthrop. Charles may commence a shareholder derivative action against Whiteglove Corporation in his name as trustee for the trust, and Hank need not be joined as a plaintiff.

Motions Under Subsection (A)

Although the second sentence of subsection (A) appears to list the exceptions to the real party in interest rule, these instances are simply illustrations of the rule, rather than exceptions to them. Thus, a party may bring an action for the use or benefit of a person who is not a party if one of the enumerated relationships is present. Although the Rule does not specify the mechanics for a motion under the Rule, a motion made by a defendant under Rule 17(A) is appropriate for challenging the basis of the plaintiff to bring an action in an Ohio court, although a motion under Rule 12(B)(6) should also be regarded as sufficient to raise the issue of whether the plaintiff is the real party in interest. The mandatory language of the Rule also provides the court with the inherent discretion to raise the issue *sua sponte*.

Illustration 17-2

Assume on the facts of Illustration 17-1 that Charles mistakenly files an action against Whiteglove Corporation in Hank's name. Whiteglove may make a motion under Rule 17(A) to challenge Hank's interest in the action and his right to maintain the action. Alternatively, Whiteglove may make a Rule 12(B)(6) motion to challenge Hank's right to bring the action.

When Plaintiff Is Not Real Party in Interest

If it is discovered that the plaintiff is not the real party in interest, subsection (A) suggests three options for the plaintiff. The plaintiff may join the person or entity in whose name an enforceable right may be maintained. The plaintiff may also withdraw and substitute the appropriate person or entity in the action. The plaintiff may also seek to have the action ratified by the person or entity in whose name the action may have been brought. Ratification may take the form of an affidavit attesting to the prosecution of the action with the knowledge and consent of the person or entity possessing the enforceable right, or by some other means that the court deems proper. The court must allow the plaintiff a reasonable time in which to join, substitute, or seek ratification of the real party in interest. Dismissal of the action is proper only after this opportunity is provided and the plaintiff fails to take any action to rectify the error.

Illustration 17-3

Assume on the facts of Illustration 17-1 that Charles, as trustee of the trust, distributes all stock from Whiteglove Corporation to Hank. Nevertheless, Charles commences a shareholder derivative action against Whiteglove in his name as trustee for the trust. In response, Whiteglove makes a motion under Rule 17(A) and challenges Charles's right to bring the action. At this point, Charles may proceed in three ways. First, Charles may join Hank as a party to the action. Charles may also withdraw from the suit and substitute Hank as the appropriate party to bring the action. Finally, Charles may seek to have the action ratified by Hank.

Infant or Incompetent Persons

Subsection (B) contains special provisions relating to the capacity of minors or incompetent persons to sue or to be sued. If an infant or incompetent person has a legal representative, the representative has the authority both to sue or to be sued on behalf of the infant or incompetent person. If no such representative exists, an infant or incompetent person may bring an action through a next friend or *guardian ad litem*. If an infant or incompetent person that has no legal representative is sued in an Ohio court, the court may appoint a *guardian ad litem* to defend the person in the action and make other orders to properly protect the interests of the infant or incompetent person.

ADDITIONAL AUTHORITY

6 WRIGHT & MILLER §§ 1541-1580
4 MOORE'S FEDERAL PRACTICE §§ 17.01-17.28
4 ANDERSON'S OHIO CIVIL PRACTICE §§ 157.05-157.11
1 KLEIN DARLING AT 17-1 to AT 17-31
3 TEREZ F 7.2.1 to F 7.2.4
3 OH. JUR. PL. AND PRAC. FORMS, ch. 22
4 MILLIGAN Forms 17-1 to 17-36
1 FINK §§ 17-1 to 17-4

LEADING CASES

Administrator Must Bring Action in Wrongful Death Action

Yardley v. W. Ohio Conference of the United Methodist Church, Inc., 138 Ohio App. 3d 872, 742 N.E.2d 723 (2000) (a wrongful death action must be brought in the name of a person appointed by a court to be the administrator, executor, or personal representative of the decedent's estate)

Appointment of Guardian

State ex rel. Robinson v. Cuyahoga County Court of Common Pleas, 75 Ohio St. 3d 431, 662 N.E.2d 798 (a court, incident to its power to try a case, may appoint a guardian ad litem, pursuant to Rule 17(B); and mandamus will not issue to compel the appointment to be vacated), *cert. denied*, 117 S. Ct. 492, 136 L. Ed. 2d 385, 65 U.S.L.W. 3369 (1996)

Definition of Real Party in Interest

First Union Natl. Bank v. Hufford, 146 Ohio App. 3d 673, 767 N.E.2d 1206 (2001) (to ascertain the real party in interest, a court must consider who would be entitled to damages)

Airborne Express, Inc. v. Systems Research Lab., 106 Ohio App. 3d 498, 666 N.E.2d 584 (1995) (a real party in interest is directly benefited or injured by the outcome of a case, and retains the substantive right to relief), *appeal not allowed*, 75 Ohio St. 3d 1411, 661 N.E.2d 759 (1996)

Expiration of Statute of Limitations

Continental Ins. Co. v. Twedell, 100 Ohio Misc.2d 25, 717 N.E.2d 1195 (M.C. 1998) (if an existing party rather than a "non-party" movant raises the issue of non-joinder of a real party in interest after the expiration of the statute of limitations, the real party in interest should be joined under Rule 17, because such joinder relates back to the date the action commenced)

Real Party in Interest; Generally

Johnson's Janitorial Serv. v. Alltel Corp., 92 Ohio App. 3d 327, 635 N.E.2d 60 (1993) (pursuant to Rule 17(A), a plaintiff may amend a complaint to name real party in interest if done in a timely manner)

Real Party in Interest Not Affirmative Defense

First Union Natl. Bank v. Hufford, 146 Ohio App. 3d 673, 767 N.E.2d 1206 (2001) (although the failure to name the real party in interest as a party plaintiff must be timely raised by the defendant, it is not an affirmative defense that must be raised in the defendant's initial responsive motion or pleading)

Standing; Substitution of Proper Party

State ex rel. Tubbs Jones v. Suster, 84 Ohio St. 3d 70, 701 N.E.2d 1002 (1998) (if a claim is asserted by one who is not the real party in interest, standing to prosecute the action is lacking even if the court has subject matter jurisdiction; the lack of standing, however, may be cured by substituting the proper party so that the court may proceed to adjudicate the matter)

CHAPTER 18

Rule 18. Joinder of Claims and Remedies

Rule 18 reads as follows:

(A) Joinder of claims. A party asserting a claim to relief as an original claim, counterclaim, cross-claim, or third-party claim, may join, either as independent or as alternate claims, as many claims, legal or equitable, as he has against an opposing party.

(B) Joinder of remedies; fraudulent conveyances. Whenever a claim is one heretofore cognizable only after another claim has been prosecuted to a conclusion, the two claims may be joined in a single action; but the court shall grant relief in that action only in accordance with the relative substantive rights of the parties. In particular, a plaintiff may state a claim for money and a claim to have set aside a conveyance fraudulent as to him, without first having obtained a judgment establishing the claim for money.

COMMENTARY

The labyrinth encompassing the joinder of claims and the joinder of parties continues with Rule 18. As noted previously, Rules 13 and 18, relating to the joinder of claims, Rules 19, 19.1, and 20, relating to the joinder of parties, and Rule 14, governing the joinder of parties and claims through third-party practice, are all interrelated, and a discussion of the complexities of any of these Rules necessarily entails reference to the others.

Despite the fact that Rule 18 is included within Title IV of the Rules, labelled "Parties," the Rule does not provide for the joinder of additional parties. Instead, parties must be properly joined under Rule 19, Rule 19.1 or Rule 20 before claims under Rule 18 may be added. Furthermore, a claim must be properly asserted under Rule 3, Rule 13, or Rule 14 before a claim under Rule 18 can be joined. This latter requirement is discussed in more detail below.

"Conditional" Claims Under Rule 18 Generally

Rule 18 furthers the liberal joinder philosophy of the Rules by allowing any party already asserting a valid claim to join as many claims as that party has against an opposing party. Although the far-reaching language of the Rule may appear to imply that the other Rules governing joinder of claims, such as Rules 13 and 14, are rendered inconsequential by Rule 18, these other Rules are still necessary for determining whether an initial claim is cognizable. Thus, claims joined under Rule 18 may be best characterized as "conditional" claims, although this terminology is not employed by the Rule. In other words, Rule 18 is triggered only when a claim is properly asserted under some other Rule. Once an original claim, counterclaim, cross-claim, or third-party claim is properly brought, Rule 18 may be used to assert any other claim against an opposing party.

Illustration 18-1

Cynthia commences an action against her neighbor Rose for property damage when Rose's terrier Perky tore up Cynthia's flower garden. Cynthia also has an unrelated breach of contract against Rose involving a joint business venture. Cynthia wishes to commence one action against Rose for both of these claims. Under Rule 18, Cynthia may join her breach of contract claim with her property damage claim once the court recognizes that the property claim is cognizable, even though the two claims are unrelated to one another.

"Conditional" claims under Rule 18 are optional, and they need not relate to the subject matter of any of the other claims. To avoid needless complication and unnecessary confusion in the action, the court may order a separate trial for "conditional" claims under Rule 42.

Illustration 18-2

Assume on the facts of Illustration 18-1 that the court determines the jury will be confused if both of Cynthia's claims are presented at the same trial. The court may thus order separate trials on the property damage claim and breach of contract claim.

Contingent Claims Allowed

Subsection (B) expressly allows a party to join contingent claims, or claims that mature upon the successful prosecution of other claims. The second sentence of this subsection is illustrative only; it provides an example of a claim that is cognizable only upon obtaining a judgment on another claim.

ADDITIONAL AUTHORITY

6 WRIGHT & MILLER §§ 1581-1600
4 MOORE'S FEDERAL PRACTICE §§ 18.01-18.23

4 Anderson's Ohio Civil Practice §§ 157.02-157.04
1 Klein Darling AT 18-1 to AT 18-7
3 Terez F 4.11.14
3 Oh. Jur. Pl. and Prac. Forms, ch. 23
4 Milligan Forms 18-1 to 18-9
1 Fink §§ 18-1 to 18-6

LEADING CASES

Class Action as Conditional Claim

Blon v. Bank One, Akron, N.A., 22 Ohio App. 3d 91, 489 N.E.2d 301 (1985) (a person joined to an action as a plaintiff or defendant may plead any and all claims available to that person, including an attempt to bring a class action, without leave of court), *rev'd*, 35 Ohio St. 3d 98, 519 N.E.2d 363 (1988)

Joinder of Related Claims

U.S. Sprint Communications Co. Ltd. Partnership v. Mr. K's Foods, Inc., 68 Ohio St. 3d 181, 624 N.E.2d 1048 (1994) (upon acquiring personal jurisdiction over a nonresident defendant for claims arising in Ohio, joinder of related claims not arising in Ohio is permitted)

CHAPTER 19

Rule 19. Joinder of Persons Needed for Just Adjudication

Rule 19 reads as follows:

(A) Persons to be joined if feasible. A person who is subject to service of process shall be joined as a party in the action if

    (1)   in his absence complete relief cannot be accorded among those already parties, or

    (2)   he claims an interest relating to the subject of the action and is so situated that the disposition of the action in his absence may

        (a)   as a practical matter impair or impede his ability to protect that interest or

        (b)   leave any of the persons already parties subject to a substantial risk of incurring double, multiple, or otherwise inconsistent obligations by reason of his claimed interest, or

    (3)   he has an interest relating to the subject of the action as an assignor, assignee, subrogor, or subrogee.

If he has not been so joined, the court shall order that he be made a party upon timely assertion of the defense of failure to join a party as provided in Rule 12(B)(7). If the defense is not timely asserted, waiver is applicable as provided in Rule 12(G) and (H). If he should join as a plaintiff but refuses to do so, he may be made a defendant, or, in a proper case, an involuntary plaintiff. In the event that such joinder causes the relief sought to exceed the jurisdiction of the court, the court shall certify the proceedings in the action to the court of common pleas.

(B) Determination by court whenever joinder not feasible. If a person as described in subdivision (A)(1), (2), or (3) hereof cannot be made a party, the court shall determine whether in equity and good conscience the action should proceed among the parties before it, or should be dismissed, the absent person being thus regarded as indispensable. The factors to be considered by the court include: first, to what extent a judgment rendered in the person's absence might be prejudicial to him or those already parties; second, the extent to which, by protective provisions in the judgment, by the shaping of relief, or other measures, the prejudice can be lessened or avoided; third, whether a judgment rendered in the person's absence will be adequate; fourth, whether the plaintiff will have an adequate remedy if the action is dismissed for nonjoinder.

(C) Pleading reasons for nonjoinder. A pleading asserting a claim for relief shall state the names, if known to the pleader, of any persons as described in subdivision (A)(1), (2), or (3) hereof who are not joined, and the reasons why they are not joined.

(D) Exception of class actions. This rule is subject to the provisions of Rule 23.

COMMENTARY

Rule 19 and Rule 19.1 govern the joinder of persons needed for just adjudication, commonly referred to as "compulsory" joinder. Rules 13 and 18, relating to the joinder of claims, Rules 19, 19.1, and 20, relating to the joinder of parties, and Rule 14, governing the joinder of parties and claims through third-party practice, are all interrelated, and a discussion of the complexities of any of these Rules necessarily entails reference to the others. Briefly, parties must be properly joined under Rule 19, 19.1, or Rule 20 before counterclaims and cross-claims under Rule 13, third-party claims under Rule 14, and "conditional" claims under Rule 18 may be considered.

It should be noted Rule 19.1 supplements Rule 19 by expanding the scope of parties to whom compulsory joinder is applicable. The wording of the title of Rule 19, "Joinder of Persons Needed for Just Adjudication," chosen to correspond to the identically-titled Federal Rule of Civil Procedure 19, is re-labeled as "Compulsory Joinder" in Rule 19.1, which, as noted above, is the common name used to identify the rule. Rule 19.1 has no analog in the Federal Rules of Civil Procedure. The difference in the titles of the Ohio Rules is not intended to reflect any difference in the operation or coverage of those Rules; in fact, the similar format and structure of the two Rules reflect the connection between the two.

As Rule 19 significantly affects the operation of class actions, subsection (D) explicitly provides that the Rule is subject to the provisions of Rule 23. This proviso should be interpreted as subjecting Rule 19 to Rule 23.1 as well.

Operation of Rule 19

The operation of Rule 19 itself is fairly straightforward. It distinguishes between "necessary" parties, *i.e.*, parties that fall into one of the three categories listed in subsection (A), and "indispensable" parties, *i.e.*, parties whose nonjoinder must result in a dismissal of the action. These denominations should not be confused with one another, as "indispensable" parties are always "necessary," but "necessary" parties may not be "indispensable."

Illustration 19-1

If Linda is determined to be a "necessary" party because her absence would prevent complete relief from being afforded among the existing parties, a further determination must then be made as to whether the action should continue. Only then, if it is determined that Linda is "indispensable" under subsection (B), will the action be dismissed.

"Necessary" Parties

Subsection (A) specifies four categories of persons that must be joined in an action: (1) persons whose absence would prevent complete relief among existing parties; (2) persons claiming an interest in the action that are situated such that a disposition of the action in their absence may, as a practical matter, impair or impede their ability to protect their interest; (3) persons claiming an interest in the action that are situated such that a disposition of the action in their absence may render an existing party subject to a substantial risk of incurring multiple or inconsistent obligations; and (4) persons having an interest relating to the subject of the action as an assignor, assignee, subrogor, or subrogee. Persons that fall into one of these four categories may be referred to as "necessary" parties; these persons must be joined in the action if a party makes a timely motion to this effect under Rule 12(B)(7) and the court can secure personal jurisdiction over them. The Rule indicates that the failure to make such a motion will result in a waiver of joinder under Rule 19.

Illustration 19-2

Tracy commences an action against Eddy's Repair Shop to recover for personal injuries suffered in a fire at the repair shop. Rather than naming Eddy's Repair Shop as a defendant in the action, Tracy sues Corporate Insurance, the insurer of Eddy's Repair Shop. However, the insurance policy covers only losses in excess of $500,000. Under Rule 19(A), Eddy's Repair Shop is considered a "necessary" party, as Tracy cannot obtain complete relief in the absence of Eddy's Repair Shop as a party to the action.

Illustration 19-3

Donna owns a life estate in a parcel of land, the remainder interest of which is owned by Rich. Donna commences an action against a tenant, Lee, for ejectment, and Lee defends on the basis that he owns the property through adverse possession. Rich should be joined in the action, as the disposition of the action may impede his ability to protect or even retain his remainder interest.

Illustration 19-4

Steel Laborers United, a union comprised of steel workers, represents the interests of the workers at Associated Steel. Under the terms of a collective bargaining agreement with Steel Laborers United, Associated Steel must run three shifts a day around the clock. A community association commences an action against Associated Steel, seeking an injunction to limit the hours in which smoke caused by the production process is discharged into the surrounding area to no more than 10 hours a day. Under Rule 19, Steel Laborers United should be joined in the action, as the grant of an injunction will expose Associated Steel to inconsistent obligations with regard to the hours of production.

If the court determines that a person is a "necessary" party, it must issue an order directing the person to be joined as a party. This order poses no particular problem if the person should be joined as a defendant in the action. However, when a "necessary" party should be aligned with the plaintiff and the party refuses to join the action, the court may order that the person be joined as a defendant and treated in the same manner as any other defendant.

Certification of Proceedings to Court of Common Pleas

In Ohio, the jurisdiction of municipal and county courts is limited to claims under $10,000 and $3000, respectively. In the event that joinder under Rule 19 results in an aggregate claim amount that divests a municipal or county court of its jurisdiction, subsection (A) provides that a record of the proceedings shall be certified and the action transferred to the court of common pleas in the county or territorial district in which the court is located.

"Involuntary Plaintiffs"

The reference to an "involuntary plaintiff" in subsection (A) is not intended to imply that any unwilling "necessary" party that should be aligned with the plaintiff can be ordered to so join. Instead, the court may order that a "necessary" party be joined as an involuntary plaintiff only in a "proper case." Such a case exists only when the absent person has a duty to allow the plaintiff to use that person's name in the action.

"Indispensable" Parties

If a person falls into one of the four categories listed in subsection (A) but over whom personal jurisdiction cannot be obtained, subsection (B) requires the court to determine whether the party is "indispensable." An "indispensable" party is a person without whom the court cannot in equity and good conscience allow the action to continue. Such a ruling would result in a dismissal of the action and compel the plaintiff to bring the action in another forum. The determination of whether a party is "indispensable" is not made until an initial determination is made regarding whether the party is "necessary" under subsection (A).

Subsection (B) lists the factors that the court should consider in making this determination: (1) the extent to which a judgment rendered in the person's absence might be prejudicial to the existing parties; (2) the degree to which the prejudice to the absent person or existing parties can be lessened or avoided through protective orders or narrowly-drawn judgments; (3) the adequacy of a judgment rendered in the person's absence; and (4) whether the existing plaintiff will have an adequate remedy if the action is dismissed for nonjoinder. Notably, the use of protective orders and judgments has proved particularly helpful in allowing courts to avoid the harsh action of dismissal. This list is not exclusive, and the court may consider other factors in determining whether an action should be dismissed because an "indispensable" person cannot be joined in the action.

Pleading Requirements of Rule 19

Subsection (C) supplements the pleading rules in Rules 8 and 9 by requiring all parties to state the known identities of all necessary and indispensable persons that are not joined in the action in their pleadings. The reasons for the nonjoinder of such persons should also be stated with particularity in the pleadings. This explication will assist the court in ruling on a motion under Rule 12(B)(7) to dismiss the action for failure to join a necessary or indispensable person.

ADDITIONAL AUTHORITY

7 WRIGHT & MILLER §§ 1601-1650

4 MOORE'S FEDERAL PRACTICE §§ 19.01-19.09

4 ANDERSON'S OHIO CIVIL PRACTICE §§ 157.12-157.151

KLEIN DARLING AT 19-1 to AT 19-25

3 TEREZ F 7.4.1 to F 7.4.4, F 7.6.3, F 16.1.9

3 OH. JUR. PL. AND PRAC. FORMS, ch. 24

1 FINK §§ 19-1 to 19-15

OHIO LITIGATION CHECKLISTS, Parties and Actions, §§ 6-8

LEADING CASES

Dismissal if Joinder Not Feasible

Malakpa v. Red Cab Co., 72 Ohio Misc. 2d 27, 655 N.E.2d 458 (C.P. 1995) (an action filed in Ohio must be dismissed if an indispensable party cannot be joined due to lack of personal jurisdiction)

Expiration of Statute of Limitations

Continental Ins. Co. v. Twedell, 100 Ohio Misc.2d 25, 717 N.E.2d 1195 (M.C. 1998) (if an existing party rather than a "non-party" movant raises the issue of non-joinder of a real party in interest after the expiration of the statute of limitations, the real party in interest should be joined under Rule 17, because such joinder relates back to the date the action commenced)

Failure to Join an Indispensable Party; Waiver

Modic v. Modic, 91 Ohio App. 3d 775, 633 N.E.2d 1151 (1993) (the defense of failure to join an indispensable party must be made in a pleading, a motion for judgment on the pleadings, or at the trial on the merits, and the failure to do so does not permit raising the defense after entry of judgment), *jurisdictional motion overruled*, 69 Ohio St. 3d 1416, 630 N.E.2d 377 (1994)

Indispensable Parties; Procedure

Evans v. Graham, 71 Ohio App. 3d 417, 594 N.E.2d 71 (1991) (upon determining that a person should be joined pursuant to Rule 19(A) and that the person is an indispensable party, the court should order the party be brought into the action or should grant leave for the amendment of complaints to add the other party)

Party Unnecessary Where Impleader Available

St. Clair Builders, Inc. v. Aetna Casualty and Surety Co., No. 65893 (8th Dist.), 1994 Ohio App. LEXIS 3350 (where the pleading party could have avoided multiple litigation by impleading the absent party pursuant to Rule 14, the absent party was not a necessary party)

Persons to Be Joined If Feasible; Dismissal

Chambers v. Stevenson, 71 Ohio App. 3d 566, 594 N.E.2d 1097 (1991) (dismissal for failure to join a necessary party is proper only when the defect complained of cannot be cured)

Waiver of Joinder

Sankin v. Melena Co., LPA, 83 Ohio App. 3d 169, 614 N.E.2d 807 (1992) (an attorney who neither filed a motion requesting joinder nor objected to joinder waived his right to raise failure to join former clients whose fees were the subject of a dispute on appeal)

CHAPTER 19.1

Rule 19.1. Compulsory Joinder

Rule 19.1 reads as follows:

(A) Persons to be joined. A person who is subject to service of process shall be joined as a party in the action, except as provided in division (B) of this rule, if the person has an interest in or a claim arising out of the following situations:

(1) Personal injury or property damage to the person or property of the decedent which survives the decedent's death and a claim for wrongful death to the same decedent if caused by the same wrongful act;

(2) Personal injury or property damage to a husband or wife and a claim of the spouse for loss of consortium or expenses or property damage if caused by the same wrongful act;

(3) Personal injury or property damage to a minor and a claim of the parent or guardian of the minor for loss of consortium or expenses or property damage if caused by the same wrongful act;

(4) Personal injury or property damage to an employee or agent and a claim of the employer or principal for property damage if caused by the same wrongful act.

If he has not been so joined, the court, subject to subdivision (B) hereof, shall order that he be made a party upon timely assertion of the defense of failure to join a party as provided in Rule 12(B)(7). If the defense is not timely asserted, waiver is applicable as provided in Rule 12(G) and (H). If he should join as a plaintiff but refuses to do so, he may be made a defendant, or, in a proper case, an involuntary plaintiff. In the event that such joinder causes the relief sought to exceed the jurisdiction of the court, the court shall certify the proceedings in the action to the court of common pleas.

(B) Exception to compulsory joinder. If a party to the action or a person described in subdivision (A) shows good cause why that person should not be joined, the court shall proceed without requiring joinder.

(C) Pleading reasons for nonjoinder. A pleading asserting a claim for relief shall state the names, if known to the pleader, of any persons as described in subdivision (A)(1), (2), (3), or (4) hereof who are not joined, and the reasons why they are not joined.

(D) Exception of class actions. This rule is subject to the provisions of Rule 23.

COMMENTARY

Rule 19.1 and Rule 19 govern compulsory joinder, though Rule 19 is titled differently. As noted previously, Rules 13 and 18, relating to the joinder of claims, Rules 19, 19.1 and 20, relating to the joinder of parties, and Rule 14, governing the joinder of parties and claims through third-party practice, are all interrelated, and a discussion of the complexities of any of these Rules entails reference to the others. Briefly, parties must be joined under Rule 19, Rule 19.1 or Rule 20 before counterclaims and cross-claims under Rule 13, third party claims under Rule 14, and "conditional" claims under Rule 18 may be considered.

It should be noted Rule 19.1 supplements Rule 19 by expanding the scope of parties to whom compulsory joinder is applicable. The wording of the title of Rule 19, "Joinder of Persons Needed for Just Adjudication," chosen to correspond to the identically-titled Federal Rule of Civil Procedure 19, is re-labeled as "Compulsory Joinder" in Rule 19.1, which, as noted above, is the common name used to identify the rule. Rule 19.1 has no analog in the Federal Rules of Civil Procedure. The difference in the titles of the Ohio Rules is not intended to reflect any difference in the operation or coverage of those Rules; in fact, the similar format and structure of the two Rules reflect the connection between the two.

As Rule 19.1 significantly affects the operation of class actions, subsection (D) explicitly provides that the Rule is subject to the provisions of Rule 23. This proviso should be interpreted as subjecting Rule 19.1 to Rule 23.1 as well.

Comparison to Rule 19

As noted, Rule 19.1 is an extension of Rule 19 in its structure and philosophy. Subsection (A), like Rule 19(A), specifies the persons who must be joined if feasible. Subsection (B) is similar to Rule 19 by allowing departure from the general rule provisions in Rule 19.1(A) as a matter of equity. Subsections (C) and (D) are also virtually identical to their counterparts in Rule 19.

Rule 19.1 broadens the scope of Rule 19 by extending the principle of compulsory joinder to the categories of persons set forth in subsection (A). These persons are not encompassed by the scope of Rule 19 and were not required to be joined in an action under prior Ohio law. Rule 19.1 reflects the reasoning articulated in the Staff Notes to Rule 19.1 that a party with a separate claim should join its claim with that of another person even though the claims are independent under substantive law and could be pursued separately. Rule 19.1 mirrors Rule 19 in that the same facts and the same wrongful act must serve as the basis for claims which are required to be joined. As with Rule 19, a motion for joinder under Rule 19.1 must be made by a party pursuant to Rule 12(B)(7) or the right of the parties to compel the joinder of another party will be waived in accordance with the provisions of subsections (G) and (H) of Rule 12.

Persons to Be Joined

Subsection (A) specifies the four categories of persons to whom the Rule is applicable and joinder is required. First, survival actions and wrongful death actions arising out of an accident causing injury to a person who later dies as a result of the injuries must be joined under Rule 19.1(A)(1). Rule 19.1(A)(2) and (3) require joinder of claims arising out of wrongful acts that cause personal injury or property damage to a spouse or minor and also provide the uninjured spouse, parent or guardian a claim for loss of consortium, expenses, or property damages. Finally, joinder is required for claims involving personal injury or property damage to an employer or agent where the employer or principal has a related claim for property damage caused by the same wrongful act.

Exception to Joinder

Subsection (B) provides a exception to compulsory joinder under Rule 19.1 for "good cause" shown. Although the circumstances under which a party would be regarded as "indispensable" under Rule 19(B) would certainly satisfy the requirements for "good cause," the Staff Notes to Rule 19.1 also indicate that there may be other circumstances in which nonjoinder may be appropriate. Accordingly, the court is provided with broader discretion to refuse to order the joinder of a compulsory party under Rule 19.1 than it is under Rule 19.

Pleading Requirements

Subsection (C) parallels Rule 19(C) in supplementing the pleading rules in Rules 8 and 9 by requiring all parties to state the known identities of all persons falling into the categories established in subsection (A). The reasons for the nonjoinder of such persons should also be stated with particularity in the pleadings. This explication will assist the court in ruling on a motion under Rule 12(B)(7) to dismiss the action for failure to join a compulsory party.

Certification of Proceedings to Court of Common Pleas

In Ohio, the jurisdiction of municipal and county courts is limited to claims under $10,000 and $3000, respectively. In the event that joinder under Rule 19 results in an aggregate claim amount that divests a municipal or county court of its jurisdiction, subsection (A) provides that a record of the proceedings shall be certified and the action transferred to the court of common pleas in the county or territorial district in which the court is located.

ADDITIONAL AUTHORITY

4 ANDERSON'S OHIO CIVIL PRACTICE §§ 157.16-157.18
1 KLEIN DARLING AT 19.1-1 to AT 19.2-12
3 TEREZ F 4.16.1 to F 4.16.11, F 4.22.5, F 4.22.6, F 7.4.7, F 16.1.9
3 OH. JUR. PL. AND PRAC. FORMS, ch. 25
4 MILLIGAN Forms 19.1-1 to 19.1-14
1 FINK §§ 19.1-1 to 19.1-5
OHIO LITIGATION CHECKLISTS, Parties and Actions, §§ 6-8

LEADING CASES

Compulsory Joinder; Purpose

Turowski v. Johnson, 68 Ohio App. 3d 704, 589 N.E.2d 462 (1990) (Rule 19.1 provides defendants the means of compelling joinder in civil suits of all parties who may have a claim against them arising out of the same controversy to avoid multiple lawsuits and inconsistent judgments), *jurisdictional motion overruled*, 62 Ohio St. 3d 1410, 577 N.E.2d 362 (1991)

Effect of Dismissing Underlying Claim

Perry v. Eagle-Picher Indus., 52 Ohio St. 3d 168, 556 N.E.2d 484 (1990) (the dismissal of a personal injury claim or failure to substitute an estate as a party plaintiff did not affect claims for loss of consortium or wrongful death)

Loss of Consortium Derivative Claim

Wiseman v. General Motors Corp., 74 Ohio Misc. 2d 111, 659 N.E.2d 889 (C.P. 1995) (a spouse's loss of consortium claim is derivative of the other spouse's claims)

CHAPTER 20

Rule 20. Permissive Joinder of Parties

Rule 20 reads as follows:

(A) **Permissive joinder.** All persons may join in one action as plaintiffs if they assert any right to relief jointly, severally, or in the alternative in respect of or arising out of the same transaction, occurrence, or succession or series of transactions or occurrences and if any question of law or fact common to all these persons will arise in the action. All persons may be joined in one action as defendants if there is asserted against them jointly, severally, or in the alternative, any right to relief in respect of or arising out of the same transaction, occurrence, or succession or series of transactions or occurrences and if any question of law or fact common to all defendants will arise in the action. A plaintiff or defendant need not be interested in obtaining or defending against all the relief demanded. Judgment may be given for one or more of the plaintiffs according to their respective rights to relief, and against one or more defendants according to their respective liabilities.

(B) **Separate trials.** The court may make such orders as will prevent a party from being prejudiced, delayed, or put to expense by the inclusion of a party against whom he asserts no claim and who asserts no claim against him, and may order separate trials or make other orders to prevent prejudice or delay.

COMMENTARY

Rule 20 governs permissive joinder, or joinder of persons that are not deemed "compulsory" parties under Rule 19 or Rule 19.1. As noted previously, Rules 13 and 18, relating to the joinder of claims, Rules 19, 19.1 and 20, relating to the joinder of parties, and Rule 14, governing the joinder of parties and claims through third-party practice, are all interrelated, and a discussion of the complexities of any of these Rules necessarily entails reference to the others. Briefly, parties must be properly joined under Rule 19 or Rule 20 before counterclaims and cross-claims under Rule 13, third-party claims under Rule 14, and "conditional" claims under Rule 18 may be considered.

Permissive Joinder Generally

Rule 20 implements the liberal joinder philosophy of the Rules by permitting joinder of parties in a broad range of cases. Unlike compulsory joinder under Rule 19 or Rule 19.1, Rule 20 contains only two restrictions on the ability of a plaintiff to join defendants: (1) an alleged right must arise out of the same transaction, occurrence, or series of transactions or occurrences; and (2) a common question of law or fact with respect to the defendants must be present in the action. Joinder under Rule 20 is always at the discretion of the parties. It should also be noted that joinder of the parties must be proper before joinder of claims against the parties can be considered. However, once the requirements of Rule 20 are satisfied and joinder of the parties is proper, a party may use the more liberal claim-joinder provisions of Rule 18 to assert unrelated claims against the joined parties.

Illustration 20-1

Peter suffers serious injuries when he is involved in an automobile collision with Doris. At the emergency room where Peter is taken after the accident, Dr. Steinberg negligently treats him, thus aggravating his injuries. Peter wishes to commence an action against both Doris and Dr. Steinberg. Under Rule 20, Peter may join both parties as defendants in one action. Peter's claims against each defendant arise out of the same series of occurrences, namely the automobile accident and subsequent medical treatment. Peter's claims against each defendant also consist of common questions of fact, namely the extent of Peter's injuries. Once the parties are properly joined, Peter may assert any unrelated claim he may have against the parties in the same action.

Separate Trials and Protective Orders Allowed

Subsection (B) provides that the court may order separate trials or make protective orders where multiple parties have been joined under Rule 20. Separate trials may prevent a party from being prejudiced or delayed in an action.

ADDITIONAL AUTHORITY

7 WRIGHT & MILLER §§ 1651-1680

4 MOORE'S FEDERAL PRACTICE §§ 20.01-20.09

4 ANDERSON'S OHIO CIVIL PRACTICE §§ 157.19-157.21

1 KLEIN DARLING AT 20-1 to AT 20-13

3 TEREZ F 7.4.1

3 OH. JUR. PL. AND PRAC. FORMS, ch. 26

4 MILLIGAN Forms 20-1 to 20-12

1 FINK §§ 20-1 to 20-9

OHIO LITIGATION CHECKLISTS, Parties and Actions, §§ 6-8

LEADING CASES

Court of Common Pleas May Not Be Joined

Dalton v. Bureau of Criminal Identification and Investigation, 39 Ohio App. 3d 123, 530 N.E.2d 35 (1987) (a court of common pleas may not be joined as a defendant under Rule 20(A))

CHAPTER 21

Rule 21. Misjoinder and Nonjoinder of Parties

Rule 21 reads as follows:

Misjoinder of parties is not ground for dismissal of an action. Parties may be dropped or added by order of the court on motion of any party or of its own initiative at any stage of the action and on such terms as are just. Any claim against a party may be severed and proceeded with separately.

COMMENTARY

Rule 21 provides the mechanism for the implementation of Rules 18-20. A party may seek to add or drop a party under Rules 19, 19.1, and 20 by making a motion to the court, or the court may so order on its own initiative. A party may also raise the issue in a responsive pleading.

The first sentence of Rule 21 states that misjoinder of parties is not a proper ground for dismissal of the action. However, dismissal of parties from the action or severance of claims against parties are appropriate actions for the court.

ADDITIONAL AUTHORITY

7 WRIGHT & MILLER §§ 1681-1700
4 MOORE'S FEDERAL PRACTICE §§ 21.01-21.06
4 ANDERSON'S OHIO CIVIL PRACTICE §§ 157.22-157.24
1 KLEIN DARLING AT 21-1 to AT 21-4
3 TEREZ F 7.4.1 to F 7.4.3
3 OH. JUR. PL. AND PRAC. FORMS, ch. 27
4 MILLIGAN Forms 21-1 to 21-26
1 FINK §§ 21-1 to 21-5
OHIO LITIGATION CHECKLISTS, Parties and Actions, §§ 6-8

LEADING CASES

Court Authority to Join Necessary Party

State ex rel. Multimedia, Inc. v. Whalen, 48 Ohio St. 3d 41, 549 N.E.2d 167

(1990) (a trial court may, *sua sponte*, join necessary parties to an action under OHIO REV. CODE § 149.43(B) when the custodian of records was not a party)

Dismissal of Selective Parties

Dalton v. Wearsh, 102 Ohio App. 3d 491, 657 N.E.2d 533 (1995) (a plaintiff who obtained an arbitration award against one defendant was not entitled to dismiss defendants against whom he failed to recover)

Statute of Limitations Bars Joinder of Plaintiff

Picciuto v. Lucas County Board of Commissioners, 69 Ohio App. 3d 789, 591 N.E.2d 1287 (1990) (when a cause of action as to a person is barred by the statute of limitations, that person may not be brought into the action as a new party defendant)

CHAPTER 22

Rule 22. Interpleader

Rule 22 reads as follows:

Persons having claims against the plaintiff may be joined as defendants and required to interplead when their claims are such that the plaintiff is or may be exposed to double or multiple liability. It is not ground for objection to the joinder that the claims of the several claimants or the titles on which their claims depend do not have a common origin or are not identical but are adverse to and independent of one another, or that the plaintiff avers that he is not liable in whole or in part to any or all of the claimants. A defendant exposed to similar liability may obtain such interpleader by way of cross-claim or counterclaim. The provisions of this rule supplement and do not in any way limit the joinder of parties permitted in Rule 20.

In such an action in which any part of the relief sought is a judgment for a sum of money or the disposition of a sum of money or the disposition of any other thing capable of delivery, a party may deposit all or any part of such sum or thing with the court upon notice to every other party and leave of court. The court may make an order for the safekeeping, payment or disposition of such sum or thing.

COMMENTARY

Rule 22 governs interpleader, a special party-joinder device. The Ohio version of interpleader is similar to the analogous device under the Federal Rules of Civil Procedure, although Ohio Rule 22 contains important clarification provisions not included in Federal Rule 22.

Interpleader Generally

Interpleader allows a person possessing money or property that is the subject of inconsistent claims, referred to as the "stakeholder," to force all persons presenting a claim for the money or property, referred to as the "claimants," to go before a single court to resolve the dispute. The device allows a stakeholder to thus avoid separate actions over the same subject matter and possibly multiple liability to different claimants.

The interpleader device is available to defendants as well as plaintiffs, a point recognized explicitly in the Rule. Defendants who satisfy the requirements of maintaining an interpleader action should invoke the provisions of the Rule by way of counterclaim or cross-claim. Although not expressly authorized by the Rule, there appears to be no reason why interpleader should not be available to defendants by way of third-party claim as well.

Requirements of Interpleader Actions

To properly understand the language and operation of Rule 22, it is helpful to differentiate the Rule from its historical analog. Under the common law, strict bills of interpleader had very rigid restrictions that prevented the use of the bills in many situations in which the suit may have been useful. These strict requirements included: (1) the same thing or debt must be claimed by all the parties against whom relief is demanded; (2) the adverse claims must be derived from a common source; (3) the plaintiff must be disinterested in the subject matter; and (4) the plaintiff must have incurred no independent liability to any of the claimants, instead remaining completely indifferent to the outcome of the action.

Under Rule 22, all four requirements have been explicitly abolished. Therefore, Rule 22 may be used when the claimants are asserting claims to differing amounts of the money or property at stake, or when the sources of the claims have distinct derivations. Furthermore, Rule 22 allows the stakeholder to also act in the capacity of a claimant. As written, the only requirement in the Rule is that the "claims [of the interpleaded parties] are such that the plaintiff is or may be exposed to double or multiple liability." Accordingly, Rule 22 may be available in a broad range of situations.

Illustration 22-1

Jemma purchases an insurance policy on the life of her husband, Antonio, from Allcounty Insurance Co., naming herself as the beneficiary. The policy contains a forfeiture clause in the event of suicide by the insured. Several months later, Antonio is killed in a suspicious shotgun incident, which is initially ruled as an accidental death by the police. Under the applicable state law, the next of kin receive the proceeds of a life insurance policy if the primary beneficiary is held criminally responsible for the death in question. Allcounty Insurance Co. may commence an interpleader action under Rule 22, naming Jemma and Antonio's sister, Maria, who is Antonio's next of kin, as claimants. Allcounty may also allege that Antonio's death was a suicide, thereby naming itself as a claimant in the action.

Interpleader Procedure

Interpleader typically occurs in two stages. Rule 22 indicates that the stakeholder who exercises control over a fund may be required to deposit with the court a sum of money or material object that is the subject of the action. In most cases, the stake will be in the form of a tangible object, such as a specific fund, life insurance policy, or stock. In many cases, such a deposit may be desired by the party seeking interpleader, who, if disinterested in the eventual outcome of the action, seeks only to have its responsibility for the property abated. In essence, a kind of escrow account is created with the court, thus relieving the party making a deposit into such an account of the responsibility for the fund or object deposited. The stakeholder then drops out of the action, leaving the claimants to establish the valid claims. If the stakeholder claims a potential interest in the property, the court may order that the stakeholder post a bond or other security in an amount sufficient to guarantee the availability of the property upon resolution of the claims.

The second stage of the action involves the determination of the competing claims of the parties. This stage of interpleader resembles ordinary actions in most respects, and all other procedural rules, such as the discovery rules, apply to this stage of interpleader as they would to ordinary actions.

ADDITIONAL AUTHORITY

7 WRIGHT & MILLER §§ 1701-1750

4 MOORE'S FEDERAL PRACTICE §§ 22.01-22.08

4 ANDERSON'S OHIO CIVIL PRACTICE §§ 158.01-158.04

1 KLEIN DARLING AT 22-1 to AT 22-12

3 TEREZ F 7.6.1 to F 7.6.5

3 OH. JUR. PL. AND PRAC. FORMS, ch. 28

4 MILLIGAN Forms 22-1 to 22-36

1 FINK §§ 22-1 to 22-8

LEADING CASES

Action on Interest Not Barred by Interpleader Action

> *Hussey v. Aetna Life Ins. Co.*, 104 Ohio App. 3d 6, 660 N.E.2d 1228 (1995) (a second suit for interest was not prevented by res judicata after judgment in an interpleader action resolved the claims to life insurance policy proceeds)

Interest on Deposit

> *Hussey v. Aetna Life Ins. Co.*, 104 Ohio App. 3d 6, 660 N.E.2d 1228 (1995) (a party who wins a judgment for damages is entitled to interest earned on the amount deposited in an interest bearing account at the direction of the court)

Res Judicata; Subrogation Claim

John Hancock Mut. Life Ins. Co. v. Bird, 69 Ohio App. 3d 206, 590 N.E.2d 336
   (1990) (a person in privity with a party to an action upon which judgment was
   entered is precluded from re-litigating an issue raised in a prior action), *dismissed*, 57 Ohio St. 3d 712, 568 N.E.2d 689 (Ohio, Jan 30, 1991)

CHAPTER 23

Rule 23. Class Actions

Rule 23 reads as follows:

(A) Prerequisites to a class action. One or more members of a class may sue or be sued as representative parties on behalf of all only if

  (1) the class is so numerous that joinder of all members is impracticable,

  (2) there are questions of law or fact common to the class,

  (3) the claims or defenses of the representative parties are typical of the claims or defenses of the class, and

  (4) the representative parties will fairly and adequately protect the interests of the class.

(B) Class actions maintainable. An action may be maintained as a class action if the prerequisites of subdivision (A) are satisfied, and in addition:

  (1) the prosecution of separate actions by or against individual members of the class would create a risk of

    (a) inconsistent or varying adjudications with respect to individual members of the class which would establish incompatible standards of conduct for the party opposing the class; or

    (b) adjudications with respect to individual members of the class which would as a practical matter be dispositive of the interests of the other members not parties to the adjudications or substantially impair or impede their ability to protect their interests; or

  (2) the party opposing the class has acted or refused to act on grounds generally applicable to the class, thereby making appropriate final injunctive relief or corresponding declaratory relief with respect to the class as a whole; or

  (3) the court finds that the questions of law or fact common to the members of the class predominate over any questions affecting only individual members, and that a class action is superior to other available methods for the fair and efficient adjudication of the controversy. The matters pertinent to the findings include:

    (a) the interest of members of the class in individually controlling the prosecution or defense of separate actions;

    (b) the extent and nature of any litigation concerning the controversy already commenced by or against members of the class;

    (c) the desirability or undesirability of concentrating the litigation of the claims in the particular forum;

    (d) the difficulties likely to be encountered in the management of a class action.

(C) Determination by order whether class action to be maintained; notice; judgment; actions conducted partially as class actions.

    (1) As soon as practicable after the commencement of an action brought as a class action, the court shall determine by order whether it is to be so maintained. An order under this subdivision may be conditional, and may be altered or amended before the decision on the merits.

    (2) In any class action maintained under subdivision (B)(3), the court shall direct to the members of the class the best notice practicable under the circumstances, including individual notice to all members who can be identified through reasonable effort. The notice shall advise each member that

        (a) the court will exclude him from the class if he so requests by a specified date;

        (b) the judgment, whether favorable or not, will include all members who do not request exclusion; and

        (c) any member who does not request exclusion may, if he desires, enter an appearance through his counsel.

    (3) The judgment in an action maintained as a class action under subdivision (B)(1) or (B)(2), whether or not favorable to the class, shall include and describe those whom the court finds to be members of the class. The judgment in an action maintained as a class action under subdivision (B)(3), whether or not favorable to the class, shall include and specify or describe those to whom the notice provided in subdivision (C)(2) was directed, and who have not requested exclusion, and whom the court finds to be members of the class.

    (4) When appropriate (a) an action may be brought or maintained as a class action with respect to particular issues, or (b) a class may be divided into subclasses and each subclass treated as a class, and the provisions of this rule shall then be construed and applied accordingly.

(D) Orders in conduct of actions. In the conduct of actions to which this rule applies, the court may make appropriate orders:

    (1) determining the course of proceedings or prescribing measures to prevent undue repetition or complication in the presentation of evidence or argument;

(2) requiring, for the protection of the members of the class or otherwise for the fair conduct of the action, that notice be given in such manner as the court may direct to some or all of the members of any step in the action, or of the proposed extent of the judgment, or of the opportunity of members to signify whether they consider the representation fair and adequate, to intervene and present claims or defenses, or otherwise to come into the action;

(3) imposing conditions on the representative parties or on intervenors;

(4) requiring that the pleadings be amended to eliminate therefrom allegations as to representation of absent persons, and that the action proceed accordingly;

(5) dealing with similar procedural matters.

The orders may be combined with an order under Rule 16, and may be altered or amended as may be desirable from time to time.

(E) Dismissal or compromise. A class action shall not be dismissed or compromised without the approval of the court, and notice of the proposed dismissal or compromise shall be given to all members of the class in such manner as the court directs.

(F) Aggregation of claims. The claims of the class shall be aggregated in determining the jurisdiction of the court.

COMMENTARY

Rule 23 governs class actions, one of the most innovative joinder devices under the Rules. Class action procedures allow an action to be brought by or against a party who is representative of a class of persons who are similarly situated to the representative party with respect to the action. Each person in the class is not formally joined in the action, but the disposition of the action is binding on them with respect to the issues in the litigation. In practice, class actions brought by plaintiffs who are representative of a class are far more frequent than actions brought by individual plaintiffs against defendant classes. However, Rule 23 applies equally to both kinds of class actions. Ohio Rule 23 is virtually identical to Federal Rule of Civil Procedure 23, with the exception of minor stylistic changes and the addition of subsection (F).

Structure of Class Actions

The structure of Rule 23 suggests a two-stage procedure in class actions. First, subsection (C)(1) directs the court to certify that the class sought to be represented has satisfied the requirements for certification under subsections (A) and (B). Second, the court conducts the proceedings, with an eye toward the considerable discretion conferred upon it in subsections (D) and (E) to make appropriate orders to protect the interests of the members of the class and to regulate the conduct of the representatives and the attorneys for the class. In many cases, a third procedural stage, after a final judgment has been entered, is also appropriate. During this stage, the court renders decisions regarding attorneys' fees, makes orders regarding the notification of the members of the class of the disposition of the action, and takes any other steps it deems proper in protecting the interests of the members of the class.

Policies of Rule 23 and Advantages of Class Actions

In general, the policies of class actions are to achieve economies of time, expense, and effort, and to promote the uniformity of decision with regard to similarly situated persons. Accordingly, class actions may be advantageous for a number of reasons. First, they avoid the inefficiencies of multiple litigation by enabling a single action to resolve the claims of a large number of persons. In addition to drastically reducing the burden of individual actions on the courts, the class action allows a large number of persons, each of whom have been damaged or harmed in some small way, to pool their resources together so that the costs of litigation do not outweigh the possible remedy.

Second, class actions provide determinacy on issues that may affect a large number of individuals. Thus, the device allows parties in a class action to reduce the risk of inconsistent obligations because of incompatible judgments in separate actions.

Subsection (F) requires that the claims of all members of a class shall be combined for purposes of determining the jurisdiction of the court. Because the jurisdiction of municipal and county courts is limited to claims under $10,000 and $3000, respectively, class actions under subsection (B)(3) will rarely arise in these courts.

Prerequisites to Class Actions Generally

Subsection (A) lists the four prerequisites that must be satisfied before an action can qualify for class action treatment under the Rule. Although courts and commentators have sometimes expressed frustration at the lack of definition of these requirements or guidance on how they are to be applied, they are perhaps best conceptualized as addressing different aspects of the class sought to be certified. The first two requirements, commonly referred to as the "numerosity" and "commonality" requirements, focus on the characteristics of the defined class. The final two requirements, the "typicality" and "adequacy of representation" requirements, focus not on the class itself, but instead on the characteristics and quality of the representatives of the class.

This interpretation is supported by the order in which the requirements are presented in the Rule. If the class itself does not satisfy the minimal numerosity and commonality requirements, the first two presented in subsection (A), it is pointless to consider whether the representatives of the class satisfy the final two requirements set forth in that subsection.

Numerosity

The numerosity requirement is intended to ensure that the class is large enough such that joinder of the individual class members would be impracticable. This determination is largely dependent on the facts and circumstances on each case, and no one number of individuals renders the class sufficiently "numerous." In some instances, 200 members may not be numerous enough, whereas 30 members may be sufficient in other circumstances.

Illustration 23-1

Two hundred taxpayers wish to commence a class action against the Ohio Tax Authority, seeking an order to compel the Authority to recognize tax deductions for several capital losses experienced by the group in the past year. Although individual actions by each of the 200 plaintiffs may be burdensome on the judicial system, the court may refuse to certify the litigation as a class action because 200 litigants is not "numerous" in light of the 4 million taxpayers residing in the state.

Illustration 23-2

Thirty female employees wish to commence a class action against Brad's Food Emporium, seeking equitable relief from sexual harassment occurring at their place of employment. Brad's Food Emporium employs a total of 75 individuals, 30 females and 45 males. The court will likely certify the litigation as a class action because a class of 30 employees is likely to be considered "numerous" under the circumstances.

Commonality

The commonality requirement, at a minimum, suggests that at least one question of law or fact must be common to all members of the class. Although this requirement is frequently considered in conjunction with the typicality requirement, the better view is that the commonality requirement dictates that the class be defined in a manner sufficient to readily identify the members of the class. Cases that have denied certification to classes on the grounds that the class was too vague should be considered as classes that did not satisfy the commonality requirement.

Illustration 23-3

As the representative of all poor persons within the city of Columbus, Frank commences an action against the Columbus police department, alleging that the department discriminates against persons based upon their economic status. Although Frank and other individual litigants may have valid claims, the court should not certify Frank's suit as a class action, as the designation of the class as "all poor persons within the city of Columbus" is too vague to satisfy the requirements of Rule 23(A).

Typicality

The typicality requirement ensures that the claims or defenses of the representative parties substantially duplicate those that would have probably been presented by the absent members of the class. If the same transaction or occurrence lies at the heart of the litigation for the representatives of the class and the individual class members, the requirement should be deemed to have been met.

Illustration 23-4

Jose commences an action against Gargantua Gold Mining Corp. as the representative of a class of all stockholders of the company. Jose alleges that Gargantua failed to provide him with a detailed prospectus of the company at the time he purchased his shares, as required by SEC regulations. Under these circumstances, the court should probably not certify Jose's suit as a class action, as it is unlikely that Jose's claim is typical of the claims of the other members of the class.

Adequacy of Representation

The adequacy of representation requirement plays an important role in the certification process. Perhaps more than any other, this requirement ensures the integrity of the court and the class action device itself by assuring that the absent class members have had an adequate opportunity to have their grievances heard. Because the disposition of the class action is binding on all members of the class, due process objections obtain when those members are not adequately represented. Factors to be considered in determining whether or not this requirement is satisfied include the characteristics of the representatives of the class, including the personal stake of the representatives in the action, and the quality, adequacy, and experience of the attorneys who will represent the class.

Illustration 23-5

Jennifer, a pilot employed by Hyskie Airlines, commences an action against Hyskie Airlines as the representative of all current and former pilots of the airline.

In the action, Jennifer alleges that Hyskie Airlines promotion practices and pension programs constitute unlawful sex discrimination in violation of Ohio law. Before the class is certified, Hyskie agrees to eliminate the offending conduct, but the parties cannot agree with regard to backpay, pension funding, or retroactive seniority. Under these circumstances, Jennifer is an inadequate representative of the pilots formerly employed by the airline because of a possible conflict of interest with regard to pension funding and distributions.

Categories of Class Actions Generally

Subsection (B) defines the three categories of class actions. After the court concludes that the requirements of subsection (A) have been satisfied, it must determine which category of class action the instant case belongs to. This categorization has implications for the procedure to be taken in the action.

Subsection (B)(1)(a)—Risk of Inconsistent Obligations

Certification under subsection (B)(1)(a) is appropriate when the prosecution of separate actions by or against individual members of the class would create a risk of inconsistent obligations or incompatible standards of conduct for the party opposing the class.

Illustration 23-6

In Springfield, a number of the municipality's bondholders would like to bring an action against the municipality seeking to have the bond issue invalidated. However, other bondholders would like to limit the issue, and still others want to enforce interest payments on the issue. Judgments in favor of each of these persons would create inconsistent obligations for the municipality, and a class action covering all of the bondholders is best-suited to a uniform resolution of the case.

Subsection (B)(1)(b)—Impairment of Interests in Separate Actions

Certification under subsection (B)(1)(b) is appropriate when the prosecution of separate actions by or against individual members of the class would, as a practical matter, be dispositive of, or substantially impair or impede the ability to protect, the interests of the other members of the class. Because of the similarity of this standard with the definition of "necessary" parties under Rule 19, class actions are excepted, in subsection (D) of that Rule, from its mandatory joinder requirement.

Illustration 23-7

Shari commences an action against Dick's Distribution Company as the representative of a class of shareholders to force the company to declare a dividend. The court should certify the suit as a class action under 23(B)(1)(b), as success in the action would be dispositive of all other shareholders' interests.

Subsection (B)(2)—Declaratory or Injunctive Relief Sought

Certification of a class under subsection (B)(2) is most suitable when the party opposing the class has acted or has refused to act in a manner that has affected the entire class. Thus, declaratory judgments or permanent injunctions are the primary remedies being sought by the representatives of the class in actions certified under this subsection. However, because of the disfavor accorded to class actions certified under subsection (B)(3), certification under subsection (B)(2) is not restricted to class actions in which the remedy sought is limited to only declaratory or injunctive relief. The representatives of the class may also seek monetary damages as an incident to the declaratory judgment or injunction.

Illustration 23-8

Ken commences a civil rights action against Diane's Grocery as the representative of a class of customers seeking injunctive relief from discrimination based on religious belief. The court should certify the suit as a class action under Rule 23(B)(2), as Diane's Grocery has discriminated against class members in a manner that has affected the entire class.

Illustration 23-9

Assume on the facts of Illustration 23-8 that the action brought by Ken seeks monetary damages as well as injunctive relief. Although class actions certified under Rule 23(B)(2) ordinarily involve requests for declaratory or injunctive relief, the court will still certify Ken's action as a Rule 23(B)(2) class action.

Subsection (B)(3)—Common Questions of Law or Fact Generally

Certification under subsection (B)(3) is the most controversial, and perhaps unfortunately, the most frequently used category for classifying class actions. To properly certify a class action under this subsection, the court is required to make two special findings in addition to the four ordinarily required.

"Dominant Commonality"

The court must first determine that questions of law or fact common to the members of the class predominate over any questions affecting only individual members. Although this requirement would appear to duplicate the commonality prerequisite of subsection (A), the commonality required for certification under subsection (B)(3) is more appropriately characterized as "dominant commonality." Such a determination, at the very least, requires the court to find that the common questions of law or fact to be resolved in the class action would be those questions that must be resolved in every individual case if the actions were brought separately.

Illustration 23-10

Cain commences an action against the city of Jefferson as the representative of a class of landowners seeking an order declaring a city regulation as a "taking" and requiring compensation be paid to each of the landowners. Although the amount of compensation to be paid to each landowner presents a separate issue, the court should certify the litigation as a class action under Rule 23(B)(3), as the question of whether the city's regulation constitutes a "taking" predominates over the question as to the amount of compensation that should be paid to each landowner.

Requirement that Class Action Be Superior to Other Methods

Next, to certify a class action under subsection (B)(3), the court must determine that a class action is superior to other available methods for the fair and efficient adjudication of the matter. Other available methods include individual actions by the members of the class, class arbitration, where available, and administrative proceedings. The Rule presents a nonexhaustive list of the factors to be considered by the court in making these determinations. They include: (1) the interest of the members of the class in maintaining individual actions compared to a single class action; (2) the extent of any litigation concerning the action that has already commenced by or against members of the class; (3) the advantages of litigating the class action in the particular court where the class action was filed, including the location of key evidence or witnesses; and (4) any administrative difficulties that are likely to be encountered in the management of a class action.

Procedural Requirements of Class Actions Generally

Subsection (C) contains certain procedural provisions that must be satisfied in all class actions. However, subsection (C) is most noted for its notification requirements in class actions certified under subsection (B)(3).

Certification of Class Actions Mandatory

Subsection (C)(1) requires the court to make a certification of the class as soon as practicable after the commencement of the action. Certification is thus mandatory, and class actions may not be maintained without findings by the court that the prerequisites of subsection (A) have been met and without a classification of the class action into one of the three categories listed in subsection (B). This certification may be conditioned upon the occurrence or fulfillment of a future event, and any certification order may be altered or amended at any time before a final judgment has been entered, including the authority conferred by subsection (C)(4) to divide the class into subclasses and treat each class as a separate class or as individual actions.

Appealability of Certification Orders

Ohio courts have taken a rather unusual approach to the question of whether certification orders of trial court with respect to class actions are immediately appealable nonwithstanding their seemingly interlocutory status. This probably should not be surprising considering the extraordinary confusion engendered by O.R.C. § 2505.02, which governs appeals of interlocutory orders.

Although an exhaustive discussion of § 2505.02 is beyond the scope of this manual, the Ohio Supreme Court has ruled that this section permits a party to take an immediate appeal of an order of a trial court denying class certification. However, an order granting class certification is not appealable under this provision, and an aggrieved defendant (in most cases, the defendant will be opposing certification of the class) must await the outcome of the litigation and a final judgment before taking an appeal on the certification issue. It should be noted that Federal Rule of Civil Procedure has recently added a subsection (f), which confers upon courts of appeals the discretion to hear appeals of grants or denials of certification orders in federal court. Defendants should thus seek to remove cases, where appropriate, to federal court when the question of class certification will be contested.

Notification of Members of a Class Certified Under Subsection (B)(3)

Subsection (C)(2) is a provision especially tailored to the constitutional considerations inherent in class actions. The disposition of class actions are, of course, binding on all members of the certified class unless those members have opted out of the class. Yet the great majority of the members of any certified class are not physically present before the court, so the procedural posture of class actions must contain additional protections to preserve the constitutional rights of these absent members to have their disputes resolved fairly in court. Because of the loosely-knit nature of classes certified under subsection (B)(3), additional protection of the constitutional rights of the absent class members is provided in subsection (C)(2). This additional protection is thought to be unnecessary in class actions certified under subsections (B)(1) or (B)(2) because of the more tightly-defined nature of such classes and the likelihood that members of those classes will be timely and correctly apprised of the existence of the class action and the possible consequences upon its disposition.

Subsection (C)(2) requires that all members of a class certified under subsection (B)(3) must be notified that they are members of a class that is the subject of a class action, that each member of the class may choose to "opt out" of the action, that every member who does not choose to "opt out" will be bound by the judgment, whether it is favorable to the class or not, and that each member of the class may be represented in the class action by an attorney of that member's own choosing. The notification must be made in the best manner practicable under the circumstances, and if the names and addresses of the members of the class can be ascertained with reasonable effort, individual notification must be made. This notification is distinct from any service of process in class actions, which generally is required only for the named representatives of the class.

Illustration 23-11

In a certified class consisting of 2000 former employees of Big Off-Blue Corp., a large computer company with annual revenues of over $2 billion, the last-known addresses of the employees satisfying the criteria of the class can be ascertained only through a search of Big Off-Blue's files. A judge is likely to order that each of the members of the class must be notified personally of the class action, as the effort and expense involved is not disproportionate to the size of the company with respect to the number of members in the class.

Contents of Judgments in Class Actions

Subsection (C)(3) provides that judgments in all class actions must include and describe those persons who the court determines are members of the class and on whom the judgment will bind. The subsection further provides that judgments in class actions certified under subsection (B)(3) must also specify or describe those persons to whom notice of the action had been provided and must specify those persons who requested exclusion from the class.

Court Management of Class Actions—Orders

Subsection (D) provides the court with substantial authority to retain control over the management of the action. This provision complements the expanded authority of the court under Rule 16. The kinds of orders contemplated for the management of class actions are identified in subsection (D), but the list is not exhaustive.

Court Management of Class Actions—Dismissals and Settlements

Subsection (E) states that class actions may not be dismissed or otherwise compromised, such as through a settlement, without the permission of the court. The court must prescribe the method in which notice of the approved settlement or dismissal is provided to members of the class. This provision reinforces the concept of the court as playing an active role in the management and overall control of class actions.

ADDITIONAL AUTHORITY

7A WRIGHT & MILLER §§ 1751-1780

7B WRIGHT & MILLER §§ 1781-1820

5 MOORE'S FEDERAL PRACTICE §§ 23.01-23.110

4 ANDERSON'S OHIO CIVIL PRACTICE §§ 158.05-158.21

1 KLEIN DARLING AT 23-1 to AT 23-17

3 TEREZ F 8.1.1 to F 8.1.3, F 8.2.1 to F 8.2.5, F 8.3.1 to F 8.3.5

3 OH. JUR. PL. AND PRAC. FORMS, ch. 29

4 MILLIGAN Forms 23-1 to 23-71

1 FINK §§ 23-1 to 23-33

OHIO LITIGATION CHECKLISTS, Parties and Actions, §§ 4, 5

LEADING CASES

Adequacy of Representation and Typicality Requirements

> *Baughman v. State Farm Mut. Auto. Ins. Co.*, 88 Ohio St. 3d 480, 727 N.E.2d 1265 (2000) (the typicality or adequacy of representation requirements are not destroyed by a unique defense unless the defense is so central to the action that it threatens to preoccupy the representative to the other class members' detriment)

Adequacy of Representation; Counsel

> *Cleveland Bd. of Educ. v. Armstrong World Indus.*, 22 Ohio Misc. 2d 18, 476 N.E.2d 397 (C.P. 1985) (the requirement of adequacy of representation by counsel is satisfied where counsel is able and experienced and where the danger of a collusive suit potentially detrimental to the interests of the class is nonexistent)

Appealability of Certification Order

> *Chamberlain v. AK Steel Corp.*, 82 Ohio St. 3d 389, 696 N.E.2d 569 (1998) (Lundberg Stratton, J., dissenting) (there is no reason why an order of a trial court denying class certification is a final appealable order because it constitutes a "special proceeding" under O.R.C. § 2505.02, whereas an order granting class certification is not a final appealable order under the same rationale)

Dayton Women's Health Ctr. v. Enix, 52 Ohio St. 3d 67, 55 N.E.2d 956 (1990) (an order determining that an action may or may not be maintained as a class action is a final appealable order), *cert. denied*, 498 U.S. 1047 (1991)

Blumenthal v. Medina Supply Co., 100 Ohio App. 3d 473, 654 N.E.2d 368 (the grant of class certification by a court is not a final appealable order), *appeal not allowed*, 72 Ohio St. 3d 1530, 649 N.E.2d 839 (1995)

Class Certification; Deferral of Motion

Jackson v. Glidden Co., 98 Ohio App. 3d 100, 647 N.E.2d 879 (1995) (a court is warranted in deferring a ruling on a motion for class certification until it has passed on motions to dismiss the complaint)

Class Certification Inappropriate

In re Kroger Co. Shareholders Litig., 70 Ohio App. 3d 52, 590 N.E.2d 391 (1990) (where substantial conflicts of interest are evident among members of a class and where the requirements of typicality and adequate representation are not met, an action should not be certified as a class action)

Class Certification; Standard on Appeal

Hamilton v. Ohio Savings Bank, 82 Ohio St. 3d 67, 694 N.E.2d 442 (1998) (denial of class certification is reversible only for an abuse of discretion)

Class Member Has No Standing to Appeal Settlement

Volante v. Harding Business College, 83 Ohio App. 3d 548, 615 N.E.2d 324 (1992) (an unnamed class member does not have standing to appeal the settlement of a class action that has been approved by the court)

Common Question of Law or Fact

Shaver v. Standard Oil Co., 68 Ohio App. 3d 783, 589 N.E.2d 1348 (1990) (common questions of law or fact must represent a substantial aspect of a class and must be capable of resolution for all members of the class in a single adjudication), *jurisdictional motion overruled*, 58 Ohio St. 3d 711, 570 N.E.2d 280 (1991), *and appeal after remand*, 89 Ohio App. 3d 52, 623 N.E.2d 602, *appeal dismissed*, 67 Ohio St. 3d 1478, 620 N.E.2d 851 (1993)

Defendant Classes; Certification Requirements

Planned Parenthood Ass'n v. Project Jericho, 52 Ohio St. 3d 56, 556 N.E.2d 157 (1990) (defendant classes may be certified pursuant to Rule 23, though the trial court must make the same affirmative findings as those required for plaintiff class actions)

Description of Class Must Be Clear

Petty v. Wal-Mart Stores, 148 Ohio App. 3d 348, 773 N.E.2d 576 (2002) (the definition of a class must be sufficiently precise so that it is administratively feasible for the court to determine whether a particular individual is a member)

Simmons v. Am. Gen. Life & Acc. Ins. Co., 140 Ohio App. 3d 503, 748 N.E.2d 122 (2000) (the requirement that there be a class will not be deemed satisfied unless the description of it is sufficiently definite so that it is administratively feasible for the court to determine whether a particular individual is a member)

Disposition of Settlement Fund

In re Miamisburg Train Derailment Litig., 92 Ohio App. 3d 304, 635 N.E.2d 46 (1993) (a court, in its discretion, may distribute funds to undercompensated plaintiffs rather than returning to defendant the amount where the defendant renounced any right or expectation of return of the unspent balance of a settlement fund), *dismissed, jurisdictional motion overruled*, 69 Ohio St. 3d 1418, 630 N.E.2d 737, *and dismissed, jurisdictional motion overruled*, 69 Ohio St. 3d 1449, 633 N.E.2d 543, *and cause dismissed*, 69 Ohio St. 3d 1492, 635 N.E.2d 381 (1994)

Dominant Commonality

Cope v. Metropolitan Life Ins. Co., 82 Ohio St. 3d 426, 696 N.E.2d 1001 (1998) (the dominant commonality, or predominance requirement, will be satisfied where generalized evidence would prove or disprove an element of the claim for each member of the class)

Findings of Fact on Certification Decisions

Hamilton v. Ohio Sav. Bank, 82 Ohio St. 3d 67, 694 N.E.2d 442 (1998) (although there is no explicit requirement in Rule 23 that the trial court make formal findings to support its decision on a motion for class certification, there are compelling policy reasons for doing so)

Inadequate Notice to Class Members

Meek v. Gem Boat Serv., 69 Ohio App. 3d 404, 590 N.E.2d 1296 (1990) (an action should not proceed as a class action where the court has failed to comply with the requirements of Rule 23(C)(2)), *jurisdictional motion overruled*, 57 Ohio St. 3d 720, 568 N.E.2d 699 (1991)

Order Limiting Discovery on Certification Motion

Burrell v. Sol Bergman Estate Jewelers, Inc., 77 Ohio App. 3d 766, 603 N.E.2d 1059 (1991) (a trial court did not abuse its discretion in limiting discovery concerning class certification issues to prevent a "fishing expedition" to discover other potential members of a class), *jurisdictional motion overruled*, 63 Ohio St. 3d 1406, 585 N.E.2d 428 (1992)

"Predominance" Requirement

Breedlove v. Ohio Dep't of Transp., 62 Ohio Misc. 2d 298, 598 N.E.2d 242 (C.P. 1991) (common questions must predominate over questions affecting individual members to permit the certification of a class)

Predominance; Satisfaction of Requirement

Cope v. Metropolitan Life Ins. Co., 82 Ohio St. 3d 126, 696 N.E.2d 1001 (1998) (a class satisfies the predominance requirement when generalized evidence exists to prove or disprove an element on a simultaneous, class-wide basis, because such proof obviates the need to examine each class member's individual position)

Rule 23(B)(2) Action Inappropriate

James v. ITT Fin. Servs., No. 64547 (8th Dist.), 1994 Ohio App. LEXIS 77 (where the primary relief requested is in the form of damages rather than an injunction, Rule 23(B)(2) is inapplicable)

Settlement of Class Action

In re Kroger Co. Shareholders Litig., 70 Ohio App. 3d 52, 590 N.E.2d 391 (1990) (in determining whether a proposed class settlement should be approved, a trial court should consider the fairness and reasonableness of the proposed settlement to all who are affected by it, the adequacy of the settlement to the class members, and whether the settlement is in the public interest)

State Law Variations Must Be Analyzed

Simmons v. Am. Gen. Life & Acc. Ins. Co., 140 Ohio App. 3d 503, 748 N.E.2d 122 (2000) (a party seeking class certification must demonstrate, through extensive analysis of state law variances, that the variations in state law do not swamp any common issues and defeat predominance)

Statute of Limitations

Beavercreek Local Sch. v. Basic, Inc., 71 Ohio App. 3d 669, 595 N.E.2d 360 (the statute of limitations is tolled upon the commencement of a class action as to all asserted members of the class until a member opts out), *motion to certify overruled*, 61 Ohio St. 3d 1431, 575 N.E.2d 219 (1991)

Subclasses

Breedlove v. Ohio Dep't of Transp., 62 Ohio Misc. 2d 298, 598 N.E.2d 242 (C.P. 1991) (where subclasses of plaintiffs would fail to qualify for subclass treatment due to predomination of individual issues and failure to meet numerosity requirements, resolution of a suit through subclasses is inappropriate)

Subsection (B)(2) Certification Improper

Logsdon v. National City Bank, 62 Ohio Misc. 2d 449, 601 N.E.2d 262 (C.P. 1991) (where the plaintiffs seek damages primarily, certification of the class pursuant to Rule 23(B)(2) is improper, because this Rule applies to classes primarily seeking final injunctive or declaratory relief)

"Superiority" Requirement

Cleveland Bd. of Educ. v. Armstrong World Indus., 22 Ohio Misc. 2d 18, 476 N.E.2d 397 (C.P. 1985) (the requirement of "superiority" means that pursuing an action as a class is "more advanced or higher, greater or more excellent than another in any respect")

Typicality Requirement Explained

Baughman v. State Farm Mut. Auto. Ins. Co., 88 Ohio St. 3d 480, 727 N.E.2d 1265 (2000) (the typicality requirement to class certification is satisfied if the claim arises from the same event, practice, or course of conduct from which the claims of other class members arise; the requirement is usually met, regardless of varying underlying fact patterns, if the same unlawful conduct was allegedly directed at or affected both the class members and the plaintiff)

Unique Defense

Hamilton v. Ohio Sav. Bank, 82 Ohio St. 3d 67, 694 N.E.2d 442 (1998) (unique defense will not destroy the typicality or adequacy of representation requirements so as to preclude class certification unless the defense is so central to the litigation that it threatens to preoccupy the class representative to the detriment of the other class members)

CHAPTER 23.1

Rule 23.1. Derivative Actions by Shareholders

Rule 23.1 reads as follows:

In a derivative action brought by one or more legal or equitable owners of shares to enforce a right of a corporation, the corporation having failed to enforce a right which may properly be asserted by it, the complaint shall be verified and shall allege that the plaintiff was a shareholder at the time of the transaction of which he complains or that his share thereafter devolved on him by operation of law. The complaint shall also allege with particularity the efforts, if any, made by the plaintiff to obtain the action he desires from the directors and, if necessary, from the shareholders and the reasons for his failure to obtain the action or for not making the effort. The derivative action may not be maintained if it appears that the plaintiff does not fairly and adequately represent the interests of the shareholders similarly situated in enforcing the right of the corporation. The action shall not be dismissed or compromised without the approval of the court, and notice of the proposed dismissal or compromise shall be given to shareholders in such manner as the court directs.

COMMENTARY

Rule 23.1 governs shareholder derivative actions, special kinds of class actions that may be brought by the stockholder of a corporation. The action is designed to provide a shareholder with the means to enforce a right of action that belongs to the corporation which the persons in control of the corporation refuse to enforce.

Illustration 23.1-1

Ely, a shareholder of Gangster Graphics Incorporated, learns that several officers of the corporation are guilty of criminal wrongdoing. Despite Ely's repeated requests that action be taken by the corporation against the wrongdoers, Gangster Graphics does not pursue the matter. Under Rule 23.1, Ely may commence a shareholder derivative action against Gangster Graphics to force the corporation to take action against the wrongdoers.

Requirements of Derivative Actions

To properly bring a shareholder derivative action under Rule 23.1, the plaintiff must allege that he was a shareholder at the time of the transaction of which he complains or that his share thereafter devolved on him by operation of law. The plaintiff must also set forth the efforts in obtaining the desired action from those persons in control of the corporation, an obligation frequently referred to as the demand requirement. Such a demand generally protects the rights of the directors and shareholders of a corporation to control the actions of the organization. In general, only when the corporation refuses to take the desired action is a shareholder derivative appropriate.

Court's Power to Dismiss

The court has the power to dismiss the action if it appears that the plaintiff does not fairly and adequately represent the interests of the other shareholders in the action. Furthermore, the Rule confers upon the court broad discretion to conduct the action in a manner it deems appropriate. The action can be dismissed only by order of the court, and only after proper notice of the pending dismissal has been provided to all other shareholders.

ADDITIONAL AUTHORITY

7C WRIGHT & MILLER §§ 1821-1860
5 MOORE'S FEDERAL PRACTICE §§ 23.1.01-23.1.17
4 ANDERSON'S OHIO CIVIL PRACTICE §§ 158.22-158.27
1 KLEIN DARLING AT 23.1-1 to AT 23.1-3
3 TEREZ F 4.23.3 to F 4.23.6
3 OH. JUR. PL. AND PRAC. FORMS, ch. 30
4 MILLIGAN Forms 23.1-1 to 23.1-36
1 FINK §§ 23.1-1 to 23.1-12

LEADING CASES

Breach of Fiduciary Duty

Grand Council v. Owens, 86 Ohio App. 3d 215, 620 N.E.2d 234 (1993) (generally, actions for breach of fiduciary duties may be brought pursuant to Rule 23.1)

Direct Cause of Action Improper

Weston v. Weston Paper & Mfg. Co., 74 Ohio St. 3d 377, 658 N.E.2d 1058 (1996) (a direct cause of action was improper where there was no separate and distinct injury to the rights of the plaintiffs)

Direct Cause of Action Proper

Yackel v. Kay, 95 Ohio App. 3d 472, 642 N.E.2d 1107 (a direct cause of action, rather than a derivative action, is appropriate where the majority shareholder of a close corporation receives excessive compensation), *appeal not allowed*, 70 Ohio St. 3d 1457, 639 N.E.2d 795 (1994)

Lack of Commonality Precludes Independent Action

Abrahamson v. Waddell, 63 Ohio Misc. 2d 270, 624 N.E.2d 1118 (C.P. 1992) (a shareholder who has suffered no injury other than that in common with other shareholders has no independent cause of action)

Representativeness of Plaintiff

HER, Inc. v. Parenteau, 147 Ohio App. 3d 285, 770 N.E.2d 105 (2002) (in evaluating whether a plaintiff in a shareholder derivative suit fairly and adequately represents the interests of similarly situated shareholders, the court should consider: (1) the economic antagonisms between the representative and the class; (2) the remedy sought by plaintiff in the action; (3) indications that the named plaintiff was not the driving force behind the litigation; (4) plaintiff's unfamiliarity with the litigation; (5) other litigation pending between the plaintiff and defendants; (6) the relative magnitude of plaintiff's personal interests as compared to his interest in the derivative action itself; (7) plaintiff's vindictiveness toward the defendants; and (8) the degree of support plaintiff was receiving from the shareholders he purports to represent)

Requirements for Maintenance of Derivative Action

Weston v. Weston Paper & Mfg. Co., 74 Ohio St. 3d 377, 658 N.E.2d 1058 (1996) (plaintiffs must specify efforts made to have directors or other shareholders take demanded action, explain why they failed in this effort, and show that they fairly and adequately represent the interests of similarly situated shareholders)

CHAPTER 24

Rule 24. Intervention

Rule 24 reads as follows:

(A) Intervention of right. Upon timely application anyone shall be permitted to intervene in an action:

    (1)   when a statute of this state confers an unconditional right to intervene; or

    (2)   when the applicant claims an interest relating to the property or transaction that is the subject of the action and the applicant is so situated that the disposition of the action may as a practical matter impair or impede the applicant's ability to protect that interest, unless the applicant's interest is adequately represented by existing parties.

(B) Permissive intervention. Upon timely application anyone may be permitted to intervene in an action:

    (1)   when a statute of this state confers a conditional right to intervene; or

    (2)   when an applicant's claim or defense and the main action have a question of law or fact in common.

    When a party to an action relies for ground of claim or defense upon any statute or executive order administered by a federal or state governmental officer or agency or upon any regulation, order, requirement or agreement issued or made pursuant to the statute or executive order, the officer or agency upon timely application may be permitted to intervene in the action. In exercising its discretion the court shall consider whether the intervention will unduly delay or prejudice the adjudication of the rights of the original parties.

(C) Procedure. A person desiring to intervene shall serve a motion to intervene upon the parties as provided in Civ. R. 5. The motion and any supporting memorandum shall state the grounds for intervention and shall be accompanied by a pleading, as defined in Civ. R. 7(A), setting forth the claim or defense for which intervention is sought. The same procedure shall be followed when a statute of this state gives a right to intervene.

COMMENTARY

Rule 24 governs intervention, a procedure through which a nonparty in an action whose interests are affected by the action may seek to become a party. The Rule strikes a balance between protecting the interests of nonparties without infringing upon the rights of the parties in the action. Historically, the procedure was divided into intervention as of right, which was applicable only in a narrow range of circumstances, and permissive intervention, which required leave of the court. Rule 24 preserves this distinction, but substantially broadens the scope of intervention as of right.

Intervention as of Right—When Appropriate

Subsection (A) provides two circumstances in which a person may intervene in an action. First, a state statute may provide for such an unconditional right to intervene in certain situations. Subsection (A)(2) sets forth the second, more frequently-encountered situation. It allows a person to intervene in an action without having to secure the court's permission if three requirements are met. Of course, the court will determine if the requirements have been met, and if the court finds that intervention as of right is not available to a person, that person may intervene in the action only with the court's permission. A determination that the requirements of subsection (A) have not been met are reviewable *de novo* by the appellate court.

Requirements Under Subsection (A)(2)

First, a person seeking to intervene under subsection (A)(2) must claim an interest relating to the property or transaction that is the subject of the action. Although the traditional operation of intervention required that the quality of the claimed interest be substantial and legally protectable, such as a property right, the Rule expands the concept to those practical interests that may not be enforceable as legally protectable ones.

Second, the intervenor must demonstrate that the disposition of the action may practically impair or impede that person's ability to subsequently protect the claimed interest. Traditionally, intervention as of right was proper only when the person seeking to intervene demonstrated that it would be legally bound by the judgment, such as through the doctrine of *res judicata*. Under the Rule, however, virtually any practical impact on the intervenor's ability to protect the interest, such as the force that a judgment may have on a subsequent action by the intervenor through the doctrine of *stare decisis*, will be sufficient.

Third, a person seeking to intervene must show that the claimed interest is not adequately represented by the existing parties in the action. In many cases, inadequate representation will be readily apparent, such as when the interests of the existing parties are hostile to that of the intervening party, or when a party who may have, at one time, adequately represented the interest of the intervening party but who has since waived the issue or has made a pretrial stipulation to its non-litigation. For example, adequate representation will usually be found to exist in class actions and actions represented by an administrator or executor.

Illustration 24-1

Thomas, the executor of an estate containing several rental properties, commences an action against the tenants of the properties seeking to void the leases and evict the tenants. Sally, a beneficiary under the will, seeks to intervene in the action to protect her interest. Although the resolution of the action will affect Sally's interest as a practical matter, the court will likely deny Sally's petition to intervene because she has made no showing that Thomas will not adequately represent the interests of all beneficiaries of the will.

Permissive Intervention Generally

Subsection (B) sets forth three circumstances in which a person may intervene with the permission of the court. When a person seeks to intervene under subsection (B), the court may consider a broad range of factors in deciding whether or not to allow the person to intervene, and the court's decision will be reversed only for an abuse of discretion.

Permissive Intervention—When Appropriate

First, a state statute may confer a conditional right to intervene in an action. As with intervention as of right, these statutes are applicable only in unusual situations.

Second, a person may seek to intervene in an action with the permission of the court when the person's potential claim or defense in a subsequent action has an issue of law or fact in common with the current action. This provision allows the court to grant intervention in a broad range of situations. However, denial of intervention is proper when it would unfairly prejudice the interests of the existing parties or when it would unduly prolong the litigation.

The second sentence of subsection (B) describes the final situation in which intervention may be granted by the court. It provides that a federal or state governmental officer or agency may seek intervention in an action when a party to the action invokes a statute, executive order, regulation, or related paper administered by that officer or agency as part of its case-in-chief or defense.

Procedure for Intervention

Subsection (C) sets forth the procedure to be used when a person seeks to intervene under either subsection (A) or (B). The person must serve a motion on all parties in the action in accordance with the service provisions of Rule 5. The motion must describe the grounds for the intervention and whether the intervention sought is permissive or as of right. The person must also file a pleading, which should delineate the claim or defense for which intervention is sought. In most cases, the pleading will be largely duplicative of the contents of the motion. The motion and pleading must, of course, be filed with the court. Although the pleading requirement appeared to be unambiguous under the Rule, a 1999 amendment reinforces the requirement by indicating that the pleading must be one of the documents listed in Rule 7(A) (in most cases, it will be a complaint). The court will then decide on the propriety of the motion and whether the person's application to intervene on the grounds specified in the motion is proper.

Timeliness of Motion

Although the Rule provides no instruction on relevant considerations in deciding whether a motion is timely, the Ohio Supreme Court has provided several factors that will assist a court in determining whether intervention is appropriate. First, a court should consider the point to which the suit had progressed. Second, a court should inquire into the purpose for which intervention is sought. Third, the court should examine the length of time preceding the application during which the proposed intervenor knew or reasonably should have known of his interest in the case. Fourth, the court should explore any prejudice to original parties due to the proposed intervenor's failure after he knew or reasonably should have known of his interest in the case to apply promptly for intervention. Finally, the court should examine all unusual circumstances militating against or in favor of intervention.

Motions to intervene under either subsection (A) or (B) must be made in a "timely" fashion. The Rule provides no guidance on what constitutes a "timely" motion, and logic implies that the same considerations in making such a determination should not be given equal weight on motions to intervene as of right and motions to intervene permissively. Specifically, the degree to which the interest of a person seeking to intervene as of right may be impaired or impeded should affect the determination whether or not the motion was timely. A denial of a motion to intervene on grounds that it is untimely is reversible only for an abuse of discretion.

ADDITIONAL AUTHORITY

7C WRIGHT & MILLER §§ 1901-1950
6 MOORE'S FEDERAL PRACTICE §§ 24.01-24.24
4 ANDERSON'S OHIO CIVIL PRACTICE §§ 155.24-155.27
1 KLEIN DARLING AT 24-1 to AT 24-26
3 TEREZ F 7.5.1 to F 7.5.3
3 OH. JUR. PL. AND PRAC. FORMS, ch. 31
4 MILLIGAN Forms 24-1 to 24-42
1 FINK §§ 24-1 to 24-10
OHIO LITIGATION CHECKLISTS, Parties and Actions, § 9

LEADING CASES

Appealability of Motion to Intervene

South Ohio Coal Co. v. Kidney, 100 Ohio App. 3d 661, 654 N.E.2d 1017 (the grant of a person's motion to intervene is a final appealable order), *appeal not allowed*, 72 Ohio St. 3d 1530, 649 N.E.2d 839 (1995)

Intervention After Expiration of Statute of Limitations

Continental Ins. Co. v. Twedell, 100 Ohio Misc.2d 25, 717 N.E.2d 1195 (M.C. 1998) (a party generally may not intervene into a cause of action after the expiration of the statute of limitations; however, an exception provides that a movant may intervene in an action after the expiration of the statute of limitations if the movant is a real party in interest, that is, a co-owner of a pending claim)

Intervention After Final Judgment

State ex rel. First New Shiloh Baptist Church v. Meagher, 82 Ohio St. 3d 501, 696 N.E.2d 1058 (1998) (intervention after final judgment has been entered is unusual and will not ordinarily be granted)

Intervention of Right; Generally

Fouche v. Denihan, 66 Ohio App. 3d 120, 583 N.E.2d 457 (1990) (to intervene as of right, a person must show an interest in the matter which is the subject of the action the disposition of which could impede the ability of that person to protect the claimed interest and that none of the parties represent his interest)

Permissive Intervention Broadly Construed

State ex rel. Superamerica Group v. Licking Cty. Bd of Elections, 80 Ohio St. 3d 182, 685 N.E.2d 507 (1997) (Rule 24 is to be liberally construed in favor of intervention, provided that all procedural requirements have been satisfied)

Pleading Required with Intervention Motion

State ex rel. Polo v. Cuyahoga County Bd. of Elections, 74 Ohio St. 3d 143, 656 N.E.2d 1277 (1995) (a motion to intervene must be accompanied by a pleading setting forth a claim or defense)

Timeliness of Intervention Motion

West Am. Ins. Co v. Dutt, 70 Ohio App. 3d 422, 591 N.E.2d 552 (1990) (a motion to intervene must be timely with regard to the statute of limitations and in the context of trial proceedings)

Timeliness of Intervention Motion; Considerations

State ex rel. First New Shiloh Baptist Church v. Meagher, 82 Ohio St. 3d 501, 696 N.E.2d 1058 (1998) (the timeliness of an intervention motion is determined by the following factors: (1) the point to which the suit had progressed; (2) the purpose for which intervention is sought; (3) the length of time preceding the application during which the proposed intervenor knew or reasonably should have known of his interest in the case; (4) the prejudice to the original parties due to the proposed intervenor's failure after he knew or reasonably should have known of his interest in the case to apply promptly for intervention; and (5) the existence of unusual circumstances militating against or in favor of intervention)

CHAPTER 25

Rule 25. Substitution of Parties

Rule 25 reads as follows:

(A) Death.

    (1)   If a party dies and the claim is not thereby extinguished, the court shall, upon motion, order substitution of the proper parties. The motion for substitution may be made by any party or by the successors or representatives of the deceased party and, together with the notice of hearing, shall be served on the parties as provided in Rule 5 and upon persons not parties in the manner provided in Rule 4 through Rule 4.6 for the service of summons. Unless the motion for substitution is made not later than ninety days after the death is suggested upon the record by service of a statement of the fact of the death as provided herein for the service of the motion, the action shall be dismissed as to the deceased party.

    (2)   In the event of the death of one or more of the plaintiffs or of one or more of the defendants in an action in which the right sought to be enforced survives only to the surviving plaintiffs or only against the surviving defendants, the action does not abate. The death shall be suggested upon the record and the action shall proceed in favor of or against the surviving parties.

(B) Incompetency. If a party is adjudged incompetent, the court upon motion served as provided in subdivision (A) of this rule shall allow the action to be continued by or against his representative.

(C) Transfer of interest. In case of any transfer of interest, the action may be continued by or against the original party, unless the court upon motion directs the person to whom the interest is transferred to be substituted in the action or joined with the original party. Service of the motion shall be made as provided in subdivision (A) of this rule.

(D) Public officers; death or separation from office.

    (1)   When a public officer is a party to an action in his official capacity and during its pendency dies, resigns, or otherwise ceases to hold office, the action does not abate and his successor is automatically substituted as a party. Proceedings following the substitution shall be in the name of the substituted party, but any misnomer not affecting the substantial rights of the parties shall be disregarded. An order of substitution may

be entered at any time, but the omission to enter such an order shall not affect the substitution.

(2) When a public officer sues or is sued in his official capacity, he may be described as a party by his official title rather than by name. The court however may require the addition of his name.

(E) Suggestion of death or incompetency. Upon the death or incompetency of a party it shall be the duty of the attorney of record for that party to suggest such fact upon the record within fourteen days after he acquires actual knowledge of the death or incompetency of that party. The suggestion of death or incompetency shall be served on all other parties as provided in Rule 5.

COMMENTARY

Rule 25 provides for the substitution of parties in the event of death, incapacity, transfer of interest, or succession of officers. In general, an action does not terminate simply because the original parties to the action no longer have the capacity to litigate the action. Rule 25 allows the action to continue by the representative of the original party or the successor in interest. The Rule does not address the actions that are extinguished by the death or incapacity of one of the parties; this is governed by the applicable substantive law.

Substitution on Death or Incapacity

If a party dies or becomes incapacitated before the action is completed, subsections (A) and (B) require the death or incapacity to be noted in the record. All parties must then be notified of the death or incapacity in accordance with the service provisions of Rule 5, and all non-parties must be notified in accordance with the service provisions of Rules 4-4.6. These non-parties are usually those who may be substituted for the deceased or incapacitated party.

The court may order the substitution of the proper party if a motion for substitution is made by a party or substituted party no later than 90 days from the date the death or incapacity is noted in the record. A copy of the motion should also be served on all other parties. Although a hearing on the substitution is contemplated by the Rule, the court has the authority to dispense with oral argument and decide the issue on the basis of the motion only or on written briefs in cases in which the issues are not complex or disputed. The court may also allow a longer period for such a motion if the substituted party can demonstrate excusable neglect for the failure to make a motion. Furthermore, if the successors in interest to the deceased party or the representatives of the incapacitated party are not readily identifiable, those persons have 90 days from the date that they are identified to file a motion under subsection (A).

Subsection (A)(2) provides that an action will not be delayed by the death of one or more of the plaintiffs or defendants if the action can continue by or against the remaining parties. Substituted parties can be added to the continuing proceedings at a later date if a proper motion is made under subsection (A).

Substitution on Transfer of Interest

Subsection (C) allows for substitution of parties for a transfer of interest made after the action has been initiated. However, this substitution is not mandatory, and the court may require that the action proceed by or against the original party. A motion for substitution should be made by the transferee in interest, and copies of the motion should be served on all other parties.

Illustration 25-1

Eve commences a breach of contract action against Hank's Electric for damages to Eve's house caused by the negligent repair of lighting fixtures. Two months later, Eve sells the house to Jane. Under Rule 25(C), Jane may make a motion for substitution so that she is allowed to recover damages to the house. However, the court, at its discretion, may require Eve to proceed with the action.

Substitution on Succession of Public Officers

Subsection (D) specifies that, in the event that a public officer is a party to an action and the person occupying that office ceases to act in that capacity, the substitution of that person's successor in that office occurs automatically. No motion is necessary to effect the substitution, and an entry in the record concerning the substitution may be made at any time during the course of the litigation. To avoid technical errors regarding the correct denomination of the parties, subsection (D)(2) allows a public officer to sue or be sued in an official capacity under a description of that person's office only. However, the court may require that the action proceed under the name of the individual occupying that office.

Attorney's Duty to Notify of Death or Incompetency

Subsection (E) imposes the primary duty of notifying the court of the death or incompetency of a party upon the attorney for that party. The notification must occur within 14 days after the attorney acquires such knowledge. However, this provision should not be construed as precluding any party from suggesting to the court the death or incompetency of one of the parties. The subsection was added simply to clarify the person who bears the primary responsibility for so notifying the court.

ADDITIONAL AUTHORITY

7C WRIGHT & MILLER §§ 1951-1960
6 MOORE'S FEDERAL PRACTICE §§ 25.01-25.50
5 ANDERSON'S OHIO CIVIL PRACTICE §§ 169.01-169.06
1 KLEIN DARLING AT 25-1 to AT 25-22
3 TEREZ F 7.3.1 to F 7.3.8
3 OH. JUR. PL. AND PRAC. FORMS, ch. 32
4 MILLIGAN Forms 25-1 to 25-44
1 FINK §§ 25-1 to 25-16

LEADING CASES

Administrator of Estate Is Real Party in Interest

Yardley v. W. Ohio Conference of the United Methodist Church, Inc., 138 Ohio App. 3d 872, 742 N.E.2d 723 (2000) (under rule requiring that every action be prosecuted in name of real party in interest, a special administrator of an estate could sue in his name as representative without joining those for whose benefit action was brought and without securing their consent)

Automatic Succession of Public Official

State ex rel. Botkins v. Laws, 69 Ohio St. 3d 383, 632 N.E.2d 897 (1994) (pursuant to Rule 25(D), a successor to a public official is automatically substituted as a party)

Creditor of Estate Substituted as Party

Yardley v. W. Ohio Conference of the United Methodist Church, Inc., 138 Ohio App. 3d 872, 742 N.E.2d 723 (2000) (creditor who had been named special administrator of decedent's estate was entitled to be substituted as plaintiff in survival action after decedent's death, even though estate's beneficiaries did not wish to continue that action)

Dismissal upon Death Without Prejudice

Lisi v. Schafer, No. 64374 (8th Dist.), 1994 Ohio App. LEXIS 72 (dismissal for failure to substitute the estate for the deceased party is without prejudice for lack of personal jurisdiction, and a new action is permitted within one year of the dismissal by OHIO REV. CODE ANN § 2305.19)

Notice of Death; Who May File

Norris v. Weir, 35 Ohio App. 3d 110, 520 N.E.2d 10 (1987) (any party may suggest the fact of death upon the record and serve a motion for substitution of parties when a party to a lawsuit dies and his attorney fails to comply with Rule 25)

Pendency of Appeal; Substitution of Party Not Allowed

Hook v. Springfield, 141 Ohio App. 3d 260, 750 N.E.2d 1162 (2001) (estate could not be substituted as a party in claimant's workers' compensation appeal where the claimant died during the pendency of appeal)

Substitution for Transfer of Interest

Ahlrichs v. Tri-Tex Corp., 41 Ohio App. 3d 207, 534 N.E.2d 1231 (1987) (parties may be substituted at the discretion of the trial court upon a finding of transfer of interest)

V
DEPOSITIONS AND DISCOVERY

CHAPTER 26

Rule 26. General Provisions Governing Discovery

Rule 26 reads as follows:

(A) Policy; discovery methods. It is the policy of these rules

    (1) to preserve the right of attorneys to prepare cases for trial with that degree of privacy necessary to encourage them to prepare their cases thoroughly and to investigate not only the favorable but the unfavorable aspects of such cases and

    (2) to prevent an attorney from taking undue advantage of his adversary's industry or efforts.

    Parties may obtain discovery by one or more of the following methods: deposition upon oral examination or written questions; written interrogatories; production of documents or things or permission to enter upon land or other property, for inspection and other purposes; physical and mental examinations; and requests for admission. Unless the court orders otherwise, the frequency of use of these methods is not limited.

(B) Scope of discovery. Unless otherwise ordered by the court in accordance with these rules, the scope of discovery is as follows:

    (1) In general. Parties may obtain discovery regarding any matter, not privileged, which is relevant to the subject matter involved in the pending action, whether it relates to the claim or defense of the party seeking discovery or to the claim or defense of any other party, including the existence, description, nature, custody, condition and location of any books, documents, or other tangible things and the identity and location of persons having knowledge of any discoverable matter. It is not ground for objection that the information sought will be inadmissible at the trial if the information sought appears reasonably calculated to lead to the discovery of admissible evidence.

    (2) Insurance agreements. A party may obtain discovery of the existence and contents of any insurance agreement under which any person carrying on an insurance business may be liable to satisfy part or all of a judgment which may be entered in the action or to indemnify or reimburse for payments made to satisfy the judgment. Information concerning the insurance agreement is not by reason of disclosure subject to comment or admissible in evidence at trial.

    (3) Trial preparation: materials. Subject to the provisions of subdivision (B)(4) of this rule, a party may obtain discovery of documents and tangible things prepared in anticipation of litigation or for trial by or for another party or by or for that other party's representative (including his attorney, consultant, surety, indemnitor, insurer, or agent) only upon a showing of good cause therefor. A statement concerning the action or its subject matter previously given by the party seeking the statement may be obtained without showing good cause. A statement of a party is

(a) a written statement signed or otherwise adopted or approved by the party, or

(b) a stenographic, mechanical, electrical, or other recording, or a transcription thereof, which is a substantially verbatim recital of an oral statement which was made by the party and contemporaneously recorded.

(4) Trial preparation: experts.

(a) Subject to the provisions of subdivision (B)(4)(b) of this rule and Rule 35(B), a party may discover facts known or opinions held by an expert retained or specially employed by another party in anticipation of litigation or preparation for trial only upon a showing that the party seeking discovery is unable without undue hardship to obtain facts and opinions on the same subject by other means or upon a showing of other exceptional circumstances indicating that denial of discovery would cause manifest injustice.

(b) As an alternative or in addition to obtaining discovery under subdivision (B)(4)(a) of this rule, a party by means of interrogatories may require any other party

(i) to identify each person whom the other party expects to call as an expert witness at trial, and

(ii) to state the subject matter on which the expert is expected to testify.

Thereafter, any party may discover from the expert or the other party facts known or opinions held by the expert which are relevant to the stated subject matter. Discovery of the expert's opinions and the grounds therefor is restricted to those previously given to the other party or those to be given on direct examination at trial.

(c) The court may require that the party seeking discovery under subdivision (B)(4)(b) of this rule pay the expert a reasonable fee for time spent in responding to discovery, and, with respect to discovery permitted under subdivision (B)(4)(a) of this rule, may require a party to pay another party a fair portion of the fees and expenses incurred by the latter party in obtaining facts and opinions from the expert.

(C) **Protective orders.** Upon motion by any party or by the person from whom discovery is sought, and for good cause shown, the court in which the action is pending may make any order that justice requires to protect a party or person from annoyance, embarrassment, oppression, or undue burden or expense, including one or more of the following:

(1) that the discovery not be had;

(2) that the discovery may be had only on specified terms and conditions, including a designation of the time or place;

(3) that the discovery may be had only by a method of discovery other than that selected by the party seeking discovery;

(4) that certain matters not be inquired into or that the scope of the discovery be limited to certain matters;

(5) that discovery be conducted with no one present except persons designated by the court;

(6) that a deposition after being sealed be opened only by order of the court;

(7) that a trade secret or other confidential research, development, or commercial information not be disclosed or be disclosed only in a designated way;

(8) that the parties simultaneously file specified documents or information enclosed in sealed envelopes to be opened as directed by the court.

If the motion for a protective order is denied in whole or in part, the court, on terms and conditions as are just, may order that any party or person provide or permit discovery. The provisions of Civ. R. 37(A)(4) apply to the award of expenses incurred in relation to the motion.

Before any person moves for a protective order under this rule, that person shall make a reasonable effort to resolve the matter through discussion with the attorney or unrepresented party seeking discovery. A motion for a protective order shall be accompanied by a statement reciting the effort made to resolve the matter in accordance with this paragraph.

(D) **Sequence and timing of discovery.** Unless the court upon motion, for the convenience of parties and witnesses and in the interests of justice, orders otherwise, methods of discovery may be used in any sequence and the fact that a party is conducting discovery, whether by deposition or otherwise, shall not operate to delay any other party's discovery.

(E) **Supplementation of responses.** A party who has responded to a request for discovery with a response that was complete when made is under no duty to supplement his response to include information thereafter acquired, except as follows:

(1) A party is under a duty seasonably to supplement his response with respect to any question directly addressed to

    (a) the identity and location of persons having knowledge of discoverable matters, and

    (b) the identity of each person expected to be called as an expert witness at trial and the subject matter on which he is expected to testify.

(2) A party who knows or later learns that his response is incorrect is under a duty seasonably to correct the response.

(3) A duty to supplement responses may be imposed by order of the court, agreement of the parties, or at any time prior to trial through requests for supplementation of prior responses.

COMMENTARY

Rule 26 is possibly the most important Rule of Civil Procedure. It defines the scope of discoverable material and establishes a background of policy against which all other discovery rules operate. In essence, Rule 26 is designed to incorporate the basic philosophy of discovery under the Rules: parties should be able to obtain all information relevant in an action that is in the possession of any person before the trial occurs, unless the information is privileged.

Rule 26 makes the discovery process the most important aspect of litigation for determining the facts and issues involved in an action. The Rule also contains a host of other provisions, including ones governing protective orders, the work-product doctrine, insurance agreements, expert witnesses, and the supplementation of responses to discovery requests.

Required Disclosures

Ohio Rule 26 does not impose on parties a duty of mandatory disclosure with regard to certain kinds of information, as does Federal Rule of Civil Procedure 26. That Rule was amended in 1993 to require all parties to provide to all other parties the specific information listed in that Rule without being served with a formal discovery request. These kinds of information are thus properly referred to as discovery disclosures, rather than discovery responses.

Under Ohio Rule 26, the information subject to mandatory disclosure in the federal system is still discoverable; however, the parties must secure such information through the usual discovery mechanisms, and no party is required to divulge any information without being requested to do so.

Note on Discovery Practice in Ohio Federal Court

Federal Rule of Civil Procedure 26 contains an "opt-out" provision in subsection (a)(1) of that Rule, which provides for alteration of the mandatory disclosure rules by stipulation of the parties or by order or local rule. As of the date of publication, the Northern District of Ohio, along with the Bankruptcy Court of the Northern District, has not opted out of these rules, and the mandatory disclosure provisions are effective. The Southern District of Ohio and Bankruptcy Court of the Southern District, however, have opted out of several provisions in Federal Rule 26. Thus, parties filing actions in the Southern District of Ohio are not required to make the mandatory initial disclosures as required under subsection (a)(1) of Federal Rule 26, though parties must still make the other required disclosures pursuant to subsections (a)(2)-(5). Parties in the Southern District are also not required to conduct a discovery conference meeting under subsection (f), and the prohibition on formal discovery before the discovery conference under subsection (d) is similarly inoperative.

° Note on Amendments to Federal Rule of Civil Procedure 26 °

The United States Supreme Court has made significant amendments to Federal Rule of Civil Procedure 26, among others, effective December 1, 2000. Although an exhaustive discussion of these amendments is beyond the scope of this manual, the amendments establish a nationally uniform policy with respect to initial disclosures, discovery conferences, and discovery practice generally. The "opt-out" provision has been eliminated, and local rules of federal courts in conflict with the Federal Courts have been rendered invalid.

Policy of Discovery

Subsection (A) of Ohio Rule 26 sets forth the overarching policy of all discovery rules. They are: (1) to preserve the right of privacy of attorneys to prepare cases thoroughly and to investigate favorable and unfavorable aspects of such cases; and (2) to prevent an attorney from profiting from the work of opposing counsel. This policy statement is substantially a restatement of that enunciated in *Hickman v. Taylor*, 329 U.S. 495 (1947).

Discovery Tools

Subsection (A) also lists the discovery tools available to parties. They include depositions, both written and oral, interrogatories, production of documents and tangible objects, entry upon land for inspection and other purposes, physical and mental examinations, and requests for admission. Rules 28-36 provide greater detail on the scope and use of these discovery tools.

Timing of Discovery; Planning Conference

The frequency of use of the various discovery devices is generally not limited except by express proscription in a Rule or unless the court orders otherwise. Subsection (D) directs that these various discovery tools may be used in any order in which the parties or their attorneys deem prudent and also that both sides in an action may conduct discovery concomitantly. Unlike Federal Rule of Civil Procedure 26, Ohio Rule 26 does not require a discovery planning meeting during which the attorneys or parties can plan the course of the discovery process in the action. However, Rule 16 is sufficiently broad to authorize such a meeting, and one may be ordered in the court's discretion.

Scope of Discovery

The scope of discovery is set forth in subsection (B). It states that "[p]arties may obtain discovery regarding any matter, not privileged, which is relevant to the subject matter involved in the pending action," and not subject to any of the exceptions stated in that subsection. This definition contemplates a broad range of discoverable information and is not limited by the list of information in subsection (B)(1).

Subsection (B)(1) states that information need not be admissible at trial to be discoverable, but only that the information be reasonably calculated to lead to the discovery of admissible evidence. Thus, objections to discovery requests on evidentiary grounds of hearsay or lack of probative value will not be sufficient to render the information undiscoverable. However, this provision should not be interpreted as permitting the discovery of all evidence that would not be admissible at trial. Objections to discovery requests on grounds of irrelevancy or privilege are proper. There must also be some demonstration by the requesting party that the discoverable information may lead to the discovery of admissible evidence.

Illustration 26-1

Andrew and Sarah witness an automobile accident that is the subject of litigation between Paul and Caroline. At Andrew's deposition, Paul's attorney asks, "Did Sarah tell you that Caroline was speeding?" Andrew replied, "Yes, Sarah said that Caroline was traveling at least 75 miles per hour." Andrew's response is hearsay and will likely be inadmissible at trial. Nevertheless, Andrew's testimony is reasonably calculated to lead to admissible evidence, namely the testimony of Sarah. Therefore, the question is within the scope of discovery as defined by Rule 26(B)(1).

Insurance Agreements

Rule 26(B)(2) provides for the discovery of any insurance agreement entered into by the parties that is germane to the action. The provision reflects the philosophy that the discovery of the existence and contents of insurance agreements before trial will aid in the realistic evaluation and settlement of actions. However, this provision should not be interpreted as providing for the admissibility of insurance agreements at trial, a point made explicit in subsection (B)(2). The admissibility of insurance agreements is generally determined according to Ohio Rule of Evidence 411, which provides that insurance is inadmissible to prove the negligent or wrongful conduct of parties.

Illustration 26-2

Assume on the facts of Illustration 26-1 that Paul requests information relating to any automobile insurance agreement entered into by Caroline at the time of the accident. Though Caroline must disclose any such agreement, the fact is subsequently inadmissible at trial to prove that Caroline was speeding.

Work-Product Doctrine

Subsection (B)(3) incorporates, in part, the decision in *Hickman v. Taylor*, 329 U.S. 495 (1947), which recognized a qualified immunity from discovery for certain kinds of information prepared in anticipation of litigation or trial—the work-product doctrine. Prior to that decision, the broad scope of discoverable information prompted some litigators to simply allow their adversaries to investigate and prepare the case for them, obtaining the materials through the liberal discovery rules. The phrase "prepared in anticipation of litigation" has generated a fair amount of interpretive difficulty, and an extended discussion is beyond the scope of this manual. Substantial bodies of case law have developed in response to specific applications of this standard, and practitioners are advised to use additional research tools on the issue.

The "free rider" problem is somewhat resolved under subsection (B)(3). It states that documents and other tangible things prepared by a party, the party's attorney, or another representative of that party in anticipation of litigation or trial are discoverable only upon a showing of "good cause." This standard is more lenient than that applicable in many other jurisdictions, including federal court, and it suggests that parties should be able to discover information upon a lesser showing than "substantial need" and "undue hardship."

Nonetheless, Ohio courts should guard against abuse of the distinction in these standards, requiring not only that a party show "cause" to discover protected information but also that the "cause" be qualitatively "good" in nature. Even if such a showing is made by a party, the disclosure is limited to information of a factual nature. The party who had originally prepared the materials is not required to disclose the notes or documents containing the mental impressions, conclusions, opinions, or legal theories of its attorney or other representative concerning the litigation.

Illustration 26-3

Raymond is injured in a boating accident. Prior to the commencement of litigation, Raymond's attorney conducts an investigation to assess the liability. of Rickity Ships, the manufacturer of the boat involved in the accident. After receiving a summons and complaint, the attorney for Rickity Ships requests a copy of the report made by Raymond's attorney. Under Rule 26(B)(3), the report is protected from discovery under the work-product doctrine. The attorney for Rickity Ships is in an excellent position to obtain a similar report by conducting her own investigation, and will probably not be able to make the requisite showing of "good cause," and the report need not be disclosed.

Waiver of Work-Product Objection

The qualified immunity from disclosure of work product prepared in anticipation of litigation or trial may be waived if a statement concerning the information has been "previously made." Subsection (B)(3) states that any party may obtain a "previously-made" statement of a party without making the required demonstration of "good cause." The Rule defines a statement as "previously made" if it is written or adopted by a party, or any recording of an oral statement by a party, including depositions.

Illustration 26-4

Assume on the facts of Illustration 26-3 that the attorney for Rickity Ships also requests the subject matter of a discussion between Raymond and his attorney concerning the investigation. If Raymond reveals a portion of this discussion at his deposition, Raymond has waived any protection afforded to his comments under Rule 26(B)(3).

Experts

Subsection (B)(4) distinguishes between experts that are retained in anticipation of litigation or for trial preparation and experts who are expected to testify at trial, though the Rule does so rather obliquely. Subsection (B)(4)(a) permits a party to discover the facts or opinions of any expert retained by a party but is not expected to testify at trial only upon a showing of special need. The party must demonstrate that it cannot, without undue hardship, obtain facts or opinions on the same subject matter through the use of other expert witnesses or through other means. This demonstration will rarely be made by a party, except possibly in circumstances where the subject matter is so highly specialized that the expert is uniquely qualified to testify on the matter. Subsection (B)(4)(c) provides for an allocation of fees paid to the expert to the respective parties.

Illustration 26-5

Assume on the facts of Illustration 26-4 that Rickity Ships retains the services of Doolittle, the original architect of the boat involved in the accident, but does not plan to call Doolittle as a witness. If Raymond can demonstrate that Doolittle has an opinion about the design of the boat so specialized that no other expert can accurately so testify, Raymond will be able to discover any report prepared by Doolittle.

Subsection (B)(4)(b) governs the discovery of facts or opinions of those experts that are expected to testify at trial. Such witnesses, and the general subject matter of their testimony, must be disclosed to any party who so requests. That party may thereafter depose those expert witnesses without making any showing of substantial need or undue hardship. Subsection (B)(4)(c) provides that a party taking a deposition under subsection (B)(4)(b) must pay the expert a reasonable fee for her time, including travel expenses to and from the deposition.

Illustration 26-6

Assume on the facts of Illustration 26-5 that Raymond plans to call Wannamaker, an expert on boating safety, as a witness. Rickity Ships may depose Wannamaker as of right, as they need not make any demonstration of specialized need of Wannamaker's testimony.

Protective Orders

Subsection (C) provides the court with broad discretion to fashion protective orders to guard against abuses of the discovery process. Although the Rules contain few express restrictions on the frequency with which a single discovery mechanism may be used by a party, the court may provide for a comprehensive discovery plan under this subsection. Grounds for granting a motion for a protective order are listed in that subsection, but the list is not exhaustive.

Before making a motion for a protective order, a party is required to confer with the affected party in an attempt to resolve the matter without court intervention. The protective order should set forth the terms or conditions under which discovery may proceed, and the failure to obey a protective order is sanctionable under Rule 37(B). The party opposing the motion for a protective order, whether or not an order is actually issued, must pay the reasonable expenses incurred by the party making the motion, including attorneys' fees, unless the court finds that the motion was substantially justified or that other circumstances would make an award of expenses and fees unjust.

Illustration 26-7

Assume on the facts of Illustration 26-6 that Raymond refuses to answer interrogatories inquiring as to the subject matter of Wannamaker's prospective testimony, and Rickity Ships makes a motion for a protective order to the court. Before making the motion, Rickity Ships must confer with Raymond and seek to resolve the matter without court intervention. If the parties are unable to resolve the matter and the court grants Rickity's motion, Raymond must pay Rickity's reasonable expenses incurred in making the motion.

Duty to Supplement Disclosures and Discovery Responses

Subsection (E) sets forth the general rule that parties are under no duty to supplement responses to discovery requests. This general rule is subject to several limitations. An implicit limitation in the Rule is that the principle applies only to those responses that were complete when they were originally made. Incomplete discovery responses must be supplemented and are sometimes sanctionable under Rule 37.

The Rule also creates three explicit exceptions to the principle explained above. First, supplementation is required with regard to any response concerning the identity and location of witnesses, including expert witnesses who are expected to testify at trial. Second, if a response to a discovery request is subsequently found to have been incorrect, as opposed to merely incomplete, that party is obligated to correct the response. Finally, a general duty to supplement prior discovery responses may be ordered by the court or agreed to by the parties at any time before trial.

ADDITIONAL AUTHORITY

8 WRIGHT & MILLER §§ 2001-2070

6 MOORE'S FEDERAL PRACTICE §§ 26.01-26.155

5 ANDERSON'S OHIO CIVIL PRACTICE §§ 159.01-159.14

2 KLEIN DARLING AT 26-1 to AT 26-6

3 TEREZ F 10.1.1 to F 10.1.9, F 10.12.1 to F 10.12.7

3 OH. JUR. PL. AND PRAC. FORMS, ch. 33

4 MILLIGAN Forms 26-1 to 26-123

1 FINK §§ 26-1 to 26-10

OHIO LITIGATION CHECKLISTS, Depositions and Discovery, § 5

LEADING CASES

Appealability of Discovery Orders

Doe v. University of Cincinnati, 42 Ohio App. 3d 227, 538 N.E.2d 419 (1988) (if the damage of a discovery order cannot be remedied by a later correction of that order, the order may be a final appealable order), *cause dismissed*, 63 Ohio St. 3d 1402, 585 N.E.2d 424 (1992)

Appealability of Protective Order

McHenry v. General Accident Ins. Co., 104 Ohio App. 3d 350, 662 N.E.2d 51 (1995) (the granting of a motion to compel production of a claims file and denial of a protective order was not a final appealable order)

Appealable Discovery Orders

Radovanic v. Cossler, 140 Ohio App. 3d 208, 746 N.E.2d 1184 (2000) (order requiring party to produce their insurance claims file in connection with party's pending motion for prejudgment interest on jury verdict awarding her damages was final and thus an appealable order)

Attorney-Client Privilege

Frank W. Schaefer, Inc. v. C. Garfield Mitchell Agency, Inc., 82 Ohio App. 3d 322, 612 N.E.2d 442 (1992) (the attorney-client privilege belongs to the client and protects only those materials involving communications between the client and attorney)

Burden on Party Opposing Discovery

Fisher v. Rose Chevrolet, 82 Ohio App. 3d 520, 612 N.E.2d 782 (1992) (a party opposing discovery must show that the requested information will not lead to the discovery of admissible evidence)

Court Discretion over Discovery Process

State ex rel. Grandview Hosp. & Med. Ctr. v. Gorman, 51 Ohio St. 3d 94, 554 N.E.2d 1297 (1990) (the trial court has inherent authority to oversee discovery, including the authority to direct an in camera inspection of records subject to privilege claims)

Disclosure of Expert Witnesses

Sindel v. Toledo Edison Co., 87 Ohio App. 3d 525, 622 N.E.2d 706 (1991) (where neither the court nor the opposing party formally requests disclosure of expert witnesses, a party has no legal obligation to disclose expert witnesses)

Exclusion of Witnesses

Vinci v. Ceraolo, 79 Ohio App. 3d 640, 607 N.E.2d 1079 (exclusion of a witness who was not disclosed as directed by Rule 26(E) is not an abuse of discretion by the trial court), *jurisdictional motion allowed*, 65 Ohio St. 3d 1434, 600 N.E.2d 678, *and cause dismissed*, 65 Ohio St. 3d 1461, 602 N.E.2d 1170 (1992)

Exclusion of Testimony Appropriate Sanction When Discovery Not Supplemented

Schafer v. RMS Realty, 138 Ohio App. 3d 244, 741 N.E.2d 155 (2000) (exclusion of testimony is appropriate sanction for failure to supplement discovery responses regarding identity of expert witnesses and subject matter on which expert is expected to testify; appellate courts are reluctant to interfere in trial court's ruling in this regard)

Expert Witnesses; Fee

Kirby v. Ahmad, 63 Ohio Misc. 2d 533, 635 N.E.2d 46 (C.P. 1994) (expert witnesses are entitled to a reasonable fee for testifying at a deposition by an adverse party, regardless of what fee is asked)

Limitations of Privilege

Springfield Local Sch. Dist. Bd. of Educ. v. Ohio Ass'n of Pub. Sch. Employees, Local 530, 106 Ohio App. 3d 855, 667 N.E.2d 458 (1995) (unless provided by the federal or Ohio Constitutions, or by a statute or case law, no privilege to refuse to testify or produce a document in a judicial proceeding at any stage of litigation is recognized)

Only Relevant Material Discoverable

Tschantz v. Ferguson, 97 Ohio App. 3d 693, 647 N.E.2d 507 (1994) (material may be discovered only if it is relevant in a particular case, but irrelevancy is determined when the information sought will not reasonably lead to the discovery of admissible evidence), *motion to certify denied*, 71 Ohio St. 3d 1476, 645 N.E.2d 1256 (1995)

Opposing Parties Expert Witness Reports Not Discoverable

Becker v. Metzger, 144 Ohio App. 3d 52, 759 N.E.2d 455 (2001) (party is not entitled to discover reports prepared by expert witnesses by opposing party where there is no showing of exceptional circumstances or undue hardship)

Protective Orders; "Good Cause"

Koval v. General Motors Corp., 62 Ohio Misc. 2d 694, 610 N.E.2d 1199 (C.P. 1990) (a party attempting to show "good cause" pursuant to Rule 26(C)(7) must show that disclosure of the information for which the protective order is sought would work a clearly defined injury to the requesting party's business)

Purpose of Sanctions

Fields v. Dailey, 68 Ohio App. 3d 33, 587 N.E.2d 400 (sanctions for discovery abuse should promote liberal discovery policies of encouraging the free flow of information and avoiding surprises at trial), *motion to certify overruled*, 56 Ohio St. 3d 703, 564 N.E.2d 707 (1990)

Subject Matter of Expert Testimony

Beavercreek Local Sch. v. Basic, Inc., 71 Ohio App. 3d 669, 595 N.E.2d 360 (1991) (the requirement that a party state the subject matter on which an expert will testify encompasses a broad scope of information under the general topic, and does not require a detailed account of the expert's possible testimony)

Work-Product Doctrine

Frank W. Schaefer, Inc. v. C. Garfield Mitchell Agency, Inc., 82 Ohio App. 3d 322, 612 N.E.2d 442 (1992) (the work-product doctrine belongs to the attorney and protects the attorney from intrusions into his private files, unless a showing of special circumstances is made)

CHAPTER 27

Rule 27. Perpetuation of Testimony—Depositions Before Action or Pending Appeal

Rule 27 reads as follows:

(A) Before action.

(1) Petition. A person who desires to perpetuate his own testimony or the testimony of another person regarding any matter that may be cognizable in any court may file a petition in the court of common pleas in the county of the residence of any expected adverse party. The petitioner shall verify that he believes the facts stated in the petition are true. The petition shall be entitled in the name of the petitioner and shall show:

(a) That the petitioner or his personal representatives, heirs, beneficiaries, successors, or assigns may be parties to an action or proceeding cognizable in a court but is presently unable to bring or defend it;

(b) The subject matter of the expected action or proceeding and his interest therein (if the validity or construction of any written instrument connected with the subject matter of the deposition may be called in question a copy shall be attached to the petition);

(c) The facts which he desires to establish by the proposed testimony and his reasons for desiring to perpetuate it;

(d) The names or, if the names are unknown, a description of the persons he expects will be adverse parties and their addresses so far as known;

(e) The names and addresses of the persons to be examined and the subject matter of the testimony which he expects to elicit from each.

The petition shall then ask for an order authorizing the petitioner to take the depositions of the persons to be examined named in the petition, for the purpose of perpetuating their testimony.

(2) Notice and service. The petitioner shall thereafter serve a notice upon each person named in the petition as an expected adverse party, together with a copy of the petition, stating that the petitioner will apply to the court, at a time and place named therein, for the order described in the petition. At least twenty-eight days before the date of hearing, unless the court upon application and showing of extraordinary circumstances prescribes a hearing on shorter notice, the notice shall be served either within or outside of this state by a method provided in Rule 4 through Rule 4.6 for service of summons, or in any other manner affording actual notice, as directed by order of the court. But if it appears to the court that an expected adverse party cannot be given actual notice, the court shall appoint a competent attorney to cross-examine the deponent; such attorney shall be allowed reasonable fees therefor which shall be taxed as costs. If any expected adverse party is a minor or incompetent the provisions of Rule 17(B) apply.

(3) **Order and examination.** If the court is satisfied that the allowance of the petition may prevent a failure or delay of justice, and that the petitioner is unable to bring or defend the contemplated action, the court shall order the testimony perpetuated, designating the deponents, the subject matter of the examination, when, where, and before whom their deposition shall be taken, and whether orally or upon written questions. The depositions may then be taken in accordance with these rules; and the court may make orders of the character provided for by Rule 34, Rule 35 and Rule 37. For the purpose of applying these rules to depositions for perpetuating testimony, each reference therein to the court in which the action is pending shall be deemed to refer to the court in which the petition for such deposition was filed.

(4) **Use of deposition.** Subject to the same limitations and objections as though the deponent were testifying at the trial in person, and to the provisions of Rule 26 and Rule 32(A) a deposition taken in accordance with this rule may be used as evidence in any action subsequently brought in any court, where the deposition is that of a party to the action, or where the issue is such that an interested party in the proceedings in which the deposition was taken had the right and opportunity for cross-examination with an interest and motive similar to that which the adverse party has in the action in which the deposition is offered. But, except where the deposition is that of a party to the action and is offered against the party, the deposition may not be used as evidence unless the deponent is unavailable as a witness at the trial.

(B) **Pending appeal.** If an appeal has been taken from a judgment of any court, a party who desires to perpetuate testimony may make a motion in the court where the action was tried, for leave to take depositions upon the same notice and service thereof as provided in (A)(2) of this rule. The motion shall show the names and addresses of the persons to be examined, the subject matter of the testimony which he expects to elicit from each, and the reasons for perpetuating their testimony. If the court is satisfied that the motion is proper to avoid a failure or delay of justice, it may make an order allowing the deposition to be taken and may make orders of the character provided for by Rule 34, Rule 35, and Rule 37. The depositions may be taken and used in the same manner and under the same conditions as are prescribed for depositions in Rule 26 and Rule 32(A).

(C) **Perpetuation by actions.** This rule does not limit the inherent power of a court to entertain an action to perpetuate testimony.

(D) **Filing of depositions.** Depositions taken under this rule shall be filed with the court in which the petition is filed or the motion is made.

(E) **Costs of deposition.** The party taking any deposition under this rule shall pay the costs thereof and of all proceedings hereunder, unless otherwise ordered by the court.

(F) **Depositions taken in other states.** A deposition taken under similar procedure of another jurisdiction is admissible in this state to the same extent as a deposition taken under this rule.

(G) **Construction of rule.** This rule shall be so construed as to effectuate the general purpose to make uniform the law of those states which have similar rules or statutes.

COMMENTARY

Rule 27(A) provides for perpetuation by petition and allows a person to use certain discovery mechanisms for the purpose of obtaining information or documents to be used in an action that has not been yet initiated. Although Rule 27 is subtitled "*Depositions* Before Action or Pending Appeal" (emphasis added) and refers to perpetuation of testimony to describe the action a person may request under the Rule, subsection (A)(3) makes clear that depositions, requests for production of documents, and requests for physical and mental examinations are all available in petitions under the Rule. Subsection (C) differentiates the Rule from "perpetuation by action," which is a civil action providing for similar kinds of requests. An action for perpetuation may be maintained under the pertinent statutory or case law, and is, of course, subject to all the procedures of the Rules incumbent on civil actions.

Depositions for Use in Future Actions

Subsection (A)(1) states that a person desiring to use a discovery mechanism for use in a future action must file a petition under Rule 27 in the court of common pleas in the county in which an expected adverse party resides. The contents of the petition should include those items that are set forth in that subsection. Although subsection (A)(1) also states that the petition should also include a request for the court to make an order authorizing the petitioner to take the desired actions, subsection (A)(2) appears to contemplate a hearing in which the formal application should be made. This is the better course of action, and the petition should simply include a request for a hearing on the matter.

Notice and Service Requirements

Subsection (A)(2) sets forth the notice and service provisions of petitions under Rule 27. Although Rule 27 requires that all persons named in the petition must be served with notice of the hearing and a copy of the petition at least 28 days before the hearing on the matter, it is not a proper objection to a Rule 27 motion that the court lacks personal jurisdiction over a person so served or that venue is improperly laid. As a Rule 27 petition is not a civil action, it is not subject to the normal criteria incumbent on civil actions.

If service of the notice and petition cannot be made with due diligence on any of the persons named in the petition, the court has the authority to direct an alternate means of service. As a hearing under Rule 27 is not a civil action, the court is not constitutionally bound by the service provisions of Rules 4-4.6. However, the court is directed to appoint an attorney for all persons not served with actual notice. The final sentence of subsection (A)(2) keys the operation of that Rule to guardianship provisions of Rule 17(B) in the event that a person named in the petition is a minor or incompetent person.

Order for Perpetuation

Under subsection (A)(3), the court may make an order for the relief requested in the petition if it finds that the perpetuation of the testimony may prevent a failure or delay of justice. The court should also determine that good cause exists for the failure of the petitioner to bring an action. Subsection (A)(4) allows depositions taken under the Rule to be used in actions involving the same subject matter in any district court in accordance with Rule 26 and Rule 32(A).

Depositions Pending Appeal

Subsection (B) is similar to subsection (A), but allows a party to make a motion to perpetuate testimony after a judgment has been entered in an action and while the action is on or awaiting appeal. The contents, notice, and manner of service of the motion is further specified in the Rule. The Rule allows the court to grant the motion under the same standard as in subsection (A), except, of course, the party is not required to show good cause why the action has not yet been initiated.

Mechanics of the Procedure

Subsection (D) requires that depositions taken under Rule 27 must be filed with the court in which the petition is filed. Furthermore, subsection (E) provides that the party taking the deposition must pay the costs of the deposition unless otherwise ordered by the court. Finally, subsection (F) simply provides that depositions taken under similar procedures in other states may be used in Ohio courts as if the deposition had been taken under Rule 27.

ADDITIONAL AUTHORITY

8 Wright & Miller §§ 2071-2080

6 Moore's Federal Practice §§ 27.01-27.52

5 Anderson's Ohio Civil Practice §§ 165.01-165.07

2 Klein Darling AT 27-1 to AT 27-20

3 Terez F 10.11.1 to F 10.11.4

3 Oh. Jur. Pl. and Prac. Forms, ch. 34

4 Milligan Forms 27-1 to 27-43

1 Fink §§ 27-1 to 27-13

Ohio Litigation Checklists, Depositions and Discovery, §§ 1-3

Ohio Litigation Checklists, Pleading and Process, §§ 1-5

LEADING CASES

Appealability of Perpetuation Order

In re Bejarano, 65 Ohio App. 3d 202, 583 N.E.2d 379 (1989) (the granting of a motion for perpetuation of testimony does not affect the substantive rights of the prospective defendant, and is not a final order appealable by the prospective defendant)

Recovery of Costs

Siders v. Reynoldsburg Sch. Dist., 99 Ohio App. 3d 173, 650 N.E.2d 150 (1994) (the costs of a deposition not used at trial were not recoverable by the plaintiff)

Standing to Bring Perpetuation Motion

In re Fraternal Order of Police, 61 Ohio Misc. 2d 135, 575 N.E.2d 535 (C.P. 1990) (a party seeking a court order for perpetuation of evidence must show it has a cognizable interest itself in the action)

CHAPTER 28

Rule 28. Persons Before Whom Depositions May be Taken

Rule 28 reads as follows:

(A) Depositions within state. Depositions may be taken in this state before: a person authorized to administer any oath by the laws of this state, a person appointed by the court in which the action is pending, or a person agreed upon by written stipulation of all the parties.

(B) Depositions outside state. Depositions may be taken outside this state before: a person authorized to administer oaths in the place where the deposition is taken, a person appointed by the court in which the action is pending, a person agreed upon by written stipulation of all the parties, or, in any foreign country, by any consular officer of the United States within his consular district.

(C) Disqualification for interest. Unless the parties agree otherwise as provided in Civ. R. 29, depositions shall not be taken before a person who:

(1) is a relative or employee of or attorney for any of the parties, or

(2) is a relative or employee of an attorney for any of the parties, or

(3) is financially interested in the action.

(D) Prohibited contracts.

(1) Any blanket contract for private court reporting services, not related to a particular case or reporting incident, shall be prohibited between a private court reporter or any other person with whom a private court reporter has a principal and agency relationship, and any attorney, party to an action, party having a financial interest in an action, or any entity providing the services of a shorthand reporter.

(2) "Blanket contract" means a contract under which a court reporter, court recorder, or court reporting firm agrees to perform all court reporting or court recording services for a client for two or more cases at a rate of compensation fixed in the contract.

(3) Negotiating or bidding reasonable fees, equal to all parties, on a case-by-case basis is not prohibited.

(4)   Division (D) of this rule does not apply to the courts or the administrative tribunals of this state.

COMMENTARY

Rule 28 governs persons before whom depositions may be taken. The Rule is interrelated with Rule 29, which governs stipulations between parties involving discovery procedure.

Depositions in Ohio

If a deposition is to be taken in Ohio, the deposition must be conducted by a person authorized to administer oaths or by a person appointed by court order or by stipulation of the parties, a point repeated in Rule 29. If a deposition is taken by telephone, Rule 30(B)(6) provides that the deposition will be considered to have occurred in the county and at the place where the deponent answers the questions.

Depositions Outside Ohio

Subsection (B) lists the four categories of persons before whom depositions outside Ohio may be taken. The first three methods mirror those established in subsection (A). The fourth method allows depositions in foreign countries to be taken before any consular officer of the United States within his consular district. As a state subject to the supremacy clause of the United States Constitution, Ohio is also bound by any treaty or convention entered into by the United States with other countries. One such treaty, the Hague Convention on the Taking of Evidence Abroad in civil or commercial matters, provides for the taking of depositions in accordance with the terms set forth therein.

Blanket Contracts with Court Reporters Prohibited

The Ohio Supreme Court added subsection (D) to Rule 28 in 2001. The provision prohibits "blanket contracts" between private court reporting services and attorneys, parties, or persons having a financial interest in the actions covered by the contract. The amendment was adopted in response to the concern that long-term financial arrangements between private court reporting services and law firms or litigants have raised the appearance of partiality and differential treatment in particular actions.

Subsection (D)(3) permits contracts between private court reporting services and attorneys, parties, or persons having a financial interest in the actions as long as lower fees may be negotiated on a case-by-case basis and the fees are the same for all parties.

In addition, under subsection (D)(4), the prohibition does not apply or extend to governmental entities, which may be required by law to obtain court reporting services on a long-term basis through competitive bidding.

ADDITIONAL AUTHORITY

8 WRIGHT & MILLER §§ 2081-2090
6 MOORE'S FEDERAL PRACTICE §§ 28.01-28.32
5 ANDERSON'S OHIO CIVIL PRACTICE § 160.08
2 KLEIN DARLING AT 28-1 to AT 28-5
3 TEREZ F 10.8.1 to F 10.8.5
3 OH. JUR. PL. AND PRAC. FORMS, ch. 35
4 MILLIGAN Forms 28-1 to 28-12
1 FINK §§ 28-1 to 28-4
OHIO LITIGATION CHECKLISTS, Depositions and Discovery, § 4

CHAPTER 29

Rule 29. Stipulations Regarding Discovery Procedure

Rule 29 reads as follows:

Unless the court orders otherwise, the parties may by written stipulation

(1) provide that depositions may be taken before any person, at any time or place, upon any notice, and in any manner and when so taken may be used like other depositions; and

(2) modify the procedures provided by these rules for other methods of discovery.

COMMENTARY

Rule 29 is a broad provision that allows the parties to enter into stipulations regarding the alteration of virtually any aspect of discovery procedure. Such stipulations allow the parties to fashion less expensive and time-consuming procedures than those provided for under the Rules or by local rule. The stipulation must be in writing and should be filed with the court. Although the court's approval is not expressly required for the parties to enter into stipulations involving discovery, the court has the authority to revoke this right of stipulation.

Stipulations Concerning Discovery Mechanisms

Clause (1) states that parties may stipulate to the manner in which depositions may be taken, including the person before whom a deposition must be taken. In this respect, Rule 29 is keyed to Rule 28, which is the general provision regarding persons before whom stipulations may be taken. Under clause (2), the parties may likewise agree to modify any other aspect of discovery procedure provided by local rule or by these Rules.

ADDITIONAL AUTHORITY

8 Wright & Miller §§ 2091-2100
6 Moore's Federal Practice §§ 29.01-29.07
2 Klein Darling AT 29-1 to AT 29-1
3 Terez F 10.8.3, F 10.9.2
3 Oh. Jur. Pl. and Prac. Forms, ch. 36

CHAPTER 30

Rule 30. Depositions Upon Oral Examination

Rule 30 reads as follows:

(A) **When depositions may be taken.** After commencement of the action, any party may take the testimony of any person, including a party, by deposition upon oral examination. The attendance of a witness deponent may be compelled by the use of subpoena as provided by Civ. R. 45. The attendance of a party deponent may be compelled by the use of notice of examination as provided by division (B) of this rule. The deposition of a person confined in prison may be taken only by leave of court on such terms as the court prescribes.

(B) **Notice of examination; general requirements; nonstenographic recording; production of documents and things; deposition of organization; deposition by telephone.**

(1) A party desiring to take the deposition of any person upon oral examination shall give reasonable notice in writing to every other party to the action. The notice shall state the time and place for taking the deposition and the name and address of each person to be examined, if known, and, if the name is not known, a general description sufficient to identify the person or the particular class or group to which the person belongs. If a subpoena duces tecum is to be served on the person to be examined, a designation of the materials to be produced shall be attached to or included in the notice.

(2) If any party shows that when the party was served with notice the party was unable, through the exercise of diligence, to obtain counsel to represent the party at the taking of the deposition, the deposition may not be used against the party.

(3) If a party taking a deposition wishes to have the testimony recorded by other than stenographic means, the notice shall specify the manner of recording, preserving, and filing the deposition. The court may require stenographic taking or make any other order to ensure that the recorded testimony will be accurate and trustworthy.

(4) The notice to a party deponent may be accompanied by a request made in compliance with Civ. R. 34 for the production of documents and tangible things at the taking of the deposition.

(5) A party, in the party's notice, may name as the deponent a public or

private corporation, a partnership, or an association and designate with reasonable particularity the matters on which examination is requested. The organization so named shall choose one or more of its proper employees, officers, agents, or other persons duly authorized to testify on its behalf. The persons so designated shall testify as to matters known or available to the organization. Division (B)(5) does not preclude taking a deposition by any other procedure authorized in these rules.

(6) The parties may stipulate in writing or the court may upon motion order that a deposition be taken by telephone. For purposes of this rule, Civ. R. 28, and Civ. R. 45(C), a deposition taken by telephone is taken in the county and at the place where the deponent is to answer questions propounded to the deponent.

(C) Examination and cross-examination; record of examination; oath; objections. Examination and cross-examination of witnesses may proceed as permitted at the trial. The officer before whom the deposition is to be taken shall put the witness on oath or affirmation and personally, or by someone acting under the officer's direction and in the officer's presence, shall record the testimony of the witness. The testimony shall be taken stenographically or recorded by any other means designated in accordance with division (B)(3) of this rule. If requested by one of the parties, the testimony shall be transcribed.

All objections made at the time of the examination to the qualifications of the officer taking the deposition, or to the manner of taking it, or to the evidence presented, or to the conduct of any party, and any other objection to the proceedings, shall be noted by the officer upon the deposition. Evidence objected to shall be taken subject to the objections. In lieu of participating in the oral examination, parties may serve written questions on the party taking the deposition and require him to transmit them to the officer, who shall propound them to the witness and record the answers verbatim.

(D) Motion to terminate or limit examinations. At any time during the taking of the deposition, on motion of any party or of the deponent and upon a showing that the examination is being conducted in bad faith or in such manner as unreasonably to annoy, embarrass, or oppress the deponent or party, the court in which the action is pending may order the officer conducting the examination to cease forthwith from taking the deposition, or may limit the scope and manner of the taking of the deposition as provided in Civ. R. 26(C). If the order made terminates the examination, it shall be resumed thereafter only upon the order of the court in which the action is pending. Upon demand of the objecting party or deponent, the taking of the deposition shall be suspended for the time necessary to make a motion for an order.

The provisions of Civ. R. 37 apply to the award of expenses incurred in relation to the motion.

(E) Submission to witness; changes; signing. When the testimony is fully transcribed, the deposition shall be submitted to the witness for examination and shall be read to or by the witness, unless examination and reading are waived by the witness and by the parties. Any changes in form or substance that the witness desires to make shall be entered upon the deposition by the officer with a statement of the reasons given by the witness for making them. The deposition shall then be signed by the witness, unless the parties by stipulation waive the signing or the witness is ill, cannot be found, or refuses to sign. If the deposition is not signed by the witness within seven days of its submission to the witness, or within such longer period, not exceeding twenty-eight days, to which the parties agree, the officer shall sign it and state on the record the fact of the waiver or of the illness or absence of the witness or the fact of the refusal to sign together with the reason, if any, given therefor; and the deposition may then be used as fully as though signed, unless on a motion to suppress the court holds that the reasons given for the refusal to sign require rejection of the deposition in whole or in part.

(F) Certification and filing by officer; exhibits; copies; notice of filing.

(1) Upon request of any party or order of the court, the officer shall transcribe the deposition. Provided the officer has retained an archival-quality copy of the officer's notes, the officer shall have no duty to retain paper notes of the deposition testimony beyond five years from the date of the deposition. The officer shall certify on the transcribed deposition that the witness was fully sworn or affirmed by the officer and that the transcribed deposition is a true record of the testimony given by the witness. If any of the parties request or the court orders, the officer shall seal the transcribed deposition in an envelope endorsed with the title of the action and marked "Deposition of (here insert name of witness)" and, upon payment of the officer's fees, promptly shall file it with the court in which the action is pending or send it by certified or express mail to the clerk of the court for filing.

Unless objection is made to their production for inspection during the examination of the witness, documents and things shall be marked for identification and annexed to and returned with the deposition. The materials may be inspected and copied by any party, except that the person producing the materials may substitute copies to be marked for identification, if the person affords to all parties fair opportunity to verify the copies by comparison with the originals. If the person producing the materials requests their return, the officer shall mark them, give each party an opportunity to inspect and copy them, and return them to the person producing them, and the materials may then be used in the same manner as if annexed to and returned with the deposition.

(2) Upon payment, the officer shall furnish a copy of the deposition to any party or to the deponent.

(3) The party requesting the filing of the deposition shall forthwith give notice of its filing to all other parties.

(G) Failure to attend or to serve subpoena; expenses.

(1) If the party giving the notice of the taking of a deposition fails to attend and proceed with the deposition and another party attends in person or by attorney pursuant to the notice, the court may order the party giving the notice to pay to the other party the amount of the reasonable expenses incurred by the other party and the other party's attorney in so attending, including reasonable attorney's fees.

(2) If the party giving the notice of the taking of a deposition of a witness fails to serve a subpoena upon the witness and the witness because of the failure does not attend, and another party attends in person or by attorney because the other party expects the deposition of that witness to be taken, the court may order the party giving the notice to pay to the other party the amount of the reasonable expenses incurred by the other party and the other party's attorney in so attending, including reasonable attorney's fees.

COMMENTARY

Rule 30 is an important Rule that sets forth the procedures to be used in scheduling and conducting oral depositions. Like many of the Rules governing discovery, Rule 30 is keyed to Rule 26, which contains general provisions governing discovery, in many respects.

When Depositions May be Taken

Under subsection (A), the permission of the court is not generally required to take the deposition of any person except for incarcerated persons. If a party wishes to take the deposition of another party, proper notice under subsection (B)(1) is all that is required to compel the party's attendance. However, if the person to be deposed is not a party to the action, subsection (A) provides that subpoenas may be issued in accordance with the provisions of Rule 45 to compel the attendance of that person at the deposition.

As noted, a party need only provide notice to an opposing party if it desires to depose that party. No subpoena or order of the court is necessary, and the failure to respond to such notice is sanctionable under Rule 37(D). However, it should be noted that the notice must include the time and place for the deposition as well as any other details concerning the deposition. For example, the failure to indicate in a notice of deposition that the party taking the deposition intends to videotape the deposition will usually justify a refusal of the deponent to participate in the deposition.

Service and Contents of Notice

Subsection (B)(1) lists the information that must be included in the notice of an intent to take oral depositions. Notice to take oral depositions must be served on every party in the action, not just the deponent. If a subpoena to produce documents is also served on a non-party deponent or a request for documents of a party deponent is properly made under Rule 34, the subpoena and request, in addition to the list of the specific materials requested, should be attached to the notice.

Recording the Deposition

The party taking the deposition has the choice of the method of recording the testimony and must pay the cost of the recording. Permission from the court or opposing parties to take depositions other than by stenographic means is not required, although the court may require stenographic taking or some other method of recording to ensure the accuracy of the recorded material. However, if a party desires to take a deposition by telephone, subsection (B)(6) provides that permission of the court or stipulation of the opposing party is required. The deposition will then be deemed to have taken place at the location where the deponent answers the questions.

If the party being deposed or a party not involved in the deposition desires that the deposition be recorded by an additional method other than stenographically or that specified in the deposition notice, subsection (B)(3) allows them to arrange for additional methods of recording the deposition at its own expense.

Depositions of Corporations

If a corporation or other organization is the subject of the deposition, the party taking the deposition need not specify in its notice the persons who will actually testify at the deposition. Instead, a description with reasonable particularity of the matters upon which the deposition is requested is sufficient. The corporation or organization must then designate those persons who will testify on behalf of the corporation or organization, and a subpoena directing a non-party corporation or organization to be deposed must contain notification to this effect. The corporation or organization may also limit the testimony of any its designated persons to certain matters, eliminating possible speculative testimony.

Illustration 30-1

Roger commences a shareholder derivative suit against the officers of Great Grape Juice, Inc., challenging the merger of Great Grape Juice, Inc. and OK Purple Cider Company. As part of his discovery, Roger wishes to depose staff accountants of Great Grape Juice Inc., but does not know the precise identity of the corporation's employees. Under Rule 30, Roger does not need to specify the precise name of the person he wishes to depose. Rather, he may notify Great Grape Juice, Inc. that he wishes to depose staff accountants who are familiar with the corporation's financial performance over the past five years. In response, Great Grape Juice, Inc. is required to designate the staff accountants who will be testifying and notify Roger of their participation.

Formal Requirements of a Deposition

Although the Rule does not set forth details as to the proper procedure for depositions, they must nonetheless be conducted before an officer or appointee according to the provisions of Rule 28 or before a person stipulated to by the parties according to the provisions of Rule 29. The deposition should generally begin with a statement on the record by the officer or appointee conducting the deposition of the officer's or appointee's name and business address, the date, time, and location of the deposition, and the name of the deponent. If audiotape, videotape, or other nonstenographic means are used to record the deposition, these items should be repeated whenever a new tape or unit of recording is used. The officer or appointee must administer the oath or affirmation on the record, and must identify all persons present at the deposition.

The officer or appointee is responsible for the administration of the oath or affirmation and the recording of the testimony, a point made explicit in subsection (C). When the deposition has been completed, the officer or appointee should so indicate on the record and repeat any stipulations entered into by the attorneys regarding the deposition.

Deposition Proceedings

The operation of the Ohio Rules of Evidence and the order of the examination of witnesses at depositions is the same as those at trial. However, some Rules of Evidence, such as Rule 210, which concerns judicial notice, and Rule 614, which concerns the calling and interrogation of witnesses by the court, are not expressly inoperative to depositions, but they are clearly inapplicable. The question of whether other deponents may attend a deposition is not resolved by Ohio Rule 30, and this is a matter that should be addressed by the parties in a stipulation before the deposition.

The final sentence of subsection (C) complements Rule 31, which governs depositions on written questions. The provision envisions the situation where additional parties may desire that the deponent respond to certain questions, but the parties or their attorneys cannot attend the deposition or the modest number of questions do not justify an appearance. Parties are thus allowed to submit written questions in a sealed envelope to the party taking the deposition, who shall give them to the officer or appointee conducting the deposition, who, in turn, will read them to the deponent.

Illustration 30-2

Assume on the facts of Illustration 30-1 that the Securities and Exchange Commission (SEC), a party who has properly intervened in the action, desires that the staff accountants answer seven brief questions. However, the SEC cannot arrange for one of its attorneys to attend the scheduled deposition. The SEC may submit written questions in a sealed envelope to Roger's attorney. In turn, Roger's attorney must give the questions to the officer conducting the deposition. This allows the SEC to have their questions answered by the accountants without scheduling an additional deposition.

Objections at Depositions Generally

At one point in time, depositions had become unduly prolonged and unfairly frustrated by lengthy objections and colloquy as to how the deponent should respond. The Rule thus directs that objections to questions posed during a deposition must be stated concisely and in a non-argumentative manner on the record. Furthermore, instructions to a deponent from the deponent's attorney not to respond to a question can, at times, be even more disruptive than objections to the question. Therefore, most objections will not operate to justify the deponent's refusal to answer the question. However, most objections to questions asked at depositions will be preserved at trial, either by operation of Rule 32 or by stipulation.

Illustration 30-3

Assume on the facts of Illustration 30-2 that the attorney for Great Grape Juice, Inc. objects to the content of a question asked by Roger's attorney on the grounds that the question is overly prejudicial to the OK Purple Cider Company. The objection does not permit the staff accountants to refuse to answer the question, and the objection will be preserved at trial.

Objections to questions at depositions or concerning depositions are best understood as falling into one of four categories: *fundamental* objections, *content* objections, *form* objections, and *procedural* objections. The distinctions between these categories are important for purposes of determining whether the objection is waived if not raised at the deposition or as soon as the error or irregularity is discovered, whether the deponent is required to answer the question in spite of the objection, and whether the objection can be cured at the deposition. These determinations are culled through an analysis of the interplay between the relevant provisions of Rule 30 and Rule 32. Although attorneys frequently stipulate at a deposition that all objections except those to the form of the question are reserved by the parties, this stipulation is rarely necessary, as the Rules operate to preserve most objections except to the form of the questions even without a stipulation. Nonetheless, such a stipulation will sometimes resolve doubt on the matter and save the parties the time and expense of an argument on the issue.

In any event, Rule 30(C) provides that "[e]vidence objected to [at a deposition] shall be taken subject to the objections." This indicates that no objection will operate to justify the refusal of a deponent to answer questions, except perhaps questions to which the answers would be privileged. If there is any doubt on the issue, the attorney for the deponent may make a motion to terminate the deposition under subsection (C) for purposes of seeking a protective order or clarification from the court.

Fundamental Objections Generally

Objections to questions to which a deponent may be instructed not to respond may be referred to as *fundamental* objections. Although Rule 30 does not expressly provide for any category of question to which a deponent is justified in refusing to answer, it is clear that several grounds justify a refusal: to preserve a privilege not expressly protected from waiver by disclosure during discovery or to discontinue the deposition to permit the deponent to make a motion under subsection (D). All other grounds for objections are not justifications for a refusal to answer, and the party taking the deposition may make a motion to the court requesting an order for the deponent to answer the question. When an attorney has instructed a deponent not to respond to a question on permissible grounds, this fact should be clearly noted in the record. Nonetheless, attorneys frequently stipulate that a deponent's refusal to answer a question or an attorney's instruction not to answer a question will be considered as a directive from the officer or appointee conducting the deposition to the deponent to answer the question and the deponent's subsequent refusal to do so.

Content Objections

Objections to questions on the grounds stated in Rule 32(D)(3)(a)—the competency of the witness or the relevancy of the evidence—and any other objection contemplated by Rule 32(B), such as hearsay, may be characterized as *content* objections. Objections on these grounds do not permit a deponent to refuse to answer the question. Although the Rules do not forbid these objections at a deposition, the necessity of doing so has been obviated by the non-waiver provisions of Rule 32. A failure to raise these objections at a deposition does not preclude a party from later raising them at trial and rendering the deposition testimony inadmissible. Nonetheless, conscientious litigators may wish to point out to their adversaries that a particular line of questioning may be clearly inadmissible, thus sparing the offending attorneys the time and effort of asking the questions. Of course, information gathered at depositions may be useful for strategic purposes even if it would be inadmissible at trial.

Form Objections

Objections to questions on grounds involving the form of the questions or the responsiveness of the answers, such as an objection that a leading question has been asked, may be referred to as *form* objections. These objections are usually cured or rectified by the parties or their attorneys at the deposition itself. The failure to raise such an objection at the deposition constitutes a waiver of the objection at trial and on appeal.

Procedural Objections

Finally, objections to any error or irregularity in the manner in which the deposition occurred, including the notice for taking a deposition, the method of recordation of the deposition, the oath or affirmation, the conduct of the parties, the location of the deposition, the officer or appointee conducting the deposition, or the preparation of the transcript or recording of the deposition, may be referred to as *procedural* objections. As with *form* objections, *procedural* objections must be raised in a timely manner at the deposition or at the time they are discovered to prevent waiver of those objections. At times, the subject of the objection may be cured at the deposition.

Illustration 30-4

If the officer or appointee fails to administer the oath to a deponent, the error may be remedied at once.

In other instances, however, the objection is properly a matter for judicial decision, such as when a person not yet joined as a party but who is expected to be so joined has a right to attend a deposition. Such an objection should be made on the record to preserve the issue at trial and on appeal.

Motion to Terminate or Limit Examinations

Subsection (D), a companion rule to Rule 26(C), allows the court to order the officer conducting the deposition to terminate the examination if two requirements are satisfied: (1) a motion to terminate the deposition must be made by the party or the party's attorney; and (2) that person must make a showing that the deposition is being conducted in bad faith or in such a manner as unreasonably to annoy, embarrass, or oppress the deponent or party. The following factors, though not exhaustive, may be considered by a court faced with a Rule 30(D) motion: the age, physical condition, and geographical location of a witness; the possible use of the deposition in a criminal trial; and prior extensive discovery on the same subject between the same parties in a state court action. It should be noted that a Rule 37(A)(2) motion to compel answers may also be utilized by an examining party to control the conduct of the examination.

Illustration 30-5

Bob sues Jill for trespassing on Bob's property. At Jill's deposition, Jill's attorney repeatedly and without justification directs Jill not to answer the questions posed by Bob, thereby frustrating the purpose of the deposition. Under Rule 30(D), Bob may interrupt the deposition and seek the court's protection. In turn, the court may instruct Jill to answer the questions and order the deposition to resume, grant Jill a protective order under Rule 26(C), or impose sanctions on Jill or her attorney under Rule 37.

Review and Signing of Transcripts

Rule 30(E) provides for a waiver by the witness and parties of submission to and reading by the witness, and a waiver of the witness's signature by the parties after submission to the witness. If a deposition is not signed within seven days after submission to the witness or within a longer period not exceeding 28 days, the officer will sign the deposition and state the fact of waiver or the reason for no signature. Subsection (E) also allows a motion to suppress an improperly signed deposition.

Illustration 30-6

Assume on the facts of Illustration 30-5 that the court instructs Jill to answer the questions posed to her and orders the deposition to resume. This time the deposition is completed with little delay. Under Rule 30, Jill is not required to review and sign the transcript unless Bob or his attorney make such a request. In an effort to prevent future problems concerning the Jill's deposition testimony, Bob requests that Jill review and sign the transcript. On November 1, the transcriptionist informs the parties that the deposition transcript is available and will be provided to each party upon request. Under Rule 30, Jill must review her testimony and sign the transcript no later than November 29. If Jill makes any changes, the transcriptionist must append the changes to the transcript and provide a copy of the amendments to each of the parties.

Filing and Certification

After all required signatures have been obtained and changes to the transcripts or recording of the deposition noted, the officer or appointee conducting the deposition is required to execute a certificate of authentication attesting that the deponents were duly sworn and that the contents of the transcript or recording of the deposition are a true record of the deponent's testimony. The certificate must be filed with the transcript or recording. The Rule also states the record of the deposition and the certificate of authenticity should be filed with the court in which the action is pending. The party taking the deposition must notify all parties of the filing of the deposition.

Exhibits

Documents, material objects, or other exhibits used at a deposition must be properly identified and attached to the record of the deposition. However, if persons in possession or control of the documents or objects desire to retain the originals, they are provided with two alternatives: they can make copies of the documents to be attached to the record of the deposition, subject to verification with the originals by any party; or, they may allow the parties to view and inspect the originals at the deposition and permit them to be marked for identification purposes, subject to later production as exhibits at trial.

Failure to Attend

Subsection (G) allows a court to order the party taking a deposition to pay the reasonable expenses, including attorneys' fees, of a party attending that deposition in two circumstances. First, if the party taking a deposition does not show up at the correct time and place of the deposition, subsection (G)(1) permits expenses of the parties attending the deposition to be charged against the absent party. Although not expressly permitted, expenses incurred by a non-party deponent when a party fails to attend a deposition should be allowed by analogy. Second, if a party fails to serve a non-party deponent with a subpoena, thereby resulting in the absence of that person, and a party relies on the notice of the taking of the deposition in attending the deposition, the reasonable expenses of attending the deposition incurred by the party relying on the notice should be paid by the party who failed to serve the subpoena.

Illustration 30-7

Dan sues Betsy for personal injuries suffered in a hunting accident. As part of discovery, Betsy wishes to depose Wanda, a passerby who witnessed the events leading to the accident. However, Betsy fails to serve Wanda with a subpoena directing Wanda to appear at Betsy's office at 9:00 A.M. on January 27. In anticipation of the deposition, Dan drives 250 miles to Betsy's office. Predictably, Wanda does not appear at Betsy's office on January 27. Under Rule 30(G), the court may order Betsy to pay the reasonable expenses of Dan in attending the deposition.

ADDITIONAL AUTHORITY

8 WRIGHT & MILLER §§ 2101-2130
7 MOORE'S FEDERAL PRACTICE §§ 30.01-30.73
5 ANDERSON'S OHIO CIVIL PRACTICE §§ 160.01-160.12
2 KLEIN DARLING AT 30-1 to AT 30-31
3 TEREZ F 10.6.1 to F 10.6.8, F 10.8.1 to F 10.8.5
3 OH. JUR. PL. AND PRAC. FORMS, ch. 37
4 MILLIGAN Forms 30-1 to 30-68
1 FINK §§ 30-1 to 30-8
OHIO LITIGATION CHECKLISTS, Depositions and Discovery, §§ 6-8, 11

LEADING CASES

Abuse of Discretion Standard

Bishop v. Ohio Bur. of Workers' Comp., 147 Ohio App. 3d 772, 768 N.E.2d 684 (2001) (a trial court's ruling on the use of the deposition of a witness is reviewed under an abuse of discretion standard)

Changes in Deposition Testimony

Wright v. Honda of Am. Mfg., 73 Ohio St. 3d 571, 653 N.E.2d 381 (1995) (a change by deponent in deposition testimony, with the original testimony, will remain in the record and will be considered by the trier of fact)

Copies and Notice of Filing

Rostorfer v. Mayfield, 72 Ohio App. 3d 515, 595 N.E.2d 481 (the court officer before whom a deposition is taken must provide each party or deponent a copy of the deposition upon payment and any party requesting the filing of the deposition must service notice of the filing to all other parties as required by Rule 5) *dismissed, jurisdictional motion overruled*, 61 Ohio St. 3d 1418, 574 N.E.2d 1090 (1991)

Cost of Deposition

Rice v. Dudick Corrosion Proof, Inc., 57 Ohio App. 3d 156, 567 N.E.2d 315 (1989) (the party taking the deposition must bear the cost of the deposition when conducted for impeachment purposes, unless there are other overriding considerations)

Deposition of Non-Party

State ex rel. the V Cos. v. Marshall, 81 Ohio St. 3d 467, 692 N.E.2d 198 (1998) (the proper procedure for securing the attendance of a non-party witness at a deposition is the issuance of a subpoena pursuant to Rule 30(A) and Rule 45(D))

Party Attendance at Deposition

Midwest Sportservice, Inc. v. Andreoli, 3 Ohio App. 3d 242, 444 N.E.2d 1050 (1981) (unless a protective order is sought, a defendant may be compelled to appear at a deposition, regardless of residency or domicile; and the failure to do so may result in the imposition of sanctions)

CHAPTER 31

Rule 31. Depositions of Witnesses Upon Written Questions

Rule 31 reads as follows:

(A) Serving questions; notice. After commencement of the action, any party may take the testimony of any person, including a party, by deposition upon written questions. The attendance of witnesses may be compelled by the use of subpoena as provided by Rule 45. The deposition of a person confined in prison may be taken only by leave of court on such terms as the court prescribes.

A party desiring to take a deposition upon written questions shall serve them upon every other party with a notice stating

(1)   the name and address of the person who is to answer them, if known, and if the name is not known, a general description sufficient to identify him or the particular class or group to which he belongs, and

(2)   the name or descriptive title and address of the officer before whom the deposition is to be taken.

A deposition upon written questions may be taken of a public or private corporation or a partnership or association in accordance with the provisions of Rule 30(B)(5).

Within twenty-one days after the notice and written questions are served, a party may serve cross questions upon all other parties. Within fourteen days after being served with cross questions, a party may serve redirect questions upon all other parties. Within fourteen days after being served with redirect questions, a party may serve recross questions upon all other parties. The court may for cause shown enlarge or shorten the time.

(B) Officer to take responses and prepare record. A copy of the notice and copies of all questions served shall be delivered by the party taking the deposition to the officer designated in the notice, who shall proceed promptly, in the manner provided by Rule 30(C), (E), and (F), to take the testimony of the witness in response to the questions and to prepare, certify, and file or mail the deposition, attaching thereto the copy of the notice and the questions received by him.

(C) Notice of filing. The party requesting the filing of the deposition shall forthwith give notice of its filing to all other parties.

COMMENTARY

Rule 31 allows parties to depose any person, party or non-party, upon written questions. Depositions upon written questions differ from oral depositions only in the manner that the questions are asked of the deponent, and not in the manner that the deponent is to respond to the questions. Persons subject to depositions upon written questions must still answer the questions orally before a person authorized or appointed to administer oaths and conduct depositions. In this way, depositions upon written questions are distinct from interrogatories, which are governed by Rule 33.

Permission of the Court Not Required

In general, leave of the court is not required to depose any person upon written question except for persons confined in prison, in which case the court may make discovery orders on terms it deems most appropriate. However, court intervention may be necessary to compel the attendance of a nonparty deponent through a subpoena, the provisions of which are set forth in Rule 45. Although Rule 31 contains no explicit limitations on the use of this discovery mechanism other than those explained here, the court has discretion, implied in Rule 26(C), to prescribe the conditions under which discovery may proceed.

Relationship to Rule 30

The provisions of Rule 31 closely parallel those of Rule 30, which govern oral depositions. The notice and leave provisions of the two Rules are identical. Notice of the deposition and copies of the written questions must be served on the person to be deposed and the officer or appointee authorized to conduct the deposition. The second paragraph of subsection (A) allows a party to take depositions upon written questions of an organization in the same manner that it may take oral depositions of that organization in accordance with Rule 30(B)(5).

Time Periods for Depositions upon Written Questions

If the person to be deposed is a party, the third paragraph of subsection (A) sets forth a 49-day period in which written questions may be cross-examined, redirected, and re-crossed. Within 21 days after being served with notice of the depositions and the list of questions, the deposed party may serve cross questions on all other parties.

Within 14 days of the receipt of the cross questions, the party may then serve redirect questions on any party to which the redirected questions may be applicable. Within 14 days of the receipt of these redirect questions, the originally deposed party may then serve recross questions. These time limitations are effective from the dates that the parties received notice of the deposition and the list of questions, not the date of the actual deposition itself. The final sentence of subsection (A) provides that these time periods may be enlarged or shortened by the court for good cause shown.

Illustration 31-1

Maggy commences a wrongful termination action against her former employer, Quincy. Maggy wishes to depose Quincy upon written questions. On February 1, Maggy serves Quincy with a notice of a deposition to be held on March 30 and a list of 18 questions to be answered at the deposition. Quincy may serve cross questions upon Maggy no later than February 22. If Quincy does so on this date, Maggy may serve redirect questions on Quincy no later than March 8. Quincy may then serve recross questions upon Maggy no later than March 22.

Procedure for Depositions upon Written Questions

The officer indicated in the notice of deposition is required to conduct the deposition in accordance with the provisions of Rule 30(C), (E), and (F). The preparation, certification, and filing requirements of officers conducting depositions upon written questions likewise parallel those of officers conducting oral questions as provided in Rule 30(F). Subsection (C) requires that the party taking the deposition shall notify all other parties when the deposition is filed with the court.

Comparison with Oral Depositions

Depositions upon written questions are not used frequently, as the inflexibility of the procedure and attenuated nature of the examination, cross-examination, redirect, and recross makes this method of discovery unwieldy. Additionally, depositions upon written questions are sometimes ineffective in assessing the demeanor of a witness when testifying. The procedure allows deponents to carefully rehearse their responses to the questions with their attorneys, as deponents must be provided with the list of the written questions before the deposition actually occurs. The primary advantage of the method is that they are cost-effective for the party taking the depositions; neither that party nor the attorney for that party is required to attend the deposition.

ADDITIONAL AUTHORITY

8 Wright & Miller §§ 2131-2140

7 MOORE'S FEDERAL PRACTICE §§ 31.01-31.17
5 ANDERSON'S OHIO CIVIL PRACTICE § 160.13
2 KLEIN DARLING AT 31-1 to AT 31-1
3 TEREZ F 10.7.1 to F 10.7.4, F 10.8.1 to F 10.8.5
3 OH. JUR. PL. AND PRAC. FORMS, ch. 37
4 MILLIGAN Forms 31-1 to 31-10
1 FINK §§ 31-1 to 31-4
OHIO LITIGATION CHECKLISTS, Depositions and Discovery, §§ 9-11

LEADING CASES

Cost of Deposition

Rice v. Dudick Corrosion Proof, Inc., 57 Ohio App. 3d 156, 567 N.E.2d 315 (1989) (the party taking the deposition must bear the cost of the deposition when conducted for impeachment purposes, unless there are other overriding considerations)

CHAPTER 32

Rule 32. Use of Depositions in Court Proceedings

Rule 32 reads as follows:

(A) **Use of depositions.** Every deposition intended to be presented as evidence must be filed at least one day before the day of trial or hearing unless for good cause shown the court permits a later filing.

At the trial or upon the hearing of a motion or an interlocutory proceeding, any part or all of a deposition, so far as admissible under the rules of evidence applied as though the witness were then present and testifying, may be used against any party who was present or represented at the taking of the deposition or who had reasonable notice thereof, in accordance with any one of the following provisions:

(1)   Any deposition may be used by any party for the purpose of contradicting or impeaching the testimony of deponent as a witness.

(2)   The deposition of a party or of anyone who at the time of taking the deposition was an officer, director, or managing agent, or a person designated under Rule 30(B)(5) or Rule 31(A) to testify on behalf of a public or private corporation, partnership or association which is a party may be used by an adverse party for any purpose.

(3)   The deposition of a witness, whether or not a party, may be used by any party for any purpose if the court finds:

(a)   that the witness is dead; or

(b)   that the witness is beyond the subpoena power of the court in which the action is pending or resides outside of the county in which the action is pending unless it appears that the absence of the witness was procured by the party offering the deposition; or

(c)   that the witness is unable to attend or testify because of age, sickness, infirmity, or imprisonment; or

(d)   that the party offering the deposition has been unable to procure the attendance of the witness by subpoena; or

(e)   that the witness is an attending physician or medical expert, although residing within the county in which the action is heard; or

(f)   that the oral examination of a witness is not required; or

(g)   upon application and notice, that such exceptional circumstances exist as to make it desirable, in the interest of justice and with due regard to the importance of presenting the testimony of witnesses orally in open court, to allow the deposition to be used.

(4) If only part of a deposition is offered in evidence by a party, an adverse party may require him to introduce all of it which is relevant to the part introduced, and any party may introduce any other parts.

Substitution of parties pursuant to Rule 25 does not affect the right to use depositions previously taken. When another action involving the same subject matter is or has been brought between the same parties or their representatives or successors in interest, all depositions lawfully taken in the one action may be used in the other as if originally taken therefor.

(B) Objections to admissibility. Subject to the provisions of subdivision (D)(3) of this rule, objection may be made at the trial or hearing to receiving in evidence any deposition or part thereof for any reason which would require the exclusion of the evidence if the witness were then present and testifying. Upon the motion of a party, or upon its own initiative, the court shall decide such objections before the deposition is read in evidence.

(C) Effect of taking or using depositions. A party does not make a person his own witness for any purpose by taking his deposition. The introduction in evidence of the deposition or any part thereof for any purpose other than that of contradicting or impeaching the deponent makes the deponent the witness of the party introducing the deposition, but this shall not apply to the use by an adverse party of a deposition as described in subdivision (A)(2) of this rule. The use of subdivision (A)(3)(e) of this rule does not preclude any party from calling such a witness to appear personally at the trial nor does it preclude the taking and use of any deposition otherwise provided by law. At the trial or hearing any party may rebut any relevant evidence contained in a deposition whether introduced by him or by any other party.

(D) Effect of errors and irregularities in depositions.

(1) As to notice. All errors and irregularities in the notice for taking a deposition are waived unless written objection stating the grounds therefor, is promptly served upon the party giving the notice.

(2) As to disqualification of officer. Objection to taking a deposition because of disqualification of the officer before whom it is to be taken is waived unless made before the taking of the deposition begins or as soon thereafter as the disqualification becomes known or could be discovered with reasonable diligence.

(3) As to taking of deposition.

(a) Objections to the competency of a witness or to the competency, relevancy, or materiality of testimony are not waived by failure to make them before or during the taking of the deposition, unless the ground of the objection is one which might have been obviated or removed if presented at that time.

(b) Errors and irregularities occurring at the oral examination in the manner of taking the deposition, in the form of the questions or answers, in the oath or affirmation, or in the conduct of parties and errors of any kind which might be obviated, removed, or cured if promptly presented, are waived unless reasonable objection thereto is made at the taking of the deposition.

(c) Objections to the form of written questions submitted under Rule 31 are waived unless served in writing upon the party propounding them within the time allowed for serving the succeeding cross or other questions and within seven days after service of the last questions authorized.

(4) **As to completion and return of deposition.** Errors and irregularities in the manner in which the testimony is transcribed or the deposition is prepared, signed, certified, sealed, indorsed, transmitted, filed, or otherwise dealt with by the officer under Rule 30 and Rule 31 are waived unless a motion to suppress the deposition or some part thereof is made with reasonable promptness after such defect is, or with due diligence might have been, ascertained.

COMMENTARY

Rule 32 governs the use of depositions at trial or other court proceedings, including hearings on motions. Although subsection (A)(3)(g) indicates a clear preference for live testimony in lieu of deposition testimony, depositions may be introduced as evidence in certain situations and with certain procedural safeguards.

Admission of Depositions at Trial; Exceptions

Subsection (A) states that all or any part of a deposition may be used at a trial, hearing, or proceeding against any party who had notice of the deposition or was present at the deposition, subject to the exceptions stated in the subsection. A party intending to use any or part of a deposition must file a copy of a transcript of the deposition with the court at least one day prior to the hearing or beginning of the trial. However, perhaps the most fundamental limitation on the admissibility of deposition testimony is the condition that it must be admissible under the Ohio Rules of Evidence, applied as if the witness were then present and testifying. The substance of this provision is repeated in subsection (B), which allows objections to the admissibility of the deposition testimony on any grounds available under the Ohio Rules of Evidence.

Rule 32 contains additional grounds upon which the opponent of deposition testimony may object and seek to have the evidence excluded. The objections contemplated in subsection (D) should be regarded either as preservations of waiver of objections to the deposition testimony or as objections to the admission of the *deposition transcript*, rather than objections to the admission of the *deposition testimony*.

When Depositions Are Allowed

Subsection (A)(1) states that depositions may be used by any party against any other party or witness for impeachment purposes. It should be noted that Ohio Rule of Evidence 801(D)(1)(a) excludes prior inconsistent statements in depositions used for impeachment purposes from its definition of hearsay, so that depositions appropriately used in this manner are presumptively admissible.

Depositions of parties or persons designated by party organizations to provide deposition testimony are admissible for any purpose under subsection (A)(2). This provision parallels Ohio Rule of Evidence 801(D)(2)(d), which excepts from its definition of hearsay those admissions of a party-opponent.

Subsection (A)(3) allows the use of a deposition of any person, whether or not that person is a party, by any party for any purpose if the court finds that any of the circumstances listed in that subsection have been met. Although those situations might be characterized as circumstances in which the witness is "unavailable," utmost care should be exercised so as not to confuse these provisions with Ohio Rule of Evidence 804(A), which sets forth, in general, a more stringent definition of "unavailability" for purposes of determining whether certain hearsay exceptions obtain. One of these exceptions covers former testimony, which includes depositions, so that if a witness is "unavailable" within the meaning of Ohio Rule of Evidence 804(A) and under Civil Rule 32(A)(3), the deposition testimony will be admissible unless some other exclusionary rule or doctrine renders it inadmissible.

Objections to Admission of Deposition Generally

As noted, Rule 32 also lists the grounds upon which the opponent of a deposition may object to its admissibility. These grounds are divided into separate categories in subsection (D). Some of these objections must be raised at or soon after the time they are discovered, whereas other kinds of objections may be raised for the first time at trial or at a hearing.

Content Objections

Objections to questions on the grounds stated in subsection (D)(3)(a)—the competency of the witness or the relevancy of the evidence—and any other objection contemplated by subsection (B), such as hearsay, may be characterized as *content* objections.

As noted, these objections are properly understood as objections to the underlying testimony of the deposition rather than objections to the deposition itself. The failure to raise these objections at a deposition does not preclude a party from later raising them at trial, unless the basis for the objection is such that it might have been remedied if raised at the deposition.

Form Objections

Objections to questions on grounds stated in subsection (D)(3)(b) relating to the form of the questions or the responsiveness of the answers, such as an objection that a leading question has been asked, may be referred to as *form* objections. These objections are usually cured or rectified by the parties or their attorneys at the deposition itself. The failure to raise such an objection at the deposition constitutes a waiver of the objection at trial and on appeal.

Procedural Objections

Objections to any error or irregularity in the manner in which the deposition occurred, including the notice for taking a deposition, the method of recordation of the deposition, the oath or affirmation, the conduct of the parties, the location of the deposition, the officer or appointee conducting the deposition, or the preparation of the transcript or recording of the deposition may be referred to as *procedural* objections. Objections falling into this category are described with greater specificity in subsection (D)(1)-(2), (D)(3)(b)-(c), and (D)(4). Like *form* objections, they must be raised in a timely manner at the deposition, when they are discovered, or within the time limits set forth in the Rule to prevent waiver of the objections.

Effect of Taking or Using Depositions

A party does not make a witness its own by taking the witness's deposition; however, by introducing the witness's testimony for any purpose other than for contradiction or impeachment, the deponent may become the witness of the party. This has implications with respect to the degree to which the party may otherwise impeach the witness under Ohio Rule of Evidence 607. Subsection (C) further provides that the deposition of a party or a person representing an entity may, pursuant to subsection (A)(2), be used for any purpose. Also, a party who has presented the deposition of a medical expert pursuant to Rule 32(A)(3)(e) is not precluded from calling the expert at trial or otherwise using the deposition as provided by law.

Use of Only Part of a Deposition

If a party offers into evidence only part of a deposition, subsection (A)(4) allows an adverse party to require the party offering the deposition as evidence to introduce any other part of the deposition that is relevant to and should in fairness be considered with the part introduced. Under the final clause of that subsection, all parties have a right to introduce any other part of the deposition originally offered as well. The first provision differs from the second, however, in that an adverse party seeking to have portions of the deposition relevant to that offered by the original party does not have to introduce those portions itself. It may actually require the offeror to introduce the portions of the deposition originally omitted. Doing so may have strategic advantages for the adverse party at trial.

Illustration 32-1

Katie commences a negligence action against Howard to recover for personal injuries suffered in an automobile accident. At trial, Katie introduces a portion of Howard's deposition that suggests Howard was driving under the influence of alcohol at the time of the accident. Under Rule 32, Howard may, of course, introduce any other part of the deposition that Katie originally offered, such as a portion of the deposition which indicates that Howard's blood alcohol content was within legal limits. However, Howard may also require Katie to introduce this portion of the deposition transcript herself in an attempt to blunt the impact of the evidence on the jury.

It is unclear whether this provision may operate to admit testimony that would otherwise be inadmissible. Under subsection (A), only those portions of the deposition that conform with the Ohio Rules of Evidence may be admitted for use at trial. However, such portions may be relevant to a part of a deposition offered into evidence by a party and thus presumptively admissible under subsection (A)(4). Whether objections to such testimony on evidentiary grounds, *e.g.*, hearsay, are contemplated under the Rule is uncertain.

A suggested resolution to the problem can be culled through an analysis of the express language of subsection (A) indicating that the general language of that subsection is to be read "in accordance" with the provisions listed in subsections (A)(1)-(4). Deposition testimony inadmissible under the Ohio Rules of Evidence should not otherwise be deemed admissible by a provision within the Rules of Civil Procedure. Instead, the function of subsections (A)(1)-(4) is merely to prescribe additional limitations on the use of deposition testimony at trial, assuming that such testimony is admissible under the Ohio Rules of Evidence. Under this view, subsection (A)(4) should be read as authorizing an unusual order of proof with respect to deposition testimony only, rather than as rendering admissible evidence which would otherwise be deemed inadmissible under applicable evidentiary rules.

Admission of Depositions Unaffected by Substitution of Parties or Subsequent Actions

Finally, subsection (A) provides that the substitution of parties under Rule 25 does not affect the rights of the parties to use and introduce into evidence depositions taken prior to the substitution. Also, depositions may be used as provided in Rule 32 in future actions, whether brought in state or federal court, between the same parties or their representatives involving the same subject matter. This prevents the necessity of taking repetitious depositions in the event that the action is voluntarily or involuntarily dismissed.

ADDITIONAL AUTHORITY

8 WRIGHT & MILLER §§ 2141-2160
7 MOORE'S FEDERAL PRACTICE §§ 32.01-32.65
5 ANDERSON'S OHIO CIVIL PRACTICE §§ 167.01-167.11
2 KLEIN DARLING AT 32-1 to AT 32-7
3 TEREZ F 10.10.1 to F 10.10.4
3 OH. JUR. PL. AND PRAC. FORMS, ch. 38
4 MILLIGAN Forms 32-1 to 32-28
1 FINK §§ 32-1 to 32-5
OHIO LITIGATION CHECKLISTS, Depositions and Discovery, § 12

LEADING CASES

Costs of Deposition

Rice v. Dudick Corrosion Proof, Inc., 57 Ohio App. 3d 156, 567 N.E.2d 315 (1989) (the party taking the deposition must bear the cost of the deposition when conducted for impeachment purposes, unless there are other overriding considerations)

Depositions in Prior Actions

Varisco v. Varisco, 91 Ohio App. 3d 542, 632 N.E.2d 1341 (1993) (appellant's failure to call the trial court's attention to the applicability of the rule governing the use of depositions taken in prior actions resulted in a waiver of the admission of those depositions)

Filing and Use of Deposition at Trial

Nice v. Marysville, 82 Ohio App. 3d 109, 611 N.E.2d 468 (1992) (a deposition intended to be used at a hearing or trial must be filed at least one day prior to the hearing or trial)

Partial Use of Deposition

Gayheart v. Dayton Power & Light Co., 98 Ohio App. 3d 220, 648 N.E.2d 72 (1994) (where only part of a deposition is read into evidence, an opposing party has the right to read the rest of it)

Prior Testimony

Green v. Toledo Hosp., 94 Ohio St. 3d 480, 764 N.E.2d 979 (2002) (prior trial testimony of a party in the same case may be submitted in a new trial as if it were deposition testimony)

Videotaped Deposition

Buchman v. Wayne Trace Local Sch. Dist. Bd. of Educ., 73 Ohio St. 3d 260, 652 N.E.2d 952 (1995) (videotape of a deposition taken by a party may be used at trial by the opposing party)

Waiver of Objection

Rigby v. Lake County, 58 Ohio St. 3d 269, 569 N.E.2d 1056 (1991) (failure to move to suppress a deposition waives right to object to the admissibility of the deposition at trial)

CHAPTER 33

Rule 33. Interrogatories to Parties

Rule 33 reads as follows:

(A) Availability; procedures for use. Any party, without leave of court, may serve upon any other party up to forty written interrogatories to be answered by the party served. A party shall not propound more than forty interrogatories to any other party without leave of court. Upon motion, and for good cause shown, the court may extend the number of interrogatories that a party may serve upon another party. For purposes of this rule, any subpart propounded under an interrogatory shall be considered a separate interrogatory.

If the party served is a public or private corporation or a partnership or association, the organization shall choose one or more of its proper employees, officers or agents to answer the interrogatories, and the employee, officer or agent shall furnish information as is known or available to the organization.

Interrogatories, without leave of court, may be served upon the plaintiff after commencement of the action and upon any other party with or after service of the summons and complaint upon the party.

Each interrogatory shall be answered separately and fully in writing under oath, unless it is objected to, in which event the reasons for objection shall be stated in lieu of an answer. When the number of interrogatories exceeds forty without leave of court, the party upon whom the interrogatories have been served need only answer or object to the first forty interrogatories. The answers are to be signed by the person making them, and the objections signed by the attorney making them. The party upon whom the interrogatories have been served shall serve a copy of the answers and objections within a period designated by the party submitting the interrogatories, not less than twenty-eight days after the service of the interrogatories or within such shorter or longer time as the court may allow. The party submitting the interrogatories may move for an order under Civ. R. 37 with respect to any objection to or other failure to answer an interrogatory.

(B) Scope and use at trial. Interrogatories may relate to any matters that can be inquired into under Civ. R. 26(B), and the answers may be used to the extent permitted by the rules of evidence.

The party calling for such examination shall not thereby be concluded but may rebut it by evidence.

An interrogatory otherwise proper is not objectionable merely because an answer to the interrogatory involves an opinion, contention, or legal conclusion, but the court may order that such an interrogatory be answered at a later time, or after designated discovery has been completed, or at a pretrial conference.

(C) Option to produce business records. Where the answer to an interrogatory may be derived or ascertained from the business records of the party upon whom the interrogatory has been served or from an examination, audit, or inspection of the business records, or from a compilation, abstract, or summary based on the business records, and the burden of deriving or ascertaining the answer is substantially the same for the party serving the interrogatory as for the party served, it is a sufficient answer to the interrogatory to specify the records from which the answer may be derived or ascertained and to afford to the party serving the interrogatory reasonable opportunity to examine, audit, or inspect the records and to make copies of the records or compilations, abstracts, or summaries from the records.

(D) Form of answers and objections to interrogatories. The party submitting interrogatories shall arrange them so that there is sufficient space after each interrogatory in which to type the answer or objections to that interrogatory. The minimum vertical space between interrogatories shall be one inch.

COMMENTARY

Interrogatories are an efficient, comparatively inexpensive discovery mechanism for ascertaining answers to basic factual questions relevant in an action. Unlike depositions, interrogatories may be served only upon other parties in the action, and not on non-party witnesses. Interrogatories should not replace depositions as a method for examining potential witnesses in an action, nor should they replace admissions as a method of establishing facts that cannot later be disputed at trial. Instead, they function as a means of acquiring basic information upon which a party may rely in formulating subsequent discovery plans. Although answers to interrogatories are not conclusively established for the purpose of presentation at trial, parties and attorneys are sanctionable under Rule 37 for providing false and misleading answers to interrogatories.

Limits on Interrogatories

Interrogatories may inquire into any matter within the scope of discovery. Rule 33(A) sets a limit of 40 on the number of interrogatories that a party may serve on any other party. This limit may be enlarged with the court's permission.

How, When, and By Whom Interrogatories Must Be Answered

Interrogatories must be answered by the parties or an officer or agent designated by a party-organization. Although the attorneys for the parties cannot answer on behalf of their clients, attorneys frequently draft proposed responses and objections, which are then reviewed and approved by their clients.

Parties have not less than 28 days from the service of the interrogatories in which to respond or note objections to the interrogatories. This time limit may be enlarged or diminished by stipulation or by order of the court. Each interrogatory must be answered completely and fully under oath, or if an interrogatory is objectionable for any reason, the objection must be set forth with specificity in lieu of a response. The answers to the interrogatories must be signed by the respondent and the attorney preparing the answers and objections. Interrogatories may be served upon the plaintiff after commencement of the action and on any other party with or after service of the summons and complaint upon the party.

Illustration 33-1

Jeff commences a tort action against Karla for personal injuries suffered when Karla attacked Jeff with a tennis racket. On September 17, Jeff serves Karla with a set of 25 interrogatories. Karla objects to interrogatory 15. Under Rule 33, Karla cannot refuse to answer all 25 interrogatories. Rather, Karla must specify the grounds for her objection and answer the interrogatories that are not objectionable. Once completed, Karla and her attorney must sign the answers and serve them upon Jeff no later than October 15.

Objections to Interrogatories

Although proper objections to interrogatories are not articulated in the Rule, they include objections that a response would place an undue financial burden on the responding party, that the interrogatories are not specific enough to enable the respondent to formulate an adequate answer, that the interrogatories are repetitious, unnecessary, outside the scope of discoverable matters or are intended to harass the responding party, or that the interrogatories ask for purely legal conclusions. With regard to this final objection, subsection (B) distinguishes among opinions relating to facts, opinions relating to the application of law to facts, and opinions relating to legal conclusions. The first two kinds of opinions are not proper grounds for objection, although the lines separating these categories of opinions are sometimes difficult to discern. Careful practitioners should instruct their clients not to respond to interrogatories that arguably ask for legal conclusions and should state this objection on the answer form. Alternatively, a practitioner may make a motion to the court seeking guidance on whether the party has proper grounds for refusing to respond to the interrogatory.

Motion to Compel a Response

If a party refuses to answer an interrogatory, the party submitting the interrogatories may make a motion to compel an answer under Rule 37(A)(2) to the court. It should be noted that Rule 37 requires a party to make a good faith attempt to confer with the opposing party and resolve the matter without court intervention before making the motion. If a motion is made, the court should consider any objection stated in conjunction with the failure to answer, if any, and make a determination on the matter. Alternatively, the court may order that the subject of the interrogatory be discussed at the next pretrial conference scheduled.

Illustration 33-2

Assume on the facts of Illustration 33-1 that Karla objects to interrogatory 23 as well, claiming that the information requested is irrelevant to the litigation. After conferring with Karla in an effort to resolve the matter, Jeff may make a motion to compel Karla to answer the interrogatory.

Use of Interrogatories at Trial

Subsection (B) states that answers to interrogatories may be used at trial to the extent permitted under the Rules of Evidence. Because a party responding to interrogatories is not subject to examination or cross-examination with regard to its responses, these answers will not satisfy the prior testimony exception to the rule excluding hearsay. Thus, parties will generally be unable to introduce their own answers to interrogatories unless the statements satisfy another exception to the evidentiary rule excluding hearsay.

Option to Produce Business Records

Subsection (C) allows a party to simply refer the party requesting an answer to an interrogatory to the business records within which the answer may be found without spending the time or incurring the expense of ascertaining the answer itself. However, a party wishing to use this option must demonstrate that the burden of ascertaining the answer is substantially the same for both parties, and must identify and specify the records within which the answers will be located. This identification and specification may, by itself, result in substantial time and expense. Of course, the party must also allow the party requesting the information to access and examine the records in question.

Form of Answers and Objections to Interrogatories

By requiring that the party submitting interrogatories provide sufficient space in which an answer or objection may be typed, subsection (D) shifts the burden of responding to boilerplate interrogatory from the party receiving the interrogatory to the party submitting the interrogatory. Thus, an attorney preparing an interrogatory should select appropriate interrogatories and structure the document in a manner such that the responding party will be relieved of the burden of retyping and responding to the questions.

ADDITIONAL AUTHORITY

8 WRIGHT & MILLER §§ 2161-2200
7 MOORE'S FEDERAL PRACTICE §§ 33.01-33.175
5 ANDERSON'S OHIO CIVIL PRACTICE §§ 161.01-161.10, 167.12
2 KLEIN DARLING AT 33-1 to AT 33-13
3 TEREZ F 4.22.3, F 4.22.4, F 10.5.1 to F 10.5.13
3 OH. JUR. PL. AND PRAC. FORMS, ch. 39
5 MILLIGAN Forms 33-1 to 33-132
1 FINK §§ 33-1 to 33-5
OHIO LITIGATION CHECKLISTS, Depositions and Discovery, §§ 13-15

LEADING CASES

Attorney Answering for Client

Inzano v. Johnston, 33 Ohio App. 3d 62, 514 N.E.2d 741 (1986) (an interrogatory directed to an individual party may not be answered by that party's attorney)

Option to Produce Business Records

Jaric, Inc. v. Chakroff, 63 Ohio App. 3d 506, 579 N.E.2d 493 (1989) (a plaintiff who responded to defendant's interrogatories by submitting a three-inch pile of documents without specifying the interrogatory that was being answered satisfied Rule 33(C))

Unsigned Interrogatory

Inzano v. Johnston, 33 Ohio App. 3d 62, 514 N.E.2d 741 (1986) (an unsigned interrogatory is not admissible as evidence at trial)

CHAPTER 34

Rule 34. Production of Documents and Things for Inspection, Copying, Testing and Entry Upon Land for Inspection and Other Purposes

Rule 34 reads as follows:

(A) **Scope.** Subject to the scope of discovery provisions of Civ. R. 26(B), any party may serve on any other party a request to produce and permit the party making the request, or someone acting on the requesting party's behalf

    (1)   to inspect and copy, any designated documents (including writings, drawings, graphs, charts, photographs, phonorecords, and other data compilation from which intelligence can be perceived, with or without the use of detection devices) that are in the possession, custody, or control of the party upon whom the request is served;

    (2)   to inspect and copy, test, or sample any tangible things that are in the possession, custody, or control of the party upon whom the request is served;

    (3)   to enter upon designated land or other property in the possession or control of the party upon whom the request is served for the purpose of inspection and measuring, surveying, photographing, testing, or sampling the property or any designated object or operation on the property.

(B) **Procedure.** Without leave of court, the request may be served upon the plaintiff after commencement of the action and upon any other party with or after service of the summons and complaint upon that party. The request shall set forth the items to be inspected either by individual item or by category and describe each item and category with reasonable particularity. The request shall specify a reasonable time, place, and manner of making the inspection and performing the related acts.

    The party upon whom the request is served shall serve a written response within a period designated in the request that is not less than twenty-eight days after the service of the request or within a shorter or longer time as the court may allow. With respect to each item or category, the response shall state that inspection and related activities will be permitted as requested, unless it is objected to, in which event the reasons for objection shall be stated. If objection is made to part of an item or category, the part shall be specified. The party submitting the request may move for an order under Civ. R. 37 with respect to any objection to or other failure to respond to the request or any part of the request, or any failure to permit inspection as requested.

A party who produces documents for inspection shall, at its option, produce them as they are kept in the usual course of business or organized and labeled to correspond with the categories in the request.

(C) Persons not parties. Subject to the scope of discovery provisions of Civ. R. 26(B) and 45(F), a person not a party to the action may be compelled to produce documents or tangible things or to submit to an inspection as provided in Civ. R. 45. A party seeking production under this division shall give reasonable notice in writing to every other party to the action. The notice shall state the time and place for production and the name and address of each person subpoenaed. A designation of the materials to be produced shall be attached to or included in the notice.

(D) Prior to filing of action.

(1) Subject to the scope of discovery provisions of Civ. R. 26(B) and 45(F), a person who claims to have a potential cause of action may file a petition to obtain discovery as provided in this rule. Prior to filing a petition for discovery, the person seeking discovery shall make reasonable efforts to obtain voluntarily the information from the person from whom the discovery is sought. The petition shall be captioned in the name of the person seeking discovery and be filed in the court of common pleas in the county in which the person from whom the discovery is sought resides, the person's principal place of business is located, or the potential action may be filed. The petition shall include all of the following:

(a) A statement of the subject matter of the petitioner's potential cause of action and the petitioner's interest in the potential cause of action;

(b) A statement of the efforts made by the petitioner to obtain voluntarily the information from the person from whom the discovery is sought;

(c) A statement or description of the information sought to be discovered with reasonable particularity;

(d) The names and addresses, if known, of any person the petitioner expects will be an adverse party in the potential action;

(e) A request that the court issue an order authorizing the petitioner to obtain the discovery.

(2) The petition shall be served upon the person from whom discovery is sought and, if known, any person the petitioner expects will be an adverse party in the potential action, by one of the methods provided in these rules for service of summons.

(3)   The court shall issue an order authorizing the petitioner to obtain the requested discovery if the court finds all of the following:

    (a)   The discovery is necessary to ascertain the identity of a potential adverse party;

    (b)   The petitioner is otherwise unable to bring the contemplated action;

    (c)   The petitioner made reasonable efforts to obtain voluntarily the information from the person from whom the discovery is sought.

COMMENTARY

Rule 34 governs production and entry requests. Production requests are requests by a party to inspect, copy, sample, or test documents or tangible things that are in the possession or control of another party. Entry requests are requests by a party to be admitted to land or other property in the possession or control of another party for the purposes of inspection, measurement, surveying, photographing, testing, or sampling the property or objects on the property. Subject to the discovery provisions of Rule 26(B) and Rule 45(F), subsection (C) allows a subpoena *duces tecum* to be served on a non-party in conjunction with Rule 45 for production and entry requests.

Serving Production or Entry Requests

To make use of this discovery mechanism, a party must serve a written request on the other party that is the subject of the request. The request must specify the documents, things, or category of documents or things that are the object of the request, and must propose a time, place, and manner for the requested actions. The request may be served upon the plaintiff after commencement of the action and on any other party with or after service of the summons and complaint upon the party. Rule 30(B)(4) provides that this request may be attached to a notice to take the party's deposition.

Responding to Production or Entry Requests

The party to whom the production or entry request is directed has not less than 28 days in which to respond to the request, subject to alteration by the court. The response should indicate the extent to which the party agrees to comply with the request, and should specifically state any objections to the request.

Objections must be made in the response to the production or entry request or they will be deemed to have been waived. The production or entry will then proceed to the extent agreed upon in the response. If an objection to a request is made or the production or entry is not permitted by the party according to the terms set forth in the response, the party submitting the request for production or entry may make a motion to compel discovery under Rule 37(A) to the court.

It should be noted that Rule 37 requires a party to make a good faith attempt to confer with the opposing party and resolve the matter without court intervention before making a motion. If a motion is made, the court should consider any objection stated in conjunction with the failure to comply with the request, if any, and make a determination on the matter.

Illustration 34-1

Annette steals a valuable painting from Tom's dining room and sells it to Ivan. Tom commences an action against Annette and Ivan to recover damages for the value of the painting, which has since been destroyed. In an effort to challenge Tom's estimate of the value of the painting, Annette serves Tom with a written request for production of a copy of the most recent appraisal of the painting on September 9. Tom must respond to the request no later than October 7.

Duty to Keep Documents Organized

The last sentence of subsection (B) was added in 1980 to ensure that the party producing documents for inspection must do so as they are kept and organized in the usual course of business. This provision was intended to prevent a party from intentionally mixing together critical documents or "smoking guns" with other documents to obfuscate the significance of the former documents.

Production of Documents Prior to Filing of an Action

Subsection (D) is unusual in that it provides a method for compelling limited discovery before the commencement of an action to learn the identity of a potential adverse party. It is thus similar to the provisions of Rule 27 with regard to perpetuation of testimony, and should be interpreted as analogous to that Rule. The petition seeking this pre-filing discovery should include the information listed in subsection (D).

The court should issue an order authorizing the request for pre-filing discovery upon the satisfaction of the requirements listed in the Rule: (1) the discovery is necessary to learn the identity of a potential adverse party; (2) the petitioner is otherwise unable to bring the contemplated action; and (3) the petitioner made reasonable efforts to obtain voluntarily the information.

ADDITIONAL AUTHORITY

8 WRIGHT & MILLER §§ 2201-2230

7 MOORE'S FEDERAL PRACTICE §§ 34.01-34.16

LEADING CASES

Income Tax Returns

Anderson v. A.C. & S., Inc., 83 Ohio App. 3d 581, 615 N.E.2d 346 (1992) (income tax returns that are obtainable by a taxpayer from the applicable government agency may be discovered, even though they are not in the taxpayer's possession), *jurisdictional motion overruled*, 66 Ohio St. 3d 1489, 612 N.E.2d 1245 (1993)

Motion to Compel Production Against Non-Party

Moellering v. Schweitzer Constr. Co., No. C-860654 (1st Dist.), 1987 Ohio App. LEXIS 8620 (production of documents requested under Rule 30(B)(4) may not be ordered by the court except against a party deponent), *rev'd sub nom Moellering v. City of Cincinnati*, 40 Ohio St. 3d 20, 530 N.E.2d 1327 (1988)

Personal Medical Records

Calihan v. Fullen, 78 Ohio App. 3d 266, 604 N.E.2d 761 (1992) (unless a local rule, adopted pursuant to Rule 16, allows a court to require the pre-trial exchange of medical records without waiving the physician-patient privilege, production of personal medical records cannot be compelled)

Sanctions

Huebner v. Miles, 92 Ohio App. 3d 493, 636 N.E.2d 348 (1993) (the court is not necessarily required to impose sanctions on an opposing party that may have entered a party's land to make a survey without complying with Rule 34), *jurisdictional motion overruled*, 69 Ohio St. 3d 1424, 631 N.E.2d 164 (1994)

CHAPTER 35

Rule 35. Physical and Mental Examination of Persons

Rule 35 reads as follows:

(A) **Order for examination.** When the mental or physical condition (including the blood group) of a party, or of a person in the custody or under the legal control of a party, is in controversy, the court in which the action is pending may order the party to submit himself to a physical or mental examination or to produce for such examination the person in the party's custody or legal control. The order may be made only on motion for good cause shown and upon notice to the person to be examined and to all parties and shall specify the time, place, manner, conditions, and scope of the examination and the person or persons by whom it is to be made.

(B) **Examiner's report.**

    (1) If requested by the party against whom an order is made under Rule 35(A) or the person examined, the party causing the examination to be made shall deliver to such party or person a copy of the detailed written report submitted by the examiner to the party causing the examination to be made. The report shall set out the examiner's findings, including results of all tests made, diagnoses and conclusions, together with like reports of all earlier examinations of the same condition. After delivery, the party causing the examination shall be entitled upon request to receive from the party against whom the order is made a like report of any examination, previously or thereafter made, of the same condition, unless, in the case of a report of examination of a person not a party, the party shows that he is unable to obtain it. The court on motion may make an order against a party to require delivery of a report on such terms as are just. If an examiner fails or refuses to make a report, the court on motion may order, at the expense of the party causing the examination, the taking of the deposition of the examiner if his testimony is to be offered at trial.

    (2) By requesting and obtaining a report of the examination so ordered or by taking the deposition of the examiner, the party examined waives any privilege he may have in that action or any other involving the same controversy, regarding the testimony of every other person who has examined or may thereafter examine him in respect of the same mental or physical condition.

(3) This subdivision, 35(B), applies to examinations made by agreement of the parties, unless the agreement expressly provides otherwise.

COMMENTARY

In actions where a physical or mental condition of a party is at issue, physical or mental examinations are often necessary to determine the degree to which the condition contributed to the liability of the parties. Rule 35 governs these kinds of examinations.

Physical and Mental Examinations Generally

Subsection (A) allows a party to request an order from the court requiring that a party or person within the legal control or custody of a party submit to a physical or mental examination. Such an order is desirable because the examination occurs before a suitably certified or licensed person chosen by the party making the request. If an examination takes place, the person examined has the right to review the contents of the report of the examiner. However, the exercise of this right has, at times, dire consequences for the person examined. Subsection (B) details these consequences.

Examinations by Stipulation

Physical and mental examinations may also be agreed upon by the parties. However, examinations that are conducted by agreement of the parties are subject to the same provisions concerning the report of the examiner that are set forth in subsection (B) as if the examination had been ordered by the court, unless the agreement between the parties provides otherwise.

Examinations by Order of the Court

Unlike many discovery mechanisms, orders for physical and mental examinations are not automatically available. The Rule states that the court may order an examination if a mental or physical condition of a party or person within the custody or legal control of a party is "in controversy." Thus, only parties or dependents of parties are subject to physical or mental examination by order of the court. Additionally, a relevant mental or physical condition must be "in controversy" before the examination can be ordered. This requirement will be satisfied when a party raises an issue of its own mental or physical condition in a pleading or other paper filed with the court. However, to properly place a physical or mental condition of an opposing party "in controversy," a party may not rest upon conclusory allegations in its pleadings. It must make some kind of affirmative showing, by affidavit or otherwise, that the condition is genuinely "in controversy."

A request for an order under subsection (A) compelling a person to submit to a physical or mental examination must be made upon motion by a party. The motion should specify the persons to be examined, the kind of examination to be taken, the time and place of the proposed examination, and the certifications of the person conducting the examination. The motion should also demonstrate that there is good cause for ordering the examination, and must notify the person to be examined and all parties of the motion. If the court is satisfied that the requirements of the Rule have been met, it will issue an order compelling the person to submit to the examination under the terms in the motion or as modified by the court.

Illustration 35-1

Barry commences a tort action against Regina for personal injuries to his lower back suffered in an automobile accident. Two weeks after Regina is served with the summons and complaint, Regina observes Barry changing a tire on his truck. Under Rule 35, Regina may make a motion to the court requesting that Barry undergo a physical examination to determine the extent of any injuries to Barry's lower back.

Report of the Examination

After the examination occurs, the party against whom the order was made or the person examined may request a copy of a written report of the examination. The report should contain all the diagnoses and conclusions of the examiner, including the results of any laboratory tests. The request for the report includes a request for any reports of earlier examinations of the same condition, whether or not conducted by the same examiner.

If such a request is made or a deposition of the examiner is taken, the person examined must turn over all reports concerning the condition in controversy, including any reports generated after the examination ordered. The party also waives any claim of privilege relating to the condition. These consequences often present a difficult choice for a party that is subject to an order for examination. That party may obtain any information resulting from the examination that may be used against it at trial, but in doing so, must reveal any similar information to the opposing party concerning the condition.

Illustration 35-2

Assume on the facts of Illustration 35-1 that the court orders Barry to submit to a physical examination. After the examination occurs, Barry may request a copy of the written report of the examination as well as any reports of earlier examinations of the same condition. In doing so, Barry waives any claim of privilege pertaining to the condition of his lower back. The doctor who performed the examination must then provide Barry with a copy of any and all reports relating to Barry's lower back.

ADDITIONAL AUTHORITY

8 WRIGHT & MILLER §§ 2231-2250
7 MOORE'S FEDERAL PRACTICE §§ 35.01-35.12
5 ANDERSON'S OHIO CIVIL PRACTICE §§ 163.01-163.08
2 KLEIN DARLING AT 35-1 to AT 35-26
3 TEREZ F 10.4.1 to F 10.4.5
3 OH. JUR. PL. AND PRAC. FORMS, ch. 41
5 MILLIGAN Forms 35-1 to 35-34
1 FINK §§ 35-1 to 35-3
OHIO LITIGATION CHECKLISTS, Depositions and Discovery, §§ 19, 20

LEADING CASES

Appealability of Court Order

Montecalvo v. Montecalvo, 126 Ohio App. 3d 377, 710 N.E.2d 379 (1999) (a court order that parties submit to physical or mental examinations is generally not a final appealable order, although, in some circumstances, a trial court's order regarding physical or mental examinations would be so intrusive as to warrant immediate appellate review)

Failure to Submit to Examination

Plemons v. Sara Lee Corp., No. 88CA42 (2nd Dist.), 1989 Ohio App. LEXIS 1227 (where a party fails to submit to a physical examination ordered by the court under Rule 35(A) and undergoes surgery before a new examination can be scheduled, dismissal of the action is appropriate), *dismissed*, 44 Ohio St. 3d 714, 542 N.E.2d 1110 (1989)

Order for Examination

Brossia v. Brossia, 65 Ohio App. 3d 211, 583 N.E.2d 978 (1989) (an order for examination can only be made upon motion and for good cause shown with the time, place, manner, condition, and scope of the examination determined by the court)

Physician-Patient Privilege; Waiver

York v. Roberts, 9 Ohio Misc. 2d 21, 460 N.E.2d 327 (C.P. 1983) (a party that requests and obtains a report of an examination ordered by the court or agreed to by the parties waives any physician-patient privilege)

Psychological Examination Does Not Affect Substantial Right

Harness v. Harness, 143 Ohio App. 3d 669, 758 N.E.2d 793 (2001) (a trial court's order requiring psychological evaluations of all parties does not affect the substantial rights of the parties is thus not appealable)

Selection of Examiner Not Solely Moving Party's Choice

Harness v. Harness, 143 Ohio App. 3d 669, 758 N.E.2d 793 (2001) (a party seeking a psychological or medical examination of another party does not have the absolute right to pick the examiner)

CHAPTER 36

Rule 36. Requests for Admission

Rule 36 reads as follows:

(A) Request for admission. A party may serve upon any other party a written request for the admission, for purposes of the pending action only, of the truth of any matters within the scope of Rule 26(B) set forth in the request that relate to statements or opinions of fact or of the application of law to fact, including the genuineness of any documents described in the request. Copies of documents shall be served with the request unless they have been or are otherwise furnished or made available for inspection and copying. The request may, without leave of court, be served upon the plaintiff after commencement of the action and upon any other party with or after service of the summons and complaint upon that party.

Each matter of which an admission is requested shall be separately set forth. The matter is admitted unless, within a period designated in the request, not less than twenty-eight days after service thereof or within such shorter or longer time as the court may allow, the party to whom the request is directed serves upon the party requesting the admission a written answer or objection addressed to the matter, signed by the party or by his attorney. If objection is made, the reasons therefor shall be stated. The answer shall specifically deny the matter or set forth in detail the reasons why the answering party cannot truthfully admit or deny the matter. A denial shall fairly meet the substance of the requested admission, and when good faith requires that a party qualify his answer or deny only a part of the matter of which an admission is requested, he shall specify so much of it as is true and qualify or deny the remainder. An answering party may not give lack of information or knowledge as a reason for failure to admit or deny unless he states that he has made reasonable inquiry and that the information known or readily obtainable by him is insufficient to enable him to admit or deny. A party who considers that a matter of which an admission has been requested presents a genuine issue for trial may not, on that ground alone, object to the request; he may, subject to the provisions of Rule 37(C), deny the matter or set forth reasons why he cannot admit or deny it.

The party who has requested the admission may move for an order with respect to the answers or objections. Unless the court determines that an objection is justified, it shall order that an answer be served. If the court determines that an answer does not comply with the requirements of this rule, it may order either that the matter is admitted or that an amended answer be served. The court may, in lieu of these orders, determine that final disposition of the request be made at a pretrial conference or at a designated time prior to trial. The provisions of Rule 37(A)(4) apply to the award of expenses incurred in relation to the motion.

(B) Effect of admission. Any matter admitted under this rule is conclusively established unless the court on motion permits withdrawal or amendment of the admission. Subject to the provisions of Rule 16 governing modification of a pretrial order, the court may permit withdrawal or amendment when the presentation of the merits of the action will be subserved thereby and the party who obtained the admission fails to satisfy the court that withdrawal or amendment will prejudice him in maintaining his action or defense on the merits. Any admission made by a party under this rule is for the purpose of the pending action only and is not an admission by him for any other purpose nor may it be used against him in any other proceeding.

(C) Form of answers and objections to requests for admissions. The party submitting requests for admissions shall arrange them so that there is sufficient space after each request for admission in which to type the answer or objections to that request for admission. The minimum vertical space between requests for admissions shall be one inch.

COMMENTARY

Rule 36 governs requests for admissions by parties. This discovery mechanism is useful because matters that are the subject of admissions are conclusively established for the purposes of that action and thus need not be proven at trial.

When and on Whom Requests for Admissions May Be Served

Requests for admission may be served only on other parties. The request may be served upon the plaintiff after commencement of the action and on any other party with or after service of the summons and complaint upon the party.

Contents of Requests for Admissions

A party may seek the admission of any statement or opinion of fact, or application of law to fact, within the scope of discovery as defined in Rule 26(B)(1), including the genuineness of any documents described and attached to the request. Each matter that

BUSINESS REPLY MAIL
FIRST-CLASS MAIL PERMIT NO. 882 CINCINNATI OH

POSTAGE WILL BE PAID BY ADDRESSEE

ANDERSON PUBLISHING CO
PO BOX 1576
CINCINNATI OH 45273-9672

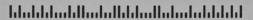

is the subject of a request for admission must be set forth separately in the request, enabling the party to respond to each matter in kind.

Responding to Requests for Admissions Generally

A party to whom requests for admission are directed has 28 days in which to respond to the requests. This time period may be lengthened or shortened by order of the court. It is crucial that parties respond to requests for admission within the proper time period, as a party will be deemed to have admitted each matter to which it does not timely respond, even if the assertion is demonstrably false. The response must be signed by the party or the attorney preparing the response.

Illustration 36-1

Lucy commences a wrongful termination action against Jonathan, alleging that she was fired because she refused to submit to Jonathan's sexual advances. On October 10, Lucy serves a request for admission upon Jonathan, requesting that Jonathan admit that he propositioned Lucy for sexual favors on five separate occasions. Jonathan has until November 7 to respond to Lucy's request for admission. If Jonathan fails to respond by that date, the actions will be deemed to have occurred, even if Jonathan did not in fact make any such proposition.

Kinds of Responses to Requests for Admission

A response to a request for admission may take one of four forms. First, the responding party may simply admit the matter that is the subject of the request. Second, the responding party may specifically deny the matter that is the subject of the request. A blanket denial is not sufficient, as the Rule states that "[a] denial shall fairly meet the substance of the requested admission." If only part of a matter can be denied, the responding party is required to specify the portion that is admitted and specifically deny the remainder.

Illustration 36-2

Assume on the facts of Illustration 36-1 that Lucy also requests that Jonathan admit that he is the owner of the business in question. Although Jonathan owns only a 60% share in the business, Jonathan may not respond with a blanket denial by claiming that Lucy's averment is "untrue." Jonathan may state that he is not the sole owner of the business, but he must also state his ownership interest in the business to fairly meet the substance of the question.

Third, a party may respond to a request by stating that the matter cannot be either admitted or denied. This kind of response is proper when a party does not object to the substance of the request, but simply cannot truthfully respond to the request one way or the other. This failure to admit or deny must be supported by specific reasons for doing so. Lack of information or knowledge is not a proper ground upon which a failure to admit or deny can be predicated, unless the party affirms that it has made a reasonable inquiry into the truth of the matter requested and still cannot truthfully admit or deny the matter. The Rule thus places a burden on the responding party to take affirmative steps toward ascertaining the truth of the matters requested. This duty parallels that placed on parties under Rule 33 in answering interrogatories.

Illustration 36-3

Assume on the facts of Illustration 36-1 that Lucy also requests that Jonathan admit that other female employees have complained about sexual harassment. Jonathan cannot deny this averment simply because he has no personal knowledge of such complaints. Rather, Jonathan must take reasonable steps to ascertain the truth of the matter. Jonathan may discharge this burden by reviewing the complaint forms on file at the business. However, if such forms are destroyed every two years, Jonathan may respond to Lucy's request by stating that the matter cannot be either admitted or denied due to a lack of information or knowledge about the matter requested.

Finally, a party may also object to the substance of a specific request for admission. An objection to a request is distinct from a denial or a failure to admit or deny, as it does not even acknowledge the propriety of the request. A party objecting to a request may do so on a variety of grounds, including privilege, the vagueness of the request, or that the request is outside the scope of discoverable information under Rule 26(B)(1). The reasons for the objection must be included in the response to the request.

Illustration 36-4

Assume on the facts of Illustration 36-3 that Jonathan believes that Lucy's request for admission is outside the scope of discoverable information because it is not relevant to the issues involved in the case. Under Rule 36, Jonathan may refuse to admit or deny the averment and object to the substance of the request.

Motions to Compel a Response

The party requesting the admissions may make a motion to the court to determine the sufficiency of the answers or to rule on an objection to a request. It should be noted that Rule 37 normally requires a party to make a good faith attempt to confer with the opposing party and resolve the matter without court intervention before making a motion. However, this good-faith requirement of Rule 37 is not applicable to requests for admission. If a motion is made, the court should rule on any answer or objection to a request, and make an order in accordance with the ruling. The court may also defer a ruling on the matter until a scheduled pretrial conference is held or until another time that the court deems appropriate.

Effects of Admissions; Amendment

Subsection (B) indicates that any matter admitted by a party is conclusively established for the purposes of that action and need not proven by the opposing party at trial. The admission does not have res judicata effect, however, and cannot be used in subsequent actions against the party making the admission. Thus, in actions that are dismissed and re-initiated for technical reasons, requests for admission should be reserved on the parties. A withdrawal or an amendment of an admission should be permitted by the court under the standards set forth in Rule 16. Thus, an amendment or withdrawal of an admission should be allowed unless the opposing party can demonstrate that an amendment or withdrawal will result in prejudice to that party.

Form of Admissions

By requiring that the party submitting requests for admissions provide sufficient space in which an answer or objection may be typed, subsection (C) shifts the burden of responding to boilerplate admissions requests from the party receiving the request to the party submitting the request. Thus, an attorney preparing a request for admission must arrange them in such a manner so as to allow sufficient space for answers.

ADDITIONAL AUTHORITY

8 WRIGHT & MILLER §§ 2251-2280
7 MOORE'S FEDERAL PRACTICE §§ 36.01-36.13
5 ANDERSON'S OHIO CIVIL PRACTICE §§ 164.01-164.07, 167.14
2 KLEIN DARLING AT 36-1 to AT 36-49
3 TEREZ F 10.2.1 to F 10.2.7
3 OH. JUR. PL. AND PRAC. FORMS, ch. 42
1 FINK §§ 36-1 to 36-4
OHIO LITIGATION CHECKLISTS, Depositions and Discovery, §§ 21, 22

LEADING CASES

Admissions Must be Signed

Outdoor Prod., Inc. v. The Deck Connection & More, Inc., 104 Ohio Misc. 2d 19, 728 N.E.2d 44 (C.P. 1999) (party's purported responses to opposing party's requests for admissions were not effective, as they had not been signed by either the party or party's counsel)

Costs on Disputable Issue

Youssef v. Jones, 77 Ohio App. 3d 500, 602 N.E.2d 1176 (1991) (even if a matter can be proved by the requesting party, the responding party should not be charged for the cost of proving the issue where the denial is based on a belief that the matter was disputable), *jurisdictional motion overruled*, 63 Ohio St. 3d 1411, 585 N.E.2d 836 (1992)

Effect of Admission; Failure to Respond

Ramsey v. Edgepark, Inc., 66 Ohio App. 3d 99, 583 N.E.2d 443 (an admission that is the result of a failure to respond to a request for admissions is a written admission satisfying the requirement of Rule 56(C)), *cause dismissed*, 53 Ohio St. 3d 712, 560 N.E.2d 780 (1990)

Failure to Respond to Request

State ex rel. Montgomery v. Maginn, 147 Ohio App. 3d 420, 770 N.E.2d 1099 (2002) (an admission arising by a party's failure to respond to a request for admissions constitutes a "written admission" for purposes of the summary judgment rule)

Dobbleacre v. Cosco, Inc., 120 Ohio App. 3d 232, 697 N.E.2d 1016 (1998) (the failure of a party to answer in a timely manner a request for admission will constitute a conclusive admission under Rule 36 and also satisfies the writing requirement of Rule 56(C))

Good Reasons to Deny Requests for Admissions

Salem Med. Arts and Dev. Corp. v. Columbiana Cty. Bd. of Revision, 82 Ohio St. 3d 193, 694 N.E.2d 1324 (1998) (that a matter was justifiably believed to be related to a genuine issue for trial is insufficient to constitute a good reason for denying a request for admissions; instead, only those matters actually determined to be in issue meet the standard of good reason to deny)

Sanctions

Salem Med. Arts and Dev. Corp. v. Columbiana Cty. Bd. of Revision, 82 Ohio St. 3d 193, 694 N.E.2d 1324 (1998) (if matters denied in a request for admission are proved at trial, a court shall award sanctions unless: (1) the request for admissions has been held to be objectionable; (2) the court finds that there was good reason for the failure to admit; or (3) the admission sought was of no substantial importance; party is not required to file a motion to compel before moving for sanctions for a bad faith denial of requests for admissions)

Timeliness of Response to Request

Sandler v. Gossick, 87 Ohio App. 3d 372, 622 N.E.2d 389 (1993) (a late response to a request for admission may be accepted by the court upon a showing of compelling circumstances)

Withdrawal of Admissions

Colopy v. Nationwide Ins. Co., No. 17019 (9th Dist.), 1995 Ohio App. LEXIS 3462 (the trial court may determine whether to allow the withdrawal of admissions)

Withdrawal of Admissions Not Permitted

Holman v. Keegan, 139 Ohio App. 3d 911, 746 N.E.2d 209 (2000) (where trial court found that plaintiff would be prejudiced if defendant were allowed to withdraw admissions within three weeks of trial date, the refusal to permit defendant to withdraw admissions of liability that arose from failure to give timely response to requests for admissions was not an abuse of discretion even though defendant had answered complaint with a general denial of liability)

CHAPTER 37

Rule 37. Failure to Make Discovery; Sanctions

Rule 37 reads as follows:

(A) **Motion for order compelling discovery.** Upon reasonable notice to other parties and all persons affected thereby, a party may move for an order compelling discovery as follows:

(1) **Appropriate court.** A motion for an order to a party or a deponent shall be made to the court in which the action is pending.

(2) **Motion.** If a deponent fails to answer a question propounded or submitted under Rule 30 or Rule 31, or a party fails to answer an interrogatory submitted under Rule 33, or if a party, in response to a request for inspection submitted under Rule 34, fails to respond that inspection will be permitted as requested or fails to permit inspection as requested, the discovering party may move for an order compelling an answer or an order compelling inspection in accordance with the request. On matters relating to a deposition on oral examination, the proponent of the question may complete or adjourn the examination before he applies for an order.

(3) **Evasive or incomplete answer.** For purposes of this subdivision an evasive or incomplete answer is a failure to answer.

(4) **Award of expenses of motion.** If the motion is granted, the court shall, after opportunity for hearing, require the party or deponent who opposed the motion or the party or attorney advising such conduct or both of them to pay to the moving party the reasonable expenses incurred in obtaining the order, including attorney's fees, unless the court finds that the opposition to the motion was substantially justified or that other circumstances make an award of expenses unjust.

If the motion is denied, the court shall, after opportunity for hearing, require the moving party or the attorney advising the motion or both of them to pay to the party or deponent who opposed the motion the reasonable expenses incurred in opposing the motion, including attorney's fees, unless the court finds that the making of the motion was substantially justified or that other circumstances make an award of expenses unjust.

If the motion is granted in part and denied in part, the court may apportion the reasonable expenses incurred in relation to the motion among the parties and persons in a just manner.

(B) Failure to comply with order.

(1) If a deponent fails to be sworn or to answer a question after being directed to do so by the court, the failure may be considered a contempt of that court.

(2) If any party or an officer, director, or managing agent of a party or a person designated under Rule 30(B)(5) or Rule 31(A) to testify on behalf of a party fails to obey an order to provide or permit discovery, including an order made under subdivision (A) of this rule and Rule 35, the court in which the action is pending may make such orders in regard to the failure as are just, and among others the following:

(a) An order that the matters regarding which the order was made or any other designated facts shall be taken to be established for the purposes of the action in accordance with the claim of the party obtaining the order;

(b) An order refusing to allow the disobedient party to support or oppose designated claims or defenses, or prohibiting him from introducing designated matters in evidence;

(c) An order striking out pleadings or parts thereof, or staying further proceedings until the order is obeyed, or dismissing the action or proceeding or any part thereof, or rendering a judgment by default against the disobedient party;

(d) In lieu of any of the foregoing orders or in addition thereto, an order treating as a contempt of court the failure to obey any orders except an order to submit to a physical or mental examination;

(e) Where a party has failed to comply with an order under Rule 35(A) requiring him to produce another for examination, such orders as are listed in subsections (a), (b), and (c) of this subdivision, unless the party failing to comply shows that he is unable to produce such person for examination.

In lieu of any of the foregoing orders or in addition thereto, the court shall require the party failing to obey the order or the attorney advising him or both to pay the reasonable expenses, including attorney's fees, caused by the failure, unless the court expressly finds that the failure was substantially justified or that other circumstances make an award of expenses unjust.

(C) Expenses on failure to admit.
If a party, after being served with a request for admission under Rule 36, fails to admit the genuineness of any documents or the truth of any matter as requested, and if the party requesting the admissions thereafter proves the genuineness of the document or the truth of the matter, he may apply to the court for an order requiring the other party to pay him the reasonable expenses incurred in making that proof, including reasonable attorney's fees. Unless the request had been held objectionable

under Rule 36(A) or the court finds that there was good reason for the failure to admit or that the admission sought was of no substantial importance, the order shall be made.

(D) **Failure of party to attend at own deposition or serve answers to interrogatories or respond to request for inspection.** If a party or an officer, director, or a managing agent of a party or a person designated under Rule 30(B)(5) or Rule 31(A) to testify on behalf of a party fails

(1) to appear before the officer who is to take his deposition, after being served with a proper notice, or

(2) to serve answers or objections to interrogatories submitted under Rule 33, after proper service of the interrogatories, or

(3) to serve a written response to a request for inspection submitted under Rule 34, after proper service of the request, the court in which the action is pending on motion and notice may make such orders in regard to the failure as are just, and among others it may take any action authorized under subsections (a), (b), and (c) of subdivision (B)(2) of this rule. In lieu of any order or in addition thereto, the court shall require the party failing to act or the attorney advising him or both to pay the reasonable expenses, including attorney's fees, caused by the failure, unless the court expressly finds that the failure was substantially justified or that other circumstances make an award of expenses unjust.

The failure to act described in this subdivision may not be excused on the ground that the discovery sought is objectionable unless the party failing to act has applied for a protective order as provided by Rule 26(C).

(E) **[Duty to resolve.]** Before filing a motion authorized by this rule, the party shall make a reasonable effort to resolve the matter through discussion with the attorney, unrepresented party, or person from whom discovery is sought. The motion shall be accompanied by a statement reciting the efforts made to resolve the matter in accordance with this section.

COMMENTARY

A party's refusal to abide by the discovery provisions of Rules 26-36 does not subject that party to sanctions under Rule 11. Instead, discovery requests, responses, objections, and motions are covered by Rule 37, which details the sanctions available to the court for violation of discovery orders and abuse of the discovery process. Rule 37 also sets forth the procedure for making a motion to compel disclosure or discovery.

Motion for Order to Compel Discovery Generally

Subsection (A) allows a party to make a motion requesting an order to compel a person to take certain actions concerning discovery. In all cases, the motion should be made to the court in which the action is pending, regardless of whether the motion concerns a party or non-party. However, before such a motion can be made, subsection (E) indicates that the movant must make a good faith attempt to confer with the opposing party and resolve the matter without court intervention.

Evasive or Incomplete Responses

Subsection (A)(3) indicates that a person cannot avoid an order to compel discovery by presenting an evasive or incomplete disclosure, answer, or response. Such a disclosure, answer, or response will treated by the court as a failure to so perform.

Illustration 37-1

Pam commences an action against Steve for the wrongful death of her husband, who was killed in a farming accident. As part of discovery, Pam serves a written interrogatory upon Steve, asking whether Steve was intoxicated at the time of the accident. In his answer to Pam's interrogatory, Steve indicated that he had "enjoyed a refreshing beverage or two" on the day in question. As this answer constitutes an evasive or incomplete disclosure and, therefore, is an insufficient response, Pam may make a motion to compel Steve to accurately and completely answer the interrogatory. Prior to doing so, however, Pam must confer with Steve or his attorney in an effort to resolve the matter without the court's intervention.

Grounds for Granting Motions for Orders to Compel Discovery

Subsection (A)(2) specifies the actions or refusals that are proper grounds for a party to make a motion for an order compelling discovery. These actions include the failure to answer a question at an oral deposition or to a deposition upon written questions, the failure to answer an interrogatory, the failure to respond to a request for production or entry, and the failure to permit an inspection or entry as requested. A motion for an order to compel a corporation or organization to designate a person to answer questions at oral depositions or to a deposition upon written questions is also contemplated by the Rule.

Motions for Orders to Compel Discovery; Expenses and Fees

Subsection (A)(4) establishes a presumption that the party against whom a motion for an order to compel discovery has been decided must pay the reasonable expenses, including attorneys' fees, of the opposing party in either making or defending the motion. The court is required to provide a party against whom costs will be assessed an opportunity to be heard to allow that party to demonstrate that their making or opposing the motion was substantially justified or that other circumstances would make an award of expenses unjust. Fees may be assessed against the person whose actions or failures to act gave rise to the motion, that person's attorney, or both.

If a motion for an order to compel discovery is granted in part and denied in part, the court, after providing the parties with an opportunity to be heard on the matter, has broad discretion to apportion the expenses of making and opposing the motion between the parties.

Illustration 37-2

Assume on the facts of Illustration 37-1 that Pam makes a motion to the court to compel Steve to answer the interrogatory. If the motion is granted by the court, Steve must pay the reasonable expenses incurred by Pam in making the motion, unless the court finds that Steve's refusal to provide a complete response was substantially justified.

Sanctions that May Be Imposed by the Court

Subsections (B)-(D) govern the kinds of sanctions that may be imposed by a court. These subsections set forth, in great detail, which sanctions may be imposed for certain discovery violations. From these subsections, it is possible to designate five categories of sanctions:

(1) an order mandating that certain facts at issue in an action will be deemed to have been conclusively established;

(2) an order forbidding a party to support or oppose certain claims or defenses, or forbidding a party to introduce certain matters into evidence;

(3) an order striking certain pleadings or parts of pleadings, staying all proceedings until the violation is rectified, dismissing an action, or entering a default judgment;

(4) contempt of court; and

(5) an order requiring the party in violation to pay the reasonable expenses, including attorneys' fees, incurred by the other parties as a result of the violation, unless the court finds that the violation was substantially justified or that other circumstances would make an award of expenses and fees unjust.

When Certain Sanctions Are Appropriate

The following is a list of discovery violations and the categories of sanctions, as enumerated above, that may be imposed by the court for the violations:

(A) If a party fails to obey a court order permitting discovery, a court order to compel discovery under Rule 37(A), sanctions (1)-(5) are available.

(B) If a party fails to obey an order to submit to a physical or mental examination under Rule 35, sanctions (1)-(3) and (5) are available. Therefore, a person who refuses to comply with an order to submit to a physical or mental examination cannot be held in contempt of court for the failure to do so, but a person may be held in contempt of court for the failure to obey an order to pay any expenses or fees incurred by other parties resulting from its refusal to comply with the order to submit to the examination.

Illustration 37-3

Theresa is ordered to submit to a mental examination pursuant to Rule 35. Notwithstanding the court order, Theresa refuses to appear for the examination, but complies with a court order directing her to pay the expenses incurred by other parties as a result of her failure to appear. Rule 37 precludes the court from holding Theresa in contempt in this situation.

(C) If a non-party fails to answer a question at a deposition after being ordered by the court to do so, only sanction (4) is available. It should be noted that Rule 45(E) also provides for contempt sanctions on non-parties who fail to obey subpoenas.

Curiously, if the conduct of a non-party deponent gives rise to a motion to compel discovery under subsection (A), that subsection allows the court to tax the reasonable expenses, including attorneys' fees, of the moving party against the non-party deponent. However, subsection (B) does not provide for this sanction against non-parties for their refusals to obey orders of the court under subsection (A). Thus, a non-party may be properly ordered to pay the reasonable expenses of a party making a motion for an order to compel discovery and may be held in contempt for the refusal to pay. However, the non-party may not be held responsible for the expenses incurred by a party for the non-party's refusal to pay the expenses incurred in making the motion to compel discovery.

(D) If a party-deponent fails to attend her own deposition, a party fails to answer interrogatories, or a party fails to respond to requests for production or entry, sanctions (1)-(3) and (5) are available. If a party fails to answer interrogatories or to respond to requests for production or entry, the party making the motion for an order to respond is subject to the good-faith conference requirement discussed in conjunction with Rule 37(A).

Additionally, the final sentence of subsection (D) creates an exception for absentee party-deponents who make a motion for a protective order under Rule 26(C) that has not been ruled upon at the time of the deposition. Ordinarily, the filing of a motion for a protective order does not serve to protect the party; the protection depends upon the court's determination on the motion. However, under this provision, the party-deponent is protected from non-attendance at a deposition in such situations.

Illustration 37-4

Harry sues Martha for repeatedly trespassing on his land. As part of discovery, Harry notifies Martha that he wishes to depose her on November 11. On November 7, Martha makes a motion to the court for a protective order. As of November 11, the court has not ruled on Martha's motion and Martha does not attend the scheduled deposition. Rule 37(D) protects Martha from any sanctions that may be imposed as a result of her non-attendance of the deposition.

Denial of a Matter Requested to Be Admitted

Subsection (C) is a special provision relating to requests for admission under Rule 36. If a party denies a matter that is later proved to be true at trial, that party is responsible for the reasonable expenses, including attorneys' fees, incurred by the opposing party in proving the truth of the matter. The inclusion of this provision amongst discovery violations is curious, as the nature of a failure to admit a fact later proved at trial is certainly not sanctionable in most situations. Thus, the provision is subject to the far-reaching exceptions stated in that subsection.

Illustration 37-5

Assume on the facts of Illustration 37-4 that Harry serves Martha with a request for admission that asks Martha to admit that she repeatedly trespassed on Harry's property over the past year. Martha promptly denies the averment. As an affirmative response to this request would be virtually dispositive of the action, the court should not assess Harry's reasonable expenses of tendering the request for admission against Martha if Harry ultimately prevails in the action, as there is a good reason for Martha's failure to make the admission.

ADDITIONAL AUTHORITY

8 Wright & Miller §§ 2281-2300

7 Moore's Federal Practice §§ 37.01-37.122

5 Anderson's Ohio Civil Practice §§ 166.01-166.10

2 Klein Darling AT 37-1 to AT 37-26

3 Terez F 10.12.1 to F 10.12.7, F 10.13.1 to F 10.13.11

3 Oh. Jur. Pl. and Prac. Forms, ch. 43

5 Milligan Forms 37-1 to 37-82

1 Fink §§ 37-1 to 37-8

Ohio Litigation Checklists, Depositions and Discovery, § 23

LEADING CASES

Adverse Judgment For Failure to Comply

Marten v. Casgar, No 93-L-115 (11th Dist.), 1994 Ohio App. LEXIS 2943 (default judgment cannot be entered except upon a showing of willfulness or bad faith)

Court Authority to Impose Sanctions

Laubsher v. Branthoover, 68 Ohio App. 3d 375, 588 N.E.2d 290 (1991) (the court, under Rule 37, may make "just" orders in response to violations of discovery rules or court orders)

Default Judgment as Sanction

American Sales, Inc. v. Boffo, 71 Ohio App. 3d 168, 593 N.E.2d 316 (default judgment may be appropriate for the failure to appear at depositions after being served with proper notice despite no prior court order compelling discovery), *jurisdictional motion overruled*, 61 Ohio St. 3d 1422, 574 N.E.2d 1092 (1991)

Destruction of Evidence

Travelers Ins. Co. v. Dayton Power & Light Co., 76 Ohio Misc. 2d 17, 663 N.E.2d 1383 (C.P. 1996) (the disposal or destruction of evidence, even by negligence or inadvertent spoliation, may be sufficient for the imposition of sanctions under Rule 37)

Dismissal as Sanction

Anderson v. A.C. & S., Inc., 83 Ohio App. 3d 581, 615 N.E.2d 346 (1992) (an action is justifiably dismissed where counsel is notified that the failure to provide discovery may result in dismissal yet persists in refusing to comply)

Evasive Responses

Shoreway Circle, Inc. v. Gerald Skoch Co., L.P.A., 92 Ohio App. 3d 823, 637 N.E.2d 355 (where a plaintiff provides only evasive and sham responses to request for discovery and continues this conduct after receiving notice of possible dismissal, a court is justified in dismissing the action), *cause dismissed*, 69 Ohio St. 3d 1466, 634 N.E.2d 226 (1994)

Exclusion of Evidence

Nickey v. Brown, 7 Ohio App. 3d 32, 454 N.E.2d 177 (1982) (a court should only exclude evidence for failure to fully answer interrogatories when clearly necessary to enforce a party's willful noncompliance or to prevent unfair surprise)

Exclusion of Expert Witness Proper Where Untimely Disclosed

Buszkiewicz v. DiFranco, 140 Ohio App. 3d 126, 746 N.E.2d 712 (2000) (party's untimely disclosure of the identity of her expert five days before trial, which was over one month after parties represented that discovery was complete and that all witnesses had been identified, warranted exclusion of the witness)

Imposition of Sanctions; Generally

Nakoff v. Fairview Gen. Hosp., 75 Ohio St. 3d 254, 662 N.E.2d 1 (1996) (the trial court has broad discretion when considering the imposition of discovery sanctions, and such rulings will be reviewed only for an abuse of discretion)

Motions in Limine as Sanction

Wright v. Structo, 88 Ohio App. 3d 239, 623 N.E.2d 694 (1993) (motions in limine may be used to exclude evidence if a party fails to serve answers to interrogatories), *cause dismissed*, 68 Ohio St. 3d 1439, 626 N.E.2d 123 (1994)

Notice Required Before Dismissal

Hillabrand v. Drypers Corp., 87 Ohio St. 3d 517, 721 N.E.2d 1029 (2000) (the requirement that all parties must be notified of the court's intention to dismiss the case because of a failure to comply with a court order is applicable to all dismissals with prejudice, including those based on a failure to comply with discovery orders)

Sanctions for Denying Requests for Admission

Salem Med. Arts and Dev. Corp. v. Columbiana Cty. Bd. of Revision, 82 Ohio St. 3d 193, 694 N.E.2d 1324 (1998) (party is not required to file a motion to compel before moving for sanctions for a bad faith denial of requests for admissions)

Scope of Sanctions

Getter v. Getter, 90 Ohio App. 3d 1, 627 N.E.2d 1043 (1993) (sanctions that exclude evidence or claims unrelated to the requested discovery are overbroad, unjust, and punitive)

Severity of Sanctions

Evans v. Smith, 75 Ohio App. 3d 160, 598 N.E.2d 1287 (1991) (ordinarily, it is the policy of courts in Ohio to impose the least severe sanction or a sanction less severe than that of dismissal of the action with prejudice)

VI
TRIALS

CHAPTER 38

Rule 38. Jury Trial of Right

Rule 38 reads as follows:

(A) Right preserved. The right to trial by jury shall be preserved to the parties inviolate.

(B) Demand. Any party may demand a trial by jury on any issue triable of right by a jury by serving upon the other parties a demand therefor at any time after the commencement of the action and not later than fourteen days after the service of the last pleading directed to such issue. Such demand shall be in writing and may be indorsed upon a pleading of the party. If the demand is endorsed upon a pleading the caption of the pleading shall state "jury demand endorsed hereon." In an action for appropriation of a right of way brought by a corporation pursuant to Article XIII, Section 5, of the Ohio Constitution, the jury shall be composed of twelve members unless the demand specifies a lesser number; and in the event of timely demand by more than one party in such action the jury shall be composed of the greater number not to exceed twelve. In all other civil actions the jury shall be composed of eight members unless the demand specifies a lesser number; and in the event of timely demand by more than one party in such actions the jury shall be composed of the greater number not to exceed eight.

(C) Specification of issues. In his demand a party may specify the issues which he wishes so tried; otherwise he shall be deemed to have demanded trial by jury for all the issues so triable. If he has demanded trial by jury for only some of the issues, any other party within fourteen days after service of the demand or such lesser time as the court may order, may serve a demand for trial by jury of any other or all of the issues of fact in the action.

(D) Waiver. The failure of a party to serve a demand as required by this rule and to file it as required by Rule 5(D) constitutes a waiver by him of trial by jury. A demand for trial by jury made as herein provided may not be withdrawn without the consent of the parties.

COMMENTARY

Rule 38, of course, does not create the right to a jury trial. Instead, article I, § 5 of the Ohio Constitution declares that "[t]he right of trial by jury shall be inviolate, except that in civil cases, law may be passed to authorize the rendering of a verdict by the concurrence of not less than three fourths of the jury."

Demand for Jury Trial

To exercise the right to jury trial in a civil action, a party must make a timely demand according to the provisions of subsection (B). The demand may be made in a pleading, or it may be the subject of a separate motion. If made by motion, it must be served on all opposing parties no later than 14 days from the date of service of the final pleading. It should be noted that Rule 15(A) allows a final pleading to be amended once as a matter of course within 28 days of service of the pleading. This provision may be used to amend one's pleading to include a jury demand if more than 14 days but less than 28 have elapsed since the pleading has been served on all the parties.

Illustration 38-1

Greg commences a negligence action against Victoria for personal injuries suffered in a hunting accident, and Victoria serves an answer on October 1. Victoria would like for the case to be decided before a jury, but she fails to make a demand for a jury trial in her answer. Victoria may make a motion for a jury trial no later than October 15, or she may amend her answer at any time before October 29, provided that the action has not yet been placed on the trial calendar.

Subsection (C) expressly provides that a party may demand a jury trial on selected issues only, and that such a demand must specify the issues so selected. For example, a defendant in a negligence action may demand a jury trial on the issue of damages only. However, this demand must still be made in a pleading or by motion within 14 days of the service of the final pleading. The party may not decide, after the issue of liability has been decided by the court, to have the issue of damages decided by a jury. If a general demand for a jury trial is made, it will be considered as a demand for a jury trial on all the issues that can be constitutionally considered by a jury. If a party demands a jury trial only on selected issues, the opposing party may, within 14 days of being served with the original jury demand, demand a jury on the remaining issues.

Number of Jurors

Subsection (B) also provides for the number of jurors in a civil action. This subsection should be read in conjunction with Rules 47 and 48, which also relate to the impaneling of a jury. Other important aspects of impaneling a jury, such as selection of the jury pool and juror challenges for cause, are governed by local rules, statute, or case law.

Subsection (B) establishes a default of eight as the number of jurors for a civil trial. This number may be reduced by a stipulation of the parties or by a single demand for a jury specifying a lesser number. If demands for a jury trial are made by more than one party, the highest number of jurors requested not to exceed eight will be used. There is no minimum number of jurors required under the Rules; however, requests for fewer than four jurors should be granted only under exceptional circumstances. It should also be noted that subsection (B) provides an exception to this general rule; a jury of 12 may be allowed in actions for appropriation of a right of way brought by a corporation pursuant to article XIII, § 5, of the Ohio Constitution. This number may likewise be modified by stipulation or request of the parties.

Waiver of Right to Jury Trial

Subsection (D) makes it clear that the right to a jury trial is waived if it is not made in accordance with the provisions of subsections (B) and (C) and Rule 5(D). The Rule also expressly provides that, once requested, a jury trial may be waived only by the express consent of all the parties.

ADDITIONAL AUTHORITY

9 WRIGHT & MILLER §§ 2301-2330
8 MOORE'S FEDERAL PRACTICE §§ 38.01-38.52
5 ANDERSON'S OHIO CIVIL PRACTICE §§ 174.01-174.08
2 KLEIN DARLING AT 38-1 to AT 38-33
3 TEREZ F 12.1.1 to F 12.1.7
4 OH. JUR. PL. AND PRAC. FORMS, ch. 44
5 MILLIGAN Forms 38-1 to 38-23
2 FINK §§ 38-1 to 38-5

LEADING CASES

Counterclaims–Jury Demand Applied

Soler v. Evans, St. Clair & Kelsey, 94 Ohio St. 3d 432, 763 N.E.2d 1169 (2002) (a general jury demand included within a complaint applies to issues raised in a compulsory counterclaim even if the complaint is later voluntarily dismissed)

Demand; New Issues of Fact

Ferguson v. Johnson, 15 Ohio App. 3d 143, 473 N.E.2d 56 (1984) (defendant had no right to a jury trial where his demand was contained in a cross claim which raised only a new theory of recovery, not a new issue of fact)

Eminent Domain Case; Jury Trial Need Not Be Requested

Wray v. Allied Indus. Dev. Corp., 138 Ohio App. 3d 362, 741 N.E.2d 238 (2000) (by failing to file a jury demand, state did not waive its constitutional and statutory right to a jury trial in an appropriation case on compensation for taking property; the right to a jury trial is automatic and Rule 38 is inapplicable)

General Jury Demand

Soler v. Evans, St. Clair & Kelsey, 94 Ohio St. 3d 432, 763 N.E.2d 1169 (2002) (if a general jury demand is made without specifying particular issues, it will be interpreted as a demand for a jury trial on all issues upon which a jury may be demanded)

Waiver; Consent of Parties

Huffer v. Cicero, 107 Ohio App. 3d 65, 667 N.E.2d 1031 (1995) (a jury demand may not be withdrawn without the consent of the parties; however, the right to object may be waived)

Waiver; In General

Valentour v. Alexander, 96 Ohio App. 3d 718, 645 N.E.2d 1292 (where neither party made a timely demand for jury trial, parties waived their right to jury trial and court was free to refer all issues to a referee), *dismissed, appeal not allowed*, 71 Ohio St. 3d 1444, 644 N.E.2d 407 (1994)

Waiver; Time

Burke v. Gammarino, 108 Ohio App. 3d 138, 670 N.E.2d 295 (1995) (party waived right to jury trial by failing to assert the right within 14 days of service of original counterclaim, even though counterclaimant subsequently amended counter-claim)

Withdrawal of Jury Demand Not Effective

Holman v. Keegan, 139 Ohio App. 3d 911, 746 N.E.2d 209 (2000) (jury trial was required in action in which a party demanded a jury trial in the original complaint and there was no stipulation among the parties to waive the demand, no determination of an involuntary waiver, and no consent by other parties of the withdrawal of the demand)

CHAPTER 39

Rule 39. Trial by Jury or by the Court

Rule 39 reads as follows:

(A) **By jury.** When trial by jury has been demanded as provided in Rule 38, the action shall be designated upon the docket as a jury action. The trial of all issues so demanded shall be by jury, unless

    (1)   the parties or their attorneys of record, by written stipulation filed with the court or by an oral stipulation made in open court and entered in the record, consent to trial by the court sitting without a jury or

    (2)   the court upon motion or of its own initiative finds that a right of trial by jury of some or all of those issues does not exist.

    The failure of a party or his attorney of record either to answer or appear for trial constitutes a waiver of trial by jury by such party and authorizes submission of all issues to the court.

(B) **By the court.** Issues not demanded for trial by jury as provided in Rule 38 shall be tried by the court; but, notwithstanding the failure of a party to demand a jury in an action in which such a demand might have been made of right, the court in its discretion upon motion may order a trial by a jury of any or all issues.

(C) **Advisory jury and trial by consent.** In all actions not triable of right by a jury

    (1)   the court upon motion or on its own initiative may try any issue with an advisory jury or

    (2)   the court, with the consent of both parties, may order a trial of any issue with a jury, whose verdict has the same effect as if trial by jury had been a matter of right.

COMMENTARY

Rule 39 complements Rule 38 in specifying the procedure to be used when a party makes a demand for a jury trial. As noted in Chapter 38, Rules 38 and 39 do not create a right to jury trial. Courts and practitioners seeking relevant case law on the right to jury trial are thus advised to consult the additional authority listed at the end of Chapter

38 rather than the commentary provided here, which focuses entirely on the procedural aspects of the Rule.

When a party has made a proper demand for a jury trial under Rule 38, subsection (A) directs the clerk of the court to enter a notation to that effect on the court's docket.

Waiver of Prior Demand for Jury Trial

Subsection (A) delineates the circumstances in which a party may waive a prior demand for a jury trial. Such a waiver must be made by all parties in writing, or by oral stipulation in open court. Upon motion or its own initiative, a court may also nullify the jury demand by finding that the right to a jury trial does not exist under the relevant case law.

Jury Trial Ordered by the Court

Subsection (B) does not enlarge the parties' right to a jury trial, but provides the court with discretion to order a jury trial on any or all of the issues when a party has failed to make such a demand. Technically, this provision does not allow the court to grant an untimely demand for a jury trial, but provides the court with the means to attain that result. All actions not tried by a jury shall be tried to the court.

The power granted to the court in subsection (B) to order a jury trial should be distinguished from the power to employ an advisory jury granted in subsection (C)(1). Subsection (B) applies only when a right to jury trial exists but is not demanded by the parties; subsection (C) applies only when a right to jury trial does not exist.

Illustration 39-1

Marcia sues Nicole for personal injuries suffered when Nicole's dog attacked Marcia. Although both parties have a right to a jury trial under applicable case law, neither party makes a jury demand by pleading or by motion. Under Rule 39(B), however, the trial judge may order a jury trial on any or all of the issues of the case.

Advisory Jury Trial

Subsection (C) is applicable only when a right to jury trial does not exist under the relevant case law for any of the parties involved in the action. This subsection further distinguishes between advisory juries and jury by consent, and the court should specify on the record which kind has been employed.

Subsection (C)(1) allows the court, upon motion or its own initiative, to employ an advisory jury when a right to jury trial does not exist for any of the parties and one or more of the parties do not consent to a jury trial under subsection (C)(2). An advisory jury does not have any actual legal authority in the action, and the court must still state its findings of fact and conclusions of law in the record so that an appellate court may review the actions of the court. The consent of the parties is not required to employ an advisory jury, and the court may, but is not required to, first request the consent of the parties to a jury by consent under subsection (C)(2).

Illustration 39-2

Assume on the facts of Illustration 39-1 that Marcia seeks only equitable relief and, under the applicable law, does not have a right to a jury trial. Under Rule 39(C)(1), the court may employ an advisory jury to assist it in the resolution of the action. The court is required neither to seek Marcia's or Nicole's consent nor to accept or reject the findings of the advisory jury.

Subsection (C) provides for a jury by consent. A jury by consent is distinguishable from an advisory jury in that the actions of a jury by consent have the same effect as would a jury demanded as of right. Obviously, all the parties must approve of a jury by consent, and a jury by consent may be requested by motion or suggested *sua sponte* by the court.

ADDITIONAL AUTHORITY

9 WRIGHT & MILLER §§ 2331-2350
8 MOORE'S FEDERAL PRACTICE §§ 39.01-39.43
5 ANDERSON'S OHIO CIVIL PRACTICE §§ 174.09-174.14
2 KLEIN DARLING AT 39-1 to AT 39-10
3 TEREZ F 12.2.1 to F 12.2.5
4 OH. JUR. PL. AND PRAC. FORMS, ch. 44
5 MILLIGAN Forms 39-1 to 39-45
2 FINK §§ 39-1 to 39-5

LEADING CASES

Advisory Jury Trial

Crane v. Cheek, 27 Ohio App. 2d 27, 272 N.E.2d 159 (1970) (court may submit questions of fact to advisory jury for determination, but court must base its judgment on its own evaluation of the evidence and not merely on the blind approval of jury findings)

Jury Trial Ordered by the Court

Gleason v. Gleason, 64 Ohio App. 3d 667, 582 N.E.2d 657 (power of trial court to order a jury trial on any issue is not absolute; if court orders jury trial over objection, there is reversible error if objecting party is prejudiced by jury trial), *jurisdictional motion overruled*, 62 Ohio St. 3d 1434, 578 N.E.2d 825 (1991)

Waiver; Amended Pleadings

Cincinnati Ins. Co. v. Gray, 7 Ohio App. 3d 374, 455 N.E.2d 1080 (1982) (once a jury trial is demanded, it may not be waived except by the exclusive method set forth in Rule 39, and the filing of an amended pleading without such a demand will not operate as a waiver)

Waiver; Burden of Proof

Carl Sectional Home, Inc. v. Key Corp., 1 Ohio App. 3d 101, 439 N.E.2d 915 (1981) (a silent record means a previously demanded jury trial right is still operative; the burden is on the party claiming a waiver to prove compliance with the requirements of Rule 39)

Waiver; In General

Huffer v. Cicero, 107 Ohio App. 3d 65, 667 N.E.2d 1031 (1995) (a jury demand may not be withdrawn without the consent of the parties; however, the right to object may be waived)

Withdrawal of Jury Demand Not Effective

Holman v. Keegan, 139 Ohio App. 3d 911, 746 N.E.2d 209 (2000) (jury trial was required in action in which a party demanded a jury trial in the original complaint and there was no stipulation among the parties to waive the demand, no determination of an involuntary waiver, and no consent by other parties of the withdrawal of the demand)

CHAPTER 40

Rule 40. Pre-Recorded Testimony

Rule 40 reads as follows:

All of the testimony and such other evidence as may be appropriate may be presented at a trial by videotape, subject to the provisions of the Rules of Superintendence.

COMMENTARY

Rule 40 governs pre-recorded trial testimony. Rule 40 makes possible the recording of all trial testimony on videotape for later presentation to a jury. Limitations on the use of testimony and evidence on videotape may be found in Rule 13 of the Rules of Superintendence for the Courts of Ohio. It should be noted, however, that any evidence presented by videotape must satisfy the requirements for admissibility established by the Ohio Rules of Evidence: relevancy, authentication, "best evidence" rule, and hearsay.

ADDITIONAL AUTHORITY

2 KLEIN DARLING AT 40-1 to AT 40-1
4 OH. JUR. PL. AND PRAC. FORMS , ch. 45
5 MILLIGAN Forms 40-1 to 40-15
2 FINK § 40-1

LEADING CASES

Videotape; Compelling Reason

> ***Fantozzi v. Sandusky Cement Prod. Co.***, 64 Ohio St. 3d 601, 597 N.E.2d 474 (1993) (error for a court to order a prerecorded videotape trial over the objections of both parties unless the court specifically indicates that factors demonstrate a compelling reason to conduct the trial by videotape and that no prejudice will be suffered by the parties)

Videotape; In General

Sowers v. Middletown Hosp., 89 Ohio App. 3d 572, 626 N.E.2d 968 (presentation of videotaped testimony is permitted only when all trial testimony is videotaped), *jurisdictional motion overruled*, 68 Ohio St. 3d 1409, 623 N.E.2d 566 (1993)

CHAPTER 41

Rule 41. Dismissal of Actions

Rule 41 reads as follows:

(A) Voluntary dismissal: effect thereof.

    (1) By plaintiff; by stipulation. Subject to the provisions of Civ. R. 23(E), Civ. R. 23.1, and Civ. R. 66, a plaintiff, without order of court, may dismiss all claims asserted by that plaintiff against a defendant by doing either of the following:

        (a) filing a notice of dismissal at any time before the commencement of trial unless a counterclaim which cannot remain pending for independent adjudication by the court has been served by that defendant;

        (b) filing a stipulation of dismissal signed by all parties who have appeared in the action.

        Unless otherwise stated in the notice of dismissal or stipulation, the dismissal is without prejudice, except that a notice of dismissal operates as an adjudication upon the merits of any claim that the plaintiff has once dismissed in any court.

    (2) By order of court. Except as provided in division (A)(1) of this rule, a claim shall not be dismissed at the plaintiff's instance except upon order of the court and upon such terms and conditions as the court deems proper. If a counterclaim has been pleaded by a defendant prior to the service upon that defendant of the plaintiff's motion to dismiss, a claim shall not be dismissed against the defendant's objection unless the counterclaim can remain pending for independent adjudication by the court. Unless otherwise specified in the order, a dismissal under division (A)(2) of this rule is without prejudice.

(B) Involuntary dismissal: effect thereof.

    (1) Failure to prosecute. Where the plaintiff fails to prosecute, or comply with these rules or any court order, the court upon motion of a defendant or on its own motion may, after notice to the plaintiff's counsel, dismiss an action or claim.

    (2) Dismissal; non-jury action. After the plaintiff, in an action tried by the court without a jury, has completed the presentation of the plaintiff's evidence, the defendant, without waiving the right to offer evidence in the event the motion is not granted, may move for a dismissal on the

309

ground that upon the facts and the law the plaintiff has shown no right to relief. The court as trier of the facts may then determine them and render judgment against the plaintiff or may decline to render any judgment until the close of all the evidence. If the court renders judgment on the merits against the plaintiff, the court shall make findings as provided in Civ. R. 52 if requested to do so by any party.

(3) **Adjudication on the merits; exception.** A dismissal under division (B) of this rule and any dismissal not provided for in this rule, except as provided in division (B)(4) of this rule, operates as an adjudication upon the merits unless the court, in its order for dismissal, otherwise specifies.

(4) **Failure other than on the merits.** A dismissal for either of the following reasons shall operate as a failure otherwise than on the merits:

(a) lack of jurisdiction over the person or the subject matter;

(b) failure to join a party under Civ. R. 19 or Civ. R. 19.1.

(C) **Dismissal of counterclaim, cross-claim, or third-party claim.** The provisions of this rule apply to the dismissal of any counterclaim, cross-claim, or third-party claim. A voluntary dismissal by the claimant alone pursuant to division (A)(1) of this rule shall be made before the commencement of trial.

(D) **Costs of previously dismissed action.** If a plaintiff who has once dismissed a claim in any court commences an action based upon or including the same claim against the same defendant, the court may make such order for the payment of costs of the claim previously dismissed as it may deem proper and may stay the proceedings in the action until the plaintiff has complied with the order.

COMMENTARY

Rule 41 provides for dismissals of actions. An action may be dismissed voluntarily either as of right or by order of the court, but an action may be dismissed involuntarily only by order of the court. The term "voluntary" as used in this Rule refers to the position occupied by the plaintiff, so that an "involuntary" dismissal is one sought by the defendant against the plaintiff. The Rule also governs the dismissal of counterclaims and cross-claims under Rule 13, third-party claims under 14, and provides for the payment of costs of previously dismissed actions. It should be noted that class actions under Rule 23, shareholder derivative actions under 23.1, and actions involving court-appointed receivers under Rule 66 may be dismissed only with the permission of the court.

Voluntary Dismissal as of Right

Subsection (A) separates voluntary dismissals, *i.e.*, dismissals sought by the plaintiff, into three types: dismissal as of right; dismissal by stipulation; and dismissal by order of the court. It should be noted that dismissal of any claim by a party will not affect the pending status of any other claim in the action. A plaintiff may dismiss an action without prejudice or order of the court at any time before the commencement of trial, unless a counterclaim has been filed by a defendant over which the court lacks jurisdiction but for the predicate initial claim.

Illustration 41-1

Ahmed sues Chandler for personal injuries suffered in a hydroplane accident. Chandler serves an answer containing a counterclaim for damages stemming from the same accident. Ahmed may dismiss the action at any time before the commencement of the trial without prejudice.

The expansiveness of the Ohio version of the Rule with respect to the time period within which a plaintiff may voluntarily dismiss an action should not be overlooked as a strategic litigation device. The Rule allows the notice of dismissal to be filed "at any time before the commencement of trial," and the court is without discretion to reject the notice unless a jurisdictionally-dependent counterclaim remains pending. Ohio courts have not adopted a clear definition of "trial" in this regard, though it is clear that hearings on motions are not considered trials. It should also be noted that Ohio's savings statute, which is set forth at OHIO REV. CODE ANN. § 2305.19, may then permit a plaintiff to recommence the action even if the statute of limitations has run.

This right of voluntary dismissal without prejudice by the plaintiff is limited to a single dismissal; a plaintiff who has previously dismissed an action based on or including the same claim in any federal or state court cannot thereafter dismiss the action under subsection (A)(1)(a) without prejudice. This doctrine is commonly referred to as the "two dismissals rule." A plaintiff in such a situation may petition the court for dismissal without prejudice under subsection (A)(2), but the circumstances in which a dismissal without prejudice would be appropriate are highly unusual.

Illustration 41-2

Assume on the facts of Illustration 41-1 that Ahmed dismisses his action against Chandler before Chandler has filed an answer. Two months later, Ahmed brings the same action against Chandler and Chandler's brother, Todd. However, Ahmed again wishes to have the matter dismissed without prejudice. Under Rule 41, Ahmed cannot unilaterally dismiss the action without prejudice with regard to Chandler. Rather, Ahmed must petition the court for dismissal without prejudice under Rule 41(A)(2).

It should be noted that the active mood of the verb in the final sentence of subsection (A)(1) circumscribes the "two dismissals rule" to prior voluntary dismissals by the plaintiff with notice under Rule 41(A)(1) or analogous provisions. Prior dismissals by order of the court or by stipulation of the parties will not operate to trigger the "two dismissals rule."

Voluntary Dismissals by Stipulation

Somewhat misleadingly, subsection (A)(1)(b) is grouped with the other kinds of "voluntary" dismissals. As noted, the term "voluntary" refers to the position of the plaintiff and implies that the defendant is opposed to such a dismissal. This subsection, on the other hand, governs dismissals by stipulation of all the parties and, as such, are both "voluntary" *and* "involuntary." All the parties to an action must agree and sign the stipulation to make it effective. Dismissals by stipulation occur frequently when parties have settled their disputes through negotiation. When this occurs, the parties should ensure that the stipulation expressly provides that the dismissal is with prejudice; otherwise, either party is free to re-file a complaint. This presumption is reversed for those parties that have previously dismissed an action based on or including the same claim in any federal or state court; dismissals by stipulation in this instance are presumed to be with prejudice unless the stipulation provides otherwise.

Illustration 41-3

Assume on the facts of Illustration 41-1 that, instead of dismissing the action as of right under subsection (A)(1)(a), Ahmed and Chandler file a stipulation of dismissal under subsection (A)(1)(b). However, their stipulation fails to indicate that the action is being dismissed "with prejudice." The stipulation does not prevent Ahmed from re-filing the complaint against Chandler. On the other hand, if, on the facts of Illustration 41-2, Ahmed having previously dismissed the action once already, Ahmed and Chandler may file a stipulation of dismissal under (A)(1)(b). This stipulation prevents Ahmed from filing the action a third time, unless the stipulation expressly states that it is entered without prejudice.

Voluntary Dismissals by Order of the Court

Subsection (A)(2) provides the court with the discretion to grant motions to dismiss by the plaintiff upon a proper showing of cause. However, this discretion is restricted in cases where the defendant has filed a counterclaim before plaintiff's motion to dismiss and the defendant objects to the motion. In this situation, the court cannot grant the motion to dismiss unless independent grounds for hearing the counterclaim exist. Otherwise, the grant of plaintiff's motion to dismiss functions as an involuntary dismissal of defendant's claim against her wishes. As with dismissals under subsection (A)(1), dismissals by the court under subsection (A)(2) are without prejudice unless otherwise specified.

Involuntary Dismissals

Subsection (B) governs involuntary dismissals, *i.e.*, dismissals sought by the defendant. Subsection (B)(3) reverses the presumption in subsection (A) that a dismissal is without prejudice unless otherwise provided; subsection (B)(3) expressly states that a dismissal made under that subsection operates as an adjudication on the merits of the case, unless otherwise specified by the court in its order. Exceptions to this presumption are found in subsection (B)(4): a dismissal of the plaintiff's action for failure to state a claim upon which relief can be granted, lack of personal jurisdiction, or failure to join a necessary or compulsory party under Rule 19 or Rule 19.1 is presumed to be without prejudice.

Dismissals against plaintiffs are drastic measures and should not be imposed by the court lightly. The Rule lists the plaintiff's failure to prosecute as an instance in which an involuntary dismissal may be appropriate; nevertheless, the court does not have unfettered discretion to dismiss an action against a plaintiff. Warnings or other sanctions are advised before a court considers outright dismissal.

Illustration 41-4

Jane commences a libel action against Hannah, but Jane fails to appear at any of the pretrial conferences and allows the action to remain on the court's docket for over 3 years without taking any further action in the case. In this situation, the court's dismissal of the action under Rule 41(B) may be appropriate. The dismissal would be with prejudice, and Jane's action against Hannah is considered to have been adjudicated on the merits.

Dismissals by the Court in Non-Jury Actions

Subsection (B)(2) governs dismissal of the plaintiff's claim at the conclusion of the plaintiff's evidence in an action tried to the court. A motion made under this subsection is akin to a directed verdict in a jury action made under Rule 50(A)(1), but it is not subject to the standards set forth in that Rule. A defendant may move for a dismissal of the action at the close of plaintiff's case-in-chief, and if the motion is granted, either party may request the court to make findings of fact and conclusions of law in accordance with Rule 52. If the motion is denied, the defendant must then proceed with its case-in-defense.

Application to Counterclaims, Cross-Claims, and Third-Party Claims

Subsection (C) indicates that the dismissal provisions of subsections (A) and (B) apply to counterclaims, cross-claims, and third-party claims. Thus, the terms "plaintiff" and "defendant" as used in the Rule do not necessarily refer to the party filing the original complaint and answer. Rather, a defendant who brings a counterclaim against a plaintiff may dismiss the counterclaim "voluntarily" under subsection (A), but may seek dismissal of the original claim brought by the plaintiff only "involuntarily" under subsection (B).

Illustration 41-5

Jason sues Chuck for personal injuries suffered in a farming accident. Chuck promptly files a counterclaim for damages to his combine. After Jason files a motion for a jury trial, Chuck decides to dismiss his counterclaim. This dismissal is considered "voluntary" under Rule 41(A) and is presumed to be without prejudice. If Chuck later pursues the counterclaim against Jason as an independent action, Jason may seek dismissal of the counterclaim "involuntarily" under Rule 41(B).

Costs

Subsection (D) provides that the court may impose costs for the previously dismissed action against a plaintiff if that plaintiff recommences the same proceeding. It should be noted that the subsection does not provide the court with the power to impose costs for the recommenced proceeding; that issue is governed by Rule 54. Additionally, subsection (D) does not provide for the imposition of costs on the plaintiff when the plaintiff does not re-file the action; that issue is likewise governed by Rule 54. Furthermore, subsection (D) does not provide the court with any authority to dismiss the second action for plaintiff's failure to pay the costs of the previously dismissed action, though subsection (D) expressly contemplates a stay of the proceedings pending compliance with the court order.

Illustration 41-6

Buck sues Rich for compensatory damages stemming from a fire in their college dorm that destroyed Buck's compact disc collection. After Rich makes a litany of threat-like Rule 12 motions, Buck is intimidated and decides to dismiss the action. Four months later, after Buck has had a chance to confer with his

---

other roommates, Buck recommences his claim against Rich. Under Rule 41(D), the court may impose upon Buck Rich's costs for bringing the earlier Rule 12 motions. Costs for Buck's pending action will be determined under Rule 54. If Buck refuses to pay these costs, the court may not dismiss Buck's action a second time *for a refusal to pay costs*. However, the court may stay the proceedings of the second action until Buck pays Rich's costs incurred in the first action. Buck may also be ultimately responsible for Rich's costs at the conclusion of the case under Rule 54.

ADDITIONAL AUTHORITY

9 WRIGHT & MILLER §§ 2361-2380

8 MOORE'S FEDERAL PRACTICE §§ 41.01-41.70

5 ANDERSON'S OHIO CIVIL PRACTICE §§ 168.01-168.09

2 KLEIN DARLING AT 41-1 to AT 41-41

3 TEREZ F 16.1.1 to F 16.1.11

4 OH. JUR. PL. AND PRAC. FORMS, ch. 46

5 MILLIGAN Forms 41-1 to 41-47

2 FINK §§ 41-1 to 41-5

OHIO LITIGATION CHECKLISTS, Trial, §§ 27-29

LEADING CASES

Collateral Issues

State ex rel. Hummel v. Sadler, 96 Ohio St. 3d 84, 771 N.E.2d 853 (2002) (despite a voluntary dismissal, the court may nonetheless retain jurisdiction over certain kinds of collateral issues not related to the merits of the action)

Contempt Proceeding Not Dismissed

Corn v. Russo, 90 Ohio St. 3d 551, 740 N.E.2d 265 (2001) (voluntary dismissal of underlying personal injury action did not divest trial court of jurisdiction over criminal contempt proceedings against an expert witness)

Counterclaims—Jury Demand Applied

Soler v. Evans, St. Clair & Kelsey, 94 Ohio St. 3d 432, 763 N.E.2d 1169 (2002) (a general jury demand included within a complaint applies to issues raised in a compulsory counterclaim even if the complaint is later voluntarily dismissed)

Dismissal of Counterclaims and Third Party Claims

Robinson v. B.O.C. Group, General Motors Corp., 81 Ohio St. 3d 361, 691

N.E.2d 667 (1998) (Rule 41(B)(1) is equally applicable to counterclaims and third party claims)

Hearing on Sanctions Collateral to Underlying Proceeding

Stone v. House of Day Funeral Serv., 140 Ohio App. 3d 713, 748 N.E.2d 1200 (2000) (although a voluntary dismissal generally divests a trial court of jurisdiction, a hearing on sanctions is considered collateral to the underlying proceedings and jurisdiction on the motion for sanctions is retained by the trial court)

Inability to Present Witness Voluntary Dismissal

Cincinnati Bar Ass'n v. Fischer, 92 Ohio St. 3d 90, 748 N.E.2d 1089 (2001) (dismissal of complaint against a party because the party was unable to present a witness did not constitute a dismissal for failure to prosecute; accordingly, the dismissal qualified as a voluntary dismissal)

Involuntary Dismissal; In General

McCann v. Lakewood, 95 Ohio App. 3d 226, 642 N.E.2d 48 (dismissal for failure to prosecute is an involuntary dismissal, and is deemed to be an adjudication on the merits), *dismissed, appeal not allowed*, 70 Ohio St. 3d 1465, 640 N.E.2d 527 (1994)

Involuntary Dismissal; Notice

Logsdon v. Nichols, 72 Ohio St. 3d 124, 647 N.E.2d 1361 (1995) (court of common pleas erred in dismissing plaintiff's action without prejudice because court did not provide required notice to plaintiff)

Rankin v. Willow Park Convalescent Home, 99 Ohio App. 3d 110, 649 N.E.2d 1320 (1994) (when court intends to order dismissal for a violation of discovery rules, court must give prior notice of its intent to dismiss with prejudice in order to give the noncomplying party one last chance to conform)

Jurisdiction-Based Dismissal Does Not Bar New Action

CTI Audio, Inc. v. Fritkin-Jones Design Group, Inc., 144 Ohio App. 3d 449, 760 N.E.2d 842 (2001) (the dismissal of an action for lack of jurisdiction does not bar the commencement of a new action on the same claim if the jurisdictional defect is cured)

Jurisdiction of Court Not Present When Action Voluntarily Dismissed

Selker & Furber v. Brightman, 138 Ohio App. 3d 710, 742 N.E.2d 203 (2000) (plaintiffs' self-executing notice of voluntary dismissal rendered cross-claim moot and deprived the trial court of jurisdiction to grant intervention, dismiss the action, and grant relief from the court-ordered dismissal)

Motion for Sanctions and Attorneys' Fees Collateral to Underlying Action

Curtis v. Curtis, 140 Ohio App. 3d 812, 749 N.E.2d 772 (2000) (while a trial court is generally divested of jurisdiction following a plaintiff's voluntary dismissal, it does not lose jurisdiction to consider properly filed motions for sanctions or for attorneys' fees)

Notice Required Before Dismissal

Hillabrand v. Drypers Corp., 87 Ohio St. 3d 517, 721 N.E.2d 1029 (2000) (the trial court may dismiss an action for failure to comply with a court order, but only after notice to party)

Standard on Appeal

D & J Co. v. Stuart, 146 Ohio App. 3d 67, 765 N.E.2d 368 (2001) (a dismissal under Rule 41 will be reversed on appeal only when the ruling is erroneous as a matter of law or is contrary to the manifest weight of the evidence)

Summary Judgment Appealable When Remaining Parties Dismissed

Denham v. New Carlisle, 86 Ohio St. 3d 594, 716 N.E.2d 184 (1999) (the granting of a motion for summary judgment becomes a final appealable order when a party against whom the motion has been granted voluntarily dismisses the remaining parties in the action)

Voluntary Dismissal; As of Right

Andrews v. Sajar Plastics, Inc., 98 Ohio App. 3d 61, 647 N.E.2d 854 (1994) (notice of dismissal is self-executing and gives plaintiff an absolute right to terminate his or her cause of action voluntarily and unilaterally at any time prior to commencement of a trial)

Voluntary Dismissal by Order of Court

Logsdon v. Nichols, 72 Ohio St. 3d 124, 647 N.E.2d 1361 (1995) (court of common pleas may consider merits of plaintiff's motion for dismissal by order of court even though court had previously approved plaintiff's dismissal without prejudice)

Voluntary Dismissal by Stipulation

Jones v. Billingham, 105 Ohio App. 3d 8, 663 N.E.2d 627 (1995) (when both parties, by stipulation, agree to dismiss their claims without prejudice, they both abandoned the claims pleaded in the action, without prejudice to claims being refiled in future actions)

Voluntary Dismissal Not Contingent upon Commencement of an Action

Robinson v. B.O.C. Group, Gen. Motors Corp., 81 Ohio St. 3d 361, 691 N.E.2d 667 (1998) (Rule 41(A) does not apply only to those who commence an action, nor does it make dismissal contingent upon commencement, as some kinds of proceedings, such as appeals in workers' compensation cases are "commenced" by a party other than the "plaintiff")

Voluntary Dismissal; Prohibition of Jurisdiction

Page v. Riley, 85 Ohio St. 3d 621, 710 N.E.2d 690 (1999) (after a trial court's unconditional dismissal of a case or after the proper voluntary dismissal of a case pursuant to Rule 41(A)(1), the trial court patently and unambiguously lacks jurisdiction to proceed, and a writ of prohibition will issue to prevent the exercise of jurisdiction)

Voluntary Dismissal; Second Notice

Logsdon v. Nichols, 72 Ohio St. 3d 124, 647 N.E.2d 1361 (1995) (second notice of dismissal operates as an adjudication on the merits and bars refiling of same claim)

Voluntary Dismissal; Worker's Compensation Claim

Kaiser v. Ameritemps, Inc., 84 Ohio St. 3d 411, 704 N.E.2d 1212 (1999) (a workers' compensation claimant may use Rule 41(A)(1)(a) to dismiss voluntarily an appeal to the court of common pleas brought by an employer under O.R.C. 4123.512)

CHAPTER 42

Rule 42. Consolidation; Separate Trials

Rule 42 reads as follows:

(A) Consolidation. When actions involving a common question of law or fact are pending before a court, that court after a hearing may order a joint hearing or trial of any or all the matters in issue in the actions; it may order some or all the actions consolidated; and it may make such orders concerning proceedings therein as may tend to avoid unnecessary costs or delay.

(B) Separate trials. The court, after a hearing, in furtherance of convenience or to avoid prejudice, or when separate trials will be conducive to expedition and economy, may order a separate trial of any claim, cross-claim, counter-claim, or third-party claim, or of any separate issue or of any number of claims, cross-claims, counterclaims, or third-party claims, or issues, always preserving inviolate the right to trial by jury.

COMMENTARY

Rule 42 provides for the consolidation and separation of trials. Such actions are within the discretion of the court, and will be reversed only upon a showing of prejudice to a party or the denial of a substantive right.

Consolidation of Trials

Subsection (A) states that a court may order the consolidation of actions involving "a common question of law or fact." The actions to be consolidated should be at the same stage in the litigation, but this commonality is not required under the Rule. Any of the trial stages may be consolidated, and a consolidation neither requires nor precludes consolidation of the other stages. Cases may be transferred to another district court for the purpose of consolidation.

Illustration 42-1

On December 30, an airplane carrying thirty passengers exploded in flames and fell to the ground. Two months later, Cynthia, the widow of one of the

---

passengers, commences a wrongful death action against Frank's Faulty Airplanes, the manufacturer of the airplane. Three months after Cynthia commences her action, Tracy, whose baggage was being transported in the airplane, commences a negligence action against Frank's Faulty Airplanes. Although the two suits were commenced at different times and involve separate claims, the court may, at its discretion, consolidate the two actions for the purposes of determining the liability of Frank's Faulty Airplanes.

Separation of Trials

Subsection (B) allows for separate trials or proceedings to avoid prejudice or where the separation will be conducive to "expedition and economy" of the action. Separation is sometimes necessary because of the ease of joining counterclaims, cross-claims, or third-party claims under the Rules. Separation of the liability and damages aspects of a trial are also contemplated by the Rule.

Illustration 42-2

Assume on the facts of Illustration 42-1 that Frank's Faulty Airplanes files a third-party complaint against Defective Devices Inc., the supplier of parts used to manufacture the airplane. Under Rule 42(B), the court may bifurcate the third-party action from the original actions of Cynthia and Tracy if the court feels that a consolidated action may prejudice the parties or confuse the jury.

ADDITIONAL AUTHORITY

9 WRIGHT & MILLER §§ 2381-2400
8 MOORE'S FEDERAL PRACTICE §§ 42.01-42.24
5 ANDERSON'S OHIO CIVIL PRACTICE §§ 172.01-172.04
2 KLEIN DARLING AT 42-1 to AT 42-3
3 TEREZ F 7.1.1 to F 7.1.52
4 OH. JUR. PL. AND PRAC. FORMS, ch. 47
5 MILLIGAN Forms 42-1 to 42-43
2 FINK §§ 42-1 to 42-5
OHIO LITIGATION CHECKLISTS, Parties and Actions, §§ 1-3
OHIO LITIGATION CHECKLISTS, Pleading and Process, §§ 15-19

LEADING CASES

Consolidation; In General

> *Jamestown Village Condo. Owners Ass'n v. Market Media Research, Inc.*, 96 Ohio App. 3d 678, 645 N.E.2d 1265 (1994) (consolidations of trials are entirely discretionary with the court; denial of consolidation is not a final appealable order)

Consolidation; Requirements

> *Waterman v. Kitrick*, 60 Ohio App. 3d 7, 572 N.E.2d 250 (1990) (before trials may be properly consolidated, the court must determine if there is sufficient commonality of issues to warrant consolidation and if the parties are substantially the same)

Separation; In General

> *Marion Production Credit Ass'n v. Cochran*, 40 Ohio St. 3d 265, 533 N.E.2d 325 (1988) (when trials are ordered on separate issues, the execution of all judgments determined upon a single claim should be stayed pending a final determination of the entire action with respect to all parties)

CHAPTER 43

Rule 43. [Reserved]

CHAPTER 44

Rule 44. Proof of Official Record

Rule 44 reads as follows:

(A) Authentication.

(1) Domestic. An official record, or an entry therein, kept within a state or within the United States or within a territory or other jurisdiction of the United States, when admissible for any purpose, may be evidenced by an official publication thereof or by a copy attested by the officer having the legal custody of the record, or by his deputy, and accompanied by a certificate that such officer has the custody. The certificate may be made by a judge of a court of record in which the record is kept or may be made by any public officer having a seal of office and having official duties in the political subdivision in which the record is kept, authenticated by the seal of his office.

(2) Foreign. A foreign official record, or an entry therein, when admissible for any purpose, may be evidenced by an official publication thereof; or a copy thereof, attested by a person authorized to make the attestation, and accompanied by a final certification as to the genuineness of the signature and official position

(a) of the attesting person or

(b) of any foreign official whose certificate of genuineness of signature and official position relates to the attestation or is in a chain of certificates of genuineness of signature and official position relating to the attestation.

A final certification may be made by a secretary of embassy or legation, consul general, consul, vice consul, or consular agent of the United States, or a diplomatic or consular official of the foreign country assigned or accredited to the United States. If reasonable opportunity has been given to all parties to investigate the authenticity and accuracy of the documents, the court may, for good cause shown,

(a) admit an attested copy without final certification or

(b) permit the foreign official record to be evidenced by an attested summary with or without a final certification.

(B) Lack of record. A written statement that after diligent search no record or entry of a specified tenor is found to exist in the records designated by the statement, authenticated as provided in subdivision (A)(1) of this rule in the case of a domestic record, or complying with the requirements of subdivision (A)(2) of this rule for a summary in the case of a foreign record, is admissible as evidence that the records contain no such record or entry.

(C) Other proof. This rule does not prevent the proof of official records or of entry or lack of entry therein by any other method authorized by law.

COMMENTARY

Subsection (A) sets forth the procedure to be used for authenticating official records of domestic or foreign governments. A domestic or foreign record may be authenticated either through an official publication of the record or through a copy of the record to which a person listed and certified in the manner prescribed in the Rule has attested to its validity. Rule 44 is intended to complement the procedures set forth in Ohio Evidence Rule 902 for self-authentication. The existence of the rule can be explained by the fact that the Rule was adopted from Federal Rule of Civil Procedure 44, which was originally adopted before the promulgation of the Federal Rules of Evidence.

Lack of Record

Behind the drafting in subsection (B) lies the simple directive that evidence of the absence of an official record to prove the nonexistence of the record may be proved by a written statement, authenticated or according to subsection (A), to that effect. Subsection (C) states that the methods of authentication listed in the Rule are not intended to supersede any other method of authentication for official records that may be provided for by statute or state law.

ADDITIONAL AUTHORITY

9 WRIGHT & MILLER §§ 2431-2440

9 MOORE'S FEDERAL PRACTICE §§ 44.01-44.07

2 KLEIN DARLING AT 44-1 to AT 44-8

3 TEREZ F 15.4.1, F 15.4.2

4 OH. JUR. PL. AND PRAC. FORMS, ch. 48

5 MILLIGAN Forms 44-1 to 44-17

2 FINK §§ 44-1 to 44-6

LEADING CASES

Authentication

State v. Morrison, 2 Ohio App. 3d 364, 442 N.E.2d 114 (1982) (certification stapled to the front of a BMV packet which contained records on defendant satisfies requirements of Rule 44 for purposes of admission into evidence)

Lack of Record

State v. Colvin, 19 Ohio St. 2d 86, 249 N.E.2d 122 (1969) (where state dental board issues a certificate indicating that no certificate to practice dentistry in the state of Ohio has been issued to any person specified in the record, the certificate shall be received as prima facie evidence in any court)

CHAPTER 44.1

Rule 44.1. Judicial Notice of Certain Law; Determination of Foreign Law

Rule 44.1 reads as follows:

(A) Judicial notice of certain law.

(1) Judicial notice shall be taken of the rules of the supreme court of this state and of the decisional, constitutional, and public statutory law of this state.

(2) A party who intends to rely on a municipal ordinance, a local rule of court, or an administrative regulation within this state shall give notice in his pleading or other reasonable written notice. The court in taking judicial notice of a municipal ordinance, a local rule of court, or an administrative regulation within this state may inform itself in such manner as it deems proper, and may call upon counsel to aid in obtaining such information. The court's determination shall be treated as a ruling on a question of law and shall be made by the court and not the jury. A court may, however, take judicial notice of its own rules or of a municipal ordinance within the territorial jurisdiction of the court without advance notice in the pleading of a party or other written notice.

(3) A party who intends to rely on the decisional, constitutional, public statutory law, rules of court, municipal ordinances, or administrative regulations of any other state, territory, and jurisdiction of the United States shall give notice in his pleading or other reasonable notice. The court in taking judicial notice of the decisional, constitutional, public statutory law, rules of court, municipal ordinances, or administrative regulations of any other state, territory, and jurisdiction of the United States may inform itself in such manner as it deems proper, and may call upon counsel to aid in obtaining such information. The court's determination shall be treated as a ruling on a question of law, and shall be made by the court and not the jury.

(B) Determination of foreign law. A party who intends to rely on the law of a foreign country shall give notice in his pleadings or other reasonable written notice. The court in determining the law of a foreign country may consider any relevant material or source, including testimony, whether or not submitted by a party. The court's determination shall be treated as a ruling on a question of law and shall be made by the court and not the jury.

COMMENTARY

Rule 44.1 provides for the judicial notice and determination of some kinds of laws, regulations, and ordinances. The determination of such law is often a proper subject for judicial notice. However, judicial notice of law, as opposed to judicial notice of facts, is expressly beyond the scope of the Ohio Rules of Evidence. The Rule also contains advance notification requirements for parties who desire to have certain categories of law admitted.

Judicial Notice of Domestic Law

The Rule makes an initial distinction between domestic and foreign law; the former may be judicially noticed at trial, whereas the latter is subject to the normal rules of admissibility as is any other evidence. The primary difference between these two avenues of admissibility is with respect to the ease and facility of proof at trial. Judicial notice is a procedure in which the court simply makes certain conclusions of law upon the suggestion of the parties. Formal proof requires the proponent of the evidence to satisfy all requirements for admissibility as set forth under the Ohio Rules of Evidence: relevancy, authentication, "best evidence" rule, and hearsay.

Subsection (A) separates domestic law into 3 categories: constitutional, statutory, case law of the state of Ohio, and rules of procedure promulgated by the Supreme Court of Ohio; all other Ohio law; and all law of other domestic jurisdictions. The first category may be judicially noticed without advance notice by the parties. The second and third categories may also be judicially noticed, but the court may enlist the assistance of counsel in taking judicial notice of these laws. Parties must also provide the court and all other parties with advance notice as to the intent to admit such law at trial. The rules of the court in which the action is pending or an ordinance of a municipality within the territorial jurisdiction of the court in which the action is pending may be judicially noticed without advance notice by any party. In any case, the court's notice of such law is regarded as a question of law and is reviewed *de novo* on appeal.

Determination of Foreign Law

Subsection (B) provides for the determination of foreign law. The Rule allows the court to consider any source or material, which need not be admissible at trial, in determining the proper interpretation of foreign law. As with laws that are judicially noticed, determination of foreign laws are regarded as questions of law and are reviewed *de novo* on appeal.

Notice of Intent to Raise Issue of Law

Rule 44.1 requires that parties who intend to raise issues of local or specialized law, law of another state, or foreign law are required to so notify both the court and the opposing parties. This notification may be done in the pleadings or in some other written paper filed with the court. This notice should provide the court with sufficient time to make any required determinations of the law at issue.

ADDITIONAL AUTHORITY

9 WRIGHT & MILLER §§ 2441-2450
9 MOORE'S FEDERAL PRACTICE §§ 44.1.01-44.1.05
2 KLEIN DARLING AT 44.1-1 to AT 44.1-16
3 TEREZ F 4.8.1 to F 4.8.3
4 OH. JUR. PL. AND PRAC. FORMS, ch. 49
5 MILLIGAN Forms 44.1-1 to 44.1-16
2 FINK §§ 44.1-1 to 44.1-5

LEADING CASES

Foreign Law; In General

In re Knotts, 109 Ohio App. 3d 267, 671 N.E.2d 1357 (1996) (trial court lacked authority to take judicial notice of previous adjudication and journal entry, as entry at issue was result of another proceeding which had different case numbers and separate dockets)

Foreign Law; Notice

D.H. Overmyer Telecasting Co. v. American Home Assurance Co., 29 Ohio App. 3d 31, 502 N.E.2d 694 (1986) (party wishing to rely on an administrative regulation must give notice in his pleading or other reasonable written notice)

Foreign Ordinances

Aurora v. Sea Lakes, Inc., 105 Ohio App. 3d 60, 663 N.E.2d 690 (court may take judicial notice of city ordinances in admissions tax challenge because city was within its territorial jurisdiction), *dismissed, appeal not allowed*, 74 Ohio St. 3d 1462, 656 N.E.2d 1298 (1995)

CHAPTER 45

Rule 45. Subpoena

Rule 45 reads as follows:

(A) Form; issuance.

(1) Every subpoena shall do all of the following:

   (a) state the name of the court from which it is issued, the title of the action, and the case number;

   (b) command each person to whom it is directed, at a time and place specified in the subpoena, to:

      (i) attend and give testimony at a trial, hearing, or deposition;

      (ii) produce documents or tangible things at a trial, hearing, or deposition;

      (iii) produce and permit inspection and copying of any designated documents that are in the possession, custody, or control of the person;

      (iv) produce and permit inspection and copying, testing, or sampling of any tangible things that are in the possession, custody, or control of the person; or

      (v) permit entry upon designated land or other property that is in the possession or control of the person for the purposes described in Civ. R. 34(A)(3).

   (c) set forth the text of divisions (C) and (D) of this rule.

A command to produce and permit inspection may be joined with a command to attend and give testimony, or may be issued separately.

A subpoena may not be used to obtain the attendance of a party or the production of documents by a party in discovery. Rather, a party's attendance at a deposition may be obtained only by notice under Civ. R. 30, and documents may be obtained from a party in discovery only pursuant to Civ. R. 34.

(2) The clerk shall issue a subpoena, signed, but otherwise in blank, to a party requesting it, who shall complete it before service. An attorney who has filed an appearance on behalf of a party in an action may also sign and issue a subpoena on behalf of the court in which the action is pending.

(3) If the issuing attorney modifies the subpoena in any way, the issuing attorney shall give prompt notice of the modification to all other parties.

(B) Service. A subpoena may be served by a sheriff, bailiff, coroner, clerk of court, constable, or a deputy of any, by an attorney at law, or by any other person designated by order of the court who is not a party and is not less than eighteen years of age. Service of a subpoena upon a person named therein shall be made by delivering a copy of the subpoena to the person, by reading it to him or her in person, or by leaving it at the person's usual place of residence, and by tendering to the person upon demand the fees for one day's attendance and the mileage allowed by law. The person serving the subpoena shall file a return of the subpoena with the clerk. If the witness being subpoenaed resides outside the county in which the court is located, the fees for one day's attendance and mileage shall be tendered without demand. The return may be forwarded through the postal service or otherwise.

(C) Protection of persons subject to subpoenas.

(1) A party or an attorney responsible for the issuance and service of a subpoena shall take reasonable steps to avoid imposing undue burden or expense on a person subject to that subpoena.

(2)

    (a) A person commanded to produce under divisions (A)(1)(b)(ii), (iii), (iv), or (v) of this rule need not appear in person at the place of production or inspection unless commanded to attend and give testimony at a deposition, hearing, or trial.

    (b) Subject to division (D)(2) of this rule, a person commanded to produce under divisions (A)(1)(b)(ii), (iii), (iv), or (v) of this rule may, within fourteen days after service of the subpoena or before the time specified for compliance if such time is less than fourteen days after service, serve upon the party or attorney designated in the subpoena written objections to production. If objection is made, the party serving the subpoena shall not be entitled to production except pursuant to an order of the court by which the subpoena was issued. If objection has been made, the party serving the subpoena, upon notice to the person commanded to produce, may move at any time for an order to compel the production. An order to compel production shall protect any person who is not a party or an officer of a party from significant expense resulting from the production commanded.

(3) On timely motion, the court from which the subpoena was issued shall quash or modify the subpoena, or order appearance or production only under specified conditions, if the subpoena does any of the following:

(a) Fails to allow reasonable time to comply;

(b) Requires disclosure of privileged or otherwise protected matter and no exception or waiver applies;

(c) Requires disclosure of a fact known or opinion held by an expert not retained or specially employed by any party in anticipation of litigation or preparation for trial as described by Civ. R. 26(B)(4), if the fact or opinion does not describe specific events or occurrences in dispute and results from study by that expert that was not made at the request of any party;

(d) Subjects a person to undue burden.

(4) Before filing a motion pursuant to division (C)(3)(d) of this rule, a person resisting discovery under this rule shall attempt to resolve any claim of undue burden through discussions with the issuing attorney. A motion filed pursuant to division (C)(3)(d) of this rule shall be supported by an affidavit of the subpoenaed person or a certificate of that person's attorney of the efforts made to resolve any claim of undue burden.

(5) If a motion is made under division (C)(3)(c) or (C)(3)(d) of this rule, the court shall quash or modify the subpoena unless the party in whose behalf the subpoena is issued shows a substantial need for the testimony or material that cannot be otherwise met without undue hardship and assures that the person to whom the subpoena is addressed will be reasonably compensated.

(D) Duties in responding to subpoena.

(1) A person responding to a subpoena to produce documents shall, at the person's option, produce them as they are kept in the usual course of business or organized and labeled to correspond with the categories in the subpoena. A person producing documents pursuant to a subpoena for them shall permit their inspection and copying by all parties present at the time and place set in the subpoena for inspection and copying.

(2) When information subject to a subpoena is withheld on a claim that it is privileged or subject to protection as trial preparation materials under Civ. R. 26(B)(3) or (4), the claim shall be made expressly and shall be supported by a description of the nature of the documents, communications, or things not produced that is sufficient to enable the demanding party to contest the claim.

(E) Sanctions. Failure by any person without adequate excuse to obey a subpoena served upon that person may be deemed a contempt of the court from which the subpoena issued. A subpoenaed person or that person's attorney who frivolously resists discovery under this rule may be required by the court to pay the reasonable expenses, including reasonable attorney's fees, of the party seeking the discovery. The court from which a subpoena was issued may impose upon a party or attorney in breach of the duty imposed by division (C)(1) of this rule an appropriate sanction, which may include, but is not limited to, lost earnings and reasonable attorney's fees.

(F) **Privileges.** Nothing in this rule shall be construed to authorize a party to obtain information protected by any privilege recognized by law, or to authorize any person to disclose such information.

COMMENTARY

The procedures for issuing, serving, and responding to a subpoena are detailed in Rule 45. Subpoenas are issued to persons who are not parties in an action, and they direct those persons to attend depositions, provide trial testimony, produce certain kinds of discoverable documents, and other kinds of actions necessary for the disposition of a civil action. The contents of Rule 45 are similar to those of, and are related to, a number of other Rules, most notably Rules 26, 30, and 37, which relate to discovery.

Form and Issuance of Subpoenas

Subpoenas may be issued by attorneys as officers of the court. Subsection (A)(2) states that blank subpoenas shall be issued by the clerk, who shall sign the subpoena. Subpoenas are usually issued by the clerk of the court in which the action is pending, though attorneys may seek to have a subpoena issued by a clerk in a judicial district in which the witness is located. If a witness is located outside the state of Ohio, of course, the issuance of a subpoena will be governed by the law of the state from which the subpoena is issued.

Attorneys are then responsible for completing the contents of the subpoena, and they must also sign it. Subsection (A)(1)(c) requires that the full text of subsections (C) and (D) be included in the subpoena to alert the persons to whom the subpoena is directed of their rights and duties under Rule 45. Attorneys are responsible for any possible abuse of a subpoena, which is actionable as a tort.

Production of Documents

Subsection (A)(1) does not require the deposition of the custodian who is in control of discoverable material. The production of such material may be compelled independent of any deposition. Similarly, the Rule authorizes a subpoena to be issued to compel the inspection of premises in the possession of a non-party.

Illustration 45-1

Samantha is the plaintiff in a toxic tort action against Olivia's Oil Refining. Samantha wishes to acquire copies of notes compiled by Wally, a former employee of Olivia's Oil Refining, while he was an employee of the company. Under Rule 45(A)(1), Samantha need not depose Wally to acquire these documents, and may simply serve upon Wally a subpoena containing a request for the production of documents.

Illustration 45-2

Assume on the facts of Illustration 45-1 that Wally's notes are stored at his summer home, which is located in a different state than the one in which Wally resides. Under Rule 45(A)(1)(b)(iii), Wally must produce the documents, though Samantha will generally be required to pay expenses associated with the procurement of the notes.

Service of Subpoenas

Subsection (B)(1) provides that a subpoena may be served by anyone 18 years or older who is not a party in the action. Service of the subpoena must be made in person or by leaving it at the residence of the person. Service is not complete until the attendance fees and mileage allowances have been tendered.

Protection of Persons Subject to Subpoenas

Subsection (C) states the rights of witnesses under the Rule. Subsection (C)(1) articulates the expanded liability of the attorney correlative to the increased powers of attorneys to issue subpoenas under subsection (A). The Rule specifies that an attorney must take reasonable steps to avoid imposing undue burden or expense on a person subject to a subpoena issued and served by that attorney.

Subsection (C)(2) reiterates the directive of subsection (A)(1) that a person who is the subject of a production or inspection request need not be present at the place of production or inspection unless that person is also directed to appear at a deposition, albeit in slightly different terms. The subsection also allows 14 days in which a person may respond to a subpoena. The subsection also protects non-parties from significant expense in complying with production requests. Subsection (C)(3) lists the grounds under which a subpoena may be quashed or modified by a court.

Duties in Responding to a Subpoena

Subsection (D) extends to non-parties the duty to organize and arrange documents that are the subject of a subpoena imposed on parties by the final sentence of Rule 34(B). Furthermore, the subsection imposes the same duty on non-parties to describe the nature of the documents that are withheld for reasons of privilege or work product doctrine that is imposed on parties under Rule 26(B)(3) or 26(B)(4). The description must be sufficient to allow the party seeking access to the documents to challenge the claim of privilege or work product doctrine before the court. A person who desires to assert a privilege or work product doctrine claim with regard to documents must also disclose that claim promptly to the attorney issuing the subpoena.

Illustration 45-3

Blake commences a breach of contract action against Patricia, alleging that Patricia misrepresented the quality of the contract goods in question. Blake serves a subpoena upon Eve, a former business associate of Patricia, requesting that Eve provide Blake with any and all documents that address the quality of the goods produced by Patricia. Eve refuses to comply with the subpoena, claiming that the documents constitute privileged information. Under Rule 45, Eve must specifically state the documents being withheld under the claim of privilege. Though not a party to the action, Eve must nonetheless specify the grounds for her claim of privilege.

Subpoenas for Out-of-State Witnesses

Rule 45 does not contain specific provisions governing the subpoena of witnesses located outside the State or the subpoena of witnesses located within Ohio for actions commenced in other states. Instead, Ohio has adopted the Uniform Act to Secure the Attendance of Witnesses from Without a State in Criminal Proceedings at OHIO REV. CODE ANN. §§ 2939.25-2939.29, which contains reciprocal provisions in both situations. An extended discussion of these statutory provisions is beyond the scope of this manual.

Contempt for Failure to Obey a Subpoena

Subsection (E) states that a person who fails to obey the terms of a subpoena without adequate excuse may be held in contempt of the court from which the subpoena was issued.

ADDITIONAL AUTHORITY

9 WRIGHT & MILLER §§ 2451-2470
9 MOORE'S FEDERAL PRACTICE §§ 45.01-45.04
5 ANDERSON'S OHIO CIVIL PRACTICE §§ 177.01-177.08

LEADING CASES

Failure to Subpoena Witness

Fletcher v. Bolz, 35 Ohio App. 3d 129, 520 N.E.2d 22 (1987) (witness may not be held liable for damages due to the failure to testify at a deposition if the witness has not been subpoenaed pursuant to Rule 45)

Notice to Opposing Parties Not Required for Subpoena Duces Tecum

Neftzer v. Neftzer, 140 Ohio App. 3d 618, 748 N.E.2d 608 (2000) (unlike analogous federal rule, Rule 45 does not expressly require notification of opposing counsel of subpoena duces tecum, although it does require the issuing attorney to give prompt notice of a modification of a subpoena to all other parties)

Party to Be Served with Subpoena

Carosella v. Conwell, 138 Ohio App. 3d 688, 742 N.E.2d 188 (2000) (Rule 45 requires that subpoenas be served on parties and not their counsel; accordingly, a failure of a party to appear pursuant to a subpoena delivered to counsel was not proper ground to grant parents' motion for new trial)

Privilege Asserted Through Motion to Quash

Neftzer v. Neftzer, 140 Ohio App. 3d 618, 748 N.E.2d 608 (2000) (assertion of privilege to suppress relevant evidence usually comes in the form of a motion to quash a subpoena)

Production of Documents

Foor v. Huntington Nat'l Bank, 27 Ohio App. 3d 76, 499 N.E.2d 1297 (1986) (pursuant to subpoena duces tecum, a court may require an attorney to produce papers, which are held under a retaining lien, provided that the former client gives security for payment of the fee secured by the retaining lien)

Protection of Persons Subject to Subpoenas

Mann v. University of Cincinnati, 824 F. Supp. 1190 (S.D. Ohio 1993) (attorney violated rule governing issuance of subpoena when he instructed subpoena recipient that the only alternative to appearing with the documents solicited was to provide the documents before the subpoena production date), *aff'd*, 152 F.R.D. 119 (6th Cir. 1997)

Foor v. Huntington Nat'l Bank, 27 Ohio App. 3d 76, 499 N.E.2d 1297 (1986) (a nonparty witness who is subject to a subpoena duces tecum may appeal an order overruling a motion to quash the subpoena because the witness would otherwise have no remedy)

Service of and Relief from Subpoenas

United States Catholic Conference v. Abortion Rights Mobilization, Inc., 487 U.S. 72, *on remand*, 885 F.2d 1020 (U.S.N.Y. 1988) (if a district court has no jurisdiction of a matter and issues a subpoena relating to matters beyond a mere determination of jurisdiction, that subpoena is void)

Service; When Valid

State v. Castle, 92 Ohio App. 3d 732, 637 N.E.2d 80 (1994) (a subpoena satisfies the service requirements when it is sent by regular mail to the witness' residence and the witness has actual knowledge of it)

Denovcheck v. Board of Trumbull County Comm'rs, 36 Ohio St. 3d 14, 520 N.E.2d 1362 (1988) (a valid service of summons has been completed where a subpoena is left at the business location of a witness and where that witness has actual knowledge of the subpoena)

Subpoenas Issued by Board of Commissioners

Cincinnati Bar Ass'n v. Adjustment Serv. Corp., 89 Ohio St. 3d 385, 732 N.E.2d 362 (2000) (a subpoena includes a subpoena duces tecum, and Rule 45 provides an adequate process to challenge subpoenas issued by the Board of Commissioners on the Unauthorized Practice of Law)

Wrong Court

City of Whitehall v. Bambi Motel, Inc., 85 Ohio St. 3d 1209, 708 N.E.2d 722 (1999) (Lundberg Stratton, J., concurring) (a court should strike a motion to quash a subpoena if it is filed with a court other than the court from which the subpoena was issued)

CHAPTER 46

Rule 46. Exceptions Unnecessary

Rule 46 reads as follows:

An exception at any stage or step of the case or matter is unnecessary to lay a foundation for review whenever a matter has been called to the attention of the court by objection, motion, or otherwise and the court has ruled thereon.

COMMENTARY

Rule 46 eliminates any requirement of formal exceptions to rulings or orders of the court to preserve the issue for appeal. However, a party must still call attention to a ruling or order in a manner sufficient to indicate to the district judge the party's position on the matter.

ADDITIONAL AUTHORITY

9 Wright & Miller §§ 2471-2480
9 Moore's Federal Practice §§ 46.01-46.03
2 Klein Darling AT 46-1 to AT 46-2
3 Terez F 14.1.1, F 14.1.2
5 Milligan Forms 46-1 to 46-2
2 Fink §§ 46-1 to 46-1

LEADING CASES

Failure to Object

> ***Carrothers v. Hunter***, 23 Ohio St. 2d 99, 262 N.E.2d 867 (1970) (a party's failure to object to errors of commission in the charge of a court to the jury does not constitute waiver of the error, and such error may be proper grounds for appeal)

Invited Error Doctrine

> ***State ex rel. Bitter v. Missig***, 72 Ohio St. 3d 249, 648 N.E.2d 1355 (1995) (under invited error doctrine, a party cannot take advantage of an error which he himself invited or induced trial court to make)

CHAPTER 47

Rule 47. Jurors

Rule 47 reads as follows:

(A) Examination of jurors. Any person called as a juror for the trial of any cause shall be examined under oath or upon affirmation as to his qualifications. The court may permit the parties or their attorneys to conduct the examination of the prospective jurors or may itself conduct the examination. In the latter event, the court shall permit the parties or their attorneys to supplement the examination by further inquiry.

(B) Challenges to jury. In addition to challenges for cause provided by law, each party peremptorily may challenge three jurors. If the interests of multiple litigants are essentially the same, "each party" shall mean "each side."

Peremptory challenges may be exercised after the minimum number of jurors allowed by the rules has been passed for cause and seated on the panel. Peremptory challenges shall be exercised alternately, with the first challenge exercised by the plaintiff. The failure of a party to exercise a peremptory challenge constitutes a waiver of that challenge. If all parties or both sides, alternately and in sequence, fail to exercise a peremptory challenge, the joint failure constitutes a waiver of all peremptory challenges.

A prospective juror peremptorily challenged by either party shall be excused and another juror shall be called who shall take the place of the juror excused and be sworn and examined as other jurors. The other party, if he has peremptory challenges remaining, shall be entitled to challenge any juror then seated on the panel.

(C) Alternate jurors. The court may direct that no more than four jurors in addition to the regular jury be called and impanelled to sit as alternate jurors. Alternate jurors in the order in which they are called shall replace jurors who, prior to the time the jury retires to consider its verdict, become or are found to be unable or disqualified to perform their duties. Alternate jurors shall be drawn in the same manner, shall have the same qualifications, shall be subject to the same examination and challenges, shall take the same oath, and shall have the same functions, powers, facilities, and privileges as the regular jurors. An alternate juror who does not replace a regular juror shall be discharged after the jury retires to consider its verdict. Each party is entitled to one peremptory challenge in addition to those otherwise allowed by law if one or two alternate jurors are to be impanelled and two peremptory challenges if three or four alternate jurors are to be impanelled. The additional peremptory challenges may be used against an alternate juror only, and the other peremptory challenges allowed shall not be used against an alternate juror.

COMMENTARY

Rule 47 provides for the selection of the jury, and should be read in conjunction with Rule 38(B) and Rule 48, which also relate the impaneling of a jury. Rule 47 contains provisions relating to voir dire, peremptory challenges, and alternate jurors. Other important aspects of impaneling a jury, such as selection of the jury pool and juror challenges for cause, are governed by local rules, statute, or case law.

Voir Dire by the Parties or by the Court

Under subsection (A), the district judge has a vast amount of discretion to decide upon the form, scope, and content of voir dire examinations. Additionally, the court has the discretion to conduct voir dire itself, or it may allow the attorneys or their parties to conduct the examination. If the court chooses to conduct voir dire itself, the Rule appears to require the court to allow the parties to submit proposed questions or to supplement the examination with additional questions. The court may refuse to ask questions proposed by the attorneys of prospective jurors, but the court should not be unreasonable in its refusal.

Peremptory Challenges

In addition to challenges for cause provided by law, subsection (B) allows the parties three peremptory challenges. Peremptory challenges have drawn the attention of the United States Supreme Court in the last decade, as at least five cases on the issue have been the subject of Supreme Court opinion. In *Batson v. Kentucky*, 476 U.S. 79 (1986), the Supreme Court held that peremptory challenges may not be exercised by the State in a criminal case on the basis of race. The ban on racially discriminatory peremptory challenges has been applied to defendants in criminal cases and to all parties in civil actions. In *J.E.B. v. Alabama ex rel. T.B.*, 511 U.S. 127 (1994), the holding of *Batson* was extended to forbid peremptory challenges on the basis of sex in selected cases.

Alternate Jurors

Subsection (C) states that a court may seat only four jurors as alternate jurors. If one or two alternate jurors are to be impaneled, each party is entitled to one more peremptory challenge; and if three or four alternate jurors are to be impaneled, each party is entitled to two more peremptory challenges. The process of selecting alternate jurors follows that of regular jurors, although alternate jurors who have not replaced regular jurors will be discharged when the jury retires to consider its verdict.

ADDITIONAL AUTHORITY

9 WRIGHT & MILLER §§ 2481-2490
9 MOORE'S FEDERAL PRACTICE §§ 47.01-47.49
5 ANDERSON'S OHIO CIVIL PRACTICE §§ 176.01-176.04
2 KLEIN DARLING AT 47-1 to AT 47-7
3 TEREZ F 15.1.1
4 OH. JUR. PL. AND PRAC. FORMS, ch. 51
5 MILLIGAN Forms 47-1 to 47-9
2 FINK §§ 47-1 to 47-3

LEADING CASES

Alternate Jurors

LeFort v. Century 21-Maitland Realty Co., 32 Ohio St. 3d 121, 512 N.E.2d 640 (1987) (where a juror is incapacitated and replaced by an alternate juror during the course of jury deliberations, a violation of Rule 47 does not require reversal where counsel knows of the substitution, raises no objections thereto, and participates in the rule-violating conduct)

Challenges for Cause

Carpenter v. Bonniway Leasing, Inc., 89 Ohio App. 3d 840, 627 N.E.2d 1030 (1993) (a juror, who stated that she would try to be fair and impartial despite a history of heart disease, was not subject to removal for cause in workers' compensation action by wife of truck driver who suffered heart attack and died in crash), *jurisdictional motion overruled*, 68 Ohio St. 3d 1430, 624 N.E.2d 1067 (1994)

Examination During Trial

McQueen v. Goldey, 20 Ohio App. 3d 41, 484 N.E.2d 712 (1984) (a court is not required to allow attorney's examination of a juror who indicates during trial that she knows one of the witnesses, and the court does not abuse its discretion by asking the juror only whether she would "pay more attention" to that witness)

Peremptory Challenges

Reitz v. Howlett, 106 Ohio App. 3d 409, 666 N.E.2d 296 (1995) (each defendant was entitled to three peremptory challenges where they retained separate counsel and filed separate answers, and where only one might have been found liable)

Voir Dire; Permissible Scope

Beavercreek Local Schools v. Basic, Inc., 71 Ohio App. 3d 669, 595 N.E.2d 360 (trial court did not abuse discretion in prohibiting plaintiff in asbestos litigation from asking detailed, individual questions of venire into such areas as smoking and use of hard hats), *motion to certify overruled*, 61 Ohio St. 3d 1431, 575 N.E.2d 219 (1991)

CHAPTER 48

Rule 48. Juries: Majority Verdict; Stipulation of Number of Jurors

Rule 48 reads as follows:

In all civil actions, a jury shall render a verdict upon the concurrence of three-fourths or more of their number. The verdict shall be in writing and signed by each of the jurors concurring therein. All jurors shall then return to court where the judge shall cause the verdict to be read and inquiry made to determine if the verdict is that of three-fourths or more of the jurors. Upon request of either party, the jury shall be polled by asking each juror if the verdict is that of the juror; if more than one-fourth of the jurors answer in the negative, or if the verdict in substance is defective, the jurors must be sent out again for further deliberation. If three-fourths or more of the jurors answer affirmatively, the verdict is complete and the jury shall be discharged from the case. If the verdict is defective in form only, with the assent of the jurors and before their discharge, the court may correct it.

The parties may stipulate that the jury shall consist of any number less than the maximum number provided by Rule 38(B). For the purpose of rendering a verdict, whenever three-fourths of the jury does not consist of an integral number, the next higher number shall be construed to represent three-fourths of the jury. For juries with less than four members, the verdict must be unanimous.

COMMENTARY

Rule 48 sets forth the rules governing the number of jurors required for a verdict in a civil action. The Rule should be read in conjunction with Rule 38(B) and Rule 47, which also relate to the impaneling of a jury. Other important aspects of impaneling a jury, such as selection of the jury pool and juror challenges for cause, are governed by local rules, statute, or case law.

Procedure for Rendering of Verdict

The Rule provides for the rendering of the verdict by the jury in writing as well as orally in open court. The verdict must be signed by those jurors concurring in the verdict, and the jurors are required to be polled as to their verdict in open court upon the request of any party. The Rule distinguishes between defects in substance in the verdict and defects in form. If the verdict is contrary to that indicated by the polling of the jurors, or three-fourths of the jury do not agree as to a single verdict, the jury must be sent back to the jury room for deliberation. Defects in form of the written verdict, such as misspellings and inadvertent omissions, may be corrected *sua sponte* by the court with the jury's permission.

Percentage of Jurors Required for Verdict

Under Rule 38(B), the maximum number of jurors in a civil action is eight, with the exception of actions for appropriation of a right of way brought by a corporation, in which case 12 jurors may be impaneled. The parties may agree to a lesser number, a point reiterated in the first sentence of the second paragraph of Rule 48.

Under Rule 48, a three-fourths majority of the jury is required to render a verdict, which will be six jurors in most cases. Unlike the number of jurors, this percentage may not be reduced by stipulation of the parties. If the jury contains four members or fewer, the verdict must be unanimous. The penultimate sentence of Rule 48 provides that the next higher whole number of jurors is required for a verdict whenever three-fourths of the number of jurors is not equivalent to a whole number. Interestingly, this produces a result where the number of jurors required to reach a verdict in a jury of eight members is the same as the number of jurors required to reach a verdict in a jury of seven members (7 jurors X .75 = 5.25 jurors, which is then rounded up to 6).

ADDITIONAL AUTHORITY

9 Wright & Miller §§ 2491-2500
9 Moore's Federal Practice §§ 48.01-48.05
5 Anderson's Ohio Civil Practice §§ 176.01, 176.05
2 Klein Darling AT 48-1 to AT 48-6
3 Terez F 15.5.1 to F 15.5.7
4 Oh. Jur. Pl. and Prac. Forms, ch. 51
5 Milligan Forms 48-1 to 48-4
2 Fink §§ 48-1 to 48-5

LEADING CASES

Correction of Verdict

Highfield v. Liberty Christian Academy, 34 Ohio App. 3d 311, 518 N.E.2d 592 (1987) (a jury polled under Rule 48 may only be asked if the verdict represents that of each juror; a party has no right to poll a jury to clarify a potential mistake in their answer to an interrogatory)

Majority Verdict

O'Connell v. Chesapeake & Ohio Ry. Co., 58 Ohio St. 3d 226, 569 N.E.2d 889 (1991) (three-fourths of jury must agree as to both negligence and proximate cause, and only those jurors who so find may participate in the apportionment of comparative negligence)

CHAPTER 49

Rule 49. Verdicts; Interrogatories

Rule 49 reads as follows:

(A) General verdict. A general verdict, by which the jury finds generally in favor of the prevailing party, shall be used.

(B) General verdict accompanied by answer to interrogatories. The court shall submit written interrogatories to the jury, together with appropriate forms for a general verdict, upon request of any party prior to the commencement of argument. Counsel shall submit the proposed interrogatories to the court and to opposing counsel at such time. The court shall inform counsel of its proposed action upon the requests prior to their arguments to the jury, but the interrogatories shall be submitted to the jury in the form that the court approves. The interrogatories may be directed to one or more determinative issues whether issues of fact or mixed issues of fact and law.

The court shall give such explanation or instruction as may be necessary to enable the jury both to make answers to the interrogatories and to render a general verdict, and the court shall direct the jury both to make written answers and to render a general verdict.

When the general verdict and the answers are consistent, the appropriate judgment upon the verdict and answers shall be entered pursuant to Rule 58. When one or more of the answers is inconsistent with the general verdict, judgment may be entered pursuant to Rule 58 in accordance with the answers, notwithstanding the general verdict, or the court may return the jury for further consideration of its answers and verdict or may order a new trial.

(C) Special verdicts abolished. Special verdicts shall not be used.

COMMENTARY

Rule 49 provides for the form of the verdict. Ohio differs from some jurisdictions in not allowing special verdicts, a technique whereby the jury determines specific questions of fact without making a determination as to which will prevail.

General Verdicts

Ordinarily, the jury returns a verdict that is in the form of a general verdict. A general verdict is simply a finding for one party or the other. The procedure for rendering the verdict is set forth in Rule 48.

The abolition of the special verdict in subsection (C), along with the mandatory language of subsection (A), creates an absolute requirement of a general verdict in civil cases tried to a jury. The failure of the jury to return a general verdict of its own accord or pursuant to instructions by the court has been deemed by the Ohio Supreme Court to be reversible almost *per se*.

Jury Interrogatories; Consistency with General Verdict

Subsection (B) authorizes the submission of interrogatories to the jury. Interrogatories are specific questions addressed to issues of fact involved in the action. The interrogatories must be in written form, and the judge is directed to instruct the jury both on their duty to return a general verdict and to provide responses to the written interrogatories. As the jury is making a determination on the ultimate question of liability between the parties in its general verdict form, subsection (B) requires the entry of judgment on the general verdict if the answers to the interrogatories are consistent with one another and with the general verdict.

Jury Interrogatories; Inconsistency with General Verdict

If the jury returns answers to the interrogatories which are consistent with one another but one or more of the answers is inconsistent with the general verdict, the court has three options. The court may enter a judgment contrary to that indicated by the general verdict but in accord with all of the answers provided to the interrogatories. Alternately, the judge may resubmit the general verdict and interrogatories to the jury for further consideration and with instructions appropriate under the circumstances. The court may also in its discretion order a new trial, although this option should rarely be utilized when the less drastic measure of resubmission of the general verdict and interrogatories to the jury has been taken. Entry of judgment on a general verdict is not permitted where one or more of the answers to the interrogatories is inconsistent with the general verdict.

Illustration 49-1

In a civil action to recover damages for intentional infliction of emotional distress caused by an accident at Howie's Deep Pockets Amusement Park, the jury returns a general verdict with interrogatories that awards $750,000 to Caroline. However, the jury's answers to the interrogatories reveal that the jury concludes that Howie's Deep Pockets Amusement Park did not intentionally cause the accident and that Caroline's emotional distress was not proximately caused by the accident at Howie's Amusement Park. Under Rule 49(B), the court may enter judgment in favor of Howie's Deep Pockets Amusement Park despite the general verdict by the jury. Alternatively, the court may resubmit the general verdict with interrogatories to the jury for further consideration or order a new trial. The judge may not ignore the answers to the interrogatories and enter judgment for Caroline despite the general verdict by the jury.

ADDITIONAL AUTHORITY

9 Wright & Miller §§ 2501-2520

9 Moore's Federal Practice §§ 49.01-49.20

5 Anderson's Ohio Civil Practice §§ 180.01-180.07

2 Klein Darling AT 49-1 to AT 49-32

3 Terez F 15.5.1 to F 15.5.7, F 15.7.1 to F 15.7.8

4 Oh. Jur. Pl. and Prac. Forms, ch. 52

5 Milligan Forms 49-1 to 49-27

2 Fink §§ 49-1 to 49-4

LEADING CASES

Ambiguous Interrogatories

Alvater v. Claycraft Co., 92 Ohio App. 3d 759, 637 N.E.2d 97 (1994) (where an interrogatory is ambiguous, the court will presume that the jury construed it in a way that is consistent with the general verdict)

Answers Inconsistent with Verdict, Other Interrogatories

Thorton v. Parker, 100 Ohio App. 3d 743, 654 N.E.2d 1282 (1995) (trial court should enter judgment in accordance with answers to interrogatories inconsistent with general verdict only when it is absolutely clear that the answer dictate such a result)

Compromise Verdicts

Airborne Express, Inc. v. Systems Research Lab., 106 Ohio App. 3d 498, 666 N.E.2d 584 (1995) (even where a compromise verdict has been rendered, jury verdict will be upheld unless there is evidence of passion, prejudice, or wanton wrong on the part of the jury)

Conflicting Verdict and Jury Interrogatories

Perez v. Falls Fin. Inc., 87 Ohio St. 3d 371, 721 N.E.2d 47 (2000) (when faced with conflicting general verdict and interrogatory answers, the trial court acted within its discretion in ordering the jury to deliberate further)

Court Approval of Jury Interrogatories

Nakoff v. Fairview Glen Hosp., 75 Ohio St. 3d 254, 662 N.E.2d 1 (1996) (court has discretion to reject interrogatories that are confusing, ambiguous, or otherwise legally objectionable)

Discretion of Court Where Verdict Conflicts with Jury Interrogatories

Colvin v. Abbey's Restaurant, Inc., 85 Ohio St. 3d 535, 709 N.E.2d 1156 (1999) (where a jury's answers to one or more special interrogatories are irreconcilable with the general verdict, the choice of whether to enter judgment in accord with the answers to interrogatories and against the general verdict, resubmit the case to the jury, or order a new trial lies within the sound discretion of the trial court)

General Verdict Mandatory

Schellhouse v. Norfolk & Western Ry. Co., 61 Ohio St. 3d 520, 575 N.E.2d 473 (1991) (the provisions of Rule 49(A) are mandatory and the court must require the jury to return a general verdict)

Inconsistent General Verdict and Interrogatory Answers

Kenney v. Fealko, 75 Ohio App. 3d 47, 598 N.E.2d 861 (1991) (procedure applicable when jury returns inconsistent general verdict and interrogatory answers applies only when jury was returning a single general verdict)

Inconsistent General Verdicts

Fulwiler v. Schneider, 104 Ohio App. 3d 398, 662 N.E.2d 82 (1995) (where general verdict is returned in favor for one of the parties, and special interrogatories are not used to determine which issue was determinative of the verdict, the court will presume that all issues were resolved in favor of the prevailing party)

Inconsistent General Verdict; Trial Court Options

Colvin v. Abbey's Restaurant, Inc., 85 Ohio St. 3d 535, 709 N.E.2d 1156 (1999) (when a jury's answers to interrogatories are inconsistent with a general verdict reached by the jury, the trial court must choose among the following options: (1) enter judgment in accordance with the interrogatory answers, (2) return the jury for further consideration of the interrogatories and the general verdict, or (3) order a new trial)

Inconsistent Interrogatories

Irvine v. Akron Beacon Journal, 147 Ohio App. 3d 428, 770 N.E.2d 1105 (2002) (when a jury returns a general verdict that is inconsistent with interrogatories, the proper procedure is to send the jury back for further deliberations, not to enter judgment on the answers to interrogatories which contradicted the general verdict)

Jury Interrogatories; In General

Freeman v. Norfolk & W. Ry. Co., 69 Ohio St. 3d 611, 635 N.E.2d 310 (1994) (when plaintiff alleges multiple acts of negligence, the jury may be asked to specify what the negligence consisted of; however, an interrogatory asking the jury to indicate "the particulars" of the negligence is improper in form)

Jury Interrogatories Mandatory upon Request

Jurgens Real Estate Co. v. R.E.D. Constr. Corp., 103 Ohio App. 3d 292, 659 N.E.2d 353 (if a party makes a timely request, a mandatory duty arises to submit written interrogatories to the jury, provided that the interrogatories are in a form that the court approves of), *appeal not allowed*, 74 Ohio St. 3d 1409, 655 N.E.2d 187 (1995)

New Trial Order Appealable

Colvin v. Abbey's Restaurant, Inc., 85 Ohio St. 3d 535, 709 N.E.2d 1156 (1999) (an order for a new trial is a final appealable order when it is issued sua sponte by the court after the jury returned a general verdict inconsistent with answers to interrogatories)

Objections to Jury Interrogatories

Boewe v. Ford Motor Co., 94 Ohio App. 3d 389, 632 N.E.2d 946 (1992) (a party's failure to object to an interrogatory constitutes a waiver of any error)

Statutory Special Verdicts Not Permitted

Holeton v. Crouse Cartage Co., 92 Ohio St. 3d 115, 748 N.E.2d 1111 (2001) (provision of Rule 49 that provides that special verdicts shall not be used prevails over workers' compensation statute to the extent that statute allowed special verdicts)

Sua Sponte Order for New Trial; Scope of Appellate Review

Colvin v. Abbey's Restaurant, Inc., 85 Ohio St. 3d 535, 709 N.E.2d 1156 (1999) (upon a trial court's sua sponte order for a new trial because a jury's answers to interrogatories are inconsistent with the jury's general verdict, the reviewing court of appeals only has jurisdiction to consider the propriety of the trial court's new-trial order.)

Two Issue Rule

Avila v. Questor Juvenile Furniture Co., 74 Ohio App. 3d 597, 599 N.E.2d 771 ("two issue rule," which precludes reversal of a jury verdict even if instruction on one issue is improper where jury renders a general verdict without interrogatories, does not apply where there is a charge on a issue upon which no such charge should have been entered), *jurisdictional motion overruled*, 62 Ohio St. 3d 1465, 580 N.E. 2d 785 (1991)

Waiver of Inconsistency Between Verdict and Interrogatories

Cooper v. Metal Sales Mfg. Corp., 104 Ohio App. 3d 34, 660 N.E.2d 1245 (1995) (a party's failure to enter a timely objection before the jury is discharged constitutes a waiver of any inconsistency between the verdict and an interrogatory)

Workers' Compensation Statute Superseded in Part

Holeton v. Crouse Cartage Co., 92 Ohio St. 3d 115, 748 N.E.2d 1111 (2001) (Rule 49, which provides that special verdicts shall not be used, supersedes workers' compensation statute to the extent that the statute allows special verdicts)

CHAPTER 50

Rule 50. Motion for a Directed Verdict and for Judgment Notwithstanding the Verdict

Rule 50 reads as follows:

(A) Motion for directed verdict.

(1) When made. A motion for a directed verdict may be made on the opening statement of the opponent, at the close of the opponent's evidence or at the close of all the evidence.

(2) When not granted. A party who moves for a directed verdict at the close of the evidence offered by an opponent may offer evidence in the event that the motion is not granted, without having reserved the right so to do and to the same extent as if the motion had not been made. A motion for a directed verdict which is not granted is not a waiver of trial by jury even though all parties to the action have moved for directed verdicts.

(3) Grounds. A motion for a directed verdict shall state the specific grounds therefor.

(4) When granted on the evidence. When a motion for a directed verdict has been properly made, and the trial court, after construing the evidence most strongly in favor of the party against whom the motion is directed, finds that upon any determinative issue reasonable minds could come to but one conclusion upon the evidence submitted and that conclusion is adverse to such party, the court shall sustain the motion and direct a verdict for the moving party as to that issue.

(5) Jury assent unnecessary. The order of the court granting a motion for a directed verdict is effective without any assent of the jury.

(B) Motion for judgment notwithstanding the verdict. Whether or not a motion to direct a verdict has been made or overruled and not later than fourteen days after entry of judgment, a party may move to have the verdict and any judgment entered thereon set aside and to have judgment entered in accordance with his motion; or if a verdict was not returned such party, within fourteen days after the jury has been discharged, may move for judgment in accordance with his motion. A motion for a new trial may be joined with this motion, or a new trial may be prayed for in the alternative. If a verdict was returned, the court may allow the judgment to stand or may reopen the judgment. If the judgment is reopened, the court shall either order a new trial or direct the entry of judgment, but no judgment shall be rendered by the court on the ground that the verdict is against the weight of the evidence. If no verdict was returned the court may direct the entry of judgment or may order a new trial.

(C) **Conditional rulings on motion for judgment notwithstanding verdict.**

    (1)   If the motion for judgment notwithstanding the verdict, provided for in subdivision (B) of this rule, is granted, the court shall also rule on the motion for a new trial, if any, by determining whether it should be granted if the judgment is thereafter vacated or reversed. If the motion for a new trial is thus conditionally granted, the order thereon does not affect the finality of the judgment. In case the motion for a new trial has been conditionally granted and the judgment is reversed on appeal, the new trial shall proceed unless the appellate court has otherwise ordered. In case the motion for a new trial has been conditionally denied, the appellee on appeal may assert error in that denial; and if the judgment is reversed on appeal, subsequent proceedings shall be in accordance with the order of the appellate court.

    (2)   The party whose verdict has been set aside on motion for judgment notwithstanding the verdict may serve a motion for a new trial pursuant to Rule 59 not later than fourteen days after entry of the judgment notwithstanding the verdict.

(D) **Denial of motion for judgment notwithstanding verdict.** If the motion for judgment notwithstanding the verdict is denied, the party who prevailed on that motion may, as appellee, assert grounds entitling him to a new trial in the event the appellate court concludes that the trial court erred in denying the motion for judgment notwithstanding the verdict. If the appellate court reverses the judgment, nothing in this rule precludes it from determining that the appellee is entitled to a new trial, or from directing the trial court to determine whether a new trial shall be granted.

(E) **Statement of basis of decision.** When in a jury trial a court directs a verdict or grants judgment without or contrary to the verdict of the jury, the court shall state the basis for its decision in writing prior to or simultaneous with the entry of judgment. Such statement may be dictated into the record or included in the entry of judgment.

COMMENTARY

Rule 50 provides for motions for a directed verdict and for a judgment notwithstanding the verdict, commonly referred to as a "motion for JNOV," representing the Latin name for the motion, *judgment non obstante veredicto*. These motions allow parties to request that the court find that it has prevailed in the action as a matter of law either before the jury retires for deliberation or after it has returned a verdict. Analogous motions in federal court are called "motions for judgment as a matter of law," though significant differences exist between the two Rules.

Motion for Directed Verdict; When Proper

Rule 50(A) allows a party to move for a directed verdict on the opening statement of the opponent, at the close of the opponent's evidence, or at the close of all the evidence, but before the jury retires for its deliberations. A motion for a directed verdict is analogous to a motion for summary judgment under Rule 56, a point to which the commonality in language in Rule 56 and subsection (A)(4) attests.

Specifically, a directed verdict is proper when the court finds that "reasonable minds could come to but one conclusion upon the evidence and that conclusion is adverse to [the non-moving] party." Such a finding should only be made after the court construes the evidence in the light most favorable to the non-moving party. The purpose of this requirement is to prevent the court from usurping the role of the jury in such an instance; it is thus said that, if reasonable minds could differ as to the proper disposition of the case, a directed verdict is not appropriate. Nonetheless, subsection (A)(5) provides that the assent of the jury is not required when the court grants a directed verdict.

A directed verdict is also appropriate when a party has failed to establish the legal sufficiency of its pleadings, as opposed to the factual sufficiency of the evidence, though this situation will rarely arise at trial. In this sense, a directed verdict is similar to a judgment on the pleadings under Rule 12(C).

However, it should be noted that the Ohio Supreme Court has consistently interpreted Rule 50(A)(4) to indicate that a directed verdict motion raises a question of what is typically referred to as the "legal sufficiency of the evidence" only, not a question of the weight of the evidence or the credibility of the witnesses. Such a view not only collapses the concepts of "legal sufficiency" with respect to the pleadings and "factual sufficiency" with respect to the evidence, it also seems to contradict the express language of Rule 50(A)(4), which requires the court to "constru[e] the evidence most **strongly** in favor of the party against whom the motion is directed" (emphasis added), a rather difficult task if the court is not to weigh the sufficiency of the evidence in the first place.

Appeal of a Directed Verdict

The nature of an appeal of a directed verdict is unsettled under Ohio law. Although some case law suggests that the court should not decide whether issues of material fact exist in a motion for a directed verdict, the express language of the Rule appears to suggest to the contrary. Furthermore, the different denomination of motions made before the case is submitted to the jury and those made after the case is submitted to the jury suggests that the two motions have differing standards of proof. The directive in subsection (B) that no motion for JNOV shall be granted on the ground that a jury verdict is against the weight of the evidence is also evidence of the distinction.

At the very least, the denial of a motion for a directed verdict on the ground that the opposing party's case is not legally sufficient should be appealable. The legal sufficiency of a party's case is not a proper issue for the jury, and error may be predicated on the trial court's failure to grant a motion to this effect. Whether the denial of a motion for directed verdict on the ground that the trial court failed to conclude that reasonable minds could arrive at but one conclusion after having construed the evidence in the light most favorable to the non-moving party is a question to which no definite answer is provided under Ohio law.

Motion for Directed Verdict; How Made

According to subsection (A)(3), the party moving for the directed verdict must state the grounds on which the motion is made. This requirement allows the opposing party an opportunity to offer proof as to a specific fact which may have been omitted from the trial inadvertently. A denial of a motion for a directed verdict functions neither as a waiver of the right to present evidence subsequent to the motion nor as a waiver of a jury trial of any issue not yet presented by the evidence. Although it is not clear under the Rule whether a motion for a directed verdict at the close of the opposing party's case sufficiently preserves the issue for appeal, careful practitioners should resolve any doubt by renewing the motion at the close of all the evidence.

Illustration 50-1

Bernard is a defendant in a libel action brought by Andrea. At the close of Andrea's case, Bernard makes a motion for a directed verdict, arguing that the statement he made was true and thus not libelous. The court denies the motion on the grounds that no evidence of truth has been yet introduced. After Bernard presents his case-in-defense, he should renew his motion for a directed verdict at the close of all the evidence to preserve the issue for appeal.

Motions for JNOV and Motions for New Trial

Rule 50(B) governs motions for judgments notwithstanding the verdict, or motions for JNOV. These motions are typically made after the trial has ended and the judgment has been entered on a jury verdict, though the Rule provides for such motions upon a hung jury. Motions for JNOV are usually joined with motions for a new trial under Rule 59, and subsections (C) and (D) set forth the various outcomes resulting from the grant or denial of these two motions.

Motions for JNOV; When Made

Motions for JNOV made under subsection (B) must be *filed* within 14 days after the entry of judgment. This period may not be enlarged by the court, as Rule 6(B), which provides for enlargement of time periods by the court generally, specifically excepts motions made under Rule 50(B) from its provisions. Motions for JNOV may also be made no later than 14 days from the date of the discharge of the jury in the event that the jury has not returned a verdict.

Under Federal Rule of Civil Procedure 50, a motion for judgment as a matter of law made before the case is submitted to the jury is an absolute condition to the similar motion after the jury returns with its verdict. This requirement stems from an idiosyncratic interpretation of the Seventh Amendment under federal case law, and the Staff Notes to Ohio Rule 50 state that no similar "directed verdict trap" exists under Ohio law. Thus, motions for JNOV may be made whether or not motions for a directed verdict were made during trial, a point made expressly in the first sentence of subsection (B).

Motions for JNOV; When Granted

The standard for granting a motion for JNOV, like the standard for a directed verdict, requires that upon any determinative issue, reasonable minds could come to but one conclusion adverse to the non-moving party based upon the submitted evidence. However, a motion for JNOV is not a substitute for a renewed directed verdict. Instead, the Staff Notes to Rule 50 indicate that the two lines of cases addressing the standards for granting motions for directed verdicts and those for granting motions for JNOV remain effective under the Rule. If the jury returns a verdict, the court is provided with three options when deciding a motion for JNOV: (1) to deny the motion, thus allowing the judgment resulting from the verdict to stand; (2) to order a new trial; or (3) to grant the motion, thus directing the entry of judgment contrary to that indicated by the verdict. If the jury does not return a verdict, the court is authorized to order a new trial or to grant the motion, thus directing the entry of judgment in accordance with that requested in the motion for JNOV.

Operation of Decisions on Motions When Appealed

Subsections (C) and (D) detail the operation of decisions on motions for JNOV and conditional decisions for motions for new trials if an appeal is taken from the action. Those subsections anticipate the four distinct situations resulting from the grant or denial of a motion for JNOV and the conditional grant or denial of a motion for a new trial. Although the Rule does not detail the operation of decisions for motion for JNOV when no motion for a new trial is made, the permutations are greatly simplified in that instance. This situation rarely arises, as experienced litigators routinely join motions for new trials with motions for JNOV. If, for some reason, motions for new trials are not made by the parties, the operation of subsections (C) and (D) can also be triggered because the court has the authority to order a new trial *sua sponte* under Rule 59(D).

Subsection (C) directs that, if a motion for JNOV is granted, the court should also rule conditionally on the motion for new trial, if one is made, and specify the grounds for conditionally ruling on that motion. Ordinarily, the grant of a motion for a new trial destroys the finality of the judgment, and prevents the immediate appeal of the judgment. However, when such a motion is granted conditionally in conjunction with the grant of a motion for JNOV, subsection (C) states that the grant of a motion for new trial does not preclude the appeal of the judgment. Instead, the grant of the motion for a new trial will be effective if the JNOV is reversed or vacated on appeal, unless the appellate court orders otherwise.

Illustration 50-2

Assume on the facts of Illustration 50-1 that the jury returns with a verdict for Kathryn. Bernard then makes a motion for JNOV, which the court grants, and joins with it a motion for a new trial, which the court conditionally grants. On review, the appellate court grants a summary reversal of the trial court's JNOV, but does not specify any other action to be taken. At this point, the trial court's conditional grant of Bernard's motion for a new trial will take effect.

If the motion for a new trial is denied conditionally in conjunction with the grant of a motion for JNOV, the order denying the motion for a new trial is appealable by the appellee. Denials of motions for new trials are not normally appealable as such under Rule 59. However, if an appellate court reverses or vacates the JNOV, the Rule authorizes the appellate court to order a new trial, notwithstanding the denial of that motion in the lower court.

Illustration 50-3

Assume on the facts of Illustration 50-2 that the court grants Bernard's motion for JNOV but conditionally denies his motion for a new trial. If Kathryn appeals the court's grant of Bernard's motion for JNOV, Bernard may cross-appeal the trial court's denial of Bernard's motion for a new trial.

Subsection (D) directs that, if a motion for JNOV is denied and that denial is appealed, the appellee may assert grounds for the first time on appeal that it is entitled to a new trial if the appellate court reverses or vacates the denial of the motion for JNOV. As noted above, the careful practitioner should make a motion for a new trial even when a jury verdict is in her favor, thereby preserving the opportunity for the court to grant a new trial in lieu of granting the motion for JNOV and rendering the contingency of subsection (D) immaterial.

Illustration 50-4

Assume on the facts of Illustration 50-3 that Bernard fails to join a motion for a new trial with his motion for JNOV. The court denies his motion and Bernard appeals. The appellate court vacates the trial court's order of Bernard's motion and is prepared to direct the trial court to enter an order granting Bernard's motion. At this point, Kathryn may argue for a new trial on grounds not advanced at trial below, thus avoiding an entirely adverse ruling on appeal.

Basis of Decision

Because the granting of either a directed verdict or JNOV signifies the substitution of the judgment of the court for that of a jury, Rule 50(E) requires the court to set forth, in writing, the grounds for granting either motion. This statement serves as the basis upon which an appeal may be taken.

ADDITIONAL AUTHORITY

9 WRIGHT & MILLER §§ 2521-2550

9 MOORE'S FEDERAL PRACTICE §§ 50.01-50.10

5 ANDERSON'S OHIO CIVIL PRACTICE §§ 178.01-178.08

2 KLEIN DARLING AT 50-1 to AT 50-99

3 TEREZ F 16.2.1, F 16.2.2, F 21.1.1, F 21.1.2

4 OH. JUR. PL. AND PRAC. FORMS, ch. 53

6 MILLIGAN Forms 50-1 to 50-27

2 FINK §§ 50-1 to 50-13

OHIO LITIGATION CHECKLISTS, Trial, §§ 23, 26

LEADING CASES

Appellate Review of Entry of Final Judgment

Waller v. Mayfield, 37 Ohio St. 3d 118, 524 N.E.2d 458 (1988) (court of appeals may not enter final judgment in favor of plaintiff upon reversing trial court's entry of directed verdict)

Appellate Review of JNOV Motions

McKenney v. Hillside Dairy Co., 109 Ohio App. 3d 164, 671 N.E.2d 1291 (1996) (standard of appellate review for motions for judgment notwithstanding the verdict is identical to that applicable to motions for a directed verdict)

Appellate Review of New Trial Motions

White Motor Corp. v. Moore, 48 Ohio St. 2d 156, 357 N.E.2d 1069 (1976) (pursuant to Rule 50(C)(1), court of appeals may "otherwise order" and reverse the trial court's implied conditional grant of a new trial when no other error appears on the record)

Directed Verdict and Summary Standard Compared

Sheets v. Norfolk S. Corp., 109 Ohio App. 3d 278, 671 N.E.2d 1364 (1996) (tests for directed verdict and summary judgment are similar in that both require the court to construe evidence most strongly in favor of the nonmoving party, the motion must be overruled unless reasonable minds can only reach the conclusion that the moving party is entitled to judgment as a matter of law; tests differ in that the court must not make an additional determination as to whether genuine issues of fact exist in deciding a motion for directed verdict)

Directed Verdict Presents Question of Law

Sommer v. Conrad, 134 Ohio App. 3d 291, 730 N.E.2d 1058 (1999) (a motion for a directed verdict presents a question of law, not a question of fact, even though in deciding such a motion it is necessary to review and consider the evidence)

Motions for Directed Verdict; In General

Wagner v. Roche Labs., 77 Ohio St. 3d 116, 671 N.E.2d 252 (1996) (a court cannot consider the weight of the evidence or the credibility of witnesses in deciding a motion for directed verdict)

Motions for JNOV; In General

Miller v. Paulson, 97 Ohio App. 3d 217, 646 N.E.2d 521 (1994) (in deciding a motion for judgment notwithstanding the verdict, court must assume the truth of plaintiff's evidence, grant plaintiff's evidence favorable interpretation, and consider as proven every material fact that the evidence tends to substantiate; court cannot consider the weight of the evidence or the credibility of witnesses)

Partial JNOV Not Appealable

State ex rel. A & D Ltd. Partnership v. Keefe, 77 Ohio St. 3d 50, 671 N.E.2d 13 (1996) (order granting the plaintiff's motion for judgment notwithstanding the verdict on the issue of liability alone is not a final appealable order)

"Reasonable Minds" Standard

Goodyear Tire & Rubber Co. v. Aetna Cas. & Sur. Co., 95 Ohio St. 3d 512, 769 N.E.2d 835 (2002) (the "reasonable minds" test for granting a directed verdict requires the court to discern only whether there exists any evidence of substantive probative value that favors the position of the non-moving party)

Renewal of Motion

Mobberly v. Hendricks, 98 Ohio App. 3d 839, 649 N.E.2d 1247 (1994) (when a party's motion for direct verdict is denied at the close of plaintiff's evidence, the party making the motion must renew the motion at the close of all evidence, or errors regarding sufficiency of evidence are waived)

Standard for Directed Verdict

Wagner v. Roche Labs., 77 Ohio St. 3d 116, 671 N.E.2d 252 (1996) ("reasonable minds" test of directed verdict requires the court to determine whether any evidence of substantial probative value in support of the claims of the party opposing the motion exists)

Standard for JNOV; In General

Cooper v. Metal Sales Mfg. Corp., 104 Ohio App. 3d 34, 660 N.E.2d 1245 (1995) (in ruling upon a motion for judgment as a matter of law, the court must deny the motion if there is substantial evidence to support the nonmoving party's position and upon which reasonable minds may differ)

Standards for Directed Verdict and Dismissal Distinct

Johnson v. Tansky Sawmill Toyota, Inc., 95 Ohio App. 3d 164, 642 N.E.2d 9 (1994) (a motion for judgment by a defendant at the close of plaintiff's case in a bench trial is a motion for dismissal and not for directed verdict; the distinction is critical, as two different standards apply)

Standards for Directed Verdict and JNOV Identical

Gallagher v. Cleveland Browns Football Co., 74 Ohio St. 3d 427, 659 N.E.2d 1232 (1996) (standards applied to motions for directed verdict and motions for judgment notwithstanding the verdict are identical)

CHAPTER 51

Rule 51. Instructions to the Jury; Objection

Rule 51 reads as follows:

(A) Instructions; error; record. At the close of the evidence or at such earlier time during the trial as the court reasonably directs, any party may file written requests that the court instruct the jury on the law as set forth in the requests. Copies shall be furnished to all other parties at the time of making the requests. The court shall inform counsel of its proposed action on the requests prior to counsel's arguments to the jury and shall give the jury complete instructions after the arguments are completed. The court also may give some or all of its instructions to the jury prior to counsel's arguments. The court need not reduce its instructions to writing.

On appeal, a party may not assign as error the giving or the failure to give any instruction unless the party objects before the jury retires to consider its verdict, stating specifically the matter objected to and the grounds of the objection. Opportunity shall be given to make the objection out of the hearing of the jury.

(B) Cautionary instructions. At the commencement and during the course of the trial, the court may give the jury cautionary and other instructions of law relating to trial procedure, credibility and weight of the evidence, and the duty and function of the jury and may acquaint the jury generally with the nature of the case.

COMMENTARY

Rule 51 sets forth the procedure by which the court instructs the jury before it retires for deliberation. The Rule contemplates the submission of proposed instructions by the parties, though the ultimate determination rests with the court.

Jury Instructions Generally

Under Rule 51, the court is required to instruct the jury after closing arguments. Attorneys for the parties or the parties themselves are allowed to submit recommended jury instructions to the court in a manner and at a time which the court deems proper. The court is not required to instruct the jury according to the recommendations of the attorneys or the parties, however, and the court must apprise the attorneys or the parties of the substance of its instructions to the jury prior to so instructing. If, however, the court fails to provide the attorneys the opportunity to object to jury instructions, the failure will not always operate to excuse the attorneys' failure to raise objections. Ohio courts have held that such an obligation remains with the attorneys regardless of the court's compliance with the third sentence of subsection (A). This enables the attorneys or the parties the opportunity to object to the proposed instructions, either in regard to the giving or failure to give a specific instruction, outside of the hearing of the jury. The attorney or party must specify the instruction objected to and the grounds for the objection. The objection need not be formal, in accordance with Rule 46, but the record should definitively indicate that attorney's opposition to the jury instructions actually given. If a party does not so object, the issue is deemed to have been waived, and the party cannot thereafter raise the issue on any post-trial motion or on appeal.

In addition, Ohio recognizes the "plain error" doctrine in this context, which permits an appellate court to overturn a verdict if the action is both obvious and prejudicial to the character of and public confidence in the proceedings of the judiciary.

> ### Illustration 51-1
>
> Anders commences a breach of warranty action against Jack's Used Cars, alleging that Jack has failed to make repairs on one of the cars sold to him. Anders and Jack both submit detailed jury instructions to the court, which adopts the instructions submitted by Anders and, after informing the parties of its decision, instructs the jury accordingly. Subsequently, the jury renders a verdict in favor of Anders. After reviewing the instructions more carefully, Jack now concludes that they contain erroneous statements of law with regard to breach of warranty actions. However, as Jack has failed to object to the jury instructions prior to the time the case was submitted to the jury, Jack is deemed to have waived his objections, and he cannot raise the issue on any post-trial motion or on appeal.

Cautionary Instructions

Under subsection (B), the court is granted discretion to familiarize the jury with the nature of the case, the law relating to trial procedure, credibility and weight of evidence, and the function and duty of the jury. Such instructions are sometimes compelled by Ohio Rule of Evidence 105 and other Rules of Evidence.

ADDITIONAL AUTHORITY

9 WRIGHT & MILLER §§ 2551-2570
9 MOORE'S FEDERAL PRACTICE §§ 51.01-51.21

5 ANDERSON'S OHIO CIVIL PRACTICE §§ 179.01-179.05
2 KLEIN DARLING AT 51-1 to AT 51-39
3 TEREZ F 18.1.1 to F 18.1.3
4 OH. JUR. PL. AND PRAC. FORMS, ch. 54
6 MILLIGAN Forms 51-1 to 51-35
2 FINK §§ 51-1 to 51-18
OHIO LITIGATION CHECKLISTS, Trial, §§ 23

LEADING CASES

Accuracy of Instructions

Sharp v. Norfolk & W. Ry. Co., 72 Ohio St. 3d 307, 649 N.E.2d 1219 (trial court must give jury instructions that constitute an accurate and complete statement of the law; inadequate jury instructions that, in effect, mislead the jury, constitutes reversible error), *order clarified*, 73 Ohio St. 3d 1429, 652 N.E.2d 801 (1995)

Failure to Give Necessary Instructions

Marshall v. Gibson, 19 Ohio St. 3d 10, 482 N.E.2d 583 (1985) (trial court's failure to instruct the jury on comparative negligence at the request of the defendant is reversible error, even where the jury renders a verdict in favor of the defendant)

Failure to Object to Interrogatory

Nelson v. Ford Motor Co., 145 Ohio App. 3d 58, 761 N.E.2d 1099 (2001) (failure to object to the submission of an interrogatory to jury constitutes a waiver of that issue on appeal)

Objections; Basis on Appeal

Leber v. Smith, 70 Ohio St. 3d 548, 639 N.E.2d 1159 (1994) (a party cannot object to a jury instruction on appeal on a different basis than its objection at trial)

Objections to Instructions

Cleveland Elec. Illuminating Co. v. Astorhurst Land Co., 18 Ohio St. 3d 268, 480 N.E.2d 794 (1985) (a party's failure to object to an erroneous jury instruction that only eight of 12 jurors had to agree on verdict, when in actuality concurrence of nine was required, precluded the party's claim of error on appeal)

Requests for Instructions

Atkinson v. International Technegroup, Inc., 106 Ohio App. 3d 349, 666 N.E.2d 257 (1995) (trial court is not required to give a party's requested jury instructions to the jury verbatim; rather, court may use its own language to communicate the same issues), *appeal not allowed*, 74 Ohio St. 3d 1525, 660 N.E.2d 744 (1996)

Waiver of Objections

Steinke v. Koch Fuels, Inc., 78 Ohio App. 3d 791, 605 N.E.2d 1341 (where a jury instruction is given at a party's request, that party waives any right to challenge the instruction on appeal), *cause dismissed*, 65 Ohio St. 3d 1440, 600 N.E.2d 682 (1992)

CHAPTER 52

Rule 52. Findings by the Court

Rule 52 reads as follows:

When questions of fact are tried by the court without a jury, judgment may be general for the prevailing party unless one of the parties in writing requests otherwise before the entry of judgment pursuant to Civ. R. 58, or not later than seven days after the party filing the request has been given notice of the court's announcement of its decision, whichever is later, in which case, the court shall state in writing the conclusions of fact found separately from the conclusions of law.

When a request for findings of fact and conclusions of law is made, the court, in its discretion, may require any or all of the parties to submit proposed findings of fact and conclusions of law; however, only those findings of fact and conclusions of law made by the court shall form part of the record.

Findings of fact and conclusions of law required by this rule and by Rule 41(B)(2) are unnecessary upon all other motions including those pursuant to Rule 12, Rule 55 and Rule 56.

An opinion or memorandum of decision filed in the action prior to judgment entry and containing findings of fact and conclusions of law stated separately shall be sufficient to satisfy the requirements of this rule and Rule 41(B)(2).

COMMENTARY

Rule 52 provides for a statement of the findings of fact in an action tried to the court. The Rule does not expressly authorize a statement of the court's conclusions of law, as such a statement is implied by Rule 54 and Rule 58 and necessary for the entry of judgment in any case. The Rule is not applicable in actions tried to a jury; such actions are instead governed by Rules 49 and 50.

Form of Verdict by the Court

When an action has tried to the court, either because none of the parties have requested a jury action or because one does not exist, the first paragraph of Rule 52 allows the court to render a judgment analogous to a general verdict rendered by a jury under Rule 49(A). Such a judgment will simply state which party has prevailed in the action. The court may elect, however, to announce its findings of fact separately from its conclusions of law as part of the judgment, in a separate opinion, or in a memorandum of decision. Such a statement is required whenever one of the parties so requests in writing before the entry of judgment or within seven days of being informed of the court's decision.

Findings of Fact

The non-prevailing party generally requests findings of fact and conclusions of law to elucidate the rationale for the court's decision, and these findings become the basis for allegation of error on appeal. On appeal, a reviewing court must affirm the findings of the trial court if it appears from an examination of the evidence as a whole that there is some evidence from which the trial court could have reached the ultimate factual conclusions supporting the judgment. It should be noted that whenever a request for findings is made after the entry of judgment, the time within which an appeal may be taken will have already begun running from the date of entry of judgment. For this reason, the preparation of findings before the entry of judgment is preferred to the preparation after the entry of judgment.

The third paragraph of Rule 52 repeats the directive stated expressly in the first sentence of the Rule that its provisions apply only in actions tried to the court. Thus, a separate statement of the findings of fact is unnecessary on motions made pursuant to Rule 12, Rule 55, and Rule 56. Rule 41(B)(2) provides for motions for involuntary dismissal of the action against the plaintiff at the close of the plaintiff's case-in-chief. In this situation, the plaintiff may request of the court a statement of the findings of fact in the action if such a motion is granted.

ADDITIONAL AUTHORITY

9 WRIGHT & MILLER §§ 2571-2600

9 MOORE'S FEDERAL PRACTICE §§ 52.01-52.63

5 ANDERSON'S OHIO CIVIL PRACTICE §§ 181.01-181.05

2 KLEIN DARLING AT 52-1 to AT 52-37

3 TEREZ F 17.1.1 to F 17.1.3

4 OH. JUR. PL. AND PRAC. FORMS, ch. 55

6 MILLIGAN Forms 52-1 to 52-22

2 FINK §§ 52-1 to 52-13

LEADING CASES

Adequate Findings and Conclusions

Strah v. Lake City Humane Soc., 90 Ohio App. 3d 822, 631 N.E.2d 165 (1993) (court complied with Rule 52 where its opinion adequately explained the basis of its judgment)

Findings and Conclusions Stated Separately

Bates v. Sherwin-Williams, 105 Ohio App. 3d 529, 664 N.E.2d 612 (1995) (court is not required to issue findings of fact where the decision is based solely upon conclusions of law)

State ex rel. Papp v. James, 69 Ohio St. 3d 373, 632 N.E.2d 889 (1994) (upon a timely request, court must issue written findings of fact and conclusions of law supporting an award of permanent custody)

Findings of Fact Not Required

State ex rel. Sharif v. Cuyahoga Cty. Ct. of Common Pleas, 85 Ohio St. 3d 375, 708 N.E.2d 718 (1999) (motions for postconviction relief and summary judgment may be decided by a court without issuing findings of fact or conclusions of law)

Inadequate Findings and Conclusions

In re Adoption of Gibson, 23 Ohio St. 3d 170, 492 N.E.2d 146 (1986) (court's failure to provide written findings of fact and conclusions of law upon timely request constitutes reversible error; an oral announcement of the decision does not satisfy the requirements of Rule 52)

Freeman v. Westland Builders, Inc., 2 Ohio App. 3d 212, 441 N.E.2d 283 (1981) (bare recital of the evidence is not a finding of fact)

Incomplete Findings; Duty of Appellate Court

Pettet v. Pettet, 55 Ohio App. 3d 128, 562 N.E.2d 929 (1988) (where separate findings of fact are neither requested nor supplied by the court, the court of appeals must affirm the judgment if an examination of the record reveals that there is some evidence to support the trial court's judgment)

Request for Findings Tolls Time for Appeal

Walker v. Doup, 36 Ohio St. 3d 229, 522 N.E.2d 1072 (1988) (when a party makes a timely request for findings of fact and conclusions of law, the period for review does not commence until the trial court files its findings of fact and conclusions of law)

Caudill v. Caudill, 71 Ohio App. 3d 564, 594 N.E.2d 1096 (1991) (the time for filing a notice of appeal is continued until the trial court issues proper findings of fact and conclusions of law)

CHAPTER 53

Rule 53. Magistrates

Rule 53 reads as follows:

(A) Appointment. A court of record may appoint one or more magistrates who shall be attorneys at law admitted to practice in Ohio. A magistrate appointed under this rule may also serve as a magistrate under Crim. R. 19 or as a traffic magistrate.

(B) Compensation. The compensation of the magistrate shall be fixed by the court, and no part of the compensation shall be taxed as costs.

(C) Reference and Powers.

(1) Order of reference.

(a) A court of record may by order refer any of the following to a magistrate:

(i) any pretrial or post-judgment motion in any case;

(ii) the trial of any case that will not be tried to a jury; and

(iii) upon the unanimous written consent of the parties, the trial of any case that will be tried to a jury.

Except as provided in division (C)(1)(a)(iii) of this rule, the effect of a magistrate's order or decision is the same regardless of whether the parties have consented to the order of reference.

(b) Subject to division (C)(1)(a)(ii) and (iii) of this rule, an order of reference may be specific to a particular case or may refer categories of motions or cases.

(c) The order of reference to a magistrate may do all of the following:

(i) specify or limit the magistrate's powers;

(ii) direct the magistrate to report only upon particular issues, do or perform particular acts, or receive and report evidence only;

(iii) fix the time and place for beginning and closing the hearings and for the filing of the magistrate's decision.

(2) General powers. Subject to the specifications and limitations stated in the order of reference, the magistrate shall regulate all proceedings in every hearing as if by the court and do all acts and take all measures necessary or proper for the efficient performance of the magistrate's duties under the order. The magistrate may do all of the following:

(a)　issue subpoenas for the attendance of witnesses and the production of evidence;

(b)　rule upon the admissibility of evidence, unless otherwise directed by the order of reference;

(c)　put witnesses under oath and examine them;

(d)　call the parties to the action and examine them under oath.

(e)　In cases involving direct or indirect contempt of court, and when necessary to obtain the alleged contemnor's presence for hearing, issue an attachment for the alleged contemnor and set bail to secure the alleged contemnor's appearance, considering the conditions of release prescribed in Crim. R. 46.

(3)　Power to enter orders.

(a)　Pretrial orders. Unless otherwise specified in the order of reference, the magistrate may enter orders without judicial approval in pretrial proceedings under Civ. R. 16, in discovery proceedings under Civ. R. 26 to 37, temporary restraining orders under Civ. R. 75(I), in hearings under Civ. R. 75(N), and other orders as necessary to regulate the proceedings.

(b)　Appeal of pretrial orders. Any person may appeal to the court from any order of a magistrate entered under division (C)(3)(a) of this rule by filing a motion to set the order aside, stating the party's objections with particularity. The motion shall be filed no later than ten days after the magistrate's order is entered. The pendency of a motion to set aside does not stay the effectiveness of the magistrate's order unless the magistrate or the court grants a stay.

(c)　Contempt in the magistrate's presence. In cases of contempt in the presence of the magistrate, the magistrate may impose an appropriate civil or criminal contempt sanction. Contempt sanctions under division (C)(3)(c) of this rule may be imposed only by a written order that recites the facts and certifies that the magistrate saw or heard the conduct constituting contempt. The contempt order shall be filed and a copy provided by the clerk to the appropriate judge of the court forthwith. The contemnor may by motion obtain immediate review of the magistrate's contempt order by a judge, or the judge or magistrate may set bail pending judicial review.

(d)　Other orders. Unless prohibited by the order of reference, a magistrate shall continue to be authorized to enter orders when authority is specifically conveyed by statute to magistrates.

    (e) **Form of magistrate's orders.** All orders of a magistrate shall be in writing, signed by the magistrate, identified as a magistrate's order in the caption, filed with the clerk, and served on all parties or their attorneys.

(D) Proceedings.

    (1)   All proceedings before the magistrate shall be in accordance with these rules and any applicable statutes, as if before the court.

    (2)   Except as otherwise provided by law, all proceedings before the magistrate shall be recorded in accordance with procedures established by the court.

(E) Decisions in referred matters. Unless specifically required by the order of reference, a magistrate is not required to prepare any report other than the magistrate's decision. Except as to those matters on which magistrates are permitted to enter orders without judicial approval pursuant to division (C)(3) of this rule, all matters referred to magistrates shall be decided as follows:

    (1) **Magistrate's decision.** The magistrate promptly shall conduct all proceedings necessary for decision of referred matters. The magistrate shall prepare, sign, and file a magistrate's decision of the referred matter with the clerk, who shall serve copies on all the parties or their attorneys.

    (2) **Findings of fact and conclusions of law.** If any party makes a request for findings of fact and conclusions of law under Civ. R. 52 or if findings and conclusions are otherwise required by law or by the order of reference, the magistrate's decision shall include findings of fact and conclusions of law. If the request under Civ. R. 52 is made after the magistrate's decision is filed, the magistrate shall include the findings of fact and conclusions of law in an amended magistrate's decision.

    (3) **Objections.**

        (a) **Time for filing.** Within fourteen days of the filing of a magistrate's decision, a party may file written objections to the magistrate's decision. If any party timely files objections, any other party may also file objections not later than ten days after the first objections are filed. If a party makes a request for findings of fact and conclusions of law under Civ. R. 52, the time for filing objections begins to run when the magistrate files a decision including findings of fact and conclusions of law.

        (b) **Form of objections.** Objections shall be specific and state with particularity the grounds of objection. If the parties stipulate in writing that the magistrate's findings of fact shall be final, they may object only to errors of law in the magistrate's decision. Any objection to a finding of fact shall be supported by a transcript of all the evidence submitted to the magistrate relevant to that fact or an affidavit of that evidence if a transcript is not available. A party shall not assign as error on appeal the court's adoption of any finding of fact or conclusion of law unless the party has objected to that finding or conclusion under this rule.

(4) **Court's action on magistrate's decision.**

(a) **When effective.** The magistrate's decision shall be effective when adopted by the court. The court may adopt the magistrate's decision if no written objections are filed unless it determines that there is an error of law or other defect on the face of the magistrate's decision.

(b) **Disposition of objections.** The court shall rule on any objections. The court may adopt, reject, or modify the magistrate's decision, hear additional evidence, recommit the matter to the magistrate with instructions, or hear the matter. The court may refuse to consider additional evidence proffered upon objections unless the objecting party demonstrates that with reasonable diligence the party could not have produced that evidence for the magistrate's consideration.

(c) **Permanent and interim orders.** The court may adopt a magistrate's decision and enter judgment without waiting for timely objections by the parties, but the filing of timely written objections shall operate as an automatic stay of execution of that judgment until the court disposes of those objections and vacates, modifies, or adheres to the judgment previously entered. The court may make an interim order on the basis of a magistrate's decision without waiting for or ruling on timely objections by the parties where immediate relief is justified. An interim order shall not be subject to the automatic stay caused by the filing of timely objections. An interim order shall not extend more than twenty-eight days from the date of its entry unless, within that time and for good cause shown, the court extends the interim order for an additional twenty-eight days.

COMMENTARY

Rule 53 provides for the appointment of magistrates, formerly referred to as "referees." Magistrates are not elected positions, and they may be removed from office by their appointing court.

Ohio Rule 53 should not be confused with Federal Rule of Civil Procedure 53, which governs masters. Masters are specialized court officers who assist juries and sometimes courts in the trial of complicated or especially arcane or abstruse issues. Masters are not authorized by the Ohio Rules, but may be provided for by local rule.

Appointment and Compensation

Magistrates may be appointed by courts of record and must be attorneys admitted to practice in Ohio. The appointing court or local rule determines the compensation of the appointed magistrate, although such compensation may not be charged as costs to the parties.

Reference and Powers

Subject to circumscription in Rule 53, the authority of magistrates is determined solely by an order of reference by a trial court. Subsection (C)(1) sets forth the circumstances under which a matter may be referred to a magistrate, as well as the court's authority to determine the scope of the magistrate's duties in the order of reference. The court's authority, through an order of reference, may also be used to limit the statutory authority of magistrates to enter orders.

The general powers of a magistrate, subject to limitations in the order of reference, are enumerated in subsection (C)(2). Any order of a magistrate must be written, signed, and identified as a magistrate's order in the caption, filed with the clerk, and served on all parties or their attorneys. Sanctions may be imposed for contempt by a written order specifying the facts and certifying that the magistrate witnessed the conduct constituting contempt.

Although the decision of a magistrate is not ordinarily effective until it is adopted by the trial court, subsection (C)(3)(a) makes an exception for pretrial motions referred to a magistrate. Such motions may be decided by a magistrate without the approval of the trial court, and the decision of the magistrate is effective immediately. An appeal of a magistrate's order on a pretrial must be filed within 10 days after it is announced, but an appeal will not stay the effectiveness of the order unless a stay is granted by the magistrate or court.

Proceedings

Proceedings before a magistrate are regarded as proceedings before a trial court. Therefore, all rules of practice and procedure, as well as any applicable statutes, apply in proceedings before a magistrate as they would before a trial court. The affirmative provision of contempt power to magistrates in subsection (C)(3)(c) reinforces this directive. All proceedings before magistrates must be recorded in a manner authorized by the trial court or by local rule.

Decisions in Referred Matters

Subsection (E) sets forth the mechanics by which matters referred to magistrates are decided. The magistrate, unless otherwise directed by the order of reference, is not required to prepare any report other than the magistrate's decision. However, a Rule 52 motion for findings of fact and conclusions of law may be made by either party either before or after the magistrate's decision has been filed. The 14-day time period for objections is preserved and begins to run only when a magistrate's decision embodying findings and conclusions is filed. In addition to the 14-day requirement, objections must be stated with particularity to preserve an issue for judicial consideration. The failure to object constitutes a waiver. Subsection (E) was amended in 1998 to ensure that the trial court actually rules upon, and not merely considers, objections to the report of a magistrate. Rulings on objections should be set forth in an order.

A magistrate's order is effective upon adoption by the court; however, the court may reject or modify the decision, hear additional evidence, recommit the matter to the magistrate with instructions or hear the matter. Unless the evidence would not have been obtained in time to present it to the magistrate, the court may refuse to hear new evidence on objections.

The court may enter judgment on the magistrate's decision without waiting for objections, though a timely objection will function as an automatic stay until the court makes a ruling. The court may also enter interim orders based on the magistrate's decision without waiting for objections so long as immediate relief is justified. Interim orders are effective for 28 days, although, for good cause shown, the period may be extended by the court for an additional 28 days.

ADDITIONAL AUTHORITY

9 Wright & Miller §§ 2601-2650

9 Moore's Federal Practice §§ 53.01-53.93

5 Anderson's Ohio Civil Practice §§ 175.01-175.05

2 Klein Darling AT 53-1 to AT 53-6

3 Terez F 15.2.1 to F 15.2.10

4 Oh. Jur. Pl. and Prac. Forms, ch. 56

6 Milligan Forms 53-1 to 53-79

2 Fink §§ 53-1 to 53-6

LEADING CASES

Adoption of Magistrate's Report Without Objections

Duganitz v. Ohio Adult Parole Auth., 92 Ohio St. 3d 556, 751 N.E.2d 1058 (2001) (court of appeals is empowered by Rule 53 to adopt decisions of magistrates without waiting for objections, where objections were untimely filed)

Appellate Review of Trial Court's Adoption of Report

State ex rel. Duncan v. Chippewa Twp. Trustees, 73 Ohio St. 3d 728, 654 N.E.2d 1254 (1995) (when a trial court adopts a magistrate's report and a party objecting to the report fails to provide the court with independent evidence and documents refuting the findings of the report, a court of appeals may only review to determine whether the trial court's application of law to its factual findings constituted an abuse of discretion)

Appointment of Magistrate Must Involve Motion or Trial

State ex rel. Allstate Ins. Co. v. Gaul, 131 Ohio App. 3d 419, 722 N.E.2d 616 (1999) (Rule 53, which governs the appointment of magistrates, does not authorize the trial court to appoint a special master for investigation purposes only; the order of appointment must refer a motion or trial to the special master)

Appointment to Master

Valentour v. Alexander, 96 Ohio App. 3d 718, 645 N.E.2d 1292 (1994) (where neither party made a timely demand for a jury trial, the court is free to refer all issues in the case to a magistrate)

Deferral by Trial Court Not Permitted

Knauer v. Keener, 143 Ohio App. 3d 789, 758 N.E.2d 1234 (2001) (the trial court may not properly defer to a magistrate in the exercise of the trial court's de novo review)

Domestic Relations Proceedings

State ex rel. Thompson v. Spon, 83 Ohio St. 3d 551, 700 N.E.2d 1281 (1998) (a magistrate may enter orders without judicial approval in pretrial hearings under Rule 75 unless otherwise specified in the reference order, and the magistrate is not required to issue findings of fact and conclusions of law with respect to these orders)

Entry and Detainer Proceedings; Rules Applicable

Miele v. Ribovich, 90 Ohio St. 3d 439, 739 N.E.2d 333 (2000) (Rule 53 applies to forcible entry and detainer proceedings insofar as it authorizes a magistrate to prepare a decision without factual findings and enables the trial court to adopt the magistrate's decision without conducting an independent analysis)

Extension of Time; Abuse of Discretion

Bernard v. Bernard, No. 97 CA 67 (5th Dist.), 1998 Ohio App. LEXIS 4014 (where a party files a request for an extension of time within the fourteen day period permitted by Rule 53 and has a valid reason for the requested extension, a trial court abuses its discretion when it denies the request)

Factual Findings of Magistrates

Ohio Edison Co. v. Gilmore, 106 Ohio App. 3d 6, 665 N.E.2d 226 (1995) (trial court may redetermine the factual findings of a magistrate based on objections to the magistrate's factual findings and a review of the transcript of proceedings before a magistrate)

Hearing Not Required on Appeal from Magistrate

Kubin v. Kubin, 140 Ohio App. 3d 367, 747 N.E.2d 851 (2000) (Rule 53 does not require trial court to hold hearing before ruling upon objections to magistrate's decision)

Magistrate Order Not Final

McCown v. McCown, 145 Ohio App. 3d 170, 762 N.E.2d 398 (2001) (a magistrate judge's order is not a final, appealable order until the trial court has ruled on the objections)

Objection to Magistrate's Decision Required for Appeal

State ex rel. Booher v. Honda of Am. Mfg., Inc., 88 Ohio St. 3d 52, 723 N.E.2d 571 (2000) (a party may not allege as error conclusions of law contained in magistrate's decision where the party failed to object in a timely fashion to those conclusions as required by Rule 53)

Plain Error Doctrine Applicable to Magistrate's Decision

Miller v. Miller, 139 Ohio App. 3d 512, 744 N.E.2d 778 (2000) (by failing to object to an element of a magistrate's decision, an appellant ordinarily waives his right to challenge it; nonetheless, the "plain error" doctrine will apply in those extremely rare cases where exceptional circumstances require its application to prevent a manifest miscarriage of justice, and where the error complained of, if left uncorrected, would have a material adverse effect on the character of, and public confidence in, judicial proceedings)

Powers of Magistrates

Takacs v. Baldwin, 106 Ohio App. 3d 196, 665 N.E.2d 736 (1995) (magistrates serve only in an advisory capacity and cannot render final judgments affecting the substantive rights of the parties), *appeal not allowed*, 74 Ohio St. 3d 1513, 659 N.E.2d 1289 (1996)

Report of Magistrate and Entry of Judgment Distinct

In re Zakov, 107 Ohio App. 3d 716, 669 N.E.2d 344 (1995) (an entry merely incorporating the recommendations of a magistrate's report does not serve as a judgment; the report and the entry of judgment must be separate and distinct instruments)

Report of Magistrates

Harbeitner v. Harbeitner, 94 Ohio App. 3d 485, 641 N.E.2d 206 (1994) (until a judge has acted upon the report, a magistrate may freely correct mistakes of fact or law contained in the report; a party waives any objection to the magistrate's alteration by failing to file a written objection with the court)

Trial Court Review of Magistrate Findings

Roberts v. Payton, 105 Ohio App. 3d 597, 664 N.E.2d 978 (1995) (where an objecting party does not submit to the trial court the affidavit or transcript of the magistrate's hearing, the scope of a trial court's review of the factual findings in a report is limited to determining whether those findings are sufficient to support the magistrate's ultimate factual findings and conclusions of law)

VII
JUDGMENT

CHAPTER 54

Rule 54. Judgment; Costs

Rule 54 reads as follows:

(A) Definition; form. "Judgment" as used in these rules includes a decree and any order from which an appeal lies as provided in section 2505.02 of the Revised Code. A judgment shall not contain a recital of pleadings, the magistrate's decision in a referred matter, or the record of prior proceedings.

(B) Judgment upon multiple claims or involving multiple parties. When more than one claim for relief is presented in an action whether as a claim, counter-claim, cross-claim, or third-party claim, and whether arising out of the same or separate transactions, or when multiple parties are involved, the court may enter final judgment as to one or more but fewer than all of the claims or parties only upon an express determination that there is no just reason for delay. In the absence of a determination that there is no just reason for delay, any order or other form of decision, however designated, which adjudicates fewer than all the claims or the rights and liabilities of fewer than all the parties, shall not terminate the action as to any of the claims or parties, and the order or other form of decision is subject to revision at any time before the entry of judgment adjudicating all the claims and the rights and liabilities of all the parties.

(C) Demand for judgment. A judgment by default shall not be different in kind from or exceed in amount that prayed for in the demand for judgment. Except as to a party against whom a judgment is entered by default, every final judgment shall grant the relief to which the party in whose favor it is rendered is entitled, even if the party has not demanded the relief in the pleadings.

(D) Costs. Except when express provision therefor is made either in a statute or in these rules, costs shall be allowed to the prevailing party unless the court otherwise directs.

COMMENTARY

Rule 54 defines a "judgment," and it sets forth some of the provisions relating to judgments. Other Rules, most notably Rule 58, also cover judgments and should be read in conjunction with Rule 54. The Rule is also the primary provision concerning costs, but as with judgments, is not the only Rule bearing upon the subject. Rules 26, 37, 41(D), 53(B), and 68 should also be consulted to determine their applicability to issues involving costs.

Definition of Judgment

Rule 54(A) keys the definition of a judgment to its appealability. It provides that a judgment is "a decree and any order from which an appeal lies as provided in section 2505.02 of the Revised Code." Other than subsection (B), Rule 54 does not otherwise address those orders or actions of the court which are appealable; this issue is predominantly governed by § 2505.02, which has been the subject of a great number of opinions and now represents one of the most confusing areas under Ohio law.

The purpose of subsection (A) should be construed narrowly; the Rule only identifies those actions of the court that are rendered appealable by the operation of a distinct source of law as "judgments." In general, only final judgments are appealable; other interlocutory orders cannot normally be appealed until the final disposition of the entire action. Because the definition of a judgment is tied to its appealability, any action that is said to be an exception to the general rule that only final judgments are appealable is nonetheless regarded as a "judgment," despite its interlocutory nature. A consent decree is a judgment.

Illustration 54-1

Gary commences a breach of contract action against Governor Adams alleging that the Governor has broken promises made during the last campaign which amount to an oral contract. Governor Adams moves the court to dismiss the claim, arguing that a state statute bars such actions on grounds of sovereign immunity. The court denies Governor Adams's motion. If a state statute provides that an immediate appeal may be taken from a denial of such a motion, the order will be considered to be a "judgment" despite the fact that the primary issues in the case have yet to be decided.

A judgment should be distinguished from an opinion. A judgment is an action of the court, whereas an opinion is simply the articulation of the court's reasons for the judgment. Judges may make judgments with or without written opinions, although some kind of explanation by the judge for the action taken is usually required.

Interrelationship of Rule 54 with Other Rules

Rule 54 speaks only to the pronouncement, or rendition, of the judgment. Rule 58 covers the entry of judgment by the court, and provides that each judgment shall be set forth on a separate document. This directive is reinforced by the final sentence of subsection (A), which states that the judgment shall not contain "a recital of pleadings, the magistrate's decision in a referred matter, or the record of prior proceedings." These matters are properly the subject of an opinion. A judgment is not effective when it is rendered, only when it is entered and recorded by the clerk according to Rule 58. Thus, the time for appeal of a judgment begins on the date that the judgment is entered and recorded on the docket, and not necessarily the date on which the judgment of the court is pronounced.

Illustration 54-2

Assume on the facts of Illustration 54-1 that the court renders a verdict in favor of Gary on April 5 and issues an opinion on the unique legal issues involved. However, the judgment is not entered and recorded by the clerk until April 10. Under these circumstances, the time within which Governor Adams may appeal the judgment begins to run on April 11.

Certification of Judgment

As noted, subsection (B) confers upon the court the authority to determine the appealability of some kinds of orders or decrees. If an action involves multiple claims or multiple parties, the court may resolve one or more of the claims or issues concerning a party without resolving the remaining claims or issues among other parties and pronounce a judgment from which an appeal lies to that effect. To do this, the judge must make both an express determination that there is no just reason for delay and a direction for the entry of judgment. This action is often referred to as certification by the court. The Rule reiterates the requirement that the judgment be certified by the court by stating that any such order not properly certified as an appealable judgment is a nonappealable interlocutory order subject to revision at any time before the final judgment is rendered.

Subsection (B) does not confer upon the court unfettered discretion to decide which orders will be appealable simply by certifying them as judgments. The standard stated in the first sentence of that subsection must be satisfied, or the certification will be reversed for an abuse of discretion. Thus, a judge cannot certify as an appealable judgment one type of relief sought on a single claim.

Illustration 54-3

In a class action suit against Toxic Chemical Corporation on a single legal theory of recovery, the plaintiff class seeks $15 million in damages. Because of the complex nature of the claim, the court orders that the action be bifurcated into liability and damages phases. If a jury returns a verdict against Toxic on the issue of liability only, Toxic may not take an appeal on the verdict until the damages issue has been resolved, absent a statute specifically authorizing such an appeal.

Judgment Awarded Not Limited to That Requested in Pleadings

Rule 54(C) simply provides that the relief sought by a party in its pleadings shall not bar that party from receiving any relief to which it is entitled, except in the case of a default judgment. This applies at any stage of the proceedings, even on remand from an appellate court. Default judgments are limited to the kinds and amount of the relief requested in the complaint.

Illustration 54-4

Assume on the facts of Illustration 54-3 that the jury concludes that the plaintiff class is entitled only to a permanent injunction. Under Rule 54(C), the judge may order a permanent injunction, even though the plaintiff class did not request that an injunction be granted.

Costs

Subsection (D) is a broad provision relating to the assessment of costs. Unlike Federal Rule of Civil Procedure 54, which distinguishes between attorneys' fees and all other costs in an action and which sets forth a detailed procedure to be used in the assignment of costs, Ohio Rule 54(D) merely establishes a presumption that the costs should be taxed against the non-prevailing party.

Although an exhaustive discussion of costs is beyond the scope of this manual, the term "costs" is statutorily defined in most cases. They typically consist of fees to which officers, witnesses, jurors, and other participants in the litigation are entitled to recover for their services. Such fees are commonly said to be "taxable" and are usually included in the judgment if granted. Attorneys' fees, of course, are not considered "costs." However, in certain kinds of statutorily-created causes of action, attorneys' fees may be taxed against an opposing party as a special item if the statutory provision so indicates.

The determination as to whether to award costs typically involves a two-step analysis. First, the court should determine whether a particular expense is included in "costs." Courts frequently speak of "personal expenses" and "litigation expenses" in this regard, with only the latter constituting "costs." This determination is relatively straightforward in the great majority of cases and for most expenses, though unusual litigation expenses are sometimes the subject of protracted argument. Conscientious litigators should ensure that the taxing of any expense other than those routinely encountered during the course of litigation is the subject of discussion and stipulation at an early pretrial conference.

The second step involves a determination by the court as to whether a litigation expense constituting a "cost" should be taxed in a particular case, and if so, against whom. Such a determination is within the discretion of the court. Although courts often lean toward awarding costs to the prevailing party, as Rule 54(D) so presumes, the language of the Rule is sufficiently broad to permit the taxing of costs against a prevailing party if the court finds that the party caused undue delay or otherwise compromised the litigation process. In addition, the proper determination as to which party has "prevailed" in a particular action will sometimes be the most complicated factor in the analysis.

ADDITIONAL AUTHORITY

10 Wright & Miller §§ 2651-2680

10 Moore's Federal Practice §§ 54.01-54.191

5 Anderson's Ohio Civil Practice §§ 182.01-182.07

2 Klein Darling AT 54-1 to AT 54-5

3 Terez F 15.6.1 to F 15.6.14

5 Oh. Jur. Pl. and Prac. Forms, ch. 66-67

6 Milligan Forms 54-1 to 54-80

2 Fink §§ 54-1 to 54-12

Ohio Litigation Checklists, Pleading and Process, §§ 15-19

LEADING CASES

Arbitration; Stay of Action

Owens Flooring Co. v. Hummel Constr. Co., 140 Ohio App. 3d 825, 749 N.E.2d 782 (2001) (trial court's order denying a stay of action pending arbitration was not a final judgment entered as to any party or claim; accordingly, the statutory provision authorizing the review of orders denying a stay of trial pending arbitration was applicable)

Costs Denied to Partially Prevailing Party

State ex rel. Reyna v. Natalucci-Persichetti, 83 Ohio St. 3d 194, 699 N.E.2d 76 (1998) (denying costs to both parties can be appropriate when neither party entirely prevails; thus, a court does not abuse its discretion in refusing to award a partially prevailing party the costs of his action)

Costs on Summary Judgment Disposition

Haller v. Borror, 107 Ohio App. 3d 432, 669 N.E.2d 17 (1995) (a court reporter fee for taking a deposition and providing a transcript is taxable under Rule 54(D) when the action is decided on summary judgment)

Definition of Judgment

Rogoff v. King, 91 Ohio App. 3d 438, 632 N.E.2d 977 (1993) (Rule 58(A) and Rule 54(A), construed together, require nothing more than a clear and concise pronouncement of the court's judgment)

Denial of Summary Judgment Motion Not Appealable

Shump v. First Continental-Robinwood Assoc., 138 Ohio App. 3d 353, 741 N.E.2d 232 (2000) (a denial of a motion for summary judgment was not a final appealable order, and therefore trial court could reconsider that decision)

Deposition Costs Disallowed

Carr v. Lunney, 104 Ohio App. 3d 139, 661 N.E.2d 246 (1995) (a court may not allow the taxing of deposition costs because no statutory authority provides for such an award)

Fees of Deposition Reporter

Williamson v. Ameritech Corp., 81 Ohio St. 3d 342, 691 N.E.2d 288 (1998) (Ohio Rev. Code Ann. § 2319.27 does not provide for the taxing of the fees for the services of a court reporter at a deposition as costs)

Interlocutory Order–Motion for Reconsideration Proper Vehicle

Drillex, Inc. v. Lake Cty. Bd. of Commrs., 145 Ohio App. 3d 384, 763 N.E.2d 204 (2001) (a motion for reconsideration is the proper procedural vehicle for obtaining relief after a ruling on an interlocutory order)

Magistrate Certification for Appeal Not Permitted

United Cos. Lending Corp. v. Robinson, 134 Ohio App. 3d 96, 730 N.E.2d 423 (1999) (Rule 54(B), which allows the entry of final judgment as to one or more but fewer than all claims or parties in an action involving multiple claims or multiple parties, requires that the court make an express determination that there is no just reason for delay; an adoption and incorporation by court of a finding by a referee, magistrate, or any other bureaucratic functionary below the trial court judge that there is no just reason for delay, standing alone, is insufficient to comply with rule)

Multiple Claims and Multiple Parties

State ex rel. Electrolert Inc. v. Lindeman, 99 Ohio App. 3d 154, 650 N.E.2d

137 (1994) (a judgment is interlocutory where it lacks Rule 54(B) language and adjudicates less than all of the claims involved in the action)

Provisional Remedy Not Subject to Certification

State ex rel. Butler Cty. Children Services Bd. v. Sage, 95 Ohio St. 3d 23, 764 N.E.2d 1027 (2002) (a provisional remedy is a remedy other than a claim for relief; therefore, an order granting or denying a provisional remedy is not subject to the requirements of Rule 54(B), which governs final judgment as to one or more but fewer than all claims for relief)

Ruling on Liability Alone Not Appealable

State ex rel. A & D Ltd. Partnership v. Keefe, 77 Ohio St. 3d, 671 N.E.2d 13 (1996) (order granting judgment notwithstanding the verdict on the issue of liability alone is not a final, appealable order)

Sua Sponte Award of Damages

Lance v. Bowe, 98 Ohio App. 3d 202, 648 N.E.2d 60 (1994) (a court may award punitive damages even where they are not requested, so long as the award does not exceed the damages claimed in the party's demand)

Summary Judgment Appealable When Remaining Parties Dismissed

Denham v. New Carlisle, 86 Ohio St. 3d 594, 716 N.E.2d 184 (1999) (the granting of a motion for summary judgment becomes a final appealable order when party against whom the motion has been granted voluntarily dismisses the remaining parties in the action)

Videotape Deposition Expenses

Cave v. Conrad, 94 Ohio St. 3d 299, 762 N.E.2d 991 (2002) (reasonable videotape deposition expenses may be taxed as costs and awarded to successful claimants on appeal from a decision of Industrial Commission in workers' compensation case)

Waiver of Damage Claims

Delaney v. Skyline Lodge, Inc., 95 Ohio App. 3d 264, 642 N.E.2d 395 (1994) (despite adequate notice of claims of compensatory and punitive damages, appellant's failure to raise the lack of any specific money demand until its motion for judgment notwithstanding the verdict constituted waiver)

CHAPTER 55

Rule 55. Default

Rule 55 reads as follows:

(A) **Entry of judgment.** When a party against whom a judgment for affirmative relief is sought has failed to plead or otherwise defend as provided by these rules, the party entitled to a judgment by default shall apply in writing or orally to the court therefor; but no judgment by default shall be entered against a minor or an incompetent person unless represented in the action by a guardian or other such representative who has appeared therein. If the party against whom judgment by default is sought has appeared in the action, he (or, if appearing by representative, his representative) shall be served with written notice of the application for judgment at least seven days prior to the hearing on such application. If, in order to enable the court to enter judgment or to carry it into effect, it is necessary to take an account or to determine the amount of damages or to establish the truth of any averment by evidence or to make an investigation of any other matter, the court may conduct such hearings or order such references as it deems necessary and proper and shall when applicable accord a right of trial by jury to the parties.

(B) **Setting aside default judgment.** If a judgment by default has been entered, the court may set it aside in accordance with Rule 60(B).

(C) **Plaintiffs, counterclaimants, cross-claimants.** The provisions of this rule apply whether the party entitled to the judgment by default is a plaintiff, a third-party plaintiff or a party who has pleaded a cross-claim or counterclaim. In all cases a judgment by default is subject to the limitations of Rule 54(C).

(D) **Judgment against this state.** No judgment by default shall be entered against this state, a political subdivision, or officer in his representative capacity or agency of either unless the claimant establishes his claim or right to relief by evidence satisfactory to the court.

COMMENTARY

Rule 55 establishes the procedures to be used when a party defaults in an action, defined as "fail[ing] to plead or otherwise defend" in the action. Although subsection (C) indicates that any party may be the object of a default judgment on claims asserted against it, a motion seeking default judgment is not the proper mechanism for a party defending a claim who desires to have the claim dismissed because the opposing party has failed to prosecute the claim. Rather, such a motion should be made in accordance with the provisions of Rule 41(B)(1).

Default Judgment Generally

Rule 55 sets forth a one-step procedure to be used by parties wishing to obtain default judgments. Unlike some kinds of default judgments in federal court, a default judgment may never be entered by the clerk, and application for all default judgments must be made orally or in writing to the court. In all cases must the relief granted as part of a default judgment be limited to that requested in the pleadings.

Default judgments are always discretionary, and the court may order additional hearings or order the party seeking the default judgment to produce evidence that would support the party's claim for relief. Under subsection (D), such evidence is required when a default judgment against Ohio or a representative of Ohio is sought by a party.

Illustration 55-1

Victoria commences a breach of contract action against Allan to recover $750 for the services provided in repairing Allan's truck. Allan fails to answer the complaint and offers no reason for his non-cooperation. Under Rule 55(A), Victoria may make a motion for default judgment to the court. Default judgment may be granted without notice to Allan, as he has not made any kind of "appearance" in the action within. However, Victoria is limited in her relief to the $750 originally demanded.

Comparison with Default Judgment in Federal Court

Although Ohio Rule 55 and its Federal analog resemble one another in several respects, significant differences remain. Whereas the Ohio version of the Rule requires only a one-step procedure for the entry of a default judgment, Federal Rule 55 employs a two-step procedure. Under the latter procedure, an entry of default is made on the record by the clerk. Such an entry does not constitute a binding judgment, however, and a motion for a default judgment must be made after the default is entered. Of course, the default judgment itself, if one is rendered, must be entered according to the provisions of Federal Rule 58. Under the Ohio default judgment procedure, both steps are collapsed into a single motion.

Notice Provision

The most important feature of subsection (A) is the seven-day notice provision to the opposing party. In this regard, the Rule distinguishes between those parties who do not make an *appearance* in the action and those parties who simply do not plead or otherwise defend. Although a default judgment may be entered against any party who has failed to plead or otherwise defend in the action, notice of the hearing on default must be provided only to those parties who make an appearance in the action, even if that party inexcusably fails to appear at trial. This provision ensures that parties will not have default judgments entered against them if they indicate any kind of desire to defend the claim. In general, a "failure to appear" is construed quite strictly, and a party who files an untimely pleading, or a party who files a motion to dismiss under Rule 12 but does not subsequently file a responsive pleading, or a party who even notifies the prosecuting party of their intention to defend a claim, must be notified of the application of default and subsequent hearing on the matter.

Illustration 55-2

Assume on the facts of Illustration of 55-1 that Allan employs an attorney, who notifies the court of Allan's intention to remove the action to federal court. However, no further appearance is made by Alan or his attorney and the court does not receive a removal notification from any federal court. Under these circumstances, the attorney's limited communication with the court should be sufficient to constitute an "appearance," and Alan must be notified at least seven days before a hearing on the matter or a default judgment is entered.

Penalty Default

The term "penalty default" is often used to refer to either an involuntary dismissal under Rule 41(B) or a default judgment rendered as a sanction under Rule 37(B)(2)(c) or Rule 37(D). The procedures set forth in those Rules, however, differ substantially from one another, and case law interpreting one of those provisions should not be construed as impacting the other.

An involuntary dismissal under Rule 41(B) may be entered only against a plaintiff for a failure to prosecute a claim or comply with the Rules or a court order. The plaintiff's failure should be documented in a specific ruling, and the plaintiff should be afforded an opportunity to explain her actions or inactions triggering the involuntary dismissal. Although Rule 41(B)(3) indicates that an involuntary dismissal will presumptively function as an adjudication on the merits of the case, thereby preempting a recommencement of the action, an involuntary dismissal does not result in a "default judgment" open to attack or execution as the term is used in the Rules. Although involuntary dismissals are not authorized as against defending parties, the provisions of Rule 55 may be used against recalcitrant or noncompliant defendants.

As noted, Rule 37(B)(2)(c) provides for a sanction of a default judgment against a party for failing to obey an order to compel discovery, and subsection (D) provides for the same sanction against a party who fails to appear at that party's own deposition. However, the notice provisions contained in Rule 55 must be complied with before a default judgment may be rendered as a sanction under Rule 37.

Setting Aside Default Judgments

Subsection (B) sets forth only one method of setting aside a default judgment, a motion for post-judgment relief under Rule 60(B). The factors listed in Rule 60 should therefore be consulted to determine whether a motion made to set aside a default judgment under that Rule should be granted.

However, at least two additional mechanisms may be used to set aside a default judgment: a motion for reconsideration and appeal. A motion for reconsideration to the court rendering the default judgment will ordinarily be denied as a matter of course unless a technical error has been discovered which has made the default judgment improper. A motion to the same effect may also be brought under Rule 60(A). An appeal of a default judgment is unlikely to succeed unless a novel or disputable issue of procedural law was instrumental in the rendering of the default judgment.

ADDITIONAL AUTHORITY

10 WRIGHT & MILLER §§ 2681-2710
10 MOORE'S FEDERAL PRACTICE §§ 55.01-55.50
5 ANDERSON'S OHIO CIVIL PRACTICE §§ 170.01-170.06
2 KLEIN DARLING AT 55-1 to AT 55-19
3 TEREZ F 11.2.1 to F 11.2.5
5 OH. JUR. PL. AND PRAC. FORMS, ch. 68
6 MILLIGAN Forms 55-1 to 55-45
2 FINK §§ 55-1 to 55-5

LEADING CASES

Action Constituting an Appearance

Miamisburg Motel v. Huntington Nat'l Bank, 88 Ohio App. 3d 117, 623 N.E.2d 163 (1993) (a party appears in an action when that party clearly expresses to the opposing party an intention and purpose to defend the suit, regardless of whether a formal pleading has been made)

Action Not Constituting an Appearance

Hrabak v. Collins, 108 Ohio App. 3d 117, 670 N.E.2d 281 (1995) (private communications between the attorneys of plaintiff and defendant do not constitute an appearance for the purposes of Rule 55(A))

Default Judgments Against the State

State ex rel. Shimola v. Cleveland, 70 Ohio St. 3d 110, 637 N.E.2d 325 (1994) (a default judgment may be entered against the state where a city does not respond to a writ of mandamus and the petitioner establishes a right to such relief)

Notice to Opposing Party

AMCA Int'l Corp. v. Carlton, 10 Ohio St. 3d 88, 461 N.E.2d 1282 (1984) (a party may not take a default judgment against an opposing party who has "appeared" absent a seven-day notice)

Setting Aside Default Judgment; In General

Blasco v. Mislik, 69 Ohio St. 3d 684, 433 N.E.2d 612 (1982) (relief from a default judgment should be denied if the moving party fails to allege any reason justifying his failure to file a timely answer and the motion for relief is not made in a timely fashion)

Setting Aside Default Judgment; Meritorious Defense

GMAC v. Deskins, 16 Ohio App. 3d 132, 474 N.E.2d 1207 (1984) (where timely relief is sought from a default judgment on the basis of a meritorious defense, any doubt in the matter should be resolved in favor of the defendant so that cases may be decided on their merits)

CHAPTER 56

Rule 56. Summary Judgment

Rule 56 reads as follows:

(A) **For party seeking affirmative relief.** A party seeking to recover upon a claim, counterclaim, or cross-claim or to obtain a declaratory judgment may move with or without supporting affidavits for a summary judgment in the party's favor as to all or any part of the claim, counterclaim, cross-claim, or declaratory judgment action. A party may move for summary judgment at any time after the expiration of the time permitted under these rules for a responsive motion or pleading by the adverse party, or after service of a motion for summary judgment by the adverse party. If the action has been set for pretrial or trial, a motion for summary judgment may be made only with leave of court.

(B) **For defending party.** A party against whom a claim, counterclaim, or cross-claim is asserted or a declaratory judgment is sought may, at any time, move with or without supporting affidavits for a summary judgment in the party's favor as to all or any part of the claim, counterclaim, cross-claim, or declaratory judgment action. If the action has been set for pretrial or trial, a motion for summary judgment may be made only with leave of court.

(C) **Motion and proceedings.** The motion shall be served at least fourteen days before the time fixed for hearing. The adverse party prior to the day of hearing may serve and file opposing affidavits. Summary judgment shall be rendered forthwith if the pleadings, depositions, answers to interrogatories, written admissions, affidavits, transcripts of evidence, and written stipulations of fact, if any, timely filed in the action, show that there is no genuine issue as to any material fact and that the moving party is entitled to judgment as a matter of law. No evidence or stipulation may be considered except as stated in this rule. A summary judgment shall not be rendered unless it appears from the evidence or stipulation, and only from the evidence or stipulation, that reasonable minds can come to but one conclusion and that conclusion is adverse to the party against whom the motion for summary judgment is made, that party being entitled to have the evidence or stipulation construed most strongly in the party's favor. A summary judgment, interlocutory in character, may be rendered on the issue of liability alone although there is a genuine issue as to the amount of damages.

(D) **Case not fully adjudicated upon motion.** If on motion under this rule summary judgment is not rendered upon the whole case or for all the relief asked and a trial is necessary, the court in deciding the motion, shall examine the evidence or stipulation properly before it, and shall if practicable, ascertain what material facts exist without controversy and what material facts are actually and in good faith controverted. The court shall thereupon make an order on its journal specifying the facts that are without controversy, including the extent to which the amount of damages or other relief is not in controversy, and directing such further proceedings in the action as are just. Upon the trial of the action the facts so specified shall be deemed established, and the trial shall be conducted accordingly.

(E) **Form of affidavits; further testimony; defense required.** Supporting and opposing affidavits shall be made on personal knowledge, shall set forth such facts as would be admissible in evidence, and shall show affirmatively that the affiant is competent to testify to the matters stated in the affidavit. Sworn or certified copies of all papers or parts of papers referred to in an affidavit shall be attached to or served with the affidavit. The court may permit affidavits to be supplemented or opposed by depositions or by further affidavits. When a motion for summary judgment is made and supported as provided in this rule, an adverse party may not rest upon the mere allegations or denials of the party's pleadings, but the party's response, by affidavit or as otherwise provided in this rule, must set forth specific facts showing that there is a genuine issue for trial. If the party does not so respond, summary judgment, if appropriate, shall be entered against the party.

(F) **When affidavits unavailable.** Should it appear from the affidavits of a party opposing the motion for summary judgment that the party cannot for sufficient reasons stated present by affidavit facts essential to justify the party's opposition, the court may refuse the application for judgment or may order a continuance to permit affidavits to be obtained or discovery to be had or may make such other order as is just.

(G) **Affidavits made in bad faith.** Should it appear to the satisfaction of the court at any time that any of the affidavits presented pursuant to this rule are presented in bad faith or solely for the purpose of delay, the court shall forthwith order the party employing them to pay to the other party the amount of the reasonable expenses which the filing of the affidavits caused the other party to incur, including reasonable attorney's fees, and any offending party or attorney may be adjudged guilty of contempt.

✧ ✧ ✧ ✧ ✧

COMMENTARY

Rule 56, which governs summary judgment, is perhaps the most recognized and analyzed Rule. Summary judgment is considered to be an efficacious method of disposing of an action when the only issues to be decided are legal ones.

Subsections (A), (B), (D), (F), (G), most of subsection (C), and the first half of subsection (E) of Rule 56 are strictly procedural in nature, and there are very few controverted issues involving those parts of the Rule. On the contrary, the third sentence of subsection (C) and the latter half of subsection (E) and the issues surrounding them are significantly more complex. For this reason, this Chapter will separate the discussion of Rule 56 accordingly.

Motions for Summary Judgment; How and When Made

Subsection (A) provides that any party presenting a claim for relief may make a motion for summary judgment on that claim at any time after the expiration of the time permitted for a responsive motion or pleading by the adverse party, ordinarily 28 days. The selection of this specific time period is intended to avoid the situation where a plaintiff files a summary judgment motion before the defendant has had an opportunity to respond to the complaint, although service of a responsive pleading before the expiration of the time period does not appear to allow a plaintiff to make a motion for summary judgment any earlier than the original date established by the 28-day waiting period. Alternatively, a party presenting a claim may move for summary judgment after being served with a motion for summary judgment by the opposing party. The motion for summary judgment may include, but is not required to include, supporting affidavits, a point reiterated several times throughout the Rule.

Subsection (B) states that a defendant or other party defending a claim is not subject to the usual 28-day restriction of subsection (A) and may file a motion for summary judgment at any time. Affidavits in support of the motion are likewise permitted, but not required. A party defending a claim may make a motion for summary judgment before filing a mandatory pleading or any other paper with the court. Although Rule 12(A) does not provide for automatic extensions of the time periods in which responsive pleadings must be served when a motion for summary judgment is made by a defending party, that subsection impliedly authorizes the court to alter the time period in an appropriate manner in these situations.

Illustration 56-1

While Jim and his wife, Sharon, are walking to the local grocery store, an automobile driven by Frank darts off the road and hits Jim. On January 5, Sharon commences a wrongful death action against Frank and requests $20 million for compensatory damages and loss of consortium. Sharon serves Frank with a summons and copy of the complaint on January 10. Under Rule 56(A), Sharon may make a motion for summary judgment at any time after February 7. If, however, Frank serves an answer on Sharon on January 20, Sharon must still wait until February 7 to file a motion for summary judgment. Under Rule 56(B), however, Frank may make a motion for summary judgment at any time, and Frank need not file an answer before making the motion. If Frank should choose to file such a motion before serving an answer, he should request, along with his motion, that his 28-day time period for serving an answer be tolled by the filing of his summary judgment motion.

The first sentence of subsection (C) appears to contemplate a hearing on every motion for summary judgment, and a hearing on the motion is strongly recommended in any event. A motion for summary judgment must be served on the opposing party at least 14 days before the date of the hearing, and the second sentence of subsection (C) allows the adverse party to submit opposing affidavits at least one day prior to the hearing.

Partial Summary Judgment

Both subsection (A) and subsection (B) allow a motion for summary judgment on all or any part of a claim. Similarly, the final sentence of subsection (C) permits a motion for summary judgment on the issue of liability alone even though there is a disputed issue of fact concerning damages. Although the Rule does not explicitly provide for the reverse situation, *i.e.*, a motion for summary judgment on the issue of damages when the liability of the parties is still in dispute, the court has the discretion to decide a motion under the authority of subsections (A) and (B).

Decisions by the court on such motions are commonly referred to as partial summary judgments, a term that is slightly misleading. The term judgment as defined in Rule 54 necessarily implies a decision or order of the court from which an appeal can be immediately taken. Motions for summary judgment on a part of a claim are normally interlocutory in character, and summary judgments on issues of liability alone are expressly designated as such.

Illustration 56-2

Assume on the facts of Illustration 56-1 that the court is prepared to find for Sharon on the issue of Frank's liability, but is unwilling to award to Sharon the full amount of her damage claims. Rule 56 allows the court to grant partial summary judgment under these circumstances. If the court does indeed grant partial summary judgment on the issue of Frank's liability, the court will allow the litigation to proceed to determine the issue of damages. However, the court's order on Frank's liability is not immediately appealable under Rule 54.

Summary Judgment and Judgment on the Pleadings Distinguished

A motion for summary judgment is different from a motion for judgment on the pleadings under Rule 12(C) or a motion to dismiss for failure to state a claim upon which relief can be granted under Rule 12(B)(6) in that the former is designed to pierce the allegations in the pleadings to determine if there truly is a factual matter in dispute. Thus, additional materials outside the pleadings are usually considered by the court in deciding on a motion for summary judgment. These motions under Rule 12 are easily converted to a motion for summary judgment simply by presenting materials other than the pleadings to the court. This conversion thus provides the parties with the ability to submit additional materials in support of or in opposition to the motion.

Supporting Materials on Motion for Summary Judgment

The party moving for summary judgment is permitted to supplement the motion with supporting affidavits under subsection (A) or (B), and the party opposing the motion is authorized to submit opposing affidavits under the second sentence of subsection (C). Under a strict reading of the Rules, additional materials, such as depositions can be submitted by the parties only with permission of the court under the third sentence of subsection (E), but these materials are usually submitted as a matter of course along with the motion by the moving party and the brief in opposition to the motion by the adverse party. Nonetheless, the court retains the discretion to disallow certain kinds of materials submitted by the parties in support of or in opposition to the motion. If the opposing party cannot obtain affidavits or additional materials necessary to oppose the motion within the time period before the hearing on the matter, subsection (F) allows the court to dismiss the motion, grant a continuance, or take any other action as it deems proper.

A 1999 amendment to the Rule deleted the "pending case" requirement with respect to transcripts of evidence submitted in support of or in opposition to a motion for summary judgment. Transcripts of evidence from other cases may be filed and and considered by the court in deciding on the motion. However, this amendment should not be construed as permitting depositions and other discovery materials from other cases to be similarly permitted. This distinction is not clear from the language of the amended rule; the affected portion of subsection (C) should probably have been amended to provide "transcripts of evidence in the pending case or from another case" to indicate the distinction.

Under subsection (E), supporting or opposing affidavits must be based on the personal knowledge of the affiant, must contain only those facts that would be admissible at trial, and must be duly sworn or certified. Subsection (G) allows the imposition of specific sanctions, including civil contempt, on parties who submit affidavits in bad faith or for the purpose of delay. Although this subsection provides for such sanctions only in conjunction with affidavits, parties who submit additional materials in bad faith or for the purpose of delay are sanctionable under Rule 37 and possibly Rule 11.

If any affidavit presented pursuant to Rule 56 is presented in bad faith or for the purpose of delay, subsection (G) provides that the court may order the party presenting such an affidavit to pay the reasonable expenses of the opposing party incurred because of the filing of these affidavits. The court may also adjudge any offending party or attorney guilty of contempt.

Case Not Fully Adjudicated on Summary Judgment Motion

The provisions of subsection (D) contemplate the situation in which the court determines that summary judgment is not appropriate with respect to all or part of a claim. In that instance, the court is directed to ascertain those facts that are not in controversy and for which a trial is not needed, and make an order establishing those facts as such. At trial, those facts are not properly within the province of the jury.

Illustration 56-3

Assume on the facts of Illustration 56-1 that Sharon files a timely motion for summary judgment and attaches affidavits which establish that Frank was driving with a blood alcohol content of three times the legal limit. Frank does not contest the accuracy of these results, but contends that the accident was caused when Jim wandered out into the street, thus causing the accident. In this situation, the trial judge may make an order establishing the fact that Frank was driving under the influence of alcohol, thereby removing determination of this uncontested fact from the jury. However, Sharon's motion for summary judgment will be denied.

Summary Judgment Standard

The circumstances in which summary judgment is appropriate are not always straightforward. The standard for granting a motion for summary judgment in subsection (C)—"there is no genuine issue as to any material fact and [ ] the moving party is entitled to judgment as a matter of law"—has been the subject of numerous opinions. These opinions appear to present two contradictory views of summary judgment. The traditional view suggests that the purpose of summary judgment is to dispose of only those cases that present only legal issues. Under this view, the court is not supposed to engage in any kind of fact-finding role, but rather is required simply to determine whether any disputed issue of fact exists.

However, this view of summary judgment appears to contradict the principle often articulated by judges and scholars that, in deciding on a motion for summary judgment, the court should view the evidence in the light most favorable to the nonmoving party. Viewing the evidence in this way necessarily implies that the court must engage in an assessment of the weight of the evidence. Proponents of this view of summary judgment suggest that the purposes of summary judgment is to weed out those cases in which a trial would be useless.

It appears as though the drafters of Ohio Rule 56 have opted for the latter view. Subsection (C) expressly states that the nonmoving party is "entitled to have the evidence or stipulation construed most strongly in his favor." Furthermore, the Rule states that summary judgment should be granted if "reasonable minds can come to but one conclusion" and this conclusion is adverse to the nonmoving party. These phrases suggest that summary judgment in favor of a party is appropriate when a directed verdict would have been granted to that party at trial under Rule 50.

Two-Part Test

The language of Rule 56 suggests a two-part test in deciding motions for summary judgment, derived from the standard for summary judgment articulated in subsection (C). *First*, the moving party must demonstrate that it is entitled to judgment as a matter of law. In this respect, a summary judgment motion is identical to a judgment on the pleadings under Rule 12(C), a view supported by the repeated statements in Rule 56 that affidavits in support of a motion for summary judgment are not required. Stated somewhat differently, if a party making a claim moves for summary judgment, it is a necessary but not sufficient condition that the movant demonstrate that it is entitled to judgment as a matter of law by alleging facts sufficient to state a cognizable claim upon which relief can be granted *and* by establishing that any affirmative defense alleged by the defending party does not sufficiently repudiate the claim.

Alternatively, if a party defending a claim moves for summary judgment, it is a necessary but sufficient condition that the movant demonstrate that it is entitled to judgment as a matter of law by establishing that the facts alleged by the party making the claim do not state a claim upon which relief can be granted *or* by establishing that the facts constituting the affirmative defense are uncontroverted. In deciding whether a party has made the requisite demonstration in this regard, disputed questions of fact are simply not relevant, and a court should properly refrain from assessing their relative weight.

Illustration 56-4

Mike brings an action against Melissa under an Ohio statute and alleges facts A, B, and C in his complaint. Melissa files an answer admitting facts A and B but denying fact C. Additionally, Melissa raises an affirmative defense by alleging facts D, E, and F, which Mike admits in a subsequent pleading. Melissa then files a motion for summary judgment on Mike's original claim, arguing that facts A, B, and C do not state a claim upon which relief can be granted. If the court agrees with Melissa, it should grant Melissa her motion, and the issue of whether fact C is a disputed issue of material fact is not relevant.

Illustration 56-5

Assume on the facts of Illustration 56-4 that in her motion for summary judgment, Melissa also argued that she is entitled to judgment on Mike's original claim because admitted facts D, E, and F constitute an affirmative defense even if Mike's complaint states a cognizable claim. If the court agrees that Mike's complaint states a claim upon which relief can be granted, it should nonetheless grant Melissa's motion if her answer states a cognizable defense. The issue of whether fact C is a disputed issue of material fact is not relevant.

Illustration 56-6

Assume on the facts of Illustration 56-5 that Mike defends Melissa's motion for summary judgment by arguing that his complaint states a sufficient claim and Melissa's defense is deficient because she has failed to allege fact G. If the court agrees with Mike, it should deny Melissa's motion for summary judgment not because fact G is a disputed issue of material fact, but rather because Melissa has not demonstrated that she is entitled to judgment as a matter of law.

Only after the court determines that the party moving for summary judgment is entitled to judgment as a matter of law should it proceed to the question of whether any genuine issue of material fact exists. If this latter question is answered in the negative, only then is summary judgment appropriate.

Relationship to Rule 12 and Rule 50

The apparent connection between the "judgment as a matter of law" part of the summary judgment standard and a judgment on the pleadings under Rule 12(C) implies a connection between the "no genuine issue as to any material fact" part of the summary judgment standard and motions for judgment notwithstanding the verdict under Rule 50. The role of additional materials outside the pleadings becomes crucial in this regard, as the court may then use these additional materials to appropriately weigh the evidence that would be presented at trial to determine if a trial would be needed.

In this way, then, summary judgment is correctly perceived as a bridge connecting the Rule 12(C) mechanism for determining the legal *sufficiency of the pleadings*—judgment as a matter of law—and the Rule 50 mechanism for determining the factual *sufficiency of the evidence*—no genuine issue of material fact exists. Only when the moving party satisfies both of these components of the standard should the court grant the motion for summary judgment.

The framers of Rule 56, however, unintentionally reversed the correct operation and application of the standard by placing the "genuine issue" component before the "judgment as a matter of law" component. The party seeking summary judgment should first demonstrate the legal sufficiency of its pleadings before demonstrating the legal insufficiency of the opposing party's evidence.

Thus, although the court is not supposed to weigh the credibility of the evidence presented by the materials outside the pleadings to determine if the moving party is entitled to judgment as a matter of law, the court *must* do so to determine if genuine issues of material fact exist. In making this latter determination, the court should also take into account the respective burdens of proof that would fall on the parties at trial and whether those parties have satisfied those burdens in their materials presented in support of or in opposition to a motion for summary judgment.

Defeating a Motion for Summary Judgment

A party may defeat a motion for summary judgment in one of three ways. First, the defending party may simply point out to the court that the moving party has simply not alleged facts sufficient to make out a cognizable claim. In other words, the defending party points out that the moving party has not demonstrated that it is entitled to a judgment as a matter of law.

Illustration 56-7

Peter is injured when the blade of a table saw with which he was working inexplicably shatters. Tommy's Tools is the manufacturer of the blade. Peter commences a products liability action against Tommy's Tools, arguing that Tommy's Tools was negligent in the design of the table saw. If Peter files a timely motion for summary judgment, Tommy's Tools may defeat the motion by simply pointing out that Peter has not alleged facts sufficient to establish that Tommy's Tools owed Peter a duty of care.

Second, the defending party may point out to the court that the moving party has made no attempt to demonstrate the legal insufficiency of the defending party's affirmative defense—another way of demonstrating that the moving party is not entitled to judgment as a matter of law.

Illustration 56-8

Assume on the facts of Illustration 56-7 that Tommy's answer alleges that Peter suffered the injuries as the result of his own negligence in using the table saw. However, if Peter fails to refute Tommy's contributory negligence defense in any manner, Tommy's Tools may defeat the summary judgment motion simply by bringing this to the court's attention.

Third, the defending party may demonstrate to the court that, even though the moving party has demonstrated the legal sufficiency of its claim, genuine issues of material fact exist which justify a trial on those issues.

Illustration 56-9

Assume on the facts of Illustration 56-8 that Tommy's Tools produces an affidavit from a witness stating that Peter disengaged the safety devices on the table saw before using it, and therefore cannot be held liable for his injuries. On the other side, Peter claims that the safety devices were not attached when he received the table saw. Under these circumstances, Tommy's Tools may defeat Peter's motion for summary judgment by pointing out that genuine issues of fact exist as to the negligence of the parties.

If a defending party chooses the third route, subsection (E) states that it "may not rest upon the mere allegations or denials of [its] pleading, but [its] response, by affidavit or as otherwise provided in this rule, must set forth specific facts showing that there is a genuine issue for trial." If a defending party does not respond in this fashion, the final sentence of subsection (E) instructs the court to enter summary judgment for the moving party, "if appropriate." This phrase was intended to ensure that summary judgment should not be granted unless the moving party first meets its burden of demonstrating that it is entitled to judgment as a matter of law.

Illustration 56-10

Assume on the facts of Illustration 56-9 that Tommy's Tools claims that Peter disengaged the safety devices before using the saw but can produce no evidence to substantiate the claim. If this is Tommy's only defense and all other facts comprising Peter's claim are uncontroverted, the court should grant Peter's motion for summary judgment.

ADDITIONAL AUTHORITY

10 WRIGHT & MILLER §§ 2711-2718
10A WRIGHT & MILLER §§ 2719-2750

11 Moore's Federal Practice §§ 56.01-56.50

5 Anderson's Ohio Civil Practice §§ 171.01-171.10

2 Klein Darling AT 56-1 to AT 56-45

3 Terez F 11.3.1 to F 11.3.3

5 Oh. Jur. Pl. and Prac. Forms, ch. 69

6 Milligan Forms 56-1 et seq.

2 Fink §§ 56-1 to 56-20

LEADING CASES

Affidavits; Failure to Object

State ex rel. Chuvalas v. Tompkins, 83 Ohio St. 3d 171, 699 N.E.2d 58 (1998) (an appellate court may properly consider affidavits attached to appellee's brief filed in that court in a merit determination where appellant waives any objection to the affidavits by not moving to strike them or otherwise specifying their alleged impropriety)

Affidavits Made with Personal Knowledge

Bonacorsi v. Wheeling & Lake Erie Ry. Co., 95 Ohio St. 3d 314, 767 N.E.2d 707 (2002) (affidavits supporting motions for summary judgment must be made with personal knowledge)

Burden of Production at Trial

State ex rel. Zimmerman v. Tompkins, 75 Ohio St. 3d 447, 663 N.E.2d 639 (1996) (summary judgment is appropriate where the nonmoving party does not produce evidence on any issue for which that party bears the burden of production at trial)

Demonstration of Genuine Issue of Material Fact

Weiland v. Benton, 108 Ohio App. 3d 512, 671 N.E.2d 295 (1996) (when the moving party supports its motion for summary judgment with evidentiary material of the type and character set out in the Rule, the nonmoving party must submit affidavits or other evidentiary material to show that there is a genuine issue of material fact)

Mayes v. Holman, 76 Ohio St. 3d 147, 666 N.E.2d 1132 (1996) (when a motion for summary judgment is properly supported, the nonmoving party cannot rest on the mere allegations of its pleading, but its response must set forth specific facts showing that there is a genuine issue of material fact)

Disputed Facts in Employment Cases

Collins v. Rizkana, 73 Ohio St. 3d 65, 652 N.E.2d 653 (1995) (issues of material fact existed as to whether an employer subjected an employee to unwanted and offensive contact and retaliated against her for refusing to deny the incidents, resulting in her constructive discharge, precluding summary judgment)

Failure to Respond "Written" Admission for Summary Judgment

State ex rel. Montgomery v. Maginn, 147 Ohio App. 3d 420, 770 N.E.2d 1099 (2002) (an admission arising by a party's failure to respond to a request for admissions constitutes a "written admission" for purposes of the summary judgment rule)

Findings of Fact Not Required

State ex rel. Sharif v. Cuyahoga Cty. Ct. of Cmn. Pleas, 85 Ohio St. 3d 375, 708 N.E.2d 718 (1999) (motions for summary judgment may be decided by a court without issuing findings of fact or conclusions of law)

Frivolous Lawsuits

Conley v. Brown Corp. of Waverly, Inc., 82 Ohio St. 3d 470, 696 N.E.2d 1085 (1998) (one solution to "frivolous" lawsuits brought pursuant to employer intentional tort theories is the use of Rule 56, which challenges the merits of a claim)

Initial Burden

Dresher v. Burt, 75 Ohio St. 3d 280, 662 N.E.2d 264 (1996) (a party seeking summary judgment on the ground that the nonmoving party cannot prove its case bears the initial burden of informing the trial court of the basis of its motion and identifying portions of the record that demonstrate the absence of genuine issues of material fact)

Motion to Compel Discovery Overruled by Ruling on Summary Judgment

Denham v. New Carlisle, 138 Ohio App. 3d 439, 741 N.E.2d 587 (2000) (grant of summary judgment for a party implicitly overruled opposing motion to compel discovery and for a continuance to respond to summary judgment motion)

Notice and Hearing Requirements

Klesch v. Ried, 95 Ohio App. 3d 664, 643 N.E.2d 571 (1994) (parties are entitled to be notified of a hearing date only where a hearing is requested by one of the parties; a trial court is not required to schedule an oral hearing in every case)

Notice Requirement Mandatory

State ex rel. Nelson v. Russo, 89 Ohio St. 3d 227, 729 N.E.2d 1181 (2000) (the court must notify all parties at least 14 days before the time fixed for hearing when it converts a motion to dismiss under Rule 12 into a motion for summary judgment under Rule 56)

Only Disputed Facts Preclude Summary Judgment

Miller v. Loral Defense Sys., 109 Ohio App. 3d 379, 672 N.E.2d 227 (1996) (only disputes over facts that might affect the outcome of a suit will properly preclude an entry of summary judgment)

Opinions in Affidavits

Wall v. Firelands Radiology, Inc., 106 Ohio App. 3d 313, 666 N.E.2d 235 (1995) (an affidavit without an averment of personal knowledge must show personal knowledge specifically; opinions in such affidavits may be considered as long as the statements comply with Rule 56 and the rules of evidence), *appeal not allowed*, 74 Ohio St. 3d 1512, 659 N.E.2d 1289 (1996)

Opposing Motions; In General

Clark Cty. Solid Waste Mgt. Dist. v. Danis Clarkco Landfill Co., 109 Ohio App. 3d 19, 671 N.E.2d 1034 (1996) (parties who must respond to a motion for summary judgment before adequate discovery is complete are required to seek their remedy through the rule allowing the court to order a continuance to conduct further discovery)

Requirement of Affidavits

Dresher v. Burt, 75 Ohio St. 3d 280, 662 N.E.2d 264 (1996) (neither party is required to submit affidavits to support a motion for summary judgment, but the moving party must point specifically to something in the record, such as pleadings, answers to interrogatories, depositions, affidavits, transcripts of evidence, to support its motion)

Shifting Burdens

Dresher v. Burt, 75 Ohio St. 3d 280, 662 N.E.2d 264 (1996) (if the moving party satisfies its initial burden of identifying portions of the record that demonstrate the lack of a genuine issue of material fact, the nonmoving party bears a reciprocal burden to set forth specific facts showing that there is a genuine issue of material fact for trial)

Standard for Summary Judgment; In General

Horton v. Harwick Chem. Corp., 73 Ohio St. 3d 679, 653 N.E.2d 1196 (1995) (in an asbestos case, summary judgment is proper under the same circumstances as in any other case, *i.e.*, when, considering the evidence as a whole, (1) no genuine issues of material fact remains, (2) the moving party is entitled to judgment as a matter of law, and (3) the evidence, construed most strongly in favor of the nonmoving party, reveals that reasonable minds could only conclude in favor of the moving party)

Standard; No Legally Sufficient Claim

Dresher v. Burt, 75 Ohio St. 3d 280, 662 N.E.2d 264 (1996) (entry of summary judgment may be rendered if the pleadings and arguments of the moving party clearly establish that the nonmoving party has no legally sufficient claim under applicable law)

Summary Judgment Inappropriate for Case Ready for Trial

State ex rel. Wilson-Simmons v. Lake Cty. Sheriffs Dept., 82 Ohio St. 3d 37, 693 N.E.2d 789 (1998) (when an action is ready to be tried on the merits at trial, a summary judgment motion is inappropriate)

Supporting Documentation

Bowmer v. Dettelbach, 109 Ohio App. 3d 680, 672 N.E.2d 1081 (1996) (court of appeals will consider documentary evidence submitted to support a motion for summary judgment even though the evidence was not submitted in accordance with a rule requiring all documents to be accompanied by personal certification)

Waiver of Issues

Gallagher v. Cleveland Browns Football Co., 74 Ohio St. 3d 427, 659 N.E.2d 1232 (1996) (although no provision in Rule 56 suggests that a party who fails to make a motion for summary judgment on a particular issue waives the right to raise the issue, judicial economy favors raising any issue on which the moving party claims entitlement to judgment as a matter of law)

CHAPTER 57

Rule 57. Declaratory Judgments

Rule 57 reads as follows:

The procedure for obtaining a declaratory judgment pursuant to Sections 2721.01 to 2721.15, inclusive, of the Revised Code, shall be in accordance with these rules. The existence of another adequate remedy does not preclude a judgment for declaratory relief in cases where it is appropriate. The court may advance on the trial list the hearing of an action for a declaratory judgment.

COMMENTARY

Although Rule 57 is directed at actions in which a declaratory judgment is the relief being sought, the Rule does not specify when a party may bring such actions. Instead, the first sentence of the Rule simply keys the procedure in declaratory relief proceedings under OHIO REV. CODE ANN. §§ 2721.01-.15, which sets forth the substantive law in this area, to the Rules. In this sense, Rule 57 should be read in conjunction with Rule 1(C), which governs exceptions to the general applicability of the Rules. Subsection (A) of Rule 1 states that the Rules apply in all civil actions in the state of Ohio, with the exceptions listed in subsection (C) of that Rule. As actions in which declaratory relief is the remedy being sought is a "special statutory proceeding" under the meaning of Rule 1(C)(7), the Rules would not apply to such actions if they would, by their nature, be clearly inapplicable. Rule 57 resolves any doubt on the issue by making the Rules expressly applicable.

Miscellaneous Provisions

The Rule also provides that courts have the authority to advance a hearing of an action for declaratory judgments on the trial calendar, but no court is required to do so. The Rule impliedly preserves the right to jury trial in actions involving requests for declaratory relief, so that the existence of such a right is determined by the underlying nature of the issues in the request for a declaratory judgment.

ADDITIONAL AUTHORITY

10A WRIGHT & MILLER §§ 2751-2780

12 Moore's Federal Practice §§ 57.01-57.104

2 Klein Darling AT 57-1 to AT 57-6

3 Terez F 4.21.2, F 7.6.1

5 Oh. Jur. Pl. and Prac. Forms, ch. 70

6 Milligan Forms 57-1 to 57-19

2 Fink §§ 57-1 to 57-6

LEADING CASES

Alternative Remedies

Ditch Landowners' Ass'n v. Joint Bd. of Huron & Seneca Cty. Comm'rs, 51 Ohio St. 3d 131, 554 N.E.2d 1324 (1990) (the "another adequate remedy" language of Rule 57 validates a declaratory judgment action even though there is an alternative but nonexclusive remedy available)

Permissible Use of Declaratory Judgment

Helman v. Hartford Fire Ins. Co., 105 Ohio App. 3d 617, 664 N.E.2d 991 (1995) (if, during discovery, an insurer uncovers facts that it believes absolve it of the duty to defend, the insurer may commence a declaratory judgment action to adjudicate its duty to defend, even if the underlying complaint alleges conduct within the scope of coverage within the policy)

CHAPTER 58

Rule 58. Entry of Judgment

Rule 58 reads as follows:

(A) Preparation; entry; effect. Subject to the provisions of Rule 54(B), upon a general verdict of a jury, upon a decision announced, or upon the determination of a periodic payment plan, the court shall promptly cause the judgment to be prepared and, the court having signed it, the clerk shall thereupon enter it upon the journal. A judgment is effective only when entered by the clerk upon the journal.

(B) Notice of filing. When the court signs a judgment, the court shall endorse thereon a direction to the clerk to serve upon all parties not in default for failure to appear notice of the judgment and its date of entry upon the journal. Within three days of entering the judgment upon the journal, the clerk shall serve the parties in a manner prescribed by Civ. R. 5(B) and note the service in the appearance docket. Upon serving the notice and notation of the service in the appearance docket, the service is complete. The failure of the clerk to serve notice does not affect the validity of the judgment or the running of the time for appeal except as provided in App. R. 4(A).

(C) Costs. Entry of the judgment shall not be delayed for the taxing of costs.

COMMENTARY

Rule 58 sets forth many of the provisions relating to judgments, including those concerning the entry of judgment. The entry of judgment should be distinguished from the rendition of judgment, which is governed by Rule 54. Accordingly, Rule 58 should be read in conjunction with these Rules.

Separate Document Requirement

Although Rule 58 does not expressly require that every judgment be embodied in a distinct document, such a practice is implied in the operation of the Rule. A judgment should be a short statement of the action taken by a judge in a particular case. Rule 58 requires that the judgment be set forth in a separate document from an opinion, order, or any other paper accompanying the rendition of the judgment. The purpose of this requirement is to clarify to the parties when the final judgment is entered, which is keyed to the running of the time for taking an appeal of the judgment. A party will be deemed to have waived the separate document requirement when the issue is not raised on appeal.

Duties of the Court

Under Rule 58, the court is required to provide for the preparation and signing of the judgment. In many instances, the court will direct the clerk to prepare the judgment, but the court may not direct the clerk to sign the judgment in lieu of the court. This requirement safeguards against the entry of erroneous or incomplete judgments. In rare cases, the court may direct the attorneys to prepare a judgment, which must thereafter be approved and signed by the court.

Duties of the Clerk

The Rule specifies two alternative sets of duties of the clerk with regard to judgments. First, the clerk is required to enter a properly prepared and signed judgment in the clerk's journal. Only the entry of judgment by the clerk will begin the running of the time in which an appeal may be taken, and a party may seek to enforce a judgment only after a judgment has been entered.

Second, the clerk is required to notify, in accordance with the provisions of Rule 5(B), all parties, except those parties against whom a default judgment has been entered, of the entry of judgment. The clerk is required to effect such service within three days of the entry of judgment, but the Rule provides that receipt of the notice by the parties is not necessary to complete the service. The validity of the judgment or the running of the time in which an appeal may be taken is not affected by the clerk's failure to provide the parties with notice of the entry of judgment except as provide by Ohio Rule of Appellate Procedure 4(A).

Entry Not Delayed by Motion for Costs

Rule 58(C) states that an entry of judgment and subsequent commencement of the time in which an appeal may be taken is not affected by motions for costs or fees under Rule 54. This provision was included to distinguish the practice in Ohio from that under Federal Rule 58, which allows the court to delay the finality of the judgment for appellate purposes until the matter of attorneys' fees is decided.

Illustration 58-1

Henry is awarded $2.5 million in a libel action against Munchausen Publishing. Before an appeal has been filed, Henry makes a motion to recover attorneys' fees under Rule 54. Under Rule 58, the finality of the judgment is not affected by Henry's motion, and the time period within which Munchausen Publishing may appeal the judgment is not tolled pending disposition of the motion.

ADDITIONAL AUTHORITY

11 Wright & Miller §§ 2781-2800

12 Moore's Federal Practice §§ 58.01-58.08

5 Anderson's Ohio Civil Practice §§ 182.06

2 Klein Darling AT 58-1 to AT 58-6

3 Terez F 15.6.1 to F 15.6.14

5 Oh. Jur. Pl. and Prac. Forms, ch. 71

6 Milligan Forms 58-1 to 58-13

2 Fink §§ 58-1 to 58-5

LEADING CASES

Formal Entry Required

City of Cleveland v. Trzebuckowski, 85 Ohio St. 3d 524, 709 N.E.2d 1148 (1999) (a conclusion or statement of judgment must be journalized formally to become appealable as a final order)

Form of Entry

In re Mitchell, 93 Ohio App. 3d 153, 637 N.E.2d 989 (1993) (a court must sign the entry of judgment; a rubber stamp is not sufficient to make it a final appealable order)

Juvenile Court Appeals

In re Anderson, 92 Ohio St. 3d 63, 748 N.E.2d 67 (2001) (the Rules of Civil Procedure and Appellate Procedure apply to the filing of a civil notice of appeal from juvenile court)

Non-Final Judgments

Horner v. Toledo Hosp., 94 Ohio App.3d 282, 640 N.E.2d 857 (1993) (Rule 58 does not require that all judgments and orders be entered on the journal; only judgments that are final orders are required to be entered on the journal)

Notation on Case File Ineffective for Entry of Judgment

State ex rel. White v. Dunkin, 80 Ohio St. 3d 335, 686 N.E.2d 267 (1998) (handwritten notation on a case file does not constitute journalization of the judgment by the clerk)

Notice of Filing

Lipscomb v. London Correctional Inst., 96 Ohio App. 3d 245, 644 N.E.2d 1079 (1994) (Appellate Rule 4(A) provides that the time for appeal of a civil case does not begin until the service of the notice under Rule 58(B) if notice is not provided within the three-day period set forth in the Rule)

Time for Filing Appeal

In re Anderson, 92 Ohio St. 3d 63, 748 N.E.2d 67 (2001) (thirty-day time limit for filing the notice of appeal does not begin to run until the later of: (1) the entry of the judgment or order appealed if the notice mandated by rule is served within three days of the entry of the judgment, or (2) service of the notice of judgment and its date of entry if service is not made on the party within the three-day period)

CHAPTER 59

Rule 59. New Trials

Rule 59 reads as follows:

(A) Grounds. A new trial may be granted to all or any of the parties and on all or part of the issues upon any of the following grounds:

(1) Irregularity in the proceedings of the court, jury, magistrate, or prevailing party, or any order of the court or magistrate, or abuse of discretion, by which an aggrieved party was prevented from having a fair trial;

(2) Misconduct of the jury or prevailing party;

(3) Accident or surprise which ordinary prudence could not have guarded against;

(4) Excessive or inadequate damages, appearing to have been given under the influence of passion or prejudice;

(5) Error in the amount of recovery, whether too large or too small, when the action is upon a contract or for the injury or detention of property;

(6) The judgment is not sustained by the weight of the evidence; however, only one new trial may be granted on the weight of the evidence in the same case;

(7) The judgment is contrary to law;

(8) Newly discovered evidence, material for the party applying, which with reasonable diligence he could not have discovered and produced at trial;

(9) Error of law occurring at the trial and brought to the attention of the trial court by the party making the application;

In addition to the above grounds, a new trial may also be granted in the sound discretion of the court for good cause shown.

When a new trial is granted, the court shall specify in writing the grounds upon which such new trial is granted.

On a motion for a new trial in an action tried without a jury, the court may open the judgment if one has been entered, take additional testimony, amend findings of fact and conclusions of law or make new findings and conclusions, and enter a new judgment.

(B) Time for motion. A motion for a new trial shall be served not later than fourteen days after the entry of the judgment.

(C) Time for serving affidavits. When a motion for a new trial is based upon affidavits they shall be served with the motion. The opposing party has fourteen days after such service within which to serve opposing affidavits, which period may be extended for an additional period not exceeding twenty-one days either by the court for good cause shown or by the parties by written stipulation. The court may permit supplemental and reply affidavits.

(D) **On initiative of court.** Not later than fourteen days after entry of judgment the court of its own initiative may order a new trial for any reason for which it might have granted a new trial on motion of a party.

The court may also grant a motion for a new trial, timely served by a party, for a reason not stated in the party's motion. In such case the court shall give the parties notice and an opportunity to be heard on the matter. The court shall specify the grounds for new trial in the order.

COMMENTARY

Rule 59 governs motions for new trials, which are typically made after the trial has ended and the judgment has been entered, though local rules may provide for the filing of these motions before a judgment has been entered. Rule 59 motions for a new trial must be *filed* within 14 days after the entry of judgment, and in this respect, are similar to motions for judgment notwithstanding the verdict under Rule 50(B). These motions are interrelated, a fact to which the cross-reference to Rule 59 in Rule 50(C) attests. Nonetheless, the standards of and procedures for motions made under Rules 59 and 50(B) are different, and should neither be confused by practitioners nor co-mingled by courts.

Extension of 14-Day Time Period Not Permitted

The 14-day time periods designated in subsections (B) and (D) of Rule 59 are strict deadlines that may not be extended by the court. Rule 6(B), which provides for the enlargement of time periods, expressly exempts these subsections from the operation of its provisions. However, the time period for the filing of affidavits under Rule 59(C) may be enlarged, as the language of the Rule expressly indicates.

Significantly, the 3-day extension of Rule 6(E) is applicable to motions under Rule 59 if the clerk notifies the parties of the entry of judgment by mail. However, Rule 59(B) expressly states that the 14-day period begins to run from the date that the judgment was entered on the docket, not the date on which the parties were notified of the entry. Because, under Rule 58(B), the clerk has up to 3 days from the entry of judgment in which to notify the parties, attorneys should be careful to ensure that motions under Rule 59 are made within the requisite 14-day period. The computations of time and final-day relief under Rule 6(A) also apply to Rule 59 motions.

Illustration 59-1

On December 14, Harris obtains a judgment against Darren for $10,000, and the clerk enters the judgment on the docket the following day, December 15. The clerk then notifies the parties of the entry of judgment by sending out notifications by mail on December 17. Under Rule 59(B), Darren has 14 days to file a motion for a new trial, but this period is extended for 3 days under Rule 6(E) because notification was made by mail. The resulting 17-day period begins on December 16, the day after the entry of judgment, and ends on January 1. However, because January 1 is a legal holiday under Rule 6(A), the deadline will be extended until the next day that is not a Saturday, Sunday, or legal holiday.

Motions to Alter or Amend a Judgment

Rule 59 does not provide for motions to alter or amend a judgment. A motion denominated as such should be treated either as a motion for a new trial under Rule 59, a motion to correct a clerical mistake under Rule 60(A), or a motion for post-judgment relief under Rule 60(B), depending upon the basis serving as the predicate for the motion. Whether such a motion is timely would therefore depend on its characterization as either a Rule 59 motion for a new trial or one of the two kinds of Rule 60 motions specified above.

Grounds for a New Trial

Rule 59 provides for the grant of a new trial by motion of a party or on the court's own initiative. The grounds for granting a new trial are specified in subsection (A)(1)-(9); however these are not exhaustive, and subsection (A) indicates that the court retains discretion to grant a new trial for good cause shown.

Motion for a New Trial Generally

Subsection (B) states that any party may make a motion for a new trial no later than 14 days after entry of the judgment. Subsection (D) states that a court, within the 14-day time period, may order a new trial on its own initiative for any reason that would justify the grant of a motion for a new trial under subsection (B). If a court chooses to order a new trial *sua sponte*, it must provide the parties with notice of its intention to do so and with an opportunity to address the adequacy or inadequacy of the judgment. The court must also specify the grounds for the order of a new trial if it chooses to do so on its own initiative.

Similarly, the situation where a court grants a motion for a new trial under subsection

(B) on grounds not advocated by the moving party is akin to ordering a new trial *sua sponte*. In this situation, the court must provide the parties with notice and an opportunity to be heard, and must also specify the grounds for the new trial in its order.

Motions for New Trials and Appeals

A motion for a new trial suspends the judgment in effect and tolls the time remaining in which an appeal may be taken. An appeal following the denial of a motion of a new trial should be an appeal on the judgment itself, not on the order denying the motion requesting the new trial. If no prejudice would result to the opposing party, an appeal from such an order should be regarded as harmless error and treated as an appeal on the judgment. When a motion for a new trial is denied, the appeals period begins again from the date of entry of the order of the court denying the motion.

Illustration 59-2

Assume on the facts of Illustration 59-1 that there is a 30-day period within which a party may appeal a final judgment. Because this period begins to run on December 16, Darren would thus have until January 14 to file an appeal. If, however, Darren makes a motion for a new trial on December 22, the 30-day time period will toll until the motion is decided. In many cases, a hearing on the motion will not be scheduled until after the original deadline for filing an appeal had no post-judgment motion been made.

Illustration 59-3

Assume on the facts of Illustration 59-1 that Darren files a timely motion for a new trial, which the court promptly denies and which Darren intends to appeal. If Darren mistakenly designates his petition as an appeal on the trial court's denial of his motion for a new trial, the appellate court should disregard the technical error and treat the appeal as if it had been made on the underlying judgment.

If the motion for a new trial under Rule 59 is granted, the judgment in effect is destroyed and an appeal may not be taken until a new judgment has been entered in accordance with the new trial.

Illustration 59-4

Assume on the facts of Illustration 59-1 that Darren files a timely motion for a new trial. If the court grants Darren's motion, the $10,000 judgment against Darren is destroyed and Harris may not appeal the grant of a new trial until a new judgment has been entered in accordance with the new trial.

There are two exceptions to the general rules governing motions for new trials discussed above. First, a prerogative writ allowing review of a grant of a motion for a new trial may be used in exceptional circumstances. Second, a grant of a motion for new trial in conjunction with a grant or denial of a motion for judgment notwithstanding the verdict under Rule 50(B) is actually a grant of a motion for a new trial conditioned upon the reversal of the grant or denial of the motion for judgment notwithstanding the verdict on appeal. Rule 50(C)(1) indicates that the grant of a motion for a new trial in such circumstances does not destroy the finality of judgment and allows an appeal to be taken immediately therefrom.

Illustration 59-5

Assume on the facts of Illustration 59-1 that Darren renews an earlier motion for judgment as a matter of law in accordance with Rule 50. In addition, Darren files a timely motion for a new trial in the event that his motion for judgment as a matter of law is denied. If the court denies his motion for judgment as a matter of law but conditionally grants the motion for a new trial, the grant of the motion for a new trial will not prevent Darren from taking an immediate appeal on the denial of the motion for judgment as a matter of law.

Affidavits with Motions for New Trials

When a party moves for a new trial under subsection (A), subsection (C) allows supporting and opposing affidavits to be filed with the motion or within the delineated time period thereafter. Although not expressly allowed under the Rule, a court should similarly allow supporting and opposing affidavits to be filed when it notifies the parties of its intention to order a new trial on its own initiative under subsection (D).

Motions Under Rule 59 and Rule 60 Distinguished

The primary difference between motions under Rule 59 and motions under Rule 60, other than the time period in which they may be made, is their effect on the finality of the judgment and whether they toll the time allowed for appeal. Motions for a new trial under Rule 59 automatically suspend the judgment and toll the time in which an appeal may be taken, at least until the motion is ruled upon.

In this sense, then, Rule 59 motions are not properly conceptualized as post-judgment motions, as the definition of a "judgment" under Rule 54 implies finality. Rule 59 motions are more properly conceived of as "motions for reconsideration as of right," requiring a court to review and re-examine the judgment that is the basis for the Rule 59 motion. Rule 60, motions, on the other hand, are true post-judgment motions, as they do not affect the finality of a judgment or the time in which an appeal of that judgment may be taken.

This distinction suggests that Rule 59 motions should be subject to less exacting scrutiny than Rule 60 motions, as the preference for finality in the federal courts and the availability of Rule 59 motions to parties in the first instance should indicate a narrower range of circumstances in which the grant of a Rule 60 motion is appropriate. The more extensive list of bases upon which a grant of a motion under Rule 59 is appropriate reflects this distinction.

ADDITIONAL AUTHORITY

11 WRIGHT & MILLER §§ 2801-2850
12 MOORE'S FEDERAL PRACTICE §§ 59.01-59.55
5 ANDERSON'S OHIO CIVIL PRACTICE §§ 184.01, 184.04, 184.05
2 KLEIN DARLING AT 59-1 to AT 59-43
3 TEREZ F 15.7.1 to F 15.7.8, F 20.1.1, F 20.2.1 to F 20.2.4, F 22.1.1 to F 22.1.4
5 OH. JUR. PL. AND PRAC. FORMS, ch. 72
6 MILLIGAN Forms 59-1 to 59-46
2 FINK §§ 59-1 to 59-25

LEADING CASES

Alternate Juror Misconduct

Koch v. Rist, 89 Ohio St. 3d 250, 730 N.E.2d 963 (2000) (it is proper for a trial court to order a new trial where an alternate juror accompanied jury into jury room during deliberations and remained there until jury reached its verdict after being dismissed at conclusion of trial)

Alternate Juror Not Permitted in Jury Room

Koch v. Rist, 89 Ohio St. 3d 250, 730 N.E.2d 963 (2000) (trial court acted within its discretion in ordering a new trial based on the extraordinary misconduct of alternate juror who, after being dismissed at conclusion of trial, accompanied jury into jury room during deliberations and remained there until jury reached its verdict)

Grounds for New Trial; Closing Argument

Sheets v. Norfolk S. Corp., 109 Ohio App. 3d 278, 671 N.E.2d 1364 (1996) (defendants were not entitled to new trial on the grounds that the plaintiffs' counsel made improper comments to the jury during closing arguments, as the defendant's counsel objected to nearly every comment and those objections were sustained)

Grounds for New Trial; Juror Conduct

Brooks v. Wilson, 98 Ohio App. 3d 301, 648 N.E.2d 552 (1994) (defendant dentist was not entitled to a new trial where a juror in a dental malpractice action questioned his dentist about issues raised in the case, as the juror obtained information already presented to him at trial), *appeal not allowed*, 71 Ohio St. 3d 1494, 646 N.E.2d 469 (1995)

Grounds for New Trial; Liability Uncontested

Iames v. Murphy, 106 Ohio App. 3d 627, 666 N.E.2d 1147 (1995) (a new trial on damages alone is usually granted only when liability is not contested)

Improper Role of Judge

Pangle v. Joyce, 76 Ohio St. 3d 389, 667 N.E.2d 1202 (1996) (in finding that the judgment rendered by the jury was contrary to existing law, the trial court impermissibly conducted a weighing of the evidence and an assessment of the credibility of witnesses)

Inadequacy or Excessiveness of Jury Verdict

Barto v. McKinley, 146 Ohio App. 3d 121, 765 N.E.2d 409 (2001) (a trial court's refusal to grant a motion for a new trial premised on the inadequacy or excessiveness of the verdict must address: (1) the amount of the verdict; and (2) whether the jury arrived at the award based on improper evidence, improper counsel, or influenced by other inappropriate conduct)

Proper Role of Judge

Bland v. Graves, 85 Ohio App. 3d 644, 620 N.E.2d 920 (1993) (judge's role in deciding whether to grant a new trial does not allow the judge to substitute his own judgment for that of the jury), *appeal after new trial*, 99 Ohio App. 3d 123, 650 N.E.2d 117 (1994), *and dismissed, appeal not allowed*, 72 Ohio St. 3d 1405, 647 N.E.2d 494 (1995)

Rehearing of Questions

Meyer v. Srivastava, 141 Ohio App. 3d 662, 752 N.E.2d 1011 (2001) (Rule 59 allows the trial judge to order a rehearing of the questions in the trial court under circumstances more favorable to their deliberate consideration than those attending the first investigation)

Standard on Appeal

Sharp v. Norfolk & W. Ry. Co., 72 Ohio St. 3d 307, 649 N.E.2d 1219 (decision on motion for new trial will be disturbed only upon a showing that a decision is unreasonable, unconscionable, or arbitrary), *order clarified*, 73 Ohio St. 3d 1429, 652 N.E.2d 801 (1995)

CHAPTER 60

Rule 60. Relief From Judgment or Order

Rule 60 reads as follows:

(A) Clerical mistakes. Clerical mistakes in judgments, orders or other parts of the record and errors therein arising from oversight or omission may be corrected by the court at any time on its own initiative or on the motion of any party and after such notice, if any, as the court orders. During the pendency of an appeal, such mistakes may be so corrected before the appeal is docketed in the appellate court, and thereafter while the appeal is pending may be so corrected with leave of the appellate court.

(B) Mistakes; inadvertence; excusable neglect; newly discovered evidence; fraud; etc. On motion and upon such terms as are just, the court may relieve a party or his legal representative from a final judgment, order or proceeding for the following reasons:

(1) mistake, inadvertence, surprise or excusable neglect;

(2) newly discovered evidence which by due diligence could not have been discovered in time to move for a new trial under Rule 59(B);

(3) fraud (whether heretofore denominated intrinsic or extrinsic), misrepresentation or other misconduct of an adverse party;

(4) the judgment has been satisfied, released or discharged, or a prior judgment upon which it is based has been reversed or otherwise vacated, or it is no longer equitable that the judgment should have prospective application; or

(5) any other reason justifying relief from the judgment.

The motion shall be made within a reasonable time, and for reasons (1), (2) and (3) not more than one year after the judgment, order or proceeding was entered or taken. A motion under this subdivision (B) does not affect the finality of a judgment or suspend its operation.

The procedure for obtaining any relief from a judgment shall be by motion as prescribed in these rules.

COMMENTARY

Correction of Clerical Mistakes

Rule 60(A) confers broad discretion on district judges to correct mistakes of a clerical nature that are found in judgments, orders, and other parts of a trial record. A clerical correction may be instigated by motion or on the court's own initiative, and notice to the parties of the correction is not required.

Motions under Rule 60(A) to correct a clerical error do not generally suspend the finality of the judgment and or toll the time period in which an appeal may be taken. If an appeal from a judgment has already been filed with the appellate court, the permission of the appeals court is required before a judge may correct a clerical error under Rule 60(A).

Motions for Post-Judgment Relief Generally

A party may also seek post-judgment relief from a judgment for the reasons listed in Rule 60(B). This list of reasons should not be regarded as an exclusive list of the bases upon which the grant of a motion for post-judgment relief would be proper, a point suggested by subsection (B)(5). The list is intended rather to indicate the grounds most commonly relied upon by parties in making motions for post-judgment relief.

Illustration 60-1

Susan commences a breach of contract action against Betsy, alleging that Betsy failed to deliver goods in a timely fashion as required by a written contract between the parties. After a cursory review of the evidence, the trial judge feels that Susan is entitled to judgment as a matter of law and wishes to enter summary judgment *sua sponte* in favor of Susan in accordance with Rule 56. However, the clerk of the court fails to notify Betsy of the judge's intention, and the requisite 14-day period for making post-judgment motions passes with nary a peep from Betsy. Under these circumstances, a motion under Rule 60(B)(1) is the appropriate course of action for Betsy, and the motion may be brought at any time within one year of the date of entry of the summary judgment.

A motion for post-judgment relief must be made within a reasonable time and, for a motion on grounds listed in clauses (1)-(3), within one year of the final judgment, order, or proceeding from which the relief is being sought. This one-year time period may not be enlarged under Rule 6(B), as Rule 6(B) expressly exempts Rule 60(B) from its operation. It should also be noted that fraud upon the court is distinguished from fraud on an opposing party as set forth in subsection (B)(3). A motion alleging fraud upon the court would fall under the residual clause in subsection (B)(5), and as such, is not subject to the one-year time limitation of fraud against an opposing party.

Appeal of Motions Under Rule 60

A grant or denial of a Rule 60(B) motion must be entered as a separate judgment according to Rule 58 and is appealable as any other judgment. However, the issue on appeal should be the grant or denial of the motion seeking post-judgment relief, not the judgment, order, or proceeding forming the basis of the Rule 60(B) motion.

Illustration 60-2

Assume on the facts of Illustration 60-1 that the judge denies Betsy's Rule 60(B)(1) motion. The court must enter the denial of the motion as a separate document from the predicate judgment. Betsy may choose to attack the court's denial of her Rule 60(B)(1) motion on appeal, but the court's grant of summary judgment in favor of Susan on substantive grounds is not a proper consideration for the appellate court at this time.

A motion for a rehearing of a Rule 60(B) motion is not restricted by the 14-day time period provisions of Rule 59; it is timely so long as it is made within the time for taking an appeal of the grant or denial of the original Rule 60(B) motion.

Illustration 60-3

Assume on the facts of Illustration 60-2 that the judge denies Betsy's Rule 60(B) motion on the grounds that it was made more than 14 days after the entry of judgment. Sensing that the judge has confused motions under Rule 60 and motions under Rule 59, Betsy is considering making a motion for a rehearing of the issue instead of appealing the issue directly to a higher court. Betsy would have more than 14 days to make this decision, as the motion for rehearing is not directed at the predicate judgment. Thus, the motion is not subject to the 14-day time limit of Rule 59 and may be made at any time within one year of the date of entry of the original summary judgment.

Motions Under Rule 60 and Rule 59 Distinguished

The primary difference between motions under Rule 60 and motions under Rule 59, other than the time period in which they may be made, is their effect on the finality of the judgment and whether they toll the time allowed for appeal. Motions for a new trial under Rule 59 automatically suspend the judgment and toll the time in which an appeal may be taken, at least until the motion is ruled upon.

In this sense, then, Rule 59 motions are not properly conceptualized as post-judgment motions, as the definition of a "judgment" under Rule 54 implies finality. Rule 59 motions are more properly conceived of as "motions for reconsideration as of right," requiring a court to review and re-examine the judgment that is the basis for the Rule 59 motion. Rule 60, motions, on the other hand, are true post-judgment motions, as they do not affect the finality of a judgment or the time in which an appeal of that judgment may be taken.

This distinction suggests that Rule 59 motions should be subject to less exacting scrutiny than Rule 60 motions, as the preference for finality in the federal courts and the availability of Rule 59 motions to parties in the first instance should indicate a narrower range of circumstances in which the grant of a Rule 60 motion is appropriate. The more extensive list of bases upon which a grant of a motion under Rule 59 is appropriate reflects this distinction.

ADDITIONAL AUTHORITY

11 Wright & Miller §§ 2851-2880
12 Moore's Federal Practice §§ 60.01-60.85
7 Moore's Federal Practice §§ 60.09-60.41
5 Anderson's Ohio Civil Practice §§ 184.01, 184.03
2 Klein Darling AT 60-1 to AT 60-71
3 Terez F 22.1.1 to F 22.1.2
5 Oh. Jur. Pl. and Prac. Forms, ch. 73
6 Milligan Forms 60-1 to 60-39
2 Fink §§ 60-1 to 60-13

LEADING CASES

Definition of Clerical Mistakes

State ex rel. Litty v. Leskovyansky, 77 Ohio St. 3d 97, 671 N.E.2d 236 (1996) ("clerical mistake" refers to a mistake or omission, mechanical in nature and apparent on the record, which does not involve a legal decision or a legal judgment)

Grounds for Relief; Change in Law

In re Estate of Reese, 106 Ohio App. 3d 340, 666 N.E.2d 252 (1995) (a change in controlling law before an action is final may be grounds for relief under Rule 60(B))

Grounds for Relief; Condition Not Fulfilled

In re Dunn, 102 Ohio App. 3d 217, 656 N.E.2d 1341 (1995) (a mother was entitled to relief under Rule 60(B) where her surrender of parental rights was with the agreement that a cousin would adopt the child, but the cousin later refused to adopt)

Grounds for Relief; Conduct of Judge

Chester Twp. v. Fraternal Order of Police, Ohio Labor Council, Inc., 102 Ohio App. 3d 404, 657 N.E.2d 348 (1995) (trial court's failure to read or consider a brief is not grounds for relief under Rule 60(B))

Grounds for Relief; Generally

Cuyahoga Support Enforcement Agency v. Guthrie, 84 Ohio St. 3d 437, 705 N.E.2d 318 (1999) (a moving party, to prevail on a Rule 60(b) motion, must demonstrate: (1) that the party has a meritorious defense or claim to present if relief is granted; (2) that the party is entitled to relief under one of the grounds stated in Rule 60(B)(1)-(5); and (3) the motion is made within a reasonable time, and, where the grounds of relief are Rule 60(B)(1)-(3), not more than one year after the judgment, order or proceeding was entered or taken)

Motions for Relief from Judgment; Timing

Strack v. Pelton, 70 Ohio St. 3d 172, 637 N.E.2d 914 (1994) (a motion for relief is not timely when it is filed more than one year after judgment and more than one year after new evidence upon which it is based became admissible)

Taylor v. Haven, 91 Ohio App. 3d 846, 633 N.E.2d 1197 (1993) (where a male appears without an attorney and admits paternity, but subsequent genetic tests exclude him as a father, a 12-year delay in bring an action for relief is not per se unreasonable)

Motion for Relief Not Substitute for Timely Appeal

Bragg v. Seidner, 92 Ohio St. 3d 87, 748 N.E.2d 532 (2001) (defendant could not use a motion for relief from judgment as a substitute for a timely appeal from judgment denying his petition for writ of habeas corpus and a motion to amend petition)

Paternity Tests

Cuyahoga Support Enforcement Agency v. Guthrie, 84 Ohio St. 3d 437, 705 N.E.2d 318 (1999) (results of a paternity test obtained after an adjudication of the existence of a parent-and-child relationship are not "newly discovered evidence" for purposes of motions under Rule 60(B))

Settlement Agreement Not Subject to Motion for Relief from Judgment

Colvin v. Abbey's Restaurant, Inc., 131 Ohio App. 3d 439, 722 N.E.2d 630 (1999) (a settlement agreement signed by the parties and filed with the court, followed by an order of dismissal, is generally not reviewable through a motion for relief from judgment)

Standard for Relief

State ex rel. Richard v. Seidner, 76 Ohio St. 3d 149, 666 N.E.2d 1134 (1996) (to obtain relief under Rule 60(B), the moving party must demonstrate that he has a meritorious defense, that he is entitled to relief under one of the grounds stated in the five subsections under the Rule, and that the motion is made within a reasonable time and, where the grounds for relief are one of the first three subsections, not more than one year after the judgment, order, or proceeding was entered or occurred)

Time for Appeal Not Extended by Motion for Relief from Judgment

State ex rel. Richard v. Cuyahoga Cty. Commrs., 89 Ohio St. 3d 205, 729 N.E.2d 755 (2000) (a motion for relief from judgment cannot be used as a means to extend the time for perfecting an appeal from the judgment or as a substitute for a timely appeal)

CHAPTER 61

Rule 61. Harmless Error

Rule 61 reads as follows:

No error in either the admission or the exclusion of evidence and no error or defect in any ruling or order or in anything done or omitted by the court or by any of the parties is ground for granting a new trial or for setting aside a verdict or for vacating, modifying or otherwise disturbing a judgment or order, unless refusal to take such action appears to the court inconsistent with substantial justice. The court at every stage of the proceeding must disregard any error or defect in the proceeding which does not affect the substantial rights of the parties.

COMMENTARY

The concept of harmless error is normally reserved for appellate review of issues. In general, an appellate court can reverse or vacate a judgment only if it finds error that would affect the outcome of the case and one or more substantial rights of the parties. Errors or defects in litigation procedures are said to be harmless when they do not justify a reproduction of the entire trial process. Rule 61 embodies this principle in the Civil Rules. In this respect, it is similar to Ohio Rule of Evidence 103(A), which incorporates the concept of harmless error, though not in express terms.

The concept of harmless error has limited application under the Civil Rules. The inclusion of Rule 61 immediately after the Rules governing motions for new trials and motions for post-judgment relief was undoubtedly intentional. When a court decides motions under Rules 59 and 60, it comes closest to playing a role akin to that of an appellate court. The notion of harmless error is thus an appropriate tool of review for district courts entertaining such motions.

ADDITIONAL AUTHORITY

11 Wright & Miller §§ 2881-2900
12 Moore's Federal Practice §§ 61.01-61.11
2 Klein Darling AT 61-1 to AT 61-1
5 Oh. Jur. Pl. and Prac. Forms, ch. 74

6 Milligan Forms 61-1 to 61-6

2 Fink §§ 61-1 to 61-5

LEADING CASES

Harmless Error; Issue Resolved by Jury

Continental Ins. Co. v. Whittington, 71 Ohio St. 3d 150, 642 N.E.2d 615 (1994) (any error in trial court's denial of a motion for summary judgment is moot or harmless if a subsequent trial on the same issues raised in the motion demonstrates that genuine issues of material fact support judgment in favor of the nonmoving party)

Harmless Error; Punitive Damage Claim

Sharp v. Norfolk & W. Ry. Co., 72 Ohio St. 3d 307, 649 N.E.2d 1219 (any error in allowing the estate of decedent to present a claim for punitive damages was harmless where no punitive damages were awarded), *order clarified*, 73 Ohio St. 3d 1429, 652 N.E.2d 801 (1995)

Jury Not Affected by Error

Craig v. Woodruff, 140 Ohio App. 3d 596, 748 N.E.2d 592 (2000) (generally, in order to find that substantial justice has been done to an appellant so as to prevent reversal of a judgment for errors occurring at the trial, the reviewing court must not only weigh the prejudicial effect of those errors but also determine that, if those errors had not occurred, the jury or other trier of the facts would probably have made the same decision)

Substantial Rights

Cappara v. Schibley, 85 Ohio St. 3d 403, 709 N.E.2d 117 (1999) (a court's error may be considered harmless only if it does not affect the substantial rights of the parties)

Substantive Rights Affected

Cunningham v. Goodyear Tire & Rubber Co., 104 Ohio App. 3d 385, 662 N.E.2d 73 (1995) (any error or defect in trial proceedings that does not affect a party's substantial right must be disregarded)

CHAPTER 62

Rule 62. Stay of Proceedings to Enforce a Judgment

Rule 62 reads as follows:

(A) **Stay on motion for new trial or for judgment.** In its discretion and on such conditions for the security of the adverse party as are proper, the court may stay the execution of any judgment or stay any proceedings to enforce judgment pending the disposition of a motion for a new trial, or of a motion for relief from a judgment or order made pursuant to Rule 60, or of a motion for judgment notwithstanding the verdict made pursuant to Rule 50.

(B) **Stay upon appeal.** When an appeal is taken the appellant may obtain a stay of execution of a judgment or any proceedings to enforce a judgment by giving an adequate supersedeas bond. The bond may be given at or after the time of filing the notice of appeal. The stay is effective when the supersedeas bond is approved by the court.

(C) **Stay in favor of the government.** When an appeal is taken by this state or political subdivision, or administrative agency of either, or by any officer thereof acting in his representative capacity and the operation or enforcement of the judgment is stayed, no bond, obligation or other security shall be required from the appellant.

(D) **Power of appellate court not limited.** The provisions in this rule do not limit any power of an appellate court or of a judge or justice thereof to stay proceedings during the pendency of an appeal or to suspend, modify, restore, or grant an injunction during the pendency of an appeal or to make any order appropriate to preserve the status quo or the effectiveness of the judgment subsequently to be entered.

(E) **Stay of judgment as to multiple claims or multiple parties.** When a court has ordered a final judgment under the conditions stated in Rule 54(B), the court may stay enforcement of that judgment until the entering of a subsequent judgment or judgments and may prescribe such conditions as are necessary to secure the benefit thereof to the party in whose favor the judgment is entered.

COMMENTARY

Rule 62 governs stays of proceedings that may be used to enforce a judgment, including executions of judgments. The Rule specifies the situations in which a court may grant various stays of proceedings. Unlike judgments in the federal system, judgments in Ohio are not subject to an automatic 10-day stay following the entry of judgment by the clerk. Parties may seek to enforce judgments entered in their favor immediately.

Stay of Proceedings on Certain Motions

Subsection (A) provides a judge with the authority to grant a stay of proceedings to enforce a judgment upon the filing of three kinds of motions: (1) whenever a motion for a new trial is made under Rule 59; (2) whenever a motion for post-judgment relief is made under Rule 60; and (3) whenever a motion for judgment notwithstanding the verdict is made under Rule 50. A bond or other security is not required to effect a stay on these motions, but may be required by the court in its discretion.

Stays of Judgment on Appeal; Bond Requirement

Subsection (B) allows an appellant to obtain a stay of a judgment pending appeal by filing a supersedeas bond in an amount sufficient to protect the opposing party. Although the language of the Rule appears to require a supersedeas bond to effect the stay, courts have dispensed with the bond requirement where, in the court's discretion, a bond was not necessary to protect the interests of the adverse parties. Subsection (C) exempts the State and its properly designated agents and officers from the supersedeas bond requirement.

Relationship to Stays By Appellate Courts

The power of the court to grant a stay neither diminishes nor enlarges the powers of the appellate courts to grant stays of judgments under the Rules of Appellate Procedure, a point expressly made in subsection (D). Ohio Rule of Appellate Procedure 7(A) provides that a stay of judgment should be sought from the district court before seeking a stay from the appellate court. The trial court retains its power over stays of judgment until the appellate court speaks on the matter.

Stays on Multiple Claims of Parties

Subsection (E) is arguably repetitive, but it makes the express point that a judgment on a claim involving multiple claims or multiple parties under Rule 54(B) may be stayed under conditions that the court deems necessary.

ADDITIONAL AUTHORITY

11 Wright & Miller §§ 2901-2920

12 MOORE'S FEDERAL PRACTICE §§ 62.01-62.332

2 KLEIN DARLING AT 62-1 to AT 62-5

3 TEREZ F 19.7.1 to F 19.7.4

5 OH. JUR. PL. AND PRAC. FORMS, ch. 75

6 MILLIGAN Forms 62-1 to 62-18.2

2 FINK §§ 62-1 to 62-6

LEADING CASES

Bureau of Workers' Compensation Not Entitled to Stay

Baker v. Ohio Bur. of Workers' Comp., 140 Ohio App. 3d 766, 749 N.E.2d 333 (2000) (Bureau of Workers' Compensation was not entitled to a stay of judgment pending appeal)

Mandamus Action; Party Entitled to Stay of Judgment

State ex rel. State Fire Marshal v. Curl, 87 Ohio St. 3d 568, 722 N.E.2d 73 (2000) (party was entitled to a stay of judgment as a matter of right pending appeal in a mandamus action; accordingly, the trial court lacked jurisdiction to either enforce the judgment or conduct contempt proceedings)

Stay of Judgment; Burden

Anderson v. Scherer, 97 Ohio App. 3d 753, 647 N.E.2d 545 (1994) (if the party seeking finality demonstrates no just reason for delay exists, the party seeking a stay of the judgment has the burden of demonstrating a reason as to why execution should be delayed), *appeal not allowed*, 71 Ohio St. 3d 1480, 645 N.E.2d 1260 (1995)

Stay Pending Appeal

Hagood v. Gail, 105 Ohio App. 3d 780, 664 N.E.2d 1373 (1995) (issuance of stay order has no effect on appealed judgment that has been fully executed), *appeal not allowed*, 74 Ohio St. 3d 1499, 659 N.E.2d 314 (1996)

CHAPTER 63

Rule 63. Disability of a Judge

Rule 63 reads as follows:

(A) During trial. If for any reason the judge before whom a jury trial has commenced is unable to proceed with the trial, another judge, designated by the administrative judge, or in the case of a single-judge division by the chief justice of the supreme court, may proceed with and finish the trial upon certifying in the record that he has familiarized himself with the record of the trial; but if such other judge is satisfied that he cannot adequately familiarize himself with the record, he may in his discretion grant a new trial.

(B) [After verdict or findings.] If for any reason the judge before whom an action has been tried is unable to perform the duties to be performed by the court after a verdict is returned or findings of fact and conclusions of law are filed, another judge designated by the administrative judge, or in the case of a single-judge division by the Chief Justice of the Supreme Court, may perform those duties; but if such other judge is satisfied that he cannot perform those duties, he may in his discretion grant a new trial.

COMMENTARY

Rule 63 provides for the substitution of a judge who has become unable to proceed in a trial due to disability, disqualification, or any other reason for withdrawal. Substitution of judges is often necessary to avoid the inconvenience of beginning a trial anew when the judge becomes unable to proceed.

Disability During Trial

Subsection (A) provides for the substitution of a judge who is unable to proceed in a jury trial. Before the substitution has been made, the Rule requires that the new judge certify familiarity with the record. If, however, the replacement judge is unable to do so, a new trial may be granted at the court's discretion. As the Rule does not provide for the substitution of judges in bench trials, and appropriately so, new trials should be granted in these situations.

Disability After Verdict or Findings

Subsection (B) provides for the substitution of a judge after a verdict has been returned or findings of fact and conclusions of law have been filed. The replacement judge's role is generally ministerial at this point in the trial, although a new trial may be granted at the judge's discretion if the judge cannot complete the necessary duties.

ADDITIONAL AUTHORITY

11 Wright & Miller §§ 2921-2930
12 Moore's Federal Practice §§ 63.01-63.74
2 Klein Darling AT 63-1 to AT 63-4
5 Oh. Jur. Pl. and Prac. Forms, ch. 76
6 Milligan Forms 63-1 to 63-13
2 Fink §§ 63-1 to 63-5

LEADING CASES

Actions of Successor Judge

Potocnik v. Sifco Indus., 103 Ohio App. 3d 560, 660 N.E.2d 510 (1995) (actions of a successor judge are voidable where the entry reassigning a case does not provide a justification for the transfer; reassignment is appropriate only when the assigned judge has a long-term absence or there is a need for immediate action in the case)

Inapplicable After Testimony Is Heard

Vergon v. Vergon, 87 Ohio App. 3d 639, 622 N.E.2d 1111 (1993) (Rule 63 does not apply to a bench trial where a judge was substituted after testimony was heard but prior to judgment or findings)

Inapplicable To Magistrates

Hartt v. Munobe, 67 Ohio St. 3d 3, 615 N.E.2d 617 (1993) (Rule 63 does not apply where a judge refers a case to a magistrate)

Journalized Entry Does Not Indicate Succession of Judge

In re Hlavsa, 139 Ohio App. 3d 871, 745 N.E.2d 1144 (2000) (administrative judge who signed notation journalizing an entry was acting ex officio as a clerk and, thus, filing and journalization notation on judgment entry was not a manifestation of another judge's intent to succeed to judgment of judge who had been suspended from the practice of law after signing judgment entry)

VIII
PROVISIONAL AND FINAL REMEDIES

CHAPTER 64

Rule 64. Seizure of Person or Property

Rule 64 reads as follows:

At the commencement of and during the course of an action, all remedies providing for seizure of person or property for the purpose of securing satisfaction of the judgment ultimately to be entered in the action are available under the circumstances and in the manner provided by law. The remedies thus available include arrest, attachment, garnishment, replevin, sequestration, and other corresponding or equivalent remedies, however designated and regardless of whether the remedy is ancillary to an action or must be obtained by independent action.

COMMENTARY

Rule 64, in conjunction with Rule 65, governs provisional remedies in Ohio courts. These remedies are intended to preserve the status quo or existing situation at the time a party brings an action. They are necessary to ensure that sufficient funds or resources of the opposing party are available to a party should the party eventually prevail and obtain a judgment in its favor.

Remedies Under Applicable Law Remain Available

Rule 64 provides simply that all provisional remedies under Ohio law, or the law of the jurisdiction in which the property in question is located, remain available to a party. The specific remedies, as well as the procedures required for the imposition of these remedies, are typically governed by statute. Rule 64 simply preserves these remedies to all parties.

ADDITIONAL AUTHORITY

11 Wright & Miller §§ 2931-2940
13 Moore's Federal Practice §§ 64.01-64.19
6 Anderson's Ohio Civil Practice §§ 204.01-204.51
2 Klein Darling AT 64-1 to AT 64-1
3 Terez F 19.2.1 to F 19.2.10
5 Oh. Jur. Pl. and Prac. Forms, ch. 77

6 MILLIGAN Forms 64-1 to 64-89
2 FINK §§ 64-1 to 64-1

LEADING CASES

Garnishment

> ***Toledo Trust Co. v. Niedzwiecki***, 89 Ohio App. 3d 745, 627 N.E.2d 616 (1993) (property held by third party is subject to garnishment to satisfy judgment debts when, at the time of the service of garnishment order, the judgment debtor has a right or title to the property)

CHAPTER 65

Rule 65. Injunctions

Rule 65 reads as follows:

(A) **Temporary restraining order; notice; hearing; duration.** A temporary restraining order may be granted without written or oral notice to the adverse party or his attorney only if

(1) it clearly appears from specific facts shown by affidavit or by the verified complaint that immediate and irreparable injury, loss or damage will result to the applicant before the adverse party or his attorney can be heard in opposition, and

(2) the applicant's attorney certifies to the court in writing the efforts, if any, which have been made to give notice and the reasons supporting his claim that notice should not be required.

The verification of such affidavit or verified complaint shall be upon the affiant's own knowledge, information or belief; and so far as upon information and belief, shall state that he believes this information to be true. Every temporary restraining order granted without notice shall be filed forthwith in the clerk's office; shall define the injury and state why it is irreparable and why the order was granted without notice; and shall expire by its terms within such time after entry, not to exceed fourteen days, as the court fixes, unless within the time so fixed the order, for good cause shown, is extended for one like period or unless the party against whom the order is directed consents that it may be extended for a longer period. The reasons for the extension shall be set forth in the order of extension. In case a temporary restraining order is granted without notice, the motion for a preliminary injunction shall be set down for hearing at the earliest possible time and takes precedence over all matters except older matters of the same character. When the motion comes on for hearing the party who obtained the temporary restraining order shall proceed with the application for a preliminary injunction and, if he does not do so, the court shall dissolve the temporary restraining order. On two days' notice to the party who obtained the temporary restraining order without notice or on such shorter notice to that party as the court may prescribe, the adverse party may appear and move its dissolution or modification, and in that event the court shall proceed to hear and determine such motion as expeditiously as the ends of justice require.

(B) Preliminary injunction.

    (1) Notice. No preliminary injunction shall be issued without reasonable notice to the adverse party. The application for preliminary injunction may be included in the complaint or may be made by motion.

    (2) Consolidation of hearing with trial on merits. Before or after the commencement of the hearing of an application for a preliminary injunction, the court may order the trial of the action on the merits to be advanced and consolidated with the hearing of the application. Even when this consolidation is not ordered, any evidence received upon an application for a preliminary injunction which would be admissible upon the trial on the merits becomes part of the record on the trial and need not be repeated upon the trial. This subdivision (B)(2) shall be so construed and applied as to save to the parties any rights they may have to trial by jury.

(C) Security. No temporary restraining order or preliminary injunction is operative until the party obtaining it gives a bond executed by sufficient surety, approved by the clerk of the court granting the order or injunction, in an amount fixed by the court or judge allowing it, to secure to the party enjoined the damages he may sustain, if it is finally decided that the order or injunction should not have been granted.

The party obtaining the order or injunction may deposit, in lieu of such bond, with the clerk of the court granting the order or injunction, currency, cashier's check, certified check or negotiable government bonds in the amount fixed by the court.

Before judgment, upon reasonable notice to the party who obtained an injunction, a party enjoined may move the court for additional security. If the original security is found to be insufficient, the court may vacate the injunction unless, in reasonable time, sufficient security is provided.

No security shall be required of this state or political subdivision, or agency of either, or of any officer thereof acting in his representative capacity.

A surety upon a bond or undertaking under this rule submits himself to the jurisdiction of the court and irrevocably appoints the clerk of the court as his agent upon whom any papers affecting his liability on the bond or undertaking may be served. His liability as well as the liability of the party obtaining the order or injunction may be enforced by the court without jury on motion without the necessity for an independent action. The motion and such notice of the motion as the court prescribes may be served on the clerk of the court who shall forthwith mail copies to the persons giving the security if their addresses are known.

(D) Form and scope of restraining order or injunction. Every order granting an injunction and every restraining order shall set forth the reasons for its issuance; shall be specific in terms; shall describe in reasonable detail, and not by reference to the complaint or other document, the act or acts sought to be restrained; and is binding upon the parties to the action, their officers, agents, servants, employees, attorneys and those persons in active concert or participation with them who receive actual notice of the order whether by personal service or otherwise.

(E) Service of temporary restraining orders and injunctions. Restraining orders which are granted ex parte shall be served in the manner provided for service of process under Rule 4 through Rule 4.3 and Rule 4.6, or in a manner directed by order of the court. If the restraining order is granted upon a pleading or motion accompanying a pleading the order may be served with the process and pleading. When service is made pursuant to Rule 4 through Rule 4.3 and Rule 4.6, the sheriff or the person designated by order of the court shall forthwith make his return.

Restraining orders or injunctions which are granted with notice may be served in the manner provided under Rule 4 through Rule 4.3 and Rule 4.6, in the manner provided in Rule 5 or in the manner designated by order of the court. When service is made pursuant to Rule 4 through Rule 4.3 and Rule 4.6, the sheriff or the person designated by order of the court shall forthwith make his return.

COMMENTARY

Rule 65, in conjunction with Rule 64, governs provisional remedies in Ohio courts. These remedies are intended to preserve the status quo or existing situation at the time an action is commenced. They are necessary to ensure that sufficient funds or resources of the opposing party are available to a party should the party eventually prevail and obtain a judgment in its favor or to preserve the status quo to ensure the efficacy of the final remedy.

Preliminary Injunctions and TROs Generally; Contempt

Rule 65 governs preliminary injunctions and temporary restraining orders (TROs), the two historical tools used by courts in equity to impose provisional remedies. These orders usually command a party to do or refrain from doing a specific act. Preliminary injunctions and TROs are enforceable through the court's contempt power, and are served in the manner provided for service of process under Rules 4-4.3 and Rule 4.6 when granted *ex parte*. When such orders are granted with notice, subsection (E) provides that service on the parties may also be made as under Rule 5 or as ordered by the court.

Civil contempt sanctions are designed to ensure compliance with the order through an appropriate form of coercion, usually in the form of fines levied upon the offending party. Criminal contempt sanctions are also designed to ensure compliance with the order, but they have the additional purpose of vindicating the court's authority through an appropriate form of punishment, usually in the form of prison sentences. Of course, when criminal contempt sanctions are imposed, the more stringent burdens of proof and procedural protections afforded to a criminal defendant apply.

Preliminary Injunctions and TROs Distinguished

Preliminary injunctions and TROs have different purposes, and one should not be used as a substitute for the other. The procedural differences in obtaining these orders specified in Rule 65 illuminate these differences. TROs are a "stopgap" measure; they are designed to preserve the status quo only until a hearing on a preliminary injunction is possible. Thus, TROs expire automatically 14 days after their issuance, unless the court orders a longer period for cause shown or the parties agree to a longer period. Preliminary injunctions typically remain in effect until the action is resolved.

Illustration 65-1

Amanda's Construction Company arrives at Lorin's home planning to bulldoze the land and prepare it for the construction of a new zoo. Lorin's attempts to convince the employees that they are at the wrong location are ignored, and the workers continue to make preparations to grade the land. Lorin is faced with an emergency situation in which there is no time to provide notice and an opportunity for Amanda's Construction Company to be heard. Thus, Lorin should be allowed to obtain a temporary restraining order that precludes the further development of his land until a hearing can be arranged. If the court grants a temporary restraining order, a hearing will be scheduled to determine whether a preliminary injunction should be issued or whether Amanda's Construction Company should be allowed to proceed with its work.

Purposes of Preliminary Injunctions and TROs

The purposes of preliminary injunctions and TROs are also distinct from those attending other kinds of provisional remedies that may be available to a party under Rule 64, such as attachment and garnishment, and should not be used as substitutes for them. Although all provisional remedies are intended to preserve the status quo, preliminary injunctions and TROs should not be issued merely to ensure that sufficient assets of the defendant are available to satisfy a judgment. Accordingly, the issuance of a TRO requires a demonstration of "immediate and irreparable injury, loss, or damage."

Illustration 65-2

Under the facts of Illustration 65-1, Lorin is threatened with an "irreparable injury" because monetary damages cannot adequately compensate him for some of the value inherent in the land, *e.g.*, the home may have been a family homestead for five generations. Simply insuring that Amanda's Construction Company may have sufficient assets to build a replacement house may be little consolation to Lorin.

Procedure for Granting a TRO

Subsection (A) details both the requirements that must be met before the issuance of a TRO and the contents of a TRO. As TROs are unusual in that they may be granted *ex parte*, the Rule contains a number of safeguards to attempt to ensure that the order is not granted erroneously: the 14-day time period limitation on the order; the immediacy and irreparability of the injury, loss, or damage; the fact that the injury, loss, or damage must "clearly appear [ ] from specific facts" in the affidavit or complaint; a showing of the reasons for the failure to provide notice to the adverse party; and the opportunity for the adverse party to appear before the expiration of the time period and to move to dissolve or modify the TRO.

TROs that extend beyond the original 14-day time period are generally treated as preliminary injunctions, and as such, should be appealable as interlocutory orders. Any additional standards that apply to preliminary injunctions also must be met. However, if the adverse party consents to an extension of the time period of a TRO, the order should not be viewed as having been converted into a preliminary injunction for purposes of appeal.

Standard for Preliminary Injunctions

Curiously, the precise standard to be used by a court in granting a motion for a preliminary injunction is not specified in Rule 65. However, it may be significant to inquire whether a kind of "irreparable injury," similar to that required in a motion for a TRO, will result if the motion is denied. The movant should also be required to demonstrate some likelihood of succeeding on the merits of the case. In addition, courts have considered the weight of possible injury to the movant compared to that of the non-movant and the threat of harm to the public interest if the injunction is issued.

Procedural Differences Between Preliminary Injunctions and TROs

The primary distinction between preliminary injunctions and TROs is that preliminary injunctions may be granted only after notice to the adverse party, a condition specified in subsection (B)(1), whereas TROs can be granted *ex parte*. A hearing on the application for a preliminary injunction is also contemplated by subsection (B)(2). However, the court must find appropriate findings of fact and conclusions of law on the matter sufficient to rule upon on appeal, and a hearing is the usual vehicle for achieving this. Hearings on preliminary injunctions may also be required by local rule.

Procedure for Deciding on Preliminary Injunction

Subsection (A) requires that, when a TRO is granted *ex parte*, hearings on motions for preliminary injunctions must be held at the earliest possible time and take precedence over all matters except for other hearings on preliminary injunctions. Subsection (B)(2) provides that the court, in its discretion, may advance the trial date and consolidate the trial with a hearing on a preliminary injunction. Such a consolidation is advantageous when it appears to the court that the issues to be resolved at the hearing on the preliminary injunction are concomitant with or overlap those to be determined at trial. If consolidation is ordered by the court, however, the parties must be given a full opportunity to present any and all evidence in the action. Subsection (B)(2) goes on to provide that, if consolidation is not ordered by the court, the parties need not re-present evidence admitted at the hearing on the preliminary injunction at the trial, unless such admission would destroy a party's rights to a jury trial.

Security

Subsection (C) clearly requires that no preliminary injunction or TRO can be granted unless a bond or other security is provided by the movant. The kind of security, as well as the amount required, is within the discretion of the court. The court also has the discretion to dispense with the necessity of a bond or other security, but should do so only after a consideration of the specific facts and circumstances involved.

The third paragraph of subsection (C) provides for a motion to post additional security. Such a motion may be necessary where the assets subject to the preliminary injunction or TRO have appreciated rapidly or where the original security is determined to have been insufficient.

The final paragraph of subsection (C) is analogous to Federal Rule 65.1. It guarantees that a party seeking to recover on a bond need not proceed against the surety through an independent action. The bond may be enforced against the surety by motion. Subsection (C), by its express terms, applies only to those bonds issued to secure property subject to a TRO or preliminary injunction.

Subsection (C) states that the clerk of the district court is appointed as agent for the surety upon whom any papers affecting the surety's liability may be served. The clerk is then required to forward copies of these papers to the surety. This procedure ensures that a party can easily and expeditiously recover on a bond when appropriate.

Form and Scope of Preliminary Injunctions and TROs

Subsection (D) generally sets forth the form and scope of the preliminary injunctions and TROs. In conjunction with the provisions of subsection (A), subsection (D) provides for specificity and exactitude in the terms and granting of a preliminary injunction or TRO.

ADDITIONAL AUTHORITY

11 WRIGHT & MILLER §§ 2941-2980

13 MOORE'S FEDERAL PRACTICE §§ 65.01-65.81

6 ANDERSON'S OHIO CIVIL PRACTICE §§ 206.01-260.13

2 KLEIN DARLING AT 65-1 to AT 65-7

3 TEREZ F 4.21.1, F 9.3.1 to F 9.3.6

5 OH. JUR. PL. AND PRAC. FORMS, ch. 78

6 MILLIGAN Forms 65-1 to 65-63

2 FINK §§ 65-1 to 65-7

OHIO LITIGATION CHECKLISTS, Pleading and Process, §§ 1-5

LEADING CASES

Bond Proceeding Not Affected by Dismissal of Action

Miller-Valentine Constr., Inc. v. Iron Workers Local Union No. 55, 138 Ohio App. 3d 134, 740 N.E.2d 701 (2000) (fact that the case was dismissed with the consent of the party against whom a temporary restraining order was issued did not affect the ability of that party to file a motion for assessment of damages on the injunction bond and seek the requisite judicial determination during that proceeding)

Consolidating Hearing with Trial

Strah v. Lake Cty. Humane Soc'y, 90 Ohio App. 3d 822, 631 N.E.2d 165 (1993) (a party is not prejudiced by impropriety in consolidating a hearing on a motion for a preliminary injunction with a trial on the merits where the party does not object and is fully prepared to proceed with trial)

Hearing Not Required on TRO Application

Hohmann, Boukis & Curtis Co., L.P.A. v. Brunn Law Firm Co., L.P.A., 138 Ohio App. 3d 693, 742 N.E.2d 192 (2000) (trial court was not required to hold hearing on application for temporary restraining order (TRO), and thus, trial court did not err in failing to receive evidence and testimony prior to denying application)

Purpose of Preliminary injunctions

Yudin v. Knight Indus., 109 Ohio App. 3d 437, 672 N.E.2d 265 (1996) (the purpose of a preliminary injunction is to preserve the status quo of the parties pending final adjudication of case upon merits)

Ruling on Issue Not Appealable Unless Injunction Is Granted

Coon v. Barnes, 95 Ohio App. 3d 349, 642 N.E.2d 449 (1994) (an order simply granting summary judgment for the plaintiff in an action seeking injunctive relief, without providing any remedy establishing the respective rights and obligations of the parties to permit compliance or enforcement, is not a final appealable order)

Scope of Restraining Orders and Injunctions

Yocono's Restaurant, Inc. v. Yocono, 100 Ohio App. 3d 11, 651 N.E.2d 1347 (1994) (an injunction covering a 15-mile radius from a specific point is not ambiguous, as it requires reference to a map)

Specificity in TRO or Injunction Required

Natl. Equity Title Agency, Inc. v. Rivera, 147 Ohio App. 3d 246, 770 N.E.2d 76 (2001) (the rule requiring a restraining order or injunction to be specific in terms and describe in reasonable detail the act or acts sought to be restrained requires sufficient detail to advise the defendants of the conduct which they are prohibited from engaging in)

Standard for Injunction; Comparative Injury Rule

Rite Aid of Ohio, Inc. v. Marc's Variety Store, Inc., 93 Ohio App. 3d 407, 638 N.E.2d 1056 (1994) (under the "comparative injury or balance of inconvenience rule," a permanent injunction will not be granted where it would cause more harm than it would avoid or where it would result in the impairment of an important public interest)

Standard for Injunction; Discretion of Court

Danis Clarkco Landfill Co. v. Clark Cty. Solid Waste Mgt. Dist., 73 Ohio St. 3d 590, 653 N.E.2d 646 (1995) (the trial court's decision to grant or deny an injunction is a matter solely within the discretion of the court)

TRO Procedure in Rule Supersedes Statutory Procedure

Cosgrove v. Grogan, 141 Ohio App. 3d 733, 753 N.E.2d 256 (2001) (an *ex parte* temporary restraining order (TRO) is available under Rule 65 despite statutory language setting forth separate procedure in a specific kinds of cases)

TROs; Immediate and Irreparable Harm

Hale v. Columbus, 63 Ohio App. 3d 368, 578 N.E.2d 881 (injunctive relief to enjoin enforcement of an ordinance is properly denied where the ordinance is determined to be a constitutional exercise of police power and the parties challenging the ordinance are unable to demonstrate that they would suffer immediate and irreparable harm), *jurisdictional motion allowed*, 56 Ohio St. 3d 708, 565 N.E.2d 604 (1990), *and cause dismissed*, 58 Ohio St. 3d 704, 569 N.E.2d 513 (1991)

TROs; Transformation to Injunctions

Turoff v. Stefanac, 16 Ohio App. 3d 227, 475 N.E.2d 189 (1984) (where both parties had notice of, were present at, and participated in the temporary restraining order hearing, the court may treat the application for a temporary restraining order as an application for a preliminary injunction)

CHAPTER 66

Rule 66. Receivers

Rule 66 reads as follows:

An action wherein a receiver has been appointed shall not be dismissed except by order of the court. Receiverships shall be administered in the manner provided by law and as provided by rules of court.

COMMENTARY

Rule 66 recognizes receivership as an additional provisional remedy that may be available to a party under Ohio law. The purpose of the Rule is to render the Rules to all actions involving receivers appointed under Ohio statutory law. The Rule also provides that an action involving a receiver cannot be settled by the parties and may be dismissed only by order of the court.

ADDITIONAL AUTHORITY

12 Wright & Miller §§ 2981-2990
13 Moore's Federal Practice §§ 66.01-66.08
6 Anderson's Ohio Civil Practice §§ 205.01-205.06
2 Klein Darling AT 66-1
3 Terez F 19.5.1, F 19.5.2
5 Oh. Jur. Pl. and Prac. Forms, ch. 79
7 Milligan Forms 66-1 to 66-44
2 Fink § 66-1

CHAPTER 67

Rule 67. [Reserved]

CHAPTER 68

Rule 68. Offer of Judgment

Rule 68 reads as follows:

An offer of judgment by any party, if refused by an opposite party, may not be filed with the court by the offering party for purposes of a proceeding to determine costs.

This rule shall not be construed as limiting voluntary offers of settlement made by any party.

COMMENTARY

Rule 68 is unusual in that it should be viewed more as a "non-Rule" than as a Rule. It contains no affirmative provisions, and was instead presumably intended to make explicit that the Ohio Supreme Court has not adopted the procedure to encourage offers of judgment by a party as set forth in Federal Rule 68.

Of course, offers of judgment or settlement offers are permitted and even encouraged in Ohio as a means of resolving disputes without consuming valuable judicial resources. Rule 68 simply provides that such offers that are rejected are not relevant in any proceeding to determine costs.

ADDITIONAL AUTHORITY

12 WRIGHT & MILLER §§ 3001-3010
13 MOORE'S FEDERAL PRACTICE §§ 68.01-68.10
2 KLEIN DARLING AT 68-1
3 TEREZ F 11.1.1, F 11.1.2
5 OH. JUR. PL. AND PRAC. FORMS, ch. 80
7 MILLIGAN Forms 68-1 to 68-2
2 FINK § 68-1

CHAPTER 69

Rule 69. Execution

Rule 69 reads as follows:

Process to enforce a judgment for the payment of money shall be a writ of execution, unless the court directs otherwise. The procedure on execution, in proceedings supplementary to and in aid of a judgment, and in proceedings on and in aid of execution shall be as provided by law. In aid of the judgment or execution, the judgment creditor or his successor in interest when that interest appears of record, may also obtain discovery from any person, including the judgment debtor, in the manner provided in these rules.

COMMENTARY

Rule 69 states that the enforcement of a judgment shall be through a writ of execution, the procurement of which is governed by Ohio statutory law. The Rule also makes available in any action to enforce a judgment all discovery mechanisms as provided in Rules 29-36 to any person who has previously secured a judgment. These discovery tools may be beneficial in situations where the property with which a judgment might be satisfied is concealed or otherwise not known to the person who has secured the judgment.

ADDITIONAL AUTHORITY

12 WRIGHT & MILLER §§ 3011-3020
13 MOORE'S FEDERAL PRACTICE §§ 69.01-69.05
6 ANDERSON'S OHIO CIVIL PRACTICE §§ 215.01-215.42
2 KLEIN DARLING AT 69-1
3 TEREZ F 19.1.1 to F 19.1.4, F 19.2.1 to F 19.2.10, F 19.3.1 to F 19.3.3
5 OH. JUR. PL. AND PRAC. FORMS, ch. 81
7 MILLIGAN Forms 69-1 to 69-159
2 FINK § 69-1

LEADING CASES

New Process Not Required upon Transfer

Slodov v. Stralka, 71 Ohio App. 3d 137, 593 N.E.2d 81 (1991) (a transferee court may issue prejudgment orders without effecting new process)

Notice to Attorney Sufficient

State ex rel. Klein v. Chorpening, 6 Ohio St. 3d 3, 450 N.E.2d 1161 (1983) (notice of proceedings in the execution of judgment in contempt is properly given where it is served upon the attorney of record for the judgment debtor)

CHAPTER 70

Rule 70. Judgment for Specific Acts; Vesting Title

Rule 70 reads as follows:

If a judgment directs a party to execute a conveyance of land, to transfer title or possession of personal property, to deliver deeds or other documents, or to perform any other specific act, and the party fails to comply within the time specified, the court may, where necessary, direct the act to be done at the cost of the disobedient party by some other person appointed by the court, and the act when so done has like effect as if done by the party. On application of the party entitled to performance, the clerk shall issue a writ of attachment against the property of the disobedient party to compel obedience to the judgment. The court may also in proper cases adjudge the party in contempt. If real or personal property is within this state, the court in lieu of directing a conveyance thereof may enter a judgment divesting the title of any party and vesting it in others, and such judgment has the effect of a conveyance executed in due form of law. When any order or judgment is for the delivery of possession, the party in whose favor it is entered is entitled to a writ of execution upon application to the clerk.

COMMENTARY

Authority of Court to Compel Performance

Rule 70 provides Ohio courts with the means to compel the performance of specific acts when the party ordered to do so refuses. Although the contempt power of the court may be sufficient to appropriately punish a disobedient party, such a finding may be little consolation to an aggrieved party who desires that the specific act be performed. Rule 70 allows the court to appoint a separate party, usually a government official, to perform the specified act. The performance by the court appointee has the same effect as if the disobedient person had performed the act.

Illustration 70-1

Susan commences a trespass action against her neighbor Ralph, alleging that Ralph planted several fruit trees on her property. The court, after granting a motion for summary judgment by Susan, orders Ralph to remove the fruit trees

---

within 14 days of the order. Ralph refuses and promptly leaves on a 25-day cruise to the Galapagos Islands. The court may then issue an order directing the Public Works Department of the local jurisdiction to remove the fruit trees. Any costs associated with this removal will also be taxed to Ralph.

Authority of Court to Vest Title in Real or Personal Property

Alternately, if the specific act ordered in the judgment is the conveyance of a piece of real or personal property, the court may divest the disobedient party of the property and vest the aggrieved party with the property by entering a judgment to that effect. Such a judgment is treated in the same manner as would a conveyance between the parties. However, this power of the court is limited to real and personal property located within the county in which the court is located. Where property is located outside the county, parties wishing to avail themselves of the relief specified in Rule 70 should register the judgment in the county in which the property is located and make a proper motion to a court within that county.

Illustration 70-2

Brenda commences a breach of contract action against Richard, alleging that Richard failed to deliver a parcel of land as required by the express terms of a written contract. The court grants a motion for summary judgment by Brenda and orders Richard to execute a deed conveying the parcel of land specified in the contract within 15 days of the order. Richard refuses and does nothing. To accomplish the conveyance, the court may direct the Recorder's Office or other government agency to issue a new deed in Brenda's name. Alternatively, the court may enter a judgment divesting Richard of the property and immediately vesting it in Brenda. A certified copy of the judgment will provide Brenda with proof of title in the property.

ADDITIONAL AUTHORITY

12 WRIGHT & MILLER §§ 3021-3030

13 MOORE'S FEDERAL PRACTICE §§ 70.01-70.04

2 KLEIN DARLING AT 70-1

3 TEREZ F 19.6.1 to F 19.6.4

5 OH. JUR. PL. AND PRAC. FORMS, ch. 82

7 MILLIGAN Forms 70-1 to 70-17

2 FINK §§ 70-1 to 70-2

LEADING CASES

Objections Waived

Sheldon v. Flinn, 89 Ohio App. 3d 490, 624 N.E.2d 1109 (1993) (although the court did not have authority under Rule 70 to interpret a deed, the party waived its objections by submitting to the proceedings)

To Whom Applicable

Tessler v. Ayer, 108 Ohio App. 3d 47, 669 N.E.2d 891 (1995) (Rule 70 is reserved for particularly obstinate parties who refused to comply with a judgment)

CHAPTER 71

Rule 71. Process in Behalf of and Against Persons Not Parties

Rule 71 reads as follows:

When an order is made in favor of a person who is not a party to the action, he may enforce obedience to the order by the same process as if he were a party; and, when obedience to an order may be lawfully enforced against a person who is not a party, he is liable to the same process for enforcing obedience to the order as if he were a party.

COMMENTARY

Rule 71 provides that non-parties may enforce orders made in their favor in the same manner as do parties. The Rule also provides for the converse situation: an order against a non-party may be enforced in the same manner as orders against parties. However, courts have tended to require that non-parties have standing to maintain an action to enforce orders in their favor. This seems to be the correct result with regard to the first clause of Rule 71, as analogy to the second clause demonstrates. Obviously, a court may not enforce an order against a non-party over whom the court has no personal jurisdiction.

It is also significant to note that non-parties should be permitted to invoke Rule 71 only when an order has been entered in their favor. Persons not signatories to a settlement agreement should have no basis upon which to seek its enforcement.

Relationship to Other Rules

Other Rules may also provide for more narrow applications to non-parties. The term "lawfully" in Rule 71 indicates that specific provisions in other Rules, such as Rule 65(D), which, in part, governs the scope of preliminary injunctions and temporary restraining orders over non-parties, take precedence over the general provisions set forth in this Rule.

ADDITIONAL AUTHORITY

12 Wright & Miller §§ 3031-3040

13 Moore's Federal Practice §§ 71.01-71.04
2 Klein Darling at 71-1
5 Oh. Jur. Pl. and Prac. Forms, ch. 83
7 Milligan Forms 71-1 to 71-2
2 Fink § 71-1

CHAPTER 72

Rule 72. [Reserved]

IX
SPECIAL PROCEEDINGS

CHAPTER 73

Rule 73. Probate Division of the Court of Common Pleas

Rule 73 reads as follows:

(A) **Applicability.** These Rules of Civil Procedure shall apply to proceedings in the probate division of the court of common pleas as indicated in this rule. Additionally, all of the Rules of Civil Procedure, though not specifically mentioned in this rule, shall apply except to the extent that by their nature they would be clearly inapplicable.

(B) **Venue.** Civ. R. 3(B) shall not apply to proceedings in the probate division of the court of common pleas, which shall be venued as provided by law. Proceedings under Chapters 2101. through 2131. of the Revised Code, which may be venued in the general division or the probate division of the court of common pleas, shall be venued in the probate division of the appropriate court of common pleas.

Proceedings that are improperly venued shall be transferred to a proper venue provided by law and division (B) of this rule, and the court may assess costs, including reasonable attorney fees, to the time of transfer against the party who commenced the action in an improper venue.

(C) **Service of summons.** Civ. R. 4 through 4.6 shall apply in any proceeding in the probate division of the court of common pleas requiring service of summons.

(D) **Service and filing of pleadings and papers subsequent to original pleading.** In proceedings requiring service of summons, Civ. R. 5 shall apply to the service and filing of pleadings and papers subsequent to the original pleading.

(E) **Service of notice.** In any proceeding where any type of notice other than service of summons is required by law or deemed necessary by the court, and the statute providing for notice neither directs nor authorizes the court to direct the manner of its service, notice shall be given in writing and may be served by or on behalf of any interested party without court intervention by one of the following methods:

(1) By delivering a copy to the person to be served;

(2) By leaving a copy at the usual place of residence of the person to be served;

(3)   By certified or express mail, addressed to the person to be served at the person's usual place of residence with instructions to forward, return receipt requested, with instructions to the delivering postal employee to show to whom delivered, date of delivery, and address where delivered, provided that the certified or express mail envelope is not returned with an endorsement showing failure of delivery;

(4)   By ordinary mail after a certified or express mail envelope is returned with an endorsement showing that it was refused;

(5)   By ordinary mail after a certified or express mail envelope is returned with an endorsement showing that it was unclaimed, provided that the ordinary mail envelope is not returned by the postal authorities with an endorsement showing failure of delivery;

(6)   By publication once each week for three consecutive weeks in some newspaper of general circulation in the county when the name, usual place of residence, or existence of the person to be served is unknown and cannot with reasonable diligence be ascertained; provided that before publication may be utilized, the person giving notice shall file an affidavit which states that the name, usual place of residence, or existence of the person to be served is unknown and cannot with reasonable diligence be ascertained;

(7)   By other method as the court may direct.

Civ. R. 4.2 shall apply in determining who may be served and how particular persons or entities must be served.

(F)   Proof of service of notice; when service of notice complete. When service is made through the court, proof of service of notice shall be in the same manner as proof of service of summons.

When service is made without court intervention, proof of service of notice shall be made by affidavit. When service is made by certified or express mail, the certified or express mail return receipt which shows delivery shall be attached to the affidavit. When service is made by ordinary mail, the prior returned certified or express mail envelope which shows that the mail was refused or unclaimed shall be attached to the affidavit.

Service of notice by ordinary mail shall be complete when the fact of mailing is entered of record except as stated in division (E)(5) of this rule. Service by publication shall be complete at the date of the last publication.

(G)   Waiver of service of notice. Civ. R. 4(D) shall apply in determining who may waive service of notice.

(H)   Forms used in probate practice. Forms used in proceedings in the probate division of the courts of common pleas shall be those prescribed in the rule applicable to standard probate forms in the Rules of Superintendence. Forms not prescribed in such rule may be used as permitted in that rule.

Blank forms reproduced for use in probate practice for any filing to which the rule applicable to specifications for printing probate forms of the Rules of Superintendence applies shall conform to the specifications set forth in that rule.

(I) **Notice of filing of judgments.** Civ. R. 58(B) shall apply to all judgments entered in the probate division of the court of common pleas in any action or proceeding in which any party other than a plaintiff, applicant, or movant has filed a responsive pleading or exceptions. Notice of the judgment shall be given to each plaintiff, applicant, or movant, to each party filing a responsive pleading or exceptions, and to other parties as the court directs.

(J) **Filing with the court defined.** The filing of documents with the court, as required by these rules, shall be made by filing them with the probate judge as the *ex officio* clerk of the court. A court may provide, by local rules adopted pursuant to the Rules of Superintendence, for the filing of documents by electronic means. If the court adopts such local rules, they shall include all of the following:

(1) any signature on electronically transmitted documents shall be considered that of the attorney or party it purports to be for all purposes. If it is established that the documents were transmitted without authority, the court shall order the filing stricken.

(2) a provision shall specify the days and hours during which electronically transmitted documents will be received by the court, and a provision shall specify when documents received electronically will be considered to have been filed.

(3) any document filed electronically that requires a filing fee may be rejected by the clerk of court unless the filer has complied with the mechanism established by the court for the payment of filing fees.

COMMENTARY

Rule 73 is an unusual Rule that contains provisions relating to the unique application of the Rules in probate actions. The Rule is not, therefore, of general applicability, and should be read within its distinctive historical and structural context. The Rule is more of "judicial statute" than a "rule," and the distinction between the scope of Rule 73 and that of the other Rules may imply a distinctive interpretational heuristic. In this sense, Rule 73 is similar to Federal Rule of Procedure 71A, which sets forth detailed provisions for use in eminent domain proceedings.

Applicability of Rules to Probate Actions

Rule 73 should be read in conjunction with Rule 1(C)(7), which states that the Rules do not apply to all special statutory proceedings to the extent that they would be clearly inapplicable. To this end, the second sentence of subsection (A) repeats this directive in the context of probate proceedings. Rule 73 also clarifies any confusion as to the applicability of certain Rules in probate proceedings. In other words, subsections (B)-(I) set forth those Rules that are applicable in all probate actions, with the variations listed in those subsections. Additionally, other Rules continue to apply in probate proceedings, but only to the extent that they are not clearly inapplicable according to subsection (A) and Rule 1(C).

Illustration 73-1

The Staff Notes to Rule 73 indicate that Rule 11 applies in probate actions and prevails over prior statutory verification requirements because the Rule is not clearly inapplicable.

Venue

For a variety of reasons, the venue provisions found in Rule 3(B) are inappropriate in probate actions. In recognition of this fact, Rule 73(B) provides that venue in probate actions continue to be determined by statute, except that actions under the designated statutory sections, including land sale actions, must be venued in the appropriate probate division of the court of common pleas. Finally, subsection (B) sets forth a basic transfer provision for probate proceedings. This is necessary because venue transfer under Rule 3(C) is linked to Rule 3(B), which is made inapplicable to probate actions by Rule 73(B).

Service of Summons and Other Papers

A formal summons may be necessary or desirable in many kinds of probate actions. In these situations, subsections (C) and (D) key the service of the summons and papers subsequent to the summons to Rules 4-4.6 and Rule 5.

Subsection (E) provides for the service of other process where a formal summons is not required by law. In this respect, the subject matter of subsection (E) is akin to Federal Rule of Civil Procedure 4.1, which provides for service of process other than a summons and has no counterpart under the Ohio Rules of Civil Procedure. Subsection (E) allows notice to be served by any interested party in an action without court involvement according to the methods listed in the Rule. Furthermore, Rule 4.2 provides additional methods of service that are expressly applicable under Rule 73(E).

Proof and Waiver of Service of Notice

Subsection (F) is necessary to provide for proof of service when service is made under subsection (E). If service is made by the court, proof of service will be in the same manner as that used for proving service of a summons under Rule 4-4.6. Where service is effected by a person without court intervention, however, subsection (F) provides for proof of service by either attaching the certified mail receipt showing delivery or by entering in the record the fact of service by ordinary mail provided that the ordinary mail envelope is not returned with an endorsement showing a failure of delivery.

Service of process other than a formal summons may be waived according to the provisions of Rule 4(D). This provision is similarly applicable to waiver of a formal summons through subsection (C)'s reference to that section.

Forms

Pursuant to subsection (H), standard probate forms, as provided for under the Ohio Rules of Superintendence, are to be used in probate proceedings. The subsection also eliminates any requirement that matters filed in probate division courts be executed under oath; instead, the signature of the person filing the matter will be sufficient.

Notice of Filing of Judgment

In 1989, Rule 58 was amended to clarify that the clerk of courts shall serve signed judgments upon parties. Subsection (I) makes clear that this duty applies to clerks in probate proceedings in the manner indicated. Thus, the plaintiff and any party that has filed a responsive pleading or a bill of exceptions must be given notice of the judgment by the clerk. The court also retains discretion to direct the clerk to notify other parties of the entry of judgment.

Electronically Filed Documents

Subsection (J) was added in 2001 as part of a group of amendments to other Rules of Procedure to establish minimum standards for the use of information systems, electronic signatures, and electronic filing. Under the Rule, local rules that provide for the electronic filing of documents may be adopted. However, local rules must contain, at a minimum, two provisions: a "signature provision" and a "time provision."

First, local rules must contain a "signature provision" that indicates that signatures on electronically transmitted documents shall be considered that of the attorney or party it purports to be for all purposes in an action. Evidence that a document filed electronically was done so without proper authority should be presented by motion, and if the court finds that such authority was absent, the filing must be stricken.

Second, local rules must contain a "time provision" that indicates the days and hours when documents may be submitted electronically and when such documents will be considered to have been filed. Local rules that provide for more than one method of electronic transmission for documents should adopt separate "time provisions" for each method.

The Rule also indicates that local rules may provide for the rejection of electronically filed documents if the appropriate filing fee has not been submitted. However, this provision is not required, and local rules may provide for the acceptance of such documents and alternative penalties, such as an increased fee.

ADDITIONAL AUTHORITY

2 Klein Darling AT 73-1 to AT 73-10
7 Milligan Forms 73-1 to 73-15
2 Fink § 73-1

LEADING CASES

Applicability of Civil Rules in Will Contests

Yancey v. Pyles, 44 Ohio App. 2d 410, 339 N.E.2d 835 (1975) (the provisions of Rule 3(A) and Rule 4 are fully applicable to proceedings brought under Ohio Revised Code § 2117.12, which governs claims against an estate)

Error to Dismiss In Lieu of Transfer

Siebenthal v. Summers, 56 Ohio App. 2d 168, 381 N.E.2d 1344 (1978) (where an action to contest a will is mistakenly filed in the general division of the court of common pleas, prejudicial error is committed if the court dismisses the complaint rather than transferring the action to the docket of the probate division)

Notice to Beneficiaries Not Required

In re Estate of Marinelli, 99 Ohio App. 3d 372, 650 N.E.2d 935 (1994) (decedent's biological father was not entitled to service of administrator's proposed distribution of wrongful death settlement proceeds; the father had notice of and appeared and testified at the hearing, and the proposed distribution was on file with the court and was available for inspection)

CHAPTER 74

Rule 74. Juvenile Proceedings [Abrogated]

CHAPTER 75

Rule 75. Divorce, Annulment, and Legal Separation Actions

Rule 75 reads as follows:

(A) Applicability. The Rules of Civil Procedure shall apply in actions for divorce, annulment, legal separation, and related proceedings, with the modifications or exceptions set forth in this rule.

(B) Joinder of parties. Civ. R. 14, 19, 19.1, and 24 shall not apply in divorce, annulment, or legal separation actions, however:

(1) A person or corporation having possession of, control of, or claiming an interest in property, whether real, personal, or mixed, out of which a party seeks a division of marital property, a distributive award, or an award of spousal support or other support, may be made a party defendant;

(2) When it is essential to protect the interests of a child, the court may join the child of the parties as a party defendant and appoint a guardian ad litem and legal counsel, if necessary, for the child and tax the costs;

(3) When child support is ordered, the court, on its own motion or that of an interested person, after notice to the party ordered to pay child support and to his or her employer, may make the employer a party defendant.

(C) Trial by court or magistrate. In proceedings under this rule there shall be no right to trial by jury. All issues may be heard either by the court or by a magistrate as the court, on the request of any party or on its own motion, may direct. Civ. R. 53 shall apply to all cases or issues directed to be heard by a magistrate.

(D) Investigation. On the filing of a complaint for divorce, annulment, or legal separation, where minor children are involved, or on the filing of a motion for the modification of a decree allocating parental rights and responsibilities for the care of children, the court may cause an investigation to be made as to the character, family relations, past conduct, earning ability, and financial worth of the parties to the action. The report of the investigation shall be made available to either party or their counsel of record upon written request not less than seven days before trial. The report shall be signed by the investigator and the investigator shall be subject to cross-examination by either party concerning the contents of the report. The court may tax as costs all or any part of the expenses for each investigation.

(E) Subpoena where custody involved. In any case involving the allocation of parental rights and responsibilities for the care of children, the court, on its own motion, may cite a party to the action from any point within the state to appear in court and testify.

(F) Judgment. The provisions of Civ. R. 55 shall not apply in actions for divorce, annulment, legal separation, or civil protection orders. For purposes of Civ. R. 54(B), the court shall not enter final judgment as to a claim for divorce, dissolution of marriage, annulment, or legal separation unless one of the following applies:

(1) The judgment also divides the property of the parties, determines the appropriateness of an order of spousal support, and, where applicable, either allocates parental rights and responsibilities, including payment of child support, between the parties or orders shared parenting of minor children;

(2) Issues of property division, spousal support, and allocation of parental rights and responsibilities or shared parenting have been finally determined in orders, previously entered by the court, that are incorporated into the judgment;

(3) The court includes in the judgment the express determination required by Civ. R. 54(B) and a final determination that either of the following applies:

(a) The court lacks jurisdiction to determine such issues;

(b) In a legal separation action, the division of the property of the parties would be inappropriate at that time.

(G) Civil protection order. A claim for a civil protection order based upon an allegation of domestic violence shall be a separate claim from a claim for divorce, dissolution of marriage, annulment, or legal separation.

(H) Relief pending appeal. A motion to modify, pending appeal, either a decree allocating parental rights and responsibilities for the care of children, or a spousal or other support order, shall be made to the trial court in the first instance, whether made before or after a notice of appeal is filed. The trial court may grant relief upon terms as to bond or otherwise as it considers proper for the security of the rights of the adverse party and in the best interests of the children involved. Civ. R. 62(B) does not apply to orders allocating parental rights and responsibilities for the care of children or a spousal or other support order. An order entered upon motion under this rule may be vacated or modified by the appellate court. The appellate court has authority to enter like orders pending appeal, but an application to the appellate court for relief shall disclose what has occurred in the trial court regarding the relief.

(I) **Temporary restraining orders.**

    (1) **Restraining order: exclusion.** The provisions of Civ. R. 65(A) shall not apply in divorce, annulment, or legal separation actions.

    (2) **Restraining order: grounds, procedure.** When it is made to appear to the court by affidavit of a party sworn to absolutely that a party is about to dispose of or encumber property, or any part thereof of property, so as to defeat another party in obtaining an equitable division of marital property, a distributive award, or spousal or other support, or that a party to the action or a child of any party is about to suffer physical abuse, annoyance, or bodily injury by the other party, the court may allow a temporary restraining order, with or without bond, to prevent that action. A temporary restraining order may be issued without notice and shall remain in force during the pendency of the action unless the court or magistrate otherwise orders.

(J) **Continuing jurisdiction.** The continuing jurisdiction of the court shall be invoked by motion filed in the original action, notice of which shall be served in the manner provided for the service of process under Civ. R. 4 to 4.6. When the continuing jurisdiction of the court is invoked pursuant to this division, the discovery procedures set forth in Civ. R. 26 to 37 shall apply.

(K) **Hearing.** No action for divorce, annulment, or legal separation may be heard and decided until the expiration of forty-two days after the service of process or twenty-eight days after the last publication of notice of the complaint, and no action for divorce, annulment, or legal separation shall be heard and decided earlier than twenty-eight days after the service of a counterclaim, which under this rule may be designated a cross-complaint, unless the plaintiff files a written waiver of the twenty-eight day period.

(L) **Notice of trial.** In all cases where there is no counsel of record for the adverse party, the court shall give the adverse party notice of the trial upon the merits. The notice shall be made by regular mail to the party's last known address, and shall be mailed at least seven days prior to the commencement of trial.

(M) **Testimony.** Judgment for divorce, annulment, or legal separation shall not be granted upon the testimony or admission of a party not supported by other credible evidence. No admission shall be received that the court has reason to believe was obtained by fraud, connivance, coercion, or other improper means. The parties, notwithstanding their marital relations, shall be competent to testify in the proceeding to the same extent as other witnesses.

(N) Allowance of spousal support, child support, and custody pendente lite.

(1) When requested in the complaint, answer, or counterclaim, or by motion served with the pleading, upon satisfactory proof by affidavit duly filed with the clerk of the court, the court or magistrate, without oral hearing and for good cause shown, may grant spousal support pendente lite to either of the parties for the party's sustenance and expenses during the suit and may make a temporary order regarding the support, maintenance, and allocation of parental rights and responsibilities for the care of children of the marriage, whether natural or adopted, during the pendency of the action for divorce, annulment, or legal separation.

(2) Counter affidavits may be filed by the other party within fourteen days from the service of the complaint, answer, counterclaim, or motion, all affidavits to be used by the court or magistrate in making a temporary spousal support order, child support order, and order allocating parental rights and responsibilities for the care of children. Upon request, in writing, after any temporary spousal support, child support, or order allocating parental rights and responsibilities for the care of children is journalized, the court shall grant the party so requesting an oral hearing within twenty-eight days to modify the temporary order. A request for oral hearing shall not suspend or delay the commencement of spousal support or other support payments previously ordered or change the allocation of parental rights and responsibilities until the order is modified by journal entry after the oral hearing.

(O) Delay of decree. When a party who is entitled to a decree of divorce or annulment is ordered to pay spousal support or child support for a child not in his or her custody, or to deliver a child to the party to whom parental rights and responsibilities for the care of the child are allocated, the court may delay entering a decree for divorce or annulment until the party, to the satisfaction of the court, secures the payment of the spousal support or the child support for the child, or delivers custody of the child to the party to whom parental rights and responsibilities are allocated.

COMMENTARY

Rule 75 clarifies the applicability of the Rules in domestic relations proceedings, those actions involving divorce, annulment, or legal separation. Although such proceedings are "civil actions," and thus within the ambit of Rule 1, the distinct nature of the kind of relief sought in such actions suggests modifications and exceptions to the application of some of the Rules. Subsection (A) makes this point explicitly.

Rule 75 contains a great many provisions, most of which are beyond the scope of this manual. However, several of the more important provisions are summarized in brief below.

Joinder

Subsection (B) states that Rules 14, 19, 19.1, and 24 are not generally applicable in domestic relations proceedings, but sets forth three exceptions to this rule. First, a person or corporation in control of property from which a party seeks a division of marital property, a distributive award, or an award of spousal support or other support is sought may be joined as a defendant. Second, a child may be joined as a party when the court determines that joinder is necessary to protect the interests of the child. Subsection (B)(2) provides for the appointment of a *guardian ad litem* or legal counsel in this situation. Finally, an employer may be joined as a party defendant where an employee is ordered to pay child support.

No Right to Jury Trial

Subsection (C) states that no right to a jury trial exists in domestic relations proceedings. However, this provision should be regarded as declaratory only, as a rule of procedure may not affect the substantive rights of parties, the right to jury trial being one of the most salient substantive rights in any action. Nonetheless, subsection (C) provides simply that all issues in these actions are to be heard by a court or, upon motion by the parties or *sua sponte*, by a magistrate if the court so directs.

Judgment

Subsection (F) was significantly expanded in 1998. Although the provisions of the prior version of the subrule are retained in the first sentence of the new version, the subsection now contains additional clarificational provisions relating to the entry of judgments in domestic relations actions.

The amended rule now provides that certification of any judgment under Rule 54(B) in a domestic relations case may not be made unless the judgment resolves all claims presented in the action (*e.g.*, divorce, property settlement, child support and custody) except those for civil protection orders. Of course, the Rule should not be construed as denying the court to enter a ruling on the civil protection order as part of the judgment on the other claims. The Rule merely prevents the immediate appeal under Rule 54(B) on a single claim in a domestic relations action except a claim for a civil protection order, which may be appealed immediately. It should be noted, in addition, that the requirements of Rule 54(B) must be satisfied in all cases.

Relief Pending Appeal

Subsection (H) provides that Rule 62(B) does not apply to actions concerning parental rights and responsibilities. Consequently, a court may modify a custody, support, or alimony order for the pendency of an appeal. An amendment to the Rule in 1997 makes clear that a motion to modify such orders should be made to the trial court during the pendency of appeal, with the decision of the court also subject to review in the appellate court. The Staff Notes to Rule 75 instruct that "[t]he trial court is the most appropriate forum to consider such a motion in the first instance, given that the trial judge is already familiar with the issues [ ] and [that] the likelihood that further factual presentations and inquiry will be necessary for the court to dispose of the motion."

Temporary Restraining Orders

Subsection (I) suspends the normal procedure for obtaining TROs set forth in Rule 65(A) and provides for its own procedure in subsection (I)(2). TROs issued under this provision differ from those issued under Rule 65(A) in two significant respects. First, a bond is not required to encumber property in a domestic relations proceeding through the issuance of a TRO, as is generally required under Rule 65. Second, TRO's under Rule 75(I)(2) typically have no specified termination date, and generally remain in effect during the entirety of the action.

Subsections (I) and (B) were amended in 2001 to clarify that those provisions apply when a party is seeking a division of marital property, a distributive award, or an award of spousal support or other support. The former language referred only to "spousal support or other support," raising questions concerning the applicability of those provisions to divisions of marital property and distributive awards. The reference to "other support" was retained to ensure that the provisions of subsection (B) and (I) are applicable to interests of other parties, such as child support.

Hearings

Subsection (K) provides for a "cooling off" period in any action requesting divorce, annulment, or legal separation. Accordingly, no hearing may be held in any such action until 42 days have expired since the summons was served on the defendant or 28 days after the last publication of notice. A shorter period, linked to the service of any counterclaim, is also set forth under the Rule, though this period may be waived.

ADDITIONAL AUTHORITY

2 Klein Darling AT 75-1 to AT 75-16
7 Milligan Forms 75-1 to 75-149
2 Fink §§ 75-1 to 75-15

LEADING CASES

Alimony and Support; Filing Requirements

Kahn v. Kahn, 42 Ohio App. 3d 61, 536 N.E.2d 678 (1987) (Rule 75 requires that the party opposing a request for temporary alimony respond to the request by counter affidavit within 14 days and/or by motion to modify within 28 days of a temporary order)

Antenuptial Agreements Enforceable

Kelm v. Kelm, 68 Ohio St. 3d 26, 623 N.E.2d 39 (1993) (if properly implemented, antenuptial agreements are enforceable)

Appointment of Guardian

Pruden-Wilgus v. Wilgus, 46 Ohio App. 3d 13, 545 N.E.2d 647 (1989) (the appointment of a guardian ad litem pursuant to Rule 75(B)(2) is within the discretion of the court)

Attorneys' Fees in Alimony Award

Gross v. Gross, 64 Ohio App. 3d 815, 582 N.E.2d 1144 (1990) (an alimony award may include a reasonable allowance for attorney fees; the decision to allow such an award to either party is within the sound discretion of the trial court and will not be overturned absent an abuse of discretion)

Bond Requirements

Davis v. Davis, 55 Ohio App. 3d 196, 563 N.E.2d 320 (1988) (Rule 75 does not allow a court to grant a stay of monetary judgment without the posting of an adequate security)

Hearing Before Expiration of Time Period

Robinette v. Robinette, 41 Ohio App. 3d 25, 534 N.E.2d 251 (1988) (Rule 75 provides that no action for divorce, annulment, or alimony may be heard and decided until the expiration of 42 days after service of process or 28 days if service is effected by publication)

Intervention Disallowed

Maher v. Maher, 64 Ohio App. 2d 22, 410 N.E.2d 1260 (1978) (an illegitimate child has no right under Rule 75(B) to intervene in a divorce action in which its natural father is the defendant and the child has no interest of a direct or intermediate nature in any particular property of the father)

Jurisdiction

Emery v. Emery, 101 Ohio App. 3d 559, 656 N.E.2d 5 (1995) (an obligor's assertion that he is not the child's father does not invoke a trial court's continuing jurisdiction to modify a support order)

Magistrates

State ex rel. Thompson v. Spon, 83 Ohio St. 3d 551, 700 N.E.2d 1281 (1998) (a magistrate may enter orders without judicial approval in pretrial hearings under Rule 75 unless otherwise specified in the reference order, and the magistrate is not required to issue findings of fact and conclusions of law with respect to these orders)

Notice of Trial By Judge

King v. King, 55 Ohio App. 2d 43, 379 N.E.2d 251 (1977) (the court, and not counsel, must give the adverse party a notice of trial as required by Rule 75)

Post-Decree Motions to Show Cause

State ex rel. Soukup v. Celebrezze, 83 Ohio St. 3d 549, 700 N.E.2d 1278 (1998) (post-decree show-cause motions filed by a party invoke both the inherent power of a domestic relations court to enforce its own orders and the court's continuing jurisdiction under Rule 75)

Relief Pending Appeal

DiLacqua v. DiLacqua, 88 Ohio App. 3d 48, 623 N.E.2d 118 (1993) (temporary support orders are reviewable after entry of a final order that disposes of the action; a legitimate purpose of temporary support order is to maintain the status quo during the pendency of the divorce proceedings)

Review of Magistrate's Findings

Wilson v. Brown, 41 Ohio App. 3d 77, 534 N.E.2d 883 (1988) (finding made by a magistrate acting under the authority granted by Rule 75(C) are interlocutory in nature, but such findings may not be set aside lightly)

Right to Jury Trial

Koepke v. Koepke, 52 Ohio App. 3d 47, 556 N.E.2d 1198 (1989) (parties have no right to a jury trial in a divorce proceeding; spouses who wish to commence a tort action separate from their divorce proceeding inadvertently lose their right to a jury trial for the tort claim when a court chooses to combine the two causes of action)

Service by Mail

Quisenberry v. Quisenberry, 91 Ohio App. 3d 341, 632 N.E.2d 916 (1993) (service by ordinary mail of wife's motions for appointment of a receiver to sell the marital property and for an order requiring her husband to vacate the marital premises was adequate to invoke the court's jurisdiction)

Service Requirements Mandatory

Satava v. Gerhard, 66 Ohio App. 3d 598, 585 N.E.2d 899 (1990) (failure to comply with the service requirements of Rule 75 precludes a court from exercising jurisdiction in an action for modification of child support)

TROs Directed at Non-Parties

Van Ho v. Van Ho, 17 Ohio App. 3d 108, 477 N.E.2d 659 (1984) (a domestic relations court may not issue a post-decree temporary restraining order affecting a person who is not a party to the action)

TROs; When Appropriate

Addy v. Addy, 97 Ohio App. 3d 204, 646 N.E.2d 513 (1994) (a restraining order is proper where the support obligor threatened at trial to quit his job and leave the state to avoid paying support)

CHAPTER 76

Rule 76. Time for Perfecting Appeal Stayed [Abrogated]

CHAPTER 77

Rule 77. [Reserved]

CHAPTER 78

Rule 78. [Reserved]

CHAPTER 79

Rule 79. [Reserved]

CHAPTER 80

Rule 80. [Reserved]

CHAPTER 81

Rule 81. References to Ohio Revised Code

Rule 81 reads as follows:

A reference in these Rules to a section of the Revised Code shall mean the section as amended from time to time including the enactment of additional sections the numbers of which are subsequent to the section referred to in the Rules.

COMMENTARY

Rule 81 is self-explanatory. The Rule is considered necessary to prevent the continual amendment of the Rules whenever changes to sections of the Ohio Revised Code that are cross-referenced in the Rules are made. To maintain the Rules' linguistic simplicity and structural elegance, references to distinct legal provisions should be interpreted in light of this interpretational heuristic.

Rule 81 is misleadingly included in Title IX of the Ohio Rules of Civil Procedure. Its prescriptions apply to all Rules, and its coupling with the miscellaneous provisions of Rules 73 and 75 should not be construed as indicating that Rule 81 applies only to those Rules. Instead, it is more appropriate to view Rule 81 in conjunction with the Rules included in Title X, entitled "General Provisions."

ADDITIONAL AUTHORITY

2 Klein Darling at 81-1
7 Milligan Forms 81-1
2 Fink § 81-1

X
GENERAL PROVISIONS

505

CHAPTER 82

Rule 82. Jurisdiction Unaffected

Rule 82 reads as follows:

These rules shall not be construed to extend or limit the jurisdiction of the courts of this state.

COMMENTARY

Rule 82 simply articulates an implied limitation contained in Article IV, § 5(B) of the Ohio Constitution that a Rule of Civil Procedure cannot "abridge, enlarge or modify any substantive right." Accordingly, Rule 82 recognizes that the jurisdiction of Ohio courts cannot be altered by the Rules. Instead, the jurisdiction of Ohio courts is provided for by Ohio statutory law and by the Ohio Constitution, and the Rules operate merely to facilitate the exercise of that jurisdiction.

ADDITIONAL AUTHORITY

12 WRIGHT & MILLER §§ 3141-3150
14 MOORE'S FEDERAL PRACTICE §§ 82.01-82.22
2 KLEIN DARLING AT 82-1 to AT 82-6
7 MILLIGAN Forms 82-1
2 FINK § 82-1

LEADING CASES

Jurisdiction Unaffected by Local Rule

Cole v. Central Ohio Transit Auth., 20 Ohio App. 3d 312, 486 N.E.2d 140 (1984) (a court's local rules pertain to procedure, not the jurisdiction of the court; thus, an erroneous referral of a case to nonbinding arbitration in accordance with local rule does not affect the jurisdiction of the court or the substantive rights of a party)

Procedural Nature of Venue

Morrison v. Steiner, 32 Ohio St. 2d 86, 290 N.E.2d 841 (1972) (delineation of proper venue is a procedural matter and is within the rule-making power of the Ohio Supreme Court)

CHAPTER 83

Rule 83. Local Rules of Practice

Rule 83 reads as follows:

(A) A court may adopt local rules of practice which shall not be inconsistent with these rules or with other rules promulgated by the Supreme Court and shall file its local rules of practice with the Clerk of the Supreme Court.

(B) Local rules of practice shall be adopted only after the court gives appropriate notice and an opportunity for comment. If a court determines that there is an immediate need for a rule, it may adopt the rule without prior notice and opportunity for comment, but promptly shall afford notice and opportunity for comment.

COMMENTARY

Rule 83 contains two separate provisions. Subsection (A) restates the power of local courts to promulgate any rule of practice or procedure regulating the conduct of civil actions. Such power is expressly granted in Article IV, § 5(B) of the Ohio Constitution. Any local rule must not, of course, conflict with one of the Ohio Rules of Civil Procedure or other rule promulgated by the Ohio Supreme Court, such as the Rules of the Supreme Court of Ohio. See *Note on Judicial Rulemaking in Ohio*, located at the beginning of this manual.

Subsection (A) was amended in 2000 to emphasize the original intent of the Rule as explained above. The amendment was also intended to reinforce the requirement that any local rule be filed with the Clerk of the Supreme Court of Ohio.

Procedure for Promulgating Local Rules

Subsection (B) sets forth the procedural requirements for the adoption of local rules. Although the Rule does not specify the procedure to be used for the public notice and comment requirements, they may be satisfied in a number of ways. A public hearing will satisfy the requirements, though the original advisory committee's note indicates that a public hearing is not required. An "advisory committee," similar to that used by the Supreme Court in drafting the Rules themselves, may also be used, as will publishing proposed rules in various state and local legal publications.

Although subsection (B) contemplates the adoption of local rules without notice or a period for public comment, the Rule specifies that such a measure should be reserved for all but the most exigent of circumstances. Public notice and comment must be provided as soon as possible following an "emergency" adoption of a local rule.

ADDITIONAL AUTHORITY

12 WRIGHT & MILLER §§ 3151-3160
14 MOORE'S FEDERAL PRACTICE §§ 83.01-83.34
2 KLEIN DARLING AT 83-1 to AT 83-5
7 MILLIGAN Forms 83-1 to 83-2
2 FINK §§ 83-1 to 83-12

LEADING CASES

Dismissal for Violation of Local Rule

Richerson v. Patten, 83 Ohio App. 3d 895, 615 N.E.2d 1136 (1992) (only flagrant, substantial disregard for local court rules can justify a dismissal on procedural grounds)

Local Rule Invalid Where Contradictory

Vance v. Roedersheimer, 64 Ohio St. 3d 552, 597 N.E.2d 153 (1992) (the "unless the court otherwise directs" language of Rule 54(D) does not allow the court to award costs to a non-prevailing party; thus, a local rule permitting such an award is invalid)

CHAPTER 84

Rule 84. Forms

Rule 84 reads as follows:

The forms contained in the Appendix of Forms which the supreme court from time to time may approve are sufficient under these rules and are intended to indicate the simplicity and brevity of statement which these rules contemplate.

COMMENTARY

The Appendix of Forms is reproduced in the Appendix of this manual. The forms exemplify the simplicity and elegance of the pleading anticipated by the Rules. In addition, Rule 84 clearly contemplates the actual use of these forms by practitioners. As only these forms are explicitly guaranteed as sufficient under the Rules, practitioners are well-advised to use these forms when appropriate.

ADDITIONAL AUTHORITY

12 WRIGHT & MILLER §§ 3161-3170
14 MOORE'S FEDERAL PRACTICE §§ 84.01-84.02
2 KLEIN DARLING AT 84-1
7 MILLIGAN Forms 84-1
2 FINK § 84-1

CHAPTER 85

Rule 85. Title

Rule 85 reads as follows:

These rules shall be known as the Ohio Rules of Civil Procedure and may be cited as "Civil Rules" or "Civ. R.—."

COMMENTARY

The Rule is self-explanatory. Throughout this manual, the Ohio Rules of Civil Procedure have been cited in this manner, or as the Ohio Rules, or simply as the Rules.

ADDITIONAL AUTHORITY

12 WRIGHT & MILLER §§ 3171-3180
14 MOORE'S FEDERAL PRACTICE §§ 85.01-85.02
2 KLEIN DARLING AT 85-1
7 MILLIGAN Forms 85-1
2 FINK § 85-1

CHAPTER 86

Rule 86. Effective Date

Rule 86 reads as follows:

(A) Effective date of original rules. These rules shall take effect on the first day of July, 1970. They govern all proceedings in actions brought after they take effect and also all further proceedings in actions then pending, except to the extent that in the opinion of the court their application in a particular action pending when the rules take effect would not be feasible or would work injustice, in which event the former procedure applies.

(B) Effective date of amendments. The amendments submitted by the Supreme Court to the General Assembly on January 15, 1971, on April 14, 1971, and on April 30, 1971, shall take effect on the first day of July, 1971. They govern all proceedings in actions brought after they take effect and also all further proceedings in actions then pending, except to the extent that in the opinion of the court their application in a particular action pending when the rules take effect would not be feasible or would work injustice, in which event the former procedure applies.

(C) Effective date of amendments. The amendments submitted by the Supreme Court to the General Assembly on January 15, 1972, and on May 1, 1972, shall take effect on the first day of July, 1972. They govern all proceedings in actions brought after they take effect and also all further proceedings in actions then pending, except to the extent that their application in a particular action pending when the rules take effect would not be feasible or would work injustice, in which event the former procedure applies.

(D) Effective date of amendments. The amendments submitted by the Supreme Court to the General Assembly on January 12, 1973, shall take effect on the first day of July, 1973. They govern all proceedings in actions brought after they take effect and also all further proceedings in actions then pending, except to the extent that their application in a particular action pending when the amendments take effect would not be feasible or would work injustice, in which event the former procedure applies.

(E) Effective date of amendments. The amendments submitted by the Supreme Court to the General Assembly on January 10, 1975 and on April 29, 1975, shall take effect on July 1, 1975. They govern all proceedings in actions brought after they take effect and also all further proceedings in actions then pending, except to the extent that their application in a particular action pending when the amendments take effect would not be feasible or would work injustice, in which event the former procedure applies.

(F) Effective date of amendments. The amendments submitted by the Supreme Court to the General Assembly on January 9, 1976 shall take effect on July 1, 1976. They govern all proceedings in actions brought after they take effect and also all further proceedings in actions then pending, except to the extent that their application in a particular action pending when the amendments take effect would not be feasible or would work injustice, in which event the former procedure applies.

(G) Effective date of amendments. The amendments submitted by the Supreme Court to the General Assembly on January 12, 1978, and on April 28, 1978, shall take effect on July 1, 1978. They govern all proceedings in actions brought after they take effect and also all further proceedings in actions then pending, except to the extent that their application in a particular action pending when the amendments take effect would not be feasible or would work injustice, in which event the former procedure applies.

(H) Effective date of amendments. The amendments submitted by the Supreme Court to the General Assembly on January 14, 1980 shall take effect on July 1, 1980. They govern all proceedings in actions brought after they take effect and also all further proceedings in actions then pending, except to the extent that their application in a particular action pending when the amendments take effect would not be feasible or would work injustice, in which event the former procedure applies.

(I) Effective date of amendments. The amendments submitted by the Supreme Court to the General Assembly on January 12, 1983 shall take effect on July 1, 1983. They govern all proceedings in actions brought after they take effect and also all further proceedings in actions then pending, except to the extent that their application in a particular action pending when the amendments take effect would not be feasible or would work injustice, in which event the former procedure applies.

(J) Effective date of amendments. The amendments submitted by the Supreme Court to the General Assembly on January 12, 1984 shall take effect on July 1, 1984. They govern all proceedings in actions brought after they take effect and also all further proceedings in actions then pending, except to the extent that their application in a particular action pending when the amendments take effect would not be feasible or would work injustice, in which event the former procedure applies.

(K) Effective date of amendments. The amendments submitted by the Supreme Court to the General Assembly on December 24, 1984 and January 8, 1985 shall take effect on July 1, 1985. They govern all proceedings in actions brought after they take effect and also all further proceedings in actions then pending, except to the extent that their application in a particular action pending when the amendments take effect would not be feasible or would work injustice, in which event the former procedure applies.

(L) **Effective date of amendments.** The amendments submitted by the Supreme Court to the General Assembly on January 9, 1986 shall take effect on July 1, 1986. They govern all proceedings in actions brought after they take effect and also all further proceedings in actions then pending, except to the extent that their application in a particular action pending when the amendments take effect would not be feasible or would work injustice, in which event the former procedure applies.

(M) **Effective date of amendments.** The amendments submitted by the Supreme Court to the General Assembly on January 14, 1988 shall take effect on July 1, 1988. They govern all proceedings in actions brought after they take effect and also all further proceedings in actions then pending, except to the extent that their application in a particular action pending when the amendments take effect would not be feasible or would work injustice, in which event the former procedure applies.

(N) **Effective date of amendments.** The amendments submitted by the Supreme Court to the General Assembly on January 6, 1989 shall take effect on July 1, 1989. They govern all proceedings in actions brought after they take effect and also all further proceedings in actions then pending, except to the extent that their application in a particular action pending when the amendments take effect would not be feasible or would work injustice, in which event the former procedure applies.

(O) **Effective date of amendments.** The amendments submitted by the Supreme Court to the General Assembly on January 10, 1991 and further revised and submitted on April 29, 1991, shall take effect on July 1, 1991. They govern all proceedings in actions brought after they take effect and also all further proceedings in actions then pending, except to the extent that their application in a particular action pending when the amendments take effect would not be feasible or would work injustice, in which event the former procedure applies.

(P) **Effective date of amendments.** The amendments filed by the Supreme Court with the General Assembly on January 14, 1992 and further revised and filed on April 30, 1992, shall take effect on July 1, 1992. They govern all proceedings in actions brought after they take effect and also all further proceedings in actions then pending, except to the extent that their application in a particular action pending when the amendments take effect would not be feasible or would work injustice, in which event the former procedure applies.

(Q) **Effective date of amendments.** The amendments submitted by the Supreme Court to the General Assembly on January 8, 1993 and further revised and filed on April 30, 1993 shall take effect on July 1, 1993. They govern all proceedings in actions brought after they take effect and also all further proceedings in actions then pending, except to the extent that their application in a particular action pending when the amendments take effect would not be feasible or would work injustice, in which event the former procedure applies.

(R) **Effective date of amendments.** The amendments submitted by the Supreme Court to the General Assembly on January 14, 1994 shall take effect on July 1, 1994. They govern all proceedings in actions brought after they take effect and also all further proceedings in actions then pending, except to the extent that their application in a particular action pending when the amendments take effect would not be feasible or would work injustice, in which event the former procedure applies.

(S) **Effective date of amendments.** The amendments to Rules 11 and 53 filed by the Supreme Court with the General Assembly on January 11, 1995 and refiled on April 25, 1995 shall take effect on July 1, 1995. They govern all proceedings in actions brought after they take effect and also all further proceedings in actions then pending, except to the extent that their application in a particular action pending when the amendments take effect would not be feasible or would work injustice, in which event the former procedure applies.

(T) **Effective date of amendments.** The amendments to Rules 4.2, 19.1, 53, 54, 59, 73, and 75 filed by the Supreme Court with the General Assembly on January 5, 1996 and refiled on April 26, 1996 shall take effect on July 1, 1996. They govern all proceedings in actions brought after they take effect and also all further proceedings in actions then pending, except to the extent that their application in a particular action pending when the amendments take effect would not be feasible or would work injustice, in which event the former procedure applies.

(U) **Effective date of amendments.** The amendments to Rules 4.1, 4.2, 4.3, 4.5, 4.6, 30, 56, 73, and 75 filed by the Supreme Court with the General Assembly on January 10, 1997 and refiled on April 24, 1997 shall take effect on July 1, 1997. They govern all proceedings in actions brought after they take effect and also all further proceedings in actions then pending, except to the extent that their application in a particular action pending when the amendments take effect would not be feasible or would work injustice, in which event the former procedure applies.

(V) Effective date of amendments. The amendments to Rules 3, 53, and 75 filed by the Supreme Court with the General Assembly on January 15, 1998 and further revised and refiled on April 30, 1998, shall take effect on July 1, 1998. They govern all proceedings in actions brought after they take effect and also all further proceedings in actions then pending, except to the extent that their application in a particular action pending when the amendments take effect would not be feasible or would work injustice, in which event the former procedure applies.

(W) Effective date of amendments. The amendments to Rules 24, 33, and 56 filed by the Supreme Court with the General Assembly on January 13, 1999 shall take effect on July 1, 1999. They govern all proceedings in actions brought after they take effect and also all further proceedings in actions then pending, except to the extent that their application in a particular action pending when the amendments take effect would not be feasible or would work injustice, in which event the former procedure applies.

(X) Effective date of amendments. The amendments to Civil Rule 83 filed by the Supreme Court with the General Assembly on January 13, 2000 and refiled on April 27, 2000 shall take effect on July 1, 2000. They govern all proceedings in actions brought after they take effect and also all further proceedings in actions then pending, except to the extent that their application in a particular action pending when the amendments take effect would not be feasible or would work injustice, in which event the former procedure applies.

(Y) Effective date of amendments. The amendments to Civil Rules 5, 11, 28, 41, 73, and 75 filed by the Supreme Court with the General Assembly on January 12, 2001, and revised and refiled on April 26, 2001, shall take effect on July 1, 2001. They govern all proceedings in actions brought after they take effect and also all further proceedings in actions then pending, except to the extent that their application in a particular action pending when the amendments take effect would not be feasible or would work injustice, in which event the former procedure applies.

COMMENTARY

Rule 86 originally provided for the determination of the effective date of the first set of Rules promulgated in 1970 and for the application of those Rules to actions then pending. Subsections (B)-(U) were added at the same time as amendments to the Rules from 1971 to 1997, and those subsections also provided for the determination of the effective dates of the amendments and their applications.

Effective Date of Amendments

This drafting technique—indicating the effective date of amendments to the Rules by amending Rule 86—was abandoned by the United States Supreme Court in 1963. In addition to highly theoretical and almost virtually academic arguments concerning the self-referential problems posed by the technique, it has been noted that it also produces a rather unwieldy and inelegant Rule. In its place, the Supreme Court began indicating the effective dates of all amendments to the Rules in its Promulgating Order submitted to Congress. Thus, additional amendments to Federal Rule 86 became unnecessary. This technique continued in use until 1988, when 28 U.S.C. § 2074 was amended to provide for effective dates of amendments to rules of "December 1 of the year in which such rule is so transmitted [to Congress] unless otherwise provided by law."

The better technique is that adopted by the United States Supreme Court in this regard. As the Ohio Constitution, in OHIO CONST. art. IV, § 5(B), sets forth the effective date for all amendments to rules of procedure established by the Ohio Supreme Court as July 1 in the year in which the rules were submitted to the Ohio General Assembly, the first sentence of subsections (A)-(U) is repetitious at best and confusing at worst. Indeed, any attempt to fashion an effective date of anything but July 1 would violate the express terms of the Ohio Constitution. Rule 86 is simply unnecessary to indicate the effective date of any amendment to the Rules, and the Ohio Supreme Court would be prudent to abrogate this needless appendage.

Applicability to Pending Actions

Although it is common experience that amendments to rules apply to actions commenced after the effective date of those amendments, the application of amendments to actions already commenced is not as clear. The final sentence of subsections (A)-(U) of Rule 86 operate as a presumption that such amendments apply to actions then pending so long as it would "not be feasible or would work injustice" to the parties. Ohio courts have substantial discretion in this regard and rarely been reversed in this regard.

As noted above, the continual accretion of subsections to Rule 86 whenever the Rules are amended is unnecessary. To indicate the usual operation of amendments to actions then pending, the Ohio Supreme Court may elect to so provide in an order to the Ohio General Assembly whenever it submits rules for approval. This practice would mimic that chosen by the United States Supreme Court when it indicates the application of amendments to actions then pending in its Promulgating Order.

A more elegant solution, however, would be the amendment of Rule 86 so that it simply reads, "All amendments to these Rules govern all proceedings in actions brought after they take effect and also all further proceedings in actions then pending, except to the extent that in the opinion of the court their application in a particular action pending when the rules take effect would not be feasible or would work injustice, in which event the former procedure applies." This would produce a Rule that is elegant in design as well as unambiguous in effect.

ADDITIONAL AUTHORITY

12 Wright & Miller §§ 3181-3200
14 Moore's Federal Practice §§ 86.01-86.03
2 Klein Darling AT 86-1 to AT 86-2
7 Milligan Forms 86-1 to 86-7
2 Fink § 86-1

APPENDIX OF OFFICIAL FORMS

(See Rule 84)

Introductory Statement

The forms which follow are intended for illustration only. They are limited in number inasmuch as no attempt is made to furnish a manual of forms.

The forms are expressly declared by Rule 84 to be sufficient under the rules. Departures from the forms shall not void papers which are otherwise sufficient, and the forms may be varied when necessary to meet the facts of a particular case.

Where appropriate, the forms assume that the action has been brought in the Court of Common Pleas, Franklin County, Ohio.

FORM 1

CAPTION AND SUMMONS

COURT OF COMMON PLEAS
FRANKLIN COUNTY, OHIO

A.B.
221 E. West Street
Columbus, Ohio 43215

      Plaintiff

    v.

C.D.
122 W. East Street
Columbus, Ohio 43214

      Defendant

No. _____

SUMMONS

To the following named defendants:

Name	Address

You have been named defendant(s) in a complaint filed in Franklin County Court of Common Pleas, Franklin County Court House, Columbus, Ohio, 43215 by

Name	Address

plaintiff(s). A copy of the complaint is attached hereto. The name and address of the plaintiff's attorney is _____

You are hereby summoned and required to serve upon the plaintiff's attorney, or upon the plaintiff, if he has no attorney of record, a copy of an answer to the complaint within twenty-eight days after service of this summons on you, exclusive of the day of service. Your answer must be filed with the Court within three days after the service of a copy of the answer on the plaintiff's attorney.

If you fail to appear and defend, judgment by default will be rendered against you for the relief demanded in the complaint.

Clerk, Court of Common Pleas
Franklin County, Ohio

Date _____

By _____
Deputy

NOTE: The caption above designates the particular paper as a "SUMMONS." The particular pleading or paper should contain an appropriate designation, thus: "COMPLAINT," "ANSWER," etc. A more specific designation in a caption is also appropriate, thus: "MOTION TO INTERVENE AS A DEFENDANT."

INSTRUCTIONS FOR PERSONAL OR RESIDENCE SERVICE

To: _____

    You are instructed to make personal-residence service [cross out one] upon the defendant(s) _____
(Name(s))

_____

at _____
(address for service, if different from body of summons)

Special instructions for server: _____

_____

RETURN OF SERVICE OF SUMMONS (PERSONAL)

Fees	
Service	$_____
Mileage	_____
Copy	_____
Docket	_____
Return	_____
Totals	$_____

I received this summons on _____, 19__, at _____ o'clock, __m. and made personal service of it upon _____ by locating him-them [cross out one] and tendering a copy summons and accompanying documents, on _____, 19__.

_____

_____
Sheriff-Bailiff-Process Server

By _____
Deputy

* * * * *

RETURN OF SERVICE OF SUMMONS (RESIDENCE)

Fees	
Service	$_____
Mileage	_____
Copy	_____
Docket	_____
Return	_____
Totals	$_____

I received this summons on _____, 19__, at _____ o'clock, __m., and made residence service of it upon the defendant(s) _____

_____

by leaving, at his-their [cross out one] usual place of residence with _____, a person of suitable age and discretion then residing therein, a copy of the summons, a copy of the complaint and accompanying documents, on _____, 19__.

_____

_____
Sheriff-Bailiff-Process Server

Date: _____   By _____
                              Deputy

RETURN OF SERVICE OF SUMMONS (FAILURE OF SERVICE)

Fees	
Service	$_____
Mileage	_____
Copy	_____
Docket	_____
Return	_____
Totals	$_____

I received this summons on _____, 19__, at _____ o'clock, __m. with instructions to make personal-residence [cross out one] service upon the defendant(s) _____ and I was unable to serve a copy of the summons upon him-them [cross out one] for the following reasons: _____

_____

_____
Sheriff-Bailiff-Process Server

Date: _____   By _____
                              Deputy

Comment: The endorsement of time of receipt by the Sheriff is required by § 311.09, R.C.

NOTE: Returns shall be made pursuant to Rule 4 through Rule 4.6 and pertinent sections of the Ohio Revised Code which are not in conflict with the Rules of Civil Procedure and which establish particular duties for the serving officer, i.e., Sections 311.08, 311.17 and 2335.31, Revised Code.

FORM 2

COMPLAINT ON A PROMISSORY NOTE

COURT OF COMMON PLEAS
FRANKLIN COUNTY, OHIO

A.B., Plaintiff	)
(address)	)
v.	)　　No. _____
C.D., Defendant	)
(address)	)　　COMPLAINT

1. Defendant on or about June 1, 19__, executed and delivered to plaintiff a promissory note, a copy of which is hereto attached as Exhibit A.

2. Defendant owes to plaintiff the amount of said note and interest.

WHEREFORE plaintiff demands judgment against defendant for the sum of _____ dollars, interest, and costs.

_____
(Attorney for Plaintiff)

_____
(Address)

NOTE: 1. The pleader should follow the form above if he has possession of a copy of the note. The pleader should attach a copy of the note to the pleading. See Rule 10(D).

2. Under the rules free joinder of claims is permitted. See Rule 8(E) and Rule 18. Consequently the claims set forth in each and all of the following forms may be joined with this complaint or with each other. Ordinarily each claim should be stated in a separate division of the complaint, and the divisions should be designated as counts successively numbered (i.e., COUNT ONE, COUNT TWO, etc.). See Rule 10(B). In particular the rules permit alternative and inconsistent pleading. See Rule 8(E)(2).

3. The attorney must sign the pleading. See Rule 11. The pleading need not be verified. See Rule 11.

FORM 2A

COMPLAINT ON A PROMISSORY NOTE
(REASON FOR OMISSION OF COPY STATED)

1. Defendant on or about June 1, 19__, executed and delivered to plaintiff a promissory note.

[in the following words and figures: (here set out the note verbatim)]

or

[whereby defendant promised to pay plaintiff or order on June 1, 19___, the sum of _____ dollars with interest thereon at the rate of _____ percent per annum].

2. Plaintiff is unable to attach a copy of the said note because (here set out the reason for failure to attach the note).

3. Defendant owes to plaintiff the amount of said note and interest.

WHEREFORE (etc. as in Form 2).

NOTE: 1. The pleader states why, under Rule 10(D), he is unable to attach a copy of the note.

2. If pleader can set forth the note verbatim from information at hand, he may do so.

3. Or pleader may plead the legal effect of the note, he being unable to attach a copy of the note.

4. This type form may be used in other situations whenever pleader is required to attach a copy of an instrument, but a copy of the instrument is not available to him.

FORM 3

COMPLAINT ON AN ACCOUNT

Defendant owes plaintiff _____ dollars according to the account hereto annexed as Exhibit A.

WHEREFORE (etc. as in Form 2).

FORM 4

COMPLAINT FOR GOODS SOLD AND DELIVERED

Defendant owes plaintiff _____ dollars for goods sold and delivered by plaintiff to defendant between June 1, 19___, and December 1, 19___.

WHEREFORE (etc. as in Form 2).

NOTE: This form may be used where the action is for an agreed price or for the reasonable value of the goods.

FORM 5

COMPLAINT FOR MONEY LENT

Defendant owes plaintiff _____ dollars for money lent by plaintiff to defendant on June 1, 19___.

WHEREFORE (etc. as in Form 2).

FORM 6

COMPLAINT FOR MONEY PAID BY MISTAKE

Defendant owes plaintiff _____ dollars for money paid by plaintiff to defendant by mistake on June 1, 19___, under the following circumstances: [here state the circumstances with particularity—see Rule 9(B)].

WHEREFORE (etc. as in Form 2).

FORM 7

COMPLAINT FOR MONEY HAD AND RECEIVED

Defendant owes plaintiff _____ dollars for money had and received from one G.H. on June 1, 19___, to be paid by defendant to plaintiff.

WHEREFORE (etc. as in Form 2).

FORM 8

COMPLAINT FOR NEGLIGENCE

1. On June 1, 19___, in a public highway called High Street in Columbus, Ohio, defendant negligently drove a motor vehicle against plaintiff who was then crossing said highway.

2. As a result plaintiff was thrown down and had his leg broken and was otherwise injured, was prevented from transacting his business, suffered great pain of body and mind, and incurred expenses for medical attention and hospitalization in the sum of one thousand dollars.

WHEREFORE plaintiff demands judgment against defendant in the sum of _____ dollars and costs.

NOTE: Since contributory negligence is an affirmative defense, the complaint need contain no allegation of due care of plaintiff.

FORM 9

COMPLAINT FOR NEGLIGENCE WHERE PLAINTIFF IS UNABLE TO DETERMINE DEFINITELY WHETHER THE PERSON RESPONSIBLE IS C.D. OR E.F. OR WHETHER BOTH ARE RESPONSIBLE AND WHERE HIS EVIDENCE MAY JUSTIFY A FINDING OF WILFULNESS OR OF RECKLESSNESS OR OF NEGLIGENCE

A.B., Plaintiff	)	
(address)	)	
v.	)	No. _____
C.D. and E.F., Defendants	)	
(addresses)	)	COMPLAINT

1. On June 1, 19__, in a public highway called High Street in Columbus, Ohio, defendant C.D. or defendant E.F., or both defendants C.D. and E.F. wilfully or recklessly or negligently drove or caused to be driven a motor vehicle against plaintiff who was then crossing said highway.

2. As a result plaintiff was thrown down and had his leg broken and was otherwise injured, was prevented from transacting his business, suffered great pain of body and mind, and incurred expenses for medical attention and hospitalization in the sum of one thousand dollars.

WHEREFORE plaintiff demands judgment against C.D. or against E.F. or against both in the sum of _____ dollars and costs.

FORM 10

COMPLAINT FOR CONVERSION

On or about December 1, 19__, defendant converted to his own use ten bonds of the _____ Company (here insert brief identification as by number and issue) of the value of _____ dollars, the property of plaintiff.

WHEREFORE plaintiff demands judgment against defendant in the sum of _____ dollars, interest, and costs.

FORM 11

COMPLAINT FOR SPECIFIC PERFORMANCE OF CONTRACT TO CONVEY LAND

1. On or about December 1, 19___, plaintiff and defendant entered into an agreement in writing a copy of which is hereto annexed as Exhibit A.

2. In accord with the provisions of said agreement plaintiff tendered to defendant the purchase price and requested a conveyance of the land, but defendant refused to accept the tender and refused to make the conveyance.

3. Plaintiff now offers to pay the purchase price.

WHEREFORE plaintiff demands (1) that defendant be required specifically to perform said agreement, (2) damages in the sum of one thousand dollars, and (3) that if specific performance is not granted plaintiff have judgment against defendant in the sum of _____ dollars.

> NOTE: The demand for relief seeks specific performance as well as ancillary damages resulting from the delay. In addition the demand for relief seeks damages in a certain sum if the court finds it impossible to grant specific performance as where, in the interim, defendant has conveyed the property to a purchaser for value without notice.

FORM 12

COMPLAINT ON CLAIM FOR DEBT AND TO SET ASIDE FRAUDULENT CONVEYANCE UNDER RULE 18(B)

A.B., Plaintiff)
(address))
  v.)   No. _____
C.D. and E.F., Defendants)
(addresses))   COMPLAINT

1. Defendant C.D. on or about _____ executed and delivered to plaintiff a promissory note a copy of which is hereto annexed as Exhibit A.

2. Defendant C.D. owes to plaintiff the amount of said note and interest.

3. Defendant C.D. on or about _____ conveyed all his property, real and personal [or specify and describe] to defendant E.F. for the purpose of defrauding plaintiff and hindering and delaying the collection of the indebtedness evidenced by the note above referred to.

WHEREFORE plaintiff demands:

(1) That plaintiff have judgment against defendant C.D. for _____ dollars and interest; (2) that the aforesaid conveyance to defendant E.F. be declared void and the judgment herein be declared a lien on said property; (3) that plaintiff have judgment against the defendants for costs.

FORM 13

COMPLAINT FOR INTERPLEADER AND DECLARATORY RELIEF

1. On or about June 1, 19___, plaintiff issued to G.H. a policy of life insurance, a copy of which is attached as Exhibit A, whereby plaintiff promised to pay to K.L. as beneficiary the sum of _____ dollars upon the death of G.H. The policy required the payment by G.H. of a stipulated premium on June 1, 19___, and annually thereafter as a condition precedent to its continuance in force.

2. No part of the premium due June 1, 19___, was ever paid and the policy ceased to have any force or effect on July 1, 19___.

3. Thereafter, on September 1, 19___, G.H. and K.L. died as the result of a collision between a locomotive and the automobile in which G.H. and K.L. were riding.

4. Defendant C.D. is the duly appointed and acting executor of the will of G.H.; defendant E.F. is the duly appointed and acting executor of the will of K.L., defendant X.Y. claims to have been duly designated as beneficiary of said policy in place of K.L.

5. Each of defendants, C.D., E.F., and X.Y. is claiming that the above-mentioned policy was in full force and effect at the time of the death of G.H.; each of them is claiming to be the only person entitled to receive payment of the amount of the policy and has made demand for payment thereof.

6. By reason of these conflicting claims of the defendants, plaintiff is in great doubt as to which defendant is entitled to be paid the amount of the policy, if it was in force at the death of G.H.

WHEREFORE plaintiff demands that the court adjudge:

(1) That none of the defendants is entitled to recover from plaintiff the amount of said policy or any part thereof.

(2) That each of the defendants be restrained from instituting any action against plaintiff for the recovery of the amount of said policy or any part thereof.

(3) That, if the court shall determine that said policy was in force at the death of G.H., the defendants be required to interplead and settle between themselves their rights to the money due under said policy, and that plaintiff be discharged from all liability in the premises except to the person whom the court shall adjudge entitled to the amount of said policy.

(4) That plaintiff recover its costs.

FORM 14

MOTION TO DISMISS, PRESENTING DEFENSES OF FAILURE TO STATE A CLAIM, OF LACK OF SERVICE OF PROCESS, AND OF LACK OF JURISDICTION UNDER RULE 12(B)

COURT OF COMMON PLEAS
FRANKLIN COUNTY, OHIO

A.B., Plaintiff	)	
(address)	)	
v.	)	No. _____
C.D. Corporation, Defendant	)	
(address)	)	MOTION TO DISMISS

The defendant moves the court as follows:

1. To dismiss the action because the complaint fails to state a claim against defendant upon which relief can be granted.

2. To dismiss the action or in lieu thereof to quash the return of service of summons on the grounds (a) that the defendant is a corporation organized under the laws of Delaware and was not and is not subject to service of process within this state, and (b) that the defendant has not been properly served with process in this action, all of which more clearly appears in the affidavits of M.N. and X.Y. hereto attached as Exhibit A and Exhibit B, respectively.

3. To dismiss the action on the ground that the court lacks jurisdiction because [here state the reasons why the court lacks jurisdiction].

_____
(Attorney for Defendant)

_____
(Address)

SERVICE OF COPY

A copy hereof was served upon X.Y., attorney for plaintiff, by mailing it to him on June 1, 19__ [or set forth other method of service upon X.Y.].

_____
(Attorney for Defendant)

(Amended, eff 7-1-71)

NOTE: 1. The form gives various examples of defenses which may be raised by motion under Rule 12(B).

2. Whether the motion should be accompanied by a notice of hearing on the motion or whether the motion should be accompanied by a memorandum brief depends upon the rules of a particular local court. See Rule 7(B) and the rules of the local court regarding motion practice.

3. All papers after the original pleading required to be served upon an opposite party shall have endorsed thereon, when filed with the court, a statement setting forth the date and method of service. See Rule 5.

FORM 15

ANSWER PRESENTING DEFENSES UNDER RULE 12(B)

A.B., Plaintiff	)	
(address)	)	No. _____
v.	)	
C.D. and E.F., Defendants	)	ANSWER, COUNTERCLAIM
(addresses)	)	AND CROSS-CLAIM

FIRST DEFENSE

The complaint fails to state a claim against defendant C.D. upon which relief can be granted.

SECOND DEFENSE

If the defendant C.D. is indebted to plaintiff for the goods mentioned in the complaint, he is indebted to him jointly with G.H. G.H. is alive, is a resident of this state, is subject to the jurisdiction of this court and can be made a party but has not been made one.

THIRD DEFENSE

Defendant C.D. admits the allegation contained in paragraphs 1 and 4 of the complaint; alleges that he is without knowledge or information sufficient to form a belief as to the truth of the allegations contained in paragraph 2 of the complaint; and denies each and every other allegation contained in the complaint.

FOURTH DEFENSE

The right of action set forth in the complaint did not accrue within _____ years next before the commencement of this action.

COUNTERCLAIM

[Here set forth any claim as a counterclaim in the manner in which a claim is pleaded in a complaint.]

CROSS-CLAIM AGAINST DEFENDANT M.N.

[Here set forth the claim constituting a cross-claim against defendant M.N. in the manner in which a claim is pleaded in a complaint.]

_____

(Attorney for Defendant, C.D.)

_____

(Address)

(Service of Copy as in Form 14)

NOTE: 1. The above form contains examples of certain defenses provided for in Rule 12(B). The first defense challenges the legal sufficiency of the complaint. It is a substitute for a motion to dismiss; that is, under former practice the issue raised by the first defense would have been raised by demurrer, and under present practice the same issue might have been raised by motion at the option of the defendant. See Rule 12(B).

2. The second defense embodies the old plea in abatement. The decision thereon, however, may, for example, well provide under Rule 19(A) or Rule 21 for the citing in of the party rather than an abatement of the action.

3. The third defense is an answer on the merits.

4. The fourth defense is one of the affirmative defenses provided for in Rule 8(C).

5. The answer also includes a counterclaim and a cross-claim. See Rule 12(B).

FORM 16

SUMMONS AGAINST THIRD-PARTY DEFENDANT

COURT OF COMMON PLEAS
FRANKLIN COUNTY, OHIO

A.B., Plaintiff (address) 　　v. C.D., Defendant and 　Third-Party Plaintiff (address) 　　v. E.F., Third-Party 　Defendant (address)	))) 　　　No. _____)))　　SUMMONS)))

To the above-named Third-Party Defendant:

You are hereby summoned and required to serve upon _____, plaintiff's attorney whose address is _____, and upon _____, who is attorney for C.D., defendant and third-party plaintiff, and whose address is _____, an answer to the third-party complaint which is herewith served upon you within twenty-eight days after the service of this summons upon you exclusive of the day of service. If you fail to do so, judgment by default will be taken against you for the relief demanded in the third-party complaint. There is also served upon you herewith a copy of the complaint of the plaintiff which you may but are not required to answer. Your answer to the third-party complaint and your answer to the plaintiff's complaint must also be filed with the court.

　　　　　　　　　　　　　　　　　　　_____
　　　　　　　　　　　　　　　　　　　　　　　　(Clerk of Court)
Date _____
　　　　　　　　　　　By _____
　　　　　　　　　　　　　　　　　　　　　　　(Deputy)

NOTE: It may be necessary, depending upon when the third-party complaint is served, to seek leave of court by motion to bring in a third-party defendant. See Rule 14(A).

FORM 16A

COMPLAINT AGAINST THIRD-PARTY DEFENDANT

COURT OF COMMON PLEAS
FRANKLIN COUNTY, OHIO

A.B., Plaintiff
(address)
   v.
C.D., Defendant and
   Third-Party Plaintiff
(address)
   v.
E.F., Third-Party
   Defendant
(address)
	No. _____
	
	THIRD-PARTY COMPLAINT

1. Plaintiff A.B. has filed against defendant C.D. a complaint, a copy of which is hereto attached as Exhibit A.

2. [Here state the grounds upon which C.D. is entitled to recover from E.F., all or part of what A.B. may recover from C.D. The statement should be framed as in an original complaint.]

WHEREFORE C.D. demands judgment against third-party defendant E.F. for all sums [make appropriate change where C.D. is entitled to only partial recovery over against E.F.] that may be adjudged against defendant C.D. in favor of plaintiff A.B.

_____
(Attorney for C.D., Third-Party Plaintiff)

_____
(Address)

NOTE: It is necessary to comply with Rule 5 regarding service of third-party papers on plaintiff.

FORM 17

MOTION TO INTERVENE AS A DEFENDANT UNDER RULE 24

COURT OF COMMON PLEAS
FRANKLIN COUNTY, OHIO

A.B., Plaintiff
(address)
   v.
C.D., Defendant
(address)
   v.
E.F., Applicant for
   Intervention
(address)
	No. _____
	
	MOTION TO INTERVENE AS
	A DEFENDANT

E.F. moves for leave to intervene as a defendant in this action in order to assert the defenses set forth in his proposed answer, of which a copy is hereto attached, on the ground that [here insert the appropriate grounds of intervention].

_____

(Attorney for E.F., Applicant for Intervention)

_____

(Address)

NOTE: (as amended effective July 1, 1999) It is necessary that a motion to intervene be accompanied by a pleading as required in Civ. R. 24(C). It is also necessary to comply with Civ. R. 5 regarding service of the motion* on the parties to the action.

* [The pleading should also be served pursuant to Rule 5.]

FORM 18

JUDGMENT ON JURY VERDICT

COURT OF COMMON PLEAS
FRANKLIN COUNTY, OHIO

A.B., Plaintiff	)	
(address)	)	
v.	)	No. _____
C.D., Defendant	)	
(address)	)	JUDGMENT

This action came on for trial before the Court and a jury, and the issues having been duly tried and the jury having duly rendered its verdict.

IT IS ORDERED AND ADJUDGED [that the plaintiff A.B. recover of the defendant C.D. the sum of _____, with interest thereon at a rate of _____ percent as provided by law, and his costs of action.]

[that the plaintiff take nothing, that the action be dismissed on the merits, and that the defendant C.D. recover of the plaintiff A.B. his costs of action.]

Dated at Columbus, Ohio, this _____ day of _____, 19__.

_____

Judge, Court of Common Pleas

JOURNALIZED this _____ day of _____, 19__.

_____

Clerk of Court

By _____ Deputy Clerk

NOTE: This form is illustrative of the judgment to be entered upon the general verdict of a jury. It deals with the cases where there is a general jury verdict awarding the plaintiff money damages or finding for the defendant, but is adaptable to other situations of jury verdicts.

FORM 19

JUDGMENT ON DECISION BY THE COURT

COURT OF COMMON PLEAS
FRANKLIN COUNTY, OHIO

A.B., Plaintiff   )
(address)   )
    v.   )   No. _____
C.D., Defendant   )
(address)   )   JUDGMENT

This action came on for [trial] [hearing] before the Court, and the issues having been duly [tried] [heard] and a decision having been duly rendered.

IT IS ORDERED AND ADJUDGED [that the plaintiff A.B. recover of the defendant C.D. the sum of _____, with interest thereon at the rate of _____ percent as provided by law, and his costs of action.]

[that the plaintiff take nothing, that the action be dismissed on the merits, and that the defendant C.D. recover of the plaintiff A.B. his costs of action.]

Dated at Columbus, Ohio, this _____ day of _____, 19__.

_____
Judge, Court of Common Pleas

JOURNALIZED this _____ day of
_____, 19__.

_____
Clerk of Court
By _____ Deputy Clerk

NOTE: This form is illustrative of the judgment to be entered upon a decision of the court. It deals with the cases of decisions by the court awarding a party only money damages or costs, but is adaptable to other decisions by the court.

FORM 20

COMPLAINT FOR DIVORCE, ALIMONY AND CUSTODY OF CHILDREN

COURT OF COMMON PLEAS
FRANKLIN COUNTY, OHIO

A.B., Plaintiff)
(address))
    v.)   No. _____
C.D., Defendant)
(address))   COMPLAINT

1. Plaintiff has been a resident of Ohio for at least *six months* immediately preceding the filing of this complaint.

2. Plaintiff and defendant were married at _____, in the State of _____, on the _____ day of _____, 19__, and there are [no] _____ children, the issue of such marriage [whose names and ages are, respectively (stating them, and as to who has custody)].

3. Plaintiff says that defendant [here set forth one or more of the statutory grounds for divorce as provided for by law].

WHEREFORE, plaintiff demands that she [he] be granted a divorce from defendant and awarded custody of their minor children; that she [he] be granted reasonable alimony and support for their minor children; [that she be restored to her former name of _____]; and for her costs herein, including a reasonable sum for her expenses and attorney's fees in this action, and for such other relief as shall be proper and necessary.

_____
(Attorney for Plaintiff)

_____
(Address)

(Amended, eff 7-1-76)

OHIO RULES OF APPELLATE PROCEDURE

Effective July 1, 1971

Complete with amendments through June 30, 2003

TITLE I
APPLICABILITY OF RULES

RULE 1. Scope of rules

(A) These rules govern procedure in appeals to courts of appeals from the trial courts of record in Ohio.

(B) Procedure in appeals to courts of appeals from the board of tax appeals shall be as provided by law, except that App. R. 13 to 33 shall be applicable to those appeals.

(C) Procedures in appeals to courts of appeals from juvenile courts pursuant to section 2505.073 of the Revised Code shall be as provided by that section, except that these rules govern to the extent that the rules do not conflict with that section.

(Amended, eff 7-1-94)

RULE 2. Law and fact appeals abolished

Appeals on questions of law and fact are abolished.

TITLE II
APPEALS FROM JUDGMENTS AND ORDERS OF COURT OF RECORD

RULE 3. Appeal as of right—how taken

(A) **Filing the notice of appeal.** An appeal as of right shall be taken by filing a notice of appeal with the clerk of the trial court within the time allowed by Rule 4. Failure of an appellant to take any step other than the timely filing of a notice of appeal does not affect the validity of the appeal, but is ground only for such action as the court of appeals deems appropriate, which may include dismissal of the appeal. Appeals by leave of court shall be taken in the manner prescribed by Rule 5.

(B) Joint or consolidated appeals. If two or more persons are entitled to appeal from a judgment or order of a trial court and their interests are such as to make joinder practicable, they may file a joint notice of appeal, or may join in appeal after filing separate timely notices of appeal, and they may thereafter proceed on appeal as a single appellant. Appeals may be consolidated by order of the court of appeals upon its own motion or upon motion of a party, or by stipulation of the parties to the several appeals.

(C) Cross appeal.

(1) Cross appeal required. A person who intends to defend a judgment or order against an appeal taken by an appellant and who also seeks to change the judgment or order or, in the event the judgment or order may be reversed or modified, an interlocutory ruling merged into the judgment or order, shall file a notice of cross appeal within the time allowed by App.R. 4.

(2) Cross appeal not required. A person who intends to defend a judgment or order appealed by an appellant on a ground other than that relied on by the trial court but who does not seek to change the judgment or order is not required to file a notice of cross appeal.

(D) Content of the notice of appeal. The notice of appeal shall specify the party or parties taking the appeal; shall designate the judgment, order or part thereof appealed from; and shall name the court to which the appeal is taken. The title of the case shall be the same as in the trial court with the designation of the appellant added, as appropriate. Form 1 in the Appendix of Forms is a suggested form of a notice of appeal.

(E) Service of the notice of appeal. The clerk of the trial court shall serve notice of the filing of a notice of appeal and, where required by local rule, a docketing statement, by mailing, or by facsimile transmission, a copy to counsel of record of each party other than the appellant, or, if a party is not represented by counsel, to the party at the party's last known address. The clerk shall mail or otherwise forward a copy of the notice of appeal and of the docket entries, together with a copy of all filings by appellant pursuant to App. R. 9(B), to the clerk of the court of appeals named in the notice. The clerk shall note on each copy served the date on which the notice of appeal was filed. Failure of the clerk to serve notice shall not affect the validity of the appeal. Service shall be sufficient notwithstanding the death of a party or a party's counsel. The clerk shall note in the docket the names of the parties served, the date served, and the means of service.

(F) Amendment of the notice of appeal. The court of appeals within its discretion and upon such terms as are just may allow the amendment of a timely filed notice of appeal.

(G) Docketing statement. If a court of appeals has adopted an accelerated calendar by local rule pursuant to Rule 11.1, a docketing statement shall be filed with the clerk of the trial court with the notice of appeal. (See Form 2, Appendix of Forms.)

The purpose of the docketing statement is to determine whether an appeal will be assigned to the accelerated or the regular calendar.

A case may be assigned to the accelerated calendar if any of the following apply:

(1) No transcript is required (e.g. summary judgment or judgment on the pleadings);

(2) The length of the transcript is such that its preparation time will not be a source of delay;

(3) An agreed statement is submitted in lieu of the record;

(4) The record was made in an administrative hearing and filed with the trial court;

(5) All parties to the appeal approve an assignment of the appeal to the accelerated calendar; or

(6) The case has been designated by local rule for the accelerated calendar.

The court of appeals by local rule may assign a case to the accelerated calendar at any stage of the proceeding. The court of appeals may provide by local rule for an oral hearing before a full panel in order to assist it in determining whether the appeal should be assigned to the accelerated calendar.

Upon motion of appellant or appellee for a procedural order pursuant to App. R. 15(B) filed within seven days after the notice of appeal is filed with the clerk of the trial court, a case may be removed for good cause from the accelerated calendar and assigned to the regular calendar. Demonstration of a unique issue of law which will be of substantial precedential value in the determination of similar cases will ordinarily be good cause for transfer to the regular calendar.

(Amended, eff 7-1-72; 7-1-77; 7-1-82; 7-1-91; 7-1-92; 7-1-94)

RULE 4. Appeal as of right—when taken

(A) Time for appeal. A party shall file the notice of appeal required by App.R. 3 within thirty days of the later of entry of the judgment or order appealed or, in a civil case, service of the notice of judgment and its entry if service is not made on the party within the three day period in Rule 58(B) of the Ohio Rules of Civil Procedure.

(B) Exceptions. The following are exceptions to the appeal time period in division (A) of this rule:

(1) Multiple or cross appeals. If a notice of appeal is timely filed by a party, another party may file a notice of appeal within the appeal time period otherwise prescribed by this rule or within ten days of the filing of the first notice of appeal.

(2) Civil or juvenile post-judgment motion. In a civil case or juvenile proceeding, if a party files a timely motion for judgment under Civ. R. 50(B), a new trial under Civ. R. 59(B), vacating or modifying a judgment by an objection to a magistrate's decision under Civ. R. 53(E)(4)(c) or Rule 40(E)(4)(c) of the Ohio Rules of Juvenile Procedure, or findings of fact and conclusions of law under Civ. R. 52, the time for filing a notice of appeal begins to run as to all parties when the order disposing of the motion is entered.

(3) Criminal post-judgment motion. In a criminal case, if a party timely files a motion for arrest of judgment or a new trial for a reason other than newly discovered evidence, the time for filing a notice of appeal begins to run when the order denying the motion is entered. A motion for a new trial on the ground of newly discovered evidence made within the time for filing a motion for a new trial on other grounds extends the time for filing a notice of appeal from a judgment of conviction in the same manner as a motion on other grounds. If made after the expiration of the time for filing a motion on other grounds, the motion on the ground of newly discovered evidence does not extend the time for filing a notice of appeal.

(4) Appeal by prosecution. In an appeal by the prosecution under Crim.R. 12(K) or Juv.R. 22(F), the prosecution shall file a notice of appeal within seven days of entry of the judgment or order appealed.

(5) Partial final judgment or order. If an appeal is permitted from a judgment or order entered in a case in which the trial court has not disposed of all claims as to all parties, other than a judgment or order entered under Civ.R. 54(B), a party may file a notice of appeal within thirty days of entry of the judgment or order appealed or the judgment or order that disposes of the remaining claims. Division (A) of this rule applies to a judgment or order entered under Civ.R. 54(B).

(C) Premature notice of appeal. A notice of appeal filed after the announcement of a decision, order, or sentence but before entry of the judgment or order that begins the running of the appeal time period is treated as filed immediately after the entry.

(D) Definition of "entry" or "entered". As used in this rule, "entry" or "entered" means when a judgment or order is entered under Civ.R. 58(A) or Crim.R. 32(C).

(Amended, eff 7-1-72; 7-1-85; 7-1-89; 7-1-92; 7-1-96; 7-1-02)

RULE 5. Appeals by leave of court in criminal cases

(A) Motion by defendant for delayed appeal. After the expiration of the thirty day period provided by App. R. 4(A) for the filing of a notice of appeal as of right in criminal cases, an appeal may be taken only by leave of the court to which the appeal is taken. A motion for leave to appeal shall be filed with the court of appeals and shall set forth the reasons for the failure of the appellant to perfect an appeal as of right. Concurrently with the filing of the motion, the movant shall file with the clerk of the trial court a notice of appeal in the form prescribed by App. R. 3 and shall file a copy of the notice of the appeal in the court of appeals.

The movant also shall furnish an additional copy of the notice of appeal and a copy of the motion for leave to appeal to the clerk of the court of appeals who shall serve the notice of appeal and the motions upon the prosecuting attorney.

(B) Motion by prosecution for leave to appeal. When leave is sought by the prosecution from the court of appeals to appeal a judgment or order of the trial court, a motion for leave to appeal shall be filed with the court of appeals within thirty days from the entry of the judgment and order sought to be appealed and shall set forth the errors that the movant claims occurred in the proceedings of the trial court. The motion shall be accompanied by affidavits, or by the parts of the record upon which the movant relies, to show the probability that the errors claimed did in fact occur, and by a brief or memorandum of law in support of the movant's claims. Concurrently with the filing of the motion, the movant shall file with the clerk of the trial court a notice of appeal in the form prescribed by App. R. 3 and file a copy of the notice of appeal in the court of appeals. The movant also shall furnish a copy of the motion and a copy of the notice of appeal to the clerk of the court of appeals who shall serve the notice of appeal and a copy of the motion for leave to appeal upon the attorney for the defendant who, within thirty days from the filing of the motion, may file affidavits, parts of the record, and brief or memorandum of law to refute the claims of the movant.

(C)(1) Motion by defendant for leave to appeal consecutive sentences pursuant to R.C. 2953.08(C). When leave is sought from the court of appeals for leave to appeal consecutive sentences pursuant to R.C. 2953.08(C), a motion for leave to appeal shall be filed with the court of appeals within thirty days from the entry of the judgment and order sought to be appealed and shall set forth the reason why the consecutive sentences exceed the maximum prison term allowed. The motion shall be accompanied by a copy of the judgment and order stating the sentences imposed and stating the offense of which movant was found guilty or to which movant pled guilty. Concurrently with the filing of the motion, the movant shall file with the clerk of the trial court a notice of appeal in the form prescribed by App.R. 3 and file a copy of the notice of appeal in the court of appeals. The movant also shall furnish a copy of the notice of appeal and a copy of the motion to the clerk of the court of appeals who shall serve the notice of appeal and the motion upon the prosecuting attorney.

(C)(2) Leave to appeal consecutive sentences incorporated into appeal as of right. When a criminal defendant has filed a notice of appeal pursuant to App. R. 4, the defendant may elect to incorporate in defendant's initial appellate brief an assignment of error pursuant to R.C. 2953.08(C), and the assignment of error shall be deemed to constitute a timely motion for leave to appeal pursuant to R.C. 2953.08(C).

(D) Determination of the motion. Except when required by the court the motion shall be determined by the court of appeals on the documents filed without formal hearing or oral argument.

(E) Order and procedure following determination. Upon determination of the motion, the court shall journalize its order and the order shall be filed with the clerk of the court of appeals, who shall certify a copy of the order and mail or otherwise forward the copy to the clerk of the trial court. If the motion for leave to appeal is overruled, except as to motions for leave to appeal filed by the prosecution, the clerk of the trial court shall collect the costs pertaining to the motion, in both the court of appeals and the trial court, from the movant. If the motion is sustained and leave to appeal is granted, the further procedure shall be the same as for appeals as of right in criminal cases, except as otherwise specifically provided in these rules.

(Amended, eff 7-1-88; 7-1-92; 7-1-94; 7-1-96)

RULE 6. Concurrent jurisdiction in criminal actions

(A) Whenever a trial court and an appellate court are exercising concurrent jurisdiction to review a judgment of conviction, and the trial court files a written determination that grounds exist for granting a petition for post-conviction relief, the trial court shall notify the parties and the appellate court of that determination. On such notification, or pursuant to a party's motion in the court of appeals, the appellate court may remand the case to the trial court.

(B) When an appellate court reverses, vacates, or modifies a judgment of conviction on direct appeal, the trial court may dismiss a petition for post-conviction relief to the extent that it is moot. The petition shall be reinstated pursuant to motion if the appellate court's judgment on direct appeal is reversed, vacated, or modified in such a manner that the petition is no longer moot.

(C) Whenever a trial court's grant of post-conviction relief is reversed, vacated, or modified in such a manner that the direct appeal is no longer moot, the direct appeal shall be reinstated pursuant to the statute. Upon knowledge that a statutory reinstatement of the appeal has occurred, the court of appeals shall enter an order journalizing the reinstatement and providing for resumption of the appellate process.

(D) Whenever a direct appeal is pending concurrently with a petition for post-conviction relief or a review of the petition in any court, each party shall include, in any brief, memorandum, or motion filed, a list of case numbers of all actions and appeals, and the court in which they are pending, regarding the same judgment of conviction.

(Effective 7-1-97)

RULE 7. Stay or injunction pending appeal—civil and juvenile actions

(A) Stay must ordinarily be sought in the first instance in trial court; motion for stay in court of appeals. Application for a stay of the judgment or order of a trial court pending appeal, or for the determination of the amount of and the approval of a supersedeas bond, must ordinarily be made in the first instance in the trial court. A motion for such relief or for an order suspending, modifying, restoring or granting an injunction during the pendency of an appeal may be made to the court of appeals or to a judge thereof, but, except in cases of injunction pending appeal, the motion shall show that application to the trial court for the relief sought is not practicable, or that the trial court has, by journal entry, denied an application, or failed to afford the relief which the applicant requested. The motion shall also show the reasons for the relief requested and the facts relied upon, and if the facts are subject to dispute the motion shall be supported by affidavits or other sworn statements or copies thereof. With the motion shall be filed such parts of the record as are relevant and as are reasonably available at the time the motion is filed. Reasonable notice of the motion and the intention to apply to the court shall be given by the movant to all parties. The motion shall be filed with the clerk of the court of appeals and normally will be considered by at least two judges of the court, but in exceptional cases where the attendance of two judges of the court would be impracticable due to the requirements of time, the application may be made to and considered by a single judge of the court on reasonable notice to the adverse party, provided, however, that when an injunction is appealed from it shall be suspended only by order of at least two of the judges of the court of appeals, on reasonable notice to the adverse party.

(B) Stay may be conditioned upon giving of bond; proceedings against sureties. Relief available in the court of appeals under this rule may be conditioned upon the filing of a bond or other appropriate security in the trial court. If security is given in the form of a bond or stipulation or other undertaking with one or more sureties, each surety submits himself or herself to the jurisdiction of the trial court and irrevocably appoints the clerk of the trial court as the surety's agent upon whom any process affecting the surety's liability on the bond or undertaking may be served. Subject to the limits of its monetary jurisdiction, this liability may be enforced on motion in the trial court without the necessity of an independent action. The motion and such notice of the motion as the trial court prescribes may be served on the clerk of the trial court, who shall forthwith mail copies to the sureties if their addresses are known.

(C) Stay in juvenile actions. No order, judgment, or decree of a juvenile court, concerning a dependent, neglected, unruly, or delinquent child, shall be stayed upon appeal, unless suitable provision is made for the maintenance, care, and custody of the dependent, neglected, unruly, or delinquent child pending the appeal.

(Amended, eff 7-1-73; 7-1-01)

RULE 8. Bail and suspension of execution of sentence in criminal cases

(A) Discretionary right of court to release pending appeal. The discretionary right of the trial court or the court of appeals to admit a defendant in a criminal action to bail and to suspend the execution of his sentence during the pendency of his appeal is as prescribed by law.

(B) Release on bail and suspension of execution of sentence pending appeal from a judgment of conviction. Application for release on bail and for suspension of execution of sentence after a judgment of conviction shall be made in the first instance in the trial court. Thereafter, if such application is denied, a motion for bail and suspension of execution of sentence pending review may be made to the court of appeals or to two judges thereof. The motion shall be determined promptly upon such papers, affidavits, and portions of the record as the parties shall present and after reasonable notice to the appellee.

(Amended, eff 7-1-75)

RULE 9. The record on appeal

(A) Composition of the record on appeal. The original papers and exhibits thereto filed in the trial court, the transcript of proceedings, if any, including exhibits, and a certified copy of the docket and journal entries prepared by the clerk of the trial court shall constitute the record on appeal in all cases. A videotape recording of the proceedings constitutes the transcript of proceedings other than hereinafter provided, and, for purposes of filing, need not be transcribed into written form. Proceedings recorded by means other than videotape must be transcribed into written form. When the written form is certified by the reporter in accordance with App. R. 9(B), such written form shall then constitute the transcript of proceedings. When the transcript of proceedings is in the videotape medium, counsel shall type or print those portions of such transcript necessary for the court to determine the questions presented, certify their accuracy, and append such copy of the portions of the transcripts to their briefs.

In all capital cases the trial proceedings shall include a written transcript of the record made during the trial by stenographic means.

(B) The transcript of proceedings; duty of appellant to order; notice to appellee if partial transcript is ordered. At the time of filing the notice of appeal the appellant, in writing, shall order from the reporter a complete transcript or a transcript of the parts of the proceedings not already on file as the appellant

considers necessary for inclusion in the record and file a copy of the order with the clerk. The reporter is the person appointed by the court to transcribe the proceedings for the trial court whether by stenographic, phonogramic, or photographic means, by the use of audio electronic recording devices, or by the use of video recording systems. If there is no officially appointed reporter, App.R. 9(C) or 9(D) may be utilized. If the appellant intends to urge on appeal that a finding or conclusion is unsupported by the evidence or is contrary to the weight of the evidence, the appellant shall include in the record a transcript of all evidence relevant to the findings or conclusion.

Unless the entire transcript is to be included, the appellant, with the notice of appeal, shall file with the clerk of the trial court and serve on the appellee a description of the parts of the transcript that the appellant intends to include in the record, a statement that no transcript is necessary, or a statement that a statement pursuant to either App.R. 9(C) or 9(D) will be submitted, and a statement of the assignments of error the appellant intends to present on the appeal. If the appellee considers a transcript of other parts of the proceedings necessary, the appellee, within ten days after the service of the statement of the appellant, shall file and serve on the appellant a designation of additional parts to be included. The clerk of the trial court shall forward a copy of this designation to the clerk of the court of appeals.

If the appellant refuses or fails, within ten days after service on the appellant of appellee's designation, to order the additional parts, the appellee, within five days thereafter, shall either order the parts in writing from the reporter or apply to the court of appeals for an order requiring the appellant to do so. At the time of ordering, the party ordering the transcript shall arrange for the payment to the reporter of the cost of the transcript.

A transcript prepared by a reporter under this rule shall be in the following form:

(1) The transcript shall include a front and back cover; the front cover shall bear the title and number of the case and the name of the court in which the proceedings occurred;

(2) The transcript shall be firmly bound on the left side;

(3) The first page inside the front cover shall set forth the nature of the proceedings, the date or dates of the proceedings, and the judge or judges who presided;

(4) The transcript shall be prepared on white paper eight and one-half inches by eleven inches in size with the lines of each page numbered and the pages sequentially numbered;

(5) An index of witnesses shall be included in the front of the transcript and shall contain page and line references to direct, cross, re-direct, and re-cross examination;

(6) An index to exhibits, whether admitted or rejected, briefly identifying each exhibit, shall be included

following the index to witnesses reflecting the page and line references where the exhibit was identified and offered into evidence, was admitted or rejected, and if any objection was interposed;

(7) Exhibits such as papers, maps, photographs, and similar items that were admitted shall be firmly attached, either directly or in an envelope to the inside rear cover, except as to exhibits whose size or bulk makes attachment impractical; documentary exhibits offered at trial whose admission was denied shall be included in a separate envelope with a notation that they were not admitted and also attached to the inside rear cover unless attachment is impractical;

(8) No volume of a transcript shall exceed two hundred and fifty pages in length, except it may be enlarged to three hundred pages, if necessary, to complete a part of the voir dire, opening statements, closing arguments, or jury instructions; when it is necessary to prepare more than one volume, each volume shall contain the number and name of the case and be sequentially numbered, and the separate volumes shall be approximately equal in length.

The reporter shall certify the transcript as correct, whether in written or videotape form, and state whether it is a complete or partial transcript, and, if partial, indicate the parts included and the parts excluded.

If the proceedings were recorded in part by videotape and in part by other media, the appellant shall order the respective parts from the proper reporter. The record is complete for the purposes of appeal when the last part of the record is filed with the clerk of the trial court.

(C) Statement of the evidence or proceedings when no report was made or when the transcript is unavailable. If no report of the evidence or proceedings at a hearing or trial was made, or if a transcript is unavailable, the appellant may prepare a statement of the evidence or proceedings from the best available means, including the appellant's recollection. The statement shall be served on the appellee no later than twenty days prior to the time for transmission of the record pursuant to App.R. 10, who may serve objections or propose amendments to the statement within ten days after service. The statement and any objections or proposed amendments shall be forthwith submitted to the trial court for settlement and approval. The trial court shall act prior to the time for transmission of the record pursuant to App.R. 10, and, as settled and approved, the statement shall be included by the clerk of the trial court in the record on appeal.

(D) Agreed statement as the record on appeal. In lieu of the record on appeal as defined in division (A) of this rule, the parties, no later than ten days prior to the time for transmission of the record pursuant to App.R. 10, may prepare and sign a statement of the case showing how the issues presented by the appeal arose and were decided in the trial court and setting forth only so many of the facts averred and proved or sought to be proved as are essential to a decision of the issues presented. If the statment conforms to the truth,

it, together with additions as the trial court may consider necessary to present fully the issues raised by the appeal, shall be approved by the trial court prior to the time for transmission of the record pursuant to App.R. 10 and shall then be certified to the court of appeals as the record on appeal and transmitted to the court of appeals by the clerk of the trial court within the time provided by App.R. 10.

(E) Correction or modification of the record. If any difference arises as to whether the record truly discloses what occurred in the trial court, the difference shall be submitted to and settled by that court and the record made to conform to the truth. If anything material to either party is omitted from the record by error or accident or is misstated therein, the parties by stipulation, or the trial court, either before or after the record is transmitted to the court of appeals, or the court of appeals, on proper suggestion or of its own initiative, may direct that omission or misstatement be corrected, and if necessary that a supplemental record be certified and transmitted. All other questions as to the form and content of the record shall be presented to the court of appeals.

(Amended, eff 7-1-77; 7-1-78; 7-1-88; 7-1-92)

RULE 10. Transmission of the record

(A) Time for transmission; duty of appellant. The record on appeal, including the transcript and exhibits necessary for the determination of the appeal, shall be transmitted to the clerk of the court of appeals when the record is complete for the purposes of appeal, or when forty days, which is reduced to twenty days for an accelerated calendar case, have elapsed after the filing of the notice of appeal and no order extending time has been granted under subdivision (C). After filing the notice of appeal the appellant shall comply with the provisions of Rule 9(B) and shall take any other action necessary to enable the clerk to assemble and transmit the record. If more than one appeal is taken, each appellant shall comply with the provisions of Rule 9(B) and this subdivision, and a single record shall be transmitted when forty days have elapsed after the filing of the final notice of appeal.

(B) Duty of clerk to transmit the record. The clerk of the trial court shall prepare the certified copy of the docket and journal entries, assemble the original papers, (or in the instance of an agreed statement of the case pursuant to Rule 9(D), the agreed statement of the case), and transmit the record upon appeal to the clerk of the court of appeals within the time stated in subdivision (A). The clerk of the trial court shall number the documents comprising the record and shall transmit with the record a list of the documents correspondingly numbered and identified with reasonable definiteness. Documents of unusual bulk or weight and physical exhibits other than documents shall not be transmitted by the clerk unless he is directed to do so by a party or by the clerk of the court of appeals. A party must make advance arrangements with the clerks for the transportation and receipt of exhibits of unusual bulk or weight.

Transmission of the record is effected when the clerk of the trial court mails or otherwise forwards the record to the clerk of the court of appeals. The clerk of the trial court shall indicate, by endorsement on the face of the record or otherwise, the date upon which it is transmitted to the court of appeals and shall note the transmission on the appearance docket.

The record shall be deemed to be complete for the purposes of appeal under the following circumstances:

(1) When the transcript of proceedings is filed with the clerk of the trial court.

(2) When a statement of the evidence or proceedings, pursuant to Rule 9(C), is settled and approved by the trial court, and filed with the clerk of the trial court.

(3) When an agreed statement in lieu of the record, pursuant to Rule 9(D), is approved by the trial court, and filed with the clerk of the trial court.

(4) Where appellant, pursuant to Rule 9(B), designates that no part of the transcript of proceedings is to be included in the record or that no transcript is necessary for appeal, after the expiration of ten days following service of such designation upon appellee, unless appellee has within such time filed a designation of additional parts of the transcript to be included in the record.

(5) When forty days have elapsed after filing of the last notice of appeal, and there is no extension of time for transmission of the record.

(6) When twenty days have elapsed after filing of the last notice of appeal, in an accelerated calendar case and there is no extension of time for transmission of the record.

(7) Where the appellant fails to file either the docketing statement or the statement required by App. R. 9(B), ten days after filing the notice of appeal.

(C) Extension of time for transmission of the record; reduction of time. Except as may be provided by local rule adopted by the court of appeals pursuant to Rule 30, the trial court for cause shown set forth in the order may extend the time for transmitting the record. The clerk shall certify the order of extension to the court of appeals. A request for extension to the trial court and a ruling by the trial court must be made within the time originally prescribed or within an extension previously granted. If the trial court is without authority to grant the relief sought, by operation of this rule or local rule, or has denied a request therefor, the court of appeals may on motion for cause shown extend the time for transmitting the record or may permit the record to be transmitted and filed after the expiration of the time allowed or fixed. If a request for an extension of time for transmitting the record has been previously denied, the motion shall set forth the denial and shall state the reasons therefor, if any were given. The court of appeals may require the record to be transmitted and the appeal to be docketed at any time within the time otherwise fixed or allowed therefor.

(D) Retention of the record in the trial court by order of the court. If the record or any part thereof is required in the trial court for use there pending the appeal, the trial court may make an order to that effect, and the clerk of the trial court shall retain the record or parts thereof subject to the request of the court of appeals, and shall transmit a copy of the order and of the docket and journal entries together with such parts of the original record as the trial court shall allow and copies of such parts as the parties may designate.

(E) Stipulation of parties that parts of the record be retained in the trial court. The parties may agree by written stipulation filed in the trial court that designated parts of the record shall be retained in the trial court unless thereafter the court of appeals shall order or any party shall request their transmittal. The parts thus designated shall nevertheless be a part of the record on appeal for all purposes.

(F) Record for preliminary hearing in the court of appeals. If prior to the time the record is transmitted a party desires to make in the court of appeals a motion for dismissal, for release, for a stay pending appeal, for additional security on the bond on appeal or on a supersedeas bond, or for any intermediate order, the clerk of the trial court at the request of any party shall transmit to the court of appeals such parts of the original record as any party shall designate.

(G) Transmission of the record when leave to appeal obtained. In all cases where leave to appeal must first be obtained all time limits for the preparation and transmission of the record hereinbefore set forth shall run from the filing of the journal entry of the court of appeals granting such leave rather than from the filing of the notice of appeal.

(Amended, eff 7-1-72; 7-1-73; 7-1-75; 7-1-76; 7-1-77; 7-1-82)

RULE 11. Docketing the appeal; filing of the record

(A) Docketing the appeal. Upon receiving a copy of the notice of appeal, as provided in App. R. 3(D) and App. R. 5, the clerk of the court of appeals shall enter the appeal upon the docket. An appeal shall be docketed under the title given to the action in the trial court, with the appellant identified as such, but if the title does not contain the name of the appellant, the appellant's name, identified as appellant, shall be added parenthetically to the title.

(B) Filing of the record. Upon receipt of the record, the clerk shall file the record, and shall immediately give notice to all parties of the date on which the record was filed. When a trial court is exercising concurrent jurisdiction to review a judgment of conviction pursuant to a petition for post-conviction relief, the clerk shall either make a duplicate record and send it to the clerk of the trial court or arrange for each court to have access to the original record.

(C) Dismissal for failure of appellant to cause timely transmission of record. If the appellant fails to cause timely transmission of the record, any appellee may file a motion in the court of appeals to dismiss the appeal. The motion shall be supported by a certificate of the clerk of the trial court showing the date and substance of the judgment or order from which the appeal was taken, the date on which the notice of appeal was filed, the expiration date of any order extending the time for transmitting the record, and by proof of service. The appellant may respond within ten days of such service.

(D) Leave to appeal. In all cases where leave to appeal must first be obtained the docketing of the appeal by the clerk of the court of appeals upon receiving a copy of the notice of appeal filed in the trial court shall be deemed conditional and subject to such leave being granted.

(Amended, eff 7-1-75; 7-1-97)

RULE 11.1 Accelerated calendar

(A) Applicability. If a court of appeals has adopted an accelerated calendar by local rule, cases designated by its rule shall be placed on an accelerated calendar. The Ohio Rules of Appellate Procedure shall apply with the modifications or exceptions set forth in this rule.

The accelerated calendar is designated to provide a means to eliminate delay and unnecessary expense in effecting a just decision on appeal by the recognition that some cases do not require as extensive or time consuming procedure as others.

(B) Record. The record on appeal, including the transcripts and the exhibits necessary for the determination of the appeal, shall be transmitted to the clerk of the court of appeals as provided by App. R. 10.

(C) Briefs. Briefs shall be in the form specified by App. R. 16. Appellant shall serve and file his brief within fifteen days after the date on which the record is filed. The appellee shall serve and file his brief within fifteen days after service of the brief of the appellant. Reply briefs shall not be filed unless ordered by the court.

(D) Oral argument. Oral argument will apply as provided by App. R. 21. If oral argument is waived, the case will be submitted to the court for disposition upon filing of appellee's brief.

(E) Determination and judgment on appeal. The appeal will be determined as provided by App. R. 11.1. It shall be sufficient compliance with App. R. 12(A) for the statement of the reason for the court's decision as to each error to be in brief and conclusionary form.

The decision may be by judgment entry in which case it will not be published in any form. (See Form 3, Appendix of Forms.)

(Effective 7-1-82)

RULE 11.2 Expedited Appeals

(A) Applicability. Appeals in actions described in this rule shall be expedited and given calendar priority over all other cases, including criminal and administrative appeals. The Ohio Rules of Appellate Procedure shall apply with the modifications or exceptions set forth in this rule.

(B) Abortion-related appeals from juvenile courts.

(1) Applicability. App. R. 11.2(B) shall govern appeals pursuant to sections 2151.85, 2505.73, and 2919.121 of the Revised Code.

(2) General rule of expedition. If an appellant files her notice of appeal on the same day as the dismissal of her complaint or petition by the juvenile court, the entire court process, including the juvenile court hearing, appeal, and decision, shall be completed in sixteen calendar days from the time the original complaint or petition was filed.

(3) Processing appeal.

(a) Immediately after the notice of appeal has been filed by the appellant, the clerk of the juvenile court shall notify the court of appeals. Within four days after the notice of appeal is filed in juvenile court, the clerk of the juvenile court shall deliver a copy of the notice of appeal and the record, except page two of the complaint or petition, to the clerk of the court of appeals who immediately shall place the appeal on the docket of the court of appeals.

(b) Record of all testimony and other oral proceedings in actions pursuant to sections 2151.85 or 2919.121 of the Revised Code may be made by audio recording. If the testimony is on audio tape and a transcript cannot be prepared timely, the court of appeals shall accept the audio tape as the transcript in this case without prior transcription. The juvenile court shall ensure that the court of appeals has the necessary equipment to listen to the audio tape.

(c) The appellant under division (B) of this rule shall file her brief within four days after the appeal is docketed. Unless waived, the oral argument shall be within five days after docketing. Oral arguments must be closed to the public and exclude all persons except the appellant, her attorney, her guardian *ad litem*, and essential court personnel.

(d) Under division (B) of this rule, "days" means calendar days and includes any intervening Saturday, Sunday, or legal holiday. To provide full effect to the expedition provision of the statute, if the last day on which a judgment is required to be entered falls on a Saturday, Sunday, or legal holiday, the computation of days shall not be extended and judgment shall be made either on the last business day before the Saturday, Sunday, or legal holiday, or on the Saturday, Sunday, or legal holiday.

(4) Confidentiality. All proceedings in appeals governed by App. R. 11.2(B) shall be conducted in a manner that will preserve the anonymity of the appellant.

Except as set forth in App. R. 11.2(B)(7), all papers and records that pertain to the appeal shall be kept confidential.

(5) Judgment entry. The court shall enter judgment immediately after conclusion of oral argument or, if oral argument is waived, within five days after the appeal is docketed.

(6) Release of records. The public is entitled to secure all of the following from the records pertaining to appeals governed by App. R. 11.2(B):

(a) The docket number;

(b) The name of the judge;

(c) The judgment entry and, if appropriate, a properly redacted opinion.

Opinions shall set forth the reasoning in support of the decision in a way that does not directly or indirectly compromise the anonymity of the appellant. Opinions written in compliance with this requirement shall be considered public records available upon request. If, in the judgment of the court, it is impossible to release an opinion without compromising the anonymity of the appellant, the entry that journalizes the outcome of the case shall include a specific finding that no opinion can be written without disclosing the identity of the appellant. Such finding shall be a matter of public record. It is the obligation of the court to remove any and all information in its opinion that would directly or indirectly disclose the identity of the appellant.

(7) Notice and hearing before release of opinion. After an opinion is written and before it is available for release to the public, the appellant must be notified and be given the option to appear and argue at a hearing if she believes the opinion may disclose her identity. Notice may be provided by including the following language in the opinion:

If appellant believes that this opinion may disclose her identity, appellant has the right to appear and argue at a hearing before this court. Appellant may perfect this right to a hearing by filing a motion for a hearing within fourteen days of the date of this opinion.

The clerk is instructed that this opinion is not to be made available for release until either of the following:

(a) Twenty-one days have passed since the date of the opinion and appellant has not filed a motion;

(b) If appellant has filed a motion, after this court has ruled on the motion.

Notice shall be provided by mailing a copy of the opinion to the attorney for the appellant or, if she is not represented, to the address provided by appellant for receipt of notice.

(8) Form 25-A. Upon request of the appellant or her attorney, the clerk shall verify on Form 25-A, as provided in the Rules of Superintendence, the date the appeal was docketed and whether a judgment has been entered within five days of that date. The completed form shall include the case number from the juvenile court and the court of appeals, and shall be filed and included as part of the record. A date-stamped copy

shall be provided to the appellant or her attorney.

(C) Adoption and parental rights appeals.

(1) Applicability. Appeals from orders granting or denying adoption of a minor child or from orders granting or denying termination of parental rights shall be given priority over all cases except those governed by App. R. 11.2(B).

(2) Record. Preparation of the record, including the transcripts and exhibits necessary for determination of the appeal, shall be given priority over the preparation and transmission of the records in all cases other than those governed by App. R. 11.2(B).

(3) Briefs. Extensions of time for filing briefs shall not be granted except in the most unusual circumstances and only for the most compelling reasons in the interest of justice.

(4) Oral argument. After briefs have been filed, the case shall be considered submitted for immediate decision unless oral argument is requested or ordered. Any oral argument shall be heard within thirty days after the briefs have been filed.

(5) Entry of judgment. The court shall enter judgment within thirty days of submission of the briefs, or of the oral argument, whichever is later, unless compelling reasons in the interest of justice require a longer time.

(D) Dependent, abused, neglected, unruly, or delinquent child appeals. Appeals concerning a dependent, abused, neglected, unruly, or delinquent child shall be expedited and given calendar priority over all cases other than those governed by App. R. 11.2(B) and (C).

(Effective 7-1-00; 7-1-01)

RULE 12. Determination and judgment on appeal

(A) Determination.

(1) On an undismissed appeal from a trial court, a court of appeals shall do all of the following:

(a) Review and affirm, modify, or reverse the judgment or final order appealed;

(b) Determine the appeal on its merits on the assignments of error set forth in the briefs under App.R. 16, the record on appeal under App.R. 9, and, unless waived, the oral argument under App.R. 21;

(c) Unless an assignment of error is made moot by a ruling on another assignment of error, decide each assignment of error and give reasons in writing for its decision.

(2) The court may disregard an assignment of error presented for review if the party raising it fails to identify in the record the error on which the assignment of error is based or fails to argue the assignment separately in the brief, as required under App.R. 16(A).

(B) Judgment as a matter of law. When the court of appeals determines that the trial court committed no error prejudicial to the appellant in any of the particulars assigned and argued in appellant's brief and that the appellee is entitled to have the judgment or final order of the trial court affirmed as a matter of law, the court of appeals shall enter judgment accordingly. When the court of appeals determines that the trial court committed error prejudicial to the appellant and that the appellant is entitled to have judgment or final order rendered in his favor as a matter of law, the court of appeals shall reverse the judgment or final order of the trial court and render the judgment or final order that the trial court should have rendered, or remand the cause to the court with instructions to render such judgment or final order. In all other cases where the court of appeals determines that the judgment or final order of the trial court should be modified as a matter of law it shall enter its judgment accordingly.

(C) Judgment in civil action or proceeding when sole prejudicial error found is that judgment of trial court is against the manifest weight of the evidence. In any civil action or proceeding which was tried to the trial court without the intervention of a jury, and when upon appeal a majority of the judges hearing the appeal find that the judgment or final order rendered by the trial court is against the manifest weight of the evidence and do not find any other prejudicial error of the trial court in any of the particulars assigned and argued in the appellant's brief, and do not find that the appellee is entitled to judgment or final order as a matter of law, the court of appeals shall reverse the judgment or final order of the trial court and either weigh the evidence in the record and render the judgment or final order that the trial court should have rendered on that evidence or remand the case to the trial court for further proceedings; provided further that a judgment shall be reversed only once on the manifest weight of the evidence.

(D) All other cases. In all other cases where the court of appeals finds error prejudicial to the appellant, the judgment or final order of the trial court shall be reversed and the cause shall be remanded to the trial court for further proceedings.

(Amended, eff 7-1-73; 7-1-92)

TITLE III
GENERAL PROVISIONS

RULE 13. Filing and service

(A) Filing. Documents required or permitted to be filed in a court of appeals shall be filed with the clerk. Filing may be accomplished by mail addressed to the clerk, but filing shall not be timely unless the documents are received by the clerk within the time fixed for filing, except that briefs shall be deemed filed on the day of mailing. If a motion requests relief which may be granted by a single judge, the judge may permit the motion to be filed with the judge, in which event the judge shall note the filing date on the motion and transmit it to the clerk. A court may provide, by local rules adopted pursuant to the Rules of Superintendence, for the filing of documents by electronic means. If the court adopts such local rules, they shall include all of the following:

(1) Any signature on electronically transmitted documents shall be considered that of the attorney or party it purports to be for all purposes. If it is established that the documents were transmitted without authority, the court shall order the filing stricken.

(2) A provision shall specify the days and hours during which electronically transmitted documents will be received by the court, and a provision shall specify when documents received electronically will be considered to have been filed.

(3) Any document filed electronically that requires a filing fee may be rejected by the clerk of court unless the filer has complied with the mechanism established by the court for the payment of filing fees.

(B) Service of all documents required. Copies of all documents filed by any party and not required by these rules to be served by the clerk shall, at or before the time of filing, be served by a party or person acting for the party on all other parties to the appeal. Service on a party represented by counsel shall be made on counsel.

(C) Manner of service. Service may be personal or by mail. Personal service includes delivery of the copy to a clerk or other responsible person at the office of counsel. Service by mail is complete on mailing.

(D) Proof of service. Documents presented for filing shall contain an acknowledgment of service by the person served or proof of service in the form of a statement of the date and manner of service and of the names of the persons served, certified by the person who made service. Documents filed with the court shall not be considered until proof of service is endorsed on the documents or separately filed.

(Amended, eff 7-1-01)

RULE 14. Computation and extension of time

(A) Computation of time. In computing any period of time prescribed or allowed by these rules, by the local rules of any court, by an order of court or by any applicable statute, the day of the act, event or default from which the designated period of time begins to run shall not be included. The last day of the period so computed shall be included, unless it is a Saturday, Sunday or a legal holiday, in which event the period runs until the end of the next day which is not a Saturday, Sunday or legal holiday. When the period of time prescribed or allowed is less than seven days, intermediate Saturdays, Sundays and legal holidays shall be excluded in the computation.

(B) Enlargement or reduction of time. For good cause shown, the court, upon motion, may enlarge or reduce the time prescribed by these rules or by its order for doing any act, or may permit an act to be done after the expiration of the prescribed time. The court may not enlarge or reduce the time for filing a notice of appeal or a motion to certify pursuant to App. R. 25. Enlargement of time to file an application to reconsider pursuant to App. R. 26(A) shall not be granted except on a showing of extraordinary circumstances.

(C) Additional time after service by mail. Whenever a party is required or permitted to do an act within a prescribed period after service of a paper upon him and the paper is served by mail, three days shall be added to the prescribed period.

(Amended, eff 7-1-94)

RULE 15. Motions

(A) Content of motions; response; reply. Unless another form is prescribed by these rules, an application for an order or other relief shall be made by motion with proof of service on all other parties. The motion shall contain or be accompanied by any matter required by a specific provision of these rules governing such a motion, shall state with particularity the grounds on which it is based and shall set forth the order or relief sought. If a motion is supported by briefs, affidavits or other papers, they shall be served and filed with the motion. Any party may file a response in opposition to a motion other than one for a procedural order [for which see subdivision (B)] within ten days after service of the motion, but motions authorized by Rule 7, Rule 8 and Rule 27 may be acted upon after reasonable notice, and the court may shorten or extend the time for responding to any motion.

(B) Determination of motions for procedural orders. Motions for procedural orders, including any motion under Rule 14(B) may be acted upon at any time, without awaiting a response thereto. Any party adversely affected by such action may request reconsideration, vacation or modification of such action.

(C) Power of a single judge to entertain motions. In addition to the authority expressly conferred by these rules or by law, and unless otherwise provided by rule or law, a single judge of a court of appeals may entertain and may grant or deny any request for relief, which under these rules may properly be sought by motion, except that a single judge may not dismiss or otherwise determine an appeal or other proceeding, and except that a court of appeals may provide by order or rule that any motion or class of motions must be acted upon by the court. The action of a single judge may be reviewed by the court.

(D) Number of copies. Three copies of all papers relating to motions shall be filed with the original, but the court may require that additional copies be furnished.

RULE 16. Briefs

(A) Brief of the appellant. The appellant shall include in its brief, under the headings and in the order indicated, all of the following:

(1) A table of contents, with page references.

(2) A table of cases alphabetically arranged, statutes, and other authorities cited, with references to the pages of the brief where cited.

(3) A statement of the assignments of error presented for review, with reference to the place in the record where each error is reflected.

(4) A statement of the issues presented for review, with references to the assignments of error to which each issue relates.

(5) A statement of the case briefly describing the nature of the case, the course of proceedings, and the disposition in the court below.

(6) A statement of facts relevant to the assignments of error presented for review, with appropriate references to the record in accordance with division (D) of this rule.

(7) An argument containing the contentions of the appellant with respect to each assignment of error presented for review and the reasons in support of the contentions, with citations to the authorities, statutes, and parts of the record on which appellant relies. The argument may be preceded by a summary.

(8) A conclusion briefly stating the precise relief sought.

(B) Brief of the appellee. The brief of the appellee shall conform to the requirements of divisions (A)(1) to (A)(8) of this rule, except that a statement of the case or of the facts relevant to the assignments of error need not be made unless the appellee is dissatisfied with the statement of the appellant.

(C) Reply brief. The appellant may file a brief in reply to the brief of the appellee, and, if the appellee has cross-appealed, the appellee may file a brief in reply to the response of the appellant to the assignments of errors presented by the cross-appeal. No further briefs may be filed except with leave of court.

(D) References in briefs to the record. References in the briefs to parts of the record shall be to the pages of the parts of the record involved; e.g., Answer p. 7, Motion for Judgment p. 2, Transcript p. 231. Intelligible abbreviations may be used. If reference is made to evidence, the admissibility of which is in controversy, reference shall be made to the pages of the transcript at which the evidence was identified, offered, and received or rejected.

(E) Reproduction of statutes, rules, regulations. If determination of the assignments of error presented requires the consideration of provisions of constitutions, statutes, ordinances, rules, or regulations, the relevant parts shall be reproduced in the brief or in an addendum at the end or may be supplied to the court in pamphlet form.

(Amended, eff 7-1-72; 7-1-92)

RULE 17. Brief of an amicus curiae

A brief of an amicus curiae may be filed only if accompanied by written consent of all parties, or by leave of court granted on motion or at the request of the court. The brief may be conditionally filed with the motion for leave. A motion for leave shall identify the interest of the applicant and shall state the reasons why a brief of an amicus curiae is desirable. Unless all parties otherwise consent, any amicus curiae shall file its brief within the time allowed the party whose position as to affirmance or reversal the amicus brief will support unless the court for cause shown shall grant leave for later filing, in which event it shall specify within what period an opposing party may answer. A motion of an amicus curiae to participate in the oral argument will be granted only for extraordinary reasons.

RULE 18. Filing and service of briefs

(A) Time for serving and filing briefs. Except as provided in App. R. 14(C), the appellant shall serve and file the appellant's brief within twenty days after the date on which the clerk has mailed the notice required by App. R. 11(B). The appellee shall serve and file the appellee's brief within twenty days after service of the brief of the appellant. The appellant may serve and file a reply brief within ten days after service of the brief of the appellee.

(B) Number of copies to be filed and served. Four copies of each brief shall be filed with the clerk, unless the court by order in a particular case shall direct a different number, and one copy shall be served on counsel for each party separately represented. If the court by local rule adopted pursuant to App. R. 13 permits electronic filing of court documents, then the requirement for filing of copies with the clerk required in this division may be waived or modified by the local rule so adopted.

(C) Consequence of failure to file briefs. If an appellant fails to file the appellant's brief within the time provided by this rule, or within the time as extended, the court may dismiss the appeal. If an appellee fails to file the appellee's brief within the time provided by this rule, or within the time as extended, the appellee will not be heard at oral argument except by permission of the court upon a showing of good cause submitted in writing prior to argument; and in determining the appeal, the court may accept the appellant's statement of the facts and issues as correct and reverse the judgment if appellant's brief reasonably appears to sustain such action.

(Amended, eff 7-1-82; 7-1-01)

RULE 19. Form of briefs and other papers

(A) Form of briefs. Briefs may be typewritten or be produced by standard typographic printing or by any duplicating or copying process which produces a clear black image on white paper. Carbon copies of briefs may not be submitted without permission of the court, except in behalf of parties allowed to proceed in forma pauperis. All printed matter must appear in at least a twelve point type on opaque, unglazed paper. Briefs produced by standard typographic process shall be bound in volumes having pages $6\frac{1}{8}$ by $9\frac{1}{4}$ inches and type matter $4\frac{1}{6}$ by $7\frac{1}{6}$ inches. Those produced by any other process shall be bound in volumes having pages not exceeding $8\frac{1}{2}$ by 11 inches and type matter not exceeding $6\frac{1}{2}$ by $9\frac{1}{2}$ inches, with double spacing between each line of text except quoted matter which shall be single spaced. Where necessary, briefs may be of such size as required to utilize copies of pertinent documents.

Without prior leave of court, no initial brief of appellant or cross-appellant and no answer brief of appellee or cross-appellee shall exceed thirty-five pages in length, and no reply brief shall exceed fifteen pages in length, exclusive of the table of contents, table of cases, statutes and other authorities cited, and appendices, if any. A court of appeals, by local rule, may adopt shorter or longer page limitations.

The front covers of the briefs, if separately bound, shall contain: (1) the name of the court and the number of the case; (2) the title of the case [see App. R. 11(A)]; (3) the nature of the proceeding in the court (e.g., Appeal) and the name of the court below; (4) the title of the document (e.g., Brief for Appellant); and (5) the names and addresses of counsel representing the party on whose behalf the document is filed.

(B) Form of other papers. Applications for reconsideration shall be produced in a manner prescribed by subdivision (A). Motions and other papers may be produced in a like manner, or they may be typewritten upon opaque, unglazed paper $8\frac{1}{2}$ by 11 inches in size. Lines of typewritten text shall be double spaced except quoted matter which shall be single spaced. Consecutive sheets shall be attached at the left margin. Carbon copies may be used for filing and service if they are legible.

A motion or other paper addressed to the court shall contain a caption setting forth the name of the court, the title of the case, the case number and a brief descriptive title indicating the purpose of the paper.

(Amended, eff 7-1-72; 7-1-97)

RULE 20. Prehearing conference

The court may direct the attorneys for the parties to appear before the court or a judge thereof for a prehearing conference to consider the simplification of the issues and such other matters as may aid in the disposition of the proceeding by the court. The court or judge shall make an order which recites the action taken at the conference and the agreements made by the parties as to any of the matters considered and which limits the issues to those not disposed of by admissions or agreements of counsel, and such order when entered controls the subsequent course of the proceeding, unless modified to prevent manifest injustice.

RULE 21. Oral argument

(A) Notice of argument. The court shall advise all parties of the time and place at which oral argument will be heard.

(B) Time allowed for argument. Unless otherwise ordered, each side will be allowed thirty minutes for argument. A party is not obliged to use all of the time allowed, and the court may terminate the argument whenever in its judgment further argument is unnecessary.

(C) Order and content of argument. The appellant is entitled to open and conclude the argument. The opening argument shall include a fair statement of the case. Counsel will not be permitted to read at length from briefs, records or authorities.

(D) Cross and separate appeals. A cross-appeal or separate appeal shall be argued with the initial appeal at a single argument, unless the court otherwise directs. If separate appellants support the same argument, they shall share the thirty minutes allowed to their side for argument unless pursuant to timely request the court grants additional time.

(E) Nonappearance of parties. If the appellee fails to appear to present argument, the court will hear argument on behalf of the appellant, if present. If the appellant fails to appear, the court may hear argument on behalf of the appellee, if his counsel is present. If neither party appears, the case will be decided on the briefs unless the court shall otherwise order.

(F) Submission on briefs. By agreement of the parties, a case may be submitted for decision on the briefs, but the court may direct that the case be argued.

(G) Motions. Oral argument will not be heard upon motions unless ordered by the court.

(H) Authorities in briefs. If counsel on oral argument intends to present authorities not cited in his brief, he shall, prior to oral argument, present in writing such authorities to the court and to opposing counsel.

(Amended, eff 7-1-72; 7-1-76)

RULE 22. Entry of judgment

(A) Form. All judgments shall be in the form of a journal entry signed by a judge of the court and filed with the clerk.

(B) Notice. When a decision is announced, the clerk shall give notice thereof by mail to counsel of record in the case.

(C) Time. Unless further time is allowed by the court or a judge thereof, counsel for the party in whose favor an order, decree or judgment is announced shall, within five days, prepare the proper journal entry and submit the entry to counsel for the opposite party. Counsel for the opposite party shall within five days after receipt of the entry (1) approve or reject the entry and

(2) forward the entry to counsel for the prevailing party for immediate submission to the court.

(D) Objections. All objections to proposed journal entries shall be in writing, and may be answered in writing. Such entry as the court may deem proper shall be approved by the court, in writing, and filed with the clerk of the court for journalization. The provisions of this rule shall not be deemed to preclude the court from sua sponte preparing and filing with the clerk for journalization its own entry. No oral arguments will be heard in the settlement of journal entries.

(E) Filing. The filing of a journal entry of judgment by the court with the clerk for journalization constitutes entry of the judgment.

(Amended, eff 7-1-72)

RULE 23. Damages for delay

If a court of appeals shall determine that an appeal is frivolous, it may require the appellant to pay reasonable expenses of the appellee including attorney fees and costs.

RULE 24. Costs

(A) Except as otherwise provided by law or as the court may order, the party liable for costs is as follows:

(1) If an appeal is dismissed, the appellant or as agreed by the parties.

(2) If the judgment appealed is affirmed, the appellant.

(3) If the judgment appealed is reversed, the appellee.

(4) If the judgment appealed is affirmed or reversed in part or is vacated, as ordered by the court.

(B) As used in this rule, "costs" means an expense incurred in preparation of the record including the transcript of proceedings, fees allowed by law, and the fee for filing the appeal. It does not mean the expense of printing or copying a brief or an appendix.

(Amended, eff 7-1-92)

RULE 25. Motion to certify a conflict

(A) A motion to certify a conflict under Article IV, Section 3(B)(4) of the Ohio Constitution shall be made in writing before the judgment or order of the court has been approved by the court and filed by the court with the clerk for journalization or within ten days after the announcement of the court's decision, whichever is the later. The filing of a motion to certify a conflict does not extend the time for filing a notice of appeal. A motion under this rule shall specify the issue proposed for certification and shall cite the judgment or judgments alleged to be in conflict with the judgment of the court in which the motion is filed.

(B) Parties opposing the motion must answer in writing within ten days after the filing of the motion. Copies of the motion, brief, and opposing briefs shall be served as prescribed for the service and filing of briefs in the initial action. Oral argument of a motion to certify a conflict shall not be permitted except at the request of the court.

(C) The court of appeals shall rule upon a motion to certify within sixty days of its filing.

(Effective 7-1-94)

RULE 26. Application for reconsideration; application for reopening

(A) Application for reconsideration. Application for reconsideration of any cause or motion submitted on appeal shall be made in writing before the judgment or order of the court has been approved by the court and filed by the court with the clerk for journalization or within ten days after the announcement of the court's decision, whichever is the later. The filing of an application for reconsideration shall not extend the time for filing a notice of appeal in the Supreme Court.

Parties opposing the application shall answer in writing within ten days after the filing of the application. Copies of the application, brief, and opposing briefs shall be served in the manner prescribed for the service and filing of briefs in the initial action. Oral argument of an application for reconsideration shall not be permitted except at the request of the court.

(B) Application for reopening. (1) A defendant in a criminal case may apply for reopening of the appeal from the judgment of conviction and sentence, based on a claim of ineffective assistance of appellate counsel. An application for reopening shall be filed in the court of appeals where the appeal was decided within ninety days from journalization of the appellate judgment unless the applicant shows good cause for filing at a later time.

(2) An application for reopening shall contain all of the following:

(a) The appellate case number in which reopening is sought and the trial court case number or numbers from which the appeal was taken;

(b) A showing of good cause for untimely filing if the application is filed more than ninety days after journalization of the appellate judgment.[;]

(c) One or more assignments of error or arguments in support of assignments of error that previously were not considered on the merits in the case by any appellate court or that were considered on an incomplete record because of appellate counsel's deficient representation;

(d) A sworn statement of the basis for the claim that appellate counsel's representation was deficient with respect to the assignments of error or arguments raised pursuant to division (B)(2)(c) of this rule and the manner in which the deficiency prejudicially affected the outcome of the appeal, which may include citations to applicable authorities and references to the record;

(e) Any parts of the record available to the applicant

and all supplemental affidavits upon which the applicant relies.

(3) The applicant shall furnish an additional copy of the application to the clerk of the court of appeals who shall serve it on the attorney for the prosecution. The attorney for the prosecution, within thirty days from the filing of the application, may file and serve affidavits, parts of the record, and a memorandum of law in opposition to the application.

(4) An application for reopening and an opposing memorandum shall not exceed ten pages, exclusive of affidavits and parts of the record. Oral argument of an application for reopening shall not be permitted except at the request of the court.

(5) An application for reopening shall be granted if there is a genuine issue as to whether the applicant was deprived of the effective assistance of counsel on appeal.

(6) If the court denies the application, it shall state in the entry the reasons for denial. If the court grants the application, it shall do both of the following:

(a) Appoint counsel to represent the applicant if the applicant is indigent and not currently represented;

(b) Impose conditions, if any, necessary to preserve the status quo during pendency of the reopened appeal.

The clerk shall serve notice of journalization of the entry on the parties and, if the application is granted, on the clerk of the trial court.

(7) If the application is granted, the case shall proceed as on an initial appeal in accordance with these rules except that the court may limit its review to those assignments of error and arguments not previously considered. The time limits for preparation and transmission of the record pursuant to App. R. 9 and 10 shall run from journalization of the entry granting the application. The parties shall address in their briefs the claim that representation by prior appellate counsel was deficient and that the applicant was prejudiced by that deficiency.

(8) If the court of appeals determines that an evidentiary hearing is necessary, the evidentiary hearing may be conducted by the court or referred to a magistrate.

(9) If the court finds that the performance of appellate counsel was deficient and the applicant was prejudiced by that deficiency, the court shall vacate its prior judgment and enter the appropriate judgment. If the court does not so find, the court shall issue an order confirming its prior judgment.

(C) [Ruling upon application for reconsideration.] If an application for reconsideration under division (A) of this rule is filed with the court of appeals, the application shall be ruled upon within forty-five days of its filing.

(Amended, eff 7-1-75; 7-1-93; 7-1-94; 7-1-97)

RULE 27. Execution, mandate

A court of appeals may remand its final decrees, judgments, or orders, in cases brought before it on appeal, to the court or agency below for specific or general execution thereof, or to the court below for further proceedings therein.

A certified copy of the judgment shall constitute the mandate. A stay of execution of the judgment mandate pending appeal may be granted upon motion, and a bond or other security may be required as a condition to the grant or continuance of the stay.

RULE 28. Voluntary dismissal

If the parties to an appeal or other proceeding shall sign and file with the clerk of the court of appeals an agreement that the proceedings be dismissed and shall pay whatever costs are due, the court shall order the case dismissed.

An appeal may be dismissed on motion of the appellant upon such terms as may be fixed by the court.

RULE 29. Substitution of parties

(A) Death of a party. If a party dies after a notice of appeal is filed or while a proceeding is otherwise pending in the court of appeals, the personal representative of the deceased party may be substituted as a party on motion filed by the representative, or by any party, with the clerk of the court of appeals. The motion of a party shall be served upon the representative in accordance with the provisions of Rule 13. If the deceased party has no representative, any party may suggest the death on the record and proceedings shall then be had as the court of appeals may direct. If a party against whom an appeal may be taken dies after entry of a judgment or order in the trial court but before a notice of appeal is filed, an appellant may proceed as if death had not occurred. After the notice of appeal is filed substitution shall be effected in the court of appeals in accordance with this subdivision. If a party entitled to appeal shall die before filing a notice of appeal, the notice of appeal may be filed by his personal representative, or, if he has no personal representative, by his attorney of record within the time prescribed by these rules. After the notice of appeal is filed, substitution shall be effected in the court of appeals in accordance with this subdivision.

(B) Substitution for other causes. If substitution of a party in the court of appeals is necessary for any reason other than death, substitution shall be effected in accordance with the procedure prescribed in subdivision (A).

(C) Public officers; death or separation from office.

(1) When a public officer is a party to an appeal or other proceeding in the court of appeals in his official capacity and during its pendency dies, resigns or otherwise ceases to hold office, the action does not abate and his successor is automatically substituted as a party. Proceedings following the substitution shall be in the name of the substituted party, but any misnomer not affecting the substantial rights of the parties shall be disregarded. An order of substitution may be entered at any time, but the omission to enter such an order shall not affect the substitution.

(2) When a public officer is a party to an appeal or other proceeding in his official capacity, he may be described as a party by his official title rather than by name, but the court may require his name to be added.

RULE 30. Duties of clerks

(A) Notice of orders or judgments. Immediately upon the entry of an order or judgment, the clerk shall serve by mail a notice of entry upon each party to the proceeding and shall make a note in the docket of the mailing. Service on a party represented by counsel shall be made on counsel.

(B) Custody of records and papers. The clerk shall have custody of the records and papers of the court. Papers transmitted as the record on appeal or review shall upon disposition of the case be returned to the court or agency from which they were received. The clerk shall preserve copies of briefs and other filings.

(Amended, eff 7-1-72)

RULE 31. [RESERVED]

RULE 32. [RESERVED]

RULE 33. [RESERVED]

RULE 34. Appointment of magistrates

(A) Original actions. Original actions in the court of appeals may be referred to a magistrate pursuant to Civ. R. 53.

(B) Appeals. When the court orders an evidentiary hearing in an appeal, the court may appoint a magistrate pursuant to Civ. R. 53 to conduct the hearing.

(C) Reference to magistrates. In any matter referred to a magistrate, all proceedings shall be governed by Civ. R. 53 and the order of reference, except that the word "judge" in Civ. R. 53 shall mean the court of appeals. An order of reference shall be signed by at least two judges of the court. Where the court has entered a general order referring a category of actions, appeals, or motions to magistrates generally, a subsequent order referring a particular action, appeal, or motion to a specific magistrate pursuant to the general order may be signed by one judge.

(Effective 7-1-97)

RULE 41. Rules of courts of appeals

(A) The courts of appeals may adopt rules concerning local practice in their respective courts that are not inconsistent with the rules promulgated by the Supreme

Court. Local rules shall be filed with the Supreme Court.

(B) Local rules shall be adopted only after the court gives appropriate notice and an opportunity for comment. If the court determines that there is an immediate need for a rule, the court may adopt the rule without prior notice and opportunity for comment, but promptly shall afford notice and opportunity for comment.

(Effective 7-1-94; Amended, eff 7-1-97)

RULE 42. Title

These rules shall be known as the Ohio Rules of Appellate Procedure and may be cited as "Appellate Rules" or "App. R. ___."

(Amended, eff 7-1-97)

RULE 43. Effective date

(A) **Effective date of rules.** These rules shall take effect on the first day of July, 1971. They govern all proceedings in actions brought after they take effect and also all further proceedings in actions then pending, except to the extent that in the opinion of the court their application in a particular action pending when the rules take effect would not be feasible or would work injustice in which event the former procedure applies.

(B) **Effective date of amendments.** The amendments submitted by the Supreme Court to the General Assembly on January 15, 1972, shall take effect on the first day of July, 1972. They govern all proceedings in actions brought after they take effect and also all further proceedings in actions then pending, except to the extent that their application in a particular action pending when the rules take effect would not be feasible or would work injustice, in which event the former procedure applies.

(C) **Effective date of amendments.** The amendments submitted by the Supreme Court to the General Assembly on January 12, 1973, and on April 30, 1973, shall take effect on July 1, 1973. They govern all proceedings in actions brought after they take effect and also all further proceedings in actions then pending, except to the extent that their application in a particular action pending when the amendments take effect would not be feasible or would work injustice, in which event the former procedure applies.

(D) **Effective date of amendments.** The amendments submitted by the Supreme Court to the General Assembly on January 10, 1975, and on April 29, 1975, shall take effect on July 1, 1975. They govern all proceedings in actions brought after they take effect and also all further proceedings in actions then pending, except to the extent that their application in a particular action pending when the amendments take effect would not be feasible or would work injustice, in which event the former procedure applies.

(E) **Effective date of amendments.** The amendments submitted by the Supreme Court to the General Assembly on January 9, 1976, shall take effect on July 1, 1976. They govern all proceedings in actions brought after they take effect and also all further proceedings in actions then pending, except to the extent that their application in a particular action pending when the amendments take effect would not be feasible or would work injustice, in which event the former procedure applies.

(F) **Effective date of amendments.** The amendments submitted by the Supreme Court to the General Assembly on January 12, 1978, shall take effect on July 1, 1978. They govern all proceedings in actions brought after they take effect and also all further proceedings in actions then pending, except to the extent that their application in a particular action pending when the amendments take effect would not be feasible or would work injustice, in which event the former procedure applies.

(G) **Effective date of amendments.** The amendments submitted by the Supreme Court to the General Assembly on January 14, 1982, shall take effect on July 1, 1982. They govern all proceedings in actions brought after they take effect and also all further proceedings in actions then pending, except to the extent that their application in a particular action pending when the amendments take effect would not be feasible or would work injustice, in which event the former procedure applies.

(H) **Effective date of amendments.** The amendments submitted by the Supreme Court to the General Assembly on December 24, 1984 and January 8, 1985 shall take effect on July 1, 1985. They govern all proceedings in actions brought after they take effect and also all further proceedings in actions then pending, except to the extent that their application in a particular action pending when the amendments take effect would not be feasible or would work injustice, in which event the former procedure applies.

(I) **Effective date of amendments.** The amendments submitted by the Supreme Court to the General Assembly on January 14, 1988, as amended, shall take effect on July 1, 1988. They govern all proceedings in actions brought after they take effect and also all further proceedings in actions then pending, except to the extent that their application in a particular action pending when the amendments take effect would not be feasible or would work injustice, in which event the former procedure applies.

(J) **Effective date of amendments.** The amendments submitted by the Supreme Court to the General Assembly on January 6, 1989, shall take effect on July 1, 1989. They govern all proceedings in actions brought after they take effect and also all further proceedings in actions then pending, except to the extent that their application in a particular action pending when the amendments take effect would not be feasible or would work injustice, in which event the former procedure applies.

(K) Effective date of amendments. The amendments submitted by the Supreme Court to the General Assembly on January 10, 1991 shall take effect on July 1, 1991. They govern all proceedings in actions brought after they take effect and also all further proceedings in actions then pending, except to the extent that their application in a particular action pending when the amendments take effect would not be feasible or would work injustice, in which event the former procedure applies.

(L) Effective date of amendments. The amendments filed by the Supreme Court with the General Assembly on January 14, 1992 and further revised and filed on April 30, 1992, shall take effect on July 1, 1992. They govern all proceedings in actions brought after they take effect and also all further proceedings in actions then pending, except to the extent that their application in a particular action pending when the amendments take effect would not be feasible or would work injustice, in which event the former procedure applies.

(M) Effective date of amendments. The amendments submitted by the Supreme Court to the General Assembly on January 8, 1993 and further revised and filed on April 30, 1993 shall take effect on July 1, 1993. They govern all proceedings in actions brought after they take effect and also all further proceedings in actions then pending, except to the extent that their application in a particular action pending when the amendments take effect would not be feasible or would work injustice, in which event the former procedure applies.

(N) Effective date of amendments. The amendments submitted by the Supreme Court to the General Assembly on January 14, 1994 and further revised and filed on April 29, 1994 shall take effect on July 1, 1994. They govern all proceedings in actions brought after they take effect and also all further proceedings in actions then pending, except to the extent that their application in a particular action pending when the amendments take effect would not be feasible or would work injustice, in which event the former procedure applies.

(O) Effective date of amendments. The amendments to Rules 4 and 5 filed by the Supreme Court with the General Assembly on January 5, 1996 and further revised and filed on April 26, 1996 shall take effect on July 1, 1996. They govern all proceedings in actions brought after they take effect and also all further

proceedings in actions then pending, except to the extent that their application in a particular action pending when the amendments take effect would not be feasible or would work injustice, in which event the former procedure applies.

(P) Effective date of amendments. The amendments to Rules 6, 11, 19, 26, 31, 32, 33, 34, 41, 42, and 43 filed by the Supreme Court with the General Assembly on January 10, 1997 and further revised and filed on April 24, 1997 shall take effect on July 1, 1997. They govern all proceedings in actions brought after they take effect and also all further proceedings in actions then pending, except to the extent that their application in a particular action pending when the amendments take effect would not be feasible or would work injustice, in which event the former procedure applies.

(Q) Effective date of amendments. The amendments to Appellate Rule 11.2 filed by the Supreme Court with the General Assembly on January 13, 2000 and refiled on April 27, 2000 shall take effect on July 1, 2000. They govern all proceedings in actions brought after they take effect and also all further proceedings in actions then pending, except to the extent that their application in a particular action pending when the amendments take effect would not be feasible or would work injustice, in which event the former procedure applies.

(R) Effective date of amendments. The amendments to Appellate Rules 7, 11.2, 13, and 18 filed by the Supreme Court with the General Assembly on January 12, 2001, and revised and refiled on April 26, 2001, shall take effect on July 1, 2001. They govern all proceedings in actions brought after they take effect and also all further proceedings in actions then pending, except to the extent that their application in a particular action pending when the amendments take effect would not be feasible or would work injustice, in which event the former procedure applies.

(S) Effective date of amendments. The amendments to Appellate Rule 4 filed by the Supreme Court with the General Assembly on January 11, 2002, and revised and refiled on April 18, 2002 shall take effect on July 1, 2002. They govern all proceedings in actions brought after they take effect and also all further proceedings in actions then pending, except to the extent that their application in a particular action pending when the amendments take effect would not be feasible or would work injustice, in which event the former procedure applies.

(Amended, eff 7-1-72; 7-1-73; 7-1-75; 7-1-76; 7-1-78; 7-1-82; 7-1-85; 7-1-88; 7-1-89; 7-1-91; 7-1-92; 7-1-93; 7-1-94; 7-1-96; 7-1-97; 7-1-00; 7-1-01; 7-1-02)

APPENDIX OF FORMS

Introductory Statement

The form which follows is intended for illustration only.

Departure from the form shall not void papers which are otherwise sufficient, and the form may be varied when necessary to meet the facts of a particular case.

FORM 1

NOTICE OF APPEAL TO A COURT OF APPEALS FROM A JUDGMENT OR APPEALABLE ORDER

COURT OF COMMON PLEAS FRANKLIN COUNTY, OHIO

A.B.,   :

221 E. West Street,   :

Columbus, Ohio 43215   :

               Plaintiff,   :   NO. _____

                 v.   :   NOTICE OF APPEAL

C.D.,   :

122 W. East Street,   :

Columbus, Ohio 43214   :

         Defendant–Appellant.   :

Notice is hereby given that C.D., defendant, hereby appeals to the Court of Appeals of Franklin County, Ohio, Tenth Appellate District (from the final judgment), from the order (describing it) entered in this action on the _____ day of _____, 19___.

                                _____

                                    (Attorney for Defendant)

                                _____

                                        (Address)

NOTE: The above form is designed for use in courts of common pleas. Appropriate changes in the designation of the court are required when the form is used for other courts.

FORM 2

DOCKETING STATEMENT
COURT OF COMMON PLEAS
FRANKLIN COUNTY, OHIO

A.B.,
221 E. West Street,
Columbus, Ohio 43215
       Plaintiff,

     v.

C.D.,
122 W. East Street,
Columbus, Ohio 43214
       Defendant.

No. CV-1981-453

DOCKETING STATEMENT

(Insert one of the following statements, as applicable):

(1) No transcript is required.

(2) The approximate number of pages of transcript ordered is _____.

(3) An agreed statement will be submitted in lieu of the record.

(4) The record was made in an administrative hearing and filed with the trial court.

(5) All parties to the appeal as shown by the attached statement approve assignment of the appeal to the accelerated calendar.

(6) The case is of a category designated for the accelerated calendar by local rule. (Specify category.)

_____

Attorney for Appellant

(Effective 7-1-82)

FORM 3

JUDGMENT ENTRY—ACCELERATED CALENDAR

TENTH DISTRICT COURT OF APPEALS
FRANKLIN COUNTY

A.B.,   :
221 East West Street,
Columbus, Ohio,   :
　　　　　　Plaintiff,   :
　　　v.   :   No. CV-1981-453
C.D.,   :
122 West East Street,
Columbus, Ohio,   :
　　　　　　Defendant.   :

JUDGMENT ENTRY

Assignment of error number one is overruled for the reason that the trial court's instruction on the burden of proof was correct. See *Jones v. State* (1980), 64 Ohio St.2d 173.

Assignment of error number two is overrruled as there was sufficient evidence presented (see testimony of Smith, R 22) to support a factual finding of agency.

The judgment of the trial court is affirmed.

_____
Judge, Presiding Judge

_____
Judge

_____
Judge

(Effective 7-1-82; amended, eff 7-1-92)

FEDERAL RULES OF CIVIL PROCEDURE

Including amendments effective December 1, 2002

I
SCOPE OF RULES—ONE FORM OF ACTION

RULE 1. Scope and Purpose of Rules

These rules govern the procedure in the United States district courts in all suits of a civil nature whether cognizable as cases at law or in equity or in admiralty, with the exceptions stated in Rule 81. They shall be construed and administered to secure the just, speedy, and inexpensive determination of every action.

RULE 2. One Form of Action

There shall be one form of action to be known as "civil action".

II
COMMENCEMENT OF ACTION; SERVICE OF PROCESS, PLEADINGS, MOTIONS, AND ORDERS

RULE 3. Commencement of Action

A civil action is commenced by filing a complaint with the court.

RULE 4. Summons

(a) Form. The summons shall be signed by the clerk, bear the seal of the court, identify the court and the parties, be directed to the defendant, and state the name and address of the plaintiff's attorney or, if unrepresented, of the plaintiff. It shall also state the time within which the defendant must appear and defend, and notify the defendant that failure to do so will result in a judgment by default against the defendant for the relief demanded in the complaint. The court may allow a summons to be amended.

(b) Issuance. Upon or after filing the complaint, the plaintiff may present a summons to the clerk for signature and seal. If the summons is in proper form, the clerk shall sign, seal, and issue it to the plaintiff for service on the defendant. A summons, or a copy of the summons if addressed to multiple defendants, shall be issued for each defendant to be served.

(c) Service with Complaint; by Whom Made.

(1) A summons shall be served together with a copy of the complaint. The plaintiff is responsible for service of a summons and complaint within the time allowed under subdivision (m) and shall furnish the person effecting service with the necessary copies of the summons and complaint.

(2) Service may be effected by any person who is not a party and who is at least 18 years of age. At the request of the plaintiff, however, the court may direct that service be effected by a United States marshal, deputy United States marshal, or other person or officer specially appointed by the court for that purpose. Such an appointment must be made when the plaintiff is authorized to proceed in forma pauperis pursuant to 28 U.S.C. § 1915 or is authorized to proceed as a seaman under 28 U.S.C. § 1916.

(d) Waiver of Service; Duty to Save Costs of Service; Request to Waive.

(1) A defendant who waives service of a summons does not thereby waive any objection to the venue or to the jurisdiction of the court over the person of the defendant.

(2) An individual, corporation, or association that is subject to service under subdivision (e), (f), or (h) and that receives notice of an action in the manner provided in this paragraph has a duty to avoid unnecessary costs of serving the summons. To avoid costs, the plaintiff may notify such a defendant of the commencement of the action and request that the defendant waive service of a summons. The notice and request

(A) shall be in writing and shall be addressed directly to the defendant, if an individual, or else to an officer or managing or general agent (or other agent authorized by appointment or law to receive service of process) of a defendant subject to service under subdivision (h);

(B) shall be dispatched through first-class mail or other reliable means;

(C) shall be accompanied by a copy of the complaint and shall identify the court in which it has been filed;

(D) shall inform the defendant, by means of a text prescribed in an official form promulgated pursuant to Rule 84, of the consequences of compliance and of a failure to comply with the request;

(E) shall set forth the date on which the request is sent;

(F) shall allow the defendant a reasonable time to return the waiver, which shall be at least 30 days from the date on which the request is sent, or 60 days from that date if the defendant is addressed outside any judicial district of the United States; and

(G) shall provide the defendant with an extra copy of the notice and request, as well as a prepaid means of compliance in writing.

If a defendant located within the United States fails to comply with a request for waiver made by a plaintiff located within the United States, the court shall impose the costs subsequently incurred in effecting service on the defendant unless good cause for the failure be shown.

(3) A defendant that, before being served with process, timely returns a waiver so requested is not required to serve an answer to the complaint until 60 days after the date on which the request for waiver of service was sent, or 90 days after that date if the defendant was addressed outside any judicial district of the United States.

(4) When the plaintiff files a waiver of service with the court, the action shall proceed, except as provided in paragraph (3), as if a summons and complaint had been served at the time of filing the waiver, and no proofs of service shall be required.

(5) The costs to be imposed on a defendant under paragraph (2) for failure to comply with a request to waive service of a summons shall include the costs subsequently incurred in effecting service under subdivision (e), (f), or (h), together with the costs, including a reasonable attorney's fee, of any motion required to collect the costs of service.

(e) Service Upon Individuals Within a Judicial District of the United States. Unless otherwise provided by federal law, service upon an individual from whom a waiver has not been obtained and filed, other than an infant or an incompetent person, may be effected in any judicial district of the United States:

(1) pursuant to the law of the state in which the district court is located, or in which service is effected, for the service of a summons upon the defendant in an action brought in the courts of general jurisdiction of the State; or

(2) by delivering a copy of the summons and of the complaint to the individual personally or by leaving copies thereof at the individual's dwelling house or usual place of abode with some person of suitable age and discretion then residing therein or by delivering a copy of the summons and of the complaint to an agent authorized by appointment or by law to receive service of process.

(f) Service Upon Individuals in a Foreign Country. Unless otherwise provided by federal law, service upon an individual from whom a waiver has not been obtained and filed, other than an infant or an incompetent person, may be effected in a place not within any judicial district of the United States:

(1) by any internationally agreed means reasonably calculated to give notice, such as those means authorized by the Hague Convention on the Service Abroad of Judicial and Extrajudicial Documents; or

(2) if there is no internationally agreed means of service or the applicable international agreement allows other means of service, provided that service is reasonably calculated to give notice:

(A) in the manner prescribed by the law of the foreign country for service in that country in an action in any of its courts of general jurisdiction; or

(B) as directed by the foreign authority in response to a letter rogatory or letter of request; or

(C) unless prohibited by the law of the foreign country, by

(i) delivery to the individual personally of a copy of the summons and the complaint; or

(ii) any form of mail requiring a signed receipt, to be addressed and dispatched by the clerk of the court to the party to be served; or

(3) by other means not prohibited by international agreement as may be directed by the court.

(g) Service Upon Infants and Incompetent Persons. Service upon an infant or an incompetent person in a judicial district of the United States shall be effected in the manner prescribed by the law of the state in which the service is made for the service of summons or other like process upon any such defendant in an action brought in the courts of general jurisdiction of that state. Service upon an infant or an incompetent person in a place not within any judicial district of the United States shall be effected in the manner prescribed by paragraph (2)(A) or (2)(B) of subdivision (f) or by such means as the court may direct.

(h) Service Upon Corporations and Associations. Unless otherwise provided by federal law, service upon a domestic or foreign corporation or upon a partnership or other unincorporated association that is subject to suit under a common name, and from which a waiver of service has not been obtained and filed, shall be effected:

(1) in a judicial district of the United States in the manner prescribed for individuals by subdivision (e)(1), or by delivering a copy of the summons and of the complaint to an officer, a managing or general agent, or to any other agent authorized by appointment or by law to receive service of process and, if the agent is one authorized by statute to receive service and the statute so requires, by also mailing a copy to the defendant, or

(2) in a place not within any judicial district of the United States in any manner prescribed for individuals by subdivision (f) except personal delivery as provided in paragraph (2)(C)(i) thereof.

(i) Serving the United States, its Agencies, Corporations, Officers, or Employees.

(1) Service upon the United States shall be effected

(A) by delivering a copy of the summons and of the complaint to the United States attorney for the district in which the action is brought or to an assistant United States attorney or clerical employee designated by the United States attorney in a writing filed with the clerk of the court or by sending a copy of the summons and of the complaint by registered or certified mail addressed to the civil process clerk at the office of the United States attorney and

(B) by also sending a copy of the summons and of the complaint by registered or certified mail to the Attorney General of the United States at Washington, District of Columbia, and

(C) in any action attacking the validity of an order of an officer or agency of the United States not made a party, by also sending a copy of the summons and of the complaint by registered or certified mail to the officer or agency.

(2)

(A) Service on an agency or corporation of the United States, or an officer or employee of the United States sued only in an official capacity, is effected by serving the United States in the manner prescribed by Rule 4(i)(1) and by also sending a copy of the summons and complaint by registered or certified mail to the officer, employee, agency, or corporation.

(B) Service on an officer or employee of the United States sued in an individual capacity for acts or omissions occurring in connection with the performance of duties on behalf of the United States—whether or not the officer or employee is sued also in an official capacity—is effected by serving the United States in the manner prescribed by Rule 4(i)(1) and by serving the officer or employee in the manner prescribed by Rule 4(e), (f), or (g).

(3) The court shall allow a reasonable time to serve process under Rule 4(i) for the purpose of curing the failure to serve:

(A) all persons required to be served in an action governed by Rule 4(i)(2)(A), if the plaintiff has served either the United States attorney or the Attorney General of the United States, or

(B) the United States in an action governed by Rule 4(i)(2)(B), if the plaintiff has served an officer or employee of the United States sued in an individual capacity.

(j) Service Upon Foreign, State, or Local Governments.

(1) Service upon a foreign state or a political subdivision, agency, or instrumentality thereof shall be effected pursuant to 28 U.S.C. § 1608.

(2) Service upon a state, municipal corporation, or other governmental organization subject to suit shall be effected by delivering a copy of the summons and of the complaint to its chief executive officer or by serving the summons and complaint in the manner prescribed by the law of that state for the service of summons or other like process upon any such defendant.

(k) Territorial Limits of Effective Service.

(1) Service of a summons or filing a waiver of service is effective to establish jurisdiction over the person of a defendant

(A) who could be subjected to the jurisdiction of a court of general jurisdiction in the state in which the district court is located, or

(B) who is a party joined under Rule 14 or Rule 19 and is served at a place within a judicial district of the United States and not more than 100 miles from the place from which the summons issues, or

(C) who is subject to the federal interpleader jurisdiction under 28 U.S.C. § 1335, or

(D) when authorized by a statute of the United States.

(2) If the exercise of jurisdiction is consistent with the Constitution and laws of the United States, serving a summons or filing a waiver of service is also effective, with respect to claims arising under federal law, to establish personal jurisdiction over the person of any defendant who is not subject to the jurisdiction of the courts of general jurisdiction of any state.

(l) Proof of Service. If service is not waived, the

person effecting service shall make proof thereof to the court. If service is made by a person other than a United States marshal or deputy United States marshal, the person shall make affidavit thereof. Proof of service in a place not within any judicial district of the United States shall, if effected under paragraph (1) of subdivision (f), be made pursuant to the applicable treaty or convention, and shall, if effected under paragraph (2) or (3) thereof, include a receipt signed by the addressee or other evidence of delivery to the addressee satisfactory to the court. Failure to make proof of service does not affect the validity of the service. The court may allow proof of service to be amended.

(m) Time Limit for Service. If service of the summons and complaint is not made upon a defendant within 120 days after the filing of the complaint, the court, upon motion or on its own initiative after notice to the plaintiff, shall dismiss the action without prejudice as to that defendant or direct that service be effected within a specified time; provided that if the plaintiff shows good cause for the failure, the court shall extend the time for service for an appropriate period. This subdivision does not apply to service in a foreign country pursuant to subdivision (f) or (j)(1).

(n) Seizure of Property; Service of Summons Not Feasible.

(1) If a statute of the United States so provides, the court may assert jurisdiction over property. Notice to claimants of the property shall then be sent in the manner provided by the statute or by service of a summons under this rule.

(2) Upon a showing that personal jurisdiction over a defendant cannot, in the district where the action is brought, be obtained with reasonable efforts by service of summons in any manner authorized by this rule, the court may assert jurisdiction over any of the defendant's assets found within the district by seizing the assets under the circumstances and in the manner provided by the law of the state in which the district court is located.

RULE 4.1. Service of Other Process

(a) Generally. Process other than a summons as provided in Rule 4 or subpoena as provided in Rule 45 shall be served by a United States marshal, a deputy United States marshal, or a person specially appointed for that purpose, who shall make proof of service as provided in Rule 4(1). The process may be served anywhere within the territorial limits of the state in which the district court is located, and, when authorized by a statute of the United States, beyond the territorial limits of that state.

(b) Enforcement of Orders: Commitment for Civil Contempt. An order of civil commitment of a person held to be in contempt of a decree or injunction issued to enforce the laws of the United States may be served and enforced in any district. Other orders in civil contempt proceedings shall be served in the state

in which the court issuing the order to be enforced is located or elsewhere within the United States if not more than 100 miles from the place at which the order to be enforced was issued.

RULE 5. Service and Filing of Pleadings and Other Papers

(a) Service: When required. Except as otherwise provided in these rules, every order required by its terms to be served, every pleading subsequent to the original complaint unless the court otherwise orders because of numerous defendants, every paper relating to discovery required to be served upon a party unless the court otherwise orders, every written motion other than one which may be heard ex parte, and every written notice, appearance, demand, offer of judgment, designation of record on appeal, and similar paper shall be served upon each of the parties. No service need be made on parties in default for failure to appear except that pleadings asserting new or additional claims for relief against them shall be served upon them in the manner provided for service of summons in Rule 4.

In an action begun by seizure of property, in which no person need be or is named as defendant, any service required to be made prior to the filing of an answer, claim, or appearance shall be made upon the person having custody or possession of the property at the time of its seizure.

(b) Making Service.

(1) Service under Rules 5(a) and 77(d) on a party represented by an attorney is made on the attorney unless the court orders service on the party.

(2) Service under Rule 5(a) is made by:

(A) Delivering a copy to the person served by:

(i) handing it to the person;

(ii) leaving it at the person's office with a clerk or other person in charge, or if no one is in charge leaving it in a conspicuous place in the office; or

(iii) if the person has no office or the office is closed, leaving it at the person's dwelling house or usual place of abode with someone of suitable age and discretion residing there.

(B) Mailing a copy to the last known address of the person served. Service by mail is complete on mailing.

(C) If the person served has no known address, leaving a copy with the clerk of the court.

(D) Delivering a copy by any other means, including electronic means, consented to in writing by the person served. Service by electronic means is complete on transmission; service by other consented means is complete when the person making service delivers the copy to the agency designated to make delivery. If authorized by local rule, a party may make service under this subparagraph (D) through the court's transmission facilities.

(3) Service by electronic means under Rule 5(b)(2)(D) is not effective if the party making service

learns that the attempted service did not reach the person to be served.

(c) Same: Numerous Defendants. In any action in which there are unusually large numbers of defendants, the court, upon motion or of its own initiative, may order that service of the pleadings of the defendants and replies thereto need not be made as between the defendants and that any cross-claim, counterclaim, or matter constituting an avoidance or affirmative defense contained therein shall be deemed to be denied or avoided by all other parties and that the filing of any such pleading and service thereof upon the plaintiff constitutes due notice of it to the parties. A copy of every such order shall be served upon the parties in such manner and form as the court directs.

(d) Filing; Certificate of Service. All papers after the complaint required to be served upon a party, together with a certificate of service, must be filed with the court within a reasonable time after service, but disclosures under Rule 26(a)(1) or (2) and the following discovery requests and responses must not be filed until they are used in the proceeding or the court orders filing:

(i) depositions,

(ii) interrogatories,

(iii) requests for documents or to permit entry upon land, and

(iv) requests for admission.

(e) Filing with the Court Defined. The filing of papers with the court as required by these rules shall be made by filing them with the clerk of court, except that the judge may permit the papers to be filed with the judge, in which event the judge shall note thereon the filing date and forthwith transmit them to the office of the clerk. A court may by local rule permit papers to be filed, signed, or verified by electronic means that are consistent with technical standards, if any, that the Judicial Conference of the United States establishes. A paper filed by electronic means in compliance with a local rule constitutes a written paper for the purpose of applying these rules. The clerk shall not refuse to accept for filing any paper presented for that purpose solely because it is not presented in proper form as required by these rules or any local rules or practices.

RULE 6. Time

(a) Computation. In computing any period of time prescribed or allowed by these rules, by the local rules of any district court, by order of court, or by any applicable statute, the day of the act, event, or default from which the designated period of time begins to run shall not be included. The last day of the period so computed shall be included, unless it is a Saturday, a Sunday, or a legal holiday, or, when the act to be done is the filing of a paper in court, a day on which weather or other conditions have made the office of the clerk of the district court inaccessible, in which event the period runs until the end of the next day which is not one

of the aforementioned days. When the period of time prescribed or allowed is less than 11 days, intermediate Saturdays, Sundays, and legal holidays shall be excluded in the computation. As used in this rule and in Rule 77(c), "legal holiday" includes New Year's Day, Birthday of Martin Luther King, Jr., Washington's Birthday, Memorial Day, Independence Day, Labor Day, Columbus Day, Veterans Day, Thanksgiving Day, Christmas Day, and any other day appointed as a holiday by the President or the Congress of the United States, or by the state in which the district court is held.

(b) Enlargement. When by these rules or by a notice given thereunder or by order of court an act is required or allowed to be done at or within a specified time, the court for cause shown may at any time in its discretion

(1) with or without motion or notice order the period enlarged if request therefor is made before the expiration of the period originally prescribed or as extended by a previous order, or

(2) upon motion made after the expiration of the specified period permit the act to be done where the failure to act was the result of excusable neglect;

but it may not extend the time for taking any action under Rules 50(b) and (c)(2), 52(b), 59(b), (d) and (e), and 60(b), except to the extent and under the conditions stated in them.

(c) Unaffected by Expiration of Term. [Rescinded Feb. 28, 1966, eff. July 1, 1966.]

(d) For Motions—Affidavits. A written motion, other than one which may be heard ex parte, and notice of the hearing thereof shall be served not later than 5 days before the time specified for the hearing, unless a different period is fixed by these rules or by order of the court. Such an order may for cause shown be made on ex parte application. When a motion is supported by affidavit, the affidavit shall be served with the motion; and, except as otherwise provided in Rule 59(c), opposing affidavits may be served not later than 1 day before the hearing, unless the court permits them to be served at some other time.

(e) Additional Time After Service under Rule 5(b)(2)(B), (C), or (D). Whenever a party has the right or is required to do some act or take some proceedings within a prescribed period after the service of a notice or other paper upon the party and the notice or paper is served upon the party under Rule 5(b)(2)(B), (C), or (D), 3 days shall be added to the prescribed period.

III
PLEADINGS AND MOTIONS

RULE 7. Pleadings Allowed; Form of Motions

(a) Pleadings. There shall be a complaint and an answer; a reply to a counterclaim denominated as such; an answer to a cross-claim, if the answer contains a cross-claim; a third-party complaint, if a person who was not an original party is summoned under the provisions of Rule 14; and a third-party answer, if a third-party complaint is served. No other pleading shall be allowed, except that the court may order a reply to an answer or a third-party answer.

(b) Motions and Other Papers.

(1) An application to the court for an order shall be by motion which, unless made during a hearing or trial, shall be made in writing, shall state with particularity the grounds therefor, and shall set forth the relief or order sought. The requirement of writing is fulfilled if the motion is stated in a written notice of the hearing of the motion.

(2) The rules applicable to captions and other matters of form of pleadings apply to all motions and other papers provided for by these rules.

(3) All motions shall be signed in accordance with Rule 11.

(c) Demurrers, Pleas, etc., Abolished. Demurrers, pleas, and exceptions for insufficiency of a pleading shall not be used.

RULE 7.1. Disclosure Statement

(a) Who Must File: Nongovernmental Corporate Party. A nongovernmental corporate party to an action or proceeding in a district court must file two copies of a statement that identifies any parent corporation and any publicly held corporation that owns 10% or more of its stock or states that there is no such corporation.

(b) Time for Filing; Supplemental Filing. A party must:

(1) file the Rule 7.1(a) statement with its first appearance, pleading, petition, motion, response, or other request addressed to the court, and

(2) promptly file a supplemental statement upon any change in the information that the statement requires.

RULE 8. General Rules of Pleading

(a) Claims for Relief. A pleading which sets forth a claim for relief, whether an original claim, counterclaim, cross-claim, or third-party claim, shall contain

(1) a short and plain statement of the grounds upon which the court's jurisdiction depends, unless the court already has jurisdiction and the claim needs no new grounds of jurisdiction to support it,

(2) a short and plain statement of the claim showing that the pleader is entitled to relief, and

(3) a demand for judgment for the relief the pleader seeks.

Relief in the alternative or of several different types may be demanded.

(b) Defenses; Form of Denials. A party shall state in short and plain terms the party's defenses to each claim asserted and shall admit or deny the averments upon which the adverse party relies. If a party is without knowledge or information sufficient to form a belief as to the truth of an averment, the party shall so state and this has the effect of a denial. Denials shall fairly meet the substance of the averments denied. When a pleader intends in good faith to deny only a part or a qualification of an averment, the pleader shall specify so much of it as is true and material and shall deny only the remainder. Unless the pleader intends in good faith to controvert all the averments of the preceding pleading, the pleader may make denials as specific denials of designated averments or paragraphs or may generally deny all the averments except such designated averments or paragraphs as the pleader expressly admits; but, when the pleader does so intend to controvert all its averments, including averments of the grounds upon which the court's jurisdiction depends, the pleader may do so by general denial subject to the obligations set forth in Rule 11.

(c) Affirmative Defenses. In pleading to a preceding pleading, a party shall set forth affirmatively accord and satisfaction, arbitration and award, assumption of risk, contributory negligence, discharge in bankruptcy, duress, estoppel, failure of consideration, fraud, illegality, injury by fellow servant, laches, license, payment, release, res judicata, statute of frauds, statute of limitations, waiver, and any other matter constituting an avoidance or affirmative defense. When a party has mistakenly designated a defense as a counterclaim or a counterclaim as a defense, the court on terms, if justice so requires, shall treat the pleading as if there had been a proper designation.

(d) Effect of Failure to Deny. Averments in a pleading to which a responsive pleading is required, other than those as to the amount of damage, are admitted when not denied in the responsive pleading. Averments in a pleading to which no responsive pleading is required or permitted shall be taken as denied or avoided.

(e) Pleading to be Concise and Direct; Consistency.

(1) Each averment of a pleading shall be simple, concise, and direct. No technical forms of pleading or motions are required.

(2) A party may set forth two or more statements of a claim or defense alternately or hypothetically, either in one count or defense or in separate counts or defenses. When two or more statements are made in the alternative and one of them if made independently would be sufficient, the pleading is not made insufficient by the insufficiency of one or more of the alternative statements. A party may also state as many separate claims or defenses as the party has regardless of consistency and whether based on legal, equitable, or maritime grounds. All statements shall be made subject to the obligations set forth in Rule 11.

(f) Construction of Pleadings.

All pleadings shall be so construed as to do substantial justice.

RULE 9. Pleading Special Matters

(a) Capacity. It is not necessary to aver the capacity

of a party to sue or be sued or the authority of a party to sue or be sued in a representative capacity or the legal existence of an organized association of persons that is made a party, except to the extent required to show the jurisdiction of the court. When a party desires to raise an issue as to the legal existence of any party or the capacity of any party to sue or be sued or the authority of a party to sue or be sued in a representative capacity, the party desiring to raise the issue shall do so by specific negative averment, which shall include such supporting particulars as are peculiarly within the pleader's knowledge.

(b) Fraud, Mistake, Condition of the Mind. In all averments of fraud or mistake, the circumstances constituting fraud or mistake shall be stated with particularity. Malice, intent, knowledge, and other condition of mind of a person may be averred generally.

(c) Conditions Precedent. In pleading the performance or occurrence of conditions precedent, it is sufficient to aver generally that all conditions precedent have been performed or have occurred. A denial of performance or occurrence shall be made specifically and with particularity.

(d) Official Document or Act. In pleading an official document or official act it is sufficient to aver that the document was issued or the act done in compliance with law.

(e) Judgment. In pleading a judgment or decision of a domestic or foreign court, judicial or quasi-judicial tribunal, or of a board or officer, it is sufficient to aver the judgment or decision without setting forth matter showing jurisdiction to render it.

(f) Time and Place. For the purpose of testing the sufficiency of a pleading, averments of time and place are material and shall be considered like all other averments of material matter.

(g) Special Damage. When items of special damage are claimed, they shall be specifically stated.

(h) Admiralty and Maritime Claims. A pleading or count setting forth a claim for relief within the admiralty and maritime jurisdiction that is also within the jurisdiction of the district court on some other ground may contain a statement identifying the claim as an admiralty or maritime claim for the purposes of Rules 14(c), 38(e), 82, and the Supplemental Rules for Certain Admiralty and Maritime Claims. If the claim is cognizable only in admiralty, it is an admiralty or maritime claim for those purposes whether so identified or not. The amendment of a pleading to add or withdraw an identifying statement is governed by the principles of Rule 15. A case that includes an admiralty or maritime claim within this subdivision is an admiralty case within 28 U.S.C. § 1292(a)(3).

RULE 10. Form of Pleadings

(a) Caption; Names of Parties. Every pleading shall contain a caption setting forth the name of the court, the title of the action, the file number, and a designation as in Rule 7(a). In the complaint the title of the action shall include the names of all the parties, but in other pleadings it is sufficient to state the name of the first party on each side with an appropriate indication of other parties.

(b) Paragraphs; Separate Statements. All averments of claim or defense shall be made in numbered paragraphs, the contents of each of which shall be limited as far as practicable to a statement of a single set of circumstances; and a paragraph may be referred to by number in all succeeding pleadings. Each claim founded upon a separate transaction or occurrence and each defense other than denials shall be stated in a separate count or defense whenever a separation facilitates the clear presentation of the matters set forth.

(c) Adoption by Reference; Exhibits. Statements in a pleading may be adopted by reference in a different part of the same pleading or in another pleading or in any motion. A copy of any written instrument which is an exhibit to a pleading is a part thereof for all purposes.

RULE 11. Signing of Pleadings, Motions, and Other Papers; Representations to Court; Sanctions

(a) Signature. Every pleading, written motion, and other paper shall be signed by at least one attorney of record in the attorney's individual name, or, if the party is not represented by an attorney, shall be signed by the party. Each paper shall state the signer's address and telephone number, if any. Except when otherwise specifically provided by rule or statute, pleadings need not be verified or accompanied by affidavit. An unsigned paper shall be stricken unless omission of the signature is corrected promptly after being called to the attention of the attorney or party.

(b) Representations to Court. By presenting to the court (whether by signing, filing, submitting, or later advocating) a pleading, written motion, or other paper, an attorney or unrepresented party is certifying that to the best of the person's knowledge, information, and belief, formed after an inquiry reasonable under the circumstances,—

(1) it is not being presented for any improper purpose, such as to harass or to cause unnecessary delay or needless increase in the cost of litigation;

(2) the claims, defenses, and other legal contentions therein are warranted by existing law or by a nonfrivolous argument for the extension, modification, or reversal of existing law or the establishment of new law;

(3) the allegations and other factual contentions have evidentiary support or, if specifically so identified, are likely to have evidentiary support after a reasonable opportunity for further investigation or discovery; and

(4) the denials of factual contentions are warranted on the evidence or, if specifically so identified, are reasonably based on a lack of information or belief.

(c) Sanctions. If, after notice and a reasonable opportunity to respond, the court determines that subdivision (b) has been violated, the court may, subject to the conditions stated below, impose an appropriate sanction upon the attorneys, law firms, or parties that have violated subdivision (b) or are responsible for the violation.

(1) *How Initiated.*

(A) By Motion. A motion for sanctions under this rule shall be made separately from other motions or requests and shall describe the specific conduct alleged to violate subdivision (b). It shall be served as provided in Rule 5, but shall not be filed with or presented to the court unless, within 21 days after service of the motion (or such other period as the court may prescribe), the challenged paper, claim, defense, contention, allegation, or denial is not withdrawn or appropriately corrected. If warranted, the court may award to the party prevailing on the motion the reasonable expenses and attorney's fees incurred in presenting or opposing the motion. Absent exceptional circumstances, a law firm shall be held jointly responsible for violations committed by its partners, associates, and employees.

(B) On Court's Initiative. On its own initiative, the court may enter an order describing the specific conduct that appears to violate subdivision (b) and directing an attorney, law firm, or party to show cause why it has not violated subdivision (b) with respect thereto.

(2) *Nature of Sanction; Limitations.* A sanction imposed for violation of this rule shall be limited to what is sufficient to deter repetition of such conduct or comparable conduct by others similarly situated. Subject to the limitations in subparagraphs (A) and (B), the sanction may consist of, or include, directives of a nonmonetary nature, an order to pay a penalty into court, or, if imposed on motion and warranted for effective deterrence, an order directing payment to the movant of some or all of the reasonable attorneys' fees and other expenses incurred as a direct result of the violation.

(A) Monetary sanctions may not be awarded against a represented party for a violation of subdivision (b)(2).

(B) Monetary sanctions may not be awarded on the court's initiative unless the court issues its order to show cause before a voluntary dismissal or settlement of the claims made by or against the party which is, or whose attorneys are, to be sanctioned.

(3) *Order.* When imposing sanctions, the court shall describe the conduct determined to constitute a violation of this rule and explain the basis for the sanction imposed.

(d) Inapplicability to Discovery. Subdivisions (a) through (c) of this rule do not apply to disclosures and discovery requests, responses, objections, and motions that are subject to the provisions of Rules 26 through 37.

RULE 12. Defenses and Objections—When and How Presented—By Pleading or Motion—Motion for Judgment on Pleadings

(a) When Presented.

(1) Unless a different time is prescribed in a statute of the United States, a defendant shall serve an answer

(A) within 20 days after being served with the summons and complaint, or

(B) if service of the summons has been timely waived on request under Rule 4(d), within 60 days after the date when the request for waiver was sent, or within 90 days after that date if the defendant was addressed outside any judicial district of the United States.

(2) A party served with a pleading stating a cross-claim against that party shall serve an answer thereto within 20 days after being served. The plaintiff shall serve a reply to a counterclaim in the answer within 20 days after service of the answer, or, if a reply is ordered by the court, within 20 days after service of the order, unless the order otherwise directs.

(3)

(A) The United States, an agency of the United States, or an officer or employee of the United States sued in an official capacity, shall serve an answer to the complaint or cross-claim—or a reply to a counterclaim—within 60 days after the United States attorney is served with the pleading asserting the claim.

(B) An officer or employee of the United States sued in an individual capacity for acts or omissions occurring in connection with the performance of duties on behalf of the United States shall serve an answer to the complaint or cross-claim—or a reply to a counterclaim—within 60 days after service on the officer or employee, or service on the United States attorney, whichever is later.

(4) Unless a different time is fixed by court order, the service of a motion permitted under this rule alters the periods of time as follows:

(A) if the court denies the motion or postpones its disposition until the trial on the merits, the responsive pleading shall be served within 10 days after notice of the court's action; or

(B) if the court grants a motion for a more definite statement, the responsive pleading shall be served within 10 days after the service of the more definite statement.

(b) How Presented. Every defense, in law or fact, to a claim for relief in any pleading, whether a claim, counterclaim, cross-claim, or third-party claim, shall be asserted in the responsive pleading thereto if one is required, except that the following defenses may at the option of the pleader be made by motion:

(1) lack of jurisdiction over the subject matter,

(2) lack of jurisdiction over the person,

(3) improper venue,

(4) insufficiency of process,

(5) insufficiency of service of process,

(6) failure to state a claim upon which relief can be granted,

(7) failure to join a party under Rule 19.

A motion making any of these defenses shall be made before pleading if a further pleading is permitted. No defense or objection is waived by being joined with one or more other defenses or objections in a responsive pleading or motion. If a pleading sets forth a claim for relief to which the adverse party is not required to serve a responsive pleading, the adverse party may assert at the trial any defense in law or fact to that claim for relief. If, on a motion asserting the defense numbered (6) to dismiss for failure of the pleading to state a claim upon which relief can be granted, matters outside the pleading are presented to and not excluded by the court, the motion shall be treated as one for summary judgment and disposed of as provided in Rule 56, and all parties shall be given reasonable opportunity to present all material made pertinent to such a motion by Rule 56.

(c) Motion for Judgment on the Pleadings. After the pleadings are closed but within such time as not to delay the trial, any party may move for judgment on the pleadings. If, on a motion for judgment on the pleadings, matters outside the pleadings are presented to and not excluded by the court, the motion shall be treated as one for summary judgment and disposed of as provided in Rule 56, and all parties shall be given reasonable opportunity to present all material made pertinent to such a motion by Rule 56.

(d) Preliminary Hearings. The defenses specifically enumerated (1)-(7) in subdivision (b) of this rule, whether made in a pleading or by motion, and the motion for judgment mentioned in subdivision (c) of this rule shall be heard and determined before trial on application of any party, unless the court orders that the hearing and determination thereof be deferred until the trial.

(e) Motion for More Definite Statement. If a pleading to which a responsive pleading is permitted is so vague or ambiguous that a party cannot reasonably be required to frame a responsive pleading, the party may move for a more definite statement before interposing a responsive pleading. The motion shall point out the defects complained of and the details desired. If the motion is granted and the order of the court is not obeyed within 10 days after notice of the order or within such other time as the court may fix, the court may strike the pleading to which the motion was directed or make such order as it deems just.

(f) Motion to Strike. Upon motion made by a party before responding to a pleading or, if no responsive pleading is permitted by these rules, upon motion made by a party within 20 days after the service of the pleading upon the party or upon the court's own initiative at any time, the court may order stricken from any pleading any insufficient defense or any redundant, immaterial, impertinent, or scandalous matter.

(g) Consolidation of Defenses in Motion. A party who makes a motion under this rule may join with it any

other motions herein provided for and then available to the party. If a party makes a motion under this rule but omits therefrom any defense or objection then available to the party which this rule permits to be raised by motion, the party shall not thereafter make a motion based on the defense or objection so omitted, except a motion as provided in subdivision (h)(2) hereof on any of the grounds there stated.

(h) Waiver or Preservation of Certain Defenses.

(1) A defense of lack of jurisdiction over the person, improper venue, insufficiency of process, or insufficiency of service of process is waived

(A) if omitted from a motion in the circumstances described in subdivision (g), or

(B) if it is neither made by motion under this rule nor included in a responsive pleading or an amendment thereof permitted by Rule 15(a) to be made as a matter of course.

(2) A defense of failure to state a claim upon which relief can be granted, a defense of failure to join a party indispensable under Rule 19, and an objection of failure to state a legal defense to a claim may be made in any pleading permitted or ordered under Rule 7(a), or by motion for judgment on the pleadings, or at the trial on the merits.

(3) Whenever it appears by suggestion of the parties or otherwise that the court lacks jurisdiction of the subject matter, the court shall dismiss the action.

RULE 13. Counterclaim and Cross-Claim

(a) Compulsory Counterclaims. A pleading shall state as a counterclaim any claim which at the time of serving the pleading the pleader has against any opposing party, if it arises out of the transaction or occurrence that is the subject matter of the opposing party's claim and does not require for its adjudication the presence of third parties of whom the court cannot acquire jurisdiction. But the pleader need not state the claim if

(1) at the time the action was commenced the claim was the subject of another pending action, or

(2) the opposing party brought suit upon the claim by attachment or other process by which the court did not acquire jurisdiction to render a personal judgment on that claim, and the pleader is not stating any counterclaim under this Rule 13.

(b) Permissive Counterclaims. A pleading may state as a counterclaim any claim against an opposing party not arising out of the transaction or occurrence that is the subject matter of the opposing party's claim.

(c) Counterclaim Exceeding Opposing Claim. A counterclaim may or may not diminish or defeat the recovery sought by the opposing party. It may claim relief exceeding in amount or different in kind from that sought in the pleading of the opposing party.

(d) Counterclaim Against the United States. These rules shall not be construed to enlarge beyond the limits now fixed by law the right to assert counterclaims or to claim credits against the United States or an officer or agency thereof.

(e) Counterclaim Maturing or Acquired After Pleading. A claim which either matured or was acquired by the pleader after serving a pleading may, with the permission of the court, be presented as a counterclaim by supplemental pleading.

(f) Omitted Counterclaim. When a pleader fails to set up a counterclaim through oversight, inadvertence, or excusable neglect, or when justice requires, the pleader may by leave of court set up the counterclaim by amendment.

(g) Cross-Claim Against Co-Party. A pleading may state as a cross-claim any claim by one party against a co-party arising out of the transaction or occurrence that is the subject matter either of the original action or of a counterclaim therein or relating to any property that is the subject matter of the original action. Such cross-claim may include a claim that the party against whom it is asserted is or may be liable to the cross-claimant for all or part of a claim asserted in the action against the cross-claimant.

(h) Joinder of Additional Parties. Persons other than those made parties to the original action may be made parties to a counterclaim or cross-claim in accordance with the provisions of Rules 19 and 20.

(i) Separate Trials; Separate Judgments. If the court orders separate trials as provided in Rule 42(b), judgment on a counterclaim or cross-claim may be rendered in accordance with the terms of Rule 54(b) when the court has jurisdiction so to do, even if the claims of the opposing party have been dismissed or otherwise disposed of.

RULE 14. Third-Party Practice

(a) When Defendant May Bring in Third Party. At any time after commencement of the action a defending party, as a third-party plaintiff, may cause a summons and complaint to be served upon a person not a party to the action who is or may be liable to the third-party plaintiff for all or part of the plaintiff's claim against the third-party plaintiff. The third-party plaintiff need not obtain leave to make the service if the third-party plaintiff files the third-party complaint not later than 10 days after serving the original answer. Otherwise the third-party plaintiff must obtain leave on motion upon notice to all parties to the action. The person served with the summons and third-party complaint, hereinafter called the third-party defendant, shall make any defenses to the third-party plaintiff's claim as provided in Rule 12 and any counterclaims against the third-party plaintiff and cross-claims against other third-party defendants as provided in Rule 13. The third-party defendant may assert against the plaintiff any defenses which the third-party plaintiff has to the plaintiff's claim. The third-party defendant may also assert any claim against the plaintiff arising out of the transaction or occurrence that is the subject matter of the

plaintiff's claim against the third-party plaintiff. The plaintiff may assert any claim against the third-party defendant arising out of the transaction or occurrence that is the subject matter of the plaintiff's claim against the third-party plaintiff, and the third-party defendant thereupon shall assert any defenses as provided in Rule 12 and any counterclaims and cross-claims as provided in Rule 13. Any party may move to strike the third-party claim, or for its severance or separate trial. A third-party defendant may proceed under this rule against any person not a party to the action who is or may be liable to the third-party defendant for all or part of the claim made in the action against the third-party defendant. The third-party complaint, if within the admiralty and maritime jurisdiction, may be in rem against a vessel, cargo, or other property subject to admiralty or maritime process in rem, in which case references in this rule to the summons include the warrant of arrest, and references to the third-party plaintiff or defendant include, where appropriate, a person who asserts a right under Supplemental Rule C(6)(b)(i) in the property arrested.

(b) When Plaintiff May Bring in Third Party. When a counterclaim is asserted against a plaintiff, the plaintiff may cause a third party to be brought in under circumstances which under this rule would entitle a defendant to do so.

(c) Admiralty and Maritime Claims. When a plaintiff asserts an admiralty or maritime claim within the meaning of Rule 9(h), the defendant or person who asserts a right under Supplemental Rule C(6)(b)(i), as a third-party plaintiff, may bring in a third-party defendant who may be wholly or partly liable, either to the plaintiff or to the third-party plaintiff, by way of remedy over, contribution, or otherwise on account of the same transaction, occurrence, or series of transactions or occurrences. In such a case the third-party plaintiff may also demand judgment against the third-party defendant in favor of the plaintiff, in which event the third-party defendant shall make any defenses to the claim of the plaintiff as well as to that of the third-party plaintiff in the manner provided in Rule 12 and the action shall proceed as if the plaintiff had commenced it against the third-party defendant as well as the third-party plaintiff.

RULE 15. Amended and Supplemental Pleadings

(a) Amendments. A party may amend the party's pleading once as a matter of course at any time before a responsive pleading is served or, if the pleading is one to which no responsive pleading is permitted and the action has not been placed upon the trial calendar, the party may so amend it at any time within 20 days after it is served. Otherwise a party may amend the party's pleading only by leave of court or by written consent of the adverse party; and leave shall be freely given when justice so requires. A party shall plead in response to an amended pleading within the time remaining for response to the original pleading or within 10 days after service of the amended pleading, whichever period may be the longer, unless the court otherwise orders.

(b) Amendments to Conform to the Evidence. When issues not raised by the pleadings are tried by express or implied consent of the parties, they shall be treated in all respects as if they had been raised in the pleadings. Such amendment of the pleadings as may be necessary to cause them to conform to the evidence and to raise these issues may be made upon motion of any party at any time, even after judgment; but failure so to amend does not affect the result of the trial of these issues. If evidence is objected to at the trial on the ground that it is not within the issues made by the pleadings, the court may allow the pleadings to be amended and shall do so freely when the presentation of the merits of the action will be subserved thereby and the objecting party fails to satisfy the court that the admission of such evidence would prejudice the party in maintaining the party's action or defense upon the merits. The court may grant a continuance to enable the objecting party to meet such evidence.

(c) Relation Back of Amendments. An amendment of a pleading relates back to the date of the original pleading when

(1) relation back is permitted by the law that provides the statute of limitations applicable to the action, or

(2) the claim or defense asserted in the amended pleading arose out of the conduct, transaction, or occurrence set forth or attempted to be set forth in the original pleading, or

(3) the amendment changes the party or the naming of the party against whom a claim is asserted if the foregoing provision (2) is satisfied and, within the period provided by Rule 4(m) for service of the summons and complaint, the party to be brought in by amendment

(A) has received such notice of the institution of the action that the party will not be prejudiced in maintaining a defense on the merits, and

(B) knew or should have known that, but for a mistake concerning the identity of the proper party, the action would have been brought against the party. The delivery or mailing of process to the United States Attorney, or United States Attorney's designee, or the Attorney General of the United States, or an agency or officer who would have been a proper defendant if named, satisfies the requirement of subparagraphs (A) and (B) of this paragraph (3) with respect to the United States or any agency or officer thereof to be brought into the action as a defendant.

(d) Supplemental Pleadings. Upon motion of a party the court may, upon reasonable notice and upon such terms as are just, permit the party to serve a supplemental pleading setting forth transactions or occurrences or events which have happened since the date of the pleading sought to be supplemented. Permission may be granted even though the original plead-ing is defective in its statement of a claim for relief or defense. If the court deems it advisable that the adverse party plead to the supplemental pleading, it shall so order, specifying the time therefor.

RULE 16. Pretrial Conferences; Scheduling; Management

(a) Pretrial Conferences; Objectives. In any action, the court may in its discretion direct the attorneys for the parties and any unrepresented parties to appear before it for a conference or conferences before trial for such purposes as

(1) expediting the disposition of the action;

(2) establishing early and continuing control so that the case will not be protracted because of lack of management;

(3) discouraging wasteful pretrial activities;

(4) improving the quality of the trial through more thorough preparation, and;

(5) facilitating the settlement of the case.

(b) Scheduling and Planning. Except in categories of actions exempted by district court rule as inappropriate, the district judge, or a magistrate judge when authorized by district court rule, shall, after receiving the report from the parties under Rule 26(f) or after consulting with the attorneys for the parties and any unrepresented parties by a scheduling conference, telephone, mail, or other suitable means, enter a scheduling order that limits the time

(1) to join other parties and to amend the pleadings;

(2) to file motions; and

(3) to complete discovery.

The scheduling order may also include

(4) modifications of the times for disclosures under Rules 26(a) and 26(e)(1) and of the extent of discovery to be permitted;

(5) the date or dates for conferences before trial, a final pretrial conference, and trial; and

(6) any other matters appropriate in the circumstances of the case.

The order shall issue as soon as practicable but in any event within 90 days after the appearance of a defendant and within 120 days after the complaint has been served on a defendant. A schedule shall not be modified except upon a showing of good cause and by leave of the district judge or, when authorized by local rule, by a magistrate judge.

(c) Subjects for Consideration at Pretrial Conferences. At any conference under this rule consideration may be given, and the court may take appropriate action, with respect to

(1) the formulation and simplification of the issues, including the elimination of frivolous claims or defenses;

(2) the necessity or desirability of amendments to the pleadings;

(3) the possibility of obtaining admissions of fact and of documents which will avoid unnecessary proof, stipu-

lations regarding the authenticity of documents, and advance rulings from the court on the admissibility of evidence;

(4) the avoidance of unnecessary proof and of cumulative evidence, and limitations or restrictions on the use of testimony under Rule 702 of the Federal Rules of Evidence;

(5) the appropriateness and timing of summary adjudication under Rule 56;

(6) the control and scheduling of discovery, including orders affecting disclosures and discovery pursuant to Rule 26 and Rules 29 through 37;

(7) the identification of witnesses and documents, the need and schedule for filing and exchanging pretrial briefs, and the date or dates for further conferences and for trial;

(8) the advisability of referring matters to a magistrate judge or master;

(9) settlement and the use of special procedures to assist in resolving the dispute when authorized by statute or local rule;

(10) the form and substance of the pretrial order;

(11) the disposition of pending motions;

(12) the need for adopting special procedures for managing potentially difficult or protracted actions that may involve complex issues, multiple parties, difficult legal questions, or unusual proof problems;

(13) an order for a separate trial pursuant to Rule 42(b) with respect to a claim, counterclaim, cross-claim, or third-party claim, or with respect to any particular issue in the case;

(14) an order directing a party or parties to present evidence early in the trial with respect to a manageable issue that could, on the evidence, be the basis for a judgment as a matter of law under Rule 50(a) or a judgment on partial findings under Rule 52(c);

(15) an order establishing a reasonable limit on the time allowed for presenting evidence; and

(16) such other matters as may facilitate the just, speedy, and inexpensive disposition of the action.

At least one of the attorneys for each party participating in any conference before trial shall have authority to enter into stipulations and to make admissions regarding all matters that the participants may reasonably anticipate may be discussed. If appropriate, the court may require that a party or its representative be present or reasonably available by telephone in order to consider possible settlement of the dispute.

(d) Final Pretrial Conference. Any final pretrial conference shall be held as close to the time of trial as reasonable under the circumstances. The participants at any such conference shall formulate a plan for trial, including a program for facilitating the admission of evidence. The conference shall be attended by at least one of the attorneys who will conduct the trial for each of the parties and by any unrepresented parties.

(e) Pretrial Orders. After any conference held pursuant to this rule, an order shall be entered reciting the

action taken. This order shall control the subsequent course of the action unless modified by a subsequent order. The order following a final pretrial conference shall be modified only to prevent manifest injustice.

(f) Sanctions. If a party or party's attorney fails to obey a scheduling or pretrial order, or if no appearance is made on behalf of a party at a scheduling or pretrial conference, or if a party or party's attorney is substantially unprepared to participate in the conference, or if a party or party's attorney fails to participate in good faith, the judge, upon motion or the judge's own initiative, may make such orders with regard thereto as are just, and among others any of the orders provided in Rule 37(b)(2)(B), (C), (D). In lieu of or in addition to any other sanction, the judge shall require the party or the attorney representing the party or both to pay the reasonable expenses incurred because of any noncompliance with this rule, including attorney's fees, unless the judge finds that the noncompliance was substantially justified or that other circumstances make an award of expenses unjust.

IV
PARTIES

RULE 17. Parties Plaintiff and Defendant; Capacity

(a) Real Party in Interest. Every action shall be prosecuted in the name of the real party in interest. An executor, administrator, guardian, bailee, trustee of an express trust, a party with whom or in whose name a contract has been made for the benefit of another, or a party authorized by statute may sue in that person's own name without joining the party for whose benefit the action is brought; and when a statute of the United States so provides, an action for the use or benefit of another shall be brought in the name of the United States. No action shall be dismissed on the ground that it is not prosecuted in the name of the real party in interest until a reasonable time has been allowed after objection for ratification of commencement of the action by, or joinder or substitution of, the real party in interest; and such ratification, joinder, or substitution shall have the same effect as if the action had been commenced in the name of the real party in interest.

(b) Capacity to Sue or be Sued. The capacity of an individual, other than one acting in a representative capacity, to sue or be sued shall be determined by the law of the individual's domicile. The capacity of a corporation to sue or be sued shall be determined by the law under which it was organized. In all other cases capacity to sue or be sued shall be determined by the law of the state in which the district court is held, except

(1) that a partnership or other unincorporated association, which has no such capacity by the law of such

state, may sue or be sued in its common name for the purpose of enforcing for or against it a substantive right existing under the Constitution or laws of the United States, and

(2) that the capacity of a receiver appointed by a court of the United States to sue or be sued in a court of the United States is governed by Title 28, U.S.C. §§ 754 and 959(a).

(c) Infants or Incompetent Persons. Whenever an infant or incompetent person has a representative, such as a general guardian, committee, conservator, or other like fiduciary, the representative may sue or defend on behalf of the infant or incompetent person. An infant or incompetent person who does not have a duly appointed representative may sue by a next friend or by a guardian ad litem. The court shall appoint a guardian ad litem for an infant or incompetent person not otherwise represented in an action or shall make such other order as it deems proper for the protection of the infant or incompetent person.

RULE 18. Joinder of Claims and Remedies

(a) Joinder of Claims. A party asserting a claim to relief as an original claim, counterclaim, cross-claim, or third-party claim, may join, either as independent or as alternate claims, as many claims, legal, equitable, or maritime, as the party has against an opposing party.

(b) Joinder of Remedies; Fraudulent Conveyances. Whenever a claim is one heretofore cognizable only after another claim has been prosecuted to a conclusion, the two claims may be joined in a single action; but the court shall grant relief in that action only in accordance with the relative substantive rights of the parties. In particular, a plaintiff may state a claim for money and a claim to have set aside a conveyance fraudulent as to that plaintiff, without first having obtained a judgment establishing the claim for money.

RULE 19. Joinder of Persons Needed for Just Adjudication

(a) Persons to be Joined if Feasible. A person who is subject to service of process and whose joinder will not deprive the court of jurisdiction over the subject matter of the action shall be joined as a party in the action if

(1) in the person's absence complete relief cannot be accorded among those already parties, or

(2) the person claims an interest relating to the subject of the action and is so situated that the disposition of the action in the person's absence may

(i) as a practical matter impair or impede the person's ability to protect that interest or

(ii) leave any of the persons already parties subject to a substantial risk of incurring double, multiple, or otherwise inconsistent obligations by reason of the claimed interest.

If the person has not been so joined, the court shall order that the person be made a party. If the person should join as a plaintiff but refuses to do so, the person may be made a defendant, or, in a proper case, an involuntary plaintiff. If the joined party objects to venue and joinder of that party would render the venue of the action improper, that party shall be dismissed from the action.

(b) Determination by Court Whenever Joinder Not Feasible. If a person as described in subdivision (a)(1)-(2) hereof cannot be made a party, the court shall determine whether in equity and good conscience the action should proceed among the parties before it, or should be dismissed, the absent person being thus regarded as indispensable. The factors to be considered by the court include: first, to what extent a judgment rendered in the person's absence might be prejudicial to the person or those already parties; second, the extent to which, by protective provisions in the judgment, by the shaping of relief, or other measures, the prejudice can be lessened or avoided; third, whether a judgment rendered in the person's absence will be adequate; fourth, whether the plaintiff will have an adequate remedy if the action is dismissed for nonjoinder.

(c) Pleading Reasons for Nonjoinder. A pleading asserting a claim for relief shall state the names, if known to the pleader, of any persons as described in subdivision (a)(1)-(2) hereof who are not joined, and the reasons why they are not joined.

(d) Exception of Class Actions. This rule is subject to the provisions of Rule 23.

RULE 20. Permissive Joinder of Parties

(a) Permissive Joinder. All persons may join in one action as plaintiffs if they assert any right to relief jointly, severally, or in the alternative in respect of or arising out of the same transaction, occurrence, or series of transactions or occurrences and if any question of law or fact common to all these persons will arise in the action. All persons (and any vessel, cargo or other property subject to admiralty process in rem) may be joined in one action as defendants if there is asserted against them jointly, severally, or in the alternative, any right to relief in respect of or arising out of the same transaction, occurrence, or series of transactions or occurrences and if any question of law or fact common to all defendants will arise in the action. A plaintiff or defendant need not be interested in obtaining or defending against all the relief demanded. Judgment may be given for one or more of the plaintiffs according to their respective rights to relief, and against one or more defendants according to their respective liabilities.

(b) Separate Trials. The court may make such orders as will prevent a party from being embarrassed, delayed, or put to expense by the inclusion of a party against whom the party asserts no claim and who asserts no claim against the party, and may order separate trials or make other orders to prevent delay or prejudice.

RULE 21. Misjoinder and Non-Joinder of Parties

Misjoinder of parties is not ground for dismissal of an action. Parties may be dropped or added by order of the court on motion of any party or of its own initiative at any stage of the action and on such terms as are just. Any claim against a party may be severed and proceeded with separately.

RULE 22. Interpleader

(1) Persons having claims against the plaintiff may be joined as defendants and required to interplead when their claims are such that the plaintiff is or may be exposed to double or multiple liability. It is not ground for objection to the joinder that the claims of the several claimants or the titles on which their claims depend do not have a common origin or are not identical but are adverse to and independent of one another, or that the plaintiff avers that the plaintiff is not liable in whole or in part to any or all of the claimants. A defendant exposed to similar liability may obtain such interpleader by way of cross-claim or counterclaim. The provisions of this rule supplement and do not in any way limit the joinder of parties permitted in Rule 20.

(2) The remedy herein provided is in addition to and in no way supersedes or limits the remedy provided by Title 28, U.S.C. §§ 1335, 1397, and 2361. Actions under those provisions shall be conducted in accordance with these rules.

RULE 23. Class Actions

(a) Prerequisites to a Class Action. One or more members of a class may sue or be sued as representative parties on behalf of all only if

(1) the class is so numerous that joinder of all members is impracticable,

(2) there are questions of law or fact common to the class,

(3) the claims or defenses of the representative parties are typical of the claims or defenses of the class, and

(4) the representative parties will fairly and adequately protect the interests of the class.

(b) Class Actions Maintainable. An action may be maintained as a class action if the prerequisites of subdivision (a) are satisfied, and in addition:

(1) the prosecution of separate actions by or against individual members of the class would create a risk of

(A) inconsistent or varying adjudications with respect to individual members of the class which would establish incompatible standards of conduct for the party opposing the class, or

(B) adjudications with respect to individual members of the class which would as a practical matter be dispositive of the interests of the other members

not parties to the adjudications or substantially impair or impede their ability to protect their interests; or

(2) the party opposing the class has acted or refused to act on grounds generally applicable to the class, thereby making appropriate final injunctive relief or corresponding declaratory relief with respect to the class as a whole; or

(3) the court finds that the questions of law or fact common to the members of the class predominate over any questions affecting only individual members, and that a class action is superior to other available methods for the fair and efficient adjudication of the controversy. The matters pertinent to the findings include:

(A) the interest of members of the class in individually controlling the prosecution or defense of separate actions;

(B) the extent and nature of any litigation concerning the controversy already commenced by or against members of the class;

(C) the desirability or undesirability of concentrating the litigation of the claims in the particular forum;

(D) the difficulties likely to be encountered in the management of a class action.

(c) Determination by Order Whether Class Action to be Maintained; Notice; Judgment; Actions Conducted Partially as Class Actions.

(1) As soon as practicable after the commencement of an action brought as a class action, the court shall determine by order whether it is to be so maintained. An order under this subdivision may be conditional, and may be altered or amended before the decision on the merits.

(2) In any class action maintained under subdivision (b)(3), the court shall direct to the members of the class the best notice practicable under the circumstances, including individual notice to all members who can be identified through reasonable effort. The notice shall advise each member that

(A) the court will exclude the member from the class if the member so requests by a specified date;

(B) the judgment, whether favorable or not, will include all members who do not request exclusion; and

(C) any member who does not request exclusion may, if the member desires, enter an appearance through counsel.

(3) The judgment in an action maintained as a class action under subdivision (b)(1) or (b)(2), whether or not favorable to the class, shall include and describe those whom the court finds to be members of the class. The judgment in an action maintained as a class action under subdivision (b)(3), whether or not favorable to the class, shall include and specify or describe those to whom the notice provided in subdivision (c)(2) was directed, and who have not requested exclusion, and whom the court finds to be members of the class.

(4) When appropriate

(A) an action may be brought or maintained as a class action with respect to particular issues, or

(B) a class may be divided into subclasses and each subclass treated as a class, and the provisions of this rule shall then be construed and applied accordingly.

(d) Orders in Conduct of Actions. In the conduct of actions to which this rule applies, the court may make appropriate orders:

(1) determining the course of proceedings or prescribing measures to prevent undue repetition or complication in the presentation of evidence or argument;

(2) requiring, for the protection of the members of the class or otherwise for the fair conduct of the action, that notice be given in such manner as the court may direct to some or all of the members of any step in the action, or of the proposed extent of the judgment, or of the opportunity of members to signify whether they consider the representation fair and adequate, to intervene and present claims or defenses, or otherwise to come into the action;

(3) imposing conditions on the representative parties or on intervenors;

(4) requiring that the pleadings be amended to eliminate therefrom allegations as to representation of absent persons, and that the action proceed accordingly;

(5) dealing with similar procedural matters.

The orders may be combined with an order under Rule 16, and may be altered or amended as may be desirable from time to time.

(e) Dismissal or Compromise. A class action shall not be dismissed or compromised without the approval of the court, and notice of the proposed dismissal or compromise shall be given to all members of the class in such manner as the court directs.

(f) Appeals. A court of appeals may in its discretion permit an appeal from an order of a district court granting or denying class action certification under this rule if application is made to it within ten days after entry of the order. An appeal does not stay proceedings in the district court unless the district judge or the court of appeals so orders.

RULE 23.1. Derivative Actions by Shareholders

In a derivative action brought by one or more shareholders or members to enforce a right of a corporation or of an unincorporated association, the corporation or association having failed to enforce a right which may properly be asserted by it, the complaint shall be verified and shall allege

(1) that the plaintiff was a shareholder or member at the time of the transaction of which the plaintiff complains or that the plaintiff's share or membership thereafter devolved on the plaintiff by operation of law, and

(2) that the action is not a collusive one to confer jurisdiction on a court of the United States which it would not otherwise have.

The complaint shall also allege with particularity the

efforts, if any, made by the plaintiff to obtain the action the plaintiff desires from the directors or comparable authority and, if necessary, from the shareholders or members, and the reasons for the plaintiff's failure to obtain the action or for not making the effort. The derivative action may not be maintained if it appears that the plaintiff does not fairly and adequately represent the interests of the shareholders or members similarly situated in enforcing the right of the corporation or association. The action shall not be dismissed or compromised without the approval of the court, and notice of the proposed dismissal or compromise shall be given to shareholders or members in such manner as the court directs.

RULE 23.2. Actions Relating to Unincorporated Associations

An action brought by or against the members of an unincorporated association as a class by naming certain members as representative parties may be maintained only if it appears that the representative parties will fairly and adequately protect the interests of the association and its members. In the conduct of the action the court may make appropriate orders corresponding with those described in Rule 23(d), and the procedure for dismissal or compromise of the action shall correspond with that provided in Rule 23(e).

RULE 24. Intervention

(a) Intervention of Right. Upon timely application anyone shall be permitted to intervene in an action:

(1) when a statute of the United States confers an unconditional right to intervene; or

(2) when the applicant claims an interest relating to the property or transaction which is the subject of the action and the applicant is so situated that the disposition of the action may as a practical matter impair or impede the applicant's ability to protect that interest, unless the applicant's interest is adequately represented by existing parties.

(b) Permissive Intervention. Upon timely application anyone may be permitted to intervene in an action:

(1) when a statute of the United States confers a conditional right to intervene; or

(2) when an applicant's claim or defense and the main action have a question of law or fact in common. When a party to an action relies for ground of claim or defense upon any statute or executive order administered by a federal or state governmental officer or agency or upon any regulation, order, requirement, or agreement issued or made pursuant to the statute or executive order, the officer or agency upon timely application may be permitted to intervene in the action. In exercising its discretion the court shall consider whether the intervention will unduly delay or prejudice the adjudication of the rights of the original parties.

(c) Procedure. A person desiring to intervene shall serve a motion to intervene upon the parties as provided in Rule 5. The motion shall state the grounds therefor and shall be accompanied by a pleading setting forth the claim or defense for which intervention is sought. The same procedure shall be followed when a statute of the United States gives a right to intervene. When the constitutionality of an act of Congress affecting the public interest is drawn in question in any action in which the United States or an officer, agency, or employee thereof is not a party, the court shall notify the Attorney General of the United States as provided in Title 28, U.S.C. § 2403. When the constitutionality of any statute of a State affecting the public interest is drawn in question in any action in which that State or any agency, officer, or employee thereof is not a party, the court shall notify the attorney general of the State as provided in Title 28, U.S.C. § 2403. A party challenging the constitutionality of legislation should call the attention of the court to its consequential duty, but failure to do so is not a waiver of any constitutional right otherwise timely asserted.

RULE 25. Substitution of Parties

(a) Death.

(1) If a party dies and the claim is not thereby extinguished, the court may order substitution of the proper parties. The motion for substitution may be made by any party or by the successors or representatives of the deceased party and, together with the notice of hearing, shall be served on the parties as provided in Rule 5 and upon persons not parties in the manner provided in Rule 4 for the service of a summons, and may be served in any judicial district. Unless the motion for substitution is made not later than 90 days after the death is suggested upon the record by service of a statement of the fact of the death as provided herein for the service of the motion, the action shall be dismissed as to the deceased party.

(2) In the event of the death of one or more of the plaintiffs or of one or more of the defendants in an action in which the right sought to be enforced survives only to the surviving plaintiffs or only against the surviving defendants, the action does not abate. The death shall be suggested upon the record and the action shall proceed in favor of or against the surviving parties.

(b) Incompetency. If a party becomes incompetent, the court upon motion served as provided in subdivision (a) of this rule may allow the action to be continued by or against the party's representative.

(c) Transfer of Interest. In case of any transfer of interest, the action may be continued by or against the original party, unless the court upon motion directs the person to whom the interest is transferred to be substituted in the action or joined with the original party. Service of the motion shall be made as provided in subdivision (a) of this rule.

(d) Public Officers; Death or Separation from Office.

(1) When a public officer is a party to an action in his official capacity and during its pendency dies, resigns, or otherwise ceases to hold office, the action does not abate and the officer's successor is automatically substituted as a party. Proceedings following the substitution shall be in the name of the substituted party, but any misnomer not affecting the substantial rights of the parties shall be disregarded. An order of substitution may be entered at any time, but the omission to enter such an order shall not affect the substitution.

(2) A public officer who sues or is sued in an official capacity may be described as a party by the officer's official title rather than by name; but the court may require the officer's name to be added.

V

DEPOSITIONS AND DISCOVERY

RULE 26. General Provisions Governing Discovery; Duty of Disclosure

(a) Required Disclosures; Methods to Discover Additional Matter.

(1) *Initial Disclosures.* Except in categories of proceedings specified in Rule 26(a)(1)(E), or to the extent otherwise stipulated or directed by order, a party must, without awaiting a discovery request, provide to other parties:

(A) the name and, if known, the address and telephone number of each individual likely to have discoverable information that the disclosing party may use to support its claims or defenses, unless solely for impeachment, identifying the subjects of the information:

(B) a copy of, or a description by category and location of, all documents, data compilations, and tangible things that are in the possession, custody, or control of the party and that the disclosing party may use to support its claims or defenses, unless solely for impeachment;

(C) a computation of any category of damages claimed by the disclosing party, making available for inspection and copying as under Rule 34 the documents or other evidentiary material, not privileged or protected from disclosure, on which such computation is based, including materials bearing on the nature and extent of injuries suffered; and

(D) for inspection and copying as under Rule 34 any insurance agreement under which any person carrying on an insurance business may be liable to satisfy part or all of a judgment which may be entered in the action or to indemnify or reimburse for payments made to satisfy the judgment.

(E) The following categories of proceedings are exempt from initial disclosure under Rule 26(a)(1):

(i) an action for review on an administrative record;

(ii) a petition for habeas corpus or other proceeding to challenge a criminal conviction or sentence;

(iii) an action brought without counsel by a person in custody of the United States, a state, or a state subdivision:

(iv) an action to enforce or quash an administrative summons or subpoena;

(v) an action by the United States to recover benefit payments;

(vi) an action by the United States to collect on a student loan guaranteed by the United States;

(vii) a proceeding ancillary to proceedings in other courts; and

(viii) an action to enforce an arbitration award. These disclosures must be made at or within 14 days after the Rule 26(f) conference unless a different time is set by stipulation or court order, or unless a party objects during the conference that initial disclosures are not appropriate in the circumstances of the action and states the objection in the Rule 26(f) discovery plan. In ruling on the objection, the court must determine what disclosures—if any—are to be made, and set the time for disclosure. Any party first served or otherwise joined after the Rule 26(f) conference must make these disclosures within 30 days after being served or joined unless a different time is set by stipulation or court order. A party must make its initial disclosures based on the information then reasonably available to it and is not excused from making its disclosures because it has not fully completed its investigation of the case or because it challenges the sufficiency of another party's disclosures or because another party has not made its disclosures.

(2) *Disclosure of Expert Testimony.*

(A) In addition to the disclosures required by paragraph (1), a party shall disclose to other parties the identity of any person who may be used at trial to present evidence under Rules 702, 703, or 705 of the Federal Rules of Evidence.

(B) Except as otherwise stipulated or directed by the court, this disclosure shall, with respect to a witness who is retained or specially employed to provide expert testimony in the case or whose duties as an employee of the party regularly involve giving expert testimony, be accompanied by a written report prepared and signed by the witness. The report shall contain a complete statement of all opinions to be expressed and the basis and reasons therefor; the data or other information considered by the witness in forming the opinions; any exhibits to be used as a summary of or support for the opinions; the qualifications of the witness, including a list of all publications authored by the witness within the preceding ten years; the compensation to be paid for the study and testimony; and a listing of any other cases in which the witness has testified as an expert at trial or by deposition within the preceding four years.

(C) These disclosures shall be made at the times and in the sequence directed by the court. In the absence of other directions from the court or stipulation by the parties, the disclosures shall be made at least 90 days before the trial date or the date the case is to be ready for trial or, if the evidence is intended solely to contradict or rebut evidence on the same subject matter identified by another party under paragraph (2)(B), within 30 days after the disclosure made by the other party. The parties shall supplement these disclosures when required under subdivision (e)(1).

(3) *Pretrial Disclosures.* In addition to the disclosures required by Rule 26(a)(1) and (2), a party must provide to other parties and promptly file with the court the following information regarding the evidence that it may present at trial other than solely for impeachment:

(A) the name and, if not previously provided, the address and telephone number of each witness, separately identifying those whom the party expects to present and those whom the party may call if the need arises;

(B) the designation of those witnesses whose testimony is expected to be presented by means of a deposition and, if not taken stenographically, a transcript of the pertinent portions of the deposition testimony; and

(C) an appropriate identification of each document or other exhibit, including summaries of other evidence, separately identifying those which the party expects to offer and those which the party may offer if the need arises.

Unless otherwise directed by the court, these disclosures must be made at least 30 days before trial. Within 14 days thereafter, unless a different time is specified by the court, a party may serve and promptly file a list disclosing (i) any objections to the use under Rule 32(a) of a deposition designated by another party under Rule 26(a)(3)(B), and (ii) any objection, together with the grounds therefor, that may be made to the admissibility of materials identified under Rule 26(a)(3)(C). Objections not so disclosed, other than objections under Rules 402 and 403 of the Federal Rules of Evidence, are waived unless excused by the court for good cause.

(4) *Form of Disclosures.* Unless the court orders otherwise, all disclosures under Rules 26(a)(1) through (3) must be made in writing, signed, and served.

(5) *Methods to Discover Additional Matter.* Parties may obtain discovery by one or more of the following methods: depositions upon oral examination or written questions; written interrogatories; production of documents or things or permission to enter upon land or other property under Rule 34 or 45(a)(1)(C), for inspection and other purposes; physical and mental examinations; and requests for admission.

(b) Discovery Scope and Limits. Unless otherwise limited by order of the court in accordance with these rules, the scope of discovery is as follows:

(1) *In General.* Parties may obtain discovery regarding any matter, not privileged, that is relevant to the claim or defense of any party, including the existence, description, nature, custody, condition, and location of any books, documents, or other tangible things and the identity and location of persons having knowledge of any discoverable matter. For good cause, the court may order discovery of any matter relevant to the subject matter involved in the action. Relevant information need not be admissible at the trial if the discovery appears reasonably calculated to lead to the discovery of admissible evidence. All discovery is subject to the limitations imposed by Rule 26(b)(2)(i), (ii), and (iii).

(2) *Limitations.* By order, the court may alter the limits in these rules on the number of depositions and interrogatories or the length of depositions under Rule 30. By order or local rule, the court may also limit the number of requests under Rule 36. The frequency or extent of use of the discovery methods otherwise permitted under these rules and by any local rule shall be limited by the court if it determines that:

(i) the discovery sought is unreasonably cumulative or duplicative, or is obtainable from some other source that is more convenient, less burdensome, or less expensive;

(ii) the party seeking discovery has had ample opportunity by discovery in the action to obtain the information sought; or

(iii) the burden or expense of the proposed discovery outweighs its likely benefit, taking into account the needs of the case, the amount in controversy, the parties' resources, the importance of the issues at stake in the litigation, and the importance of the proposed discovery in resolving the issues.

The court may act upon its own initiative after reasonable notice or pursuant to a motion under Rule 26(c).

(3) *Trial Preparation: Materials.* Subject to the provisions of subdivision (b)(4) of this rule, a party may obtain discovery of documents and tangible things otherwise discoverable under subdivision (b)(1) of this rule and prepared in anticipation of litigation or for trial by or for another party or by or for that other party's representative (including the other party's attorney, consultant, surety, indemnitor, insurer, or agent) only upon a showing that the party seeking discovery has substantial need of the materials in the preparation of the party's case and that the party is unable without undue hardship to obtain the substantial equivalent of the materials by other means. In ordering discovery of such materials when the required showing has been made, the court shall protect against disclosure of the mental impressions, conclusions, opinions, or legal theories of an attorney or other representative of a party concerning the litigation.

A party may obtain without the required showing a statement concerning the action or its subject matter previously made by that party. Upon request, a person not a party may obtain without the required showing a statement concerning the action or its subject matter previously made by that person. If the request is refused, the person may move for a court order. The provisions of Rule 37(a)(4) apply to the award of expenses incurred in relation to the motion. For purposes of this paragraph, a statement previously made is

(A) a written statement signed or otherwise adopted or approved by the person making it, or

(B) a stenographic, mechanical, electrical, or other recording, or a transcription thereof, which is a substantially verbatim recital of an oral statement by the person making it and contemporaneously recorded.

(4) *Trial Preparation: Experts.*

(A) A party may depose any person who has been identified as an expert whose opinions may be presented at trial. If a report from the expert is required under subdivision (a)(2)(B), the deposition shall not be conducted until after the report is provided.

(B) A party may, through interrogatories or by deposition, discover facts known or opinions held by an expert who has been retained or specially employed by another party in anticipation of litigation or preparation for trial and who is not expected to be called as a witness at trial, only as provided in Rule 35(b) or upon a showing of exceptional circumstances under which it is impracticable for the party seeking discovery to obtain facts or opinions on the same subject by other means.

(C) Unless manifest injustice would result,

(i) the court shall require that the party seeking discovery pay the expert a reasonable fee for time spent in responding to discovery under this subdivision; and

(ii) with respect to discovery obtained under subdivision (b)(4)(B) of this rule the court shall require the party seeking discovery to pay the other party a fair portion of the fees and expenses reasonably incurred by the latter party in obtaining facts and opinions from the expert.

(5) *Claims of Privilege or Protection of Trial Preparation Materials.* When a party withholds information otherwise discoverable under these rules by claiming that it is privileged or subject to protection as trial preparation material, the party shall make the claim expressly and shall describe the nature of the documents, communications, or things not produced or disclosed in a manner that, without revealing information itself privileged or protected, will enable other parties to assess the applicability of the privilege or protection.

(c) Protective Orders. Upon motion by a party or by the person from whom discovery is sought, accompanied by a certification that the movant has in good faith conferred or attempted to confer with other affected parties in an effort to resolve the dispute without court action, and for good cause shown, the court in which the action is pending or alternatively, on matters relating to a deposition, the court in the district where the deposition is to be taken may make any order which justice requires to protect a party or person from annoyance, embarrassment, oppression, or undue burden or expense, including one or more of the following:

(1) that the disclosure or discovery not be had;

(2) that the disclosure or discovery may be had only on specified terms and conditions, including a designation of the time or place;

(3) that the discovery may be had only by a method of discovery other than that selected by the party seeking discovery;

(4) that certain matters not be inquired into, or that the scope of the disclosure or discovery be limited to certain matters;

(5) that discovery be conducted with no one present except persons designated by the court;

(6) that a deposition, after being sealed, be opened only by order of the court;

(7) that a trade secret or other confidential research, development, or commercial information not be revealed or be revealed only in a designated way; and

(8) that the parties simultaneously file specified documents or information enclosed in sealed envelopes to be opened as directed by the court.

If the motion for a protective order is denied in whole or in part, the court may, on such terms and conditions as are just, order that any party or other person provide or permit discovery. The provisions of Rule 37(a)(4) apply to the award of expenses incurred in relation to the motion.

(d) Timing and Sequence of Discovery. Except in categories of proceedings exempted from initial disclosure under Rule 26(a)(1)(E), or when authorized under these rules or by order or agreement of the parties, a party may not seek discovery from any source before the parties have conferred as required by Rule 26(f). Unless the court upon motion, for the convenience of parties and witnesses and in the interests of justice, orders otherwise, methods of discovery may be used in any sequence, and the fact that a party is conducting discovery, whether by deposition or otherwise, does not operate to delay any other party's discovery.

(e) Supplementation of Disclosures and Responses. A party who has made a disclosure under subdivision (a) or responded to a request for discovery with a disclosure or response is under a duty to supplement or correct the disclosure or response to include information thereafter acquired if ordered by the court or in the following circumstances:

(1) A party is under a duty to supplement at appropriate intervals its disclosures under subdivision (a) if the party learns that in some material respect the information disclosed is incomplete or incorrect and if the additional or corrective information has not otherwise been made known to the other parties during the discovery process or in writing. With respect to testimony of an expert from whom a report is required under subdivision (a)(2)(B) the duty extends both to information contained in the report and to information provided through a deposition of the expert, and any additions or other changes to this information shall be disclosed by the time the party's disclosures under Rule 26(a)(3) are due.

(2) A party is under a duty seasonably to amend a prior response to an interrogatory, request for production, or request for admission if the party learns that the response is in some material respect incomplete or incorrect and if the additional or corrective information has not otherwise been made known to the other parties during the discovery process or in writing.

(f) Conference of Parties; Planning for Discovery. Except in categories of proceedings exempted from initial disclosure under Rule 26(a)(1)(E) or when otherwise ordered, the parties must, as soon as practicable and in any event at least 21 days before a scheduling conference is held or a scheduling order is due under Rule 16(b), confer to consider the nature and basis of their claims and defenses and the possibilities for a prompt settlement or resolution of the case, to make or arrange for the disclosures required by Rule 26(a)(1), and to develop a proposed discovery plan that indicates the parties' views and proposals concerning:

(1) what changes should be made in the timing, form, or requirement for disclosures under Rule 26(a), including a statement as to when disclosures under Rule 26(a)(1) were made or will be made;

(2) the subjects on which discovery may be needed, when discovery should be completed, and whether discovery should be conducted in phases or be limited to or focused upon particular issues;

(3) what changes should be made in the limitations on discovery imposed under these rules or by local rule, and what other limitations should be imposed; and

(4) any other orders that should be entered by the court under Rule 26(c) or under Rule 16(b) and (c).

The attorneys of record and all unrepresented parties that have appeared in the case are jointly responsible for arranging the conference, for attempting in good faith to agree on the proposed discovery plan, and for submitting to the court within 14 days after the conference a written report outlining the plan. A court may order that the parties or attorneys attend the conference in person. If necessary to comply with its expedited schedule for Rule 16(b) conferences, a court may by local rule (i) require that the conference between the parties occur fewer than 21 days before the scheduling conference is held or a scheduling order is due under Rule 16(b), and (ii) require that the written report outlining the discovery plan be filed fewer than 14 days after the conference between the parties, or excuse the parties from submitting a written report and permit them to report orally on their discovery plan at the Rule 16(b) conference.

(g) Signing of Disclosures, Discovery Requests, Responses, and Objections.

(1) Every disclosure made pursuant to subdivision (a)(1) or subdivision (a)(3) shall be signed by at least one attorney of record in the attorney's individual name, whose address shall be stated. An unrepresented party shall sign the disclosure and state the party's address. The signature of the attorney or party constitutes a

certification that to the best of the signer's knowledge, information, and belief, formed after a reasonable inquiry, the disclosure is complete and correct as of the time it is made.

(2) Every discovery request, response, or objection made by a party represented by an attorney shall be signed by at least one attorney of record in the attorney's individual name, whose address shall be stated. An unrepresented party shall sign the request, response, or objection and state the party's address. The signature of the attorney or party constitutes a certification that to the best of the signer's knowledge, information, and belief, formed after a reasonable inquiry, the request, response, or objection is:

(A) consistent with these rules and warranted by existing law or a good faith argument for the extension, modification, or reversal of existing law;

(B) not interposed for any improper purpose, such as to harass or to cause unnecessary delay or needless increase in the cost of litigation; and

(C) not unreasonable or unduly burdensome or expensive, given the needs of the case, the discovery already had in the case, the amount in controversy, and the importance of the issues at stake in the litigation.

If a request, response, or objection is not signed, it shall be stricken unless it is signed promptly after the omission is called to the attention of the party making the request, response, or objection, and a party shall not be obligated to take any action with respect to it until it is signed.

(3) If without substantial justification a certification is made in violation of the rule, the court, upon motion or upon its own initiative, shall impose upon the person who made the certification, the party on whose behalf the disclosure, request, response, or objection is made, or both, an appropriate sanction, which may include an order to pay the amount of the reasonable expenses incurred because of the violation, including a reasonable attorney's fee.

RULE 27. Depositions Before Action or Pending Appeal

(a) Before Action.

(1) *Petition.* A person who desires to perpetuate testimony regarding any matter that may be cognizable in any court of the United States may file a verified petition in the United States district court in the district of the residence of any expected adverse party. The petition shall be entitled in the name of the petitioner and shall show:

1, that the petitioner expects to be a party to an action cognizable in a court of the United States but is presently unable to bring it or cause it to be brought,

2, the subject matter of the expected action and the petitioner's interest therein,

3, the facts which the petitioner desires to establish

by the proposed testimony and the reasons for desiring to perpetuate it,

4, the names or a description of the persons the petitioner expects will be adverse parties and their addresses so far as known, and

5, the names and addresses of the persons to be examined and the substance of the testimony which the petitioner expects to elicit from each, and shall ask for an order authorizing the petitioner to take the depositions of the persons to be examined named in the petition, for the purpose of perpetuating their testimony.

(2) *Notice and Service.* The petitioner shall thereafter serve a notice upon each person named in the petition as an expected adverse party, together with a copy of the petition, stating that the petitioner will apply to the court, at a time and place named therein, for the order described in the petition. At least 20 days before the date of hearing the notice shall be served either within or without the district or state in the manner provided in Rule 4(d) for service of summons; but if such service cannot with due diligence be made upon any expected adverse party named in the petition, the court may make such order as is just for service by publication or otherwise, and shall appoint, for persons not served in the manner provided in Rule 4(d), an attorney who shall represent them, and, in case they are not otherwise represented, shall cross-examine the deponent. If any expected adverse party is a minor or incompetent the provisions of Rule 17(c) apply.

(3) *Order and Examination.* If the court is satisfied that the perpetuation of the testimony may prevent a failure or delay of justice, it shall make an order designating or describing the persons whose depositions may be taken and specifying the subject matter of the examination and whether the depositions shall be taken upon oral examination or written interrogatories. The depositions may then be taken in accordance with these rules; and the court may make orders of the character provided for by Rules 34 and 35. For the purpose of applying these rules to depositions for perpetuating testimony, each reference therein to the court in which the action is pending shall be deemed to refer to the court in which the petition for such deposition was filed.

(4) *Use of Deposition.* If a deposition to perpetuate testimony is taken under these rules or if, although not so taken, it would be admissible in evidence in the courts of the state in which it is taken, it may be used in any action involving the same subject matter subsequently brought in a United States district court, in accordance with the provisions of Rule 32(a).

(b) Pending Appeal. If an appeal has been taken from a judgment of a district court or before the taking of an appeal if the time therefor has not expired, the district court in which the judgment was rendered may allow the taking of the depositions of witnesses to perpetuate their testimony for use in the event of further proceedings in the district court. In such case the party who desires to perpetuate the testimony may make a motion in the district court for leave to take the depositions, upon the same notice and service thereof as if the action was pending in the district court. The motion shall show

(1) the names and addresses of persons to be examined and the substance of the testimony which the party expects to elicit from each;

(2) the reasons for perpetuating their testimony.

If the court finds that the perpetuation of the testimony is proper to avoid a failure or delay of justice, it may make an order allowing the depositions to be taken and may make orders of the character provided for by Rules 34 and 35, and thereupon the depositions may be taken and used in the same manner and under the same conditions as are prescribed in these rules for depositions taken in actions pending in the district court.

(c) **Perpetuation by Action.** This rule does not limit the power of a court to entertain an action to perpetuate testimony.

RULE 28. Persons Before Whom Depositions May Be Taken

(a) **Within the United States.** Within the United States or within a territory or insular possession subject to the jurisdiction of the United States, depositions shall be taken before an officer authorized to administer oaths by the laws of the United States or of the place where the examination is held, or before a person appointed by the court in which the action is pending. A person so appointed has power to administer oaths and take testimony. The term officer as used in Rules 30, 31 and 32 includes a person appointed by the court or designated by the parties under Rule 29.

(b) **In Foreign Countries.** Depositions may be taken in a foreign country

(1) pursuant to any applicable treaty or convention, or

(2) pursuant to a letter of request (whether or not captioned a letter rogatory), or

(3) on notice before a person authorized to administer oaths in the place where the examination is held, either by the law thereof or by the law of the United States, or

(4) before a person commissioned by the court, and a person so commissioned shall have the power by virtue of the commission to administer any necessary oath and take testimony.

A commission or a letter of request shall be issued on application and notice and on terms that are just and appropriate. It is not requisite to the issuance of a commission or a letter of request that the taking of the deposition in any other manner is impracticable or inconvenient; and both a commission and a letter of request may be issued in proper cases. A notice or commission may designate the person before whom the deposition is to be taken either by name or descriptive title. A letter of request may be addressed "To the Appropriate Authority in [here name the country]."

When a letter of request or any other device is used pursuant to any applicable treaty or convention, it shall be captioned in the form prescribed by that treaty or convention. Evidence obtained in response to a letter of request need not be excluded merely because it is not a verbatim transcript, because the testimony was not taken under oath, or because of any similar departure from the requirements for depositions taken within the United States under these rules.

(c) **Disqualification for Interest.** No deposition shall be taken before a person who is a relative or employee or attorney or counsel of any of the parties, or is a relative or employee of such attorney or counsel, or is financially interested in the action.

RULE 29. Stipulations Regarding Discovery Procedure

Unless otherwise directed by the court, the parties may by written stipulation

(1) provide that depositions may be taken before any person, at any time or place, upon any notice, and in any manner and when so taken may be used like other depositions, and

(2) modify other procedures governing or limitations placed upon discovery, except that stipulations extending the time provided in Rules 33, 34, and 36 for responses to discovery may, if they would interfere with any time set for completion of discovery, for hearing of a motion, or for trial, be made only with the approval of the court.

RULE 30. Depositions upon Oral Examination

(a) **When Depositions May Be Taken; When Leave Required.**

(1) A party may take the testimony of any person, including a party, by deposition upon oral examination without leave of court except as provided in paragraph (2). The attendance of witnesses may be compelled by subpoena as provided in Rule 45.

(2) A party must obtain leave of court, which shall be granted to the extent consistent with the principles stated in Rule 26(b)(2), if the person to be examined is confined in prison or if, without the written stipulation of the parties,

(A) a proposed deposition would result in more than ten depositions being taken under this rule or Rule 31 by the plaintiffs, or by the defendants, or by third-party defendants;

(B) the person to be examined already has been deposed in the case; or

(C) a party seeks to take a deposition before the time specified in Rule 26(d) unless the notice contains a certification, with supporting facts, that the person to be examined is expected to leave the United

States and be unavailable for examination in this country unless deposed before that time.

(b) Notice of Examination: General Requirements; Method of Recording; Production of Documents and Things; Deposition of Organization; Deposition by Telephone.

(1) A party desiring to take the deposition of any person upon oral examination shall give reasonable notice in writing to every other party to the action. The notice shall state the time and place for taking the deposition and the name and address of each person to be examined, if known, and, if the name is not known, a general description sufficient to identify the person or the particular class or group to which the person belongs. If a subpoena duces tecum is to be served on the person to be examined, the designation of the materials to be produced as set forth in the subpoena shall be attached to, or included in, the notice.

(2) The party taking the deposition shall state in the notice the method by which the testimony shall be recorded. Unless the court orders otherwise, it may be recorded by sound, sound-and-visual, or stenographic means, and the party taking the deposition shall bear the cost of the recording. Any party may arrange for a transcription to be made from the recording of a deposition taken by nonstenographic means.

(3) With prior notice to the deponent and other parties, any party may designate another method to record the deponent's testimony in addition to the method specified by the person taking the deposition. The additional record or transcript shall be made at that party's expense unless the court otherwise orders.

(4) Unless otherwise agreed by the parties, a deposition shall be conducted before an officer appointed or designated under Rule 28 and shall begin with a statement on the record by the officer that includes

    (A) the officer's name and business address;

    (B) the date, time, and place of the deposition;

    (C) the name of the deponent;

    (D) the administration of the oath or affirmation to the deponent; and

    (E) an identification of all persons present.

If the deposition is recorded other than stenographically, the officer shall repeat items (A) through (C) at the beginning of each unit of recorded tape or other recording medium. The appearance or demeanor of deponents or attorneys shall not be distorted through camera or sound-recording techniques. At the end of the deposition, the officer shall state on the record that the deposition is complete and shall set forth any stipulations made by counsel concerning the custody of the transcript or recording and the exhibits, or concerning other pertinent matters.

(5) The notice to a party deponent may be accompanied by a request made in compliance with Rule 34 for the production of documents and tangible things at the taking of the deposition. The procedure of Rule 34 shall apply to the request.

(6) A party may in the party's notice and in a subpoena name as the deponent a public or private corporation or a partnership or association or governmental agency and describe with reasonable particularity the matters on which examination is requested. In that event, the organization so named shall designate one or more officers, directors, or managing agents, or other persons who consent to testify on its behalf, and may set forth, for each person designated, the matters on which the person will testify. A subpoena shall advise a non-party organization of its duty to make such a designation. The persons so designated shall testify as to matters known or reasonably available to the organization. This subdivision (b)(6) does not preclude taking a deposition by any other procedure authorized in these rules.

(7) The parties may stipulate in writing or the court may upon motion order that a deposition be taken by telephone or other remote electronic means. For the purposes of this rule and Rules 28(a), 37(a)(1), and 37(b)(1), a deposition taken by such means is taken in the district and at the place where the deponent is to answer questions.

(c) Examination and Cross-Examination; Record of Examination; Oath; Objections. Examination and cross-examination of witnesses may proceed as permitted at the trial under the provisions of the Federal Rules of Evidence except Rules 103 and 615. The officer before whom the deposition is to be taken shall put the witness on oath or affirmation and shall personally, or by someone acting under the officer's direction and in the officer's presence, record the testimony of the witness. The testimony shall be taken stenographically or recorded by any other method authorized by subdivision (b)(2) of this rule. All objections made at the time of the examination to the qualifications of the officer taking the deposition, to the manner of taking it, to the evidence presented, to the conduct of any party, or to any other aspect of the proceedings shall be noted by the officer upon the record of the deposition; but the examination shall proceed, with the testimony being taken subject to the objections. In lieu of participating in the oral examination, parties may serve written questions in a sealed envelope on the party taking the deposition and the party taking the deposition shall transmit them to the officer, who shall propound them to the witness and record the answers verbatim.

(d) Schedule and Duration; Motion to Terminate or Limit Examination.

(1) Any objection during a deposition must be stated concisely and in a non-argumentative and non-suggestive manner. A person may instruct a deponent not to answer only when necessary to preserve a privilege, to enforce a limitation directed by the court, or to present a motion under Rule 30(d)(4).

(2) Unless otherwise authorized by the court or stipulated by the parties, a deposition is limited to one day of seven hours. The court must allow additional time consistent with Rule 26(b)(2) if needed for a fair examination of the deponent or if the deponent or another person, or other circumstance, impedes or delays the examination.

(3) If the court finds that any impediment, delay, or other conduct has frustrated the fair examination of the deponent, it may impose upon the persons responsible an appropriate sanction, including the reasonable costs and attorney's fees incurred by any parties as a result thereof.

(4) At any time during a deposition, on motion of a party or of the deponent and upon a showing that the examination is being conducted in bad faith or in such manner as unreasonably to annoy, embarrass, or oppress the deponent or party, the court in which the action is pending or the court in the district where the deposition is being taken may order the officer conducting the examination to cease forthwith from taking the deposition, or may limit the scope and manner of the taking of the deposition as provided in Rule 26(c). If the order made terminates the examination, it may be resumed thereafter only upon the order of the court in which the action is pending. Upon demand of the objecting party or deponent, the taking of the deposition must be suspended for the time necessary to make a motion for an order. The provisions of Rule 37(a)(4) apply to the award of expenses incurred in relation to the motion.

(e) Review by Witness; Changes; Signing. If requested by the deponent or a party before completion of the deposition, the deponent shall have 30 days after being notified by the officer that the transcript or recording is available in which to review the transcript or recording and, if there are changes in form or substance, to sign a statement reciting such changes and the reasons given by the deponent for making them. The officer shall indicate in the certificate prescribed by subdivision (f)(1) whether any review was requested and, if so, shall append any changes made by the deponent during the period allowed.

(f) Certification and Delivery by Officer; Exhibits; Copies.

(1) The officer must certify that the witness was duly sworn by the officer and that the deposition is a true record of the testimony given by the witness. This certificate must be in writing and accompany the record of the deposition. Unless otherwise ordered by the court, the officer must securely seal the deposition in an envelope or package indorsed with the title of the action and marked "Deposition of [here insert name of witness]" and must promptly send it to the attorney who arranged for the transcript or recording, who must store it under conditions that will protect it against loss, destruction, tampering, or deterioration. Documents and things produced for inspection during the examination of the witness must, upon the request of a party, be marked for identification and annexed to the deposition and may be inspected and copied by any party, except that if the person producing the materials desires to retain them the person may

(A) offer copies to be marked for identification and annexed to the deposition and to serve thereafter as originals if the person affords to all parties fair opportunity to verify the copies by comparison with the originals or

(B) offer the originals to be marked for identification, after giving to each party an opportunity to inspect and copy them, in which event the materials may then be used in the same manner as if annexed to the deposition.

Any party may move for an order that the original be annexed to and returned with the deposition to the court, pending final disposition of the case.

(2) Unless otherwise ordered by the court or agreed by the parties, the officer shall retain stenographic notes of any deposition taken stenographically or a copy of the recording of any deposition taken by another method. Upon payment of reasonable charges therefor, the officer shall furnish a copy of the transcript or other recording of the deposition to any party or to the deponent.

(3) The party taking the deposition shall give prompt notice of its filing to all other parties.

(g) Failure to Attend or to Serve Subpoena; Expenses.

(1) If the party giving the notice of the taking of a deposition fails to attend and proceed therewith and another party attends in person or by attorney pursuant to the notice, the court may order the party giving the notice to pay to such other party the reasonable expenses incurred by that party and that party's attorney in attending, including reasonable attorney's fees.

(2) If the party giving the notice of the taking of a deposition of a witness fails to serve a subpoena upon the witness and the witness because of such failure does not attend, and if another party attends in person or by attorney because that party expects the deposition of that witness to be taken, the court may order the party giving the notice to pay to such other party the reasonable expenses incurred by that party and that party's attorney in attending, including reasonable attorney's fees.

RULE 31. Depositions upon Written Questions

(a) Serving Questions; Notice.

(1) A party may take the testimony of any person, including a party, by deposition upon written questions without leave of court except as provided in paragraph (2). The attendance of witnesses may be compelled by the use of subpoena as provided in Rule 45.

(2) A party must obtain leave of court, which shall be granted to the extent consistent with the principles stated in Rule 26(b)(2), if the person to be examined is confined in prison or if, without the written stipulation of the parties,

(A) a proposed deposition would result in more than ten depositions being taken under this rule or Rule 30 by the plaintiffs, or by the defendants, or by third-party defendants;

(B) the person to be examined has already been deposed in the case; or

(C) a party seeks to take a deposition before the time specified in Rule 26(d).

(3) A party desiring to take a deposition upon written questions shall serve them upon every other party with a notice stating

(1) the name and address of the person who is to answer them, if known, and if the name is not known, a general description sufficient to identify the person or the particular class or group to which the person belongs, and

(2) the name or descriptive title and address of the officer before whom the deposition is to be taken.

A deposition upon written questions may be taken of a public or private corporation or a partnership or association or governmental agency in accordance with the provisions of Rule 30(b)(6).

(4) Within 14 days after the notice and written questions are served, a party may serve cross questions upon all other parties. Within 7 days after being served with cross questions, a party may serve redirect questions upon all other parties. Within 7 days after being served with redirect questions, a party may serve recross questions upon all other parties. The court may for cause shown enlarge or shorten the time.

(b) Officer to Take Responses and Prepare Record. A copy of the notice and copies of all questions served shall be delivered by the party taking the deposition to the officer designated in the notice, who shall proceed promptly, in the manner provided by Rule 30(c), (e), and (f), to take the testimony of the witness in response to the questions and to prepare, certify, and file or mail the deposition, attaching thereto the copy of the notice and the questions received by the officer.

(c) Notice of Filing. When the deposition is filed the party taking it shall promptly give notice thereof to all other parties.

RULE 32. Use of Depositions in Court Proceedings

(a) Use of Depositions. At the trial or upon the hearing of a motion or an interlocutory proceeding, any part or all of a deposition, so far as admissible under the rules of evidence applied as though the witness were then present and testifying, may be used against any party who was present or represented at the taking of the deposition or who had reasonable notice thereof, in accordance with any of the following provisions:

(1) Any deposition may be used by any party for the purpose of contradicting or impeaching the testimony of deponent as a witness, or for any other purpose permitted by the Federal Rules of Evidence.

(2) The deposition of a party or of anyone who at the time of taking the deposition was an officer, director, or managing agent, or a person designated under Rule 30(b)(6) or 31(a) to testify on behalf of a public or private corporation, partnership or association or governmental agency which is a party may be used by an adverse party for any purpose.

(3) The deposition of a witness, whether or not a party, may be used by any party for any purpose if the court finds:

(A) that the witness is dead; or

(B) that the witness is at a greater distance than 100 miles from the place of trial or hearing, or is out of the United States, unless it appears that the absence of the witness was procured by the party offering the deposition; or

(C) that the witness is unable to attend or testify because of age, illness, infirmity, or imprisonment; or

(D) that the party offering the deposition has been unable to procure the attendance of the witness by subpoena; or

(E) upon application and notice, that such exceptional circumstances exist as to make it desirable, in the interest of justice and with due regard to the importance of presenting the testimony of witnesses orally in open court, to allow the deposition to be used.

A deposition taken without leave of court pursuant to a notice under Rule 30(a)(2)(C) shall not be used against a party who demonstrates that, when served with the notice, it was unable through the exercise of diligence to obtain counsel to represent it at the taking of the deposition; nor shall a deposition be used against a party who, having received less than 11 days notice of a deposition, has promptly upon receiving such notice filed a motion for a protective order under Rule 26(c)(2) requesting that the deposition not be held or be held at a different time or place and such motion is pending at the time the deposition is held.

(4) If only part of a deposition is offered in evidence by a party, an adverse party may require the offeror to introduce any other part which ought in fairness to be considered with the part introduced, and any party may introduce any other parts. Substitution of parties pursuant to Rule 25 does not affect the right to use depositions previously taken; and, when an action has been brought in any court of the United States or of any State and another action involving the same subject matter is afterward brought between the same parties or their representatives or successors in interest, all depositions lawfully taken and duly filed in the former action may be used in the latter as if originally taken therefor. A deposition previously taken may also be used as permitted by the Federal Rules of Evidence.

(b) Objections to Admissibility. Subject to the provisions of Rule 28(b) and subdivision (d)(3) of this rule, objection may be made at the trial or hearing to receiving in evidence any deposition or part thereof for any reason which would require the exclusion of the evidence if the witness were then present and testifying.

(c) Form of Presentation. Except as otherwise directed by the court, a party offering deposition testimony pursuant to this rule may offer it in stenographic or nonstenographic form, but, if in nonstenographic form, the party shall also provide the court with a transcript of the portions so offered. On request of any party in a case tried before a jury, deposition testimony offered other than for impeachment purposes shall be presented in nonstenographic form, if available, unless the court for good cause orders otherwise.

(d) Effect of Errors and Irregularities in Depositions.

(1) *As to Notice.* All errors and irregularities in the notice for taking a deposition are waived unless written objection is promptly served upon the party giving the notice.

(2) *As to Disqualification of Officer.* Objection to taking a deposition because of disqualification of the officer before whom it is to be taken is waived unless made before the taking of the deposition begins or as soon thereafter as the disqualification becomes known or could be discovered with reasonable diligence.

(3) *As to Taking of Deposition.*

(A) Objections to the competency of a witness or to the competency, relevancy, or materiality of testimony are not waived by failure to make them before or during the taking of the deposition, unless the ground of the objection is one which might have been obviated or removed if presented at that time.

(B) Errors and irregularities occurring at the oral examination in the manner of taking the deposition, in the form of the questions or answers, in the oath or affirmation, or in the conduct of parties, and errors of any kind which might be obviated, removed, or cured if promptly presented, are waived unless seasonable objection thereto is made at the taking of the deposition.

(C) Objections to the form of written questions submitted under Rule 31 are waived unless served in writing upon the party propounding them within the time allowed for serving the succeeding cross or other questions and within 5 days after service of the last questions authorized.

(4) *As to Completion and Return of Deposition.* Errors and irregularities in the manner in which the testimony is transcribed or the deposition is prepared, signed, certified, sealed, indorsed, transmitted, filed, or otherwise dealt with by the officer under Rules 30 and 31 are waived unless a motion to suppress the deposition or some part thereof is made with reasonable promptness after such defect is, or with due diligence might have been, ascertained.

RULE 33. Interrogatories to Parties

(a) Availability. Without leave of court or written stipulation, any party may serve upon any other party written interrogatories, not exceeding 25 in number including all discrete subparts, to be answered by the party served or, if the party served is a public or private corporation or a partnership or association or governmental agency, by any officer or agent, who shall furnish such information as is available to the party. Leave to serve additional interrogatories shall be granted to the extent consistent with the principles of Rule 26(b)(2). Without leave of court or written stipulation, interrogatories may not be served before the time specified in Rule 26(d).

(b) Answers and Objections.

(1) Each interrogatory shall be answered separately and fully in writing under oath, unless it is objected to, in which event the objecting party shall state the reasons for objection and shall answer to the extent the interrogatory is not objectionable.

(2) The answers are to be signed by the person making them, and the objections signed by the attorney making them.

(3) The party upon whom the interrogatories have been served shall serve a copy of the answers, and objections if any, within 30 days after the service of the interrogatories. A shorter or longer time may be directed by the court or, in the absence of such an order, agreed to in writing by the parties subject to Rule 29.

(4) All grounds for an objection to an interrogatory shall be stated with specificity. Any ground not stated in a timely objection is waived unless the party's failure to object is excused by the court for good cause shown.

(5) The party submitting the interrogatories may move for an order under Rule 37(a) with respect to any objection to or other failure to answer an interrogatory.

(c) Scope; Use at Trial. Interrogatories may relate to any matters which can be inquired into under Rule 26(b)(1), and the answers may be used to the extent permitted by the rules of evidence.

An interrogatory otherwise proper is not necessarily objectionable merely because an answer to the interrogatory involves an opinion or contention that relates to fact or the application of law to fact, but the court may order that such an interrogatory need not be answered until after designated discovery has been completed or until a pre-trial conference or other later time.

(d) Option to Produce Business Records. Where the answer to an interrogatory may be derived or ascertained from the business records of the party upon whom the interrogatory has been served or from an examination, audit or inspection of such business records, including a compilation, abstract or summary thereof, and the burden of deriving or ascertaining the answer is substantially the same for the party serving the interrogatory as for the party served, it is a sufficient answer to such interrogatory to specify the records from which the answer may be derived or ascertained and to afford to the party serving the interrogatory reasonable opportunity to examine, audit or inspect such records and to make copies, compilations, abstracts or summaries. A specification shall be in sufficient detail to permit the interrogating party to locate and to identify, as readily as can the party served, the records from which the answer may be ascertained.

RULE 34. Production of Documents and Things and Entry Upon Land for Inspection and Other Purposes

(a) Scope. Any party may serve on any other party a request

(1) to produce and permit the party making the request, or someone acting on the requestor's behalf, to inspect and copy, any designated documents (including writings, drawings, graphs, charts, photographs, phonorecords, and other data compilations from which information can be obtained, translated, if necessary, by the respondent through detection devices into reasonably usable form), or to inspect and copy, test, or sample any tangible things which constitute or contain matters within the scope of Rule 26(b) and which are in the possession, custody or control of the party upon whom the request is served; or

(2) to permit entry upon designated land or other property in the possession or control of the party upon whom the request is served for the purpose of inspection and measuring, surveying, photographing, testing, or sampling the property or any designated object or operation thereon, within the scope of Rule 26(b).

(b) Procedure. The request shall set forth, either by individual item or by category, the items to be inspected and describe each with reasonable particularity. The request shall specify a reasonable time, place, and manner of making the inspection and performing the related acts. Without leave of court or written stipulation, a request may not be served before the time specified in Rule 26(d).

The party upon whom the request is served shall serve a written response within 30 days after the service of the request. A shorter or longer time may be directed by the court or, in the absence of such an order, agreed to in writing by the parties, subject to Rule 29. The response shall state, with respect to each item or category, that inspection and related activities will be permitted as requested, unless the request is objected to, in which event the reasons for the objection shall be stated. If objection is made to part of an item or category, the part shall be specified and inspection permitted of the remaining parts. The party submitting the request may move for an order under Rule 37(a) with respect to any objection to or other failure to respond to the request or any part thereof, or any failure to permit inspection as requested.

A party who produces documents for inspection shall produce them as they are kept in the usual course of business or shall organize and label them to correspond with the categories in the request.

(c) Persons Not Parties. A person not a party to the action may be compelled to produce documents and things or to submit to an inspection as provided in Rule 45.

RULE 35. Physical and Mental Examinations of Persons

(a) Order for Examination. When the mental or physical condition (including the blood group) of a party or of a person in the custody or under the legal control of a party, is in controversy, the court in which the action is pending may order the party to submit to a physical or mental examination by a suitably licensed or certified examiner or to produce for examination the person in the party's custody or legal control. The order may be made only on motion for good cause shown and upon notice to the person to be examined and to all parties and shall specify the time, place, manner, conditions, and scope of the examination and the person or persons by whom it is to be made.

(b) Report of Examiner.

(1) If requested by the party against whom an order is made under Rule 35(a) or the person examined, the party causing the examination to be made shall deliver to the requesting party a copy of the detailed written report of the examiner setting out the examiner's findings, including results of all tests made, diagnoses and conclusions, together with like reports of all earlier examinations of the same condition. After delivery the party causing the examination shall be entitled upon request to receive from the party against whom the order is made a like report of any examination, previously or thereafter made, of the same condition, unless, in the case of a report of examination of a person not a party, the party shows that the party is unable to obtain it. The court on motion may make an order against a party requiring delivery of a report on such terms as are just, and if an examiner fails or refuses to make a report the court may exclude the examiner's testimony if offered at trial.

(2) By requesting and obtaining a report of the examination so ordered or by taking the deposition of the examiner, the party examined waives any privilege the party may have in that action or any other involving the same controversy, regarding the testimony of every other person who has examined or may thereafter examine the party in respect of the same mental or physical condition.

(3) This subdivision applies to examinations made by agreement of the parties, unless the agreement expressly provides otherwise. This subdivision does not preclude discovery of a report of an examiner or the taking of a deposition of the examiner in accordance with the provisions of any other rule.

RULE 36. Requests for Admission

(a) Request for Admission. A party may serve upon any other party a written request for the admission, for purposes of the pending action only, of the truth of any matters within the scope of Rule 26(b)(1) set forth in the request that relate to statements or opinions of fact or of the application of law to fact, including the genuineness of any documents described in the request. Copies of documents shall be served with the request unless they have been or are otherwise furnished or made available for inspection and copying. Without leave of court or written stipulation, requests for admission may not be served before the time specified in Rule 26(d).

Each matter of which an admission is requested shall be separately set forth. The matter is admitted unless, within 30 days after service of the request, or within such shorter or longer time as the court may allow or as the parties may agree to in writing, subject to Rule 29, the party to whom the request is directed serves upon the party requesting the admission a written answer or objection addressed to the matter, signed by the party or by the party's attorney. If objection is made, the reasons therefor shall be stated. The answer shall specifically deny the matter or set forth in detail the reasons why the answering party cannot truthfully admit or deny the matter. A denial shall fairly meet the substance of the requested admission, and when good faith requires that a party qualify an answer or deny only a part of the matter of which an admission is requested, the party shall specify so much of it as is true and qualify or deny the remainder. An answering party may not give lack of information or knowledge as a reason for failure to admit or deny unless the party states that the party has made reasonable inquiry and that the information known or readily obtainable by the party is insufficient to enable the party to admit or deny. A party who considers that a matter of which an admission has been requested presents a genuine issue for trial may not, on that ground alone, object to the request; the party may, subject to the provisions of Rule 37(c), deny the matter or set forth reasons why the party cannot admit or deny it.

The party who has requested the admissions may move to determine the sufficiency of the answers or objections. Unless the court determines that an objection is justified, it shall order that an answer be served. If the court determines that an answer does not comply with the requirements of this rule, it may order either that the matter is admitted or that an amended answer be served. The court may, in lieu of these orders, determine that final disposition of the request be made at a pre-trial conference or at a designated time prior to trial. The provisions of Rule 37(a)(4) apply to the award of expenses incurred in relation to the motion.

(b) Effect of Admission. Any matter admitted under this rule is conclusively established unless the court on motion permits withdrawal or amendment of the admission. Subject to the provision of Rule 16 governing amendment of a pre-trial order, the court may permit withdrawal or amendment when the presentation of the merits of the action will be subserved thereby and the party who obtained the admission fails to satisfy the court that withdrawal or amendment will prejudice that party in maintaining the action or defense on the merits. Any admission made by a party under this rule is for the purpose of the pending action only and is not an admission for any other purpose nor may it be used against the party in any other proceeding.

RULE 37. Failure to Make Disclosure or Cooperate in Discovery: Sanctions

(a) Motion For Order Compelling Disclosure or Discovery. A party, upon reasonable notice to other parties and all persons affected thereby, may apply for an order compelling disclosure or discovery as follows:

(1) *Appropriate Court.* An application for an order to a party shall be made to the court in which the action is pending. An application for an order to a person who is not a party shall be made to the court in the district where the discovery is being, or is to be, taken.

(2) *Motion.*

(A) If a party fails to make a disclosure required by Rule 26(a), any other party may move to compel disclosure and for appropriate sanctions. The motion must include a certification that the movant has in good faith conferred or attempted to confer with the party not making the disclosure in an effort to secure the disclosure without court action.

(B) If a deponent fails to answer a question propounded or submitted under Rules 30 or 31, or a corporation or other entity fails to make a designation under Rule 30(b)(6) or 31(a), or a party fails to answer an interrogatory submitted under Rule 33, or if a party, in response to a request for inspection submitted under Rule 34, fails to respond that inspection will be permitted as requested or fails to permit inspection as requested, the discovering party may move for an order compelling an answer, or a designation, or an order compelling inspection in accordance with the request. The motion must include a certification that the movant has in good faith conferred or attempted to confer with the person or party failing to make the discovery in an effort to secure the information or material without court action. When taking a deposition on oral examination, the proponent of the question may complete or adjourn the examination before applying for an order.

(3) *Evasive or Incomplete Disclosure, Answer, or Response.* For purposes of this subdivision an evasive or incomplete disclosure, answer, or response is to be treated as a failure to disclose, answer, or respond.

(4) *Expenses and Sanctions.*

(A) If the motion is granted or if the disclosure or requested discovery is provided after the motion was filed, the court shall, after affording an opportunity to be heard, require the party or deponent whose conduct necessitated the motion or the party or attorney advising such conduct or both of them to pay to the moving party the reasonable expenses incurred in making the motion, including attorney's fees, unless the court finds that the motion was filed without the movant's first making a good faith effort to obtain the disclosure or discovery without court action, or that the opposing party's nondisclosure, response, or objection was substantially justified, or that other circumstances make an award of expenses unjust.

(B) If the motion is denied, the court may enter

any protective order authorized under Rule 26(c) and shall, after affording an opportunity to be heard, require the moving party or the attorney filing the motion or both of them to pay to the party or deponent who opposed the motion the reasonable expenses incurred in opposing the motion, including attorney's fees, unless the court finds that the making of the motion was substantially justified or that other circumstances make an award of expenses unjust.

(C) If the motion is granted in part and denied in part, the court may enter any protective order authorized under Rule 26(c) and may, after affording an opportunity to be heard, apportion the reasonable expenses incurred in relation to the motion among the parties and persons in a just manner.

(b) Failure to Comply With Order.

(1) *Sanctions by Court in District Where Deposition is Taken.* If a deponent fails to be sworn or to answer a question after being directed to do so by the court in the district in which the deposition is being taken, the failure may be considered a contempt of that court.

(2) *Sanctions by Court in Which Action Is Pending.* If a party or an officer, director, or managing agent of a party or a person designated under Rule 30(b)(6) or 31(a) to testify on behalf of a party fails to obey an order to provide or permit discovery, including an order made under subdivision (a) of this rule or Rule 35, or if a party fails to obey an order entered under Rule 26(f), the court in which the action is pending may make such orders in regard to the failure as are just, and among others the following:

(A) An order that the matters regarding which the order was made or any other designated facts shall be taken to be established for the purposes of the action in accordance with the claim of the party obtaining the order;

(B) An order refusing to allow the disobedient party to support or oppose designated claims or defenses, or prohibiting that party from introducing designated matters in evidence;

(C) An order striking out pleadings or parts thereof, or staying further proceedings until the order is obeyed, or dismissing the action or proceeding or any part thereof, or rendering a judgment by default against the disobedient party;

(D) In lieu of any of the foregoing orders or in addition thereto, an order treating as a contempt of court the failure to obey any orders except an order to submit to a physical or mental examination;

(E) Where a party has failed to comply with an order under Rule 35(a) requiring that party to produce another for examination, such orders as are listed in paragraphs (A), (B), and (C) of this subdivision, unless the party failing to comply shows that that party is unable to produce such person for examination.

In lieu of any of the foregoing orders or in addition thereto, the court shall require the party failing to obey the order or the attorney advising that party or both to pay the reasonable expenses, including attorney's fees, caused by the failure, unless the court finds that the failure was substantially justified or that other circumstances make an award of expenses unjust.

(c) Failure to Disclose; False or Misleading Disclosure; Refusal to Admit.

(1) A party that without substantial justification fails to disclose information required by Rule 26(a) or 26(e)(1), or to amend a prior response to discovery as required by Rule 26(e)(2), is not, unless such failure is harmless, permitted to use as evidence at a trial, at a hearing, or on a motion any witness or information not so disclosed. In addition to or in lieu of this sanction, the court, on motion and after affording an opportunity to be heard, may impose other appropriate sanctions. In addition to requiring payment of reasonable expenses, including attorney's fees, caused by the failure, these sanctions may include any of the actions authorized under Rule 37(b)(2)(A), (B), and (C) and may include informing the jury of the failure to make the disclosure.

(2) If a party fails to admit the genuineness of any document or the truth of any matter as requested under Rule 36, and if the party requesting the admissions thereafter proves the genuineness of the document or the truth of the matter, the requesting party may apply to the court for an order requiring the other party to pay the reasonable expenses incurred in making that proof, including reasonable attorney's fees. The court shall make the order unless it finds that

(A) the request was held objectionable pursuant to Rule 36(a), or

(B) the admission sought was of no substantial importance, or

(C) the party failing to admit had reasonable ground to believe that the party might prevail on the matter, or

(D) there was other good reason for the failure to admit.

(d) Failure of Party to Attend at Own Deposition or Serve Answers to Interrogatories or Respond to Request for Inspection. If a party or an officer, director, or managing agent of a party or a person designated under Rule 30(b)(6) or 31(a) to testify on behalf of a party fails

(1) to appear before the officer who is to take the deposition, after being served with a proper notice, or

(2) to serve answers or objections to interrogatories submitted under Rule 33, after proper service of the interrogatories, or

(3) to serve a written response to a request for inspection submitted under Rule 34, after proper service of the request,

the court in which the action is pending on motion may make such orders in regard to the failure as are just, and among others it may take any action authorized under subparagraphs (A), (B), and (C) of subdivision (b)(2) of this rule. Any motion specifying a failure under clause (2) or (3) of this subdivision shall include a certification that the movant has in good faith conferred or attempted to confer with the party failing to answer or respond in an effort to obtain such answer or response without court action. In lieu of any order or in addition thereto, the court shall require the party failing to act or the attorney advising that party or both to pay the reasonable expenses, including attorney's fees, caused by the failure unless the court finds that the failure was substantially justified or that other circumstances make an award of expenses unjust.

The failure to act described in this subdivision may not be excused on the ground that the discovery sought is objectionable unless the party failing to act has a pending motion for a protective order as provided by Rule 26(c).

(e) [Abrogated.]

(f) [Repealed.]

(g) Failure to Participate in the Framing of a Discovery Plan. If a party or a party's attorney fails to participate in good faith in the development and submission of a proposed discovery plan as required by Rule 26(f), the court may, after opportunity for hearing, require such party or attorney to pay to any other party the reasonable expenses, including attorney's fees, caused by the failure.

VI
TRIALS

RULE 38. Jury Trial of Right

(a) Right Preserved. The right of trial by jury as declared by the Seventh Amendment to the Constitution or as given by a statute of the United States shall be preserved to the parties inviolate.

(b) Demand. Any party may demand a trial by jury of any issue triable of right by a jury by

(1) serving upon the other parties a demand therefor in writing at any time after the commencement of the action and not later than 10 days after the service of the last pleading directed to the issue, and

(2) filing the demand as required by Rule 5(d).

Such demand may be indorsed upon a pleading of the party.

(c) Same: Specification of Issues. In the demand a party may specify the issues which the party wishes so tried; otherwise the party shall be deemed to have demanded trial by jury for all the issues so triable. If the party has demanded trial by jury for only some of the issues, any other party within 10 days after service of the demand or such lesser time as the court may order, may serve a demand for trial by jury of any other or all of the issues of fact in the action.

(d) Waiver. The failure of a party to serve and file a demand as required by this rule constitutes a waiver by the party of trial by jury. A demand for trial by jury made as herein provided may not be withdrawn without the consent of the parties.

(e) Admiralty and Maritime Claims. These rules shall not be construed to create a right to trial by jury of the issues in an admiralty or maritime claim within the meaning of Rule 9(h).

RULE 39. Trial by Jury or by the Court

(a) By Jury. When trial by jury has been demanded as provided in Rule 38, the action shall be designated upon the docket as a jury action. The trial of all issues so demanded shall be by jury, unless

(1) the parties or their attorneys of record, by written stipulation filed with the court or by an oral stipulation made in open court and entered in the record, consent to trial by the court sitting without a jury or

(2) the court upon motion or of its own initiative finds that a right of trial by jury of some or all of those issues does not exist under the Constitution or statutes of the United States.

(b) By the Court. Issues not demanded for trial by jury as provided in Rule 38 shall be tried by the court; but, notwithstanding the failure of a party to demand a jury in an action in which such a demand might have been made of right, the court in its discretion upon motion may order a trial by a jury of any or all issues.

(c) Advisory Jury and Trial by Consent. In all actions not triable of right by a jury the court upon motion or of its own initiative may try any issue with an advisory jury or, except in actions against the United States when a statute of the United States provides for trial without a jury, the court, with the consent of both parties, may order a trial with a jury whose verdict has the same effect as if trial by jury had been a matter of right.

RULE 40. Assignment of Cases for Trial

The district courts shall provide by rule for the placing of actions upon the trial calendar

(1) without request of the parties or

(2) upon request of a party and notice to the other parties or

(3) in such other manner as the courts deem expedient.

Precedence shall be given to actions entitled thereto by any statute of the United States.

RULE 41. Dismissal of Actions

(a) Voluntary Dismissal: Effect Thereof.

(1) *By Plaintiff; By Stipulation.* Subject to the provisions of Rule 23(e), of Rule 66, and of any statute of the United States, an action may be dismissed by the plaintiff without order of court

(i) by filing a notice of dismissal at any time before service by the adverse party of an answer or of a motion for summary judgment, whichever first occurs, or

(ii) by filing a stipulation of dismissal signed by all parties who have appeared in the action.

Unless otherwise stated in the notice of dismissal or stipulation, the dismissal is without prejudice, except that a notice of dismissal operates as an adjudication upon the merits when filed by a plaintiff who has once dismissed in any court of the United States or of any state an action based on or including the same claim.

(2) *By Order of Court.* Except as provided in paragraph (1) of this subdivision of this rule, an action shall not be dismissed at the plaintiff's instance save upon order of the court and upon such terms and conditions as the court deems proper. If a counterclaim has been pleaded by a defendant prior to the service upon the defendant of the plaintiff's motion to dismiss, the action shall not be dismissed against the defendant's objection unless the counterclaim can remain pending for independent adjudication by the court. Unless otherwise specified in the order, a dismissal under this paragraph is without prejudice.

(b) Involuntary Dismissal: Effect Thereof. For failure of the plaintiff to prosecute or to comply with these rules or any order of court, a defendant may move for dismissal of an action or of any claim against the defendant. Unless the court in its order for dismissal otherwise specifies, a dismissal under this subdivision and any dismissal not provided for in this rule, other than a dismissal for lack of jurisdiction, for improper venue, or for failure to join a party under Rule 19, operates as an adjudication upon the merits.

(c) Dismissal of Counterclaim, Cross-Claim, or Third-Party Claim. The provisions of this rule apply to the dismissal of any counterclaim, cross-claim, or third-party claim. A voluntary dismissal by the claimant alone pursuant to paragraph (1) of subdivision (a) of this rule shall be made before a responsive pleading is served or, if there is none, before the introduction of evidence at the trial or hearing.

(d) Costs of Previously-Dismissed Action. If a plaintiff who has once dismissed an action in any court commences an action based upon or including the same claim against the same defendant, the court may make such order for the payment of costs of the action previously dismissed as it may deem proper and may stay the proceedings in the action until the plaintiff has complied with the order.

RULE 42. Consolidation; Separate Trials

(a) Consolidation. When actions involving a common question of law or fact are pending before the court, it may order a joint hearing or trial of any or all the matters in issue in the actions; it may order all the actions consolidated; and it may make such orders concerning proceedings therein as may tend to avoid unnecessary costs or delay.

(b) Separate Trials. The court, in furtherance of convenience or to avoid prejudice, or when separate trials will be conducive to expedition and economy, may order a separate trial of any claim, cross-claim, counterclaim, or third-party claim, or of any separate issue or of any number of claims, cross-claims, counterclaims, third-party claims, or issues, always preserving inviolate the right of trial by jury as declared by the Seventh Amendment to the Constitution or as given by a statute of the United States.

RULE 43. Taking of Testimony

(a) Form. In every trial, the testimony of witnesses shall be taken in open court, unless a federal law, these rules, the Federal Rules of Evidence, or other rules adopted by the Supreme Court provide otherwise. The court may, for good cause shown in compelling circumstances and upon appropriate safeguards, permit presentation of testimony in open court by contemporaneous transmission from a different location.

(b) [Abrogated.]

(c) [Abrogated.]

(d) Affirmation in Lieu of Oath. Whenever under these rules an oath is required to be taken, a solemn affirmation may be accepted in lieu thereof.

(e) Evidence on Motions. When a motion is based on facts not appearing of record the court may hear the matter on affidavits presented by the respective parties, but the court may direct that the matter be heard wholly or partly on oral testimony or deposition.

(f) Interpreters. The court may appoint an interpreter of its own selection and may fix the interpreter's reasonable compensation. The compensation shall be paid out of funds provided by law or by one or more of the parties as the court may direct, and may be taxed ultimately as costs, in the discretion of the court.

RULE 44. Proof of Official Record

(a) Authentication.

(1) *Domestic.* An official record kept within the United States, or any state, district, or commonwealth, or within a territory subject to the administrative or judicial jurisdiction of the United States, or an entry therein, when admissible for any purpose, may be evidenced by an official publication thereof or by a copy attested by the officer having the legal custody of the record, or by the officer's deputy, and accompanied by a certificate that such officer has the custody. The certificate may be made by a judge of a court of record of the district or political subdivision in which the record is kept, authenticated by the seal of the court, or may be made by any public officer having a seal of office and having official duties in the district or political subdivision in which the record is kept, authenticated by the seal of the officer's office.

(2) *Foreign.* A foreign official record, or an entry therein, when admissible for any purpose, may be evidenced by an official publication thereof; or a copy thereof, attested by a person authorized to make the

attestation, and accompanied by a final certification as to the genuineness of the signature and official position

(i) of the attesting person, or

(ii) of any foreign official whose certificate of genuineness of signature and official position relates to the attestation or is in a chain of certificates of genuineness of signature and official position relating to the attestation.

A final certification may be made by a secretary of embassy or legation, consul general, vice consul, or consular agent of the United States, or a diplomatic or consular official of the foreign country assigned or accredited to the United States. If reasonable opportunity has been given to all parties to investigate the authenticity and accuracy of the documents, the court may, for good cause shown,

(i) admit an attested copy without final certification or

(ii) permit the foreign official record to be evidenced by an attested summary with or without a final certification.

The final certification is unnecessary if the record and the attestation are certified as provided in a treaty or convention to which the United States and the foreign country in which the official record is located are parties.

(b) Lack of Record. A written statement that after diligent search no record or entry of a specified tenor is found to exist in the records of his office, designated by the statement, authenticated as provided in subdivision (a)(1) of this rule in the case of a domestic record, or complying with the requirements of subdivision (a)(2) of this rule for a summary in the case of a foreign record, is admissible as evidence that the records contain no such record or entry.

(c) Other Proof. This rule does not prevent the proof of official records or of entry or lack of entry therein by any other method authorized by law.

RULE 44.1. Determination of Foreign Law

A party who intends to raise an issue concerning the law of a foreign country shall give notice by pleadings or other reasonable written notice. The court, in determining foreign law, may consider any relevant material or source, including testimony, whether or not submitted by a party or admissible under the Federal Rules of Evidence. The court's determination shall be treated as a ruling on a question of law.

RULE 45. Subpoena

(a) Form; Issuance.

(1) Every subpoena shall

(A) state the name of the court from which it is issued; and

(B) state the title of the action, the name of the court in which it is pending, and its civil action number; and

(C) command each person to whom it is directed to attend and give testimony or to produce and permit inspection and copying of designated books, documents or tangible things in the possession, custody or control of that person, or to permit inspection of premises, at a time and place therein specified; and

(D) set forth the text of subdivisions (c) and (d) of this rule.

A command to produce evidence or to permit inspection may be joined with a command to appear at trial or hearing or at deposition, or may be issued separately.

(2) A subpoena commanding attendance at a trial or hearing shall issue from the court for the district in which the hearing or trial is to be held. A subpoena for attendance at a deposition shall issue from the court for the district designated by the notice of deposition as the district in which the deposition is to be taken. If separate from a subpoena commanding the attendance of a person, a subpoena for production or inspection shall issue from the court for the district in which the production or inspection is to be made.

(3) The clerk shall issue a subpoena, signed but otherwise in blank, to a party requesting it, who shall complete it before service. An attorney as officer of the court may also issue and sign a subpoena on behalf of

(A) a court in which the attorney is authorized to practice; or

(B) a court for a district in which a deposition or production is compelled by the subpoena, if the deposition or production pertains to an action pending in a court in which the attorney is authorized to practice.

(b) Service.

(1) A subpoena may be served by any person who is not a party and is not less than 18 years of age. Service of a subpoena upon a person named therein shall be made by delivering a copy thereof to such person and, if the person's attendance is commanded, by tendering to that person the fees for one day's attendance and the mileage allowed by law. When the subpoena is issued on behalf of the United States or an officer or agency thereof, fees and mileage need not be tendered. Prior notice of any commanded production of documents and things or inspection of premises before trial shall be served on each party in the manner prescribed by Rule 5(b).

(2) Subject to the provisions of clause (ii) of subparagraph (c)(3)(A) of this rule, a subpoena may be served at any place within the district of the court by which it is issued, or at any place without the district that is within 100 miles of the place of the deposition, hearing, trial, production, or inspection specified in the subpoena or at any place within the state where a state statute or rule of court permits service of a subpoena issued by a state court of general jurisdiction sitting in the place of the deposition, hearing, trial, production, or inspection specified in the subpoena. When a statute of the United States provides therefor, the court upon proper application and cause shown may authorize the

service of a subpoena at any other place. A subpoena directed to a witness in a foreign country who is a national or resident of the United States shall issue under the circumstances and in the manner and be served as provided in Title 28, U.S.C. § 1783.

(3) Proof of service when necessary shall be made by filing with the clerk of the court by which the subpoena is issued a statement of the date and manner of service and of the names of the persons served, certified by the person who made the service.

(c) Protection of Persons Subject to Subpoenas.

(1) A party or an attorney responsible for the issuance and service of a subpoena shall take reasonable steps to avoid imposing undue burden or expense on a person subject to that subpoena. The court on behalf of which the subpoena was issued shall enforce this duty and impose upon the party or attorney in breach of this duty an appropriate sanction, which may include, but is not limited to, lost earnings and a reasonable attorney's fee.

(2) (A) A person commanded to produce and permit inspection and copying of designated books, papers, documents or tangible things, or inspection of premises need not appear in person at the place of production or inspection unless commanded to appear for deposition, hearing or trial.

(B) Subject to paragraph (d)(2) of this rule, a person commanded to produce and permit inspection and copying may, within 14 days after service of the subpoena or before the time specified for compliance if such time is less than 14 days after service, serve upon the party or attorney designated in the subpoena written objection to inspection or copying of any or all of the designated materials or of the premises. If objection is made, the party serving the subpoena shall not be entitled to inspect and copy the materials or inspect the premises except pursuant to an order of the court by which the subpoena was issued. If objection has been made, the party serving the subpoena may, upon notice to the person commanded to produce, move at any time for an order to compel the production. Such an order to compel production shall protect any person who is not a party or an officer of a party from significant expense resulting from the inspection and copying commanded.

(3) (A) On timely motion, the court by which a subpoena was issued shall quash or modify the subpoena if it

(i) fails to allow reasonable time for compliance;

(ii) requires a person who is not a party or an officer of a party to travel to a place more than 100 miles from the place where that person resides, is employed or regularly transacts business in person, except that, subject to the provisions of clause (c)(3)(B)(iii) of this rule, such a person may in order to attend trial be commanded to travel from any such place within the state in which the trial is held, or

(iii) requires disclosure of privileged or other protected matter and no exception or waiver applies, or

(iv) subjects a person to undue burden.

(B) If a subpoena

(i) requires disclosure of a trade secret or other confidential research, development, or commercial information, or

(ii) requires disclosure of an unretained expert's opinion or information not describing specific events or occurrences in dispute and resulting from the expert's study made not at the request of any party, or

(iii) requires a person who is not a party or an officer of a party to incur substantial expense to travel more than 100 miles to attend trial,

the court may, to protect a person subject to or affected by the subpoena, quash or modify the subpoena or, if the party in whose behalf the subpoena is issued shows a substantial need for the testimony or material that cannot be otherwise met without undue hardship and assures that the person to whom the subpoena is addressed will be reasonably compensated, the court may order appearance or production only upon specified conditions.

(d) Duties in Responding to Subpoena.

(1) A person responding to a subpoena to produce documents shall produce them as they are kept in the usual course of business or shall organize and label them to correspond with the categories in the demand.

(2) When information subject to a subpoena is withheld on a claim that it is privileged or subject to protection as trial preparation materials, the claim shall be made expressly and shall be supported by a description of the nature of the documents, communications, or things not produced that is sufficient to enable the demanding party to contest the claim.

(e) Contempt. Failure by any person without adequate excuse to obey a subpoena served upon that person may be deemed a contempt of the court from which the subpoena issued. An adequate cause for failure to obey exists when a subpoena purports to require a nonparty to attend or produce at a place not within the limits provided by clause (ii) of subparagraph (c)(3)(A).

RULE 46. Exceptions Unnecessary

Formal exceptions to rulings or orders of the court are unnecessary; but for all purposes for which an exception has heretofore been necessary it is sufficient that a party, at the time the ruling or order of the court is made or sought, makes known to the court the action which the party desires the court to take or the party's objection to the action of the court and the grounds therefor; and, if a party has no opportunity to object to a ruling or order at the time it is made, the absence of an objection does not thereafter prejudice the party.

RULE 47. Selection of Jurors

(a) Examination of Jurors. The court may permit the parties or their attorneys to conduct the examination of prospective jurors or may itself conduct the examination. In the latter event, the court shall permit the parties or their attorneys to supplement the examination by such further inquiry as it deems proper or shall itself submit to the prospective jurors such additional questions of the parties or their attorneys as it deems proper.

(b) Peremptory Challenges. The court shall allow the number of peremptory challenges provided by 28 U.S.C. § 1870.

(c) Excuse. The court may for good cause excuse a juror from service during trial or deliberation.

RULE 48. Number of Jurors – Participation in Verdict

The court shall seat a jury of not fewer than six and not more than twelve members and all jurors shall participate in the verdict unless excused from service by the court pursuant to Rule 47(c). Unless the parties otherwise stipulate,

(1) the verdict shall be unanimous and

(2) no verdict shall be taken from a jury reduced in size to fewer than six members.

RULE 49. Special Verdicts and Interrogatories

(a) Special Verdicts. The court may require a jury to return only a special verdict in the form of a special written finding upon each issue of fact. In that event the court may submit to the jury written questions susceptible of categorical or other brief answer or may submit written forms of the several special findings which might properly be made under the pleadings and evidence; or it may use such other method of submitting the issues and requiring the written findings thereon as it deems most appropriate. The court shall give to the jury such explanation and instruction concerning the matter thus submitted as may be necessary to enable the jury to make its findings upon each issue. If in so doing the court omits any issue of fact raised by the pleadings or by the evidence, each party waives the right to a trial by jury of the issue so omitted unless before the jury retires the party demands its submission to the jury. As to an issue omitted without such demand the court may make a finding; or, if it fails to do so, it shall be deemed to have made a finding in accord with the judgment on the special verdict.

(b) General Verdict Accompanied by Answer to Interrogatories. The court may submit to the jury, together with appropriate forms for a general verdict, written interrogatories upon one or more issues of fact the decision of which is necessary to a verdict. The court shall give such explanation or instruction as may be necessary to enable the jury both to make answers to the interrogatories and to render a general verdict, and the court shall direct the jury both to make written answers and to render a general verdict. When the general verdict and the answers are harmonious, the appropriate judgment upon the verdict and answers shall be entered pursuant to Rule 58. When the answers are consistent with each other but one or more is inconsistent with the general verdict, judgment may be entered pursuant to Rule 58 in accordance with the answers, notwithstanding the general verdict, or the court may return the jury for further consideration of its answers and verdict or may order a new trial. When the answers are inconsistent with each other and one or more is likewise inconsistent with the general verdict, judgment shall not be entered, but the court shall return the jury for further consideration of its answers and verdict or shall order a new trial.

RULE 50. Judgment as a Matter of Law in Jury Trials; Alternative Motion for New Trial; Conditional Rulings

(a) Judgment as a Matter of Law.

(1) If during a trial by jury a party has been fully heard on an issue and there is no legally sufficient evidentiary basis for a reasonable jury to find for that party on that issue, the court may determine the issue against that party and may grant a motion for judgment as a matter of law against that party with respect to a claim or defense that cannot under the controlling law be maintained or defeated without a favorable finding on that issue.

(2) Motions for judgment as a matter of law may be made at any time before submission of the case to the jury. Such a motion shall specify the judgment sought and the law and the facts on which the moving party is entitled to the judgment.

(b) Renewing Motion for Judgment After Trial; Alternative Motion for New Trial. If, for any reason, the court does not grant a motion for judgment as a matter of law made at the close of all the evidence, the court is considered to have submitted the action to the jury subject to the court's later deciding the legal questions raised by the motion. The movant may renew its request for judgment as a matter of law by filing a motion no later than 10 days after entry of judgment— and may alternatively request a new trial or join a motion for a new trial under Rule 59. In ruling on a renewed motion, the court may:

(1) if a verdict was returned:

(A) allow the judgment to stand,

(B) order a new trial, or

(C) direct entry of judgment as a matter of law; or

(2) if no verdict was returned;

(A) order a new trial, or

(B) direct entry of judgment as a matter of law.

(c) Granting Renewed Motion for Judgment as a Matter of Law; Conditional Rulings; New Trial Motion

(1) If the renewed motion for judgment as a matter of law is granted, the court shall also rule on the motion for a new trial, if any, by determining whether it should be granted if the judgment is thereafter vacated or reversed, and shall specify the grounds for granting or denying the motion for the new trial. If the motion for a new trial is thus conditionally granted, the order thereon does not affect the finality of the judgment. In case the motion for a new trial has been conditionally granted and the judgment is reversed on appeal, the new trial shall proceed unless the appellate court has otherwise ordered. In case the motion for a new trial has been conditionally denied, the appellee on appeal may assert error in that denial; and if the judgment is reversed on appeal, subsequent proceedings shall be in accordance with the order of the appellate court.

(2) Any motion for a new trial under Rule 59 by a party against whom judgment as a matter of law is rendered shall be filed no later than 10 days after entry of the judgment.

(d) Same: Denial of Motion for Judgment as a Matter of Law. If the motion for judgment as a matter of law is denied, the party who prevailed on that motion may, as appellee, assert grounds entitling the party to a new trial in the event the appellate court concludes that the trial court erred in denying the motion for judgment. If the appellate court reverses the judgment, nothing in this rule precludes it from determining that the appellee is entitled to a new trial, or from directing the trial court to determine whether a new trial shall be granted.

RULE 51. Instructions to Jury: Objection

At the close of the evidence or at such earlier time during the trial as the court reasonably directs, any party may file written requests that the court instruct the jury on the law as set forth in the requests. The court shall inform counsel of its proposed action upon the requests prior to their arguments to the jury. The court, at its election, may instruct the jury before or after argument, or both. No party may assign as error the giving or the failure to give an instruction unless that party objects thereto before the jury retires to consider its verdict, stating distinctly the matter objected to and the grounds of the objection. Opportunity shall be given to make the objection out of the hearing of the jury.

RULE 52. Findings by the Court; Judgment on Partial Findings

(a) Effect. In all actions tried upon the facts without a jury or with an advisory jury, the court shall find the facts specially and state separately its conclusions of law

thereon, and judgment shall be entered pursuant to Rule 58; and in granting or refusing interlocutory injunctions the court shall similarly set forth the findings of fact and conclusions of law which constitute the grounds of its action. Requests for findings are not necessary for purposes of review. Findings of fact, whether based on oral or documentary evidence, shall not be set aside unless clearly erroneous, and due regard shall be given to the opportunity of the trial court to judge of the credibility of the witnesses. The findings of a master, to the extent that the court adopts them, shall be considered as the findings of the court. It will be sufficient if the findings of fact and conclusions of law are stated orally and recorded in open court following the close of the evidence or appear in an opinion or memorandum of decision filed by the court. Findings of fact and conclusions of law are unnecessary on decisions of motions under Rule 12 or 56 or any other motion except as provided in subdivision (c) of this rule.

(b) Amendment. On a party's motion filed no later than 10 days after entry of judgment, the court may amend its findings–or make additional findings–and may amend the judgment accordingly. The motion may accompany a motion for a new trial under Rule 59. When findings of fact are made in actions tried without a jury, the sufficiency of the evidence supporting the findings may be later questioned whether or not in the district court the party raising the question objected to the findings, moved to amend them, or moved for partial findings.

(c) Judgment on Partial Findings. If during a trial without a jury a party has been fully heard on an issue and the court finds against the party on that issue, the court may enter judgment as a matter of law against that party with respect to a claim or defense that cannot under the controlling law be maintained or defeated without a favorable finding on that issue, or the court may decline to render any judgment until the close of all the evidence. Such a judgment shall be supported by findings of fact and conclusions of law as required by subdivision (a) of this rule.

RULE 53. Masters

(a) Appointment and Compensation. The court in which any action is pending may appoint a special master therein. As used in these rules, the word "master" includes a referee, an auditor, an examiner, and an assessor. The compensation to be allowed to a master shall be fixed by the court, and shall be charged upon such of the parties or paid out of any fund or subject matter of the action, which is in the custody and control of the court as the court may direct; provided that this provision for compensation shall not apply when a United States magistrate judge is designated to serve as a master. The master shall not retain the master's report as security for the master's compensation; but when the party ordered to pay the compensation allowed by the court does not pay it after notice and within the time prescribed by the court, the master is entitled to a writ of execution against the delinquent party.

(b) Reference. A reference to a master shall be the exception and not the rule. In actions to be tried by a jury, a reference shall be made only when the issues are complicated; in actions to be tried without a jury, save in matters of account and of difficult computation of damages, a reference shall be made only upon a showing that some exceptional condition requires it. Upon the consent of the parties, a magistrate judge may be designated to serve as a special master without regard to the provisions of this subdivision.

(c) Powers. The order of reference to the master may specify or limit the master's powers and may direct the master to report only upon particular issues or to do or perform particular acts or to receive and report evidence only and may fix the time and place for beginning and closing the hearings and for the filing of the master's report. Subject to the specifications and limitations stated in the order, the master has and shall exercise the power to regulate all proceedings in every hearing before the master and to do all acts and take all measures necessary or proper for the efficient performance of the master's duties under the order. The master may require the production before the master of evidence upon all matters embraced in the reference, including the production of all books, papers, vouchers, documents, and writings applicable thereto. The master may rule upon the admissibility of evidence unless otherwise directed by the order of reference and has the authority to put witnesses on oath and may examine them and may call the parties to the action and examine them upon oath. When a party so requests, the master shall make a record of the evidence offered and excluded in the same manner and subject to the same limitations as provided in the Federal Rules of Evidence for a court sitting without a jury.

(d) Proceedings.

(1) *Meetings.* When a reference is made, the clerk shall forthwith furnish the master with a copy of the order of reference. Upon receipt thereof unless the order of reference otherwise provides, the master shall forthwith set a time and place for the first meeting of the parties or their attorneys to be held within 20 days after the date of the order of reference and shall notify the parties or their attorneys. It is the duty of the master to proceed with all reasonable diligence. Either party, on notice to the parties and master, may apply to the court for an order requiring the master to speed the proceedings and to make the report. If a party fails to appear at the time and place appointed, the master may proceed ex parte or, in the master's discretion, adjourn the proceedings to a future day, giving notice to the absent party of the adjournment.

(2) *Witnesses.* The parties may procure the attendance of witnesses before the master by the issuance and service of subpoenas as provided in Rule 45. If without adequate excuse a witness fails to appear or give evidence, the witness may be punished as for a contempt and be subjected to the consequences, penalties, and remedies provided in Rules 37 and 45.

(3) *Statement of Accounts.* When matters of accounting are in issue before the master, the master may prescribe the form in which the accounts shall be submitted and in any proper case may require or receive in evidence a statement by a certified public accountant who is called as a witness. Upon objection of a party to any of the items thus submitted or upon a showing that the form of statement is insufficient, the master may require a different form of statement to be furnished, or the accounts or specific items thereof to be proved by oral examination of the accounting parties or upon written interrogatories or in such other manner as the master directs.

(e) Report.

(1) *Contents and Filing.* The master shall prepare a report upon the matters submitted to the master by the order of reference and, if required to make findings of fact and conclusions of law, the master shall set them forth in the report. The master shall file the report with the clerk of the court and serve on all parties notice of the filing. In an action to be tried without a jury, unless otherwise directed by the order of reference, the master shall file with the report a transcript of the proceedings and of the evidence and the original exhibits. Unless otherwise directed by the order of reference, the master shall serve a copy of the report on each party.

(2) *In Non-Jury Actions.* In an action to be tried without a jury the court shall accept the master's findings of fact unless clearly erroneous. Within 10 days after being served with notice of the filing of the report any party may serve written objections thereto upon the other parties. Application to the court for action upon the report and upon objections thereto shall be by motion and upon notice as prescribed in Rule 6(d). The court after hearing may adopt the report or may modify it or may reject it in whole or in part or may receive further evidence or may recommit it with instructions.

(3) *In Jury Actions.* In an action to be tried by a jury the master shall not be directed to report the evidence. The master's findings upon the issues submitted to the master are admissible as evidence of the matters found and may be read to the jury, subject to the ruling of the court upon any objections in point of law which may be made to the report.

(4) *Stipulation as to Findings.* The effect of a master's report is the same whether or not the parties have consented to the reference; but, when the parties stipulate that a master's findings of fact shall be final, only questions of law arising upon the report shall thereafter be considered.

(5) *Draft Report.* Before filing the master's report a master may submit a draft thereof to counsel for all parties for the purpose of receiving their suggestions.

(f) Application to Magistrate Judge. A magistrate judge is subject to this rule only when the order referring a matter to the magistrate judge expressly provides that the reference is made under this rule.

VII
JUDGMENT

RULE 54. Judgments; Costs

(a) Definition; Form. "Judgment" as used in these rules includes a decree and any order from which an appeal lies. A judgment shall not contain a recital of pleadings, the report of a master, or the record of prior proceedings.

(b) Judgment Upon Multiple Claims or Involving Multiple Parties. When more than one claim for relief is presented in an action, whether as a claim, counterclaim, cross-claim, or third-party claim, or when multiple parties are involved, the court may direct the entry of a final judgment as to one or more but fewer than all of the claims or parties only upon an express determination that there is no just reason for delay and upon an express direction for the entry of judgment. In the absence of such determination and direction, any order or other form of decision, however designated, which adjudicates fewer than all the claims or the rights and liabilities of fewer than all the parties shall not terminate the action as to any of the claims or parties, and the order or other form of decision is subject to revision at any time before the entry of judgment adjudicating all the claims and the rights and liabilities of all the parties.

(c) Demand for Judgment. A judgment by default shall not be different in kind from or exceed in amount that prayed for in the demand for judgment. Except as to a party against whom a judgment is entered by default, every final judgment shall grant the relief to which the party in whose favor it is rendered is entitled, even if the party has not demanded such relief in the party's pleadings.

(d) Costs; Attorneys' Fees.

(1) *Costs Other than Attorneys' Fees.* Except when express provision therefor is made either in a statute of the United States or in these rules, costs other than attorneys' fees shall be allowed as of course to the prevailing party unless the court otherwise directs; but costs against the United States, its officers, and agencies shall be imposed only to the extent permitted by law. Such costs may be taxed by the clerk on one day's notice. On motion served within 5 days thereafter, the action of the clerk may be reviewed by the court.

(2) *Attorneys' Fees.*

(A) Claims for attorneys' fees and related nontaxable expenses shall be made by motion unless the substantive law governing the action provides for the recovery of such fees as an element of damages to be proved at trial.

(B) Unless otherwise provided by statute or order of the court, the motion must be filed no later than 14 days after entry of judgment; must specify the judgment and the statute, rule, or other grounds entitling the moving party to the award; and must state the amount or provide a fair estimate of the amount sought. If directed by the court, the motion shall also disclose the terms of any agreement with respect to fees to be paid for the services for which claim is made.

(C) On request of a party or class member, the court shall afford an opportunity for adversary submissions with respect to the motion in accordance with Rule 43(e) or Rule 78. The court may determine issues of liability for fees before receiving submissions bearing on issues of evaluation of services for which liability is imposed by the court. The court shall find the facts and state its conclusions of law as provided in Rule 52(a).

(D) By local rule the court may establish special procedures by which issues relating to such fees may be resolved without extensive evidentiary hearings. In addition, the court may refer issues relating to the value of services to a special master under Rule 53 without regard to the provisions of subdivision (b) thereof and may refer a motion for attorneys' fees to a magistrate judge under Rule 72(b) as if it were a dispositive pretrial matter.

(E) The provisions of subparagraphs (A) through (D) do not apply to claims for fees and expenses as sanctions for violations of these rules or under 28 U.S.C. § 1927.

RULE 55. Default

(a) Entry. When a party against whom a judgment for affirmative relief is sought has failed to plead or otherwise defend as provided by these rules and that fact is made to appear by affidavit or otherwise, the clerk shall enter the party's default.

(b) Judgment. Judgment by default may be entered as follows:

(1) *By the Clerk.* When the plaintiff's claim against a defendant is for a sum certain or for a sum which can by computation be made certain, the clerk upon request of the plaintiff and upon affidavit of the amount due shall enter judgment for that amount and costs against the defendant, if the defendant has been defaulted for failure to appear and is not an infant or incompetent person.

(2) *By the Court.* In all other cases the party entitled to a judgment by default shall apply to the court therefor; but no judgment by default shall be entered against an infant or incompetent person unless represented in the action by a general guardian, committee, conservator, or other such representative who has appeared

therein. If the party against whom judgment by default is sought has appeared in the action, the party (or, if appearing by representative, the party's representative) shall be served with written notice of the application for judgment at least 3 days prior to the hearing on such application. If, in order to enable the court to enter judgment or to carry it into effect, it is necessary to take an account or to determine the amount of damages or to establish the truth of any averment by evidence or to make an investigation of any other matter, the court may conduct such hearings or order such references as it deems necessary and proper and shall accord a right of trial by jury to the parties when and as required by any statute of the United States.

(c) Setting Aside Default. For good cause shown the court may set aside an entry of default and, if a judgment by default has been entered, may likewise set it aside in accordance with Rule 60(b).

(d) Plaintiffs, Counterclaimants, Cross-Claimants. The provisions of this rule apply whether the party entitled to the judgment by default is a plaintiff, a third-party plaintiff, or a party who has pleaded a cross-claim or counterclaim. In all cases a judgment by default is subject to the limitations of Rule 54(c).

(e) Judgment Against the United States. No judgment by default shall be entered against the United States or an officer or agency thereof unless the claimant establishes a claim or right to relief by evidence satisfactory to the court.

RULE 56. Summary Judgment

(a) For Claimant. A party seeking to recover upon a claim, counterclaim, or cross-claim or to obtain a declaratory judgment may, at any time after the expiration of 20 days from the commencement of the action or after service of a motion for summary judgment by the adverse party, move with or without supporting affidavits for a summary judgment in the party's favor upon all or any part thereof.

(b) For Defending Party. A party against whom a claim, counterclaim, or cross-claim is asserted or a declaratory judgment is sought may, at any time, move with or without supporting affidavits for a summary judgment in the party's favor as to all or any part thereof.

(c) Motion and Proceedings Thereon. The motion shall be served at least 10 days before the time fixed for the hearing. The adverse party prior to the day of hearing may serve opposing affidavits. The judgment sought shall be rendered forthwith if the pleadings, depositions, answers to interrogatories, and admissions on file, together with the affidavits, if any, show that there is no genuine issue as to any material fact and that the moving party is entitled to a judgment as a matter of law. A summary judgment, interlocutory in character, may be rendered on the issue of liability alone although there is a genuine issue as to the amount of damages.

(d) Case Not Fully Adjudicated on Motion. If on motion under this rule judgment is not rendered upon the whole case or for all the relief asked and a trial is necessary, the court at the hearing of the motion, by examining the pleadings and the evidence before it and by interrogating counsel, shall if practicable ascertain what material facts exist without substantial controversy and what material facts are actually and in good faith controverted. It shall thereupon make an order specifying the facts that appear without substantial controversy, including the extent to which the amount of damages or other relief is not in controversy, and directing such further proceedings in the action as are just. Upon the trial of the action the facts so specified shall be deemed established, and the trial shall be conducted accordingly.

(e) Form of Affidavits; Further Testimony; Defense Required. Supporting and opposing affidavits shall be made on personal knowledge, shall set forth such facts as would be admissible in evidence, and shall show affirmatively that the affiant is competent to testify to the matters stated therein. Sworn or certified copies of all papers or parts thereof referred to in an affidavit shall be attached thereto or served therewith. The court may permit affidavits to be supplemented or opposed by depositions, answers to interrogatories, or further affidavits. When a motion for summary judgment is made and supported as provided in this rule, an adverse party may not rest upon the mere allegations or denials of the adverse party's pleading, but the adverse party's response, by affidavits or as otherwise provided in this rule, must set forth specific facts showing that there is a genuine issue for trial. If the adverse party does not so respond, summary judgment, if appropriate, shall be entered against the adverse party.

(f) When Affidavits are Unavailable. Should it appear from the affidavits of a party opposing the motion that the party cannot for reasons stated present by affidavit facts essential to justify the party's opposition, the court may refuse the application for judgment or may order a continuance to permit affidavits to be obtained or depositions to be taken or discovery to be had or may make such other order as is just.

(g) Affidavits Made in Bad Faith. Should it appear to the satisfaction of the court at any time that any of the affidavits presented pursuant to this rule are presented in bad faith or solely for the purpose of delay, the court shall forthwith order the party employing them to pay to the other party the amount of the reasonable expenses which the filing of the affidavits caused the other party to incur, including reasonable attorney's fees, and any offending party or attorney may be adjudged guilty of contempt.

RULE 57. Declaratory Judgments

The procedure for obtaining a declaratory judgment pursuant to Title 28, U.S.C. § 2201, shall be in accordance with these rules, and the right to trial by jury may be demanded under the circumstances and in the manner provided in Rules 38 and 39. The existence of another adequate remedy does not preclude a judgment for declaratory relief in cases where it is appropriate. The court may order a speedy hearing of an action for a declaratory judgment and may advance it on the calendar.

RULE 58. Entry of Judgment

(a) Separate Document.

(1) Every judgment and amended judgment must be set forth on a separate document, but a separate document is not required for an order disposing of a motion:

(A) for judgment under Rule 50(b);

(B) to amend or make additional findings of fact under Rule 52(b);

(C) for attorney fees under Rule 54;

(D) for a new trial, or to alter or amend the judgment, under Rule 59; or

(E) for relief under Rule 60.

(2) Subject to Rule 54(b):

(A) unless the court orders otherwise, the clerk must, without awaiting the court's direction, promptly prepare, sign, and enter the judgment when:

(i) the jury returns a general verdict,

(ii) the court awards only costs or a sum certain, or

(iii) the court denies all relief;

(B) the court must promptly approve the form of the judgment, which the clerk must promptly enter, when:

(i) the jury returns a special verdict or a general verdict accompanied by interrogatories, or

(ii) the court grants other relief not described in Rule 58(a)(2).

(b) Time of Entry. Judgment is entered for purposes of these rules:

(1) if Rule 58(a)(1) does not require a separate document, when it is entered in the civil docket under Rule 79(a), and

(2) if Rule 58(a)(1) requires a separate document, when it is entered in the civil docket under Rule 79(a) and when the earlier of these events occurs:

(A) when it is set forth on a separate document, or

(B) when 150 days have run from entry in the civil docket under Rule 79(a).

(c) Cost or Fee Awards.

(1) Entry of judgment may not be delayed, nor the time for appeal extended, in order to tax costs or award fees, except as provided in Rule 58(c)(2).

(2) When a timely motion for attorney fees is made under Rule 54(d)(2), the court may act before a notice of appeal has been filed and has become effective to order that the motion have the same effect under Federal Rule of Appellate Procedure 4(a)(4) as a timely motion under Rule 59.

(d) Request for Entry. A party may request that judgment be set forth on a separate document as required by Rule 58(a)(1).

RULE 59. New Trials; Amendment of Judgments

(a) Grounds. A new trial may be granted to all or any of the parties and on all or part of the issues

(1) in an action in which there has been a trial by jury, for any of the reasons for which new trials have heretofore been granted in actions at law in the courts of the United States; and

(2) in an action tried without a jury, for any of the reasons for which rehearings have heretofore been granted in suits in equity in the courts of the United States.

On a motion for a new trial in an action tried without a jury, the court may open the judgment if one has been entered, take additional testimony, amend findings of fact and conclusions of law or make new findings and conclusions, and direct the entry of a new judgment.

(b) Time for Motion. Any motion for a new trial shall be filed no later than 10 days after entry of the judgment.

(c) Time for Serving Affidavits. When a motion for new trial is based on affidavits, they shall be filed with the motion. The opposing party has 10 days after service to file opposing affidavits, but that period may be extended for up to 20 days, either by the court for good cause or by the parties' written stipulation. The court may permit reply affidavits.

(d) On Court's Initiative; Notice; Specifying Grounds. No later than 10 days after entry of judgment the court, on its own, may order a new trial for any reason that would justify granting one on a party's motion. After giving the parties notice and an opportunity to be heard, the court may grant a timely motion for a new trial for a reason not stated in the motion. When granting a new trial on its own initiative or for a reason not stated in a motion, the court shall specify the grounds in its order.

(e) Motion to Alter or Amend Judgment. Any motion to alter or amend a judgment shall be filed no later than 10 days after entry of the judgment.

RULE 60. Relief From Judgment or Order

(a) Clerical Mistakes. Clerical mistakes in judgments, orders or other parts of the record and errors therein arising from oversight or omission may be corrected by the court at any time of its own initiative or on the motion of any party and after such notice, if any, as the court orders. During the pendency of an appeal, such mistakes may be so corrected before the appeal is docketed in the appellate court, and thereafter while the appeal is pending may be so corrected with leave of the appellate court.

(b) Mistakes; Inadvertence; Excusable Neglect; Newly Discovered Evidence; Fraud, Etc. On motion and upon such terms as are just, the court may relieve a party or a party's legal representative from a final judgment, order, or proceeding for the following reasons:

(1) mistake, inadvertence, surprise, or excusable neglect;

(2) newly discovered evidence which by due diligence could not have been discovered in time to move for a new trial under Rule 59(b);

(3) fraud (whether heretofore denominated intrinsic or extrinsic), misrepresentation, or other misconduct of an adverse party;

(4) the judgment is void;

(5) the judgment has been satisfied, released, or discharged, or a prior judgment upon which it is based has been reversed or otherwise vacated, or it is no longer equitable that the judgment should have prospective application; or

(6) any other reason justifying relief from the operation of the judgment.

The motion shall be made within a reasonable time, and for reasons (1), (2), and (3) not more than one year after the judgment, order, or proceeding was entered or taken. A motion under this subdivision (b) does not affect the finality of a judgment or suspend its operation. This rule does not limit the power of a court to entertain an independent action to relieve a party from a judgment, order, or proceeding, or to grant relief to a defendant not actually personally notified as provided in Title 28, U.S.C. § 1655, or to set aside a judgment for fraud upon the court. Writs of coram nobis, coram vobis, audita querela, and bills of review and bills in the nature of a bill of review, are abolished, and the procedure for obtaining any relief from a judgment shall be by motion as prescribed in these rules or by an independent action.

RULE 61. Harmless Error

No error in either the admission or the exclusion of evidence and no error or defect in any ruling or order or in anything done or omitted by the court or by any of the parties is ground for granting a new trial or for setting aside a verdict or for vacating, modifying, or otherwise disturbing a judgment or order, unless refusal to take such action appears to the court inconsistent with substantial justice. The court at every stage of the proceeding must disregard any error or defect in the proceeding which does not affect the substantial rights of the parties.

RULE 62. Stay of Proceedings to Enforce a Judgment

(a) Automatic Stay; Exceptions–Injunctions, Re-ceiverships, **and Patent Accountings.** Except as stated herein, no execution shall issue upon a judgment nor shall proceedings be taken for its enforcement until the expiration of 10 days after its entry. Unless otherwise ordered by the court, an interlocutory or final judgment in an action for an injunction or in a receivership action, or a judgment or order directing an accounting in an action for infringement of letters patent, shall not be stayed during the period after its entry and until an appeal is taken or during the pendency of an appeal. The provisions of subdivision (c) of this rule govern the suspending, modifying, restoring, or granting of an injunction during the pendency of an appeal.

(b) Stay on Motion for New Trial or for Judgment. In its discretion and on such conditions for the security of the adverse party as are proper, the court may stay the execution of or any proceedings to enforce a judgment pending the disposition of a motion for a new trial or to alter or amend a judgment made pursuant to Rule 59, or of a motion for relief from a judgment or order made pursuant to Rule 60, or of a motion for judgment in accordance with a motion for a directed verdict made pursuant to Rule 50, or of a motion for amendment to the findings or for additional findings made pursuant to Rule 52(b).

(c) Injunction Pending Appeal. When an appeal is taken from an interlocutory or final judgment granting, dissolving, or denying an injunction, the court in its discretion may suspend, modify, restore, or grant an injunction during the pendency of the appeal upon such terms as to bond or otherwise as it considers proper for the security of the rights of the adverse party. If the judgment appealed from is rendered by a district court of three judges specially constituted pursuant to a statute of the United States, no such order shall be made except

(1) by such court sitting in open court or

(2) by the assent of all the judges of such court evidenced by their signatures to the order.

(d) Stay Upon Appeal. When an appeal is taken the appellant by giving a supersedeas bond may obtain a stay subject to the exceptions contained in subdivision (a) of this rule. The bond may be given at or after the time of filing the notice of appeal or of procuring the order allowing the appeal, as the case may be. The stay is effective when the supersedeas bond is approved by the court.

(e) Stay in Favor of the United States or Agency Thereof. When an appeal is taken by the United States or an officer or agency thereof or by direction of any department of the Government of the United States and the operation or enforcement of the judgment is stayed, no bond, obligation, or other security shall be required from the appellant.

(f) Stay According to State Law. In any state in which a judgment is a lien upon the property of the judgment debtor and in which the judgment debtor is entitled to a stay of execution, a judgment debtor is entitled, in the district court held therein, to such stay as would be accorded the judgment debtor had the action been maintained in the courts of that state.

(g) Power of Appellate Court Not Limited. The provisions in this rule do not limit any power of an appellate court or of a judge or justice thereof to stay proceedings during the pendency of an appeal or to suspend, modify, restore, or grant an injunction during the pendency of an appeal or to make any order appropriate to preserve the status quo or the effectiveness of the judgment subsequently to be entered.

(h) Stay of Judgment as to Multiple Claims or Multiple Parties. When a court has ordered a final judgment under the conditions stated in Rule 54(b), the court may stay enforcement of that judgment until the entering of a subsequent judgment or judgments and may prescribe such conditions as are necessary to secure the benefit thereof to the party in whose favor the judgment is entered.

RULE 63. Inability of a Judge to Proceed

If a trial or hearing has been commenced and the judge is unable to proceed, any other judge may proceed with it upon certifying familiarity with the record and determining that the proceedings in the case may be completed without prejudice to the parties. In a hearing or trial without a jury, the successor judge shall at the request of a party recall any witness whose testimony is material and disputed and who is available to testify again without undue burden. The successor judge may also recall any other witness.

VIII
PROVISIONAL AND FINAL REMEDIES

RULE 64. Seizure of Person or Property

At the commencement of and during the course of an action, all remedies providing for seizure of person or property for the purpose of securing satisfaction of the judgment ultimately to be entered in the action are available under the circumstances and in the manner provided by the law of the state in which the district court is held, existing at the time the remedy is sought, subject to the following qualifications:

(1) any existing statute of the United States governs to the extent to which it is applicable;

(2) the action in which any of the foregoing remedies is used shall be commenced and prosecuted or, if removed from a state court, shall be prosecuted after removal, pursuant to these rules.

The remedies thus available include arrest, attachment, garnishment, replevin, sequestration, and other corres-

ponding or equivalent remedies, however designated and regardless of whether by state procedure the remedy is ancillary to an action or must be obtained by an independent action.

RULE 65. Injunctions

(a) Preliminary Injunction.

(1) *Notice.* No preliminary injunction shall be issued without notice to the adverse party.

(2) *Consolidation of Hearing With Trial on Merits.* Before or after the commencement of the hearing of an application for a preliminary injunction, the court may order the trial of the action on the merits to be advanced and consolidated with the hearing of the application. Even when this consolidation is not ordered, any evidence received upon an application for a preliminary injunction which would be admissible upon the trial on the merits becomes part of the record on the trial and need not be repeated upon the trial. This subdivision (a)(2) shall be so construed and applied as to save to the parties any rights they may have to trial by jury.

(b) Temporary Restraining Order; Notice; Hearing; Duration. A temporary restraining order may be granted without written or oral notice to the adverse party or that party's attorney only if

(1) it clearly appears from specific facts shown by affidavit or by the verified complaint that immediate and irreparable injury, loss, or damage will result to the applicant before the adverse party or that party's attorney can be heard in opposition, and

(2) the applicant's attorney certifies to the court in writing the efforts, if any, which have been made to give the notice and the reasons supporting the claim that notice should not be required.

Every temporary restraining order granted without notice shall be indorsed with the date and hour of issuance; shall be filed forthwith in the clerk's office and entered of record; shall define the injury and state why it is irreparable and why the order was granted without notice; and shall expire by its terms within such time after entry, not to exceed 10 days, as the court fixes, unless within the time so fixed the order, for good cause shown, is extended for a like period or unless the party against whom the order is directed consents that it may be extended for a longer period. The reasons for the extension shall be entered of record. In case a temporary restraining order is granted without notice, the motion for a preliminary injunction shall be set down for hearing at the earliest possible time and takes precedence of all matters except older matters of the same character; and when the motion comes on for hearing the party who obtained the temporary restraining order shall proceed with the application for a preliminary injunction and, if the party does not do so, the court shall dissolve the temporary restraining order. On 2 days' notice to the party who obtained the temporary restraining order without notice or on such shorter notice to that party as the court may prescribe, the adverse party may appear and move its dissolution or modification and in that event the court shall proceed to hear and determine such motion as expeditiously as the ends of justice require.

(c) Security. No restraining order or preliminary injunction shall issue except upon the giving of security by the applicant, in such sum as the court deems proper, for the payment of such costs and damages as may be incurred or suffered by any party who is found to have been wrongfully enjoined or restrained. No such security shall be required of the United States or of an officer or agency thereof.

The provisions of Rule 65.1 apply to a surety upon a bond or undertaking under this rule.

(d) Form and Scope of Injunction or Restraining Order. Every order granting an injunction and every restraining order shall set forth the reasons for its issuance; shall be specific in terms; shall describe in reasonable detail, and not by reference to the complaint or other document, the act or acts sought to be restrained; and is binding only upon the parties to the action, their officers, agents, servants, employees, and attorneys, and upon those persons in active concert or participation with them who receive actual notice of the order by personal service or otherwise.

(e) Employer and Employee; Interpleader; Constitutional Cases. These rules do not modify any statute of the United States relating to temporary restraining orders and preliminary injunctions in actions affecting employer and employee; or the provisions of Title 28, U.S.C. § 2361, relating to preliminary injunctions in actions of interpleader or in the nature of interpleader; or Title 28, U.S.C. § 2284, relating to actions required by Act of Congress to be heard and determined by a district court of three judges.

(f) Copyright Impoundment. This rule applies to copyright impoundment proceedings.

RULE 65.1. Security: Proceedings Against Sureties

Whenever these rules, including the Supplemental Rules for Certain Admiralty and Maritime Claims, require or permit the giving of security by a party, and security is given in the form of a bond or stipulation or other undertaking with one or more sureties, each surety submits to the jurisdiction of the court and irrevocably appoints the clerk of the court as the surety's agent upon whom any papers affecting the surety's liability on the bond or undertaking may be served. The surety's liability may be enforced on motion without the necessity of an independent action. The motion and such notice of the motion as the court prescribes may be served on the clerk of the court, who shall forthwith mail copies to the sureties if their addresses are known.

RULE 66. Receivers Appointed by Federal Courts

An action wherein a receiver has been appointed shall not be dismissed except by order of the court. The practice in the administration of estates by receivers or by other similar officers appointed by the court shall be in accordance with the practice heretofore followed in the courts of the United States or as provided in rules promulgated by the district courts. In all other respects the action in which the appointment of a receiver is sought or which is brought by or against a receiver is governed by these rules.

RULE 67. Deposit in Court

In an action in which any part of the relief sought is a judgment for a sum of money or the disposition of a sum of money or the disposition of any other thing capable of delivery, a party, upon notice to every other party, and by leave of court, may deposit with the court all or any part of such sum or thing, whether or not that party claims all or any part of the sum or thing. The party making the deposit shall serve the order permitting deposit on the clerk of the court. Money paid into court under this rule shall be deposited and withdrawn in accordance with the provisions of Title 28, U.S.C. §§ 2041, and 2042; the Act of June 26, 1934, c. 756, § 23, as amended (48 Stat. 1236, 58 Stat. 845), U.S.C., Title 31, § 725v; or any like statute. The fund shall be deposited in an interest-bearing account or invested in an interest-bearing instrument approved by the court.

RULE 68. Offer of Judgment

At any time more than 10 days before the trial begins, a party defending against a claim may serve upon the adverse party an offer to allow judgment to be taken against the defending party for the money or property or to the effect specified in the offer, with costs then accrued. If within 10 days after the service of the offer the adverse party serves written notice that the offer is accepted, either party may then file the offer and notice of acceptance together with proof of service thereof and thereupon the clerk shall enter judgment. An offer not accepted shall be deemed withdrawn and evidence thereof is not admissible except in a proceeding to determine costs. If the judgment finally obtained by the offeree is not more favorable than the offer, the offeree must pay the costs incurred after the making of the offer. The fact that an offer is made but not accepted does not preclude a subsequent offer. When the liability of one party to another has been determined by verdict or order or judgment, but the amount or extent of the liability remains to be determined by further proceedings, the party adjudged liable may make an offer of judgment, which shall have the same effect as an offer made before trial if it is served within a reasonable time not less than 10 days prior to the commencement of hearings to determine the amount or extent of liability.

RULE 69. Execution

(a) In General. Process to enforce a judgment for the payment of money shall be a writ of execution, unless the court directs otherwise. The procedure on execution, in proceedings supplementary to and in aid of a judgment, and in proceedings on and in aid of execution shall be in accordance with the practice and procedure of the state in which the district court is held, existing at the time the remedy is sought, except that any statute of the United States governs to the extent that it is applicable. In aid of the judgment or execution, the judgment creditor or a successor in interest when that interest appears of record, may obtain discovery from any person, including the judgment debtor, in the manner provided in these rules or in the manner provided by the practice of the state in which the district court is held.

(b) Against Certain Public Officers. When a judgment has been entered against a collector or other officer of revenue under the circumstances stated in Title 28, U.S.C. § 2006, or against an officer of Congress in an action mentioned in the Act of March 3, 1875, ch. 130, § 8 (18 Stat. 401), U.S.C., Title 2, § 118, and when the court has given the certificate of probable cause for the officer's act as provided in those statutes, execution shall not issue against the officer or the officer's property but the final judgment shall be satisfied as provided in such statutes.

RULE 70. Judgment for Specific Acts; Vesting Title

If a judgment directs a party to execute a conveyance of land or to deliver deeds or other documents or to perform any other specific act and the party fails to comply within the time specified, the court may direct the act to be done at the cost of the disobedient party by some other person appointed by the court and the act when so done has like effect as if done by the party. On application of the party entitled to performance, the clerk shall issue a writ of attachment or sequestration against the property of the disobedient party to compel obedience to the judgment. The court may also in proper cases adjudge the party in contempt. If real or personal property is within the district, the court in lieu of directing a conveyance thereof may enter a judgment divesting the title of any party and vesting it in others and such judgment has the effect of a conveyance executed in due form of law. When any order or judgment is for the delivery of possession, the party in whose favor it is entered is entitled to a writ of execution or assistance upon application to the clerk.

RULE 71. Process in Behalf of and Against Persons Not Parties

When an order is made in favor of a person who is not a party to the action, that person may enforce obedience to the order by the same process as if a party; and, when obedience to an order may be lawfully enforced against a person who is not a party, that person is liable to the same process for enforcing obedience to the order as if a party.

IX
APPEALS [Abrogated]

IX
SPECIAL PROCEEDINGS

RULE 71A. Condemnation of Property

(a) Applicability of Other Rules. The Rules of Civil Procedure for the United States District Courts govern the procedure for the condemnation of real and personal property under the power of eminent domain, except as otherwise provided in this rule.

(b) Joinder of Properties. The plaintiff may join in the same action one or more separate pieces of property, whether in the same or different ownership and whether or not sought for the same use.

(c) Complaint.

(1) *Caption.* The complaint shall contain a caption as provided in Rule 10(a), except that the plaintiff shall name as defendants the property, designated generally by kind, quantity, and location, and at least one of the owners of some part of or interest in the property.

(2) *Contents.* The complaint shall contain a short and plain statement of the authority for the taking, the use for which the property is to be taken, a description of the property sufficient for its identification, the interests to be acquired, and as to each separate piece of property a designation of the defendants who have been joined as owners thereof or of some interest therein. Upon the commencement of the action, the plaintiff need join as defendants only the persons having or claiming an interest in the property whose names are then known, but prior to any hearing involving the compensation to be paid for a piece of property, the plaintiff shall add as defendants all persons having or claiming an interest in that property whose names can be ascertained by a reasonably diligent search of the records, considering the character and value of the property involved and the interests to be acquired, and also those whose names have otherwise been learned. All others may be made defendants under the designation "Unknown Owners." Process shall be served as provided in subdivision (d) of this rule upon all defendants, whether named as defendants at the time of the commencement of the

action or subsequently added, and a defendant may answer as provided in subdivision (e) of this rule. The court meanwhile may order such distribution of a deposit as the facts warrant.

(3) *Filing.* In addition to filing the complaint with the court, the plaintiff shall furnish to the clerk at least one copy thereof for the use of the defendants and additional copies at the request of the clerk or of a defendant.

(d) Process.

(1) *Notice; Delivery.* Upon the filing of the complaint the plaintiff shall forthwith deliver to the clerk joint or several notices directed to the defendants named or designated in the complaint. Additional notices directed to defendants subsequently added shall be so delivered. The delivery of the notice and its service have the same effect as the delivery and service of the summons under Rule 4.

(2) *Same; Form.* Each notice shall state the court, the title of the action, the name of the defendant to whom it is directed, that the action is to condemn property, a description of the defendant's property sufficient for its identification, the interest to be taken, the authority for the taking, the uses for which the property is to be taken, that the defendant may serve upon the plaintiff's attorney an answer within 20 days after service of the notice, and that the failure so to serve an answer constitutes a consent to the taking and to the authority of the court to proceed to hear the action and to fix the compensation. The notice shall conclude with the name of the plaintiff's attorney and an address within the district in which action is brought where the attorney may be served. The notice need contain a description of no other property than that to be taken from the defendants to whom it is directed.

(3) *Service of Notice.*

(A) Personal Service. Personal service of the notice (but without copies of the complaint) shall be made in accordance with Rule 4 upon a defendant whose residence is known and who resides within the United States or a territory subject to the administrative or judicial jurisdiction of the United States.

(B) Service by Publication. Upon the filing of a certificate of the plaintiff's attorney stating that the attorney believes a defendant cannot be personally served, because after diligent inquiry within the state in which the complaint is filed the defendant's place of residence cannot be ascertained by the plaintiff or, if ascertained, that it is beyond the territorial limits of personal service as provided in this rule, service of the notice shall be made on this defendant by publication in a newspaper published in the county where the property is located, or if there is no such newspaper, then in a newspaper having a general circulation where the property is located, once a week for not less than three successive weeks. Prior to the last publication, a copy of the notice shall also be mailed to a defendant who cannot be personally served as provided in this rule but whose place of residence is then known. Unknown owners may be served by publication in like manner by a notice addressed to "Unknown Owners." Service by publication is complete upon the date of the last publication. Proof of publication and mailing shall be made by certificate of the plaintiff's attorney, to which shall be attached a printed copy of the published notice with the name and dates of the newspaper marked thereon.

(4) *Return; Amendment.* Proof of service of the notice shall be made and amendment of the notice or proof of its service allowed in the manner provided for the return and amendment of the summons under Rule 4.

(e) Appearance or Answer. If a defendant has no objection or defense to the taking of the defendant's property, the defendant may serve a notice of appearance designating the property in which the defendant claims to be interested. Thereafter, the defendant shall receive notice of all proceedings affecting it. If a defendant has any objection or defense to the taking of the property, the defendant shall serve an answer within 20 days after the service of notice upon the defendant. The answer shall identify the property in which the defendant claims to have an interest, state the nature and extent of the interest claimed, and state all the defendant's objections and defenses to the taking of the property. A defendant waives all defenses and objections not so presented, but at the trial of the issue of just compensation, whether or not the defendant has previously appeared or answered, the defendant may present evidence as to the amount of the compensation to be paid for the property, and the defendant may share in the distribution of the award. No other pleading or motion asserting any additional defense or objection shall be allowed.

(f) Amendment of Pleadings. Without leave of court, the plaintiff may amend the complaint at any time before the trial of the issue of compensation and as many times as desired, but no amendment shall be made which will result in a dismissal forbidden by subdivision (i) of this rule. The plaintiff need not serve a copy of an amendment, but shall serve notice of the filing, as provided in Rule 5(b), upon any party affected thereby who has appeared and, in the manner provided in subdivision (d) of this rule, upon any party affected thereby who has not appeared. The plaintiff shall furnish to the clerk of the court for the use of the defendants at least one copy of each amendment and shall furnish additional copies on the request of the clerk or of a defendant. Within the time allowed by subdivision (e) of this rule a defendant may serve an answer to the amended pleading, in the form and manner and with the same effect as there provided.

(g) Substitution of Parties. If a defendant dies or becomes incompetent or transfers an interest after the defendant's joinder, the court may order substitution of the proper party upon motion and notice of hearing. If the motion and notice of hearing are to be served upon a person not already a party, service shall be made as provided in subdivision (d)(3) of this rule.

(h) Trial. If the action involves the exercise of the power of eminent domain under the law of the United States, any tribunal specially constituted by an Act of Congress governing the case for the trial of the issue of just compensation shall be the tribunal for the determination of that issue; but if there is no such specially constituted tribunal any party may have a trial by jury of the issue of just compensation by filing a demand therefor within the time allowed for answer or within such further time as the court may fix, unless the court in its discretion orders that, because of the character, location, or quantity of the property to be condemned, or for other reasons in the interest of justice, the issue of compensation shall be determined by a commission of three persons appointed by it.

In the event that a commission is appointed the court may direct that not more than two additional persons serve as alternate commissioners to hear the case and replace commissioners who, prior to the time when a decision is filed, are found by the court to be unable or disqualified to perform their duties. An alternate who does not replace a regular commissioner shall be discharged after the commission renders its final decision. Before appointing the members of the commission and alternates the court shall advise the parties of the identity and qualifications of each prospective commissioner and alternate and may permit the parties to examine each such designee. The parties shall not be permitted or required by the court to suggest nominees. Each party shall have the right to object for valid cause to the appointment of any person as a commissioner or alternate. If a commission is appointed it shall have the powers of a master provided in subdivision (c) of Rule 53 and proceedings before it shall be governed by the provisions of paragraphs (1) and (2) of subdivision (d) of Rule 53. Its action and report shall be determined by a majority and its findings and report shall have the effect, and be dealt with by the court in accordance with the practice, prescribed in paragraph (2) of subdivision (e) of Rule 53. Trial of all issues shall otherwise be by the court.

(i) Dismissal of Action.

(1) *As of Right.* If no hearing has begun to determine the compensation to be paid for a piece of property and the plaintiff has not acquired the title or a lesser interest in or taken possession, the plaintiff may dismiss the action as to that property, without an order of the court, by filing a notice of dismissal setting forth a brief description of the property as to which the action is dismissed.

(2) *By Stipulation.* Before the entry of any judgment vesting the plaintiff with title or a lesser interest in or possession of property, the action may be dismissed in whole or in part, without an order of the court, as to any property by filing a stipulation of dismissal by the plaintiff and the defendant affected thereby; and, if the parties so stipulate, the court may vacate any judgment that has been entered.

(3) *By Order of the Court.* At any time before compensation for a piece of property has been determined and paid and after motion and hearing, the court may dismiss the action as to that property, except that it shall not dismiss the action as to any part of the property of which the plaintiff has taken possession or in which the plaintiff has taken title or a lesser interest, but shall award just compensation for the possession, title or lesser interest so taken. The court at any time may drop a defendant unnecessarily or improperly joined.

(4) *Effect.* Except as otherwise provided in the notice, or stipulation of dismissal, or order of the court, any dismissal is without prejudice.

(j) Deposit and its Distribution. The plaintiff shall deposit with the court any money required by law as a condition to the exercise of the power of eminent domain; and, although not so required, may make a deposit when permitted by statute. In such cases the court and attorneys shall expedite the proceedings for the distribution of the money so deposited and for the ascertainment and payment of just compensation. If the compensation finally awarded to any defendant exceeds the amount which has been paid to that defendant on distribution of the deposit, the court shall enter judgment against the plaintiff and in favor of that defendant for the deficiency. If the compensation finally awarded to any defendant is less than the amount which has been paid to that defendant, the court shall enter judgment against that defendant and in favor of the plaintiff for the overpayment.

(k) Condemnation Under a State's Power of Eminent Domain. The practice as herein prescribed governs in actions involving the exercise of the power of eminent domain under the law of a state, provided that if the state law makes provision for trial of any issue by jury, or for trial of the issue of compensation or both, that provision shall be followed.

(l) Costs. Costs are not subject to Rule 54(d).

RULE 72. Magistrate Judges; Pretrial Orders

(a) Nondispositive Matters. A magistrate judge to whom a pretrial matter not dispositive of a claim or defense of a party is referred to hear and determine shall promptly conduct such proceedings as are required and when appropriate enter into the record a written order setting forth the disposition of the matter. Within 10 days after being served with a copy of the magistrate judge's order, a party may serve and file objections to the order; a party may not thereafter assign as error a defect in the magistrate judge's order to which objection was not timely made. The district judge to whom the case is assigned shall consider such objections and shall modify or set aside any portion of the magistrate judge's order found to be clearly erroneous or contrary to law.

(b) Dispositive Motions and Prisoner Petitions. A magistrate judge assigned without consent of the parties to hear a pretrial matter dispositive of a claim or defense of a party or a prisoner petition challenging the conditions of confinement shall promptly conduct such proceedings as are required. A record shall be made of all evidentiary proceedings before the magistrate judge, and a record may be made of such other proceedings as the magistrate judge deems necessary. The magistrate judge shall enter into the record a recommendation for disposition of the matter, including proposed findings of fact when appropriate. The clerk shall forthwith mail copies to all parties.

A party objecting to the recommended disposition of the matter shall promptly arrange for the transcription of the record, or portions of it as all parties may agree upon or the magistrate judge deems sufficient, unless the district judge otherwise directs. Within 10 days after being served with a copy of the recommended disposition, a party may serve and file specific, written objections to the proposed findings and recommendations. A party may respond to another party's objections within 10 days after being served with a copy thereof. The district judge to whom the case is assigned shall make a de novo determination upon the record, or after additional evidence, of any portion of the magistrate judge's disposition to which specific written objection has been made in accordance with this rule. The district judge may accept, reject, or modify the recommended decision, receive further evidence, or recommit the matter to the magistrate judge with instructions.

RULE 73. Magistrate Judges; Trial by Consent and Appeal

(a) Powers; Procedure. When specially designated to exercise such jurisdiction by local rule or order of the district court and when all parties consent thereto, a magistrate judge may exercise the authority provided by Title 28, U.S.C. § 636(c) and may conduct any or all proceedings, including a jury or nonjury trial, in a civil case. A record of the proceedings shall be made in accordance with the requirements of Title 28, U.S.C. § 636(c)(5).

(b) Consent. When a magistrate judge has been designated to exercise civil trial jurisdiction, the clerk shall give written notice to the parties of their opportunity to consent to the exercise by a magistrate judge of civil jurisdiction over the case, as authorized by Title 28, U.S.C. § 636(c). If, within the period specified by local rule, the parties agree to a magistrate judge's exercise of such authority, they shall execute and file a joint form of consent or separate forms of consent setting forth such election.

A district judge, magistrate judge, or other court official may again advise the parties of the availability of the magistrate judge, but, in so doing, shall also advise the parties that they are free to withhold consent without adverse substantive consequences. A district judge or magistrate judge shall not be informed of a party's response to the clerk's notification, unless all parties have consented to the referral of the matter to a magistrate judge.

The district judge, for good cause shown on the judge's own initiative, or under extraordinary circumstances shown by a party, may vacate a reference of a civil matter to a magistrate judge under this subdivision.

(c) Appeal. In accordance with Title 28, U.S.C. § 636(c)(3), appeal from a judgment entered upon direction of a magistrate judge in proceedings under this rule will lie to the court of appeals as it would from a judgment of the district court.

(d) [Abrogated.]

RULE 74. [Abrogated.]

RULE 75. [Abrogated.]

RULE 76. [Abrogated.]

X
DISTRICT COURTS AND CLERKS

RULE 77. District Courts and Clerks

(a) District Courts Always Open. The district courts shall be deemed always open for the purpose of filing any pleading or other proper paper, of issuing and returning mesne and final process, and of making and directing all interlocutory motions, orders, and rules.

(b) Trials and Hearings; Orders in Chambers. All trials upon the merits shall be conducted in open court and so far as convenient in a regular court room. All other acts or proceedings may be done or conducted by a judge in chambers, without the attendance of the clerk or other court officials and at any place either within or without the district; but no hearing, other than one ex parte, shall be conducted outside the district without the consent of all parties affected thereby.

(c) Clerk's Office and Orders by Clerk. The clerk's office with the clerk or a deputy in attendance shall be open during business hours on all days except Saturdays, Sundays, and legal holidays, but a district court may provide by local rule or order that its clerk's office shall be open for specified hours on Saturdays or particular legal holidays other than New Year's Day, Birthday of Martin Luther King, Jr., Washington's Birthday, Memorial Day, Independence Day, Labor Day, Columbus Day, Veterans Day, Thanksgiving Day, and Christmas Day. All motions and applications in the clerk's office for issuing mesne process, for issuing final process to enforce and execute judgments, for entering defaults or judgments by default, and for other proceedings which do not require allowance or order of the court are grantable of course by the clerk; but the clerk's action may be suspended or altered or rescinded by the court upon cause shown.

(d) Notice of Orders or Judgments. Immediately upon the entry of an order or judgment the clerk shall serve a notice of the entry in the manner provided for in Rule 5(b) upon each party who is not in default for failure to appear, and shall make a note in the docket of the service. Any party may in addition serve a notice of such entry in the manner provided in Rule 5(b) for the service of papers.

RULE 78. Motion Day

Unless local conditions make it impracticable, each district court shall establish regular times and places, at intervals sufficiently frequent for the prompt dispatch of business, at which motions requiring notice and hearing may be heard and disposed of; but the judge at any time or place and on such notice, if any, as the judge considers reasonable may make orders for the advancement, conduct, and hearing of actions.

To expedite its business, the court may make provision by rule or order for the submission and determination of motions without oral hearing upon brief written statements of reasons in support and opposition.

RULE 79. Books and Records Kept by the Clerk and Entries Therein

(a) Civil Docket. The clerk shall keep a book known as "civil docket" of such form and style as may be prescribed by the Director of the Administrative Office of the United States Courts with the approval of the Judicial Conference of the United States, and shall enter therein each civil action to which these rules are made applicable. Actions shall be assigned consecutive file numbers. The file number of each action shall be noted on the folio of the docket whereon the first entry of the action is made. All papers filed with the clerk, all process issued and returns made thereon, all appearances, orders, verdicts, and judgments shall be entered chronologically in the civil docket on the folio assigned to the action and shall be marked with its file number. These entries shall be brief but shall show the nature of each paper filed or writ issued and the substance of each order or judgment of the court and of the returns showing execution of process. The entry of an order or judgment shall show the date the entry is made. When in an action trial by jury has been properly demanded or ordered the clerk shall enter the word "jury" on the folio assigned to that action.

(b) Civil Judgments and Orders. The clerk shall keep, in such form and manner as the Director of the Administrative Office of the United States Courts with the approval of the Judicial Conference of the United States may prescribe, a correct copy of every final judg-

ment or appealable order, or order affecting title to or lien upon real or personal property, and any other order which the court may direct to be kept.

(c) Indices; Calendars. Suitable indices of the civil docket and of every civil judgment and order referred to in subdivision (b) of this rule shall be kept by the clerk under the direction of the court. There shall be prepared under the direction of the court calendars of all actions ready for trial, which shall distinguish "jury actions" from "court actions."

(d) Other Books and Records of the Clerk. The clerk shall also keep such other books and records as may be required from time to time by the Director of the Administrative Office of the United States Courts with the approval of the Judicial Conference of the United States.

RULE 80. Stenographer; Stenographic Report or Transcript as Evidence

(a) [Abrogated. Dec. 27, 1946, eff. March 19, 1948.]

(b) [Abrogated. Dec. 27, 1946, eff. March 19, 1948.]

(c) Stenographic Report or Transcript as Evidence. Whenever the testimony of a witness at a trial or hearing which was stenographically reported is admissible in evidence at a later trial, it may be proved by the transcript thereof duly certified by the person who reported the testimony.

XI
GENERAL PROVISIONS

RULE 81. Applicability in General

(a) Proceedings to which the Rules Apply.

(1) These rules do not apply to prize proceedings in admiralty governed by Title 10, U.S.C., §§ 7651-7681. They do not apply to proceedings in bankruptcy to the extent provided by the Federal Rules of Bankruptcy Procedure.

(2) These rules are applicable to proceedings for admission to citizenship, habeas corpus, and quo warranto, to the extent that the practice in such proceedings is not set forth in statutes of the United States, the Rules Governing Section 2254 Cases, or the Rules Governing Section 2255 Proceedings, and has heretofore conformed to the practice in civil actions.

(3) In proceedings under Title 9, U.S.C., relating to arbitration, or under the Act of May 20, 1926, ch. 347, § 9 (44 Stat. 585), U.S.C., Title 45, § 159, relating to boards of arbitration of railway labor disputes, these rules apply only to the extent that matters of procedure are not provided for in those statutes. These rules apply to proceedings to compel the giving of testimony or production of documents in accordance with a subpoena issued by an officer or agency of the United

States under any statute of the United States except as otherwise provided by statute or by rules of the district court or by order of the court in the proceedings.

(4) These rules do not alter the method prescribed by the Act of February 18, 1922, ch. 57, § 2 (42 Stat. 388), U.S.C., Title 7, § 292; or by the Act of June 10, 1930, ch. 436, § 7 (46 Stat. 534), as amended, U.S.C., Title 7, § 499g(c), for instituting proceedings in the United States district courts to review orders of the Secretary of Agriculture; or prescribed by the Act of June 25, 1934, ch. 742, § 2 (48 Stat. 1214), U.S.C., Title 15, § 522, for instituting proceedings to review orders of the Secretary of the Interior; or prescribed by the Act of February 22, 1935, ch. 18, § 5 (49 Stat. 31), U.S.C., Title 15, § 715d(c), as extended, for instituting proceedings to review orders of petroleum control boards; but the conduct of such proceedings in the district courts shall be made to conform to these rules so far as applicable.

(5) These rules do not alter the practice in the United States district courts prescribed in the Act of July 5, 1935, ch. 372, §§ 9 and 10 (49 Stat. 453), as amended, U.S.C., Title 29, §§ 159 and 160, for beginning and conducting proceedings to enforce orders of the National Labor Relations Board; and in respects not covered by those statutes, the practice in the district courts shall conform to these rules so far as applicable.

(6) These rules apply to proceedings for enforcement or review of compensation orders under the Longshoremen's and Harbor Workers' Compensation Act, Act of March 4, 1927, c. 509, §§ 18, 21 (44 Stat. 1434, 1436), as amended, U.S.C., Title 33, §§ 918, 921, except to the extent that matters of procedure are provided for in that Act. The provisions for service by publication and for answer in proceedings to cancel certificates of citizenship under the Act of June 27, 1952, c. 477, Title III, c. 2, § 340 (66 Stat. 260), U.S.C., Title 8, § 1451, remain in effect.

(7) [Abrogated. April 30, 1951, eff. August 1, 1951.]

(b) Scire Facias and Mandamus. The writs of scire facias and mandamus are abolished. Relief heretofore available by mandamus or scire facias may be obtained by appropriate action or by appropriate motion under the practice prescribed in these rules.

(c) Removed Actions. These rules apply to civil actions removed to the United States district courts from the state courts and govern procedure after removal. Repleading is not necessary unless the court so orders. In a removed action in which the defendant has not answered, the defendant shall answer or present the other defenses or objections available under these rules within 20 days after the receipt through service or otherwise of a copy of the initial pleading setting forth the claim for relief upon which the action or proceeding is based, or within 20 days after the service of summons upon such initial pleading, then filed, or within 5 days after the filing of the petition for removal, whichever period is longest. If at the time of removal all necessary pleadings have been served, a party entitled to

trial by jury under Rule 38 shall be accorded it, if the party's demand therefor is served within 10 days after the petition for removal is filed if the party is the petitioner, or if not the petitioner within 10 days after service on the party of the notice of filing the petition. A party who, prior to removal, has made an express demand for trial by jury in accordance with state law, need not make a demand after removal. If state law applicable in the court from which the case is removed does not require the parties to make express demands in order to claim trial by jury, they need not make demands after removal unless the court directs that they do so within a specified time if they desire to claim trial by jury. The court may make this direction on its own motion and shall do so as a matter of course at the request of any party. The failure of a party to make demand as directed constitutes a waiver by that party of trial by jury.

(d) [Abrogated. Dec. 29, 1948, eff. Oct. 20, 1949.]

(e) Law Applicable. Whenever in these rules the law of the state in which the district court is held is made applicable, the law applied in the District of Columbia governs proceedings in the United States District Court for the District of Columbia. When the word "state" is used, it includes, if appropriate, the District of Columbia. When the term "statute of the United States" is used, it includes, so far as concerns proceedings in the United States District Court for the District of Columbia, any Act of Congress locally applicable to and in force in the District of Columbia. When the law of a state is referred to, the word "law" includes the statutes of that state and the state judicial decisions construing them.

(f) References to Officer of the United States. Under any rule in which reference is made to an officer or agency of the United States, the term "officer" includes a district director of internal revenue, a former district director or collector of internal revenue, or the personal representative of a deceased district director or collector of internal revenue.

RULE 82. Jurisdiction and Venue Unaffected

These rules shall not be construed to extend or limit the jurisdiction of the United States district courts or the venue of actions therein. An admiralty or maritime claim within the meaning of Rule 9(h) shall not be treated as a civil action for the purposes of Title 28, U.S.C. §§ 1391-1392.

RULE 83. Rules by District Courts; Judge's Directives

(a) Local Rules

(1) Each district court, acting by a majority of its district judges, may, after giving appropriate public notice and an opportunity for comment, make and amend

rules governing its practice. A local rule shall be consistent with–but not duplicative of–Acts of Congress and rules adopted under 28 U.S.C. §§ 2072 and 2075, and shall conform to any uniform numbering system prescribed by the Judicial Conference of the United States. A local rule takes effect on the date specified by the district court and remains in effect unless amended by the court or abrogated by the judicial council of the circuit. Copies of rules and amendments shall, upon their promulgation, be furnished to the judicial council and the Administrative Office of the United States Courts and be made available to the public.

(2) A local rule imposing a requirement of form shall not be enforced in a manner that causes a party to lose rights because of a nonwillful failure to comply with the requirement.

(b) Procedures When There is No Controlling Law. A judge may regulate practice in any manner consistent with federal law, rules adopted under 28 U.S.C. §§ 2072 and 2075, and local rules of the district. No sanction or other disadvantage may be imposed for noncompliance with any requirement not in federal law, federal rules, or the local district rules unless the alleged violator has been furnished in the particular case with actual notice of the requirement.

RULE 84. Forms

The forms contained in the Appendix of Forms are sufficient under the rules and are intended to indicate the simplicity and brevity of statement which the rules contemplate.

RULE 85. Title

These rules may be known and cited as the Federal Rules of Civil Procedure.

RULE 86. Effective Date

(a) [Effective Date of Original Rules]. These rules will take effect on the day which is 3 months subsequent to the adjournment of the second regular session of the 75th Congress, but if that day is prior to September 1, 1938, then these rules will take effect on September 1, 1938. They govern all proceedings in actions brought after they take effect and also all further proceedings in actions then pending, except to the extent that in the opinion of the court their application in a particular action pending when the rules take effect would not be feasible or would work injustice, in which event the former procedure applies.

(b) Effective Date of Amendments. The amendments adopted by the Supreme Court on December 27, 1946, and transmitted to the Attorney General on January 2, 1947, shall take effect on the day which is three months subsequent to the adjournment of the first regular session of the 80th Congress, but, if that day is prior to September 1, 1947, then these amendments shall take effect on September 1, 1947. They govern all proceedings in actions brought after they take effect and also all further proceedings in actions then pending, except to the extent that in the opinion of the court their application in a particular action pending when the amendments take effect would not be feasible or would work injustice, in which event the former procedure applies.

(c) Effective Date of Amendments. The amendments adopted by the Supreme Court on December 29, 1948, and transmitted to the Attorney General on December 31, 1948, shall take effect on the day following the adjournment of the first regular session of the 81st Congress.

(d) Effective Date of Amendments. The amendments adopted by the Supreme Court on April 17, 1961, and transmitted to the Congress on April 18, 1961, shall take effect on July 19, 1961. They govern all proceedings in actions brought after they take effect and also all further proceedings in actions then pending, except to the extent that in the opinion of the court their application in a particular action pending when the amendments take effect would not be feasible or would work injustice, in which event the former procedure applies.

(e) Effective Date of Amendments. The amendments adopted by the Supreme Court on January 21, 1963, and transmitted to the Congress on January 21, 1963, shall take effect on July 1, 1963. They govern all proceedings in actions brought after they take effect and also all further proceedings in actions then pending, except to the extent that in the opinion of the court their application in a particular action pending when the amendments take effect would not be feasible or would work injustice, in which event the former procedure applies.

TABLE TO CALCULATE NUMBER OF DAYS

This table can be used to calculate the number of days between dates. For example, 120 days from May 10 (Day 130) is September 7 (Day 250). For dates that extend into a second calendar year, simply subtract 365 from the sum of the two numbers. For example, 120 days from December 26 (Day 360) is April 25 (Day 115 [480-365]). Leap years must have 1 day added to every computation after February 28 of that year.

Date	Jan.	Feb.	Mar.	Apr.	May	June	July	Aug.	Sep.	Oct.	Nov.	Dec.
1	1	32	60	91	121	152	182	213	244	274	305	335
2	2	33	61	92	122	153	183	214	245	275	306	336
3	3	34	62	93	123	154	184	215	246	276	307	337
4	4	35	63	94	124	155	185	216	247	277	308	338
5	5	36	64	95	125	156	186	217	248	278	309	339
6	6	37	65	96	126	157	187	218	249	279	310	340
7	7	38	66	97	127	158	188	219	250	280	311	341
8	8	39	67	98	128	159	189	220	251	281	312	342
9	9	40	68	99	129	160	190	221	252	282	313	343
10	10	41	69	100	130	161	191	222	253	283	314	344
11	11	42	70	101	131	162	192	223	254	284	315	345
12	12	43	71	102	132	163	193	224	255	285	316	346
13	13	44	72	103	133	164	194	225	256	286	317	347
14	14	45	73	104	134	165	195	226	257	287	318	348
15	15	46	74	105	135	166	196	227	258	288	319	349
16	16	47	75	106	136	167	197	228	259	289	320	350
17	17	48	76	107	137	168	198	229	260	290	321	351
18	18	49	77	108	138	169	199	230	261	291	322	352
19	19	50	78	109	139	170	200	231	262	292	323	353
20	20	51	79	110	140	171	201	232	263	293	324	354
21	21	52	80	111	141	172	202	233	264	294	325	355
22	22	53	81	112	142	173	203	234	265	295	326	356
23	23	54	82	113	143	174	204	235	266	296	327	357
24	24	55	83	114	144	175	205	236	267	297	328	358
25	25	56	84	115	145	176	206	237	268	298	329	359
26	26	57	85	116	146	177	207	238	269	299	330	360
27	27	58	86	117	147	178	208	239	270	300	331	361
28	28	59	87	118	148	179	209	240	271	301	332	362
29	29		88	119	149	180	210	241	272	302	333	363
30	30		89	120	150	181	211	242	273	303	334	364
31	31		90		151		212	243		304		365

OHIO COURT SYSTEM

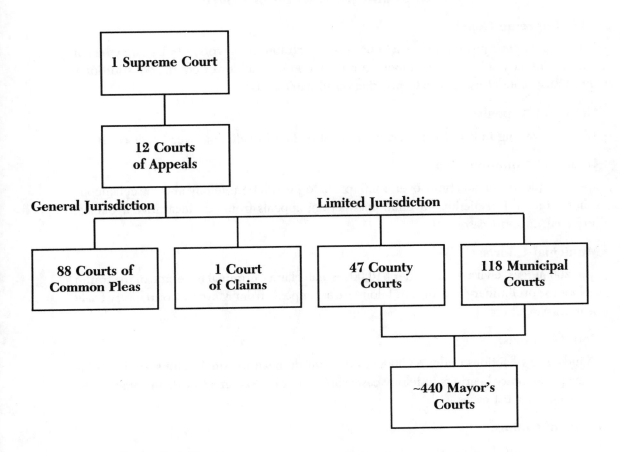

Notes and Jurisdiction of Courts

Ohio Supreme Court:

7 justices; original jurisdiction in actions seeking extraordinary writs, admission to the bar and disciplinary actions; final appellate jurisdiction over all lower courts; constitutional questions; mandatory appellate jurisdiction in capital cases.

Courts of Appeals:

12 judges sitting in 3-judge panels; general appellate jurisdiction over lower courts.

Courts of Common Pleas:

app. 370 judges; civil actions over $500; probate jurisdiction; felony and miscellaneous other criminal jurisdiction; juvenile jurisdiction; appeals from administrative agencies; jury trials in most cases.

Municipal Courts:

app. 200 judges; civil actions under $10,000; small claims; criminal misdemeanors; traffic violations; preliminary hearings in felony cases; appeals from Mayor's Courts; jury trials in most cases.

County Courts:

55 judges; civil actions under $3,000; criminal misdemeanors; small claims; traffic violations; preliminary hearings in felony cases; appeals from Mayor's Courts in some cases; jury trials in most cases.

Court of Claims:

judges rotate on temporary assignment by Supreme Court; actions against the state; miscellaneous other civil cases; jury trials in some cases.

Mayor's Courts:

app. 440 mayors; some criminal misdemeanor; first offense DWI/DUI; traffic violations; no jury trials.

APPELLATE DISTRICT MAP OF OHIO *

Ohio State Court Clerks

Supreme Court
30 E. Broad St.
Columbus, OH 43215-3414
Clerk: Marcia J. Mengel
614.466.5201

Court Administration: Stephan W. Stover
Admin. Director
Supreme Court of Ohio
30 E. Broad St., 3d Fl.
Columbus 43266-0419
614.466.2653

Adams County
110 W. Main St., Rm 244
West Union, OH 45693-1391
Clerk of Courts: Gary K. Gardner
Phone: 937.544.2344
Fax: 937.544.8911

Allen County
330 N. Elizabeth St.
P.O. Box 1243
Lima, OH 45802
Clerk of Courts: Anne E. Geiger
Phone: 419.223.8512
Fax: 419.222.8427

Ashland County
W. Second St.
P.O. Box 365
Ashland, OH 44805
Clerk of Courts: Juanita Wright
Phone: 419.282.4242
Fax: 419.281.8315

Ashtabula County
25 W. Jefferson St.
Jefferson, OH 44047-1027
Clerk of Courts: Carol A. Mead
Phone: 440.576.3637
Fax: 440.576.2819

Athens County
Court St.
P.O. Box
Athens, OH 45701
Clerk of Courts: Christie Mitchell
Phone: 740.592.3242
Fax: 740.592.3282

Auglaize County
201 S. Willipie St.
P.O. Box 409
Wapakoneta, OH 45895-0409
Clerk of Courts: Sue Ellen Kohler
Phone: 419.738.4219
Fax: 419.738.4280

Belmont County
Courthouse
Main Street
St. Clairsville, OH 43950
Clerk of Courts: Randy L. Marple
Phone: 740.695.212., ext. 252
Fax: 740.695.2121, ext. 280

Brown County
Courthouse
Administrative Bldg.
Georgetown, OH 45121
Clerk of Courts: Danny L. Pride
Phone: 937.378.3100
Fax: 937.378.4212

Butler County
Courthouse
Hamilton, OH 45011
Clerk of Courts: Cindy Carpenter
Phone: 513.887.3282
Fax: 513.887.3089

Carroll County
P.O. Box 367
Carrollton, OH 44615
Clerk of Courts: Janet Unkefer
Phone: 330.627.5282
Fax: 330.627.6656

Champaign County
200 N. Main St.
Urbana, OH 43078
Clerk of Courts: Dianne Coder
Phone: 937.653.2746
Fax: 937.653.7696

Clark County
101 N. Limestone St.
Springfield, OH 45502
Clerk of Courts: Ronald Vincent
Phone: 937.328.2458
Fax: 937.328.2436

Clermont County
289 Main St.
Batavia, OH 45103
Clerk of Courts: David R. Caudill, Jr.
Phone: 513.732.7560
Fax: 513.732.7831

Clinton County
46 S. South St.
Wilmington, OH 45177
Clerk of Courts: JoAnn M. Curliss
Phone: 937.382.2316
Fax: 937.383.3455

Columbiana County
105 Market St.
P.O. Box 349
Lisbon, OH 44432
Clerk of Courts: Anthony J. Dattilio
Phone: 330.424.7777
Fax: 330.424.3960

Coshocton County
318 Main St.
Coshocton, OH 43812
Clerk of Courts: Irene Crouso Miller
Phone: 740.622.1459
Fax: 740.622.1154

Crawford County
112 E. Mansfield St.
P.O. Box 470
Bucyrus, OH 44820
Clerk of Courts: Patricia J. Caldwell
Phone: 419.562.2766
Fax: 419.562.8011

Cuyahoga County
Justice Center
1200 Ontario St.
Cleveland, OH 44113
Clerk of Courts: Gerald E. Fuerst
Phone: 216.443.7950
Fax: 216.443.6868

Darke County
2nd Fl., Courthouse
504 S. Broadway
Greenville, OH 45331
Clerk of Courts: Cindy Pike
Phone: 937.547.7335
Fax: 937.547.7305

Defiance County
221 Clinton St.
P.O. Box 716
Defiance, OH 43512
Clerk of Courts: Jean Ziegler
Phone: 419.782.1936
Fax: 419.784.2761

Delaware County
Courthouse, 2nd Fl.
91 N. Sandusky St.
Delaware, OH 43015
Clerk of Courts: Betty J. Porter
Phone: 614.368.1850
Fax: 614.368.1849

Erie County
323 Columbus Ave.
Sandusky, OH 44870
Clerk of Courts: Barbara J. Johnson
Phone: 419.627.7705
Fax: 419.624.6873

Fairfield County
224 E. Main St.
P.O. Box 370
Lancaster, OH 43130
Clerk of Courts: Ron Balser
Phone: 740.687.7030
Fax: 740.687.0158

Fayette County
110 E. Court St.
Washington Court House, OH 43160
Clerk of Courts: Larry L. Long
Phone: 740.335.6371
Fax: 740.333.3530

Franklin County
369 S. High St., 3rd Fl.
Columbus, OH 43215
Clerk of Courts: Jesse D. Oddi
Phone: 614.462.3600
Fax: 614.462.4325

Fulton County
Courthouse, Rm. 203
210 S. Fulton Street
Wauseon, OH 43567
Clerk of Courts: Mary Gype
Phone: 419.337.9230
Fax: 419.337.9293

Gallia County
12 Locust St., Rm. 1290
Gallipolis, OH 45631
Clerk of Courts: Noreen M. Saunders
Phone: 740.446.4612, ext. 221
Fax: 740.446.4804

Geauga County
100 Short Court
Chardon, OH 44024
Clerk of Courts: Denise M. Kaminski
Phone: 440.285.2222, ext. 2380
Fax: 440.285.3603

Greene County
45 N. Detroit St.
Xenia, OH 45385
Clerk of Courts: Terri A. Mazur
Phone: 937.376.5290
Fax: 937.376.5309

Guernsey County
801 Wheeling Ave.
D-300
Cambridge, OH 43725
Clerk of Courts: Teresa A. Dankovic
Phone: 740.432.9230
Fax: 740.432.7807

Hamilton County
1000 Main St., Rm. 375
Cincinnati, OH 45202-4860
Clerk of Courts: James Cissell
Phone: 513.632.8283
Fax: 513.763.4860

Hancock County
300 S. Main St.
Findlay, OH 45840
Clerk of Courts: Carolyn A. Schimmel
Phone: 419.424.7037
Fax: 419.424.7801

Hardin County
Public Sq., 3rd Flr.
Kenton, OH 43326
Clerk of Courts: Lori J. Stevenson
Phone: 419.674.2278/2281
Fax: 419.674.2273

Harrison County
100 W. Market St.
Cadiz, OH 43907
Clerk of Courts:
Dianne L. Mazeroski-Milliken
Phone: 740.942.8863
Fax: 740.942.4693

Henry County
P.O. Box 71
Napoleon, OH 43545
Clerk of Courts: Betty Huddle
Phone: 419.592.5886
Fax: 419.592.4575

Highland County
P.O. Box 821
Hillsboro, OH 45133
Clerk of Courts: Paulette Donley
Phone: 937.393.957
Fax: 937.393.6878

Hocking County
1 Main St.
P.O. Box 108
Logan, OH 43138
Clerk of Courts: Peggy Beery
Phone: 740.385.2616
Fax: 740.385.1822

Holmes County
Courthouse, Ste. 306
1 East Jackson St.
Millersburg, OH 44654-1329
Clerk of Courts: Dorcas L. Miller
Phone: 330.674.1876
Fax: 330.674.0289

Huron County
Courthouse
2 East Main St.
Norwalk, OH 44857-1534
Clerk of Courts: Kathleen L. Walcher
Phone: 419.668.5113
Fax: 419.663.4048

Jackson County
226 East Main St.
Jackson, OH 45640
Clerk of Courts: Robert F. Walton
Phone: 740.286.2006
Fax: 740.286.4061

Jefferson County
301 Market St.
P.O. Box 1326
Steubenville, OH 43952
Clerk of Courts: Joseph G. Hamrock
Phone: 740.283.8583

Knox County
111 East High Street
Mt. Vernon, OH 43050
Clerk of Courts: Nancy R. Vail
Phone: 740.393.6788
Fax: 740.392.3533

Lake County
47 N. Park Place
P.O. Box 490
Paineville, OH 44077-0490
Clerk of Courts: Lynne L. Mazeika
Phone: 440.350.2657
Fax: 440.350.2585

Lawrence County
P.O. Box 208
Ironton, OH 45638
Clerk of Courts: Dale Burcham
740.533.4355
Phone: 800.942.5202/800.743.2470
Fax: 740.533.4387

Licking County
P.O. Box 4370
Newark, OH 43055-4370
Clerk of Courts: Larry R. Brown
Phone: 740.349.6171
Fax: 740.349.6945

Logan County
101 S. Main, Rm. 12
Bellefontaine 43311-2097
Clerk of Courts: Dottie Tuttle
Phone: 937.599.7275
Fax: 937.599.7251

Lorain County
308 Second St.P.O. Box 749
Elyria, OH 44036
Clerk of Courts: Donald J. Rothgery
Phone: 440.329.5536
Fax: 440.329.5404

Lucas County
800 Adams St., 3rd Fl.
Toledo, OH 43624
Clerk of Courts: Harry Barlos
Phone: 419.245.4484
Fax: 419.245.4487

Madison County
1 North Main Street
P.O. Box 227
London, OH 43140
Clerk of Courts: Marie Parks
Phone: 614.852.9776

Mahoning County
120 Market St.
Youngstown, OH 44503
Clerk of Courts: Anthony Vivo
Phone: 330.740.2103
Fax: 330.740.2105

Marion County
100 North Main St.
Marion, OH 43301-1823
Clerk of Courts: Kelly J. Davids
Phone: 614.387.8128
Fax: 614.383.1190

Medina County
93 Public Square
Medina, OH 44256
Clerk of Courts: Kathleen E. Fortney
Phone: 330.725.9721
Fax: 330.764.8454

Meigs County
Court St., 3rd Fl.
P.O. Box 151
Pomeroy, OH 45769
Clerk of Courts: Larry E. Spencer
Phone: 740.992.2693
Fax: 740.992.2270

Mercer County
101 North Main St.
P.O. Box 28
Celina, OH 45822-0028
Clerk of Courts: James J. Highley
Phone: 419.586.6461
Fax: 419.586.5826

Miami County
Safety Bldg., 3rd Fl.
201 W. Main St.
Troy, OH 45373
Clerk of Courts: (Mr.) Jan A. Mottinger
Phone: 937.332.6855
Fax: 937.332.7069

Monroe County
101 N. Main St., Rm. 39
Woodsfield, OH 43793
Clerk of Courts: Kitty Bolon Kahrig
Phone: 740.472.0761
Fax: 740.472.5156

Montgomery County
41 N. Perry St., Rm. 106
Dayton, OH 45422
Clerk of Courts: Craig L. Zimmers
Phone: 937.496.7623
Fax: 937.496.7627

Morgan County
Courthouse
19 East Main St.
McConnelsville, OH 43756
Clerk of Courts: Mary E. Gessel
Phone: 740.962.4752
Fax: 740.962.4522

Morrow County
48 E. High St.
Mt. Gilead, OH 43338
Clerk of Courts: Mary J. Evans
Phone: 419.947.2085
Fax: 419.947.5421

Muskingum County
401 Main St.
P.O. Box 268
Zanesville, OH 43702-0268
Clerk of Courts: Todd A. Bickle
Phone: 740.455.7104
Fax: 740.455.7177

Noble County
350 Courthouse
Caldwell, OH 43724
Clerk of Courts: Roger Smith
Phone: 740.732.4408
Fax: 740.732.5702

Ottawa County
Courthouse, Rm. 107
315 Madison St.
Port Clinton, OH 43452
Clerk of Courts: JoAn C. Monnett
Phone: 419.734.6753
Fax: 419.734.6552

Paulding County
Courthouse, 1st Fl.
115 N. Williams St.
Paulding, OH 45879
Clerk of Courts: Eleanor Edwards
Phone: 419.399.8210
Fax: 419.399.8299

Perry County
105 Main St.
P.O. Box 67
New Lexington, OH 43764
Clerk of Courts: Kay Burns
Phone: 740.342.1022
Fax: 740.342.5527

Pickaway County
207 S. Court St.P.O. Box 270
Circleville, OH 43113
Clerk of Courts: Sharon K. Cline
Phone: 740.474.5231
Fax: 740.477.3976

Pike County
Courthouse, 2nd Fl.
100 E. Second St.
Waverly, OH 45690
Clerk of Courts: John E. Williams
Phone: 740.947.2715
Fax: 740.947.5065

Portage County
Courthouse
P.O. Box 1035
Ravenna, OH 44266-1035
Clerk of Courts: Delores E. Reed
Phone: 330.297.3644
Fax: 330.297.4554

Preble County
Courthouse, 3rd Fl.
100 E. Main St.
Eaton, OH 45320
Clerk of Courts: Christopher B. Washington
Phone: 937.456.8160
Fax: 937.456.9548

Putnam County
245 E. Main St., STE. 106
Ottaw, OH 45875-1956
Clerk of Courts: Mary E. Wiener
Phone: 419.523.3110
Fax: 419.523.5284

Richland County
50 Park Ave. E.
P.O. Box 127
Mansfield, OH 44901-0127
Clerk of Courts: Phillip E. Scott
Phone: 419.774.5543
Fax: 419.774.5547

Ross County
Courthouse
2 N. Paint St.
Chillicothe, OH 45601
Clerk of Courts: Robert L. Harken
Phone: 740.773.2330
Fax: 740.773.2334

Sandusky County
100 N. Park Ave.
Fremont, OH 43420
Clerk of Courts: Linda S. Connors
Phone: 419.334.6161
Fax: 419.334.6164

Scioto County
Courthouse, Rm. 205
602 7th St.
Portsmouth, OH 45662
Clerk of Courts: Mildred E. Thompson
Phone: 740.355.8218
Fax: 740.354.2057

Seneca County
103 S. Washington St.
Tiffin, OH 44883-2352
Clerk of Courts: Carol R. Cleveland
Phone: 419.447.0671
Fax: 419.443.7919

Shelby County
P.O. Box 809
Sidney, OH 45365-0809
Clerk of Courts: Judith A. Snodgrass
Phone: 937.498.7221
Fax: 937.498.7824

Stark County
110 Central Plaza South
Suite 160
Canton, OH 44702
Clerk of Courts: Phil G. Giavasis
Phone: 330.438.0795
Fax: 330.438.0853

Summit County
53 Univ. Ave., 2nd Fl.
Akron, OH 44308-1662
Clerk of Courts: Diana Zaleski
Phone: 330.643.2211
Fax: 330.643.2213

Trumbull County
Adm. Bldg., 5th Fl.
160 High St. N.W.
Warren, OH 44481
Clerk of Courts: Margaret O'Brien
Phone: 330.675.2561
Fax: 330.675.2563

Tuscarawas County
125 E. High Ave., Rm. 230
P.O. Box 628
New Philadelphia, OH 44663
Clerk of Courts: Rockne W. Clarke
Phone: 330.364.8811, ext. 243
Fax: 330.343.4682

Union County
P.O. Box 605
Marysville, OH 43040
Clerk of Courts: Paula Pyers Warner
Phone: 937.645.3006
Fax: 937.645.3162

Van Wert County
P.O. Box 366
Van Wert, OH 45891
Clerk of Courts: Carol Speelman
Phone: 419.238.1022
Fax: 419.238.4760

Vinton County
Courthouse
100 E. Main St.
McArthur, OH 45651
Clerk of Courts: Lisa A. Gilliland
Phone: 740.596.3001
Fax: 740.596.4702

Warren County
500 Justice Dr.
P.O. Box 238
Lebanon, OH 45036
Clerk of Courts: James L. Spaeth
Phone: 513.933.1120
Fax: 513.933.2965

Washington County
Courthouse
205 Putnam St.
Marietta, OH 45750
Clerk of Courts: Judy R. Van Dyk
Phone: 740.373.6623, x229
Fax: 740.373.2085

Wayne County
107 W. Liberty St.

P.O. Box 507
Wooster, OH 44691
Clerk of Courts: Carol S. White
Phone: 330.287.5590
Fax: 330.287.5427

Williams County
One Courthouse Sq.
Bryan, OH 43506
Clerk of Courts: Sharon Miller
Phone: 419.636.1551
Fax: 419.636.7877

Wood County
One Courthouse Sq.
P.O. Box 829
Bowling Green, OH 43402
Clerk of Courts: Rebecca E. (Becky) Bhaer
Phone: 419.354.9281

Wyandot County
Courthouse, Rm. 31
Upper Sandusky, OH 43351-1493
Clerk of Courts: Ann S. Dunbar
Phone: 419.294.1432
Fax: 419.294.6414

Ohio Federal Court Clerks

Northern District of Ohio
(Ms.) Geri M. Smith
102 U.S. Courthouse
201 Superior Ave.
Cleveland, OH 44114-1201
Phone: 216.522.4355
Fax: 216.522.2140

114 U.S. Courthouse
1716 Spielbusch Ave.
Toledo, OH 43624-1347
Phone: 419.259.6412

337 Fed. Bldg. & U.S. Courthouse
125 Market Street
Youngstown, OH 44503-1787
Phone: 330.746.1726

568 U.S. Courthouse
2 South Main Street
Akron, OH 44308-1876
Phone: 330.375.5707

Bankruptcy Court Clerk, Northern District of Ohio
Beth A. Ferguson
3001 Key Tower
127 Public Square
Cleveland, OH 44114-1309
Phone: 216.522.4373 (general info)
Phone: 216.522.4373, ext. 3035 (clerk)

455 U.S. Courthouse
2 South Main St.
Akron, OH 44308
Phone: 330.375.5840

411 U.S. Courthouse
1716 Speilbusch Ave.
Toledo, OH 43624
Phone: 419.259.6440

Federal Building
201 Cleveland Ave. SW
Canton, OH 44702
Phone: 330.489.4426

P.O. Box 147
U.S. Courthouse
125 Market St.
Youngstown, OH 44501
Phone: 330.746.7027

Southern District of Ohio
Clerk:
Kenneth J. Murphy
260 U.S. Courthouse
85 Marconi Blvd.
Columbus, OH 43215
Phone: 614.469.5835
Fax: 614.469.5953

326 Potter Stewart U.S. Courthouse
100 E. Fifth Street
Cincinnati, OH 45202
Phone: 513.564.7500
Fax: 513.564.7505

P.O. Box 970
Mid-City Station
Dayton, OH 45402
Phone: 937.225.2896
Fax: 937.225.2716

Bankruptcy Court Clerk, Southern District of Ohio
Michael D. Webb
120 W. Third Street
Dayton, OH 45402
Phone: 937.225.2516, ext. 347

Kenneth Jordon, Deputy-in-Charge
Atrium Two, Ste. 800
221 E. Fourth Street
Cincinnati, OH 45202
Phone: 513.684.2572, ext. 138

Keith Brown, Deputy-in-Charge
170 N. High Street
Columbus, OH 43215-2403
Phone: 614.469.6638, ext. 236

Other Important Ohio Addresses and Phone Numbers

Governor
Robert Taft II
77 S. High, 30th Fl.
Columbus 43266-0601
Phone: 614.466.3555

Secretary of State
J. Kenneth Blackwell
30 E. Broad St., 14th Fl.
Columbus 43266-0418
Phone: 614.466.2655

Main State Capitol
Phone: 614.466.2000

Vital Statistics
Div. Of Vital Stat.
Dep't of Health
65 S. Front Street
Columbus 43215
Phone: 614.466.2533

Attorney General
Betty D. Montgomery
State Office Tower
30 E. Broad St.
Columbus 43266-0410
Phone: 614.466.3376

Corporate Phone Numbers for Ohio

General Information (Corp)
Phone: 614.466.3910

Certification Desk
Phone: 614.466.1776
Fax: 614.466.2892

Corporations Section
Phone: 614.466.3910

General Information (UCC)
Phone: 614.466.3623

Name Availability
Phone: 614.466.0590

UCC Section
Phone: 614.466.3623

State Court Websites

The Supreme Court of Ohio
www.sconet.state.oh.us/

Supreme Court Decisions
www.sconet.state.oh.us/rod/Opinions/List.asp